WORLD HISTORY

Fourth Edition

Dennis Bollinger, PhD

Greenville, South Carolina

Note: The fact that materials produced by other publishers may be referred to in this volume does not constitute an endorsement of the content or theological position of materials produced by such publishers. Any references and ancillary materials are listed as an aid to the student or the teacher and in an attempt to maintain the accepted academic standards of the publishing industry.

World History
Fourth Edition

Dennis Bollinger, PhD

Contributing Authors
Carl Abrams, PhD
Nathan Lentfer, MA
Dennis Peterson, MS
Bryan Smith, PhD

Editor
Manda Kalagayan, MEd

Bible Integration
Brian Collins, PhD
Bryan Smith, PhD

Cover
Michael Asire

Book Design
Michael Asire

Page Layout
Charity Taft

Project Coordinator
Dan Berger

Permissions
Sylvia Gass
Brenda Hansen
Ashley Hobbs
Joyce Landis

Illustration
Preston Gravely Jr.
David Schuppert

Photograph credits appear on pages 592–96.

Produced in cooperation with the Bob Jones University Division of Social Science
of the College of Arts and Science

Greenville, South Carolina 29614

Printed in the United States of America

ISBN: 978-1-60682-118-3

Printing numbers 15 14 13 12 11 10 9 8 7 6 5 4 3 2

GIVE EAR,

O my people, to my law:
Incline your ears to the words of my mouth.
I will open my mouth in a parable:
I will utter dark sayings of old:
Which we have heard and known,
and our fathers have told us.
We will not hide them from their children,

SHEWING TO THE GENERATION TO COME

The **PRAISES** of the Lord,
And his **STRENGTH**,
And his **WONDERFUL WORKS** that he hath done.

For he established a testimony in Jacob,
and appointed a law in Israel,
which he commanded our fathers,
that they should make them known to their children:

THAT THE GENERATION TO COME MIGHT KNOW THEM,

even the children which should be born;
who should arise and declare them to their children:
THAT THEY MIGHT SET THEIR HOPE IN GOD,
AND NOT FORGET THE WORKS OF GOD,
BUT KEEP HIS COMMANDMENTS.

PSALM 78:1-7

CONTENTS

Unit VI The European World

Unit VII The Modern World

FEATURES OF THE BOOK

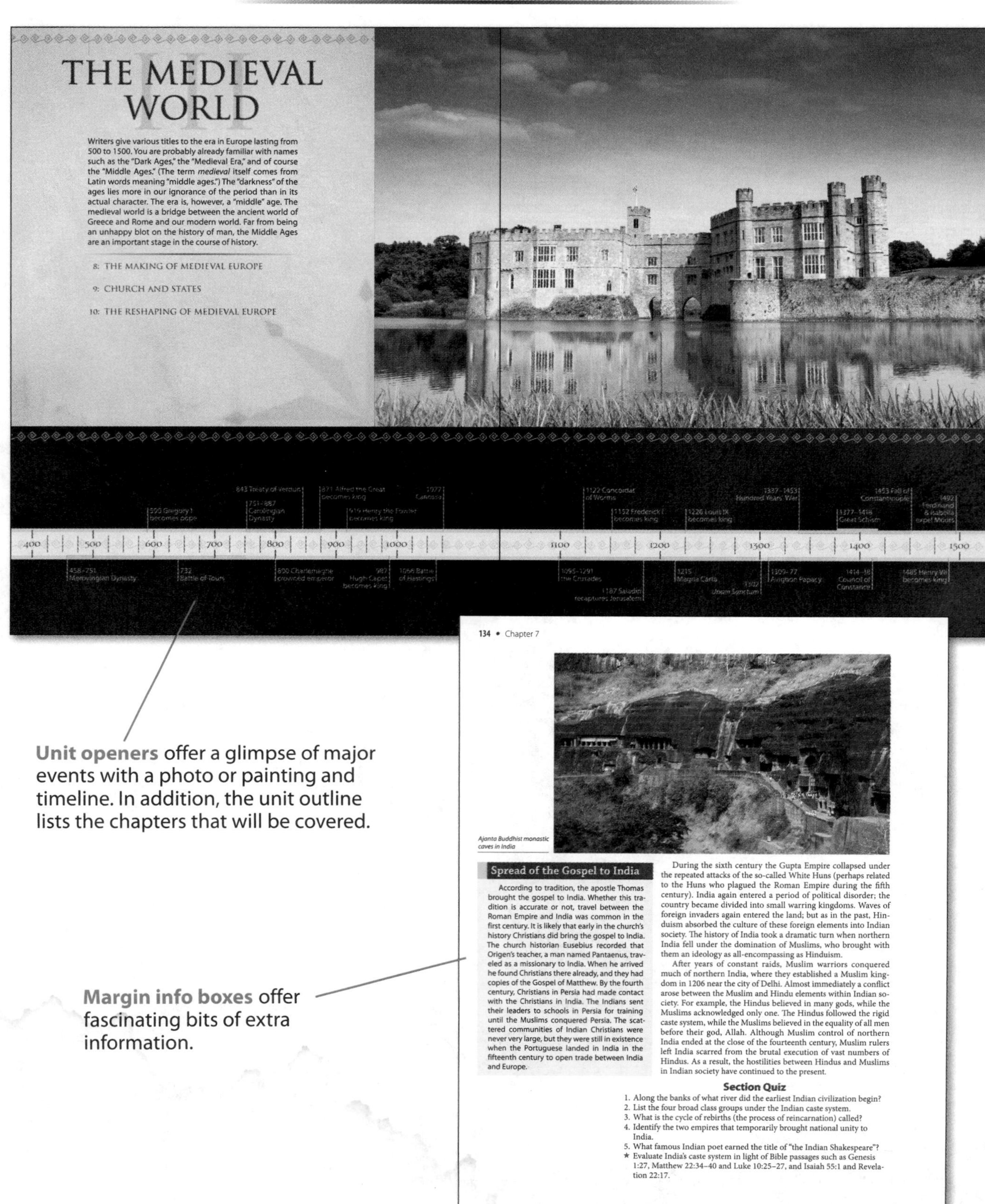

THE MEDIEVAL WORLD

Writers give various titles to the era in Europe lasting from 500 to 1500. You are probably already familiar with names such as the "Dark Ages," the "Medieval Era," and of course the "Middle Ages." (The term *medieval* itself comes from Latin words meaning "middle ages.") The "darkness" of the ages lies more in our ignorance of the period than in its actual character. The era is, however, a "middle" age. The medieval world is a bridge between the ancient world of Greece and Rome and our modern world. Far from being an unhappy blot on the history of man, the Middle Ages are an important stage in the course of history.

Unit openers offer a glimpse of major events with a photo or painting and timeline. In addition, the unit outline lists the chapters that will be covered.

134 • Chapter 7

Ajanta Buddhist monastic caves in India

Spread of the Gospel to India

According to tradition, the apostle Thomas brought the gospel to India. Whether this tradition is accurate or not, travel between the Roman Empire and India was common in the first century. It is likely that early in the church's history Christians did bring the gospel to India. The church historian Eusebius recorded that Origen's teacher, a man named Pantaenus, traveled as a missionary to India. When he arrived he found Christians there already, and they had copies of the Gospel of Matthew. By the fourth century, Christians in Persia had made contact with the Christians in India. The Indians sent their leaders to schools in Persia for training until the Muslims conquered Persia. The scattered communities of Indian Christians were never very large, but they were still in existence when the Portuguese landed in India in the fifteenth century to open trade between India and Europe.

During the sixth century the Gupta Empire collapsed under the repeated attacks of the so-called White Huns (perhaps related to the Huns who plagued the Roman Empire during the fifth century). India again entered a period of political disorder; the country became divided into small warring kingdoms. Waves of foreign invaders again entered the land; but as in the past, Hinduism absorbed the culture of these foreign elements into Indian society. The history of India took a dramatic turn when northern India fell under the domination of Muslims, who brought with them an ideology as all-encompassing as Hinduism.

After years of constant raids, Muslim warriors conquered much of northern India, where they established a Muslim kingdom in 1206 near the city of Delhi. Almost immediately a conflict arose between the Muslim and Hindu elements within Indian society. For example, the Hindus believed in many gods, while the Muslims acknowledged only one. The Hindus followed the rigid caste system, while the Muslims believed in the equality of all men before their god, Allah. Although Muslim control of northern India ended at the close of the fourteenth century, Muslim rulers left India scarred from the brutal execution of vast numbers of Hindus. As a result, the hostilities between Hindus and Muslims in Indian society have continued to the present.

Section Quiz

1. Along the banks of what river did the earliest Indian civilization begin?
2. List the four broad class groups under the Indian caste system.
3. What is the cycle of rebirths (the process of reincarnation) called?
4. Identify the two empires that temporarily brought national unity to India.
5. What famous Indian poet earned the title of "the Indian Shakespeare"?

★ Evaluate India's caste system in light of Bible passages such as Genesis 1:27, Matthew 22:34–40 and Luke 10:25–27, and Isaiah 55:1 and Revelation 22:17.

Margin info boxes offer fascinating bits of extra information.

Amazing **color artwork** helps the students "see" the sites, people, and events discussed in the text.

The Roman Forum

interests of the common people. By crying out **"Veto!"** ("I forbid!"), the tribunes could stop unjust acts of patrician officials.

In the past, patrician judges had taken advantage of the plebeians, who were not familiar with the traditions that made up Rome's unwritten laws. However, continued pressure from the plebeians finally forced the patricians to put the Roman laws into writing. Around 450 BC these laws were written down on twelve tablets and hung in the **Roman Forum**, the section of the city that was the center of government. Now all could know the law. Likewise, the law was to be applied equally to all. Young boys in the republic memorized the whole code as part of their school work. These tablets of law, called the **Law of Twelve Tables**, became the foundation of Roman civil law.

Gradually the plebeians improved their political and social standing in the republic. They gained the right to hold public offices which had previously been held only by the patricians. A few plebeians even became senators. Debtor slavery was abolished, and the law against intermarriage between plebeians and patricians was repealed. In 287 BC the plebeian assembly, now called the **Tribal Assembly**, gained the power to pass laws binding upon all the people of Rome—patricians as well as plebeians.

As the result of these two centuries of struggle, the plebeians officially gained social and political equality with the patricians. The peaceful changes seemed to make the republic more representative of the people. But as the distinctions between patricians and plebeians began to disappear, a new class distinction began to develop—the rich versus the poor. Wealthy plebeians and patricians formed a new alliance that maintained control of the Senate and held the reins of power in the republic.

Section Quiz

1. In what year was the Roman Republic founded?
2. What was the most powerful body within the governmental structure of the republic?
3. What power did tribunes exercise over unjust acts of patrician officials?

Terms in bold type draw attention to important facts, ideas, people, or definitions.

One-sixth to one-third of the arable land was set apart as the lord's **demesne** (dih MAYN)—the land reserved for the lord; the rest was allotted to the villagers. The village peasants often worked together to plow the land, sow the seed, and harvest the crops since no one peasant had enough equipment or oxen to do the job alone. The open fields were divided into long, narrow strips. In each field, a villager farmed one or more of these strips. Often the lord's demesne was not a separate field but rather the most fertile strips in each open field.

During the early Middle Ages, most manors employed a **two-field system** of farming. In this system villagers planted crops on half of the cultivated land, leaving the other half to lie fallow for a year to recover its fertility. The following year, they reversed the procedure.

Later a **three-field system** came into common use, especially in northern Europe. This system established a pattern of rotating planting among three fields. In the spring the peasants planted one field with barley, oats, or beans; in the fall they planted a second field with rye or wheat. The third field remained uncultivated for one year. This rotation of crops increased the long-term productivity of the land as one crop replaced the nutrients that a previous crop had consumed.

The population on even the smallest manors reflected the medieval class structure: clergy, nobility, and peasantry. While throughout the Middle Ages the highest social status belonged to the clergy and the nobility, every person on the manor had specific duties. The parish priest cared for the religious needs of the villagers, while the local lord provided protection and justice. The peasants worked to provide for the physical and nutritional needs of everyone on the manor.

A small percentage of the people on the manor were **freemen**. These were the more privileged peasants who served as manorial officials or skilled laborers, such as blacksmiths, millers, and carpenters. Some freemen owned their own land, but others rented land from the lord of the manor. Freemen did not have the same obligations as the average peasant. For example, freemen were often exempt from laboring in the lord's fields. Furthermore, they had the freedom to leave the manor. Although they had greater privileges, the freemen's living conditions differed little from those of average peasants.

Below: Blacksmith
Bottom: Grist mill
Bottom right: Water wheel used to power the grist mill

Vivid **color photographs** take students on a visual tour of the cultures they'll be learning about.

General feature boxes provide a more detailed look at a person, event, or concept mentioned in the text.

Chinese Characters

When God scattered Noah's descendants throughout the world (Gen. 11:1–9), they carried with them a knowledge of man's earliest history. They knew of Creation, the Fall, and the Flood. Those who migrated to China seem to have preserved some of these truths in their writing system. Since most Chinese characters tell a story, we can break down the more complex characters into simpler ones and discover the meaning of each part.

禁
to forbid

林
wood/tree

示
God

For example, the Chinese character for "to forbid" tells the story of God's command to Adam in Genesis 2:16–17. God planted two special trees in the Garden of Eden: the tree of life and the tree of knowledge of good and evil. God commanded Adam not to eat of the tree of the knowledge of good and evil but gave him permission to eat fruit from any other tree in the garden. It is interesting to note, therefore, that the character "to forbid" is made up of the symbol for "wood" or "tree" (notice that two are indicated) and one of the basic Chinese symbols for God. (This character for God also had the idea of "to command" or "to express.")

The scriptural idea of sacrifice (the killing of a spotless animal) is also found in Chinese writing. The word "to sacrifice" is made up of four major parts: "ox" or "cattle," "sheep," "beautiful" or "unblemished," and "spear" (the weapon by which the animal was killed).

義
righteous

羊
lamb

我
me

Closely associated with the idea of sacrifice is the concept of righteousness. The character that means "righteous" or "righteousness" is made up of the symbol for "lamb" and the symbol for "me." Notice that when the two characters are combined to create the word *righteous*(ness), the lamb is placed over the person. In the same manner, Christ, who is the perfect Lamb of God, covers our sins with His blood.

Another interesting study is the character for "boat" or "ship." It is made up of the symbol for "small vessel," the symbol for the number eight, and the symbol that means "person," "population," or "mouth." The largest boat built in antiquity (as far as we know) was the ark. It saved Noah and his family—a total of eight persons.

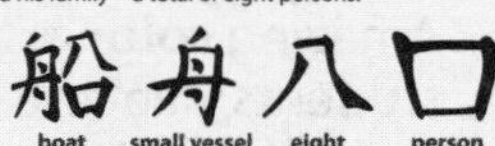

The written Chinese language indicates that at some time in the past the Chinese knew God's truth. Although most Chinese people today do not have access to the Scriptures, the written language preserves not only the truth of man's sin but also the wonderful fact of God's saving grace.

teaching. He believed that through proper conduct man could solve the problems of society and live in complete happiness. His disciples recorded and expanded upon his teaching, developing a system of ethics that became a major influence on Chinese culture.

Fundamental to Confucius's teaching was his belief in five basic human relationships: father and son, elder and younger brothers, husband and wife, friend and friend, and ruler and subjects. Confucius believed that maintaining proper relationships in these five areas would bring harmony and order to society. In addition, he placed great confidence in China's past, trusting it as the basis and guide for human behavior. From the ancients he derived the fundamental principle for all human relationships: "What you do not want done to yourself, do not do to others."

The major defect in Confucius's teaching was his neglect of the most important relationship of all—man and God. Only as we fulfill our duties and responsibilities to God are we able to properly relate to our fellow men. God's Word commands us to love God with our whole being and to love our neighbors as much as we love ourselves (Matt. 22:37–39). Only by living in obedience to God is man able to fulfill God's teaching found in Luke 6:31: "As ye would that men should do to you, do ye also to them likewise."

Xingtan Pavilion where Confucius lectured to his disciples

The historical books of the Bible center on the nations of Israel, Egypt, Babylon, Persia, Greece, and Rome. However, at the same time that these empires flourished, other equally splendid empires developed in India, China, and Africa. In the centuries following the ministry of the apostles, the gospel also spread to these parts of the world. There is little evidence that Christianity thrived initially in these regions. Recently, however, Christianity has begun to grow in Asia and Africa more quickly than in many other regions of the globe. Therefore, understanding the history of these cultures is important for Christians.

Sunrise in Africa

I. India

India is a land of great diversity. In its **topography** (the physical features of a land), climate, and population, it is a study in contrasts. This triangular subcontinent extends from southern Asia into the Indian Ocean, forming a giant peninsula. Its terrain varies from subtropical rainforest to barren deserts, from low coastal plains to the highest mountain range in the world, the Himalayas. Between the rugged mountain regions in the north and the coastal plains and tropical plateaus of the south lie fertile valleys watered by two great river systems, the Indus and the Ganges. Like the Mesopotamian and Egyptian cultures, the earliest Indian civilization began along riverbanks. The first inhabitants of India probably settled in river valleys along the Indus and Ganges Rivers.

These people must have felt secure from invaders and foreign influences. They were protected by tall mountain ranges in the north and by seas on the east and west. But despite these natural barriers, India did not remain an isolated land. Throughout its history, merchants, foreign invaders, and wandering tribes crossed the mountains along India's northwestern border (through such mountain passes as the Khyber) and settled in the fertile river valleys. As a result, India became a land of many peoples, customs, and languages. From the diverse elements within Indian society, a unique culture developed.

Early Civilization

India derives its name from the Indus River, along whose fertile banks the earliest Indian civilization flourished (ca. 2300 BC). Much of our limited knowledge of this civilization has come from excavations of two of its leading cities: Mohenjo-Daro (moh HEN joh DAH roh) and Harappa (huh RAP uh). These were carefully planned cities with wide, straight streets lined with brick houses. Evidence indicates that these cities had elaborate drainage and sewer systems that were more advanced than those in most modern-day Indian villages. Although a great distance separates India and the Near East, the early inhabitants of India carried on trade with Egypt and Mesopotamia. We know from archaeological evidence that the Indus civilization ended suddenly—perhaps by enemy invasion. It was at this time that a warlike people called the **Aryans** migrated into the Indus Valley.

The Aryans came from central Asia sometime after 1500 BC and subdued the non-Aryan people of northwest India. Many historians believe that the Aryans were

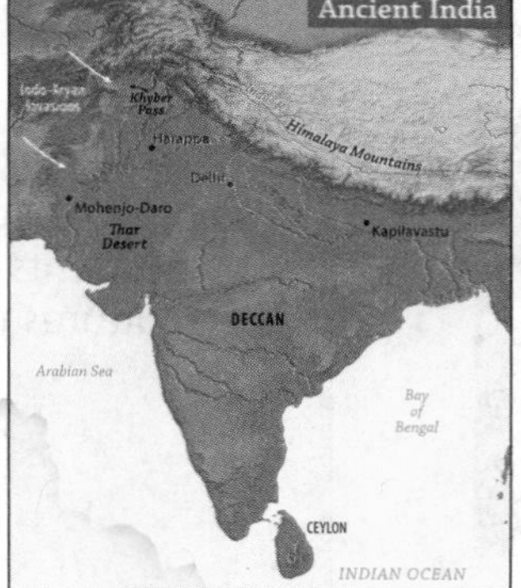

Maps help the students visualize geographic locations.

86 • Chapter 5

failed to realize, however, that these things were not really free. (The necessary funds came out of the public treasury.) Civil war often erupted as rival generals fought to gain the emperor's crown. For example, from AD 235 to 285 Rome had twenty-six different emperors. Of these, twenty-five died a violent death.

Section Quiz

1. What was the period of peace in the Mediterranean world lasting from 31 BC to AD 180 called?
2. List three titles or names by which Octavian was called.
3. What did Octavian institute within the empire in order to provide for fairer taxing of provinces? How often did he order this to take place?
4. How did many of the self-seeking, corrupt emperors of the late empire win the favor of the people?

★ Both Augustus and Christ gave moral laws to men. Why were the citizens of Augustus's kingdom unable to obey his law while the citizens of Christ's kingdom were (and are) able to obey His?

II. Roman Culture and Achievement

As Rome expanded from a small city to a large empire, it came into contact with a wide variety of people and cultures. Rome borrowed, copied, modified, and preserved many elements of these cultures, blending its own values and traditions with those of the Near Eastern and Greek cultures. Rome, a melting pot of ancient cultures, was able to hold together an empire of diverse peoples.

Greek culture influenced almost every aspect of Roman life. A Roman poet of the first century BC wrote, "Conquered Greece took captive her rude conqueror [Rome] and carried its arts to backward Italy." Rome was actually far from "backward," but the Romans did learn much from the Greeks. The Romans were more practical than the Greeks. While the Greeks built with an eye for beauty, the Romans built with an eye for usefulness. The Greeks made significant contributions in art and philosophy; the Romans, in law and politics.

Contribution to Law

One of the most valuable and enduring of Rome's achievements was its system of justice. Rome protected the individual rights and property of its citizens. The New Testament writer Luke points out that it was "not the manner of the Romans to deliver any man to die, before that he which is accused have the accusers face to face, and have licence [opportunity] to answer for himself concerning the crime laid against him" (Acts 25:16). The Romans believed that all citizens should have equal rights before the law. Cicero, the famous orator of the republic, wrote: "The legal rights at least of those who are citizens of the same commonwealth ought to be equal. For what is a State except an association or partnership in justice?"

The legal codes of many modern European countries include principles based on Roman law. Even the American system of justice has benefited from Rome's example. Here are some Roman legal principles. Do you notice any similarity between these and America's laws?

- Justice is a constant, unfailing disposition to give everyone his legal due.
- Liberty is a possession on which no evaluation can be placed.
- Freedom is beloved above all things.
- The burden of proof is on the party affirming, not on the party denying.

Section quizzes provide reinforcement to help the students remember what they have learned so far. In addition, a critical thinking question challenges the students to combine details and demonstrate higher thinking skills.

The Roman Empire • 105

Chapter 5 Review

Making Connections

1–3. How did Octavian seek to improve Roman government and society? List three specific ways.

4–5. Why did the Roman government persecute Christians? List two reasons.

Developing History Skills

1. Why did the Roman Empire decline?
2. Based on Acts 16:37–38, 19:38–41, and 25:7–12, what were the rights of a Roman citizen? How do these compare with the rights of an American citizen?

Thinking Critically

1. How did God use the Jews, Greeks, and Romans to prepare the world for the coming of His Son?
2. Arius taught that Christ did not always exist but that He was created by God the Father. Using John 1:1–4 and Colossians 2:8–9, refute this heresy.

Living in God's World

1. Defend the claim that the life, death, and Resurrection of Jesus constitute the turning point of human history.

People, Places, and Things to Know

Pax Romana
princeps
Augustus
Cicero
Virgil
Horace
Ovid
Livy
Juvenal
Tacitus
Galen
Ptolemy
geocentric theory
aqueducts
Epicurean
Lucretius
Seneca
Stoicism
Marcus Aurelius
pontifex maximus
synagogues
Septuagint
Jesus the Christ
Pontius Pilate
Tiberius
crucifixion
gospel
Stephen
Paul
Nero
Diocletian
Edict of Milan
Constantine
Arius
Council of Nicaea
Theodosius I
monasticism
patriarchs
Huns
Visigoths
Alaric
Attila
Vandals

The **Chapter Review** asks students to think in terms of higher learning, including understanding, analyzing, evaluating, and creating.

HOW TO USE THIS BOOK

Units and Chapters

World History is divided into seven units. The main theme of each unit is presented in a brief summary and timeline and illustrated by a two-page color picture. Each unit in turn contains from two to six chapters. These begin with a brief introduction and an outline of the period to be studied. The chapters are divided into main sections and subsections. For instance, one of the main sections in Chapter 2 is Mesopotamia. The first subsection under this is Sumerian Civilization. Often subsections are further divided to help you quickly identify the major topics of discussion.

Section Quizzes

At the end of each major section of a chapter is a section quiz. The numbered questions are primarily recall questions designed to test your understanding of the material you have just read. The final question is a critical thinking question that requires you to analyze, evaluate, or apply information from the section in order to answer the question. There are normally three to four section quizzes in each chapter. In addition, if a section is unusually long, a section quiz will be inserted in the middle as well as at the end.

Chapter Reviews

Each chapter ends with a review section that should help you study the chapter and demonstrate your ability to analyze and apply the chapter content. The Chapter Review is divided into five parts: Making Connections, Developing History Skills, Thinking Critically, Living in God's World, and People, Places, and Terms to Know.

1. Questions from Making Connections help you recall what you have read in the chapter and demonstrate understanding by combining details to answer the questions.
2. Questions from Developing History Skills help you develop skills in applying and analyzing information in the chapter.
3. Questions from Thinking Critically help you develop skill in evaluating information in the chapter.
4. Questions from Living in God's World help you develop creative skill through a practical application of information in the chapter.
5. People, Places, and Terms to Know are listed in the order in which they appear in the text. You should be able to define, identify, or state the importance of the terms depending on their context in the chapter. All of the terms in this list are in boldface type in the text.

Illustrations, Charts, Timelines, and Maps

Each illustration and chart in the book has been included to aid you in your understanding of world history. Take time to look at these and read the captions associated with them. The timelines will help you place events in a broader historical context. The maps will help you visualize the size and location of various countries or regions.

Highlights

Each chapter has a number of interesting articles contained in feature boxes. Not only will these help to broaden your knowledge of history, but many will also make your reading of *World History* more exciting. If you are curious, for instance, about how we got our calendar or how during World War II the United States knew ahead of time that the Japanese were going to attack Midway, you will be able to read all about it in these boxes.

Dates

In your reading of this *World History* textbook, you will encounter many dates. We do not intend for you to memorize all of them. The dates are provided so that you will be able to fit people and events into a time frame. In addition, there are some facts you need to know about dates.

How to use BC and AD

Today it is customary to label events that happened before the birth of Christ BC (meaning "before Christ") and events that happened after His birth AD ("Anno Domini," Latin for "in the year of our Lord"). BC is written after a date (e.g., 509 BC), and AD typically appears before the date (e.g., AD 70). However, we do not write AD next to a date unless it might be confused with a BC date. Therefore, when you see a date in the book without BC after it or AD before it, you may assume it is AD. Some contemporary writers use "Before the Common Era" (BCE) and "Common Era" (CE) for their dating schemes to stand for BC and AD, respectively.

How to count in BC

The dates of events before the birth of Christ are much like the countdown of a rocket launch (10, 9, 8, . . . 3, 2, 1). Ancient civilizations, of course, did not count backward like this. But because of the historical significance of the birth of Christ, we today date ancient events from the number of years before His birth.

How to recognize an approximate date

Because of incomplete historical records, it is sometimes impossible to establish an exact date for a historical event. When this is the case, we express an approximate date by placing the abbreviated form of circa (Latin for "around") before the date (e.g., ca. 1446).

How to understand dates printed after a person's name

The dates in parentheses after a person's name usually indicate his lifespan. Dates for monarchs or popes, however, are often the dates they held office. The abbreviation *r.* before a date stands for "ruled" (e.g., r. 1307–78). If a question mark appears after a date, it means we are uncertain about the time of a person's birth or death—for example, John Wycliffe (1320?–1384).

How to determine in what century an event took place

The first century includes the years 1 to 100; the second, 101 to 200; the third, 201 to 300; and so on. The twenty-first century will therefore be from 2001 to 2100. The same procedure is used for establishing centuries BC. Can you determine the centuries for the following dates? 586 BC, ca. 1446, 1900.

Pronunciation Key

Vowels				Consonants			
symbol	**example**	**symbol**	**example**	**symbol**	**example**	**symbol**	**example**
a	cat = KAT	aw	all = AWL	k	cat = KAT	th	thin = THIN
a-e	cape = KAPE	o	potion = PO shun	g	get = GET	*th*	then = *TH*EN
ay	paint = PAYNT	oa	don't = DOANT	j	gentle = JEN tul	zh	fusion = FYOO zhun
e	jet = JET	o-e	groan = GRONE				
eh	spend = SPEHND	oh	own = OHN				
ee	fiend = FEEND	u	some = SUM				
i	swim = SWIM	uh	abet = uh BET				
ih	pity = PIH tee	oo	crew = CROO				
eye	icy = EYE see	*oo*	push = P*OO*SH				
i-e	might = MITE	ou	loud = LOUD				
ah	cot = KAHT	oy	toil = TOYL				
ar	car = KAR						

The pronunciation key used in this text is designed to give the reader a self-evident, acceptable pronunciation for a word as he reads it from the page. For more accurate pronunciations, the reader should consult a good dictionary.

Stress: Syllables with primary stress appear in LARGE CAPITAL letters. Syllables with secondary stress and one-syllable words appear in SMALL CAPITAL letters. Unstressed syllables appear in lowercase letters. Where two or more words appear together, hyphens separate the syllables within each word. For example, the pronunciation of Omar Khayyam appears as (OH-mar kie-YAHM).

THE ANCIENT WORLD

I

Every story has a beginning, and a well-crafted story progresses toward a climax. Indeed, a talented writer will carefully build up to his climax, arranging the details of the plot so that the climax will have the greatest possible effect on the reader. Ancient history, the subject of this first unit, builds toward such a climax. In steady succession, empires rise and fall, each new empire appearing even greater and more extensive than the last. Finally, with the Roman Empire, ancient history reached its climax—but not with the empire itself. The Roman Empire provided the setting for the turning point of history, the death and Resurrection of Jesus Christ: "But when the fullness of the time was come, God sent forth his Son, made of a woman, made under the law, to redeem them that were under the law, that we might receive the adoption of sons" (Gal. 4:4–5).

2166 Abraham born

1446 Hebrew Exodus from Egypt

3000 BC | 2500 BC | 2000 BC | 1500 BC | 1000 BC

753 Rome founded
605–586 Hebrew captivity in Babylon begins
509–31 Roman Republic
431–404 Peloponnesian War
336 Alexander the Great becomes king of Macedonia
44 Julius Caesar assassinated
31 BC–AD 180 Pax Romana
31 Battle of Actium
6–4 Birth of Jesus Christ
70 Romans destroy Jerusalem
306 Constantine becomes a co-emperor
325 Council of Nicaea
500 BC
0
AD 500

1

FOUNDATIONS OF WORLD HISTORY

I. The Study of World History

II. The Beginnings of World History

A building cannot be stronger than its foundation. This statement is certainly true in architecture, and it is also true in the study of history. Every telling of history—whether by a grandfather at a fireside or by a college professor in front of a classroom—is based on a number of "foundation stones." This chapter will talk about the foundational concepts that form the basis for this study of world history. One foundation is the method that a historian uses to understand the past. A faulty approach to doing historical research will lead to faulty conclusions. Another foundation is the world's earliest events. These events are foundational because they form the bedrock on which all the rest of world history is built.

I. The Study of World History

The Historian and His Task

History is the inquiry into what has happened in the past and why it has happened. But how do historians know what happened in the past? Historians act a lot like detectives. They search for clues that they hope will unlock the secrets of the past. These clues, or resources, provide the raw material of historical study. By collecting, analyzing, and interpreting this material, the historian can produce an account of the past that others may use.

The Historian's Resources

The resources that historians use are of two basic kinds. First, historians examine **primary sources**, which are records produced during the time period being studied and often produced by the people involved in the events being studied. Second, historians study **secondary sources**, which are records that explain or interpret primary sources. Obviously, historians prefer to base their work on primary sources, though for some periods they are not able to do so. Primary sources may be derived from three basic historical resources: artifacts, tradition, and written records.

Primary Sources	Secondary Sources
Manuscripts of Bach's choral pieces	Article analyzing the music of Bach
Emancipation Proclamation	Biography of Abraham Lincoln
Poems by American Puritans	Books about the Puritans
Memoirs of Napoleon	Essay on military tactics

Artifacts

The historian studies **artifacts** to learn about the background and culture of a people. Artifacts are objects made by man. They may be small relics, towering monuments, or priceless works of art. Most artifacts are simple, everyday items. Pottery, tools, weapons, furniture, clothing, coins, and jewelry unearthed by archaeologists (those who search for and study the artifacts of the past) give us valuable information about everyday life in past centuries.

The historian also derives information from architecture. He considers, for example, the pyramids in Egypt, the Acropolis in Athens, the Colosseum in Rome, the Great Wall in China, the Mayan temples in Central America, the soaring cathedrals in Europe, the Taj Mahal in India, or the towering skyscrapers of New York City. These impressive structures reflect the creative skill that God has given to men as well as the character of the people who built them.

As a historical artifact, these Mayan pyramids contain important clues for understanding the culture that produced them.

Even works of art aid the historian in understanding the past. Statues, drawings, paintings, and tapestries—"pictures of the past"—depict the customs, beliefs, hobbies, fashions, and ways of life of past generations.

Tradition

Think of your own family's history. You may be able to trace your heritage back many generations. How did you learn about your family's past? Most likely this information was passed down by parents or grandparents who talked of the "good old days." Such oral communication was the earliest method of transmitting historical information. It is called **tradition**, which is simply the handing down of information by word of mouth from generation to generation. Over the centuries tradition has taken many forms. Legends, ballads, folk songs, and tales are but a few of these forms. But tradition is more than the reciting of songs and stories about the past. It includes the imparting of religious beliefs, family heritage, and social customs.

Written Records

Because word-of-mouth information can easily be forgotten or distorted, people have written down their accounts of the past to preserve a more accurate record for future generations. These **written records** are abundant and diverse. They include private letters, inventory lists, inscriptions, diaries, and journals. Historians also use information preserved in family and church records, in lists of kings and dynasties, and in political and legal documents. They gain insight into the thoughts, attitudes, and feelings of past generations by examining their works of literature. They also make use of historical works—detailed accounts of people, places, and events written during the period being investigated. These are valuable tools in understanding the past.

Of the three kinds of primary sources, written records are by far the most important to the historian. Artifacts usually give only a sketchy testimony to the past that can be interpreted in very different ways. Tradition tends to offer detailed accounts, but since these accounts are subject to the embellishing of hundreds (sometimes thousands) of retellings, the testimony it yields is often not reliable. However, written records produced by those who lived during the period give a clearer testimony than artifacts, and since they do not have to be retold generation after generation, they are far more reliable than tradition. The great importance of written records is demonstrated by the fact that most historians consider it impossible to write a reliable history of a period unless written records are available.

A portion of Thucydides' History of the Peloponnesian War

The Historian's Use of His Resources

Producing a historical account, however, involves more than just collecting primary and secondary sources. The historian must also make proper use of what he has amassed. He does this, first of all, by **evaluation of historical sources**. He examines a given record for its internal consistency and believability. Then he compares that record to others like it, examining their points of agreement and disagreement. Having exposed the strengths and weaknesses of what is available to him, the historian is ready for the next step—**historical synthesis**. In this step he gathers the useful information he has found in his investigations and weaves that information together into a narrative of the past. The narrative he produces constitutes the vast majority of his history. But the historian's task is not yet complete. He must also engage in **historical**

interpretation. He needs to interpret the events he records by integrating into that account what he believes is the meaning and significance of the events. He must not simply state what happened; he must also explain why it happened and how that explanation remains significant for humans today. Once the historian has completed the steps of evaluation, synthesis, and interpretation, his work is ready to be studied, critiqued, and perhaps received by those who desire to know more about the subject of his work.

The Historian's Philosophy

In working through the previously mentioned steps, the historian realizes right away that he is limited. He cannot know everything about the past. Furthermore, he cannot (and should not) record every bit of knowledge that is available about a given subject. He must select the events and facts that he will record. After selecting his information, he must then decide which areas will receive more emphasis. Some facts and events require several pages of description while others need only a paragraph. Decisions about selection and emphasis are driven by a historian's philosophy of life—how he answers life's most important questions. Where did the universe come from? Why is it here? Where is this world headed? These are questions that humans can answer only by faith. A historian's faith—whether the faith of a Hindu, Muslim, atheist, or Christian—will profoundly shape his telling of history.

Studying History with a Christian Worldview

The Bible gives Christians a **worldview**, a perspective from which they may examine and interpret the universe and everything in it. The **Christian worldview** presented in the Bible is composed of three central truths: (1) God made the world and everything in it; (2) this world has fallen into a sad and broken condition because of human sin; and (3) God is working to redeem this world to Himself. The paragraphs that follow are our attempt to show you how this Christian worldview shapes our telling of history and how it enables us to face with confidence the limits of historical research.

Divine Control of History

The Bible teaches that God has planned all of human history. This biblical teaching is often referred to as the doctrine of **divine providence**. There is no event that is out of God's control or that does not help to accomplish His purpose for this world.

Nebuchadnezzar's Babylon was the glory of the ancient world.

One of the best demonstrations of this truth in Scripture is found in the book of Daniel. At that time in history, God's people found themselves a conquered nation living in exile in the great Neo-Babylonian exile. But Israel's captivity did not mean God had lost control. When the ruler of the Neo-Babylonian Empire spoke with pride of his achievements, God struck his mind with a strange malady that caused him to think he was an animal. After seven years, God healed him. Then Nebuchadnezzar confessed of the God of the Bible, "He doeth according to his will in the army of heaven, and among the inhabitants of the earth: and none can stay his hand, or say unto him, What doest thou?" (Dan. 4:35). All who are able to think and reason clearly about history should arrive at the same conclusion. The Christian God is the One Who "worketh all things after the counsel of his own will" (Eph. 1:11).

The reality of divine providence affects our study of history in two important ways. First, it reminds us that we should be historical optimists. As we learn about the problems of the past (and there are more than anyone can count), we will be tempted to become very pessimistic about human history. But the fact that God is in control teaches us that we have no good reason to despair about the condition or direction of our world. Divine providence does not deny that the world is evil; it does, however, deny that the world is out of control.

Second, divine providence encourages us to develop the habit of studying history with God's will in mind. The Christian should regularly ask himself, "What was God doing in this part of history?" Certainly we face limitations in seeking to answer this question. Aside from the history recorded in the Bible, historians do not have revelation about God's purposes. The historian may not even have all of the information about what happened. The historian may compare events to Scripture and conclude that certain events benefited the spread of the gospel or strengthened the church whereas other events brought about times of chastening for God's people.

Man's Fall into Sin

We cannot understand history unless we understand what the Christian worldview teaches regarding the source of the world's problems. Ultimately, it is not scarcity, disease, social inequality, or lack of education that is to blame for pain in the world. The problem lies within each of us. Our world is a troubled place because of our fall into sin. Because our first parents disobeyed and were cursed, all of us are sinful. An understanding of human sinfulness will prevent the Christian from having an overly optimistic view about past generations. He will resist the temptation to accept an unrealistic picture of the past. The Christian can also evaluate the morality of historical actions, not merely by the standards of the time or by his personal preferences but by the moral standards of Scripture.

Where Is This World Headed?

To express despair over the wickedness of our society, we often ask, "Where is this world headed?" Christians, however, should not despair. The world is wicked, but we know that it is still God's world and that in His plan it has a glorious future. Isaac Watts's hymn "Jesus Shall Reign" eloquently reminds the believer that this world is headed for Redemption because of the coming kingdom of Jesus Christ. This hymn is based on Psalm 72.

Jesus shall reign where'er the sun
Doth his successive journeys run;
His kingdom stretch from shore to shore,
Till moons shall wax and wane no more.

People and realms of every tongue
Dwell on His love with sweetest song;
And infant voices shall proclaim
Their early blessings on His name.

Where He displays His healing power,
Death and the curse are known no more;
In Him the tribes of Adam boast
More blessings than their father lost.

Redemption in Christ as the Goal of History

We have already mentioned that God is in control of history. We have even suggested that Christians should study history attempting to discern what God has been doing in the past. We cannot, of course, discern God's working unless we know the final goal that He is guiding this world toward. We cannot suggest *what* God may have done in the past unless we first know *why* He has chosen to be in control in the first place. Repeatedly, Scripture teaches that God is in control of history to redeem this world to Himself through the work of His Son. Or to state it more fully, God has planned all that happens in order to establish Christ's kingdom on earth so that through that kingdom He may declare His own glory (Rom. 11:36; 1 Cor. 15:28; Eph. 1:10). The goal of human history is Redemption in Christ.

A historian may not be able to determine God's purpose in specific historical events. However, the Christian historian should begin by considering the historical details of the event in addition to the fact that God is in control. Believers, including historians, can rest in the knowledge that God's ultimate goal is to glorify Himself through redeeming a people. History will conclude with the Father establishing a kingdom of redeemed sinners to be ruled by His Son.

A Final Word About Studying History

As we think about our Christian worldview and how it affects our investigation of the past, we conclude that **history** is the study of the record of the past acts of God and man on earth from its creation to the present, based on the best surviving evidence. Our primary purpose for presenting to you a Christian view of history is not to enable you to do well on standardized tests or to make you appear educated before unbelievers (though we believe that if this book is used properly both will result). Our primary goal is to accomplish what the biblical historians sought to accomplish. When the psalmist Asaph introduced his survey of Israelite history, he told his readers, "I will utter dark sayings of old: which we have heard and known, and our fathers have told us. We will not hide them from their children, shewing to the generation to come the praises of the Lord . . . that they might set their hope in God, and not forget the works of God, but keep his commandments" (Ps. 78:2-4, 7).

If you are trusting in Christ for salvation from sin, then you are part of the next generation of the people of God. We sincerely hope that this year of studying world history will motivate you to set your hope in God. He has never failed His people, and He will not begin to do so in your generation. May the chapters that follow give you hundreds of reasons to live in obedience to His commands, and may they open your eyes to the ways in which God can use you to extend the kingdom of His Son. Some of you may exercise great influence on the future course of history. Many of you will have a small sphere of influence. But all of you will have influence, and that influence will have meaning and will be significant. May the history books of the next century be filled with hope because you used your influence for the glory of God.

Section Quiz

1. How do primary and secondary sources differ?
2. What are the three steps a historian must go through in order to produce a historical account?
3. What drives a historian's decisions about selection and emphasis?
4. What question should Christians regularly ask themselves as they study various periods in history?
5. What is the goal of human history?

★ Define *history*.

II. The Beginnings of World History

The first pages in most world history textbooks are some of the most difficult to get through. They deal with events in the very-distant past for which historians have only sketchy records. Paragraph after paragraph presents impersonal accounts of human-like groups struggling to move their race toward civilization.

The Bible's opening chapters present a very different account of long ago. Genesis 1–11 is anything but impersonal. It tells the story of individuals known to us by name: Adam, Eve, Cain, Abel, Noah, to name a few. More importantly, however, these chapters introduce us to history's most important person. This person too we know by name—**Yahweh**, the only true God. And unlike the cautious presentation of most history books, the Bible's record is bold, going far beyond the "shadowy past" to a time when there were no cities, no farms, no humans, and no earth.

Creation

The Bible begins where it must: "In the beginning God—." Before the universe was made, there was God and God alone. If the universe came about by chance—as many have claimed—its inhabitants are not responsible to anyone. But if the world has been made by an almighty God—as the Bible claims—then this Supreme Being holds the title deed to every galaxy, every planet, and every human. All are responsible to honor and obey the One Who has graciously chosen to let them exist.

The longnose hawkfish is just one of the billions of creatures that came into being when God simply said, "Let the waters bring forth."

God completed His world simply by speaking. In six days the earth went from nothing to a dark, watery sphere to a beautiful inhabited world that God Himself could describe as "very good" (Gen. 1:31). And God accomplished all this work with only a series of commands. Yahweh's voice of command is more than law. It determines what is and what will be. Although rebels within His creation may seem to triumph, He will in His own time prove to all that He alone is victorious, "for he spake, and it was done; he commanded and it stood fast" (Ps. 33:9).

The Climax of Creation—The Human Race

The climax of God's creative work came after He made the land animals on the sixth day. To that point, all that God had made came into existence with some form of the impersonal command "Let there be." Just before His final creation, however, God expressed special interest in what He was about to do: "Let us make man" (Gen. 1:26).

Mankind's Distinction

The reason for this special interest was that man was to be God's great masterpiece. Unlike the mammoth whales of the ocean, the majestic peaks of the mountains, and the brilliant stars scattered throughout the huge expanse of space, man would be made in God's own image: "So God created man in his own image, in the image of God created he him; male and female created he them" (Gen. 1:27). The **image of God** in man is all of the qualities that set humans apart from the rest of creation and that reflect part of God's own personality. Like God, humans would possess the characteristics of reason, moral consciousness, spiritual desire, sociability, and emotion, to name only a few similarities. By mirroring part of His own being in man's, God set in this creature's soul both the desire and the ability to know Him intimately. The other

Prehistoric Peoples?

Most world history textbooks offer an evolutionary account of the beginnings of our race. These accounts are called "prehistory" because they took place before humans developed writing. For these periods there are only artifacts: tools, clothing, weapons, and skeletons. These scant pieces of evidence are supposed to tell a story millions of years in length.

According to this view of the past, hominids (early humanlike creatures) first lived in East Africa as far back as three to four million years ago. From this time to about 10,000 BC is called the Early Stone Age (or the Paleolithic Age) because humans during this period used very simple stone tools. From the early hominids evolved the species Homo erectus ("upright human"). These hominids had more advanced tools than their predecessors, and they were the first to leave Africa for Asia and Europe. About 250,000 years ago, another human species arose, Homo sapiens ("wise human"). All humans today are members of this species.

Toward the end of the Early Stone Age, two kinds of Homo sapiens are said to have become prominent. In the caves of Europe and Southwest Asia, Neanderthals lived from about 130,000 BC to 35,000 BC. Their significant contribution to human history was the great care that they took in burying their dead. Anthropologists believe that this practice is the first indication of belief in life after death—and thus some take it as the first evidence of religion in human history. About 35,000 years ago, the Cro-Magnons arose in Europe. These humans made advancements in tools and weapons. But perhaps their most interesting advancements were in art. Paintings by Cro-Magnons have been found in the caves of Spain and southern France.

The period from 10,000 BC to about 4,000 BC is called the New Stone Age (or the Neolithic Age). The most significant development during this period was the agricultural revolution. Prior to this time, humans had been hunter-gatherers. They wandered from place to place hunting animals for food. But somehow, during the New Stone Age, humans learned that if certain seeds were planted, they could grow into edible plants. As agriculture and the domestication of animals developed, humans began settling down in permanent communities. These communities became the forerunners of the cities of antiquity. With the founding of the first cities between 4,000 and 3,000 BC, human civilization began.

It is difficult to imagine an account more at odds with biblical history. The Bible presents the human race as intelligent and able to engage in agricultural pursuits from its earliest times. Art and religion did not take millennia to develop. Toward the end of our race's first day, the first man spontaneously authored a poem (Gen. 2:23), and both man and woman spoke daily with God while in the Garden of Eden (Gen. 3:8). But the greatest problem with evolutionary accounts is that they attempt to show that humans came into being apart from God. In so doing, they remove from the history of our race the Person Who gives our race meaning and significance. God has made us in His image; therefore, we have dignity, and therefore we can know peace and happiness only as we serve and love Him. Without Him we are nothing, and without Him in our history, our history has no meaning.

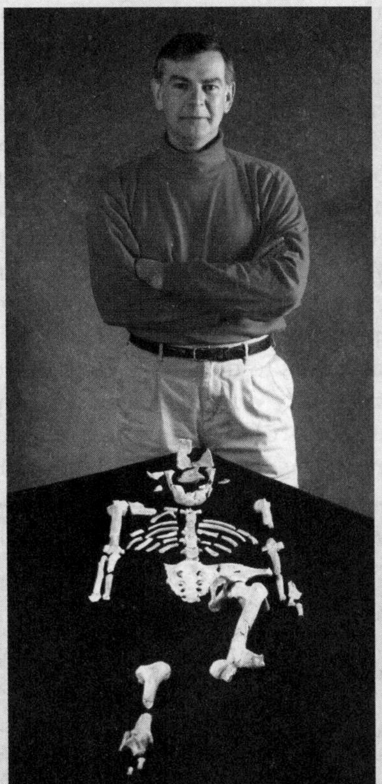

Top: *Mary Leakey, one of the most influential paleontologists of the twentieth century, convinced the scientific community that hominids first appeared in Africa rather than Asia.*

Middle: *Don Johanson, while excavating in Ethiopia in 1974, discovered what is considered an early hominid skeleton. He named it "Lucy" after a famous Beatles song. The skeleton (considered two or three million years old) is one of the most complete ever found.*

Bottom: *Though primitive to the untrained eye, the cave paintings attributed to Cro-Magnons show remarkable artistic sensitivity and skill.*

creatures praise God for being the mighty Creator. Man, however, is privileged to praise Him for being both Creator and Friend.

Mankind's Purpose

The image of God in man also equipped the human race to fulfill its calling on earth. God did not make humans simply with the ability to fellowship with Him; He also made them with a job to do. After making the first man and woman, God told them, "Be fruitful, and multiply, and replenish the earth, and subdue it: and have dominion over the fish of the sea, and over the fowl of the air, and over every living thing that moveth upon the earth" (Gen. 1:28). This first command from God, often called the **Creation Mandate**, reveals mankind's reason for being.

The Meaning of the Creation Mandate—The central command of Genesis 1:28 is the command to "subdue" the earth by exercising "dominion" over it. Whether the part in question is a tomato or Niagara Falls, humans are called by God to imagine and implement prudent ways to tame the earth and make it useful.

To exercise good and wise dominion requires all sorts of knowledge and skill—knowledge of science, math, technology, language, and history, to name a few. These areas of human endeavor are not found explicitly in Genesis 1–2, but they are implied in the Creation Mandate. Properly understood, the Creation Mandate is not a command about fish and birds only. It is a command about pursuing the advancement of culture—the physical and mental environment developed through human thought and labor.

Historians who reject the Bible's history usually assert that humans had to evolve over thousands of years before they were capable of changing their environment. The Bible, however, teaches that human management of the environment—one of the leading themes of world history—goes back to our race's first day. At that time God placed in man's heart the desire and the ability to pursue every aspect of culture. This pursuit was never meant to serve man's selfishness or pride. It was to be God's way of declaring His glory through us. All of creation exists to declare God's glory (Rom. 11:36). But humans are special. The stars glorify God by declaring the greatness of His power and creativity. Humans glorify God by being like Him and imitating His deeds. He is the infinite Lord of the universe; we are the finite lords of His earth.

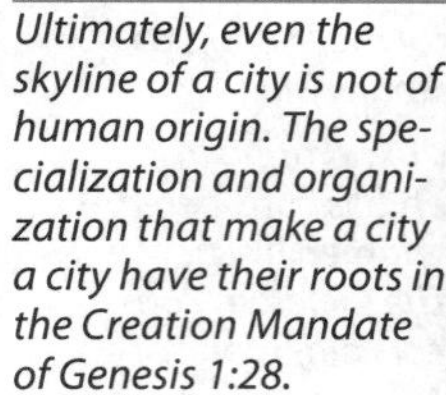

Ultimately, even the skyline of a city is not of human origin. The specialization and organization that make a city a city have their roots in the Creation Mandate of Genesis 1:28.

The Creation Mandate and Civilization—Central to the study of world history is the study of civilization. The word **civilization** comes from a Latin word (*civitas*) meaning "city," and it refers to human culture lived in cities or under their influence. Historically, a city is more than a place where many people live. It is a complex cultural institution in which humans share core values and a desire to improve the quality of their existence through specialization and organization.

Specialization refers to the division of labor that is part of the culture of every city. Individuals can specialize in a given endeavor necessary for human existence. The benefit of specialization is that individuals no longer need to do everything for themselves. Some specialize in food production, some in education, some in housing, some in the making of tools, and so forth; and each one benefits from the achievements of the others. To keep the network of specialization from unraveling, organization is necessary. This **organization** refers to a system of rules, regulations, and accountability that governs all who take part in the functions of the city. The results of specialization and organization are great advancements in science, technology, government, language, art, philosophy, and the accumulation of wealth.

It is important for Christians to realize that the city is ultimately not a human invention. Civilization—the object of study in this course—has its roots in the Creation Mandate. The specialization and organization that make a city a city are suggested in the opening commands of Genesis 1:28: "Be fruitful, and multiply, and replenish the earth, and subdue it." God recognized that the earth was a huge, complex place. If humans were to exercise the kind of dominion that would glorify Him, there would need to be a network of humans working together to maximize the usefulness of God's world. While it is true that the first city was still many years away (the first mention of a city is in Genesis 4:17), God intended from the beginning that civilization—and the enrichment that it brings—be part of human experience. It is not by accident that the Bible closes with saints in a city—the new Jerusalem.

The Fall

Adam and his wife, whom he later named **Eve** (Gen. 3:20), were part of a wonderful paradise. The best aspect of it for Adam and Eve was not the beauty of the garden or the pleasures of a perfect marriage. Their greatest joy must have come from the relationship they had with their Creator. Genesis 3:8 indicates that Yahweh came regularly to visit with Adam and Eve, perhaps much like a parent spending time with a child. There was no fear and no danger. God and His highest creation enjoyed unbroken, holy communion.

Like this plum, the fruit of the tree of the knowledge of good and evil looked beautiful and delicious.

The First Sin

All of this changed in a moment. When God called the human race to govern the earth, He called it also to govern itself. God had prohibited Adam and Eve from eating from the tree of the knowledge of good and evil (Gen. 2:16-17). This divine demand for self-control was taken by Satan as an opportunity to tempt the first woman to sin.

After listening to Satan's lies, Eve found herself doubting the only person Who is completely trustworthy and trusting the person who can never be trusted. She was then ready to commit the act that would change the world: "She took of the fruit thereof, and did eat, and gave also unto her husband with her: and he did eat" (Gen. 3:6).

The Consequences of Sin

Immediately Adam and Eve became painfully aware that they had made the wrong decision. The consequences of their sinful choice affected both their inner being and their physical existence. As the apostle Paul explained centuries later, the consequences of that choice have been passed on to all humans: "Wherefore, as by one man sin entered into the world, and death by sin; and so death passed upon all men, for that all have sinned" (Rom. 5:12).

Twisted Affections

Since God had made the man and the woman good, they originally obeyed God's most basic moral command naturally. They naturally loved God with their entire being and loved each other as much as themselves (cf. Mark 12:30–31). But when they chose to disobey, these affections became twisted. As a result, humans love themselves supremely, and they cannot bring themselves to love God or their fellow humans as they should. This central moral defect has characterized all of human culture ever since. The history of science, technology, art, politics, religion, and philosophy all bear the tragic marks of mankind's inability to love as he was meant to love.

Thwarted Dominion

God had made Adam and Eve to have dominion over the earth. Just as they had rebelled against God, so God made the earth rebel against them: "Cursed is the ground for thy sake. . . . Thorns and thistles shall it bring forth to thee" (Gen. 3:17–18). In this struggle Adam—along with all his offspring—was destined for defeat. Though called to subdue the earth, he would in the end be subdued by it: "In the sweat of thy face shalt thou eat bread, till thou return unto the ground; for out of it wast thou taken: for dust thou art, and unto dust shalt thou return" (v. 19).

The couple's most tragic punishment came last. Because they were now sinners, Adam and Eve were no longer fit to enjoy the bliss of the garden and the unhindered fellowship with God that it provided. Yahweh expelled them from paradise and stationed angels with flaming swords at its entrance. To gain the knowledge of good and evil, our first parents chose to disobey God. They got what they wanted; they lost what they had.

Redemption

In the middle of this devastating tragedy, God gave our race a glimmer of hope. While pronouncing His curse on Satan and the serpent he used, God offered a glimpse of the gracious salvation He had planned for mankind: "I will put enmity between thee [Satan] and the woman, and between thy seed and her seed; it shall bruise thy head, and thou shalt bruise his heel" (Gen. 3:15). Had it not been for this verse, there would have been no need of another. The human race had chosen its own destruction by sinning. But God revealed only moments after confronting this sin that those made in His image would have the hope of future triumph.

The Two "Seeds"

God promised both the serpent and the woman a "seed," or a group of descendants. Most likely, the **seed of the serpent** is a phrase referring primarily to Satan but also to humans yet to be born who would prove to have the same deceptive, God-defying nature that Satan evidenced that day in the garden. The **seed of the woman**, on the other hand, refers primarily to Christ but also includes future humans who are united to Him in faith.

The Central Conflict of History

Genesis 3:15 is the Bible's thesis statement for human history. Man had been called to exercise dominion over God's creation. But because of sin there would now be two dominions: the seed of the woman and the seed of the serpent. God predicted that these two seeds were destined for conflict ("enmity"). Through the long centuries ahead, Satan's offspring would wound the followers of Yahweh many times. Often Satan's bruising of God's people would seem more like fatal blows to the head than injuries to the foot. And at such times Satan and his followers would seem to go on with no injuries at all. During these periods—and there would be many—the seed of the woman would be able to discern God's working in the world only through eyes of faith. Yahweh had promised victory for His followers, but that victory would be many battles away.

Rome's Colosseum hosted many battles and became the scene of much bloodshed. Its current state of ruin reminds us of the end of all human civilizations.

Moral Decay and Judgment

The effects of sin on humanity did not take long to manifest themselves. Within the first generation after Adam and Eve, one son, Cain, murdered his brother Abel.

Cain went on to father a line of descendants whose activities are in many ways typical of human history. The Cainites, it seems, were the first to live in civilization. The first city mentioned in Scripture was built by Cain. The specialization that is always part of city life was carried on by Cain's descendants. Jabal worked in agriculture as a herdsman. Jubal labored in the arts, making musical instruments. And Tubal-cain worked in industry, producing all sorts of objects made of brass and iron. Whether they realized it or not, they were living out the implications of the Creation Mandate. They had been fruitful and therefore had multiplied over the face of the earth. Through specialization and organization, they had raised up the earliest human civilization.

The city of Jericho is thought to be the oldest city built after the Flood that has been excavated. This stone structure may have been used as an altar.

Nevertheless, their civilization was not pleasing to God. Their sin was not building and maintaining a city. Their sin was attempting to live out the Creation Mandate independent of God. Perhaps the best summary statement in Genesis for the problem with Cainite culture is the verse that introduces us to that culture: "And Cain went out from the presence of the Lord, and dwelt in the land of Nod" (Gen. 4:16). Living apart from the will and love of Yahweh was one of the core values that held Cainite civilization together.

Seth and His Seed

The story of Cain and his descendants is only part of the history of mankind after the Fall. God gave Adam and Eve another son. Eve named him **Seth** ("appointed"). She explained, "God . . . hath appointed me another seed instead of Abel" (Gen. 4:25). Seth proved to be a spiritual as well as a physical replacement for Abel. Just as Abel worshiped God in an acceptable manner, so Seth fathered a line of people who were known to "call upon the name of the Lord" (v. 26). Through Seth, the seed of the woman increased and prospered.

The Sethites, however, did not remain true to their God. Because of the reality of death, a godly people cannot remain godly unless it passes on to each new generation its love and devotion to God. At some point in their history, the Sethites allowed their children to intermarry with the Cainites. The Bible explains that Seth's descendants ("the sons of God") were attracted to the Cainite women ("the daughters of men") because "they were fair" (Gen. 6:2). As the previous generations of godly Sethites died and were replaced by the children of religiously mixed marriages, the line of Seth was transformed. Soon the

Artist's rendering of what the ark may have looked like. The foil in the back would have kept the ark facing the wind and the waves.

behavior of Seth's descendants was no different from that of Cain's people. The entire race became morally corrupt. Eventually, as the Bible declares, "every imagination of the thoughts of [man's] heart was only evil continually" (v. 5).

The Great Flood

Since the earth was no longer serving its purpose, God determined to remake His world. God was now preparing to cover the whole earth with a great flood. One man remained a committed worshiper of his Creator. **Noah** rejected the corrupting influences of the world and, like Enoch, "walked with God" (Gen. 6:9). To Noah God revealed His plan for the survival of the human race. He instructed Noah to build a massive ark. God told Noah that when he completed this project, he was to take his family and representatives of the animal kingdom into the ark, where they would be safe. Noah and his family obeyed. God held back His judgment for 120 years (Gen. 6:3). The human race had more than a century to repent and accept the promise of life offered through the ark. But in the end only Noah, his wife, his three sons, and their wives entered the ark. At the predetermined moment, the "foundations of the great deep" were broken up, and torrents of rain fell to the earth. It rained for forty days, and by the time it stopped, the entire earth was covered in water. The almighty Creator had caused the earth to return to its original state. Once again it was "without form, and void" (Gen. 1:2).

A Second Beginning

As the flood waters receded, the ark came to rest on the Ararat mountain range. As Noah left the ark, he entered a world newly reborn. The contaminating vestiges of the old world had been purged away. But sin still resided in the human heart.

One of Noah's earliest actions after the Flood was less than noble. He became intoxicated from the fruit of his own vineyard and fell asleep naked in his tent. This failure became the backdrop for one of history's most important

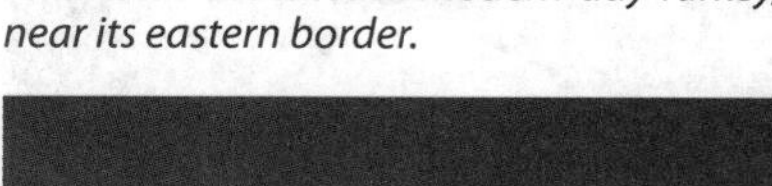

Mt. Ararat is located in modern-day Turkey, near its eastern border.

moments. Noah's son **Ham** saw his father in his shameful stupor and talked about him to his brothers, **Shem** and **Japheth**. Having proper respect and love for their father, these two sons entered Noah's tent with their backs turned and covered him with a garment.

Noah's Prophecy

When Noah realized what had happened, he punished Ham by placing a curse on **Canaan**, one of Ham's sons: "Cursed be Canaan; a servant of servants shall he be unto his brethren" (Gen. 9:25). But recognizing the noble deed of the other two sons, Noah blessed Shem and Japheth. He first spoke of Shem's future: "Blessed be the Lord God of Shem; and Canaan shall be his servant" (v. 26). Thus Noah indicated that Shem's future blessing would consist in his descendants' special relationship to Yahweh and that God would use the curse on Canaan to benefit Shem. Concerning Japheth, Noah prophesied, "God shall enlarge Japheth, and he shall dwell in the tents of Shem" (v. 27). Japheth would be blessed with wealth and power, and he would find additional blessing by sharing in Shem's blessing.

Here God suggested that Shem would somehow play a special role in the triumph of the seed of the woman. This triumph is foreshadowed in the curse on Canaan. The Canaanites, who eventually settled in a land they named for their ancestor, would end up serving the descendents of Shem. It should not surprise us, therefore, to find that much of biblical history traces God's working among the Hebrews, descendants of Shem, in a land that God took from the Canaanites.

Babel and Its Consequences

As years passed into decades, mankind once again multiplied and began to fill the earth. Civilization reemerged as city-building began again. But mankind did not want to establish many different civilizations. The race desired to live together and form a single, unified society.

At this time all of mankind spoke the same language. It was not difficult, therefore, for people to organize themselves. They gathered in the land of Shinar (probably located in southeastern Mesopotamia) and began to build the city that would later be called **Babel**. Central to this city was to be a magnificent tower, which would serve as this civilization's religious center. The reasons they gave for this undertaking are revealing: "Let us build us a city and a tower, whose top may reach unto heaven; and let us make us a name, lest we be scattered abroad upon the face of the whole earth" (Gen. 11:4).

The tower of Babel may have looked something like this reconstructed ziggurat.

God did not feel threatened by what was happening at Babel. But rather than unleashing His righteous anger, He chose to restrain our race's ability to do evil. He confused the minds of those at Babel so that they could no longer communicate with one another. In that hour, long ago, the complex and confusing differences among human languages were born.

The Rise of Nations

The human race eventually reorganized itself into people groups, each having a common language. It was probably during this period that the first nations arose. A **nation** is a very large group of people (usually including many cities) who have in common the same land area and the same language. Genesis 10 is

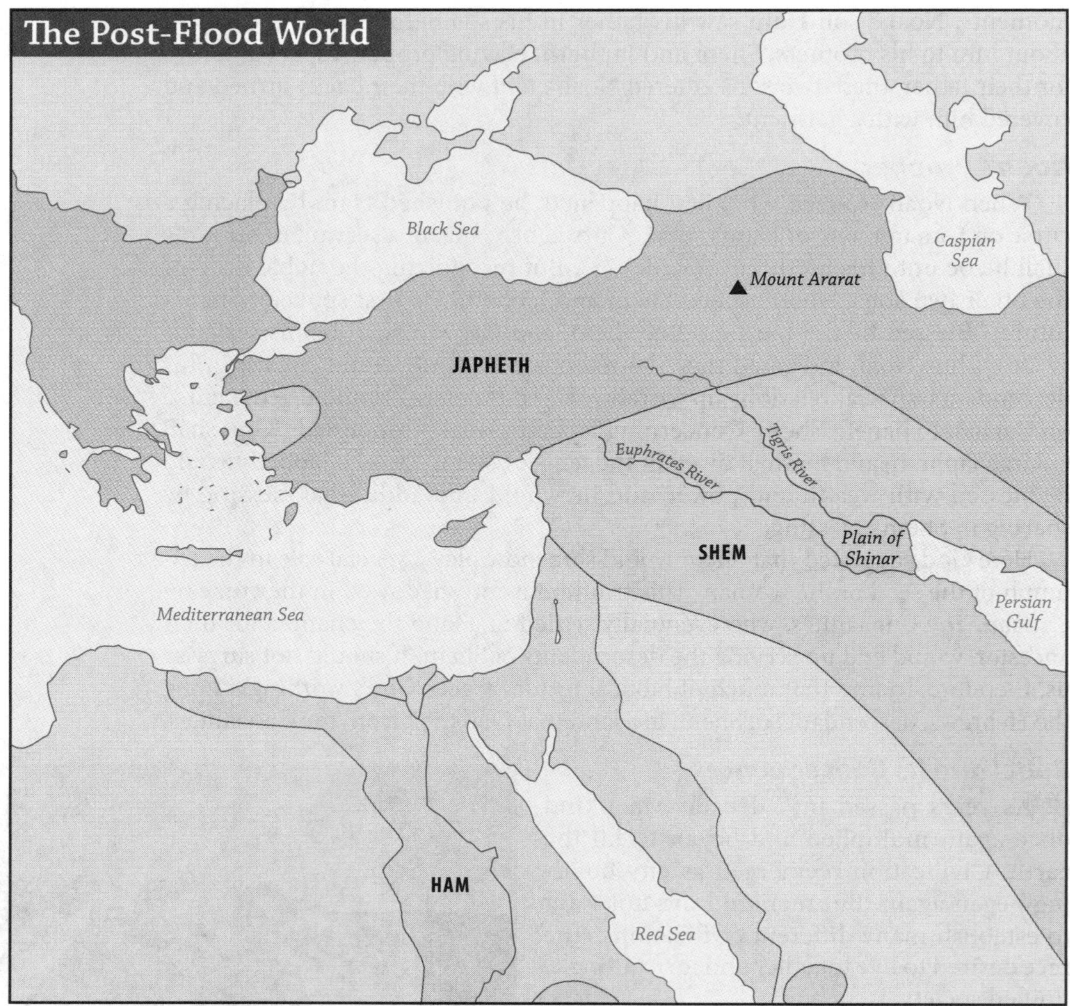

often referred to as the Bible's **Table of Nations** because it lists the descendants of Shem, Ham, and Japheth according to the nations that arose from their families. There we learn that Japheth's descendants founded nations in eastern Europe. Ham's descendants founded nations in eastern Asia and Africa. And Shem's descendants founded nations to the east and north of Ham's descendants.

Much of the rest of human history would be the story of one nation after another attempting to reestablish the ideal that the men of Babel sought. But as one nation would begin to succeed in setting up a man-centered one-world civilization, another would rise up and overthrow it. God manifests His mercy to our race beyond merely meeting humans' daily needs. His mercy is also evident in the decline and fall of great civilizations. By bringing them to an end before they gain permanent, worldwide authority, He restrains man from much of the destructive sinfulness of which he is capable.

Section Quiz

1. Who is history's most important person?
2. What detail in the Bible's account of Creation indicates that humans are God's great masterpiece?
3. Where does the Creation Mandate appear in Scripture, and what does this command include?
4. What is the chief inward effect of the Fall?
5. Where in the Bible do you find the thesis statement for human history?

★ Why was the Cainite civilization a wicked civilization?

Chapter 1 Review

Making Connections

1-4. Briefly outline the history of man from the birth of Seth to the Flood.

5. List the civilizations and kings mentioned in the book of Daniel. From the following references, name the kings Daniel served (Dan. 1:1; 5:1–2; 6:1–2; 10:1).

Developing History Skills

1. What can be learned about the land of Egypt from the prophecy of its destruction in Isaiah 19:1–10?

Thinking Critically

1. How are the rise and fall of empires a blessing from God?

Living in God's World

1. Write a brief essay about why you as a Christian should study history.
2. Write a brief essay that discusses why God chose to work out the plan of Redemption in history rather than simply redeeming Adam and Eve immediately after their sin.

People, Places, and Things to Know

primary sources
secondary sources
artifacts
tradition
written records
evaluation of historical sources
historical synthesis
historical interpretation
worldview
Christian worldview
divine providence
history
Yahweh
image of God
Creation Mandate
civilization
specialization
organization
Adam
Eve
seed of the serpent
seed of the woman
Seth
Noah
Ham
Shem
Japheth
Canaan
Babel
nation
Table of Nations

2

EARLY CIVILIZATIONS

The Plain of Gennesaret below the Arbel Cliffs

Israel is unique among the nations. All other nations followed after false gods, but God chose Israel to bring his blessings to these other nations. This blessing came primarily through the revelation that God gave to Israelite prophets (much of which is now preserved in the Old Testament). During this period of history, Israel was also to bless the nations by obeying God's Law. When the other nations saw the wisdom of God's law, they would be drawn to worship Israel's God. Sadly, aside from a few brief, shining moments in the reigns of David and Solomon, Israel failed at this mission. The nations which Israel was to bless became instruments of God to judge His wayward people.

Karnak Temple ruins

I. Mesopotamia

After God scattered the nations at the Tower of Babel, many of the descendants of Ham and Shem remained and settled in the fertile region of the Tigris and Euphrates Rivers (Gen. 10:6–32). Later the Greeks described this region with the word ***Mesopotamia*** (MES uh puh TAY mee uh), meaning the "land between the rivers." By about 3000 BC the people in the southern part of this area had established the Sumerian culture.

Sumerian Civilization

Sumer consisted of about a dozen independent city-states that had no political unity but possessed a similar culture. The cities fought constantly among themselves, each trying to gain dominance over the others. The Sumerians believed that their cities belonged to the gods. For this reason the temple was not only a place of worship but also the center of education, government, and trade. Each city had its own ruler, usually a priest, who acted as the representative of the gods.

The Sumerians' religion was a clear rejection of the one true God. They, along with almost all other civilizations until the coming of Christ, were committed to **polytheism** (belief in many gods). The fact that they were polytheistic even though they were historically near to the Flood and the witness of Noah testifies the truth of Romans 1:20–21. False religion does not result from a desire to find and know the true God. It is an attempt to replace the testimony to this God, found everywhere in this world, with a works religion.

Cuneiform

Much of what we know about Sumer has come from the discovery of thousands of clay tablets bearing **cuneiform** (KYOO nee uh form), the earliest known form of writing. Using a wedge-shaped stylus (a split reed), the Sumerians made impressions on tablets of wet clay, which they later baked until hard. They could express ideas by the manner in which they arranged these wedge-shaped impressions. Young men learned this complex writing in a formal educational system. Teachers were called "school-fathers," and the students were called "school-sons." Sumerian boys also studied the Sumerians' numerical system—a system based not on ten like ours today, but on the number sixty.

Early cuneiform tablet

Farming and Architecture

The major occupation of the Sumerians was farming. They built an elaborate network of canals and dikes to provide irrigation for their crops. Although agriculture was the basis of their economy, the people lived in fortified cities. They built their homes and public buildings with baked clay bricks. Temple towers called **ziggurats** (ZIG uh rats) are outstanding examples of Sumerian architecture. These impressive pyramid-like structures had terraces at different levels along their exterior. The bricks used in these buildings were often glazed in different colors.

Reconstructed ziggurat at Ur

Sargon

Near the end of Sumerian dominance, a new people migrated to the northern Sumerian cities. They adopted much of the Sumerian culture. At the same time, they began to assert their own influence on the cities in which they settled. Around 2270 BC the ruler **Sargon** came to power in the city-state of Kish. Sargon conquered other city-states and established the first known **empire**—the rule of one people over another. Making the city of Akkad his capital, he created a united kingdom—the Akkadian (uh KAY dee un) Empire—which stretched from the Persian Gulf to northern Mesopotamia. Under Sargon, the king's authority surpassed that of the priests. The people were encouraged to view the king as a god.

About a century after Sargon's death, the city of Ur rose to prominence. This powerful city-state may have been the same Ur that is mentioned in Genesis 11:31 as the birthplace of Abraham, the father of the Hebrew people. But whether "Ur of the Chaldees" (as the Bible calls it) was the well-known city of southern Mesopotamia is ultimately of little importance. What is important to know and remember is that the world into which Abraham was born was a world dominated by polytheism and idolatry. God revealed Himself to Abraham around 2100 BC. When He called Abraham to move out of Ur, He was not simply telling Abraham to leave his home. God was also telling him to leave his way of life—probably the only way of life Abraham had known.

Sumerian Contributions

By 2000 BC the Sumerian civilization had disappeared. However, aspects of its culture continued in later civilizations. For example, the Amorites, Hittites, Assyrians, and Persians used cuneiform. Roman architects adopted Sumerian building techniques such as the arch. Even today we use Sumerian inventions: the wheel, the division of a circle into 360 degrees, and the division of hours and minutes into sixty units. These influences testify of Sumerian knowledge and technological skill.

Amorite Civilization

Weakened by a series of wars with its neighbors, the Sumerian civilization, centered at Ur, fell to Amorite invaders. The Amorites established what is now referred to as the "Old Babylonian" Empire. Its capital was the city of Babylon (BAB uh lun), one of the greatest cities of the ancient world. The history of this city began shortly after the Flood, when Nimrod established a kingdom

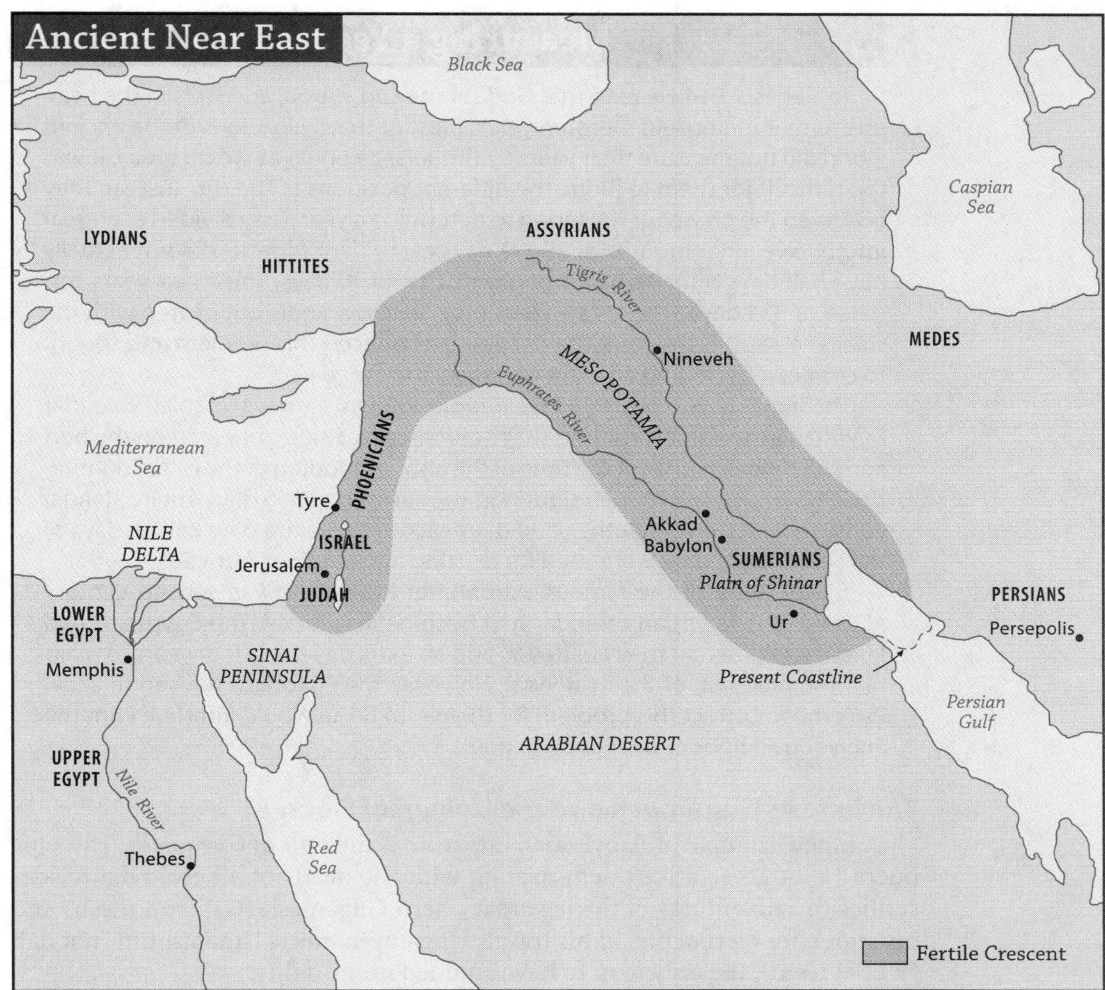

that included Babylon (Gen. 10:10). The Tower of Babel may have been built near this city.

Hammurabi (1795?–1750 BC)

The sixth king of the Amorites, **Hammurabi** (HAH moo RAH bee), united the land of Mesopotamia under his rule. He was a successful military leader and an able administrator. His large staff assisted in the building and maintenance of the canals for irrigation, in the collection of taxes, and in the administrative and business matters of the kingdom.

Hammurabi is best remembered for his code of laws. He developed this legal code by compiling, organizing, and simplifying existing laws. Hammurabi's code became the standard of judgment in moral, social, domestic, and commercial matters throughout the empire.

"To cause justice to prevail in the land, to destroy the wicked and the evil, that the strong might not oppress the weak"—this inscription introduced the 282 laws set forth in the code. Hammurabi had the code engraved in stone pillars and placed throughout the kingdom so that everyone would know the law. However, Hammurabi's law was arbitrary because the penalty for a particular offense varied with the social class of the offender. For example, if a man of the wealthy class broke a bone of a member of his own social class, his own bone was to be broken. If, however, such a man broke the bone of a commoner, he had only to pay a fine. Another flaw of Hammurabi's code was that it placed a higher value on property than on human life.

Stele containing Hammurabi's law code; the carving portrays the Babylonian god Shamash presenting the law to Hammurabi.

Measuring a Year

In Genesis 1:14 we read that God set the sun, moon, and stars in the heavens so that man could measure years. Most of the civilizations of the ancient world did not measure their years by the solar calendar as we do today. It was too difficult for them to judge the different positions of the sun. Instead they observed the phases of the moon to determine a year. They divided each year into twelve lunar months of 29 1/2 days each. Their months did not actually have half days but alternated between 29 and 30 days. Thus their years consisted of 354 days. After a few years they were markedly out of step with the solar year of 365 1/4 days. The Babylonians noticed this problem and sought to correct it by adding an extra month every few years.

The Egyptians were the first people known to have a solar calendar. Egyptian astronomers noticed that a certain star, Sirius, appeared on the horizon just before sunrise at the time of the annual flooding of the Nile. Counting the days between two such sightings, they arrived at 365 days. Their calendar consisted of twelve months of 30 days each plus 5 extra days called "days of the year." These days were used for feasting and religious festivals.

By the time of the famous astronomer Ptolemy in the second century AD, even the Egyptian calendar had become inaccurate. The Egyptians had failed to realize that they needed to add an extra day every four years to maintain the precision of their calendar. However, the Egyptians refused to allow Ptolemy to correct this problem for them—to do so would interfere with the ancient traditions of the Egyptian gods.

The Epic of Gilgamesh *and the Universal Flood*

A noted example of Babylonian literature is the *Epic of Gilgamesh*. This epic poem (a long narrative poem dealing with the deeds of a heroic figure) describes the adventures of the legendary hero Gilgamesh (GIL guh mesh) and his search for eternal life. In his travels Gilgamesh meets Utnapishtim (oot nah PEESH teem), the only man to have attained immortality.

One of the most interesting sections of the poem is Utnapishtim's account of how Ea, one of the gods, delivered him from a universal flood. Ea warned him that Enlil, one of the other gods, was angry and was planning to cover the earth with water. He told Utnapishtim to tear down his house and build a boat. Utnapishtim was also to take "the seed of all living things" aboard his boat.

Having built a boat, Utnapishtim gathered aboard his family, the craftsmen who helped him, and the animals of the field. The rains and flood raged for six days and nights and subsided on the seventh day.

Most ancient civilizations had similar legends. In all of these stories, a great flood destroys the human race except for a Noah-like figure through whom the human race is preserved. For the Christian, these similarities simply confirm the truth of the biblical account of Noah and the universal Flood (Gen. 6–8). The differences between these legends and the biblical record should be viewed as the result of mankind's tendency to mix truth with error. It is instructive to note that one of the most obvious differences between these ancient flood legends and Scripture is who is at fault for the deluge. While Genesis states clearly that man and his wickedness are to blame, the ancient legends tend to blame the caprice and selfishness of the gods. As the apostle Paul stated centuries later, when unbelieving human culture is confronted with the truth about itself, it tends to "hold [suppress] the truth in unrighteousness" (Rom. 1:18).

Amorite Accomplishments

The Amorites are also noted for their trade in gold, silver, tin, and textiles. They worked with algebra and geometry and made important contributions to the field of **astronomy** (the study of celestial bodies). However, they refused to acknowledge that "the heavens declare the glory of God" (Ps. 19:1). Instead of trusting God's control over the events of life, the Amorites resorted to a false method of interpreting human events and destiny by the position of the planets and stars—a practice that is called **astrology**.

Lacking able leadership after the death of Hammurabi, the Amorite civilization declined in both power and influence. Invaders came into the land and seized control of the territory of this once powerful kingdom.

Section Quiz

1. What did the Greeks call the fertile region between the Tigris and Euphrates Rivers?
2. What is the name of the Sumerian wedge-shaped form of writing?
3. Who established the first known empire? What became his capital city?
4. The Amorite civilization was centered in what capital city?
5. What is the difference between astronomy and astrology?

✯ What role did rivers play in ancient civilizations?

II. Egypt

Egypt is a desert land. Had it not been for the dry climate, the remains of Egypt—the monuments, the documents, and even the bodies of its rulers—would have crumbled or decayed long ago. Because so much has been preserved from this ancient civilization, we can learn a great deal about its fascinating history and culture.

The land of Egypt has served as another type of "preserver." God used Egypt as a special place of preservation for His people. The descendants of Abraham journeyed to Egypt to escape a severe famine in their land. They went with God's promise: "Fear not to go down into Egypt; for I will there make of thee a great nation" (Gen. 46:3). Centuries later Mary and Joseph with the Christ child likewise found safety in Egypt as they fled from the threats of King Herod (Matt. 2:13–21).

The Land of Egypt

Ancient Egypt was not the square-shaped territory that we call Egypt today. It was the narrow strip of land along the banks of the Nile River. It was about 750 miles long but in many places less than twelve miles wide. Because the Nile flows northward from the southern plateau, the southern region is called "Upper Egypt" and the northern region "Lower Egypt." These were really two entirely different lands. Upper Egypt lay close against the Nile, completely cut off from the outside world by desert to the east and west and by rapids (called "cataracts") to the south. Lower Egypt, on the other hand, spread out across the Nile Delta in easy contact with other nations by way of the Mediterranean Sea and the Sinai Peninsula.

One Greek historian called Egypt the "gift of the river." He was right. If there were no Nile, there would have been no Egypt. Because there was almost no rain there, only the Nile held back

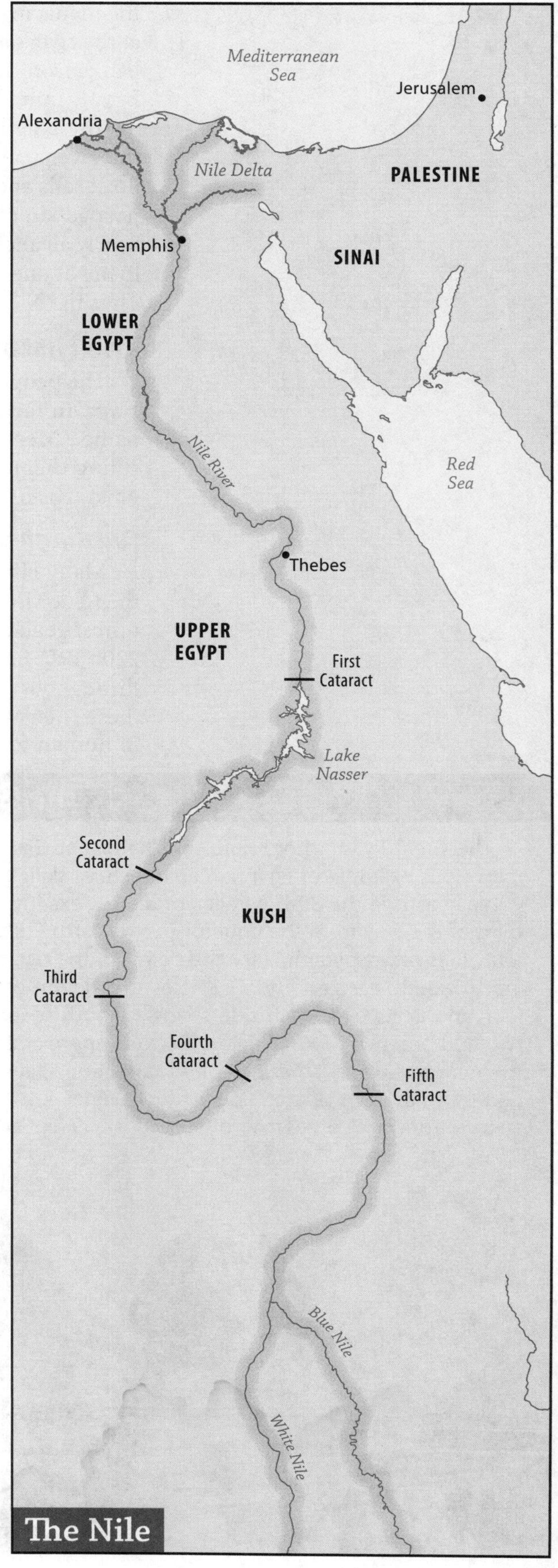

The Nile

the menacing desert wasteland. The river rose and fell every year. As the snow at the river's source in the mountains melted every spring, the river flooded its banks from June through August. This flooding deposited tons of rich silt on Egypt, annually providing fertile soil for the crops.

The Nile was also important as a highway. Boats at the northern end of the river (called the "delta" after the triangular Greek letter delta, Δ) could hoist sails and let the winds from the north push them upriver. To return they needed simply to drop their sails and let the current carry them back. Since nearly all ancient Egyptians lived on the banks of the river, it was easy for those living at one end of the kingdom to communicate with those at the other end. Thus the Nile greatly contributed to a unified Egypt.

The History of Egypt

The people of Egypt were descended from Mizraim, the son of Noah's son Ham. In fact, the Hebrews called Egypt "Mizraim." Around 3000 BC a man named **Menes** (MEE neez) united the two lands of Upper and Lower Egypt, ruling them from a capital that he called "White Walls" (later named Memphis). Historians refer to this time as the Early Dynastic Period.

Old Kingdom

Many Historians divide ancient Egyptian history into three major phases: the Old, Middle, and New Kingdoms. These phases are separated by times of unrest generally known as intermediate periods. The Old Kingdom (ca. 2700–2200 BC) has been called "The Age of the Pharaohs." There were **pharaohs** throughout all of ancient Egyptian history, of course, but in the Old Kingdom these rulers were especially powerful. The people considered them to be gods in human form. As "gods" they owned all of Egypt and used it for their own

The Great Pyramid

The Great Pyramid of Khufu (or Cheops) at Giza is a marvelous example of Egyptian architectural skill. It sits virtually astride the 30th parallel, or almost exactly one-third of the way from the equator to the North Pole. All four sides of the pyramid face the points of the compass (north, south, east, and west). It rises to a height of 481 feet, and at its base each side spans a length of nearly two and one-half football fields. It covers approximately thirteen acres, and amazingly, its foundation is almost perfectly flat from side to side; its level varies less than an inch from one corner to another over 1,069 feet away. In its construction the Egyptians used over two million stone blocks, the average weight of each being two and one-half tons. These mammoth blocks were so well placed that between some of them it is impossible to insert the blade of a knife. While the white limestone that graced its exterior has long since been stripped away (to be used in other building projects), the Great Pyramid remains a monument to the genius of the ancient Egyptians.

purposes. It was during this time that the great pyramids were built—huge tombs attesting to the splendor and might of the pharaohs. The most famous pharaoh of this age was **Khufu** (KOO foo), or Cheops, who built the Great Pyramid at Giza. Its construction required thousands of men working for twenty years.

Middle Kingdom

After a time of rebellion called "The First Intermediate Period," the Middle Kingdom, also known as "The Age of the People," began (ca. 2040–1783 BC). Aware of the social unrest that preceded them, the Egyptian pharaohs of this period directed their attention to projects that would benefit the country as a whole. As a result, the Middle Kingdom was characterized by peace and construction. For example, the Egyptians built irrigation canals and systems of ponds to store the Nile's waters for use in the dry season.

It was during this time of peace that the Israelites moved to Egypt (Gen. 46–50). God used the influence of Joseph (Abraham's great-grandson) to save the Egyptians from starvation and to provide a haven for the children of Israel during a time of famine (Gen. 47:1–6). The Israelites stayed in the land of Egypt for 430 years, from 1876 to 1446 BC (Exod. 12:40–41). During that time their numbers grew from seventy to over two million.

After the Middle Kingdom, in what has been called "The Second Intermediate Period," a foreign people called the Hyksos (HIK sose) came into the land and eventually became its rulers. It is not known exactly who they were or how they became so powerful. Many believe the Egyptians learned the art of war from the Hyksos. Evidently the Hyksos brought with them horses, chariots, and bronze weapons. It seems that the Hyksos were also responsible for beginning the enslavement of the Hebrews.

New Kingdom

Egypt eventually expelled the Hyksos and restored an Egyptian to the throne. This New Kingdom (ca. 1570–1075 BC) is also called "The Age of the Empire" because it was in this age that Egypt became a great power in the Near East. The pharaohs became "warrior-kings." They extended their control to Palestine, Syria, and the lands of the Nile (that is, to the south). In this age Upper Egypt became more important. As a result, Thebes became the Egyptian capital.

There are several pharaohs in this age that are of particular interest. One of the early rulers of the New Kingdom was **Hatshepsut** (hat SHEP soot), the first known woman ruler of Egypt. She may have been the "daughter of Pharaoh" who discovered Moses in the bulrushes and raised him as her own son (Exod. 2:5–10). Her rule was a peaceful one, and during her reign Egypt carried on extensive trade with nearby nations.

Hatshepsut's reign was followed by that of **Thutmose III** (thoot MO suh), regarded as the greatest Egyptian warrior-king. Under Thutmose, the Egyptian armies conquered Palestine and Syria, extending Egyptian rule all the way to the Euphrates River. One modern historian called Thutmose the "Napoleon of Egypt." Moses, another great leader, lived at this time. But Moses, by faith, "refused to be called the son of Pharaoh's daughter; choosing rather to suffer affliction with the people of God, than to enjoy the pleasures of sin for a season" (Heb. 11:24–25).

Thutmose III

Why Is There No Egyptian Record?

The Egyptians left no record of the Israelites in their land or the events of the Exodus. This leads some to doubt the accuracy of God's Word in the Book of Exodus. However, the Egyptians did not record losses in battle or invasions by other countries. Rather, they recorded victories and conquests. Therefore, it would have been out of character for them to record the fact that a large number of people they had enslaved had been led to freedom by an omnipotent God.

We should also note that the archaeological research for the era and location of the Israelite occupation is still underdeveloped. Future research could reveal evidence affirming the biblical account.

If current Egyptology is correct, Thutmose III was the pharaoh who refused to allow the children of Israel to go. He finally yielded after God sent ten plagues upon the land of Egypt (Exod. 7:8–11:10, 12:29–36). However, Pharaoh changed his mind and pursued the Hebrew people. God overwhelmed Pharaoh's chariots and horsemen by returning the waters of the Red Sea upon them (Exod. 14).

About a century and a half after the Hebrews left Egypt, **Rameses II** came to power. During his long reign, Egyptian rulers once again embarked on building mammoth temples and monuments. Egypt gradually declined from its rank as a Near Eastern power after his death.

The Culture of Egypt

The social structure of ancient Egypt was shaped like a pyramid: at the top was the pharaoh, supremely powerful; below him were the priests and nobles; then came the merchants, the common people, and the foreign slaves, in that order.

Most Egyptians were poor, but anyone from a lower class—even a foreign slave—could rise to a higher class if he gained the pharaoh's favor. This scenario

King Tut

Golden burial mask of Tutankhamen

About the middle of the fourteenth century BC, a nine-year-old boy named Tutankhamen became the pharaoh of Egypt. After a reign of ten years, he died and was buried in the Valley of the Kings at Thebes. The Egyptians stored great treasures in his tomb, as they did for every pharaoh. They did their best to conceal the burial sites of their pharaohs, but sooner or later most of them were plundered. Shortly after Tutankhamen's death, grave robbers broke into his tomb and stole many of the smaller precious objects that had been placed there. Even so, Tutankhamen's tomb remained nearly intact. Rock chips from another building project nearby soon covered his tomb; it remained forgotten until the twentieth century.

In 1922 British archaeologists Howard Carter and the Earl of Carnarvon found the tomb after many years of digging in the valley. Many experts consider this the greatest archaeological discovery of all time: no Egyptian tomb had ever been found in such a marvelous state of preservation. Over a period of eight years, Carter and his assistants removed, catalogued, and restored several thousand objects found in the tomb. (Carnarvon had died in 1923.) Carter and other archaeologists were amazed at the great wealth that they found—especially because Tutankhamen was a relatively unimportant pharaoh. They could only imagine what might have been buried in the tombs of Egypt's great pharaohs.

The discovery of the Rosetta Stone enabled Jean Champollion to read Egyptian hieroglyphics.

is illustrated by Joseph, a Hebrew slave who became the second most powerful man in Egypt.

Unlike women in other ancient cultures, Egyptian women were especially favored in their society. For example, women could own property and operate a business. They could also occupy religious positions as priestesses. As we have seen, one woman even became a great pharaoh.

The legacy left by the Egyptian civilization is truly great. The Egyptians made important advances in the field of medicine—they increased the knowledge of anatomy and prescribed drugs as remedies for diseases. They also developed a solar calendar, dividing the year into 365 days. They used a form of picture writing called **hieroglyphics** (HY er uh GLIF iks) and developed a type of paper made from reeds of the papyrus plant. (It is from the word *papyrus* that we get our word *paper*.) They drew upon their understanding of geometry and astronomy to build the pyramids, some of the most amazing architectural achievements of the ancient world.

The Egyptian religion was polytheistic. The people considered the pharaohs to be gods, but there were many other gods as well: animals, natural forces, and especially the Nile itself. The most important gods were Amen and Ra (who later became one god, Amen-Ra, the sun-god), and Osiris and Isis, the husband and wife who ruled the underworld.

The Egyptians believed that after death they would be judged according to their works. If their works were good enough, they would spend their afterlife in a place of peace—fishing, hunting, and relaxing. The pharaohs' tombs and those of other important men were filled with objects for them to enjoy in the next world. However, the Egyptians believed that these pleasures could not be enjoyed unless the body was preserved. Thus they developed the practice of embalming, or preserving, corpses. Today mummies of the Egyptians lie in museums, preserved by the embalmer's skill and centuries of desert dryness.

Tomb of Rameses VI

The greatness of ancient Egypt is no more. After the New Kingdom, Egypt fell successively to the Assyrians, the Persians, the Greeks, and the Romans. God's reasons for judging the Egyptians are stated in many different places in the Old Testament. In addition to their worship of false gods, the Egyptians were condemned for their pride, a vice that has often kept people and nations from repenting and trusting the true God: "Thus saith the Lord God; Behold, I am against thee, Pharaoh king of Egypt...which hath said, My river is my own, and I have made it for myself" (Ezek. 29:3). Such arrogance ultimately leads to divine humiliation: "[Egypt] shall be the basest of the kingdoms; neither shall it exalt itself any more above the nations" (v. 15). But in God's judgment He does not forget His mercy. The Bible also speaks of a coming day of blessing for Egypt (Isa. 19:22).

Section Quiz

1. To what river was a Greek historian referring when he called Egypt the "gift of the river"?
2. List the three major periods of ancient Egyptian history.
3. Who is called the "Napoleon of Egypt"?
4. Who was atop the social structure of ancient Egypt?
5. What technique did the Egyptians develop to preserve corpses?

★ How would you explain the lack of archaeological evidence for Israel's sojourn in Egypt?

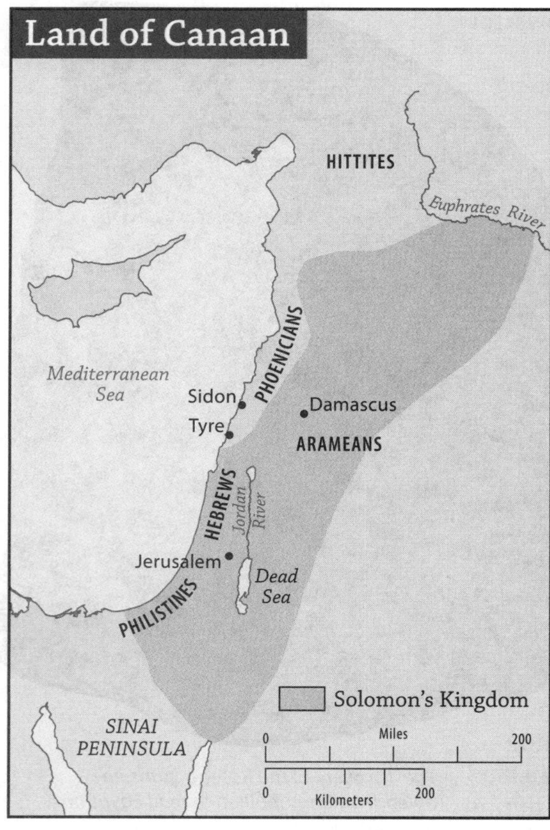

III. Land of Canaan

The land of Canaan was named for Canaan, one of Ham's sons. Most of the inhabitants of Canaan were descendants of this son of Ham. This land is very important to the story of God's working in mankind and was the land of promise for God's chosen people, the Israelites. "Every place that the sole of your foot shall tread upon, that have I given unto you. . . . From the wilderness and this Lebanon even unto the great river, the river Euphrates, all the land of the Hittites, and unto the great sea [Mediterranean] toward the going down of the sun, shall be your coast" (Josh. 1:3–4). After leaving Egypt, the children of Israel wandered in the wilderness for forty years before they reached the Promised Land. As the Hebrew people entered the land, they encountered numerous peoples. Three of them—the Hittites, the Phoenicians (fih NEESH unz), and the Arameans (AIR uh MEE unz) (or Syrians)—interacted with the Hebrew people and made notable contributions to the culture of the ancient world.

The Hittites

Before the twentieth century little was known about the Hittites. Many people did not even believe that they had ever existed because the Old Testament was the only source of information concerning them. The Hittites were the descendants of Heth, the son of Canaan and the grandson of Ham (Gen. 10:15). Biblical references to the Hittites include Abraham's purchase of a burial site from Ephron the Hittite (Gen. 23:1–20; 25:7–10) and King David's murder of Uriah the Hittite to cover up his sin with Bathsheba (2 Sam. 11:3–27).

Archaeological discoveries around the turn of the twentieth century confirmed the existence of the Hittite Empire. The Hittites may have begun to settle in Asia Minor about 2000 BC. They were not ruled by priests or gods like the Sumerians and Egyptians. The Hittite king was the commander of the army. His power rested upon the support of the chief warriors. Controlling rich supplies of iron ore, the Hittites excelled in the production of iron. With their military skill and their work in iron, they became feared by other people.

Using iron weapons and horse-drawn chariots, the Hittites extended their empire throughout Asia Minor and into the **Fertile Crescent** (which takes its name from the crescent-shaped fertile region encompassing Mesopotamia and the land of Canaan). They raided the Amorite capital of Babylon and later took control of Syria. This expansion brought them into conflict with the Egyptian empire, which was also expanding into that area. Constant fighting between the Hittites and the Egyptians weakened them both and led to their mutual decline. This event gave the Phoenicians, the Arameans, and the Hebrews an opportunity to establish independent kingdoms. Once a major power in Asia Minor and the northern Fertile Crescent, the Hittites were absorbed by more advanced cultures and gradually passed into obscurity.

Hittite statue of a bull

The Phoenicians

In Ezekiel 27:3–4 and verse 33, the prophet Ezekiel described the city of Tyre as proud and enamored with acquiring wealth. For more than a thousand years, Tyre was the leading city-state of Phoenicia. Containing many independent city-states, Phoenicia was located along the eastern coast of the Mediterranean Sea (where Lebanon is today). The Phoenicians were a Canaanite people. The earliest Phoenician city was probably Sidon, founded by Canaan's firstborn son, Sidon (Gen. 10:15).

Merchants of the Mediterranean

The Phoenicians appeared around 2000 BC and became the greatest merchants of their day. With their large merchant fleet, they traded with areas all around the Mediterranean Sea—Egypt, Greece, Sicily, Spain, and North Africa. Spices, fine linen, wheat, cattle, horses, ivory, gold, precious stones, and tin (used to harden copper) were just some of the items handled by these traders.

The Phoenicians also gained great wealth through two valuable natural resources. The first was a type of mollusk (a sea animal similar to a snail) found off the Phoenician coast. The Phoenicians obtained a purple dye from this sea animal. Purple-dyed cloth became one of their chief exports. (The word *Phoenicia* comes from the Greeks, who called the Phoenicians the "purple people" or the "traders of purple.") The second natural resource was the cedar and fir trees found in the Lebanon mountains. Phoenicia supplied the cedars that King Solomon used to build the temple in Jerusalem. In fact, Solomon used many precious materials from the commercial city of Tyre in building the temple (1 Kings 5).

In their travels Phoenician merchants sailed to the farthest reaches of the Mediterranean Sea and to Britain; some historians believe they sailed around Africa and possibly even traveled west to the North American continent. The Phoenicians planted colonies all along the Mediterranean coastline. Colonies such as Carthage would later reach greater heights than the Phoenician cities in Palestine.

Top: Mollusk
Bottom: Cedar tree in Lebanon

The Phoenician Alphabet

The Phoenicians are believed to be the originators of the alphabet. By the eleventh century BC, the cuneiform writing of the Sumerians and the hieroglyphics of the Egyptians had been in use for centuries. The Phoenicians developed uniform symbols to stand for distinct sounds. By arranging letters representing sounds, they could form an almost infinite number of words. Writing then became simple enough for most people to understand. The Greeks and the Romans later adapted this alphabet for their own use and passed it on to future generations.

The City of Tyre

Phoenician independence was lost during the ninth and eighth centuries BC as the Assyrians invaded the territory along the coast and exacted tribute from the wealthy city-states. However, Tyre, the leading Phoenician city-state, continued to thrive, its trade unhampered by the Assyrians. Long before the Assyrian invasion, Tyre had expanded to an island about a half mile off the coast. From this island fortress it was safe from land attack. Massive walls around the island city and a strong navy protected Tyre from sea attack as well.

The wealth and prosperity of Tyre was short-lived. The people of Tyre and the other Phoenician cities rejected the knowledge of the true God by worshiping **Baal,** one of the Canaanites' gods. The Phoenicians were also largely responsible for the growth of paganism in Israel. It was Jezebel, the daughter of the king of Sidon, who married King Ahab and introduced Baal-worship in

Ruins of Tyre

Israel. Because of Tyre's great commerce, pride entered the people's hearts. The prophet Ezekiel addressed them, "Thine heart is lifted up because of thy riches" (Ezek. 28:5). Tyre also laughed at the calamity of the people of God when Nebuchadnezzar destroyed Jerusalem. For these reasons the prophet Ezekiel declared that God would cause many nations to destroy this city (Ezekiel 26:3–5).

In addition, Ezekiel foretold that Nebuchadnezzar, king of Babylon, would come and besiege the city (Ezek. 26:7–11). Nebuchadnezzar did come, and he besieged Tyre for thirteen years. He destroyed the mainland portion of the city but failed to destroy the island portion. Alexander the Great, more than two hundred years later, continued the fulfillment of this prophecy regarding Tyre's removal as a commercial power. By pushing the ruins of mainland Tyre into the sea, Alexander's men built a causeway out to the island city. His forces conquered the city, killing thousands and taking many thousands captive. The plunder of Tyre continued in the centuries to follow.

The Arameans

Syria (or Aram) is often called the "crossroads of civilizations." Through the centuries this land has been the link between Asia and Africa, the "melting pot" of the Middle Eastern cultures, and the passageway of conquering armies. The Arameans, called Syrians in the King James Version, were descendants of Aram the son of Shem (Gen. 10:22). They settled throughout Syria and northern Mesopotamia. Around 1000 BC the Arameans established a number of small independent states. Although of little political importance, this people had a profound effect on the ancient world in other ways.

As the Phoenicians created a commercial empire by sea, the Arameans established one by land. Damascus, one of the oldest continuously inhabited cities in the world, became a capital of international trade. It was centrally located among the land routes of the Near East. Aramean camel caravans transported goods throughout the ancient world.

To facilitate trade, the language of the Arameans, called Aramaic, was used as a "go-between" language among the nations of the Fertile Crescent. Later, Aramaic became the common spoken language of the entire region. This is probably the language that Jesus and His disciples spoke.

The Israelites were the neighbors of the Arameans. David and Solomon conquered many of the Aramean cities, but with the division of the Hebrew nation after Solomon, constant fighting took place between the Arameans and the Hebrews. God used the Arameans to punish His people (2 Kings 13:3). Later, because of the wickedness of the people of Damascus, God pronounced the destruction of the Aramean civilization (Amos 1:3–5). In 732 BC the Assyrians crushed Damascus and took the people away as captives.

The Hebrews

The Call of Abraham

"Get thee out of thy country, and from thy kindred, and from thy father's house, unto a land that I will shew thee: and I will make of thee a great nation, and I will bless thee, and make thy name great; and thou shalt be a blessing: and I will bless them that bless thee, and curse him that curseth thee: and in thee shall all families of the earth be blessed" (Gen. 12:1–3). With these words God called **Abraham** out of Mesopotamian paganism and set in motion a series of events that will one day culminate in the second coming of His Son to earth in triumph, glory, and peace. In this call God made a covenant with Abraham (called the **Abrahamic Covenant**) that expresses very briefly God's plan for redeeming His fallen world to Himself. The covenant is composed of three basic promises. First, God promised Abraham a great seed, or group of descendants. This seed would grow to become a mighty nation from which God would raise up the Messiah (Hebrew for "the anointed one"). The Messiah would bless God's people by saving them from their sins and ruling over them in goodness and justice. Second, God promised to give Abraham's seed a land to live in, the land of Canaan. Third, God promised that, through this seed and through this land, He would bless all the peoples of the earth. This final promise is, for the Christian, the summary statement for human history. It is a declaration that finds its earliest expression in God's promise to the Serpent in Eden: "I will put enmity between thee and the woman, and between thy seed and her seed; it shall bruise thy head, and thou shalt bruise his heel" (Gen. 3:15). And it finds its consummation in history's greatest "Hallelujah": "The kingdoms of this world are become the kingdoms of our Lord, and of his Christ; and he shall reign for ever and ever" (Rev. 11:15). The story of our race is the story of how God is working to make the disobedient kingdoms of this world the kingdom of His Messiah, His own Son.

Abraham was born in 2166 BC. When God called him (ca. 2091 BC), Abraham was himself an idolater (cf. Josh. 24:2–3). God chose Abraham not because he was a better person than the other inhabitants of Ur but because He is a gracious God. He told Abraham that he would be the father of a great nation, even though his wife could not have children and the land God brought him to was occupied by other people groups. Despite these obstacles, Abraham believed God and obeyed. In time God fulfilled His promise by providing the aged Abraham with a son, Isaac, through whom the chosen line was to come. This line of blessing continued through Isaac's son Jacob. The descendants of these patriarchs are called the children of Israel, taking their name from Jacob, whose name God changed to Israel.

Bondage in Egypt

Jacob and his family went down into Egypt to escape a famine in Canaan. God had already provided for His people in Egypt by giving **Joseph** (one of Jacob's sons) a place of leadership. It was in Egypt that God revealed through Jacob that the future nation of Israel would be composed of twelve tribes, each descending from one of Jacob's twelve sons (Gen. 49). The most important of these tribes, Jacob revealed, would be **Judah**. From this patriarch Israel's kings would come, the greatest of these kings being the Messiah Himself (v. 10). In Egypt Jacob's descendants became a numerous people—the Israelites. Once a place of refuge and prosperity for the Israelites, Egypt became a place of hardship. A pharaoh who did not remember (or acknowledge) what Joseph had done for Egypt inflicted heavy burdens on the Hebrew people. God remembered his people, however, and raised up **Moses** to lead them from the land of bondage to the Promised Land. The children of Israel left Egypt in 1446 BC and crossed the Red Sea bound for the land of Canaan.

Mount Sinai

The Covenant at Sinai

One of the most important events in Hebrew history occurred in the wilderness at Mount Sinai (Exod. 19–20). There God established Israel as a theocracy—a people governed directly by God. God established His covenant with the children of Israel, promising to be ever present with them. God governed His people by communicating His will through leaders He ordained, such as Moses and Joshua. The centerpiece of the covenant at Sinai was the law of God. God's law gave them instruction, guidelines, and judgments in moral, civil, and ceremonial matters. God's law provides for all time a perfect moral standard by which men can distinguish right from wrong.

Divisions of Hebrew History

I. Patriarchal	2166–1876 BC
II. Egyptian	1876–1446 BC
III. Wilderness	1446–1406 BC
IV. Conquest	1406–1389 BC
V. Judges	1389–1050 BC
VI. United Kingdom	1050–930 BC
VII. Divided Kingdom	930–586 BC
VIII. Exile	586–538 BC
IX. Persian	538–332 BC
X. Hellenistic	332–168 BC
XI. Maccabean	168–63 BC
XII. Roman	63 BC–AD 70

The Conquest of Canaan

Though blessed with the very presence of God, the children of Israel often chose to sin. This was illustrated when Moses sent twelve spies into Canaan to search out the land (Num. 13:1–16). As the reports came back that the land was filled with giants and walled cities, the people forgot God's promises and rebelled against the Lord out of fear. Because of this rebellion, the children of Israel had to wander in the wilderness. That generation died along the way, never inhabiting the Promised Land (Num. 14:20–35). After forty years the next generation of the children of Israel crossed over the Jordan River into the land "flowing with milk and honey." Under a new leader, **Joshua**, they began their conquest of the land of Canaan. Jewish forces destroyed Jericho and Ai and defeated the many different peoples of the land. Then they divided the land among the twelve tribes of Israel (Josh. 14–22).

The Judges

After the death of Joshua, "every man did that which was right in his own eyes" (Judges 17:6, 21:25). God had intended that the Hebrew people demonstrate to the ancient world that there is but one living God. In an age dominated by polytheism, He wanted them to be sincerely committed to **monotheism** (belief in only one God). But the children of Israel turned from the true God to worship the false gods of the Canaanites. Because of their disobedience, God raised up enemies to oppress Israel. This oppression caused the children of Israel to turn back to God and cry out for mercy. God heard their cries and raised up leaders, called judges, through whom He ruled His people and delivered them from their oppressors (Judges 2:16–18).

During the judgeship of Samuel, the Israelites again rejected God's rule, desiring a human king to rule over them instead (1 Sam. 8:4–8). Saul became the first king of Israel. He united all the tribes of Israel under his leadership and led Israel in victories over the Philistines and the Amalekites. Nevertheless, he failed to obey the commands of God, and God rejected him as king (1 Sam. 15).

David and Solomon

God chose **David**, a man "after God's own heart," as the next king. From his family the promised Messiah would come. King David firmly established the Hebrew kingdom. He conquered Israel's enemies, enlarged Israel's borders, and established peace throughout the land. Jerusalem, the "city of David," became the center of worship and government for the Hebrew kingdom (2 Sam. 5:6–10).

The kingdom of Israel reached its peak during the reign of David's son **Solomon**. Visiting dignitaries, such as the Queen of Sheba, marveled at the wealth

Remains of the entrance to Solomon's fortress at Megiddo

and wisdom of this Hebrew king (1 Kings 10:1–13). Supplied with materials from Phoenicia, Solomon built the magnificent temple of God that his father David had planned. Before the end of Solomon's reign, however, he began to permit the worship of false gods in Israel. God, therefore, revealed to Solomon that He would judge Israel by dividing the nation in two.

Division and Judgment

God used Solomon's oppressive taxation policy to bring this division about. Following the death of Solomon, the Hebrew people came to Rehoboam, the new king, and begged him to lower their taxes. Rehoboam decided to increase the taxes instead (1 Kings 12:1–15). Outraged at this decision, the ten northern tribes of Israel rebelled and made Jeroboam their king. The southern tribes of Benjamin and Judah became the kingdom of Judah, remaining loyal to Rehoboam and the house of David (1 Kings 12:19–24).

The Hebrew nation, now divided, lost the greatness and peace achieved under the reigns of David and Solomon. Wickedness increased among both the people of Israel and the people of Judah. Peace was replaced by strife and constant warfare. Isaiah and Jeremiah, as well as other prophets, warned God's people of coming judgment, but their warnings went unheeded.

Judgment came upon the disobedient people of God. In 722 BC the Assyrians destroyed Samaria (the capital of the northern kingdom of Israel) and carried its people away captive. The Chaldeans (kal DEE unz) under Nebuchadnezzar (r. 605–562 BC) destroyed Jerusalem in 586 BC and carried many of the Jews back to Babylon. This period of exile, known as the **Babylonian Captivity**, lasted seventy years.

Nevertheless, God did not forsake His people, and He did not forget the Abrahamic Covenant. God raised up the Persians to free His people and restore them once again to their land. By renewing His promise of a seed for Abraham and of a land for that seed, God was keeping alive His promise to bless all the nations of the earth through the coming of the Messiah.

Section Quiz

1. What two major weapons did the Hittites use as they expanded their empire into Asia Minor?
2. What language served as a "go-between," or international language, among the people of the Fertile Crescent?
3. Name the three promises that make up the Abrahamic Covenant.
4. What is special about the third promise?
5. Define *theocracy*.

★ God promised to bless David (2 Samuel 7) and Solomon (1 Kings 3). Which promise was unconditional?

IV. Near Eastern Empires

"The most High ruleth in the kingdom of men, and giveth it to whomsoever he will, and setteth up over it the basest of men" (Dan. 4:17). God uses nations to accomplish His purpose in history. We can see in the ancient world how God used the Assyrians and the Chaldeans as instruments of judgment on the Hebrews. In a similar manner God used the Persians to preserve the Jews. Even so, these kingdoms were not excused from the consequences of their own wickedness. God's judgment eventually fell on them too.

The Assyrian Empire

The Assyrians created the largest empire the world had seen prior to 550 BC. For centuries they dwelt in northern Mesopotamia along the Tigris River, but

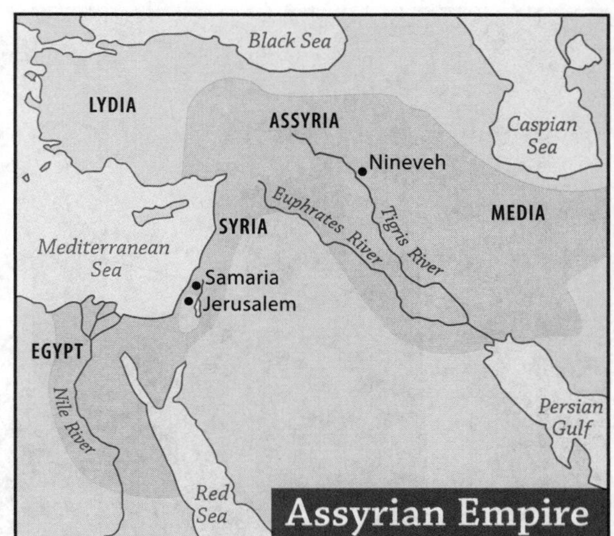

Assyrian Empire

by the eighth century BC they had built a vast empire that encompassed the Fertile Crescent, Egypt, and part of Asia Minor. Nineveh, the city built by Nimrod shortly after the Flood (Gen. 10:11), became the capital city of the empire.

The Assyrians were indebted to the previous Mesopotamian cultures; their gods, language, art, architecture, science, and literature were in large part adapted from the Sumerian and Amorite cultures. The Assyrians preserved many contributions of the earlier civilizations and spread these accomplishments throughout the ancient world by their military conquests.

Assyrian military might was unmatched by any other civilization of the day. The Assyrian army was equipped with iron weapons, siege towers, battering rams, and war chariots. Its well-trained foot soldiers, spearmen, archers, and cavalry wreaked havoc on the people of the Near East. They terrorized nations with threats of destruction, hoping to gain their submission without the use of force. They earned a reputation for fierceness and cruelty—it was not uncommon for them to butcher, mutilate, burn at the stake, or skin alive their defeated foes. They also practiced mass deportation—removing conquered people from their own land and settling them in a foreign country.

God's Judgment

God used this ungodly, war-loving people as His instrument for venting His wrath against sinful nations and to chasten His disobedient people. In Isaiah 10:5–6 God described Assyria as a rod and staff in His hand that He would use to punish Israel.

Under Tiglathpileser (tig lath puh LEE zer), the Assyrians captured the Aramean capital of Damascus. Ten years later, in 722 BC, the Assyrian army led by **Sargon II** destroyed Samaria and took captive the ten northern tribes of Israel (2 Kings 17). Later, Assyrian armies invaded Egypt and seized much of its territory.

Mercy and Judgment

The Assyrians did not acknowledge God and were not aware of His workings. They became arrogant because of their conquests. Under **Sennacherib** (sih NAK er ib) they tried to take Jerusalem during the reign of King Hezekiah. As the Assyrians prepared to take the city, the agents of Sennacherib, standing outside the walls of Jerusalem, boasted of the conquests and might of the Assyrian army (2 Kings 18:13–35). But God through His prophet Isaiah pronounced: "I will punish the fruit of the stout heart of the king of Assyria, and the glory of his high looks. For he saith, By the strength of my hand I have done it, and by my wisdom; for I am prudent" (Isa. 10:12–13). God sent the Angel of the Lord, who killed 185,000 men of Sennacherib's army as they slept (2 Kings 19:35). Sennacherib went home in defeat and was murdered by two of his own sons.

Although the Assyrians were among the most ruthless people of the ancient world, God showed mercy to them. God sent Jonah to Nineveh to preach repentance: "Arise, go to Nineveh, that great city, and cry against it; for their wickedness is come up before me" (Jon. 1:2). As this heathen city "turned from their evil way" (Jon. 3:10), God turned away His wrath. What a great example of God's mercy!

The people of Nineveh, however, eventually returned to their wicked ways, and God's mercy turned to wrath (Nah. 1–3). In 612 BC Chaldean and Median armies completely destroyed Nineveh and brought the Assyrian Empire to an end.

Reconstruction of the Ishtar Gate of Babylon

The Chaldean Empire

Nebuchadnezzar of Babylon

Babylon was one of the oldest and grandest of all the cities of the ancient world. Empires had come and gone, but Babylon had remained. Babylon had been the capital of previous civilizations, but not until the sixth century BC did it reach the height of its glory.

Shortly before 1000 BC a group of Semitic people, the Chaldeans, began to settle around Babylon. Lacking unity, they were constantly subdued by Assyrian kings. Later, however, the Chaldeans allied themselves with the Medes and helped destroy Nineveh in 612 BC. During the reign of **Nebuchadnezzar** (neb uh kud NEZ er), the "New Babylonian" Empire reached it height.

The ancient world was amazed at the sudden rise to power of the Chaldeans. Jeremiah, the prophet of the Lord, explained Nebuchadnezzar's success. Jeremiah declared that God had given Nebuchadnezzar control over many kingdoms, for a period of time, to accomplish His will (Jer. 27:5–7).

God used Nebuchadnezzar, whom He called His "servant," to punish other nations for their disobedience to Him. For example, in 605 BC Nebuchadnezzar defeated the Egyptian armies under Pharaoh Necho, who tried to conquer Syria and Palestine. Likewise, God allowed Nebuchadnezzar to destroy Jerusalem as previously stated. The dispersion of the Jewish people is known as the **Diaspora**, or "scattering." Under Nebuchadnezzar, the Chaldeans briefly became the masters of the Fertile Crescent.

Nebuchadnezzar is remembered not only for his military accomplishments but also for building up Babylon as "the glory of kingdoms, the beauty of the Chaldees' excellency" (Isa. 13:19). The ancient Greek historian Herodotus said of Babylon, "In magnificence there is no other city that approaches it." Inner and outer walls, some of which were said to tower over three hundred feet, surrounded the city. According to Herodotus, the walls were so thick that chariots, two abreast, could ride on top of them. The city was further protected by a moat surrounding the outside walls.

The Babylonian "hanging gardens" were one of the wonders of the ancient world. The gardens were probably built by Nebuchadnezzar for his Median wife, who missed the trees and flowers of her homeland. Supported by brick arches, these terraced gardens, containing tropical plants and trees, were the pride of ancient Babylon. The river Euphrates, which ran under the wall and through the midst of the city, watered the gardens and provided a water supply for the city.

Astronomy

The Chaldeans continued the interest in astronomy that had been popular during the Amorite civilization and made additional contributions to the field. They charted the positions of planets and stars, named constellations, and predicted eclipses. As did others who preceded and followed them, they accepted the belief that the position of the sun in relationship to the stars and planets influenced human destiny.

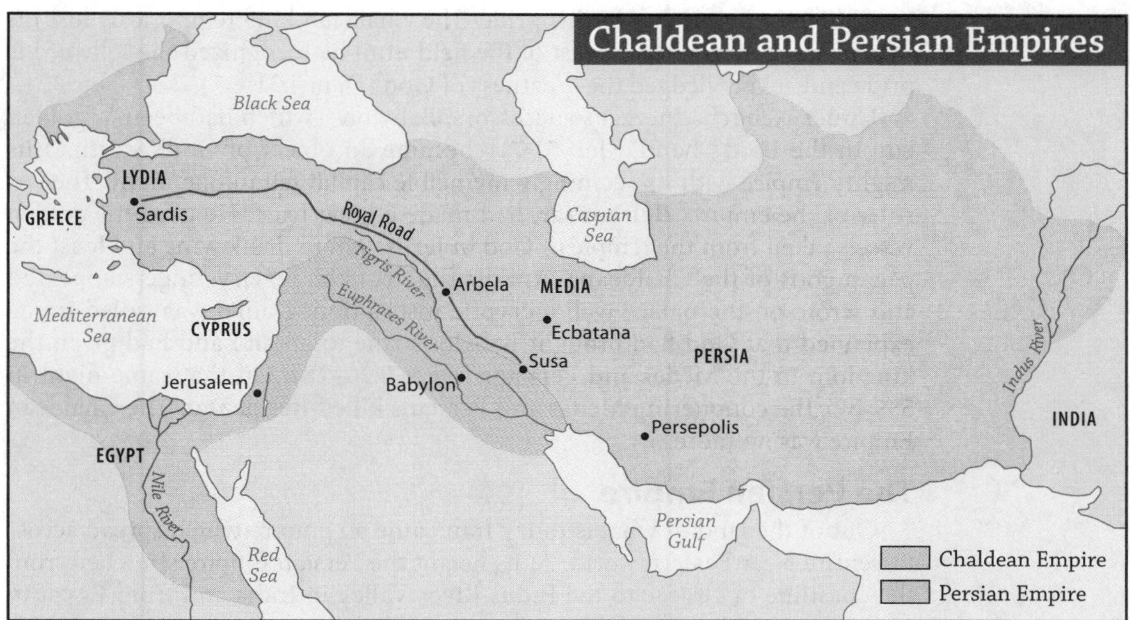

From the book of Daniel, we learn that the "wise men"—astrologers, magicians, and sorcerers—had an important place in Chaldean society. The king often called upon them for advice. Although they claimed the power to interpret dreams and tell the future, these so-called wise men were false prophets. Time and again they proved themselves unable to interpret the king's dreams (Dan. 2:10–11; 5:8). On one occasion Daniel came before King Nebuchadnezzar and said, "The secret which the king hath demanded cannot the wise men, the astrologers, the magicians, the soothsayers, shew unto the king; but there is a God in heaven that revealeth secrets, and maketh known . . . what shall be in the latter days" (Dan. 2:27–28).

God's Wrath

The glories of the Chaldean Empire did not last even a century. Nebuchadnezzar had learned of God's power from the Hebrew captive Daniel. But he viewed his accomplishment out of a heart of pride. Nebuchadnezzar said, "Is not this great Babylon, that I have built for the house of the kingdom by the might of my power, and for the honour of my majesty?" (Dan. 4:30). God

Belshazzar as Co-Ruler

The Bible is silent about events in Babylon occurring between chapters four and five of the book of Daniel. Through secular sources we know that several people struggled to gain control of Babylon following the death of Nebuchadnezzar. In chapter five of Daniel's book we read of the last person to sit on the throne of the Chaldean Empire—King Belshazzar. Following the writing on the wall, Belshazzar offered to give third place in the kingdom to anyone who could interpret the cryptic message. For many years skeptics pointed to this as an error in the Bible. However, modern research has revealed that Belshazzar was co-ruler with his father, Nabonidus. Thus, the next position that Belshazzar could offer was the third position of rule over the Chaldean Empire. This is another example of the fact that although the Bible does not provide us with every detail of history, whenever the Bible speaks of a historical event, it is always accurate.

judged Nebuchadnezzar for his pride. The Chaldean king temporarily lost his throne and became like a beast of the field until he recognized the folly of his pride and acknowledged the greatness of God (Dan. 4:31–37).

Under Nebuchadnezzar's successors, Babylon—which had been a "golden cup in the Lord's hand" (Jer. 51:7)—became an object of God's wrath. This mighty empire with its seemingly invincible capital fell in one night. The co-ruler of the empire, **Belshazzar**, had made a great feast. He used the golden vessels taken from the temple of God in Jerusalem to drink wine and toast the pagan gods of the Chaldeans. Amidst the drunken revelry, fingers appeared and wrote on the palace wall a cryptic inscription. Daniel was called in; he explained that God had brought Babylon's rule to an end and had given the kingdom to the Medes and Persians (Dan. 5:26–28). On that same night in 539 BC, the conquering Medes and Persians killed Belshazzar. The Chaldean Empire was no more.

The Persian Empire

Out of the land of what is today Iran came an empire which spread across the entire Near Eastern world. At its height the Persian Empire stretched from the coastline of Greece to the Indus River Valley in India and from Egypt to Mesopotamia. The rise of this great empire was hastened in the mid-sixth century BC by the Persian defeat of the Medes, Lydians, and Chaldeans.

Cyrus the Great

The Persian king **Cyrus** was one of the greatest conquerors who ever lived. Cyrus rose to power among the Persian tribes in the southern region of the Median Empire (see map). After the Assyrian Empire fell in 612 BC, the Medes had control of the land north and east of Mesopotamia. Cyrus took advantage of a rebellion in the Median army and conquered the Median capital of Ecbatana in 549 BC. As he extended his conquests into Asia Minor, he came into contact with the Lydians.

Artist's rendering of Cyrus the Great

The western region of Asia Minor bordering the Aegean Sea was the homeland of the Lydians. Here rich mineral resources, especially gold, were found in abundance. This land was the supposed home of King Midas, who had the legendary touch of gold. The most important contribution made by the Lydians to the ancient world was the use of coinage as an international medium of exchange. Prior to this time, the barter system (the exchange of one commodity for another) was used. The Persians, Greeks, and Romans later adopted coinage.

The Lydian king Croesus (KREE sus) confronted Cyrus and the advancing Persian army, suffering defeat in 546 BC. Unlike the Assyrians, who had difficulties ruling their vast empire because of their harsh treatment of conquered peoples, Cyrus was a wise and merciful conqueror. He allowed his defeated enemies some measure of self-rule, tolerated their religious beliefs, and restored captive peoples to their homeland. Instead of killing Croesus, Cyrus took him as a prisoner and allowed him to enjoy the life of the Persian royal court.

Persia and the Nation of Israel

The Bible refers to Cyrus as the "Lord's anointed." Isaiah, a prophet from Judah, some one hundred and fifty years before Cyrus's birth, prophesied Cyrus's rule and impact on Israel (Isa. 45:1, 4). God used Cyrus to free His people from their captivity in Babylon. As God had used the Assyrians and Chaldeans to punish Israel and Judah, He used Persia to reestablish His repentant people in their land. Isaiah 45:13 describes how Cyrus would not only allow the Jews to return to their land but also direct them to rebuild the Temple of God in Jerusalem (see also Ezra 1:2–3).

Through the Persians, God protected and provided for His chosen people. It was through Esther and the Persian king Xerxes (ZURK seez), called Ahasuerus (uh HAZ yoo EER us) in the Bible, that God delivered the Jews from the wicked plot of Haman. Later under Artaxerxes I (AR tuh ZURK seez), Nehemiah was allowed to return to Jerusalem to help rebuild the walls (Neh. 2:1–8).

The Persian Postal System

"Nothing mortal travels so fast as these Persian messengers. The entire plan is a Persian invention; and this is the method of it. Along the whole line of road there are men (they say) stationed with horses, in number equal to the number of days which the journey takes, allowing a man and horse to each day; and these men will not be hindered from accomplishing at their best speed the distance which they have to go, either by snow, or rain, or heat, or by the darkness of night."

Herodotus, The History of Herodotus, *trans. George Rawlinson, 98.*

Persian Government

The Persians developed an effective organization to rule the vast territories that they had conquered. The empire was divided into provinces called **satrapies**. Each province was overseen by a satrap, or governor, who was appointed by the Persian king. It seems that Darius the Mede, an important character in Daniel 5 and 6, was one of these satraps whom Cyrus had appointed to rule for him in the city of Babylon. The king had secret police, known as the "king's eyes," that kept the king informed of matters that took place in each province.

An excellent network of roads facilitated trade and travel throughout the empire. The primary road of the empire—the Royal Road—ran for 1,677 miles from Susa (one of the Persian capitals) to Sardis near the Aegean Sea. These roads aided the Persian mail service, which was similar to the American pony express. The book of Esther gives us an example of this mail system in action. When Xerxes made the decree to protect the Jews from Haman's evil plot, he sent letters throughout the provinces telling of his decision (Esther 8:3–10).

Top: The ruins of the ancient city of Persepolis. It was the residence of the Persian kings from the time of Darius I (521–486 BC) until its destruction by the armies of Alexander the Great in 330 BC.
Bottom: The ruins of Persepolis. In the foreground is the treasure house, right behind the Palace of Darius.

Persian Culture

Much of Persian culture was adopted from previous civilizations. The Persians borrowed the idea of coinage and gold currency from the Lydians. Their early writing system was the Sumerian cuneiform. Phoenicians and Greeks supplied Persia with its navy. The Persians also popularized the Egyptian calendar.

The religion of ancient Persia was founded by and took its name from the religious leader **Zoroaster** (ZOR oh as ter), who lived during the sixth century BC. Zoroaster rejected the polytheism prevalent in much of the ancient world and instituted the worship of one god, Ahura Mazda. The sacred writings of Zoroastrianism, called the ***Avesta***, consist of myths, regulations, and hymns of praise. Zoroaster taught that good and evil are two opposing forces; the world was their battleground. Every man takes part in this struggle, Zoroaster taught, for he serves either the forces of good or the forces of evil. Like so many of the world's false religions, Zoroastrianism held that at the end of life one would be assured of eternal happiness if his good works outweighed his evil.

The Persian Empire continued some two hundred years after the death of Cyrus. Under **Darius the Great**, the empire reached its height, expanding all the way to Greece, where the Persian expansion was halted. Although the Greeks stopped the Persian advance, the Persians continued to rule the ancient world until a new world conqueror, Alexander the Great, created an even greater empire toward the close of the fourth century BC.

Section Quiz

1. What city became the capital of the Assyrian Empire?
2. What prophet was sent by God to Nineveh to preach repentance?
3. What term describes the scattering of the Jewish people by Nebuchadnezzar?
4. What was the religion of ancient Persia? What was the name of its sacred writings?
5. Under what ruler did the Persian Empire expand all the way to Greece?

✯ How does the biblical prophecy of Cyrus demonstrate the accuracy of Scripture?

Chapter 2 Review

Making Connections

1. How did the Sumerians and other civilizations carry out aspects of the Creation Mandate?
2. Why was Hammurabi's Code inferior to the law given to Moses?
3. What was the long-term effect of the Hyksos invasion of Egypt?
4. Why did many people doubt the existence of the Hittite civilization until the twentieth century?
5. How did God use Gentile leaders, including Nebuchadnezzar and Cyrus, to serve Him?

Developing History Skills

1. Compare the Ten Commandments (Exodus 20) with David's sins recorded in 2 Samuel 11. Which commandments did he break? What were the historical consequences?
2. Read Psalm 9:17 and provide examples of how this biblical principle has been demonstrated by civilizations mentioned in this chapter.

Thinking Critically

1. Evaluate this statement: "The Bible is not an accurate record of historical events." Provide examples to support your evaluation.
2. Why did God allow wicked nations to subjugate His people? Refer to passages such as Isaiah 10:5-6 and 2 Kings 17 in your answer.

Living in God's World

1. The Old Testament provides a behind-the-scenes look at why God ordered certain historical events the way He did. Can Christians discern God's purposes in historical events that are not addressed in Scripture? What are some principles the Christian historian can use in attempting to do this?

People, Places, and Things to Know

Mesopotamia
polytheism
cuneiform
ziggurats
Sargon
empire
Hammurabi
Epic of Gilgamesh
astronomy
astrology
Menes
pharaohs
Khufu
Hatshepsut
Thutmose III
Ramses II
hieroglyphics
Fertile Crescent
Baal
Abraham
Abrahamic Covenant
Joseph
Judah
Moses
Joshua
monotheism
David
Solomon
Babylonian Captivity
Sargon II
Sennacherib
Nebuchadnezzar
Diaspora
Belshazzar
Cyrus
satrapies
Zoroaster
Avesta
Darius the Great

3

THE GREEK CIVILIZATION

I. The Early Greek World

II. Greek City-States

III. The Fateful Century

IV. Alexander's Empire

V. Greek Culture

The Acropolis in Athens

The Bible states that after the Flood the descendants of Javan (one of Japheth's sons) journeyed westward from Mesopotamia and settled in the islands of the nations (Gen. 10:4–5). This phrase may include the land we now call Greece. This land is a mountainous peninsula in the eastern Mediterranean. Between it and Asia Minor lies the island-dotted Aegean Sea. This land along the Aegean Sea formed the cradle of Greek civilization. Geography influenced Greek history from its very beginning. Mountains made farming difficult, but abundant natural harbors encouraged the Greeks to become seafarers. Furthermore, the rugged terrain hindered communication among the Greek cities, causing them to remain isolated. As a result, the Greeks developed a spirit of independence and local patriotism and became known for their love of individualism and self-sufficiency.

Island in the Sea of Crete

I. The Early Greek World

Aegean Civilizations

Archaeologists have found remains of two remarkable civilizations, the Minoan and Mycenaean, which preceded the Greek civilization in the Aegean region. Although these civilizations did not last long, they left a permanent stamp on later Greek culture.

Crete

The earliest center of civilization in the Aegean region was located on the island of Crete. By 2000 BC the **Minoan civilization** (named after the legendary King Minos) flourished on the island. Through their trade and colonization, the Minoans came into contact with the people of the Fertile Crescent. The Minoans established trade routes with the Egyptians, who desired Cretan olive oil and fine pottery. Many scholars believe that the Philistines, who troubled the Hebrew people in Palestine, were colonists from this Cretan civilization.

The grand palace at Knossos, the capital city, gives us an indication of the wealth and achievement of the Minoans. The palace had hundreds of rooms and covered several acres. Flush toilets, bathtubs, and piped water were some of the "modern" conveniences found there. The beautiful carvings, pottery, and frescoes (painting done on wet plaster walls) found among the ruins of the palace reflect the Minoan love for beauty.

The Lion Gate, entrance into the fortified citadel of Mycenae

Mycenae

At Mycenae (my SEE nee) on the mainland of Greece, another center of Aegean culture emerged. The **Mycenaean civilization** was established by invaders from the north. Much of the Mycenaean knowledge of art, building, and commerce came from the Minoan culture. When Knossos was destroyed around 1400 BC (possibly by the Mycenaeans), Mycenae became the leading commercial center of the Aegean region.

While the Minoan culture displayed a love for beauty, the Mycenaean culture reflected the military fervor of its people. Its palaces were built on high hills and fortified with massive walls. Rival kings fought constantly. The Mycenaeans expanded their trade through sea raids, piracy, and colonization.

A major commercial rival of Mycenae was the city of Troy. Located on the western coast of Asia Minor, Troy sat on a hill overlooking the Hellespont (HEL us pahnt), the strait that separates Asia Minor from Europe. (See the map on p. 43.) This strategic site linked the land trade of the Fertile Crescent with the sea trade of the Aegean world.

According to Greek legend, the Mycenaeans went to war against the city of Troy. After ten years of bitter struggle, Troy finally fell to the Mycenaeans. They had gained entrance to the city by use of the fabled Trojan horse. The glory of Mycenae was short-lived, however. Around 1200 BC, invaders called the **Dorians** came down from the north and conquered the main Mycenaean fortresses. The Dorian invasion marked the decline of the Mycenaean civilization and ushered in a new period of Greek history.

The Greek Dark Ages

The period from 1150 to 750 BC is known as the "Dark Ages" of Greek history. During this period there were new intruders in the land. They neglected

The Trojan War

According to ancient Greek legend, the Trojan War began when a Trojan prince named Paris abducted Helen, the wife of a Spartan king. The Greeks set sail for Troy when Paris refused to release her. The war lasted for ten years before the Greeks came up with an ingenious plan to capture Troy. They built a huge wooden horse as a "peace offering"; fully armed Greek soldiers hid within the belly of the horse. Once they were in place, the remaining Greeks closed the trapdoor and rolled the huge horse up to the city walls. They then withdrew in their ships to a place out of sight of Troy to await darkness, when they would return to the city. Thinking that the Greeks had finally left their land, the Trojans took the horse into the city and celebrated their good fortune. The celebration made the Trojans drunk and careless and enabled the Greek soldiers inside the horse to open the trapdoor, slip out, kill the drunken guards, and open the city gates to the returning Greek army. In just a few hours, the Greeks were able to burn and sack the city. We remember this event whenever we refer to a "Trojan horse" or when we repeat the familiar saying "Beware of Greeks bearing gifts."

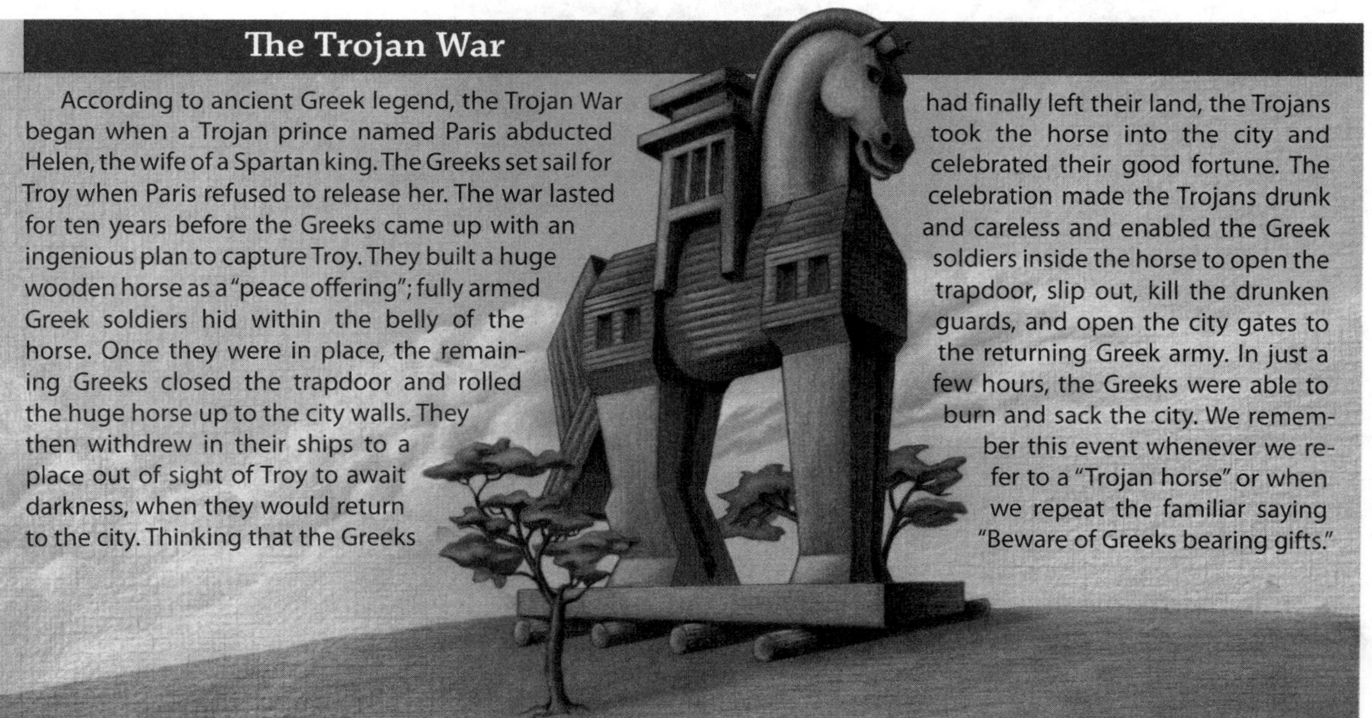

Schliemann and Troy

Heinrich Schliemann (SHLEE mahn) (1822–1890), the son of a Protestant clergyman, developed a love for the stories of ancient heroes. As a boy, Schliemann had been thrilled as his father told him in a simple and dramatic way about the Trojan War. The stories so fascinated him that Schliemann talked about them regularly. Many of the children his age laughed at him, but young Heinrich determined that one day he would find Troy.

After his commercial ventures had made him a millionaire, Schliemann retired from business and devoted himself to his lifelong ambition—finding Troy. Few scholars in the nineteenth century believed that Troy or even Homer ever existed. Schliemann, however, did not listen to their opinions. He received permission from the Turkish government to carry out excavations.

He first went to the place where Troy was believed by some to be located. Upon reaching the spot, Schliemann was troubled; the landscape was different from that described by Homer. Using the topographical information found in the *Iliad* as a guide, Schliemann found a site about three miles from the sea coast which seemed to harmonize with Homer's description. He hired workmen, and the digging began. After three years of work, Schliemann found not just one city of Troy but nine cities, each built upon the ruins of the previous city. His childhood dream had at last come true.

Excerpt from Homer

Tell me, O Muse, of that ingenious hero [Odysseus] who traveled far and wide after he had sacked the famous town of Troy. Many cities did he visit, and many were the nations with whose manners and customs he was acquainted; moreover, he suffered much by sea while trying to save his own life and bring his men safely home.

(Homer, Odyssey, 1)

the great palace fortresses, once the centers of culture in the Aegean world. Instead they adopted a simpler life in local villages and encouraged little contact with areas outside the Aegean region. Despite the decline of the Minoan and Mycenaean civilizations, the Greek Dark Ages did witness the blending of the distinctive elements in the Aegean world into a common Greek culture.

Our knowledge of the Greek Dark Ages rests largely on the epic poems, the *Iliad* and the *Odyssey*, attributed to the Greek poet **Homer**. Because Homer's poems provide nearly the only glimpse of the early Greek way of life, historians have also called this period the "Homeric Age." With stories of heroic figures, brutal warfare, and adventurous exploits, Homer describes the shaping of Greek culture. Values such as dignity, strength, valor, bravery, generosity, and wisdom as expressed in the lives of Homer's characters are the qualities the Greeks honored most.

Statue of Athena

Greek Mythology

Greek mythology played a dominant role in shaping Greek culture during the Homeric Age. The Greeks devised stories (myths) to explain their beliefs about life, the world, and their gods. According to Greek mythology, the twelve chief gods and goddesses dwelt on Mount Olympus, the heaven of the gods. **Zeus**, the "king of gods and man," was the ruler of Mount Olympus. His son, Apollo, was the god of the sun, music, and medicine. **Athena**, patron of the city of Athens, was the goddess of wisdom. Ruling over the sea and earthquakes was the god Poseidon, Zeus's brother. The Greeks believed in many gods, all of whom were endowed with certain human characteristics (***anthropomorphic***, "having human form or attributes"); yet these gods also possessed extraordinary powers and immortality.

According to Greek mythology, the gods had power to both help and harm man. Zeus, for example, often expressed his anger with men by sending lightning bolts to earth. Because these gods were the invention of sinful men, it is not surprising that they exhibited human sins: they were immoral, impatient, whimsical, unjust, and deceitful. The apostle Paul probably had Greek polytheism especially in mind when he said that the Gentiles were guilty before God because they had "changed the glory of the uncorruptible God into an image made like to corruptible man" (Rom. 1:23). Even so, the Greeks sought the favor of these gods through prayers and sacrifices. How different was the Greek religion from that of the Hebrew people, who worshiped the one true God.

In honor of Zeus, the Greeks held national religious festivals every four years at Olympia, the site of a temple of Zeus. Physical contests, thought to please the gods, became the chief feature of these festivals. The Olympic Games, as they became known, attracted competitors from all over the Aegean world. Each participant represented his home city. The intense competition indicated the high regard the Greeks had for physical prowess. To attain physical perfection was the ultimate goal of every athlete. The games became so popular that the Olympiad, the four-year interval between the games, became a Greek means of dating historical events. The Olympic Games were a rare example of cooperation between the Greek city-states.

Section Quiz

1. Where was the earliest center of civilization located in the Aegean region?
2. What Aegean culture displayed a love for military pursuits?
3. What ancient city did Heinrich Schliemann discover?
4. From what two epic poems do we get a glimpse of Greek life during the period from 1150 to 750 BC? To whom are these poems attributed?
5. What athletic contests began as an attempt to please the Greek gods through physical prowess?

★ Why did the isolation of the Greek city-states result in a spirit of independence and a love of individualism?

II. Greek City-States

Role

Though they shared the same language, customs, and religious beliefs, the Greeks lacked political unity. The Nile River in Egypt had brought the Egyptian people together and had encouraged their political unification. In sharp contrast, the mountains of Greece tended to isolate the Greek city-states, thus hindering national unity.

The Greeks usually built their cities at the foot of a hill. For protection, they would construct a fortress at the top of the hill, to which they could flee when under attack. They called their city a "**polis**," and the fortified hill, an "acropolis" (from *acro*, meaning "high").

The polis, or "city-state," was the basic political unit of Greece. Although relatively small, Greek city-states exercised powers usually associated with national states. The ultimate source of authority, protection, and livelihood for an individual Greek was his city.

The Greek Word *Polis*

The Greek word *polis* had many interesting meanings. It not only referred to a city with its buildings but also included the people and their government. Today we use this Greek word in much the same way.

Greek Usage	Our Usage
"City government"	We talk about *politics*.
"City governor"	We talk about a *politician*.
"A citizens' assembly"	We call it the *polity* or *body politic*.
"City"	Some U.S. cities have the word *polis* at the end of their names. For example: • Indianapolis—"city of Indiana" • Minneapolis—"city of water" • Annapolis—"city of Anne" (named for Queen Anne of England, 1702–1714)

Government

The Greek city-states experienced four basic forms of government. The earliest form was a **monarchy**, "rule (archy) by one (mono)," which was prominent during the Homeric Age. The king received advice from a council of nobles and a popular assembly. Gradually the council of nobles assumed the king's powers and ruled as the privileged class. This "rule of a few," called an **oligarchy** (AHL ih gar kee), produced great tension between the wealthy noble class and the lower classes.

The dissatisfaction and unrest of the lower classes often led to **tyranny**. At the head of this government was a tyrant who gained complete control of the government—usually by force. A tyrant was not necessarily a corrupt ruler, as our modern conception of that word implies. He often championed the cause of the common people and brought about reform that allowed more people to participate in government.

A unique political contribution of the Greeks was the development of **democracy**, rule by the people. Under a democratic government, qualified adult male citizens could share in the responsibility of ruling the city.

Limited Democracy

While the development of rule by the people in some Greek city-states was remarkable, it needs to be understood in its historical context. Half the population was immediately excluded because only males could vote. The remaining half was reduced considerably by a number of qualifications; for instance, only citizens could vote, and the minimum voting age was twenty. Other restrictions ensured that only a minority of males in a Greek city-state qualified as citizens. For example, slaves and most of the lower class were not eligible for citizenship. In some cities, having a Greek father and foreign mother disqualified a man from citizenship. In many cities the man had to be the son of a citizen in order to qualify for citizenship. On rare occasions, a man might be granted citizenship by a quorum of citizens as a reward for a major contribution to the city. Therefore, early Greek democracy was clearly a limited democracy with minority participation. Yet it remains a remarkable achievement for this period in history.

Development

The period from 750 to 500 BC in Greek history saw the development of the Greek city-states. Important in later Greek history, the city-states of Sparta and Athens represented two opposing political systems and ways of life. Other Greek city-states were to follow the example and leadership of either Sparta or Athens.

Sparta

Sparta was located in the southern part of Greece on the peninsula called the Peloponnesus (PEL uh puh NEE sus). Conquered by the Dorians, Sparta's inhabitants were made slaves, or **Helots** (HEL uts). The new rulers of Sparta conquered surrounding areas, reducing many of the inhabitants to slave status. Soon the Helots outnumbered the Spartans. In constant fear of an uprising, the Spartans created a thoroughly militaristic state.

The way of life at Sparta centered on the training of warriors. The highest goal of any Spartan was to be the best warrior for the Spartan state. Sparta controlled all aspects of its citizens' lives in order to maintain an army ready for battle. Spartan elders determined whether babies were healthy enough to be reared. An unhealthy baby would be left on a hillside to die. When boys reached the age of seven, the state took them from their homes and placed them in army barracks, where they underwent rigorous physical training to make them into fit warriors. They were beaten so that they would learn to endure pain. They were encouraged to steal in order to prove their resourcefulness. At the age of twenty, they became a part of the Spartan army but were not full citizens of the Spartan state until they reached the age of thirty. Even then they had to eat and sleep in the army camp instead of at home; they had to be prepared to fight at all times.

Spartan girls went through similar training so that they might learn the same Spartan spirit. Their discipline included running, jumping, and boxing. Their chief goal was to become strong mothers, rearing warriors for the state. Spartan women reportedly sent their sons and husbands off to battle with the words "Return with your shields or on them."

Greek Colonization

Greek settlement was not restricted to the land we call Greece. From about 750 to 550 BC, the Greeks established colonies throughout the Mediterranean world. The most important Greek colony in the western Mediterranean was the city of Syracuse on the island of Sicily. In fact, the Greeks established so many colonies on Sicily and in southern Italy that the area became known as Magna Graecia (Great Greece). Some colonies were founded to alleviate overcrowding, some were founded as trading posts, and some were founded as places to send the undesirable members of society.

The colonization procedure was as follows: A mother city—called a metropolis—would choose a leader (often a noble) to direct the expedition. After listening to the reports of merchants, the leader then chose a site for the colony. When final preparations had been made, the colonists, taking with them a small amount of soil as well as fire from the altars of the mother city, boarded the ships and set sail.

Once the colonists arrived at their destination, the leader assigned land and established various laws and religious rites. (Sometimes the people even worshiped their leader after his death in honor of his services to the colony.) Finally, when the colonists were securely settled, they broke their ties with the metropolis. The new city-state was on its own.

Ragusa, Sicily

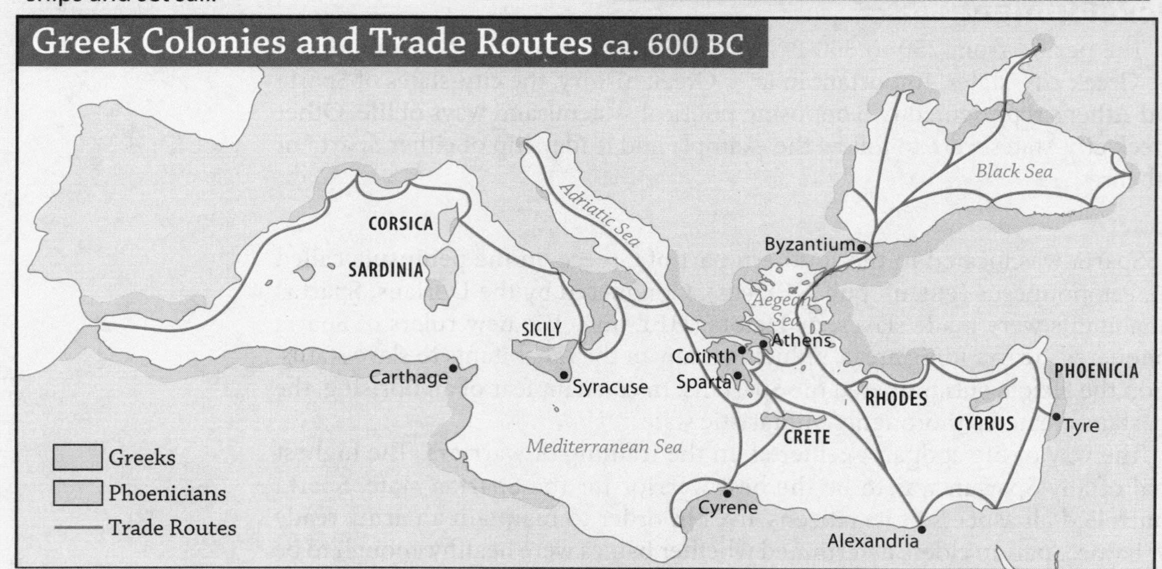

Sparta became the champion of the oligarchical form of government. A board of five Spartan nobles guarded against changes in the Spartan society and any harmful outside influences that would disrupt the *status quo* (existing state of affairs). To ensure the continuing success of the military state, the Spartans often used force or intimidation to help establish oligarchies in neighboring city-states. These city-states organized the **Peloponnesian League**, with Sparta at its head. Its purpose was to thwart the advance of the democratic principles fostered by the Athenians.

Athens

Life in Athens contrasted sharply with the rigid, disciplined life of Sparta. Sparta became associated with militarism, isolation, oligarchy, and glorification of the state. Athens, however, nurtured creativity, commercial endeavors, democracy, and individualism. The Athenians maintained the creative and intellectual heritage of the Minoan and Mycenaean civilizations.

Like other Greek city-states, Athens was ruled by a king during the Homeric Age. Later the noble class rose in power and established an oligarchy. Power was vested in a council of nobles, with the chief magistrate, or **archon**, being elected from the nobility. As the nobles gained more and more power, hostility arose between them and the common people.

Under the leadership of the statesman **Solon**, Athens took a step toward democracy. Solon assumed the office of archon around 594 BC. Charting a moderate course in Athenian affairs, he provided economic and political stability during a time of tension and hostility. Although Solon was of the noble class, he instituted reforms that helped the common man. For example, he forbade the practice of making debtors into slaves. He also created the Council of Four Hundred, which gave representation to all sections of Athens.

Greek countryside and harbor. The mountainous terrain of Greece contributed to the political fragmentation of Greek civilization.

The moderate policies that Solon instituted satisfied neither political side. After Solon's death tension mounted again between the nobles and the common people. Tyrants supporting the cause of the lower classes arose and seized control of the government. They initiated reforms and reorganized the government to allow greater citizen participation. It was not until the fifth century BC under the leadership of Pericles (PARE ih kleez) that Athens established a "rule of the people."

Section Quiz

1. What was the basic political unit of Greece?
2. List and define the four basic forms of government found in the Greek city-states.
3. What two Greek city-states represented two opposing ways of life within Greek society?
4. What Greek city-state was characterized by creativity, commercial endeavors, democracy, and individualism?

☆ Why did the moderate policies of Solon fail to satisfy either the nobles or the common people?

III. The Fateful Century

The Persian Wars

At the outset of the fifth century BC, the westward advance of the Persian Empire threatened Greek independence and isolation. The Persians, expanding into Asia Minor, conquered the Lydians as well as the Greek colonies located along the coast bordering the Aegean Sea. The Greek colonies were well treated by the Persians, but the Greeks, who valued independence and self-sufficiency, could not tolerate Persian authority. With the support of Athens, the Greek colonies rebelled and overthrew Persian rule.

Under King **Darius I** the Persians not only crushed the revolt but also sought to punish Athens for its part in the rebellion. (This is the same Darius that is mentioned in Ezra 6:1, 6–12. God used his government to aid immensely in the reconstruction of the temple of God at Jerusalem.) In 490 BC a Persian force landed at the Bay of Marathon, about twenty-five miles north of Athens. Though outnumbered and seemingly doomed for destruction, the Athenian army marched out to meet the mighty Persian army.

Herodotus's Account of the Battle of Marathon

So when the battle was set in array . . . instantly the Athenians . . . charged the barbarians [Persians] at a run. Now the distance between the two armies was little short of [one mile]. The Persians, therefore, when they saw the Greeks coming on at speed, made ready to receive them, although it seemed to them the Athenians were bereft of their senses, and bent upon their own destruction; for they saw a mere handful of men coming on at a run without either horsemen or archers. Such was the opinion of the barbarians; but the Athenians in close array fell upon them, and fought in a manner worthy of being recorded.

Herodotus, The History of Herodotus, *trans. George Rawlinson, 6. 112.*

Surprised by the Greek charge, the Persians were unable to fully use their cavalry, on which they heavily relied. Instead, they found themselves engaged in hand-to-hand combat; they were no match for the physical strength and battle skill of the Greek soldiers. The Greeks won a decisive victory.

Battle of Thermopylae

Furious over this setback, Darius, according to legend, appointed a slave to sit at his feet and say to him each day, "Master, remember the Athenians!" Darius organized a full-scale invasion of Greece but died before it could be carried out. **Xerxes**, his son, renewed the struggle. He amassed a great invasion force of men, ships, and supplies. Crossing the Hellespont on a bridge made of boats, the Persian army marched toward Greece.

In 480 BC the Persians, accompanied by their large fleet of ships, made their way down the Greek coast. The Greeks differed on how best to defend their cities. The Spartans suggested that the Greeks mass their forces across the Corinthian isthmus and defend the Peloponnesus. The Athenians objected to this plan because it would leave Athens exposed to the Persian army. The Greeks finally decided to take their stand at the mountain pass of Thermopylae (thur MOP uh lee), north of most of the city-states. (See the map of the Persian Wars found on p. 51.)

At Thermopylae a force of about seven thousand Greeks confronted the advancing Persian army. According to Herodotus, who could never resist

Modern view of the pass at Thermopylae. The road on the right was built where the beach would have been at the time of this battle.

The Hellespont Bridge

To move his army across the Hellespont from Asia Minor to Greece, Xerxes attempted a seemingly impossible feat: to build two bridges over which his army and its supplies could pass. Under the direction of Phoenician and Egyptian engineers, his men anchored a total of 674 ships in two lines across the mile-wide waterway. After tying the ships together with ropes, they laid down a plank roadway across their decks. On the planks they laid brush, which they covered with dirt, pressed down to make a solid surface. The process was nearly completed when a storm destroyed both bridges. The furious Xerxes had the chief engineers beheaded and then had the Hellespont beaten with 300 lashes! Then, under the direction of a Greek engineer, the Persians built two new bridges in the same way. In late May 480 BC, Xerxes dedicated the bridges by throwing a golden cup, a golden bowl, and a war sword into the water. Then, taking several days, the army marched across one bridge, while the supply wagons used the other. Xerxes and the Persian army were now on the European continent, a step closer to their confrontation with the Greeks.

improving a story, the Persians numbered about three million. It was more likely that they numbered about two hundred thousand. Though outnumbered, the Greeks had a good position, since only a small number of the Persian army could advance through the narrow pass at one time. The Persians attacked three times but could not take the pass. Then a Greek traitor showed the Persians another way through the mountains. When the Greeks realized that they were almost surrounded, they retreated, but three hundred Spartans along with several hundred Greeks from Thespiae and Thebes remained to hold the pass. These Greek soldiers fought to the death. According to Herodotus "they defended themselves to the last, such as still had swords using them, and the others resisting with their hands and teeth" (Herodotus, 7, 225). A monument at the spot bore these words: "Tell them in Sparta, passerby, that here, obedient to their orders, we lie."

Battle of Salamis Bay

Once past the Greek barrier, the Persians swept on to Athens. Xerxes burned it to the ground. The Athenians had left the city, realizing that they would not be able to defend it. They withdrew to an island called Salamis, just off the coast.

Hoping to exploit Xerxes' desire for a quick victory, Themistocles (thuh MIS tuh kleez), the leader of Athens, devised a trap. He sent a trusted slave to Xerxes with the story that the Greeks were frightened and were planning to escape in the morning by sailing northward. The slave also suggested that if Xerxes were to send his ships into the strait between the mainland and Salamis, he would be able to block their escape. The next morning Xerxes ordered his fleet, with many of his soldiers on board, to attack the Greeks. The Persians entered the strait just as Themistocles had hoped. But the rising morning tide made their

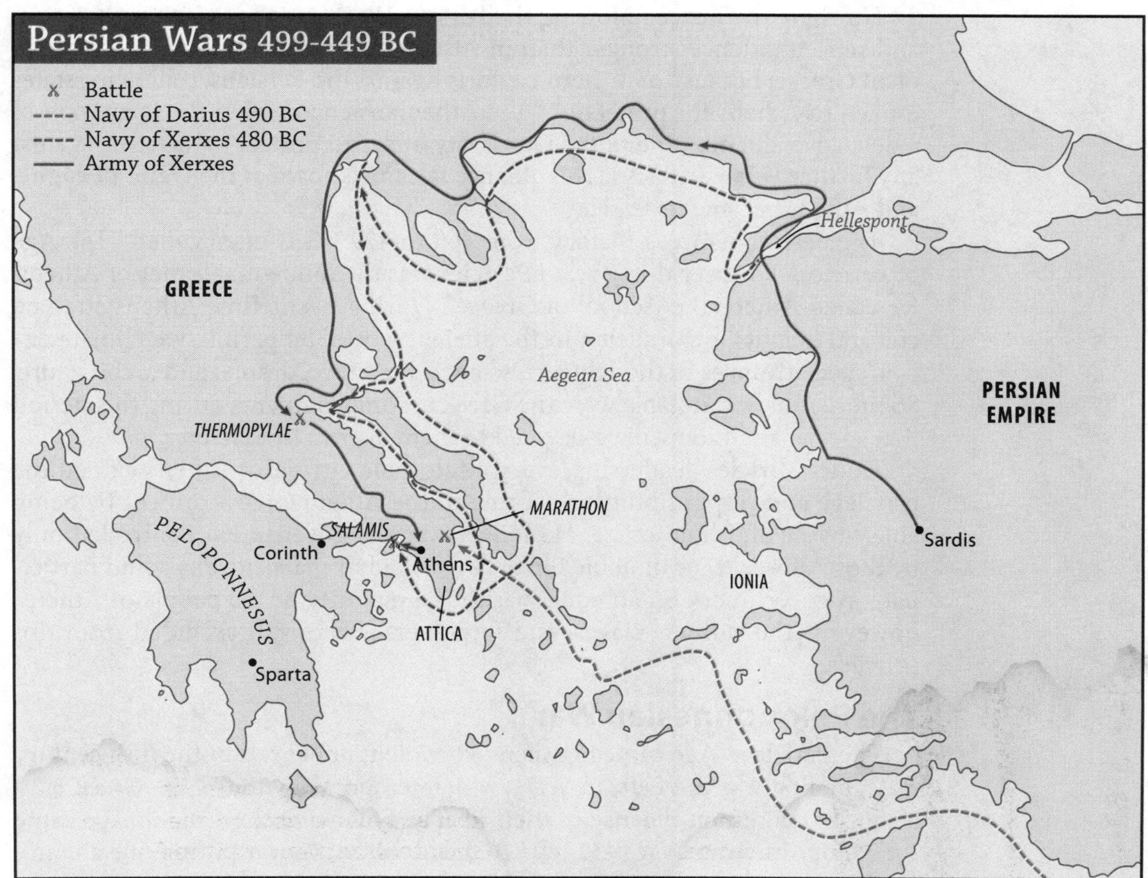

large ships hard to maneuver. As the Persian sailors struggled to steer their crafts, the Greeks launched their ships from the beaches of Salamis. The small, easily maneuvered Greek crafts created great confusion as they rammed and sank many Persian vessels. From a high vantage point overlooking the bay, Xerxes watched as the Greeks carried the day.

The following year the Greeks, led by Sparta, defeated a sizable Persian army that had remained in northern Greece. Although they had stopped the Persian invasion force, the Greeks did little to weaken the vast Persian Empire. The Persians continued to interfere in Greek affairs for two hundred years following the war. Yet the Greeks maintained their hard-fought independence. Freedom bolstered the Greek spirit, furthered the growth of democracy, and encouraged Greek creativity. The way was prepared for the "Golden Age" of Greece—a period of great cultural achievement.

Pericles on the Athenian Democracy

Our form of government does not enter into rivalry with the institutions of others. We do not copy our neighbors, but are an example to them. It is true that we are called a democracy, for the administration is in the hands of the many and not of the few. But while the law secures equal justice to all alike in their private disputes, the claim of excellence is also recognized; and when a citizen is in any way distinguished, he is preferred to the public service, not as a matter of privilege, but as the reward of merit. Neither is poverty a bar, but a man may benefit his country whatever be the obscurity of his condition.

Thucydides, *trans. Benjamin Jowett, 2.37.*

The Periclean Age

Nowhere in Greece following the Persian Wars was the spirit of patriotism and self-confidence stronger than in Athens. It became the leading city-state of all Greece; because of its heroic efforts against the Persians, other city-states looked to Athens for protection. The Athenians encouraged the formation of a defensive alliance among the Greek city-states to protect themselves against any further Persian attacks. This alliance became known as the **Delian League**, and Athens became its leader.

The period of Greek history from 460 to 429 BC is often called "The Age of Pericles." For over thirty years **Pericles** was the influential leader of Athens. He called Athens the "school of Greece." During his lifetime Athens attained cultural heights unparalleled in the ancient world. Its permissive climate encouraged advances in thought, art, science, literature, drama, and architecture. So numerous and notable were the Greek accomplishments during this period that special attention will be devoted to them later in this chapter.

Under Pericles' leadership every adult male citizen of Athens gained the privilege and responsibility of sharing in the Athenian government by being able to vote and hold office. No longer was the government controlled only by those of wealth or of noble birth. Now all adult male citizens could participate in government on an equal basis. The majority of the people of Athens, however—the women, slaves, and foreigners—were still excluded from this privilege.

The Peloponnesian War

The Periclean Age came between two violent upheavals in the fifth century BC. The first was the Persian Wars, which temporarily united the Greek city-states in a common defense of their liberty. Following the Golden Age came the **Peloponnesian War** (431–404 BC), a devastating war pitting one alliance of Greek city-states against another. As Athens had grown in influence and wealth, it began to transform the Delian League into an Athenian empire. Sparta became alarmed over the commercial and political power Athens had acquired. The tension between these two rivals and their allies finally flamed into war.

The war has been likened to a struggle between an elephant and a whale. Sparta's strength rested in its land army whereas Athens and its large fleet reigned supreme on the sea. Early in the war a devastating plague wiped out a large portion of the population of Athens, including its leading citizen, Pericles. Though weakened by these losses, Athens continued to fight. Sparta eventually gained the upper hand by forming an alliance with the Persians and was finally able to bring Athens to its knees by destroying the Athenian fleet.

Although Sparta emerged victorious, it had nothing but problems after the war. City-states that had looked to Sparta for deliverance from Athenian domination now found themselves under a greater oppressor. Democratic governments were replaced with oligarchies. The Greeks who had experienced freedom found it difficult to submit to Spartan oligarchical rule. Constant uprisings reduced Sparta's control over the Greek city-states, leaving them disunited once again.

Section Quiz

1. What eastern civilization threatened the Greeks at the outset of the fifth century?
2. At what battle did an unorthodox charge by the Greeks help them to win a decisive victory?
3. Across what body of water did Xerxes make a bridge of boats to move his army?
4. Who was the influential leader of Athens during its Golden Age?
5. Which group of city-states emerged as victors in the Peloponnesian War?

★ Why did Sparta's victory in the Peloponnesian War not lead to peace?

IV. Alexander's Empire

Rise of Macedonia

North of Greece was Macedonia, inhabited by a people related to the Greeks. King **Philip II** united Macedonia under his rule and extended his kingdom into Greece. Many Greek city-states supported Philip, hoping that he would bring unity to their land. Some resisted him, fearing that their freedom would be lost under Macedonian rule. The weakened and divided Greek city-states were no match for the well-organized army of Philip.

Philip's appreciation for Greek culture led him to treat his many subjects with great tolerance. He hoped to gain Greek support for an invasion of the Persian Empire, the Greeks' constant enemy. But in 336 BC, before he could fulfill his plans, Philip was assassinated. His son **Alexander** assumed the throne at the age of twenty. As a boy, Alexander had been taught by one of the greatest Greek philosophers, Aristotle, who had instilled in him a love for Greek culture. With his conquering armies he carried this culture to the far reaches of the Near Eastern world.

Alexander the Great

Alexander's Conquests

With amazing speed Alexander led his army across Asia Minor and confronted the Persian army, led by

King **Darius III**. In the heat of one battle, Darius fled, leaving behind his wife, mother, and children to be taken captive by Alexander. Alexander took Syria, destroyed the city of Tyre (see p. 30), and marched unopposed into Egypt. The final blow to the Persian Empire came as Alexander, near the Tigris River, defeated the larger army of Darius. Alexander had accomplished what he had set out to do—avenge the Persian invasion of Greece and become the king of Asia.

But his thirst for conquest was not yet satisfied. He marched all the way to India and would have gone beyond, but his weary army refused to go farther. They had been gone for eight years and had marched over eleven thousand miles. Alexander sulked for several days over the unwillingness of his army to continue. Although he had conquered almost all the known world of his day, his achievements had not brought any lasting satisfaction to his heart. How often men have tried to satisfy their soul's desires by seeking the fleeting pleasures of this world. Alexander probably would not have been satisfied even if he had conquered the whole world. God's Word says, "For what is a man profited, if he shall gain the whole world, and lose his own soul? or what shall a man give in exchange for his soul?" (Matt. 16:26).

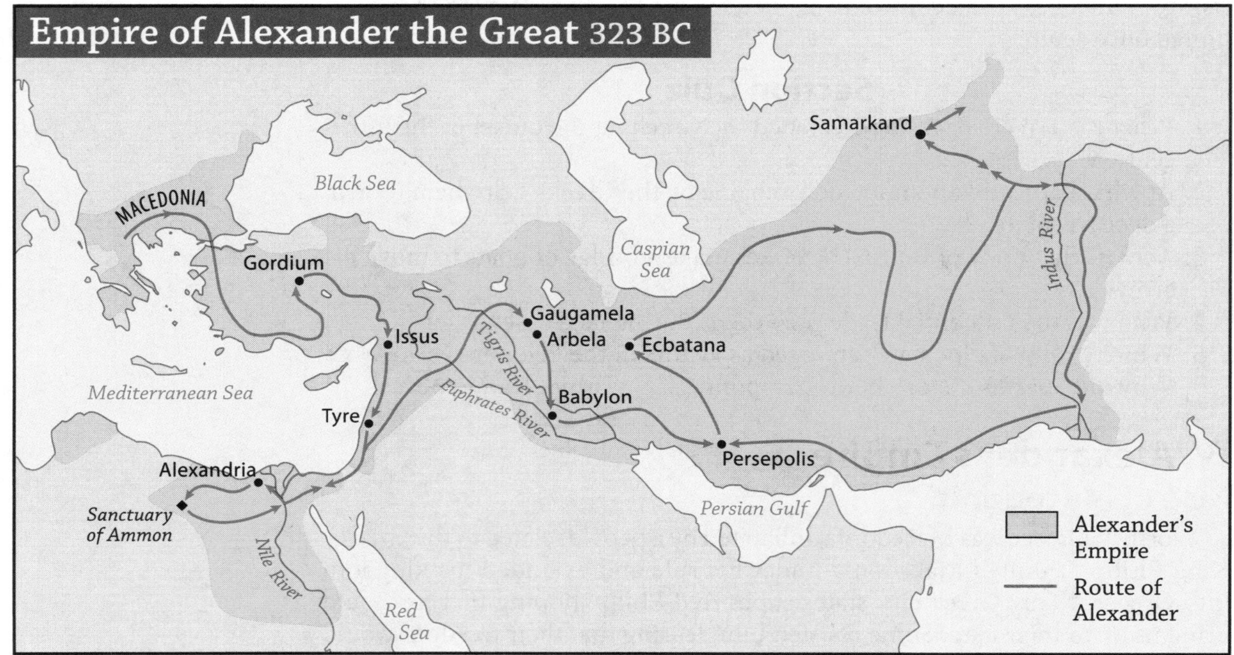

Empire Divisions

In 323 BC, at the height of his power, Alexander died of a fever; he had not yet reached his thirty-third birthday. Over two hundred years before Alexander's death, God's prophet Daniel had foretold that Alexander's empire would be divided into four kingdoms (Dan. 8:21–22; 11:4). Because Alexander left no plans for a successor to his empire, his chief generals fought among themselves to determine who would rule. Four generals emerged victorious and declared themselves kings over portions of the empire; thus Daniel's prophetic vision was fulfilled.

These new kings fought one another as each tried to restore the whole empire under his own rule. From the families of three of Alexander's generals came dynasties that ruled portions of the former empire until the time of the Roman conquests: the Ptolemies (TOL uh meez) in Egypt, the Seleucids (sih LOO sidz) in Syria and Persia, and the Antigonids (an TIG uh nidz) in Macedonia and Greece.

Alexander will be remembered as one of the world's greatest military leaders. His empire spread across the ancient world from Greece to India and included most of the capitals of earlier civilizations. He founded cities that became centers of learning and culture. Some of these he named after himself, such as Alexandria in Egypt. Through his conquests he spread the Greek culture and language to the East. Although his empire disintegrated soon after his death, the Greek culture remained a vital part of the ancient world.

Section Quiz

1. Over what kingdom did Philip II rule?
2. Who was the teacher of Alexander the Great who instilled in his young pupil a love for Greek culture?

3–5. List the three ruling families that ruled portions of Alexander's empire after his death. Identify the region over which each family ruled.

★ Why did Greek culture spread throughout the Middle East, North Africa, and Asia Minor?

V. Greek Culture

The Essence

The culture of a civilization is a reflection of the values and character of its people. The Greeks cultivated an appreciation for beauty, freedom, justice, truth, and knowledge. They exalted the person who had a creative spirit, versatile talents, a thirst for knowledge, physical ability, and a zest for life. The Greek respect for such qualities as self-control, restraint, balance, and moderation is evident in the Greek motto: "Nothing in excess, and everything in proportion." These were the qualities that characterized much of Hellenic culture. Sadly, because the Greeks rejected the true God, they also embraced idolatry in place of worshipping the living God and human philosophy in place of absolute truth.

The term **Hellenic** is used to describe Greek culture. The Greeks called themselves Hellenes and their land Hellas. The height of Hellenic culture occurred during the Golden Age of Athens. The spirit of independence and self-sufficiency, bolstered by the defeat of the Persians, produced the flowering of Hellenic culture in Athens. Most of the Greek men whose achievements history remembers lived in this city.

Ancient Greece has been called the cradle of Western culture. Greek culture left a lasting imprint on the Western world. The Greeks set forth many of the basic concepts of science, mathematics, and philosophy. Greek literature, architecture, and sculpture became models that later civilizations imitated.

Although the Greek army never conquered the world, Greek culture did conquer a large portion of it. Alexander's conquests spread the Greek language and way of life throughout much of the ancient world. As a result, Hellenic culture mixed with the cultures of the East. A new culture emerged; it was no longer just Hellenic, meaning "Greek," but **Hellenistic**, "like the Greek."

Hellenistic culture permeated the Near East from the time of Alexander until the coming of the Romans in the first century BC. Its influence was so great that this period is known as the Hellenistic Age. Hellenistic culture united the peoples of the Near East by blending their arts, religions, philosophies, and customs. The Hellenistic Age brought the East and West together in learning, in government, and in trade.

Grecian urn

The Expression

Focus on Man

"Wonders are many on earth, and the greatest of these is man." To the Greeks the ability to think and reason made man unique. His "humanity" was thus worthy of special study. The Greeks were among the first to begin the formal study of human thought and culture, called the **humanities**. Philosophers and scientists praised the human mind and its reasoning powers. Greek literature dealt with how man lives and acts. The goal of physical activity was to develop the human body toward physical perfection. Greek art focused on the human form.

The Greeks stressed the dignity and uniqueness of man. They assumed a great truth: man is the highest of created beings (Gen. 1:26–28). However, they looked upon man's uniqueness apart from God, glorifying the "creature more than the Creator" (Rom. 1:25). As a result they perverted this noble truth into a form of humanism. They did not accept God's creation of man in His own image; therefore, they praised man for his ability rather than praising the God Who gave man that ability. Similarly, they did not acknowledge their responsibility to their Creator. Instead they believed that "man is the measure [judge] of all things."

Interest in Philosophy

Throughout history men have sought answers to the basic questions of life: (1) Where did I come from? (2) Why am I here? (3) Where am I going? and (4) What is the highest good in life? Early in their history the Greeks developed many myths to help them answer these questions. Following the sixth century BC, however, many people lost confidence in these myths. Men called **philosophers**, "lovers of wisdom," tried to find the answers to these questions through man's reasoning ability. They believed that the highest good was to seek truth and attain knowledge. This, they hoped, would enable men to live properly.

The Greeks believed in the basic goodness of man. They trusted in man's wisdom as a guide for their behavior and as a means for finding happiness. They did not understand that "the wisdom of this world is foolishness with God. . . . The Lord knoweth the thoughts of the wise, that they are vain. Therefore let no man glory in men" (1 Cor. 3:19–21). The Greeks relied on man's reasoning ability in their search for wisdom. However, God's Word says that "the fear of the Lord is the beginning of wisdom: and the knowledge of the holy is understanding" (Prov. 9:10).

***Thales of Miletus (ca. 640–546 BC)*—Thales** (THAY leez) is often called the Father of Philosophy. Among the Greeks, Thales was one of the first who sought to explain the origin of the universe in natural terms. He concluded that water was the original substance of all things. He and other early philosophers did not deal with the questions of ethics—what is right and wrong. This was left to later philosophers, the most famous of whom are Socrates, Plato, and Aristotle.

Socrates

***Socrates (ca. 470–399 BC)*—Socrates** (SAHK ruh teez), a contemporary of Pericles, lived in Athens during its Golden Age. This snub-nosed man with bulging eyes devoted his life to seeking truth and teaching men how to conduct their lives. He took as his motto "Know thyself." According to Socrates, "The unexamined life is not worth living."

Socrates was not a writer but a teacher. We know what he taught by what his students wrote about him. His method of teaching involved the asking of leading questions followed by the analyzing of the students' answers. Socrates believed that truth (absolutes) could be attained

Jacques Louis David, The Death of Socrates, *Metropolitan Museum of Art, New York*

through human reason. To Socrates virtue was knowledge, and ignorance produced evil. Thus, reason was the best guide to good behavior.

Many in Athens objected to Socrates' questioning of some of the fundamental institutions of the city. They accused him of corrupting the youth and rejecting the gods of Athens. He was tried and condemned to death. Refusing to flee, Socrates calmly drank the cup of hemlock (poison) by which the sentence of death was to be carried out. He died at the age of seventy in the midst of his followers.

Plato (ca. 427–347 BC)—The most famous pupil of Socrates was **Plato** (PLAY toh). He established a school of philosophy and science called the Academy, located in Athens. In the *Republic*, he devised one of the first plans for an ideal society and government. Although Plato lived in democratic Athens, he realized that too much liberty and freedom without restraint often leads to **anarchy** (the breakdown of government and order). He stated that the "excess of liberty, whether in states or individuals, seems only to pass into excess of slavery."

In his works Plato discussed what he considered the nature of true reality. He determined that something would have to be permanent (eternal) if it were to be truly real. Since nothing in this world is permanent, Plato concluded that

Was Plato a Christian?

Throughout church history many Christians have seen parallels between Plato's philosophy and Christianity. But most often this is a result of misunderstanding Scripture. Some might see in 2 Corinthians 4:18, "For the things which are seen are temporal; but the things which are not seen are eternal," a parallel between Plato and Paul. But Plato's point was that the unseen world is the real world and the seen world is only a representation. The Bible, however, presents the world of human experience as real—temporal, yes, but not unreal. Plato also had a very un-Christian view of the unseen world. He had no conception of a personal God who loves mankind and is working to redeem the human race from its sinfulness. Plato's ideas made the concept of a bodily resurrection and a restored earth laughable to the Greeks. Some historians claim that the New Testament reflects the philosophy of Plato. But such claims are based on superficial similarities.

true reality lies outside the physical world. The things on earth are mere shadows, or imperfect reflections, of their eternal counterparts, or "forms," in the unseen realm of eternity.

Aristotle (384–322 BC)—The last of the three famous Greek philosophers was **Aristotle** (EHR uh stot ul). Aristotle was not an Athenian like the other two but came to Athens from northern Greece. At the age of eighteen, he began his study at Plato's Academy. Plato called his most famous student "the mind of the school." Like Plato, Aristotle has had a continuing impact on Western thought through his writings. Aristotle, as we learned earlier, was also the tutor of Alexander the Great, and he instilled in the young prince an appreciation for Greek culture.

Aristotle

Unlike Plato, Aristotle believed that reality was in the physical world. Therefore, he developed wide interests in many fields. He wrote treatises on politics, biology, physics, art, drama, mathematics, and ethics. He is best remembered for his works on logic, which are collectively called the *Organon* ("Instrument"). To aid man's reasoning ability, Aristotle developed the **syllogism**, a three-step logical process of thinking. The following is a good example: (1) All Greeks are human; (2) Aristotle is a Greek; (3) Therefore, Aristotle is human.

Epicureans and Stoics—The Epicurean (ep ih kyoo REE un) and Stoic philosophies emerged shortly after the death of Alexander the Great. **Epicurus** believed that great happiness and pleasure could be achieved through the avoidance of pain and fear. **Zeno**, the founder of Stoicism, taught that the affairs of men and the universe were ordered by fixed laws. Man must accept his fate and live a life of duty and self-control. These philosophies had greater impact on the Roman world than on the Hellenistic world. (See p. 94) When the apostle Paul visited Athens in the first century AD, certain Epicurean and Stoic philosophers mocked him because his preaching concerning the resurrection (Acts 17:18, 32) contradicted their teaching.

Contributions to Science, Medicine, and Mathematics

The questions raised by the Greek philosophers concerning man and his world encouraged others to seek natural or logical explanations through observation. Even before the Golden Age, **Pythagoras** (pih THAG er us), a philosopher and mathematician of the sixth century BC, had concluded that the universe could be explained in mathematical terms. His geometric theorem, the Pythagorean Theorem, is still studied by students taking geometry.

Excerpts from the Hippocratic Oath

I swear . . . that I will carry out, according to my ability and judgment, this oath, and this [written contract]. . . . I will use treatments to help the sick according to my ability and judgment, but never with a view to injury and wrong-doing. Neither will I administer a poison to anybody when asked to do so, nor will I suggest such a course. Similarly I will not give to a woman a pessary to cause an abortion. But I will keep pure and holy both my life and my art. . . . Now if I carry out this oath, and break it not, may I gain forever reputation among all men for my life and for my art; but if I transgress it and [break it], may the opposite befall me.

Hippocrates (ca. 460–ca. 377 BC), the famed physician of the Golden Age, is known as the Father of Medicine. After studying in Athens, Hippocrates became a wandering physician who traveled throughout Greece and Macedonia. Contrary to common Greek myths which held that disease was the punishment of the gods, Hippocrates (hih PAHK ruh teez) taught that every illness has a natural cause. He rejected magic and superstition and instead recommended rest and proper diet as the proper treatments. He wrote manuals that preserved his findings for other physicians.

Euclid (YOO klid) has often been called the Father of Geometry. He founded a school of mathematics in Alexandria, Egypt. His textbook, *Elements*, continues to be the basis for geometry textbooks today. The Greek inventor and mathematician Archimedes (ar kuh MEE deez), born in the Greek colony of Syracuse, was known throughout the Hellenistic world for his many discoveries. One of his discoveries was the principle of the lever, the practical value of which is illustrated today by the raising of a car with a jack. Proud of his discovery of the laws of levers, he once boasted, "Give me a spot to stand on and a lever long enough, and I will move the earth." The Greek astronomer and geographer **Eratosthenes** (ehr uh TAHS thuh neez) determined the circumference of the globe with amazing accuracy by using the geometry that Euclid popularized. He also formulated the lines of longitude and latitude that are still used today on maps. The belief that the earth is round was established by the Greeks some seventeen centuries before Columbus.

Achievement in Literature

History—We get our word *history* from the Greek word meaning "inquiry." The Greeks believed that men could learn lessons from the past to help them live in the present. **Herodotus**, the Father of History, wrote his history of the Persian Wars in the hope of "preserving from decay the remembrance of what men have done, and of preventing the great and wonderful actions of the Greeks and the Barbarians from losing their due need of glory, and withal to put on record what were their grounds of feud." Although Herodotus tried to present an accurate history, his work contains many myths and exaggerations and an obvious bias toward the Greeks.

Thucydides on the Writing of History

Of the events of the war I have not ventured to speak from any chance information, nor according to any notion of my own; I have described nothing but what I either saw myself, or learned from others of whom I made the most careful and particular inquiry. The task was a laborious one, because eyewitnesses of the same occurrences gave different accounts of them, as they remembered or were interested in the actions of one side or the other. And very likely the strictly historical character of my narrative may be disappointing to the ear. But if he who desires to have before his eyes a true picture of the events which have happened, and of the like events which may be expected to happen hereafter in the order of human things, shall pronounce what I have written to be useful, then I shall be satisfied. My history is an everlasting possession, not a prize composition which is heard and forgotten.

Thucydides, *vol. 1, 1.22.*

Thucydides (thoo SID ih deez), a contemporary of Herodotus, wrote the *History of the Peloponnesian War*, a more accurate and objective record than Herodotus's work. Although Thucydides was an Athenian and fought briefly for Athens during the war with Sparta, he did not let his personal affections influence his account of the war.

Drama—The Greek achievement in literature was unsurpassed in the ancient world. Homer's epic poems are the monuments of early Greek literature. Later the Greeks excelled in poetic drama. An outgrowth of religious festivals, drama became an important part of Greek life. In Athens, for example, several days were set aside each year for the drama festivals. Shops were closed and schools had a holiday as the entire population of the city attended the outdoor performances. The Greeks held contests to determine the best plays and actors.

Greek drama provided more than just entertainment. The plays educated the Greek people in religious beliefs, moral behavior, and civic pride. Both tragedy and comedy were among the favorite forms of Greek drama. **Sophocles** (SAHF uh kleez), a writer of tragedy, and **Aristophanes** (ehr ih STAHF uh neez), a writer of comedy, were among the most famous of the Greek dramatists. Many of the Greek dramas are still enjoyed today; their analysis of human behavior is just as penetrating today as it was in ancient Greece.

Excellence in Art

The Greeks excelled in many forms of art; the most highly prized are their urns, sculpture, and temples. Grecian urns are among the most beautiful ever fashioned. On the exteriors of these graceful forms, the Greeks painted scenes of everyday life, battles, athletic competitions, and activities of their gods.

Greek sculpture falls into three main periods: archaic, classical, and Hellenistic. In the archaic period, Greek sculpture shows a strong Egyptian influence. Figures stand stiff and expressionless, their fists clenched by their sides. From these somewhat crude forms Greek sculpture gradually became more realistic. This change came about during the classical period, a period when Greek sculpture reached its highest achievement. Through their sculpture the Greeks sought to represent the ideal man. In the Hellenistic period Greek sculpture lost its simple beauty. Its calm self-confidence was replaced by a frenzied emotional tone.

The Golden Age of Greek culture (see p. 52) was also the "golden" or "classical" age of Greek architecture. The Greek building style became a standard of excellence that later generations copied. Nothing better reflects the beauty of Greek architecture than the buildings of the Athenian Acropolis. During the Persian Wars, Xerxes had destroyed Athens, but under Pericles new and more beautiful buildings were erected. Formerly a fortress for refuge, the Athenian Acropolis became the site of temples to the Greek gods. The most spectacular of these temples is the Parthenon. We can get a glimpse of its former beauty and grandeur today, even in its ruined state.

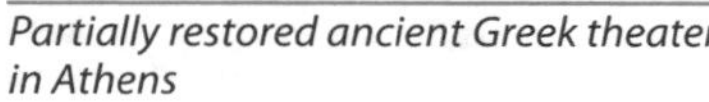

Partially restored ancient Greek theater in Athens

Top: The Parthenon in Athens, temple dedicated to the Greek goddess Athena
Bottom: The Porch of Maidens on the Acropolis of Athens, one of the finest examples of Greek statuary

The Athenians dedicated the building to the city's patron goddess, Athena. During the days of Pericles, a forty-foot-high gold and ivory statue of Athena stood inside the temple. The building itself is rectangular in shape and is supported by towering columns in beautiful symmetry. The Greeks gave it the appearance of solidity and symmetry through the subtle use of optical illusions. The steps leading to the entrance are slightly curved at the center; this feature gives the eye the illusion of their being flat. (If they were truly flat, they would appear to dip.) The columns are placed closer together at the sides of the building than at the middle. This spacing gives the appearance of regularity. Likewise, the floor rises gently at the center, giving the whole the appearance of a swelling, living edifice.

The **Parthenon** is a symbol of the cultural achievement of the Greek civilization. It is also a symbol of the spiritual blindness of the Greek people. The apostle Paul visited Athens some five hundred years after its "Golden Age." He preached against the idolatrous practices that the Parthenon and the statue of Athena represented.

Greek Architectural Orders

From the columns and capitals (the head or top of a column) of Greek buildings, we can distinguish three styles or orders of architecture: (1) the Doric style with solid, strong masculine-looking features; (2) the Ionic style with its splendor and graceful elements and its scroll-shaped capital; and (3) the Corinthian style, whose capitals were richly carved and ornately designed.

Section Quiz

1. What was the name given to the new culture that emerged in the Near East that mixed Greek culture with the cultures of the East?
2. What philosopher developed the three-step logical process of thinking called a syllogism?
3. Who is known as the Father of Medicine?
4. Who was the more objective historian: Herodotus or Thucydides?
5. Identify the three styles of Greek architecture.

✯ Why would some modern physicians be opposed to following the principles found in the Hippocratic Oath?

Chapter 3 Review

Making Connections

1–3. List three differences between the Spartan and Athenian societies.

4. Explain the difference between Hellenic and Hellenistic.

Developing History Skills

1. Why did Athens rather than Sparta become the cultural center of the Greek city-states during the Golden Age?

Thinking Critically

1. Use the first chapter of Romans to provide a biblical explanation for the gods worshiped by the Greeks.
2. Use Acts 17:22–34 and 1 Corinthians 1:22–31 to provide a guide for Christians studying Greek philosophy.

Living in God's World

1. The Greeks emphasized the need for balance in making ethical distinctions. They also taught that the key to morality was developing character, specifically by using the mind to exercise control over the emotions. What should a Christian think of this approach to morality?
2. Provide biblical answers to the great philosophical questions: (1) Where did I come from? (2) Why am I here? (3) Where am I going? and (4) What is the highest good in life?

People, Places, and Things to Know

Minoan civilization
Mycenaean civilization
Dorians
Homer
Zeus
Athena
anthropomorphic
polis
monarchy
tyranny
democracy
Helots
Peloponnesian League
archon
Solon
Darius I
Xerxes
Delian League
Pericles
Peloponnesian War
Philip II
Alexander
Darius III
Hellenic
Hellenistic
humanities
philosophers
Thales
Socrates
Plato
anarchy
Aristotle
syllogism
Epicurus
Zeno
Pythagoras
Hippocrates
Euclid
Eratosthenes
Herodotus
Thucydides
Sophocles
Aristophanes
Parthenon

4

THE ROMAN REPUBLIC

Roman aqueduct at Caesarea

Today if you were to travel in Spain, France, Britain, Italy, Greece, Asia Minor, Palestine, Egypt, or North Africa, you could find roads built almost two thousand years ago by the Romans. In fact, some of the modern roads in these lands are built on top of the firm and deep base of the old Roman roads. The Romans constructed a network of roads that connected the far corners of their vast empire with their capital city. This led to the saying, "All roads lead to Rome."

In a figurative sense, the road of ancient Western history also leads us to Rome. Rome was the culmination of ancient Western civilization. Despite its power and influence, Rome was deeply bound in spiritual darkness. It readily embraced the pagan gods and false teaching of its many conquered peoples.

The road of God's plan for the ages leads us to Rome as well. God chose to send His Son, Jesus Christ, into the world when the Roman civilization was at its height. God had been at work in history preparing the world for the coming of the Savior. It could be said that the Roman world was the cradle of Christianity. From the Roman province of Judea, the truth of the gospel spread to every part of the empire—on Roman roads.

I. Beginning of Roman Civilization

Geographic Features

The land of Italy, centrally located in the Mediterranean world, was the heart of the Roman Empire. Shaped like a boot, the Italian Peninsula extends into the Mediterranean Sea between the lands of Greece and Spain. At the southern tip of Italy is the island of Sicily, which nearly joins Italy with North Africa.

Geographic obstacles did not hamper the Romans as they did the Greeks. Because of the lack of good soil, the Greeks looked to the sea for their livelihood. However, the soil and climate of Italy were more suitable for farming. The mountains in Greece divided the Greek people and hindered their political unity. The Apennine (AP uh NINE) Mountains, which run down the middle of the Italian Peninsula, are less rugged than the mountains of Greece and did not hamper the growth of trade and travel among the people of Italy. From the Italian Peninsula, the Romans expanded their territory to include all the land surrounding the Mediterranean Sea. It is little wonder that the Romans would later call the Mediterranean ***Mare Nostrum***, which means "our sea."

Early Inhabitants

The earliest inhabitants of the Italian Peninsula had come from across the Alps and had settled in northern Italy. Many of these early settlers—called Latins—moved south and settled in Latium, a plain lying south of the Tiber River near the western coast of Italy. From this region arose a civilization that would one day rule the entire Mediterranean world.

Portions of Italy were also inhabited by the Phoenicians, Greeks, and **Etruscans**. Both the Phoenicians and the Greeks were known in the ancient world for their sea trade and colonization. Phoenicia established colonies on Sicily and along the coast of North Africa. (The Phoenician colony of Carthage in North Africa later rivaled Rome for mastery of the western Mediterranean world.) The Greeks established independent colonies on the island of Sicily also, as well as along the coast of southern Italy.

Most people have never heard of the Etruscans. They came to Italy around 800 BC and established one of Italy's earliest civilizations. Little is known of their origin, although some historians believe they came from the East, possibly from Asia Minor. The Etruscans settled along Italy's western coast, just north of the Tiber River. They soon became trade competitors with the Greeks living in Italy. The Etruscans learned much about Greek myths, architecture, sculpture, and language. It is possible that the Etruscans first introduced Greek culture to the Romans. Much of later Roman culture would reflect Greek tradition and customs.

The Founding of Rome

The city of Rome began on the banks of the Tiber River, about fifteen miles from the seacoast. Here trade routes that ran along the western coast of Italy crossed the river. At this point the river was easy to ford. People from Latium began to settle on the hills that overlooked this spot. A colony of Latin people established a village on the Palatine Hill near the Tiber. Soon other Latin villages were founded on the surrounding hills. Sometime during the eighth century BC, seven of these villages formed a league—the "**League of the Seven Hills**." This was the beginning of the city of Rome.

Like the Greeks, the Romans developed legends to explain their early history. According to Roman tradition, Rome was founded in 753 BC by the twin brothers **Romulus** and **Remus**. The legend tells how a relative of Romulus and Remus usurped the throne and ordered the two babes, who were of royal descent, to be drowned. The infants were placed in a basket and thrown into the Tiber River to die. But a wolf saved the boys and cared for them until a shepherd found them and took them in. As young men Romulus and Remus allegedly returned to found a city near the place where the wolf had discovered them. While marking out the boundaries for the city, Romulus killed Remus in a burst of jealous anger. Romulus was said to have founded the city of Rome, named it after himself, and become its first king.

Roman Roads

One of the most important factors in Rome's conquest and control of vast areas of land was its system of roads. Roman engineers constructed over fifty thousand miles of main roads, along with two hundred thousand miles of other roads. The first and most famous road, constructed in 312 BC, is the Appian Way, which runs over one hundred miles from Rome to Capua. It was along this road that the apostle Paul traveled on his journey to Rome (Acts 28:14–15). The roads were built in four or five layers, called strata (from which we get our word *street*). After surveyors had planned the road's course, laborers dug down three to five feet to a solid foundation. Occasionally construction began with a layer of sand, called pavimentum, to even out the surface. Then came the main layers: first, a bed of small rocks, from ten inches to two feet thick; next, a layer of finer concrete, about a foot thick on the sides and eighteen inches thick in the middle (thus providing an arched pavement for water runoff); lastly, a layer from six inches to two feet thick consisting of large paving stones fitted closely together to provide a smooth ride. This final layer was set into the still moist concrete below. The finished road, anywhere from eight to twenty-four feet wide, was strong enough to bear the weight of the Roman armies as they traveled to the farthest reaches of the empire. The layers made the surface slightly resilient, or flexible, so that it would not crack and break up as our modern roads sometimes do. Drains kept water, which would also harm the roads, out of the way. The Romans built the main roads primarily as highways to speed their armies on their way. However, these roads were later used by the early Christians as they carried the gospel throughout the Roman world.

Via Appia Antica*; a section of the Appian Way near Rome*

Early Society and Government

Ancient Roman home at Pompeii

The basic unit of early Roman society was the family. The family consisted of a small community—self-sufficient and self-ruled. It included not only the father, wife, and children, but also all the people who lived in the household, such as slaves. (Even property was considered to be part of the family.) The father (***pater*** in Latin) was the sole authority over the family, and his control extended to every aspect of family life. He ruled his family without interference from the state. The father was in charge of the family's worship and dispensed discipline and law, holding even the power of life and death over members of his household.

Romans took great pride in their family heritage. Parents taught their children the values of loyalty, submission to authority, self-control, and duty. Rome's strong families coupled with the patriotism and hardworking spirit of its people provided the foundation for its greatness.

The family also provided the basis for larger social groups. A number of families from a common ancestor are called a **clan**. Likewise, a number of clans united by common beliefs and living in a particular region are called a **tribe**.

Early Roman society consisted of two social classes. They differed greatly from each other in the social and political privileges of their members. The wealthy landholders and noble families made up the aristocratic class (a privileged class) called the **patricians**. They held the highest positions in the early Roman society. The majority of the people, however, belonged to the so-called inferior class called the **plebeians** (plee BEE unz). These were the "common people"—the farmers, traders, and craftsmen.

The early government of Rome was a monarchy. The king served as the chief priest, the commander of the army, and the administrator of justice. The king's authority was called the **imperium**. A small bundle of rods which enclosed an axe, called the **fasces**, symbolized his power. The king was probably elected by the people through a popular assembly that also bestowed the imperium on the newly elected king. The king often sought advice on official matters from a council of clan leaders known as the Senate.

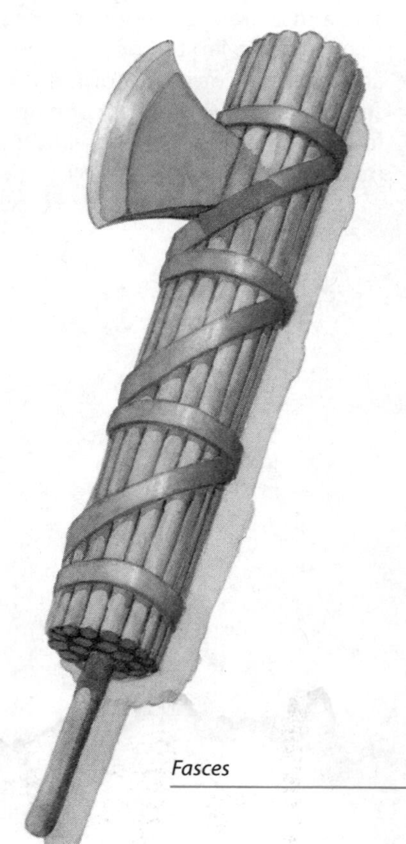
Fasces

Section Quiz

1. What did the Romans call the Mediterranean Sea?
2. According to tradition, in what year was the city of Rome founded?
3. According to legend, what two brothers founded Rome?
4. What were the two main social classes of ancient Rome?
5. What became the symbol of the king's authority in early Roman society?

★ How did the family unit play a significant role in the development of early Rome?

II. The Early Roman Republic

Establishment

About a century after the founding of Rome, the Etruscans crossed the Tiber River from the north and conquered the Latin villages. During the period of Etruscan rule, Rome grew from a weak league of villages to become the leading Latin city. As the influence of Rome increased, so did the Roman nobility's hatred for the Etruscan monarch. In 509 BC they overthrew the king. In the place of the monarchy, they established a new form of government called

What Is a Republic?

A republic is a form of government in which voting citizens control the power of government through elected officials under law. The word comes from the Latin *res publica*, which literally means "a public thing." The Romans believed that while kings often advanced themselves and their families, a republic would best protect the interests of the people. There have been many different forms of republics in history. In some only a small portion of the people have held full citizenship and have thus been able to vote. In others the vast majority of the people have had this privilege. You are probably most familiar with the word *republic* in connection with the government of the United States. The framers of the American Constitution feared government by monarchy or oligarchy because rulers under these types of governments often abused their powers and oppressed the people. Likewise, these men feared pure democracy because it might lead to mob rule. They studied the Roman Republic and saw the wisdom of a government that blended the elements of monarchy, oligarchy, and democracy into one government under written law. The framers of the Constitution recognized the biblical truth that men are evil by nature and therefore cannot be trusted. For this reason they valued a limited government that would keep any one man or group of men from obtaining absolute power. Many of the principles of government found in the American Constitution came from the model of the Roman Republic.

a **republic**. Under the Roman Republic the administration of government was divided among three governing branches: the consuls, the Senate, and the assemblies.

Two elected **consuls** (government officials) replaced the king and held the imperium. They supervised the everyday affairs of government, commanded the Roman army, and served as the supreme judges of the land. Power was equally divided between the consuls; one could not act without the consent of the other. Each consul served only a one-year term at a time. The shortness of the term prevented a consul from becoming too powerful. During the early years of the republic, members of the patrician class held the office of consul almost exclusively.

The **Senate** became the most important and most powerful body of the republic. Though the Senate was intended to serve the interests of all the people of Rome, it soon became an aristocratic body that safeguarded the powers of the patrician class. The Senate was composed of three hundred members who were appointed for life by the consuls. The permanency of the Senate resulted in an increase of its powers beyond its early advisory role. It controlled the government's finances, passed laws, and supervised the foreign affairs of the republic.

The republic also had assemblies through which the people could express their views. Wealth, birth, and the place of one's residence determined the membership and voting procedures of these various assemblies. The chief assembly of the early republic was the **Assembly of Centuries**. This assembly voted on legislation submitted by the consuls, made declarations of war, and elected high-ranking government officials. However, the Senate had veto power over the acts passed by this assembly.

Struggle Within the Republic

The patrician nobles who expelled the Etruscan king took firm control of the government. Patricians held the consulships, dominated the Senate and assemblies, made most of the laws, and controlled the courts. In contrast, the plebeians had few social privileges and virtually no voice in government. They were excluded from holding public office, and marriage between plebeians and patricians was forbidden. For failing to repay loans, plebeians could lose their property and even be sold into slavery.

For two centuries following the founding of the republic, the plebeians struggled to gain political and social equality. During these two centuries, Rome was constantly waging war against its neighbors in Italy. Because the patricians could not handle the burden of war alone, they had to rely more and more on the common people to help in fighting these wars. As the plebeians shared in the dangers of fighting, they wanted to share in the privilege of being represented in the government. By threatening to desert the army, the plebeians gradually gained concessions from the patricians.

One of the first concessions gained by the plebeians was the right to have their own assembly and elected officials. They met as the Council of Plebeians and passed resolutions called **plebiscites**. These were binding only on the plebeians, however, and not on the patrician class. The Council of Plebeians elected ten men to the office of **tribune**. The tribunes protected the rights and

The Roman Forum

interests of the common people. By crying out **"Veto!"** ("I forbid!"), the tribunes could stop unjust acts of patrician officials.

In the past, patrician judges had taken advantage of the plebeians, who were not familiar with the traditions that made up Rome's unwritten laws. However, continued pressure from the plebeians finally forced the patricians to put the Roman laws into writing. Around 450 BC these laws were written down on twelve tablets and hung in the **Roman Forum**, the section of the city that was the center of government. Now all could know the law. Likewise, the law was to be applied equally to all. Young boys in the republic memorized the whole code as part of their school work. These tablets of law, called the **Law of Twelve Tables**, became the foundation of Roman civil law.

Gradually the plebeians improved their political and social standing in the republic. They gained the right to hold public offices which had previously been held only by the patricians. A few plebeians even became senators. Debtor slavery was abolished, and the law against intermarriage between plebeians and patricians was repealed. In 287 BC the plebeian assembly, now called the **Tribal Assembly**, gained the power to pass laws binding upon all the people of Rome—patricians as well as plebeians.

As the result of these two centuries of struggle, the plebeians officially gained social and political equality with the patricians. The peaceful changes seemed to make the republic more representative of the people. But as the distinctions between patricians and plebeians began to disappear, a new class distinction began to develop—the rich versus the poor. Wealthy plebeians and patricians formed a new alliance that maintained control of the Senate and held the reins of power in the republic.

Section Quiz

1. In what year was the Roman Republic founded?
2. What was the most powerful body within the governmental structure of the republic?
3. What power did tribunes exercise over unjust acts of patrician officials?

4. What was the name of the Roman law that was written down and placed in the Roman Forum?
5. What was the name of the plebeian assembly that gained the power to pass laws binding on all the people of Rome, regardless of their social class?

★ Why did the political changes and increased power of some plebeians not end the struggle for power in Rome?

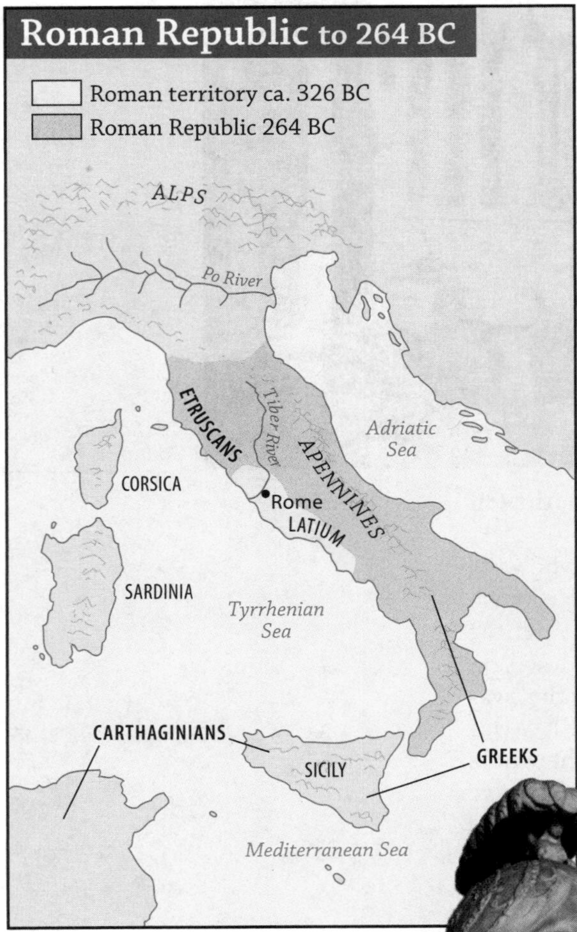

Roman Republic to 264 BC

III. The Mediterranean—A Roman Sea

The Romans had not originally set out to conquer the world. But through constant warfare from 509 to 133 BC, Rome grew from an important city along the Tiber River into the largest empire of the ancient world. How did this expansion take place?

Rome—The Master of Italy

During the years of internal struggles between the patricians and the plebeians, Rome was also involved in external struggles with its neighbors in Italy. Under Etruscan rule Rome became the leading Latin city. With the expulsion of the Etruscan king in 509 BC, other Latin cities joined with Rome in a defensive alliance for protection against the Etruscans. Just as the members of the Delian League had revolted against the growing power of Athens, so the Latin cities, fearful of the growing power of Rome, revolted. Rome defeated the Latin cities, securing a strong position in central Italy, and later acquired the land to the north by defeating the Etruscans.

Rome soon began expanding into southern Italy, threatening the Greek colonies located there. The Greek colonies feared Roman conquest and appealed to **Pyrrhus**, a distant relative of Alexander the Great, for help. With the aid of war elephants (the "tanks" of ancient warfare), Pyrrhus defeated the Romans twice. In gaining the second victory, however, Pyrrhus's army suffered such great losses that he reportedly exclaimed, "Another such victory and I shall be ruined." Since that time, a "Pyrrhic victory" has referred to a victory whose costs outweighed any advantage that may have been gained. Pyrrhus returned to Greece when Rome, joined by another Greek rival, further weakened his force. With Pyrrhus back in Greece, Rome was able to conquer all of southern Italy.

By 265 BC Rome controlled all of the Italian Peninsula. Its task now was to rule effectively a land that included Latins, Etruscans, and Greeks. Unlike most conquering peoples, the Romans treated their conquered subjects with mercy and fairness instead of force and oppression. As long as they did not rebel against Roman authority, Rome's subjects lived in relative peace. To many of its conquered subjects in Italy, Rome granted citizenship—the right to vote and hold office. To others Rome allowed a great degree of local independence. Although Rome did not demand tribute (payment of money or grain showing submission) from the conquered states within Italy, it did require them to furnish troops to help Rome fight wars. The protection of Roman law and the stability and prosperity that Rome brought to the Italian Peninsula secured the loyalty of its subjects and allies.

Pyrrhus

Rome—The Master of the Western Mediterranean

Rome's conquest of the Italian Peninsula brought it into conflict with Carthage, another power in the Western world. This rival of Rome, located in North Africa, possessed good harbors, rich mining resources, and the best navy in the western Mediterranean. While Phoenicia, the mother country of Carthage, grew weak as a result of Assyrian and Chaldean conquests, Carthage built its own empire in the West. Its empire included the North African coast, southern Spain, the islands of Sardinia and Corsica, and part of the island of Sicily.

Between 264 and 146 BC, Rome and Carthage fought each other in three wars. Both cities controlled much territory in the western Mediterranean. Both were expanding rapidly. In addition, Rome and Carthage were competing commercially for control of trade in the Mediterranean. This rivalry, which was built on both jealousy and fear, led to a series of wars known as the Punic Wars. (*Punici* was the Roman word for Phoenicians.)

Differences Between Carthage and Rome

The Carthaginians naturally are superior at sea both in efficiency and equipment, because seamanship has long been their national craft, . . . but as regards military service on land the Romans are much more efficient. . . . The troops [the Carthaginians] employ are foreign and mercenary [hired for pay], whereas those of the Romans are native of the soil and citizens. So that in this respect also we must pronounce the political system of Rome to be superior to that of Carthage, the Carthaginians continuing to depend for the maintenance of their freedom on the courage of mercenary force but the Romans on their own valour and on the aid of their allies. Consequently even if they happen to be worsted at the outset, the Romans redeem defeat by final success, while it is the contrary with the Carthaginians. For the Romans, fighting as they are for their country and their children, never can abate their fury but continue to throw their whole hearts into the struggle until they get the better of their enemies.

Polybius, The Histories, *6.52.*

The First Punic War (264–241 BC)

The First Punic War was fought over control of the island of Sicily. The Romans feared the Carthaginians would become too strong on the island. A powerful rival force could control the waters between Sicily and Italy and thus hinder Roman trade in the Mediterranean. Sicily could also become a base for a Carthaginian attack on southern Italy. The only way Rome could stop Carthage was to break its naval supremacy.

Using the design of a captured Carthaginian warship, Rome began to build a navy of its own. Although Rome soon possessed the same ships, Roman sailors could not match the experience and skill of the Carthaginians. So Rome developed new tactics for fighting at sea. Up to that time, naval battles were won by ramming and sinking the enemy's vessels. Rome substituted soldiers for experienced sailors. When an enemy ship came near, a plank was dropped (like a drawbridge) so that its spiked tip fastened to the deck of the enemy's ship. Armed Roman soldiers then crossed over and captured the ship. By this method Rome crippled the navy of Carthage.

Rome endured many setbacks, including the destruction of much of the Roman fleet by fierce storms. In addition, Roman military and diplomatic blunders prolonged the war. However, Rome finally defeated Carthage by overcoming its naval supremacy. Growing weary from the long war, Carthage sued for peace in 241 BC. Terms of the settlement included Roman control

Italian coastline along the Mediterranean Sea. A strong navy was vital for Rome's defense of its coasts and trade routes.

of Sicily and the requirement that Carthage pay for Roman losses.

The Second Punic War (218–201 BC)

Carthage recovered from its defeat in the First Punic War and extended its control over much of Spain. In 219 BC Carthage attacked a Roman ally, a Spanish town on the Mediterranean coast. The city fell after an eight-month siege, and a second war broke out between Carthage and Rome. Rome, which now had the superior navy, planned to isolate Carthage's forces in Spain. By sending one army to Spain and another to Carthage, Rome hoped for a quick end to the war against the divided Carthaginian forces. This strategy might have worked had it not been for a young Carthaginian commander named **Hannibal**.

Historians have likened Hannibal to Alexander the Great. His effective leadership and tactical skills won the devotion of his soldiers. This military genius devised strategies that are still being studied by army experts today. (Some of his tactics were used in tank battles during World War II.) Hannibal realized that his only hope of success was to invade Italy and capture Rome. By invading Italy, he planned to present himself as liberator of Rome's conquered allies and give them an opportunity to break with Rome and gain their freedom. Without the soldiers and resources supplied by its allies, Rome could be conquered—so Hannibal thought.

Hannibal

With cavalry, elephants, and some forty thousand men, Hannibal set out from Spain. He marched his army over the rugged, snow-covered Alps and into northern Italy. The dangerous mountain passes, wintry weather, and attacks from mountain tribes combined to cut his army by about half and left him with only a few supplies and elephants. Nevertheless, he surprised the Romans. They had believed it impossible for any army to cross the Alps—especially during the winter. During the next fifteen years, Hannibal brilliantly led his outnumbered army to many victories in Italy.

Battle of Cannae—In the spring of 216 BC, the Romans suffered one of the worst defeats in their long history. At Cannae (KAN ee), a small town southeast of Rome, the Roman legions confronted Hannibal's army. Because the Romans outnumbered his army almost two to one, Hannibal had to rely on superior battle tactics. He arranged his forces in the same fashion as the Roman troops—cavalry units on the flanks and infantry at the center. But unlike the Roman line, Hannibal's line bulged forward at the center, inviting the Romans to attack there. The Roman infantry charged the center of Hannibal's line, hoping to break it and divide the Carthaginian forces. While the outside of Hannibal's line held its ground, the center (according to plan) retreated, drawing the advancing Romans into a U-shaped pocket. The Romans soon found themselves hemmed in by the enemy on three sides. Meanwhile, Hannibal's cavalry, which had routed Rome's cavalry, circled around and attacked the rear of the Roman infantry. The surrounded Roman army was almost completely wiped out. Estimates vary, but Hannibal may have lost six thousand men, while the Romans may have lost around sixty thousand men. A generation passed before Rome recovered from this terrible defeat.

Following the Battle of Cannae, the situation looked very grim for the Romans, who had suffered numerous defeats at the hands of Hannibal. To make matters worse, Rome had to contend with a new Carthaginian ally, Macedonia, and suppress Syracuse, a powerful Greek city on Sicily that revolted against Rome. Despite these advantages, Hannibal was unable to conquer the city of Rome. He lacked the heavy siege equipment needed to break down Rome's walls. Furthermore, he gained few recruits from the people he freed from Roman rule. Rome's fair and generous treatment of its subjects encouraged them to remain loyal to Rome.

Scipio—The turning point in the war came through the daring strategy of a young Roman commander named Scipio (SIP ee oh). A member of a powerful family, he became the most famous Roman of his time. After defeating the Carthaginian forces in Spain, he could have moved his army into Italy to take on Hannibal. But instead he crossed over to North Africa and prepared to attack Carthage. Hannibal, who had not lost a battle in Italy, was ordered back home to defend Carthage. By the time he arrived, the Romans had already gained the advantage. Not even the leadership of Hannibal could stop Scipio and the Roman legions. At the Battle of Zama (202 BC), the Romans defeated the Carthaginian army. Carthage surrendered and was forced to give up all its territory outside of North Africa, reduce its fleet to only ten vessels, and pay a great sum to Rome for war damages. Rome was now the master of the western Mediterranean world.

The Siege of Syracuse

When Rome attacked Syracuse during the Second Punic War, the Roman commander Marcellus expected to capture the city with only a five-day siege. However, the Romans found their land-and-sea attack repulsed by a variety of unusual war machines. The land forces were met by stones and other objects hurled from great distances. The naval attack faced catapults hurling large stones. Syracuse also used cranes, some of which dropped huge stones on the ships, while others with chains and iron claws picked ships up and tipped them over or smashed them on the rocks along the shore. The inventor and director of all this advanced war machinery was Syracuse's most famous mathematician, Archimedes. So effective was his defense that the Romans became bogged down in a stalemate. In 212 BC Rome finally captured Syracuse by sending a small group of soldiers who scaled the walls at night and entered the outer city. After killing the guards on duty, the Romans opened the city gates to a larger Roman force. The Syracusans were defeated, in part, because they so trusted in their machines that they were unprepared to use their more conventional weapons.

The Third Punic War (149–146 BC)

Fifty years after the Second Punic War, many Romans became fearful and jealous of the recovering prosperity of Carthage. One man especially, the Roman senator Cato, sought to arouse the Roman people to take action against Rome's old rival. No matter what the topic of debate was in the Senate, Cato

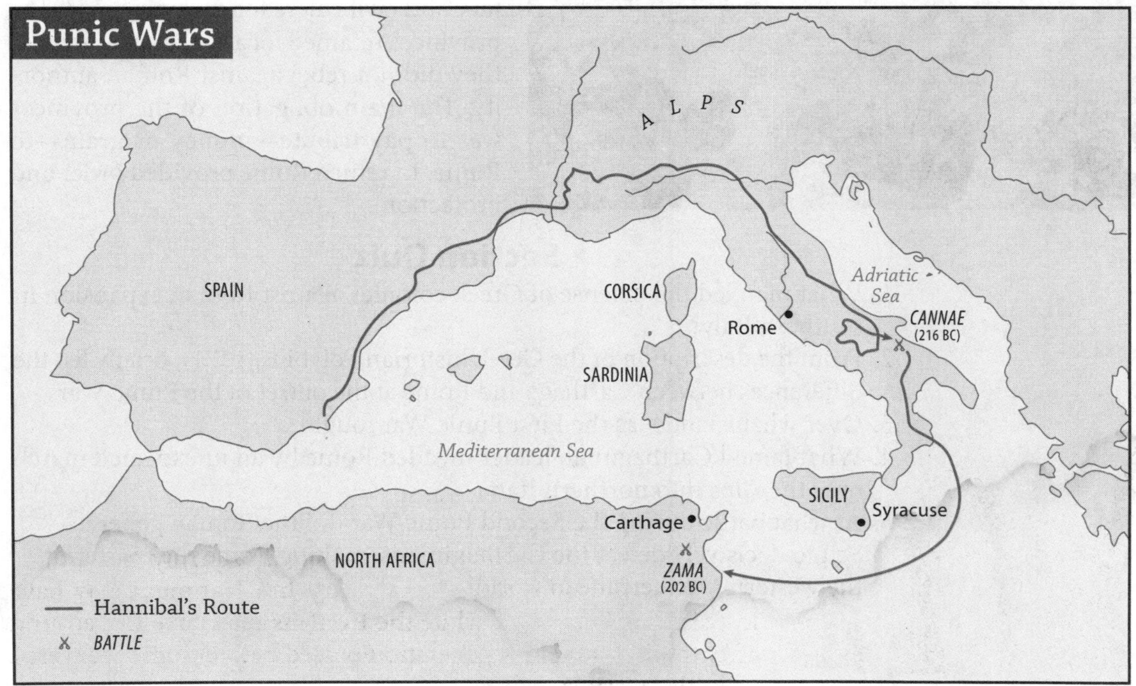

ended all his speeches with the statement, "but I declare that Carthage must be destroyed." When Carthage broke one of the provisions of its treaty with Rome, Rome harshly demanded that the Carthaginians move their city ten miles inland. Since such a move would mean the death of this commercial center, the citizens decided to fight instead. But the Carthaginians were no match for the Romans. After a three-year siege, the Romans captured the city and destroyed it. They sold the surviving inhabitants into slavery and turned the land around Carthage into a new Roman province called Africa.

Rome—The Master of the Eastern Mediterranean

After the Second Punic War, Rome turned its attention to the eastern portion of the Mediterranean. Here the kingdoms carved out of Alexander the Great's empire—Macedonia, Syria, and Egypt—were engaged in a power struggle of their own. Because Macedonia had joined Carthage against Rome during the Second Punic War, Rome sent its legions to deal with Macedonia after Carthage had been defeated. With Macedonia weakened by its wars with Rome, the king of Syria marched into Asia Minor, crossed the Hellespont, and invaded the kingdom of Macedonia. Rome met this challenge by soundly defeating the Syrian armies. Egypt, the weakest of the three remnants of Alexander's empire, thought it best to make an alliance with Rome. With this completed, Rome became the master of the entire Mediterranean world. The prophet Daniel's visions were fulfilled as the kingdoms of Alexander's generals fell to the Roman Empire (Dan. 7:6–7; 8:8).

Ruins at Carthage

At first, Rome allowed its eastern conquests a certain amount of self-government. But because of constant uprisings and petty rivalries, Rome reorganized its holdings throughout the Mediterranean into provinces. Governors appointed by the Roman Senate administered these provinces and served as the chief military and civil rulers for each province. The provinces retained local freedom as long as they did not rebel against Roman authority. The main obligation of the provinces was to pay tribute—money or grain—to Rome. In return Rome provided order and protection.

Section Quiz

1. What man led the defense of Greek colonies against Roman expansion in southern Italy?
2. From the description of the Greek historian Polybius (p. 71), briefly list the differences between Carthage and Rome at the outset of the Punic Wars.
3. Over what island was the First Punic War fought?
4. What famed Carthaginian leader invaded Rome by an unexpected march over the Alps into northern Italy?
5. At what battle during the Second Punic War did the Roman general Scipio decisively defeat the Carthaginians, making Rome the master of the western Mediterranean world?

IV. Decline into a Dictatorship

By the first century BC, Rome was the greatest power in the Mediterranean world. Nevertheless, during the last two centuries before Christ, the very foundation of the republic was shaken—not by any foreign enemy but by problems that arose within the republic as a result of unintended consequences of Roman expansion.

Problems

The economic and military backbone of the early republic was the hardworking citizen-farmer. During the period of Roman expansion, the greatest military burden as well as economic hardships fell on the small farmers. Many of them lost their land. When these citizen-farmers returned from fighting Rome's wars, they faced numerous obstacles. Some of them lacked the money needed to get their land back in shape; others were unable to pay their back taxes and thus lost their farms to the government. Those who were able to grow crops were unable to compete with the large farms of the wealthy aristocrats or with the cheap grain imported from the new Roman territories. In poverty and in debt, small farmers sold their land (usually for a cheap price) and sought jobs in the cities or as tenant farmers. But jobs were hard to find because of the increased number of slaves that were brought into Italy following Rome's conquests. Landless and unemployed, the citizen-farmers became dissatisfied and restless. Their self-reliant spirit broke down, and many turned to the government for help.

But they received no help from the government. Since its early years, the republic had undergone many changes in order to provide equal rights and privileges for all Roman citizens. The Tribal Assembly, which represented the common people, had greatly increased in power. But no sooner had these gains been achieved than the Punic Wars broke out. The common people failed to assume the responsibilities they had struggled so long to gain. They relied instead on the more experienced and stronger leadership of the Senate to see them through times of crisis. Thus, during the period of the Roman conquests, the Senate was able to increase its power and again dominate the republic.

The conditions that devastated the poor provided opportunities for increased prosperity for the already wealthy landholders, whose interests the Senate represented. Many of these wealthy landowners expanded their own estates by buying out the small farmers. They also controlled large tracts of land in the new Roman provinces. Aristocratic senators, once concerned for the best interests of the republic, tended to become selfish and pleasure loving. The pleas for reform from the masses of unemployed and landless went unheeded by the majority in the Senate, whose self-centered interests opposed any change. The Senate was unwilling to address the social and economic problems at home.

The corruption in the government at Rome spread to the Roman provinces. Many of the provincial governors appointed by the Senate used their powers for their own selfish gains. One of the greatest abuses was in the collection of taxes that each province paid to Rome. Roman officials often made agreements with men called **publicans** to collect taxes in a given province. The publicans would

Publicans

The reader of Scripture may be familiar with the term *publican*. These tax collectors were despised. Yet the New Testament records many publicans who trusted Christ. First, we read of the repentance and baptism of publicans in response to John the Baptist's preaching (Luke 3:12). Then we find that Jesus chose Matthew, a publican, to be one of His twelve disciples (Matthew 9, Mark 2, and Luke 5). We read that publicans came to hear Jesus preach (Luke 15:1)—that He even ate with them (Mark 2:16, Luke 5:30). In fact, Jesus makes a remarkable statement in Matthew 21:32. He tells the Pharisees (the religious leaders of the day) that publicans and other sinners are entering the kingdom of heaven and not them! We read again of Jesus loving these reviled people in Luke 19 when He calls to a publican sitting in a sycamore tree, who was watching Jesus pass by. This tax collector received Him with joy and was never the same again.

It is a testimony to the power of the gospel that even these most detested people received His message and were transformed like any other sinner.

agree to pay a fixed amount to Rome. Whatever they collected above this fixed sum they could keep for themselves. In return for a percentage of the extra money received, some senators and governors made deals to see that certain men were appointed publicans. Soon the publicans were among the most detested people in the Roman territories; they had become rich, but at the expense of the people. These abuses were still part of Roman society during the time of Jesus and His disciples in the first century AD.

Failure of Reform

The poor found champions for their cause in the brothers **Tiberius** and **Gaius Gracchus** (GRAK us). The Gracchi (GRAK eye; plural form of Gracchus) were from one of the noble families of Rome. Their father had been a consul, and their grandfather was Scipio, who had led Rome to victory in the Second Punic War. Elected as a tribune in 133 BC, Tiberius strove for reforms in the republic and became the spokesman for the common man.

Tiberius's Support for the Citizen-Soldiers

The wild beasts that roam over Italy . . . have every one of them a cave or lair to lurk in; but the men who fight and die for Italy enjoy the common air and light, indeed, but nothing else; houseless and homeless they wander about with their wives and children. . . . They fight and die to support others in wealth and luxury, and though they are styled masters of the world, they have not a single clod of earth that is their own.

Quoted in Plutarch, Parallel Lives, *trans. Bernadotte Perrin, "Tiberius Gracchus," 9.*

Tiberius proposed changes in Rome's land policy. For years wealthy aristocrats had monopolized the lands gained through Rome's conquests. Tiberius wanted these "public lands" to be divided among the poor. He also sought to limit the amount of public land controlled by any one person. Although the Tribal Assembly adopted his reforms, his proposals gained him powerful enemies. Wealthy landholders foresaw their own financial ruin, and senators disliked his reviving the powers of the Tribal Assembly. When Tiberius sought reelection as a tribune—an act contrary to Roman tradition at that time—angry senators killed him and three hundred of his followers. The murderers then threw the bodies into the Tiber River.

When Gaius became tribune in 123 BC, he sought to carry on his brother's land reform measures. He also proposed that the government sell grain at low prices to the poor. But the Senate undermined the popular support of Gaius by offering its own programs. (The Senate, however, had no intention of carrying through with these reforms.) During a riot carefully planned by his enemies, Gaius lost his life. Some accounts say he committed suicide to keep from falling into the hands of the senatorial forces. Once again the Senate had prevailed.

Civil War

In the early years of the republic, the Senate, in order to preserve the stability of the government, met the challenges of the plebeians by granting concessions. In response to the new challenge of the Gracchi brothers, the Senate abandoned peaceful measures and resorted to violence to preserve the power and wealth of the aristocrats. The failure of the Senate to deal with reform for the poor further weakened the republic. The disorder of the Roman state finally led to civil war.

The Roman Army

In his conquest of the ancient world, Alexander the Great relied on the Greek military formation called the "phalanx." This formation packed hundreds of men into a tight wedge with their long spears facing forward. The phalanx was very powerful and almost impossible to defeat on level ground. But it had one weakness that made it almost useless to the Romans: it could not maneuver. It could march forward or backward, but because the men and spears were tightly intertwined, it could not turn easily. Because Rome's enemies used a number of different fighting tactics, Rome needed a formation that could adapt to many different situations. Thus, Rome invented the "legion." Each legion (about five thousand men) was divided into several groups. Up front was a line of "skirmishers," carrying short spears. Next came two lines of soldiers, marching in groups called centuries. Each century, which was headed by a centurion, stood in a checkerboard formation with the other centuries. These soldiers carried heavier spears. Behind all these soldiers came a line of men carrying heavy thrusting spears with which they could mow down the enemy. As the front lines tired, they could retreat through the gaps in the checkerboard formation and rest behind the last line. There were two advantages to this formation. First, it was much more maneuverable than the phalanx, so it could adjust more easily to variations in the land and the enemy's formations. Second, the men could move in and out more easily, fight more freely, and get rest if they needed it.

The First Civil War

In the first century BC, three civil wars shook the very foundations of Rome, exposing the corruption in Roman society. The rivalry between the Tribal Assembly and the Senate gave occasion for the outbreak of the first civil war.

Following the deaths of the Gracchi brothers, the common people found a new champion for their cause in **Marius** (155?–86 BC). Marius was a well-known military hero who had gained fame for victories in North Africa and Europe. He reorganized the dwindling Roman army, allowing the poor and landless to enlist for long terms of service. He promised them a share in the spoils of war—land and money. Up to this time citizens served in the army out of loyalty for their country. Now Marius created a "professional" army, one that served for financial gain rather than for a patriotic cause. Their devotion to the commander of the army was greater than their devotion to Rome. This shift in loyalty would later be the undoing of Rome as generals used their armies to further their own interests rather than those of the people and the state.

Expansion of the Roman Republic

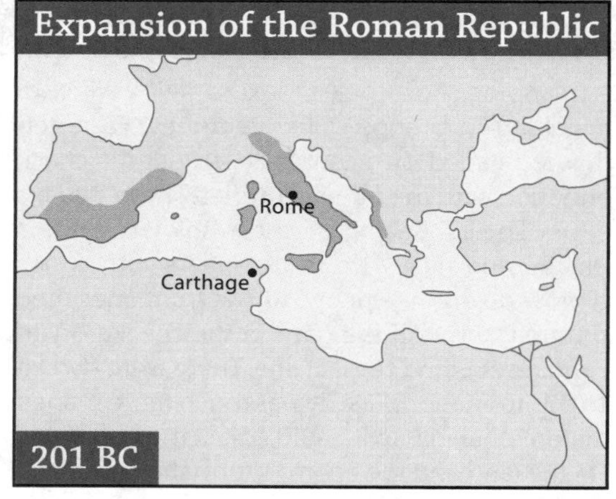

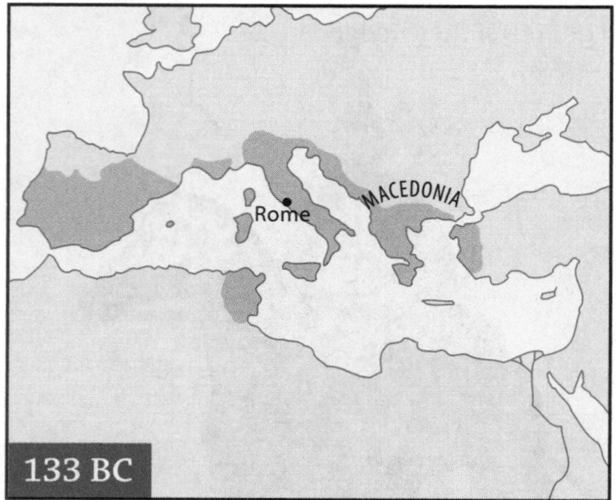

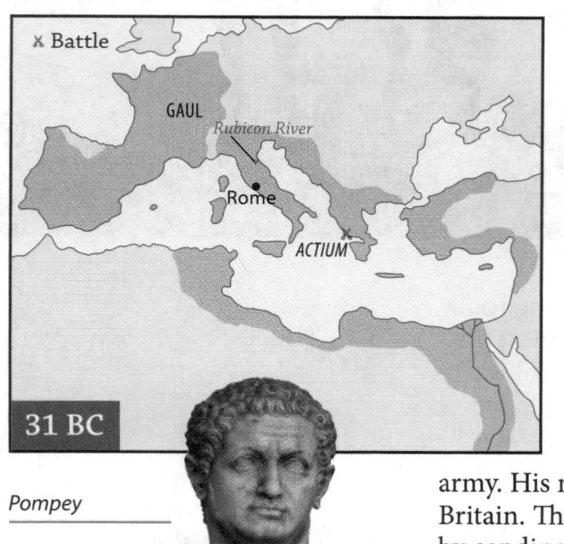

Pompey

In 88 BC war broke out in Asia Minor. The Senate appointed **Sulla** (138–78 BC), a general who was sympathetic to the senatorial side, to command the Roman army in the east. The Tribal Assembly, however, rejected the Senate's choice and appointed Marius instead. The years that followed saw much bloodshed as the tension between the Tribal Assembly and the Senate, fueled by the rivalry between Marius and Sulla, developed into civil war. In the end Sulla emerged victorious.

Sulla had himself declared dictator. He then set about reorganizing the Roman government. He hoped to restore stability and order by reviving the power and prestige of the Senate. The influence of the Tribal Assembly and the tribunes was now all but gone. With the power of the Senate firmly established, Sulla resigned as dictator. The Senate, however, was unable to maintain control of the government.

The Second Civil War

Though the first civil war ended with the Senate triumphant over the Tribal Assembly, it was obvious that a powerful man at the head of the army could control the state. Ambitious men sought to gain that control. The people, weary of economic and political crises, were willing to exchange their freedom for temporary relief.

Crassus and **Pompey**, two commanders who served in Sulla's army, competed with one another for fame and power after Sulla's death. Crassus was one of the richest men of Rome. He added military glory to his riches by raising an army and defeating a slave revolt that had threatened the Italian Peninsula. But his military glory was surpassed by that of Pompey, who had many conquests in the east. He had turned Asia Minor, Syria, and Palestine into Roman provinces. He also rid the Mediterranean Sea of pirates.

The wide accomplishments of both Crassus and Pompey, however, failed to win them the popular support that **Julius Caesar** received. This young leader, nephew of the popular Marius, undertook ambitious projects to win the public favor. Caesar (100–44 BC) was a wise politician who knew how to sway the common people in order to accomplish his aims. Crassus, Pompey, and Caesar each wanted to be sole ruler of Rome. None, though, had sufficient power to assume complete control: Crassus had the money, Pompey had the support of the Senate, and Caesar had the favor of the common people. So in 60 BC, they formed an alliance called a **triumvirate** (try UM ver it; "rule of three men") to rule Rome together.

Caesar used his position to get himself appointed governor of Gaul (modern France). There he trained a well-disciplined and loyal army. His military campaigns led him through Gaul and across the channel to Britain. Though away from Rome, he kept his name before the Roman people by sending written accounts of his military accomplishments back to Rome. These published accounts, his *Commentaries on the Gallic War,* made him the talk of Rome. Jealous of Caesar's growing strength and popularity, Pompey sought the help of the Senate to weaken his rival. (Crassus had died in war in Asia.) When the Senate ordered Caesar to return to Rome and disband his army, Caesar crossed the Rubicon (a river in northern Italy) and marched his army toward Rome. By this act Caesar declared war on Pompey and the Senate. ("Crossing the Rubicon" has come to mean making a fateful decision from which there is no turning back.)

Plutarch's Account of Caesar's Death

Those who had prepared themselves for the murder bared each of them his dagger, and Caesar, hemmed in on all sides, whichever way he turned confront[ed] blows of weapons. . . . When he saw that Brutus had drawn his dagger, he pulled his toga down over his head and sank, either by chance or because pushed there by his murderers, against the pedestal on which the statue of Pompey stood. And the pedestal was drenched with his blood, so that one might have thought that Pompey himself was presiding over this vengence upon his enemy, who now lay prostrate at his feet, quivering from a multitude of wounds.

Plutarch, Parallel Lives, *"Caesar," 66.*

Pompey and members of the Senate fled to Greece to give themselves time to raise an army to battle Caesar. When the two armies finally met, Pompey's forces were no match for Caesar's seasoned veterans. Pompey fled to Egypt, where he was later killed. With power firmly in his hands, Caesar had himself proclaimed dictator for life.

Julius Caesar

Caesar accomplished many reforms during his short rule. He curbed the corruption of the provincial governments, established colonies for the landless army veterans, granted citizenship to many non-Italians living in Rome's new colonies, and initiated many public works programs. He also established the calendar that is the basis for our modern-day calendar year of 365¼ days.

Although popular with the people, Caesar had enemies among the nobles and senators. Some were former followers of Pompey; others feared Caesar's growing power and the impact of his reforms. On the "**Ides**" (fifteenth) **of March** in **44 BC**, a group of conspirators assassinated Caesar in the Senate chamber.

The Third Civil War

A third civil war broke out after Caesar's death to determine the next ruler. Caesar's friend and right-hand man, Mark Antony, teamed with Octavian (Caesar's nephew and only male relative) to capture and punish Caesar's murderers. Octavian and Antony then divided the Roman territory in half—Octavian ruling in the west and Antony (who had fallen under the charm of Cleopatra, the queen of Egypt) ruling in the east. Each man, however, was too ambitious to share power with the other. Again war was used to settle the question of who was to be sole ruler of Rome. In **31 BC**, off the coast of Greece, Octavian's navy won a decisive victory over Antony and Cleopatra at the Battle of Actium. Antony and Cleopatra fled the battle, realizing their cause was lost. They both later committed suicide. Octavian, only thirty-one years of age, then ruled the entire Roman world.

With Octavian, one era of Roman history ended and a new one began. Historians have called the period from the Battle of Actium (31 BC) to the Fall of Rome (AD 476) the Roman Empire. Rome did not become an empire during these years; it had already built a vast empire under the republic. But beginning with Octavian (some say with Julius Caesar), Rome was no longer a republic—a "public matter"—but was transformed into a government ruled by an **imperator** (an ancient title given to the commander of a victorious army). During this period, which lasted nearly five hundred years,

How the Romans Measured Time

The Romans had two different ways of measuring time. First, they divided the daylight hours into twelve equal parts. (This meant that the "hours" were longer in the summer than in the winter.) Second, the Romans invented a water clock, which kept time in much the same manner as our modern clocks. However, these water clocks were so inaccurate that the Roman philosopher Seneca once observed that it was easier to find two philosophers who agreed than it was to find two water clocks that agreed. It is interesting to note that our use of a.m. *(ante meridiem)* and p.m. *(post meridiem)* comes from the Roman system of counting hours from the middle of the day.

In numbering their years, the Romans started counting from the founding of Rome. After the year number, they wrote A.U.C. *(ad urbe condita)*, which means "from the foundation of the city." Their years had 355 days, and even though the calendar was periodically corrected, it was still out of step with the sun. So when Julius Caesar ruled Rome, he asked astronomers to help him set the calendar straight. Upon their recommendations, he decreed that the year 707 A.U.C. (46 BC) would have 445 days. This was done so that the Roman year would once again match the solar year. In Roman history that year was known as the "Year of Confusion."

Thus began the Julian calendar, which remained in use for the next sixteen hundred years. Instead of ten months, each year then had twelve months that alternated between thirty and thirty-one days. Even today we still use the same names for the months that the Romans did. The only difference is that the Romans began their year with March and ended with February.

Perhaps you have always wondered why February has only twenty-eight days when the rest of the months have thirty or thirty-one days. According to tradition, Julius Caesar named the month of July after himself; because he did not want his month to have fewer days than any other, he took a day from February and added it to July, making a total of thirty-one days. Later, when Octavian named the month of August after himself, he also took a day from February so that his month would be just as long as Julius's month.

January—Named after Janus, the Roman god of gates and doors

February—From the Latin word that means to "purify." February was originally the last month of the year. It was during this month that the Romans purified themselves in preparation for the festivals that marked the beginning of the new year.

March—Named after Mars, the Roman god of war

April—From the Latin word that means "to open." April was originally the second month of the year.

May—Two possible sources of the name: (1) named after Maia, the Roman goddess of spring, or (2) from the Latin word that referred to older men (majores); the month of May was sacred to these older men.

June—Two possible sources of the name: (1) named after Juno, the Roman goddess of marriage, or (2) from the Latin word that referred to young men (juniores); the month of June was sacred to these young men.

July—Named by Julius Caesar after himself (It was his birth month.)

August—Named by Caesar Augustus (Octavian) after himself

September—Means "the seventh month"

October—Means "the eighth month"

November—Means "the ninth month"

December—Means "the tenth month"

imperators (from which we get our words *empire* and *emperor*) ruled with supreme power. This period of history will be the focus of the next chapter.

Section Quiz

1. What task did the publicans perform in Roman society?
2. What were the names of the two brothers who became spokesmen for reform in the later days of the republic?
3. Who were the two generals who fought in the First Civil War? Identify which one had the backing of the Senate and which one the backing of the Tribal Assembly.
4. Who were the three rulers of the triumvirate?
5. At what place and in what year did Octavian defeat Antony in the Third Civil War?

★ Did the three civil wars set a pattern for the duration of the existence of the Roman Empire? Support your answer.

Chapter 4 Review

Making Connections

1-3. List the key players in each of the civil wars, the victor, and the condition of the republic at the end of each.

4-5. List two steps by which the plebeians gained a voice in the Roman government.

Developing History Skills

1. What parallels do you see between the conditions contributing to the fall of the Roman Republic and the present conditions in the United States?

Thinking Critically

1. What made the Roman Republic strong? What made it weak?

Living in God's World

1. Western civilizations in the modern era have often modeled their governments on the Roman Republic. From a Christian perspective, is it wise to imitate a pagan government that had no knowledge of Christ or the gospel?
2. Should civic-minded Christians emphasize virtues and character to hold their own societies together? Explain.

People, Places, and Things to Know

Mare Nostrum
Etruscans
League of the Seven Hills
Romulus
Remus
pater
clan
tribe
patricians
plebeians
imperium
fasces
republic
consuls
Senate
Assembly of Centuries
plebiscites
tribune
veto
Roman Forum
Law of Twelve Tables
Tribal Assembly
Pyrrhus
Hannibal
Battle of Cannae
Scipio
publicans
Tiberius and Gaius Gracchus
Marius
Sulla
Crassus
Pompey
Julius Caesar
triumvirate
"Ides" of March (March 15, 44 BC)
31 BC
imperator

5

The Roman Empire

Detail of Christ Leaving the Praetorium *by Gustave Doré from the Bob Jones University Collection*

ישוע הנצרי מלך היהודים
ΙΗΣΟΥΣ ΝΑΖΩΡΑΙΟΣ Ο ΒΑΣΙΛΕΥΣ ΤΩΝ ΙΟΥΔΑΙΩΝ
IESUS NAZARÆUS REX ILLE IUDÆORUM

JESUS OF NAZARETH KING OF THE JEWS—By the command of Pontius Pilate, this inscription was placed on the cross on which Jesus died. Under this sign the long-awaited Messiah—the son of Abraham, Judah, and David—suffered for the sins of His people. But who were His people? The words of this sign would seem to indicate that they were Jews only. But the fact that these words were written not just in Hebrew but also in Greek and Latin would seem to suggest something else—something that is taught everywhere in Scripture. When God called Abraham, He promised that all nations would be blessed in him (Gen. 12:3). When Isaiah prophesied the coming of God's Servant, he foresaw One Who would "bring forth judgment for the Gentiles" and Who would serve as "a light of the Gentiles" (Isa. 42:6). And when Jesus revealed Himself to the Jews, John the Baptist proclaimed, "Behold, the lamb of God, which taketh away the sin of the world" (John 1:29). In this chapter we will see the beginnings of the fulfillment of God's promise to bless all nations through His Son. We will also see how God used the cultures of the Jews, Greeks, and Romans to prepare the human race to face the turning point of history—the life, death, and Resurrection of Jesus. This divine preparation culminated with the Roman Empire. This was the time when the world was made ready, when the "fulness of the time was come" (Gal. 4:4).

I. *Pax Romana*

Octavian's rule brought a period of peace to the Mediterranean world that lasted from 31 BC to AD 180. During these two centuries the Roman Empire reached its height: its boundaries encircled the Mediterranean Sea and included parts of the old Persian Empire in the east as well as most of western Europe and Britain. In contrast to the period of civil wars that preceded Octavian's reign, the first two centuries of the empire were marked for the most part by internal harmony and unity. Trade prospered, travel and communications improved, and cultural activities flourished. The western ancient world experienced a period of peace and prosperity known as the ***Pax Romana*** ("Roman Peace"). Nevertheless, this was in a sense an artificial peace. Won by war and maintained by force, it did not long endure. But during the *Pax Romana*, the Author of Peace—Jesus—was born. By His death on the cross, He secured for mankind a true and lasting peace. He said, "Peace I leave with you, my peace I give unto you: not as the world giveth, give I unto you. Let not your heart be troubled, neither let it be afraid" (John 14:27). Of Him the prophet Isaiah foretold, "For unto us a child is born, unto us a son is given: and the government shall be upon his shoulder: and his name shall be called Wonderful, Counsellor, The mighty God, The everlasting Father, The Prince of Peace. Of the increase of his government and peace there shall be no end, upon the throne of David, and upon his kingdom, to order it, and to establish it with judgment and with justice from henceforth even for ever" (Isa. 9:6–7). The world still awaits the fulfillment of this promise, but God began to fulfill it when Jesus was born King of the Jews in an eastern region of the Roman Empire.

Augustus

Augustus: The "First Citizen" of Rome

With his defeat of Antony and Cleopatra at the Battle of Actium, Octavian brought an end to a century of civil war. He returned to Rome as the triumphant ruler of the Roman world, much as Julius Caesar had two decades earlier. But unlike Julius Caesar, who had made himself dictator for life, Octavian announced in 27 BC his desire to restore the republic. He voluntarily chose to share his powers with the Senate. This division of power had existed during the republic. He took the title ***princeps*** (PRIN keps), or "first citizen." This title was popular among the common people because it conveyed the idea that he was one of them and not a noble. But in fact, the Roman government was a monarchy disguised as a republic. In his position as the head of the army, Octavian maintained firm control of the government. He was the first Roman ruler to be called an emperor—a title also given to his many successors.

We find in the New Testament (Luke 2:1) two other titles or names of Octavian: *Caesar* and *Augustus*. Caesar was Octavian's family name—he was the great-nephew and adopted son of Julius Caesar. (The term *caesar* later became a political title used by many Roman emperors.) He is best remembered by the name **Augustus**. The Senate conferred this title on him when he restored the republic. It was a title of divinity, expressing honor and majesty usually associated only with the Roman gods.

Augustus and the *Pax Romana*

During Augustus's reign (27 BC–AD 14), the entire Mediterranean world enjoyed economic prosperity. Agriculture remained the livelihood of most of the people. But the unity and stability maintained during the *Pax Romana* also encouraged the growth of trade. Rome established a stable currency of gold and silver coins, which traders could use as a medium of exchange almost anywhere in the empire. Rome freed the Mediterranean Sea of piracy and provided for safe travel in Roman territory. Ease of communication also aided trade. Greek and later Latin became almost universal languages. Not only did trade flourish within the empire, but trade also extended to the world outside the empire. The Romans imported such luxury items as silks, spices, and jewels from India and China; they brought in gold and ivory from Africa. During the *Pax Romana* the material wealth of Rome reached its peak.

In addition to prosperity and peace, Augustus's reign brought stability and order to Roman government and society. Attempting to restore honesty and efficiency in government, Augustus placed ability above social class when selecting government officials. He removed unqualified, self-seeking men from office and replaced them with well-qualified officials paid by the state. He created a police and fire service for the city of Rome. In addition, he established a postal service and undertook major building programs.

Augustus also sought to abolish corruption in the provincial governments. He reorganized the provinces of the empire, placing some under the supervision of the Senate and others under his own supervision. To provide fairer methods of taxing the provinces, Augustus ordered a census-taking throughout the empire every fourteen years. From the Scriptures we know that Augustus ordered such a census around the time of the birth of Jesus: "And it came to pass in those days, that there went out a decree from Caesar Augustus, that all the world should be taxed [registered]" (Luke 2:1).

Augustus correctly realized that a civilization is only as strong as the moral character of its people. Therefore, he sought social reforms to revive the traditional Roman virtues of duty, discipline, and hard work. He encouraged the passage of laws that promoted family life and rewarded families that had many children. Other laws punished immorality and placed limits on extravagant

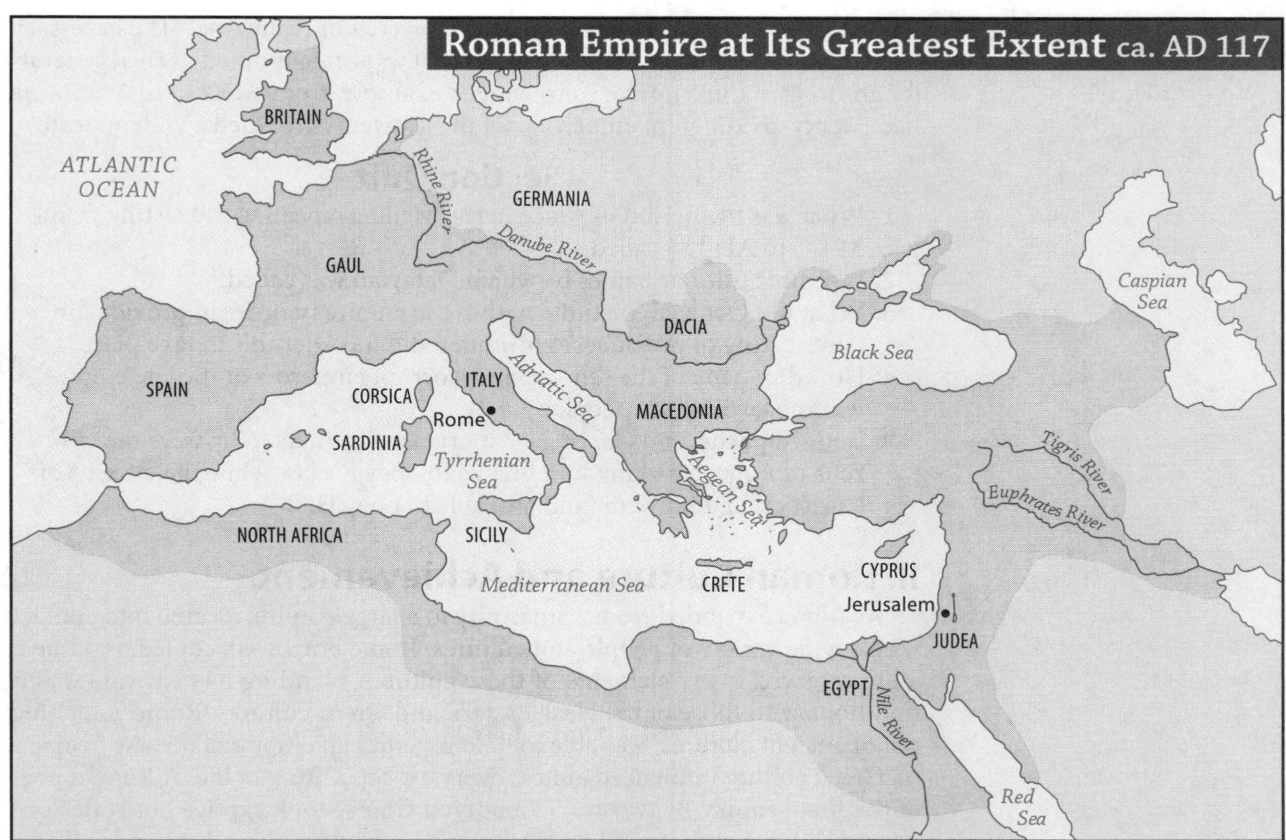

living. Despite the laws, Augustus's moral reforms failed. Moral behavior without love for God is not true morality. God's most basic moral command is that humans love Him with their entire being (Mark 12:30–31). If a culture—or an individual—refuses to love the God Who made the world and preserves it every day, its attempts at morality will never rise above hypocrisy and selfishness. In time such a culture will fall into a low moral condition that will shock and offend the very people responsible for the moral decline. It is instructive to note that the Bible's most extensive description of the moral deterioration of Gentile culture is found in a letter written to Christians living in Rome (Rom. 1:18–32). Laws ought to provide an atmosphere for proper living and may restrain improper behavior (Rom. 13:1–7), but no law can make sinful people good. True moral reform does not come from outward conformity to good laws but from an inward change in people's lives produced by faith in Jesus and His saving power (Eph. 2:1–10).

Successors of Augustus

Though Augustus established an effective and well-organized government, he left no plan for choosing a successor. For nearly a half century after his death, men who were in some way related to Julius Caesar occupied the imperial office. Most of these men led wicked lives and squandered the wealth of Rome on their own selfish pleasures. In spite of incompetent leadership, the "Roman peace" continued—it was held intact by the might of the Roman army. Toward the end of the first century, the Roman army began to elevate its favorite generals to the office of emperor. These emperors were men of proven ability. During most of the second century, they provided strong leadership for Rome.

Nevertheless, too much power placed in the hands of ambitious and self-seeking men often leads to corruption. The emperors won popular favor by providing "free" grain and amusements for the people of Rome. The Romans failed to realize, however, that these things were not really free. (The necessary funds came out of the public treasury.) Civil war often erupted as rival generals fought to gain the emperor's crown. For example, from AD 235 to 285 Rome had twenty-six different emperors. Of these, twenty-five died a violent death.

Section Quiz

1. What was the period of peace in the Mediterranean world lasting from 31 BC to AD 180 called?
2. List three titles or names by which Octavian was called.
3. What did Octavian institute within the empire in order to provide for fairer taxing of provinces? How often did he order this to take place?
4. How did many of the self-seeking, corrupt emperors of the late empire win the favor of the people?

✯ Both Augustus and Christ gave moral laws to men. Why were the citizens of Augustus's kingdom unable to obey his law while the citizens of Christ's kingdom were (and are) able to obey His?

II. Roman Culture and Achievement

As Rome expanded from a small city to a large empire, it came into contact with a wide variety of people and cultures. Rome borrowed, copied, modified, and preserved many elements of these cultures, blending its own values and traditions with those of the Near Eastern and Greek cultures. Rome, a melting pot of ancient cultures, was able to hold together an empire of diverse peoples.

Greek culture influenced almost every aspect of Roman life. A Roman poet of the first century BC wrote, "Conquered Greece took captive her rude conqueror [Rome] and carried its arts to backward Italy." Rome was actually far from "backward," but the Romans did learn much from the Greeks. The Romans were more practical than the Greeks. While the Greeks built with an eye for beauty, the Romans built with an eye for usefulness. The Greeks made significant contributions in art and philosophy; the Romans, in law and politics.

Contribution to Law

One of the most valuable and enduring of Rome's achievements was its system of justice. Rome protected the individual rights and property of its citizens. The New Testament writer Luke points out that it was "not the manner of the Romans to deliver any man to die, before that he which is accused have the accusers face to face, and have licence [opportunity] to answer for himself concerning the crime laid against him" (Acts 25:16). The Romans believed that all citizens should have equal rights before the law. Cicero, the famous orator of the republic, wrote: "The legal rights at least of those who are citizens of the same commonwealth ought to be equal. For what is a State except an association or partnership in justice?"

The legal codes of many modern European countries include principles based on Roman law. Even the American system of justice has benefited from Rome's example. Here are some Roman legal principles. Do you notice any similarity between these and America's laws?

- Justice is a constant, unfailing disposition to give everyone his legal due.
- Liberty is a possession on which no evaluation can be placed.
- Freedom is beloved above all things.
- The burden of proof is on the party affirming, not on the party denying.

- In inflicting penalties, the age and inexperience of the guilty party must be taken into account.
- No one [is] to be convicted on suspicion alone . . . [for it is] better for the crime of a guilty person to be left unpunished than for an innocent person to be condemned.
- The credibility of witnesses should be carefully weighed.
- In case of equal [conflicting] claims, the party in possession ought to be considered in the stronger position.
- Every individual is subjected to treatment in accordance with his own action, and no one is made the inheritor of the guilt of another.

Naphtali Lewis and Meyer Reinhold, eds., Roman Civilization: Selected Readings, *2nd ed., vol. 2, 535–50.*

Latin Literature and Language

The Romans modeled their literature after Greek examples. As they studied in Greece or under Greek tutors, many Romans fell under the influence of Greek literature and literary style. But they added their own literary ideas and spirit to what they borrowed from the Greeks and thereby created a distinct literature of their own.

Latin literature expresses the life and history of the Roman people. Although Latin literature lacks the originality of Greek literature, the Romans produced some literary masterpieces that are still studied and appreciated today.

Cicero

The greatest Latin literature was produced during the lifetimes of two of Rome's most famous citizens—Cicero and Augustus. **Cicero** (106–43 BC) dominated the first half of this literary age. He was not only one of the leading political figures of the late republic but also an outstanding scholar, author, lawyer, and statesman. An eloquent and effective speaker, he won acclaim as the greatest orator of his day. A master of Latin prose, he influenced later Roman writers and students of Latin literature.

The peaceful, stable conditions established during Augustus's reign (27 BC–AD 14) fostered another outpouring of literary activity. Optimism, patriotism, and appreciation for traditional Roman values dominated Latin literature. Roman writers of the Augustan Age best expressed these feelings through poetry.

Poetry of the Augustan Age

Often called the "Homer of Rome," **Virgil** (70–19 BC) is considered the greatest Roman poet. He glorified Rome in his epic poem the *Aeneid* (uh NEE id), one of the most widely read Latin literary works. Virgil modeled the *Aeneid* after Homer's great epic poems the *Iliad* and the *Odyssey*. But while Homer's works stressed the virtues of the Greek ideal man, Virgil's work exalted Rome as the ideal state.

After the death of Virgil, his close friend **Horace** (65–8 BC) became the "Poet of the Augustan Age." In a poem written in praise of Augustus, he (like Virgil before him) spoke of the triumph of Rome.

Yet Horace did not overlook the seeds of decay in Roman society. He warned of the danger of luxury and ease: "As riches grow, care follows, and a thirst for more and more." Horace praised the simple virtues of morality, justice, courage, and moderation. In his satires (works using ridicule or wit to correct or

Ovid

Livy on the Value of History

What chiefly makes the study of history wholesome and profitable is this, that you behold the lessons of every kind of experience set forth as on a conspicuous monument; from these you may choose for yourself and for your own state what to imitate, from these mark for avoidance what is shameful in the conception and shameful in the result.

Livy, History of Rome, *pref.*

expose human folly or vice), he described the many follies of contemporary Roman society. For example, he wrote: "This is a fault common to all singers, that among their friends they are never inclined to sing when asked [but] unasked they never desist."

The poetry of **Ovid** (40 BC–AD 17) is quite different from the poetry of Virgil and Horace. Ovid wrote about mythology and love. His best-known work, *Metamorphoses*, is a collection of over two hundred myths of the ancient world. He skillfully blended these tales to form one continuous story. Ovid became popular among Rome's upper class because of his poetic stories of love and romance. However, his lack of discretion and self-restraint was out of step with the emperor's program for moral reform. Augustus banned Ovid's works from Rome's three public libraries and even exiled him from the city.

History

The historian **Livy** (59 BC–AD 17), who also lived during the Augustan Age, wrote a lengthy history of Rome. In some 142 volumes, he provides an interesting narrative of the men and events of Roman history from the founding of the city through the end of the republic. Although Livy drew from many unreliable legends, his work offers valuable insight into early Roman customs and history. He saw the traditional virtues and patriotism of the Roman people as the foundation of Rome's greatness.

Later Roman Writers

The mood of Roman writers changed after the death of Augustus. Latin writers of the first century AD were more critical and pessimistic than their predecessors. The poet **Juvenal** wrote bitter satires on the loose morals and social problems of the empire.

> And when could you find more vices abounding?
> When did the gullet of greed open wider?
> When did the dice draw more to the tables?
> They don't bring their wallets along,
> They bring a whole safety deposit box.
>
> *Juvenal,* Satires, *trans. L. R. Lind, 1.93–96.*

Juvenal longed for a return to the days of the republic. He was not alone. The famed historian **Tacitus** favored the old republic over life under the self-centered emperors. His work *Annals* is a valuable but pessimistic history of Rome from the death of Augustus to the reign of Nero. In *Germania*, Tacitus gives us a rare glimpse of the lifestyle of the Germanic peoples, who later conquered the Western Roman Empire. He contrasts the simple virtues and customs of the "barbarians" with the corrupt morals of Rome's upper class.

The importance of Latin did not diminish after the collapse of the Roman Empire. Latin continued as the dominant language of medieval Europe—in learning, government, and religion. From Latin many of the native (or common) languages of Europe arose. Latin was the "parent" of the Romance languages—Italian, French, Spanish, Portuguese, and Rumanian. Although English is not a Romance language, thousands of English words are of Latin origin.

Greek Contributions

During the *Pax Romana*, centers of Greek learning, such as Alexandria, Egypt, flourished. Plutarch (45–125) was probably the most famous Greek writer in the Roman Empire. He wrote biographies that compared the lives of important Greek and Roman men. His *Parallel Lives of Illustrious Greeks and Romans* is not only an excellent literary work but also the source of valuable

Pompeii

On the afternoon of August 24, AD 79, Mount Vesuvius (a volcano about 125 miles south of Rome) violently erupted. Having no advance warning, few of the residents of the nearby city of Pompeii had time to flee. Many died from breathing poisonous gases and fumes. Others were trapped in their houses by the deadly shower of hot cinders and ashes. In three days the entire city was completely buried by a thick layer of volcanic ash, and the city of Pompeii passed from memory.

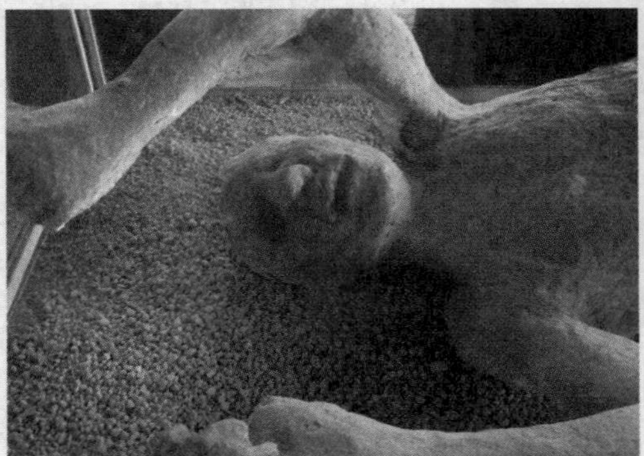

The site of the city was rediscovered in 1748. Archaeological excavations since that time have uncovered much of Pompeii. The city has been so well preserved that we can almost "relive" that fateful day over nineteen hundred years ago. Through their excavations, archaeologists have gained many insights into everyday life in Pompeii. They have uncovered many houses, complete with what were once beautiful gardens, furniture, utensils, colorful wall paintings, and even "beware-of-the-dog" signs and doghouses. In the city squares are walls covered with political posters and advertisements. City streets are lined with shops of all kinds—cloth dyers, cobblers, tanners, potters, surgeons, metal smiths, and many others. There is even a bakery with loaves of bread still in the oven.

In the process of their excavations, the archaeologists also found mysterious air pockets inside the hardened ash. Curious, they filled the air pockets with plaster of Paris. After the plaster dried and the surrounding ash could be removed, the archaeologists realized that the air pockets were forms of the men and women who had been buried by ash during the eruption. When the bodies later decomposed, only air pockets remained in the ash. The plaster casts are a graphic portrayal of the final agonies of the citizens of Pompeii.

The sudden destruction of Pompeii stands as a sobering reminder to all students of history. Human life is fragile and fleeting. As James said long ago, "Ye know not what shall be on the morrow. For what is your life? It is even a vapour, that appeareth for a little time, and then vanisheth away" (James 4:14). We should attempt to live each day aware of our mortality, remembering that at any moment we may leave this life and be ushered into the presence of God.

The dome of the Pantheon in Rome, rebuilt by the Emperor Hadrian ca. 125 AD

historical information. Advances in medicine continued under the work of the Greek physician **Galen**. Experimenting with animals, Galen studied the lungs, heart, arteries, and blood. His encyclopedia, a collection of the medical ideas of the ancient world, became the accepted medical authority of the Middle Ages. The Alexandrian astronomer and mathematician **Ptolemy** (ca. 85–ca. 165) promoted the theory that the earth was the center of the universe. He taught that the sun, moon, and planets revolved around the earth. Though based on false assumptions, his **geocentric** (earth-centered) **theory** of the universe went unchallenged for almost fourteen centuries.

Art and Architecture

As Roman generals returned from their conquests, they brought captured art and artists back to Rome. Greek art became so popular among the Romans that they commissioned artists to make copies of Greek statues. But not all Roman art was imitative. The Romans excelled in portrait busts (head and shoulder statues). These popular statues portrayed Roman heroes, honored statesmen, and valiant soldiers. Unlike Greek sculpture, most Roman statues are realistic. Some even show warts, scars, and wrinkles. The Romans also excelled in relief sculpture (sculpture in which figures project out from a flat background). Realistic reliefs adorned gigantic monuments—triumphal arches and columns—that the Roman emperors built to commemorate their conquests. The reliefs on these monuments gave a visual story of Rome's military exploits.

Even in ruins, these monuments attest to Roman engineering skill. The Romans used new building techniques as well as techniques borrowed from other cultures. Arches and vaults strengthened with concrete enabled Roman engineers to create large indoor spaces enclosed by massive domes. The Romans built **aqueducts** to supply water to many of their cities. Some aqueducts carried over fifty million gallons daily. They also built bridges and an extensive network of roads. Public baths and large amphitheaters provided relaxation and entertainment for many Romans throughout the empire. Unlike Greek buildings, which are known for their simple beauty, Roman buildings are distinguished by their large size, durability, and practicality.

Roman aqueduct

The Roman Games

The Romans flocked to arenas throughout the empire to see their favorite events—chariot races, gladiator contests, and wild beast fights. At the Circus Maximus in Rome, over a quarter of a million people gathered regularly to watch the chariot races. At the Roman Colosseum they delighted in the brutal struggles of the gladiators and wild beasts. The victors in these life-and-death contests became instant public heroes. In many of these arenas, Christians died for their faith as they were slain by the gladiator's sword, thrown to the wild beasts, or burned at the stake. These bloody "amusements" were staged by the Roman emperors to win the public favor and keep the unemployed masses of Rome out of mischief.

Seneca's Account of the Roman Games

I chanced to stop in a midday show [of gladiators], expecting fun, wit, and some relaxation, when men's eyes take respite from the slaughter of their fellow men. It was just the reverse. The preceding combats were merciful by comparison; now all the trifling is put aside and it is pure murder. . . . In the morning men are thrown to the lions and the bears, at noon they are thrown to their spectators. "Kill him! Lash him! Burn him! Why does he meet the sword so timidly? Why doesn't he kill boldly? Why doesn't he die game? Whip him to meet his wounds!" And when the show stops for intermission, "Let's have men killed meanwhile! Let's not have nothing going on!"

Quoted in F. F. Bruce, New Testament History, *42.*

The Colosseum

The Roman Colosseum is probably the most famous example of Rome's architectural genius. Shaped much like a football stadium, this mammoth structure originally towered over 160 feet high and covered six acres of land. Unlike modern stadiums, however, the Colosseum granted free admission.

Construction of the building began during the reign of the emperor Vespasian and ended in AD 80 during the reign of his son Titus. Father and son were from the Flavian family; therefore, the new stadium was originally called the Flavian Amphitheater. Since the amphitheater had been built on the site of Nero's home, the emperor Hadrian (117–38) erected a large statue (colossus) of Nero outside the building. It is for this reason that the Flavian Amphitheater soon came to be called the Colosseum.

When filled to capacity, the Colosseum could hold nearly fifty thousand people. Spectators poured in through the many numbered gates and took their places in the stadium based on their social class. To increase spectator comfort, workers positioned awnings on top of the stadium wall to give relief from the hot sun. During lunch breaks (these spectacles often lasted all day) the people could buy food and drink at the stadium.

All the activity took place on the large oval floor of the Colosseum. This floor was made of wood and covered with sand. In fact, our word *arena* is the Latin word for sand. Parts of the floor could be quickly raised and lowered to bring up wild animals from their cages below.

When the Colosseum was first built, engineers constructed the underground support system from wood and designed the system so that workers could assemble and disassemble it as needed. When the wooden floor along with this support system and the machines that moved the various elevators were removed, the lower chamber of the arena could be flooded in order to reenact famous naval battles. However, once the wooden supports were replaced with brick and concrete supports, flooding was no longer possible.

The "actors" in all these bloody spectacles were usually criminals or war captives. However, professional gladiators also fought in the arena. In addition, Christians may have been martyred for Christ in the Colosseum, although evidence to substantiate this popular tradition has proven to be elusive.

The Maison Carrée, a beautiful Roman temple at Nîmes, France, was built in honor of the grandsons of Caesar Augustus.

Religious Beliefs

Roman religious beliefs gradually changed during Rome's history. In the early days of the republic, the Romans worshipped gods of nature. Many of the planets in our solar system bear the names of these Roman gods: Mercury, Venus, Mars, Jupiter, Saturn, and Neptune. As the Romans came into contact with the Greeks, they associated their gods with the mythical gods of Mount Olympus. But like the Greeks, many Romans grew dissatisfied with the old gods and turned to philosophy to find happiness and meaning in life. The Romans had little concern for the abstract ideas of Greek philosophy; but in two Greek philosophies—Epicureanism and Stoicism—they discovered practical guidelines for living.

Epicureanism

The **Epicurean** philosophy may be summed up by the following:

There is nothing to fear in God.
There is nothing to be alarmed about in death.
Good is easily obtained.
Evil is easily endured.

The founder of this philosophy, Epicurus, taught that true happiness comes only as man frees his mind from fear and his body from pain. Epicurus believed happiness rested in the virtues of simple pleasure and peace of mind. He rejected the ideas of an afterlife and divine judgment. For him, happiness was to be found only in this life.

The poet **Lucretius** (99–55 BC) was probably the greatest expounder of Epicureanism in the Roman world. In his philosophical poem *On the Nature of Things*, Lucretius preserved the teachings of Epicurus. He hoped to reform the declining moral standards of the republic. However, many Romans interpreted

Minerva

Greek and Roman Deities

Greek Deity	Function	Roman Deity
Zeus	King of the gods	Jupiter
Hera	Queen of the gods, wife of Zeus	Juno
Ares	God of war	Mars
Apollo	God of the sun, the arts, and medicine	Apollo
Aphrodite	Goddess of love and beauty	Venus
Athena	Goddess of wisdom	Minerva
Hermes	Messenger of the gods, god of commerce and travel	Mercury
Poseidon	God of the sea	Neptune
Kronos	God of agriculture	Saturn
Artemis	Goddess of the moon	Diana
Eros	God of love	Cupid

the Epicurean teaching "seek happiness as the only good" as meaning they could do anything that would bring them pleasure. What was intended to restore Rome's traditional values became the excuse for the worst excesses of behavior.

Stoicism

The Stoic philosophy had a stronger and more lasting impact on Roman society than Epicureanism. One of the leading Stoics of the Roman Empire was **Seneca** (3 BC–65 AD), the tutor of the emperor Nero and an outstanding writer and thinker. Seneca saw **Stoicism** as the solution to Rome's moral decline.

Marcus Aurelius

Stoicism teaches that the highest good is the pursuit of the virtues of courage, dignity, duty, simplicity of life, and service to fellow men. Stoics believed in the brotherhood of man and the moral responsibility of each individual to his society. By proper living, man could bring himself into harmony with the divine law that governs the universe and directs his fate. The Stoics were sincere in their efforts, but they were sincerely mistaken; good behavior does not make a person good in the sight of God. It does not change the fact that he is a sinner.

Another eminent Roman devoted to Stoicism was the emperor **Marcus Aurelius**—scholar, philosopher, administrator, and last of the so-called Good Emperors of Rome. (His death in AD 180 marked the end of the *Pax Romana*.) Known as the "philosopher-king," Marcus Aurelius expressed the Stoic ideals in his book *Meditations*, a collection of personal reflections.

Eastern Influence

With the large number of peoples and lands embraced by the Roman Empire came a great variety of religious beliefs and ideas. From the East came the "mystery religions" that won popular acceptance among the Romans. These religions, based on polytheism and mythology, promised immortality to those who performed secret and mysterious ceremonies. Rome tolerated these foreign religious beliefs as long as the people acknowledged that the Roman emperor was a god too.

Also from the East came the practice of emperor-worship. The Roman emperor held the title ***pontifex maximus*** ("greatest priest"). In this office, he interpreted the will of the gods in the affairs of state. People expressed their loyalty and patriotism to the state by worshiping the emperor. Although Christians were loyal to the state, the government persecuted them because they did not worship the emperor—their first loyalty was to God for He alone is worthy of worship.

Section Quiz

1. What culture greatly influenced Roman culture?
2. Who was called the "Homer of Rome"?
3. What city was covered by the volcanic ash of Mount Vesuvius and not rediscovered until the mid-eighteenth century?
4. What was the name of the man and his theory that stated that the earth was the center of the universe?
5. Who was a leading Stoic philosopher of the Roman Empire and also tutor to an emperor? Which emperor was his pupil?

★ Why did Epicurean philosophy fail to help raise the declining moral standards of the Roman Empire?

III. The Introduction of Christianity

The World Made Ready

God directed the affairs of men and civilizations in ancient times to make the world ready for the coming of His Son and the spread of the gospel. Roman society at the time of Christ was characterized by safe travel and social and political stability. The widely known Greek language made possible the easy exchange of ideas. While these factors would aid the spread of Christianity, other factors would encourage the popular acceptance of Christianity. The moral decay throughout the empire demonstrated the inability of human religions and philosophies to satisfy the longings of man's soul and to provide a worthy standard of moral behavior. Into this climate of despair, God sent His Son, Who alone could satisfy that hunger and teach people how to live.

God used the Greeks and the Romans, but the Jews were His special people. Though often disobedient and rebellious against God, they preserved the knowledge and worship of the one true God in the midst of a heathen world. They offered the hope of the coming Messiah and through their sacrifices testified to the sinfulness of man and his need of reconciliation to God.

Ruins of an ancient synogogue in northern Israel, near the Lebanese border

The Babylonians destroyed Jerusalem in 586 BC and exiled thousands of Jews from their homeland. Separated from the temple in Jerusalem, these "scattered" Jews built new centers of worship called **synagogues.** (Jewish Christians later visited these centers of worship to preach the gospel message.) Like many other peoples, the Jews came under the influence of Hellenistic culture. Many Jews embraced the Greek culture and language. A group of scholars translated the Hebrew Old Testament into Greek because many Jews could no longer understand the Hebrew language. This translation is called the **Septuagint** (SEP too uh jint). Through this translation, both Hellenistic Jews and Gentiles could learn the moral standard of God's law and of the coming Messiah.

Modern-day Bethlehem—the birthplace of Christ

The Turning Point of History

At the completion of His work of preparation, God sent **Jesus the Christ** ("the Anointed One") as a sacrifice to redeem fallen man from his sinful condition and to provide eternal life to those who, by faith, trust in Him. The Bible states that "when the fulness of the time was come, God sent forth his Son, made of a woman, made under the law, to redeem them that were under the law, that we might receive the adoption of sons" (Gal. 4:4–5).

Jesus was born in Judea during the reign of the emperor Caesar Augustus. The events of His earthly life and ministry are recorded in the four Gospels (Matthew, Mark, Luke, and John). At the age of thirty, Jesus began His public ministry—preaching, teaching, and working miracles—demonstrating to all by word and deed that He was the promised Messiah, the Son of God.

However, most Jews rejected Jesus as their Messiah. The apostle John tells us that "he came unto his own, and his own received him not" (John 1:11). Instead, the Jews looked for a messiah who would free them from Roman oppression and establish the glorious kingdom foreshadowed by the reign of Solomon. The true Messiah's kingdom would right all wrongs and establish justice on the earth. But this itself is not good news for sinners. Unless the problem of sin is dealt with, no human can be part of the Messiah's kingdom. Jesus Himself said, "Except a man be born again, he cannot see the kingdom of God" (John 3:3). To make this new birth possible, the Messiah had to die a bloody and humiliating death. The Old Testament foretold His coming in Isaiah 53.

Since Jesus came to save people from sin, His preaching was filled with calls for men and women everywhere to admit their sinfulness and follow Him. The thesis of much of His preaching was the bold statement, "The kingdom of God is at hand: repent ye, and believe the gospel" (Mark 1:15). Jesus did not exempt the Jewish religious leaders from His preaching: "Woe unto you, scribes and Pharisees, hypocrites! for ye are like unto whited sepulchres, which indeed appear beautiful outward, but are within full of dead men's bones" (Matt. 23:27).

Ecce Homo *("Behold the Man") painting by Antonio Ciseri*

These religious leaders were offended by such preaching, and they plotted to have Jesus killed. They paid one of Jesus' disciples—Judas Iscariot—to betray Him. Then the religious leaders brought Him before the Roman governor **Pontius Pilate**, charging that He was working to overthrow Roman rule. They said that since He claimed to be the Messiah, the King of the Jews, He was setting Himself up in opposition to the Roman emperor **Tiberius** (14–37). Although Pilate found no fault in Jesus, he desired to maintain the peace and avoid a possible rebuke from Tiberius (John 19:12–13). Giving in to the Jewish demands, he sentenced Jesus to death by **crucifixion**.

But three days later, Jesus' tomb was empty. Some claimed that His followers had stolen the body. His followers themselves, however, gave a very different explanation. They said that when they came to the tomb on the third day (not to steal the body but to anoint it with perfume), they found that Jesus was already gone. An angel confronted them with good news: "Fear not ye: for I know that ye seek Jesus, which was crucified. He is not here: for he is risen, as he said" (Matt. 28:5–6).

The significance of this event cannot be overstated. When God raised Jesus from the dead, He proved that the life and death of this Man from Nazareth do indeed constitute the turning point of history. Up to that point, the nations of the earth were spiraling downward into depravity and destruction. But with the Resurrection Jesus was exalted to rule from heaven as the Davidic King until the Father subdued all His enemies (Acts 2:30–36). The apostles and early Christians traveled throughout the world preaching the good news of the kingdom of God (Acts 8:4), often referred to as the **gospel**. Those who repented of their sins and submitted to Jesus as Lord and Messiah received forgiveness of sins and were transferred from the kingdom of darkness into the kingdom of Christ (Acts 2:36; Col. 1:13). One day the kingdom of this world will become the kingdom of the Lord and of His Messiah (Rev. 11:15), and Jesus will reign over the world in righteousness from the new Jerusalem forever.

The Spread of the Gospel

"All power is given unto me in heaven and in earth. Go ye therefore, and teach all nations, baptizing them in the name of the Father, and of the Son, and of the Holy Ghost" (Matt. 28:18–19). With these words, Jesus Christ charged His disciples to teach all the nations (not just the Jewish nation) how to be forgiven of sin and how to live in obedience to their Maker. This is a command for Christian disciples of every age. For centuries the followers of Christ carried the gospel to many parts of the world. Conditions were favorable for the rapid expansion of the Christian faith. It was not until the nineteenth century that the missionary outreach of Christianity again experienced such favorable conditions. The initial spread of Christianity beyond its Jewish cradle was greatly aided by two events: Jewish persecution of Christians and the conversion of Paul.

Jewish Persecution

Jerusalem was the center of the early church. Christ told His disciples, "Ye shall be witnesses unto me both in Jerusalem, and in all Judaea, and in Samaria, and unto the uttermost part of the earth" (Acts 1:8). Through the disciples' preaching, thousands of Jews at Jerusalem turned from their unbelief and trusted in Jesus Christ as their Savior. But as the number of believers grew, so did the opposition of Jewish religious leaders. They began to persecute the Christians, imprisoning many of the disciples and stoning **Stephen**—the first Christian martyr. But the persecution at Jerusalem only served to spread the Christian faith, scattering Christians and their gospel message throughout Judea and Samaria.

Remnant of a Roman road near Tarsus

The Apostle Paul

Paul (AD ca. 5–ca. 67), originally named Saul, was born into a Jewish home in Tarsus (in present-day Turkey). He inherited Roman citizenship, received one of the best educations a Jew could obtain, and became a Pharisee (one of the strictest of the Jewish religious sects). His religious zeal initially made him a persecutor of the Christian church. But one day on his way to Damascus, Saul, the fervent persecutor, became a zealous Christian (Acts 9:1–6).

The Destruction of Jerusalem (AD 70)

After the destruction of Jerusalem by Nebuchadnezzar in 586 BC, Judea was under the rule of foreign powers—first the Chaldeans, then the Persians, Alexander the Great, the Ptolemies, the Seleucids, and finally the Romans. The Jews tolerated foreign rule as long as they could maintain their religious freedom and administer their own local affairs. But the Jews grew dissatisfied with Roman rule as the Roman governors of Judea gradually became more oppressive and insensitive to the strong religious beliefs of the Jews.

In AD 66 Jewish discontent flared into open rebellion. The Jewish historian Josephus, who later recorded the conflict between the Jews and the Romans, warned the Jews of the folly of armed resistance against the mighty Romans. But the Jews failed to heed his advice. Roman legions were quickly dispatched to suppress the Jewish insurrection. In AD 70 the war came to a climax as the Roman legions under their commander Titus breached the walls of Jerusalem, looted the temple, and destroyed the city. God had fulfilled Jesus' prophecy of Jerusalem's destruction (Matt. 24:2; Luke 19:44) and judged the Jews for their rejection of the Messiah. The Jews lost their homeland and became wanderers among the nations of the earth—objects of ridicule and persecution. Nevertheless, they retained their distinctiveness as a people and the promise in Romans 11 that Israel as a nation will be spiritually restored when the Jews accept Jesus as their Messiah.

The Arch of Titus in Rome, constructed soon after his death, commemorates his capture of Jerusalem.

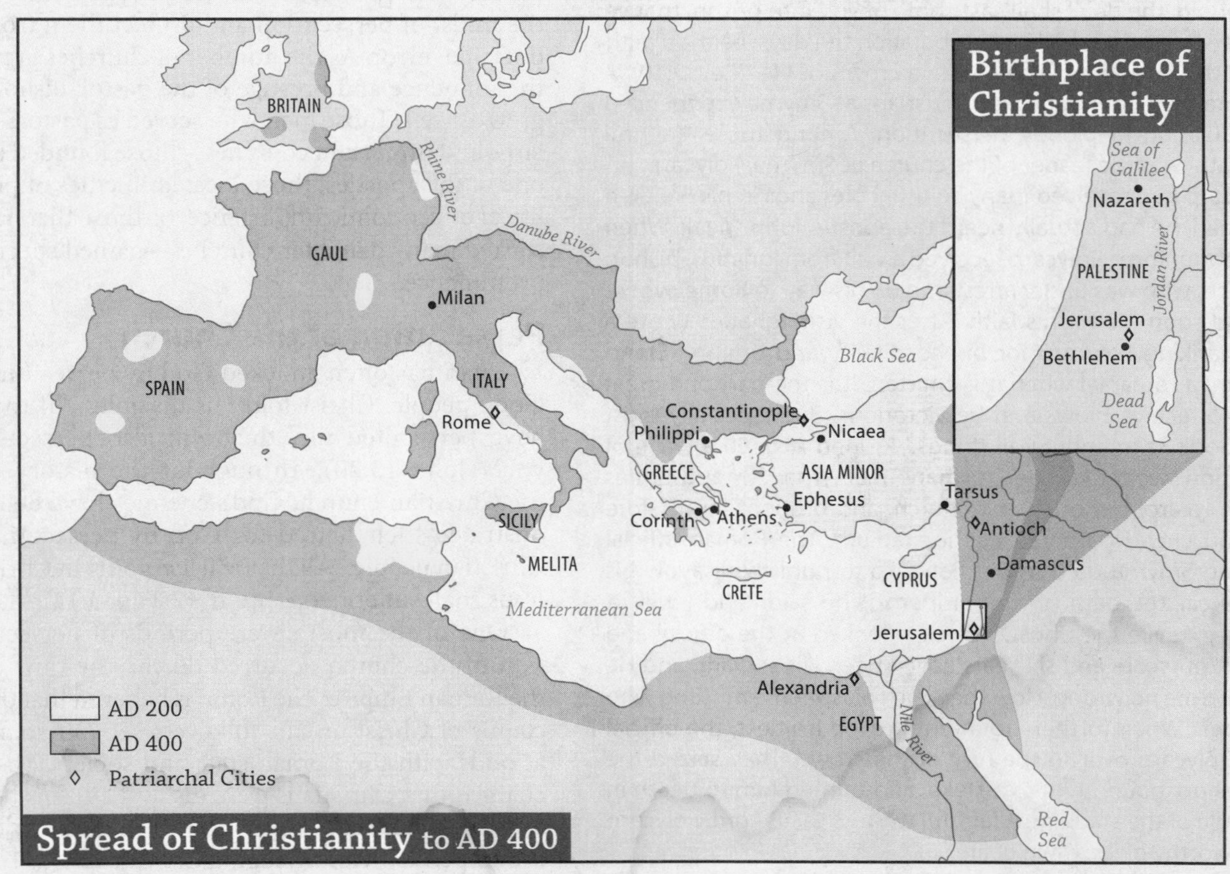

Spread of Christianity to AD 400

Perhaps no person has exceeded Paul in the impact of his work for Christ. The Holy Spirit inspired him, as He also inspired certain other men of his day (such as Peter, Luke, John, and others) to write part of the New Testament Scriptures. Paul wrote more books than any other biblical writer; most of the New Testament epistles (letters) were written by him. Through his missionary endeavors, Paul introduced the gospel to a large portion of the Roman world. He traveled thousands of miles on Roman roads preaching the gospel and establishing churches in Asia Minor, Macedonia, and Greece. The success of Paul's labors among the Gentiles demonstrated that the gospel was for all people—not just for the Jews.

Church Organizational Development

The organization of the early church was very simple. Christians met in private homes for fellowship and worship. They gathered to read portions of God's Word, pray, sing songs of praise, and partake of the Lord's Supper. As the number of believers multiplied, the apostles recognized that they could not minister to all the physical and spiritual needs in the church. Therefore, they appointed "seven men of honest report, full of the Holy Ghost and wisdom" to take care of the daily business of the church. This delegation of responsibility allowed the apostles to devote more time and effort to praying and to the preaching of the Word (Acts 6:1–6).

The earliest leaders of the church were the apostles, who were chosen directly by Christ. As the church spread and the apostles died, Christian leaders chose men of faith and experience to administer the affairs of the local assemblies. When difficult times arose, congregations looked to their pastor-bishops to provide stable leadership in the midst of persecution and protect them from doctrinal error. As the number of churches grew, the influence and prestige of the pastor-bishops grew as well. Those men who served as pastors of large and important churches—those founded by one of the apostles, those located in cities of political or economic importance, or those that had started many daughter churches—gained special prominence.

Polycarp: "Faithful unto Death"

In his message to the church at Smyrna in Asia Minor, Jesus said, "Behold, the devil shall cast some of you into prison, that ye may be tried; and ye shall have tribulation ten days: be thou faithful unto death, and I will give thee a crown of life" (Rev. 2:10). A little more than fifty years later, Christians at Smyrna experienced that tribulation in bloody persecution. Among those "faithful unto death" was the leader of the church at Smyrna, Polycarp.

Polycarp had received many spiritual blessings in his life. As a young man, he had actually heard the apostle John speak. When he was about forty, Polycarp received a visit from Ignatius, bishop of Antioch, who was under arrest and on his way to Rome, where he would soon die for his faith. After the visit, Ignatius wrote a letter, thanking Polycarp for his hospitality and urging, "Stand thou firm, as an anvil when it is smitten. It is the part of a great athlete to receive blows and be victorious. But especially must we for God's sake endure all things." Around AD 160 a wave of persecution swept over the Christians in Smyrna. City authorities seized Polycarp, bishop of the church, and brought him before a howling crowd gathered at the stadium. The Roman official governing Smyrna tried to get Polycarp to publicly disavow his faith. "Swear the oath [to the emperor]," he said, "and I will release thee; revile the Christ." Polycarp looked at the official and replied, "Fourscore and six years have I been His servant, and He hath done me no wrong. How then can I blaspheme my King who saved me?" When further argument proved fruitless, the official turned Polycarp over to the fury of the crowd. They seized the aged bishop, bound him to a stake, and burned him to death in the middle of the stadium. A faithful witness to his Lord, Polycarp proved worthy of "a crown of life."

Persecution of the Church

Satan has often attacked God by persecuting God's people. Christ told His disciples, "If they have persecuted me, they will also persecute you" (John 15:20). Throughout the history of the Christian church, God's enemies have demonstrated their hatred for God by persecuting Christian people. "All that will live godly in Christ Jesus shall suffer persecution" (2 Tim. 3:12).

One of the most severe periods of persecution of the church occurred during the time of the Roman Empire. The Romans believed that the claims of Christ on His followers set Christians at odds with the Roman state and society. They charged that Christians were disloyal citizens because they refused to burn incense on the altars of the emperors, acknowledging Caesar as Lord. The

Romans, who worshiped many different gods, opposed the exclusive claims of Christians: "Neither is there salvation in any other: for there is none other name under heaven given among men, whereby we must be saved" (Acts 4:12).

The Romans considered Christians "social misfits" and Christianity a threat to their way of life. Christians did not attend the so-called amusements of the arenas, celebrate the pagan festivals, or indulge in the many other vices of the day. Because Christians separated themselves from these public activities, the Romans branded them "haters of humanity." They resented the Christians' fervent desire to tell others about Christ and became alarmed over the rapid growth of the Christian church. Christians became the scapegoats for many of the evils that plagued the empire, from fires to earthquakes.

Nero

The first official Roman persecution of Christianity began under the emperor **Nero** (r. 54–68). He accused the Christians of setting fire to Rome, although he himself may have been responsible. What followed was a hideous display of cruelty and death. The Roman historian Tacitus records that Christians were "torn by dogs, or were nailed to crosses, or were doomed to the flames and burnt, to serve as nightly illumination, when daylight had expired."

From the time of Nero until AD 250, the persecution of Christians was sporadic and confined to small areas. However, beginning in 250, persecution became empire-wide. Thousands of Christians—both the young and the old—met death by sword, crucifixion, wild beasts, fire, and burning oil. But they had the steadfast confidence that it is better to "fear him which is able to destroy both soul and body in hell" than to fear "them which kill the body, but are not able to kill the soul" (Matt. 10:28).

Diocletian

The last and most widespread Roman persecution occurred during the reign of the emperor **Diocletian** (r. 284–305). In successive waves of edicts, Diocletian dismissed Christian soldiers from the army and ordered the destruction of Christian churches and the burning of copies of the Scriptures. Later a co-emperor ordered all Christians to sacrifice to the pagan gods under pain of torture and death.

Catacombs in Rome where Christians buried their dead

The Romans expected persecution to cause Christians to renounce their faith and deter others from converting to Christianity. Yet even as Romans persecuted the Christians, the Christian church grew numerically and became spiritually purified. More than a hundred years before the final persecution, one Christian writer had declared, "The blood of the martyrs is the seed of the Church."

From Imperial Persecution to Acceptance

In 313 one of the most significant events in the history of the Christian church occurred. With the **Edict of Milan**, the Roman emperor

Constantine

Constantine (r. 306–37) made Christianity legal, ending almost three centuries of Roman persecution of Christians. Just a year earlier, before a crucial battle with a rival for the emperor's throne, Constantine said he saw in the sky a vision of a shining cross that bore the inscription "By this sign, conquer!" Upon defeating his foe, Constantine publicly embraced Christianity, attributing his military success to the Christian God. We do not know what Constantine's true motives were for adopting the Christian faith or whether he truly became a believer. But we do know that his outward acceptance of Christianity dramatically changed the history of the church. Rome, previously a persecutor of the church, became the protector and patron of the church. Constantine restored church property that had been confiscated under the Diocletian persecution, made Sunday a legal holiday, contributed funds for new church buildings, and encouraged others to embrace Christianity.

Once threatened by persecution, Christians now found themselves protected by Roman law, favored by the Roman emperor, and granted privileges by the Roman state. The emperor tried to help the church sort through a major doctrinal difficulty. When a heretic by the name of **Arius** disrupted the unity of the church by challenging the deity of Christ, Constantine intervened and called for a general council of church leaders to settle this doctrinal controversy. In 325, the **Council of Nicaea**, presided over by Constantine, affirmed Christ's deity and the doctrine of the Trinity; it also branded Arianism a heresy. As the emperors became more involved in church matters, the church gained more favor and power in the Roman world. At the end of the fourth century, Christianity became the official and exclusive religion of the Roman state by edict of the emperor **Theodosius I** (r. 379–95).

As a result of the freedom and privileges granted by the Roman government, the church grew rapidly in membership and material prosperity. This position of favor, however, contributed to a decline in the purity of the church's membership, practices, and doctrine. Great numbers of people joined the church—some because they embraced the truth, others because it was the popular thing to do. Although Christianity triumphed over the pagan religions of Rome, some pagan ideas and practices crept into the church. One such practice was **monasticism**, which exercised a strong influence on the church from the fourth century to the end of the Middle Ages. Roman and Orthodox churches borrowed monasticism from Eastern pagan religions. Because of the moral and economic decay of the Roman Empire and the growing worldliness of the church, many sought escape from the turmoil and evil of the world by living apart from society. Monasteries developed to organize the growing numbers of men and women who sincerely believed that the greatest form of piety was to withdraw from the world, practice strict discipline, and carry out religious exercises such as prayer and denial of physical comforts. However, sincere motives did not change the scriptural teaching that Christians are to resist the evil of the present age by living a Christlike life in the world and evangelizing those who do not believe.

Christianity was born in obscurity on the edge of the Roman Empire. Within three hundred years Christianity prevailed and even won the favor of the

Growth of Church Hierarchy

The organization of the church became more complex as the church grew numerically. By the fourth century, the church had a definite hierarchical (HY er AR kih kul) structure—levels of authority among the pastor-bishops and churches in the empire. The organization of the church followed the pattern of the political and geographic divisions of the Roman Empire rather than the New Testament example. The smallest division was the parish, served by a pastor. Next was the diocese (DY uh sis) or district, a territorial division supervised by a bishop and comprising a number of parishes within and around a city. An archbishop administered a number of dioceses called a province. The patriarchates formed the largest administrative districts of the church. The **patriarchs** were the bishops of the most important cities of the empire—Jerusalem, Alexandria, Rome, Antioch, and Constantinople (the new capital founded by Constantine). This position had the most prestige and authority within the church. At first the patriarchs were all of equal rank, but over a period of time the patriarch of Rome began to insist that he be called the "first among equals."

emperor. With the end of persecution, Christian theologians had the opportunity to defend and define the doctrines of the Trinity and person of Christ. They did not recognize every error, and many false doctrines began to creep into local congregations. But God had established His church, and even in the darkest periods He raised up people who remained faithful to Him.

Section Quiz

1. What is the term for the centers of worship established by the Jews who were scattered abroad?
2. Why did the Jewish religious leaders reject Jesus as their Messiah?
3. What is the gospel?
4. Which emperor made Christianity a legal religion in the empire? Which emperor made Christianity the official religion of the empire?
5. What heresy challenged the deity of Christ? At what council in 325 was the truth of Christ's deity affirmed?

★ How is the message of the coming of Christ's kingdom both bad news and good news?

IV. Collapse of the Roman Empire

Reason for Decline

In the third century a series of political, economic, and social crises shook the foundations of the empire. Signs of internal weakness and decay were already present within the empire. In the fourth and fifth centuries, barbarian invaders entered Roman territory, and Rome was too weak to expel them. What were the reasons for this decline and the eventual collapse of the Roman Empire?

One important reason was Rome's political disorder. By the third century, Rome could no longer boast of a strong and stable government. Inefficiency and waste had accompanied the sharp rise in the size of the government. Rome also suffered from unstable leadership. The Romans had never adopted a definite plan for choosing a successor to the emperor. Hence, ambitious generals plotted and struggled to gain control of the government. As the army became increasingly involved in political affairs, armies were quick to elevate a military leader to emperor to bring stability or to gain rewards. If the army became dissatisfied with an emperor, it could remove him from power and put someone else in his place. In many cases war broke out between different legions as each tried to secure the emperor's throne for its own commander. Political turmoil, assassination, and civil war became commonplace. The army, once the protector of the Roman state, controlled the state in order to satisfy its own greed.

Closely associated with Rome's political problems were its economic troubles. The cost of maintaining an increasingly large army to defend its extensive borders, as well as the expenses of a huge government bureaucracy, drained the Roman treasury. To solve the economic crisis, the government attempted to raise revenue by increasing the tax burden on the people. In addition, emperors reduced the silver content in the Roman coins, adding cheaper metals instead. As the value of coinage declined, prices rose. This inflation was aggravated by Rome's one-sided trade with India and China, which depleted the empire's gold and silver supplies. Because Roman money became almost worthless, the barter system replaced the use of money. Trade slackened, shops closed, and poverty increased. Confidence in the economic future of Rome all but collapsed.

Moral decay was another factor in the decline of Rome. As we saw in the previous chapter, Rome's strength during its early history was due in large part to the virtues of its citizens—their discipline, patriotism, self-denial, hard work, and respect for authority. However, the moral decay that began during the days of the republic continued during the *Pax Romana*. Contentment was replaced by self-indulgence. Christians' opposition to the violent games and the immorality that engulfed the Roman Empire made them stand out in this increasingly pagan society. People looked to the government to supply free grain and public amusements, which further contributed to the large economic burden on the empire. Family life disintegrated, divorce and immorality abounded, and superstition increased. Once the backbone of Rome, a hard-working patriotic citizen became difficult to find.

Reform and Reorganization Attempts

By the end of the third century, the Roman Empire was at the point of collapse. But two powerful emperors, Diocletian and Constantine, introduced effective reforms that delayed the fall of the empire for almost two centuries. While earlier emperors tried to work within the framework of the old institutions of the republic, Diocletian and Constantine wielded supreme authority over the state in their attempts to restore order and stability to the empire.

In 284 Diocletian defeated other contenders, and his army proclaimed him emperor of Rome. Diocletian proved to be an able administrator and organizer and reshaped the political structure of the empire. He concluded that the empire was too large for one man to rule effectively. Therefore, he chose a co-emperor, known as an augustus, to rule the western half of the empire while he ruled in the east. Diocletian's plan called for each co-emperor (augustus) to appoint an assistant, called a caesar, to help the augustus and to become his successor. Diocletian divided the empire into four large administrative divisions, called prefectures, which were to be ruled by the two co-emperors and the two caesars. Through these measures, Diocletian brought temporary stability to the government.

Ancient Roman coins

Diocletian also introduced strong measures to combat Rome's economic problems. To curb inflation, he set maximum prices on goods and services. Anyone selling an item above the price limit could be put to death. He tried to revive confidence in Rome's monetary system by introducing new gold and silver coins. He also reformed the tax system, but the people still suffered under an excessive tax burden. In each instance, Diocletian's measures to solve Rome's economic worries involved greater government control and regulation. As a result, his measures only added to the problems they were intended to solve.

When Diocletian retired from office in 305, his system of joint rule fell apart. Civil war broke out among those he had appointed to succeed him and his co-emperor. After eight years of struggle, Constantine emerged victorious. He became the sole ruler of the empire and continued Diocletian's economic reforms. Constantine also followed Diocletian's example by ruling from the eastern half of the Roman Empire. He selected the site of the ancient city of Byzantium (bih ZAN shee um) to build his "New Rome," which became known as Constantinople. However, this move to the east only served to weaken the already struggling western half of the empire.

Diocletian and Constantine had prepared the way for the division of the Roman Empire into two empires. This division became permanent in 395 when Emperor Theodosius I divided the empire between his two sons. The Western Roman Empire fell to barbarian invaders soon after this separation. The Eastern Roman Empire, later called the Byzantine Empire, endured for another thousand years, as we shall see in Chapter 6.

Barbarian Invasions

During the latter years of the Roman Republic, growing numbers of Germanic peoples moved down from northern Europe and settled along Rome's borders. These people were divided into independent tribes such as the Angles, Saxons, Franks, Vandals, and Goths. Roman historians described the Germanic tribes as courageous but restless, given to much drinking and gambling, yet possessing many simple virtues. The Romans called these people "barbarians," a term they used to describe all those outside the empire who did not share in the Greek or Roman cultures.

Rome greatly increased the size of its army in an effort to protect its borders from barbarian intruders. At first Rome had a hard time finding recruits for this frontier army. To solve the problem, some emperors allowed the most "Romanized" of the Germanic tribes to settle within Roman territory to serve as a buffer between Rome and other barbarian tribes. Other emperors allowed barbarians to enlist in the army. Gradually, this foreign element in Rome's army became the primary means of protecting the empire against the more restless tribes outside its borders.

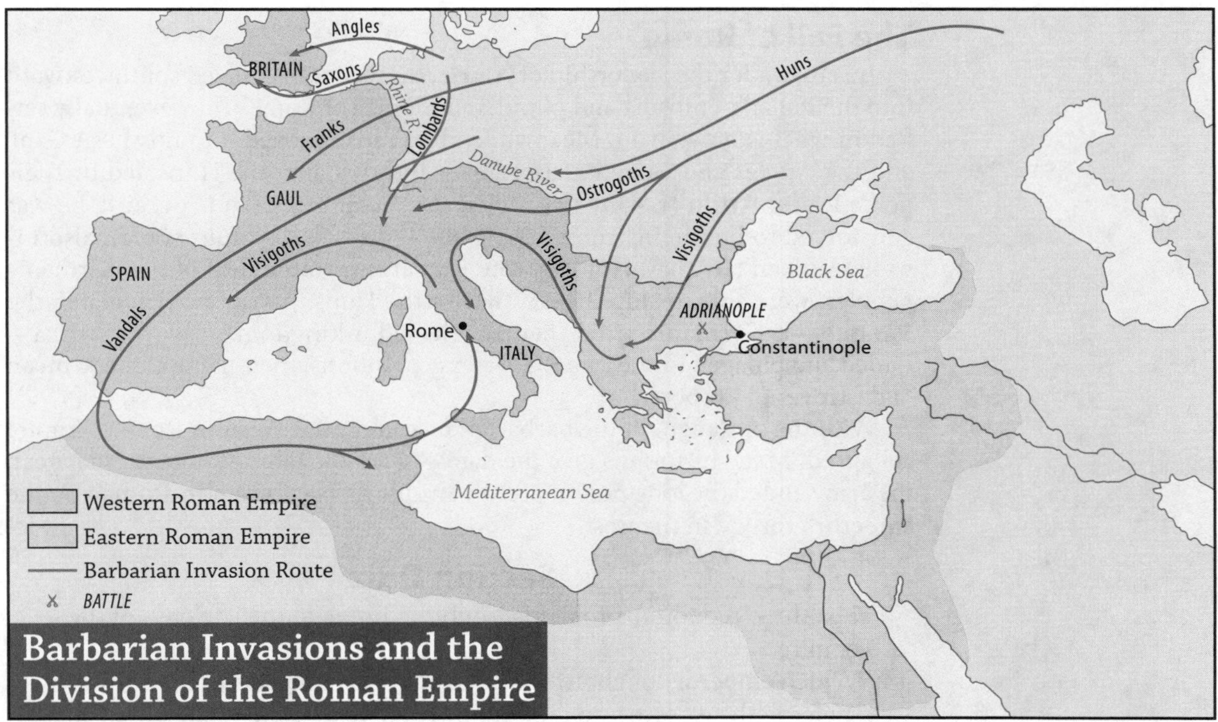

Barbarian Invasions and the Division of the Roman Empire

Out of the Far East in the late fourth century came a new threat to Rome's security—the **Huns**. This fierce nomadic tribe, which had menaced the Chinese empire for centuries, now moved across Asia into Europe, bringing terror and destruction on all who were in its path. The advance of the dreaded Huns prompted many Germanic tribes to seek refuge in Roman territory.

One such tribe was the **Visigoths**, who crossed the Danube River and settled in the eastern part of the Roman Empire. Following mistreatment by Roman officials, the Visigoths rebelled. In order to put down the revolt, the emperor led the Roman army against the Visigoths. At the Battle of Adrianople in 378, the Visigoths soundly defeated the Roman army and killed the emperor. This was obviously a disaster for Rome: its legions, thought to be invincible, had fallen in defeat before a barbarian people.

Augustine of Hippo

Augustine (354–430), an outstanding figure of the early church, lived to see the empire's decline and barbarian assaults on Rome.

In 410 barbarian invaders attacked the city of Rome. Pagan Romans blamed this disaster on the Christians. They said that the gods were punishing Rome for abandoning the old ways of worship. Augustine answered this charge in his greatest work, *The City of God.* He said that all human history is the story of two cities representing opposing ways of life. One is the city of man, the home of sinful, unsaved men. The other is the city of God, namely His church. God's purpose in history is to build His city by saving men from sin. These two cities exist side by side in this life but will be separated by God at the final judgment. The city of man and its citizens will go to the destruction reserved for sinners. Citizens of the city of God will go to eternal glory and bliss with Him. With this in mind, Augustine said that we should not look at individual historical events as demonstrating the favor or disfavor of some god. Instead we should see in every event the hand of the true God directing the course of history for His purpose and glory.

The Fall of Rome

In 410, under the leadership of **Alaric**, the Visigoths moved southwestward into the Italian peninsula and plundered the city of Rome. They eventually settled in what is now Spain. Meanwhile, the Franks moved into northern Gaul, and the Angles and Saxons crossed over into Britain. The Huns, led by their fierce leader **Attila** (r. 433–453; called the "scourge of God" because he was considered to be the instrument of God's wrath on a sinful people), also invaded Roman territory. However, the Romans, with the help of the Germanic peoples, were able to stop the advance of the Huns. Just a few years later, the **Vandals**—a Germanic tribe that established a kingdom in North Africa—raided and pillaged Rome again. To later generations, their name came to mean "a destroyer of property."

With the onslaught of the barbarian invasions, the Western Roman Empire collapsed. Many historians give the date 476 for the fall of Rome. In that year, the army ended the long period of Roman rule by placing a non-Roman on the emperor's throne in the west.

Section Quiz

1. List three economic problems troubling Rome in the late days of the empire.
2. Which emperor sought to solve the political problems of the empire by dividing the empire into four administrative divisions called prefectures?
3. Which emperor divided the empire between his two sons, leading to the division of the Roman Empire into two separate empires?
4. What did the Romans call the Germanic peoples who settled along the borders of the empire and threatened the security of the empire?
5. In what year did the Western Roman Empire collapse, when a non-Roman was placed on the imperial throne?

Chapter 5 Review

Making Connections

1–3. How did Octavian seek to improve Roman government and society? List three specific ways.

4–5. Why did the Roman government persecute Christians? List two reasons.

Developing History Skills

1. Why did the Roman Empire decline?
2. Based on Acts 16:37–38, 19:38–41, and 25:7–12, what were the rights of a Roman citizen? How do these compare with the rights of an American citizen?

Thinking Critically

1. How did God use the Jews, Greeks, and Romans to prepare the world for the coming of His Son?
2. Arius taught that Christ did not always exist but that He was created by God the Father. Using John 1:1–4 and Colossians 2:8–9, refute this heresy.

Living in God's World

1. Defend the claim that the life, death, and Resurrection of Jesus constitute the turning point of human history.

People, Places, and Things to Know

Pax Romana
princeps
Augustus
Cicero
Virgil
Horace
Ovid
Livy
Juvenal
Tacitus
Galen
Ptolemy
geocentric theory
aqueducts
Epicurean
Lucretius
Seneca
Stoicism
Marcus Aurelius
pontifex maximus
synagogues
Septuagint
Jesus the Christ
Pontius Pilate
Tiberius
crucifixion
gospel
Stephen
Paul
Nero
Diocletian
Edict of Milan
Constantine
Arius
Council of Nicaea
Theodosius I
monasticism
patriarchs
Huns
Visigoths
Alaric
Attila
Vandals

THE EASTERN WORLD

Medieval Europeans thought of Asia as a mysterious place. This unit progresses eastward from Rome into the mysterious, alluring Orient as well as southward to the continent of Africa. Beginning with the Byzantine Empire (a blending of Eastern and Western culture), we will move to the Middle East (the realm of Islam), to the faraway lands of India and China, and finally to a brief examination of early African civilizations. What seemed strange and incomprehensible to the medieval Europeans will become familiar to us.

ca. 1500–500 Aryan Civilization

483 Siddhartha Gautama (Buddha) dies

221 BC–AD 206 Ch'in Dynasty

2500 BC | 2000 BC | 1500 BC | 1000 BC | 500 BC | 0

476–1453 Byzantine Empire
618–907 T'ang Dynasty
622 Muhammad flees to Medina
661–750 Umayyad Caliphate
960–1279 Sung Dynasty
1200–1500 Mali Empire
1368–1644 Ming Dynasty
AD 500
AD 1000
AD 1500
AD 2000

6

The Byzantine & Islamic Empires

In 476 the Roman Empire collapsed in the West. It endured in the East, however, for another thousand years. This Eastern Roman Empire became known as the **Byzantine** (BIZ un teen) **Empire**. The Byzantine civilization was a blending of the cultural heritage of ancient Greece and the cultures of the Near East. Byzantine culture strongly influenced the people of Russia and southeastern Europe.

The growth of Christ's kingdom continued here in the East as it did in the West. And the spiritual contamination that was common in the West was also common in the East. Christ had promised that His kingdom would grow in this manner. He taught His disciples that the kingdom of heaven would be like a mustard seed once it is planted. It would start out very small but would experience amazing growth (Matt. 13:31–32). Christ also revealed that this kingdom would be like a field of wheat into which an enemy plants many weeds (Matt. 13:24–30). Much of the story of our race from the Resurrection of Christ to the present is the working out of these two truths. God is at work in the earth growing the kingdom of His Son, and this kingdom is constantly being corrupted by people whose faith in Christ is counterfeit.

But God allows more than just artificiality to challenge Christ's kingdom. He also raises up rival movements. During the seventh century Islam arose in the desert land of Arabia. Its zealous followers, Muslims, spread their faith through military conquest; they built an empire that stretched from Spain to India. At the same time, they forged a remarkable civilization by combining their own customs and traditions with the arts and learning of the people they conquered. This chapter will trace the beginnings, growth, and interaction of the Byzantine and Islamic civilizations.

I. The Byzantine Civilization

The Rise of "New Rome"

In 330 the emperor Constantine formally dedicated a new capital for the Roman Empire. He called the city "**New Rome**," but it became more widely known as Constantinople, "Constantine's City." This "second Rome" was ideally located on a peninsula that juts out into the waters of the Bosporus, a narrow strait that separates southeastern Europe from Asia Minor. Constantinople was the meeting place of East and West, the vital link in both land and sea trade routes. Wealth from all over the world passed through its port.

The name of Constantinople, ancient capital of the Byzantine Empire, was changed to Istanbul by the Turkish government in 1930.

In addition to being a flourishing commercial center, Constantinople also became an important political and religious center. After the days of Constantine, Roman emperors continued to live there. When the emperor Theodosius formally divided the empire into two parts (see p. 104), the city became the permanent capital of the Eastern Roman Empire. It was also recognized as one of the five major patriarchates of the Christian church.

While the Eastern Roman Empire continued to prosper, conditions in the western empire steadily declined. During the fourth and fifth centuries, barbarian tribes threatened Rome's borders. The weak western empire crumbled under the onslaught, but the richer and stronger eastern empire was able to withstand the attacks. Constantinople, the "queen of the Mediterranean," became the foremost city of the empire.

The Byzantine Empire took its name from the ancient Greek city Byzantium, on which Constantinople was built. The inhabitants of this empire still considered themselves Romans, and in many respects their civilization was a continuation of the Roman Empire. In addition to having many of the same customs and traditions, the eastern empire retained the political and legal structures of ancient Rome. But Byzantine culture was influenced even more by the Hellenistic culture that still permeated the region; it was more Greek than Roman, more Asiatic than European. While a more civilized way of life declined in the West, it endured and flourished in the East under the Byzantine Empire.

The Reign of Justinian

The first great period of Byzantine history and culture came during the reign of the emperor **Justinian** (juh STIN ee un; r. 527–65). He rose from humble origins to become one of the most famous Byzantine emperors. However, he owed much of his success to the timely counsel and strong will of his wife, **Theodora**. In 532 a riot broke out in Constantinople, threatening to topple Justinian from power. This riot flamed into a popular uprising, named the **Nika Revolt** after the people's battle cry: "Nika!" ("Conquer!"). Justinian was about to flee the capital and admit defeat when Theodora's bold advice encouraged him to stay:

> My opinion then is that the present time, above all others, is inopportune for flight, even though it bring safety. . . . For one who has been an emperor it is unendurable to be a fugitive. May I never be separated from this purple [sign of royalty]. . . . If, now, it is your wish to save yourself, O Emperor, there is no difficulty. For we have much money, and there is the sea, here the boats. However consider whether it will not come about after you have been saved that you would gladly exchange that safety for death. For as for myself, I approve a certain ancient saying that royalty is a good burial-shroud.
>
> *Procopius,* History of the Wars, *trans. H. B. Dewing, 1.24.*

This was the turning point in Justinian's reign. He remained in the capital, used loyal members of the army to kill thousands of insurrectionists, and crushed the revolt. In this manner Justinian firmly established himself as emperor.

Justinian and Theodora

Justinian then turned his attention to his chief objective: restoring the greatness of the Roman Empire. To accomplish this goal, he sought to recover the Roman territory in the West that had fallen into the hands of barbarian tribes. For over two decades Justinian's generals led military campaigns throughout the Mediterranean world. His forces defeated the Vandals in North Africa, captured Italy from the Ostrogoths, and penetrated the southern portion of the Visigoth kingdom in Spain. Justinian's conquests extended the boundaries of the Byzantine Empire to their greatest extent; nevertheless, he was unable to recover all the land once held by Rome.

One of the most enduring achievements of the Byzantine Empire was the preservation of Roman law. By the sixth century, the reliable Roman legal system had become a complex and disorganized mass of legal opinions. Its many laws were often confusing and contradictory. Like the New Testament Pharisees, the Romans had created so many regulations that they almost forgot the foundational concepts of truth and justice. For this reason Justinian appointed a commission of ten scholars to compile, reorganize, and condense the vast body of law that had accumulated from the days of ancient Rome. Their work resulted in the **Justinian Code**, a systematic arrangement of laws that clarified Roman legal principles. This code preserved the heritage of the Roman legal system, which was to provide a foundation on which most modern European nations would build their political and legal systems.

Justinian's reign marked a golden age of Byzantine culture. Like Constantine, he desired to restore the grandeur of ancient Rome. Sparing no expense, he initiated an extensive building program to construct churches, public buildings, aqueducts, and roads both in the capital city and throughout the empire. He also patronized Byzantine art. From this period comes the finest example of Byzantine architecture, the Church of **Hagia Sophia** (HAH-juh so-FEE-uh), meaning "Holy Wisdom."

Justinian and Eastern Orthodoxy

In addition to organizing laws and constructing architectural marvels, Justinian sent missionaries from the Eastern Orthodox Church to other lands. Nubia, a country located south of Egypt, was one of those lands. Later we will see the Nubians hindering the spread of Islam.

Hagia Sophia

Byzantine Empire at its Height 6th Century

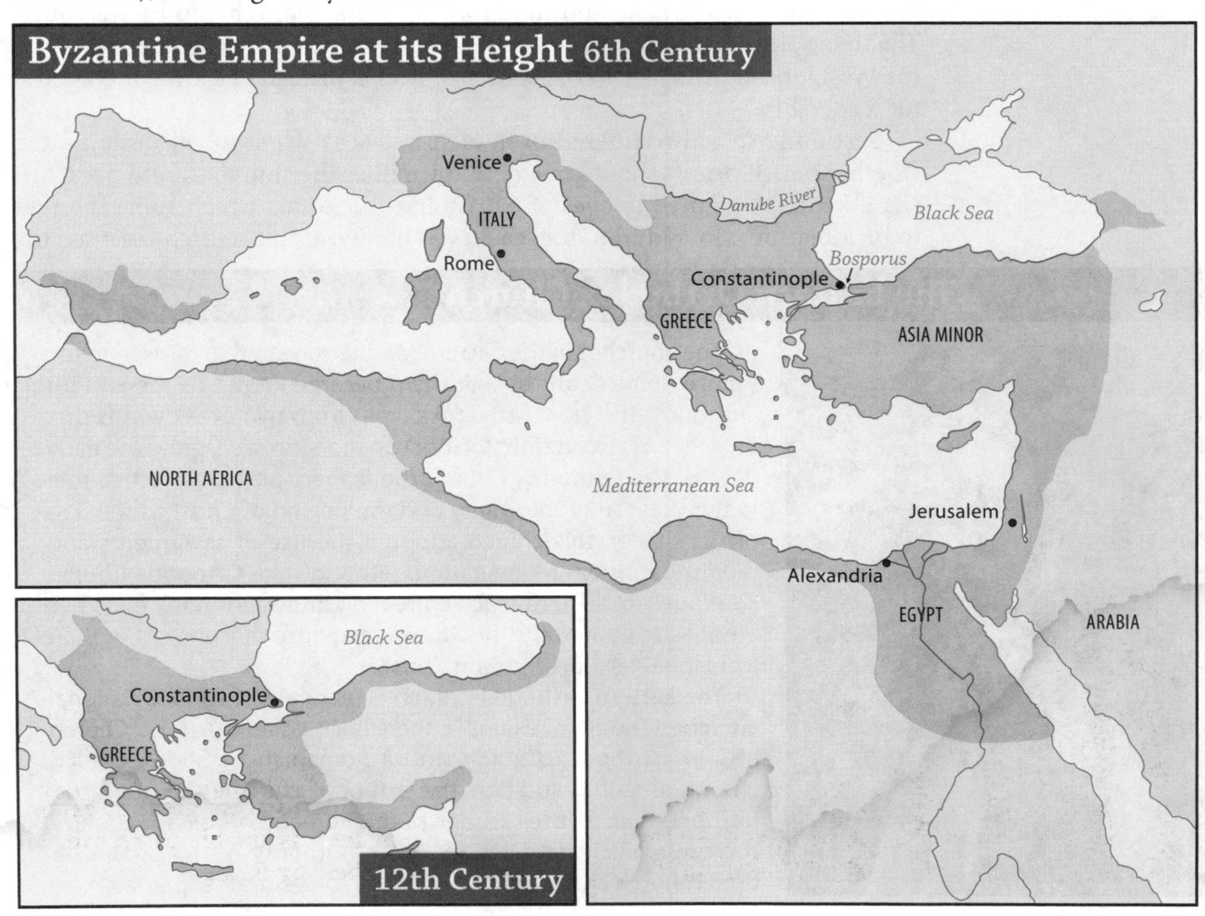

Even so, Justinian left his successors with an empire beset by many problems. In his attempts to reclaim the West, he had neglected the defense of the empire's eastern and northern borders. Likewise, his costly military campaigns, coupled with his massive building program, left the empire financially drained. Thus it may be said that Justinian took the Byzantine Empire to the height of glory but left it at the brink of ruin.

Eastern and Western Churches Separate

When Constantine founded "New Rome," he established not only a new political capital but also a new religious center. He desired Constantinople to be a Christian city, a "new Jerusalem." Under his influence, Christianity became the favored religion of the Roman Empire. It was quite natural for "Constantine's City" to rise to a place of honor in the structure of the organized church; it became one of the five patriarchal cities, second only to Rome in prestige. The bishop of Rome became the most important religious leader in the West; the patriarch of Constantinople held that position in the East.

Each church developed a distinctive character. In the West the organized church incorporated into the Christian faith a reliance on tradition alongside Scripture, the teaching that one is born again through baptism, a set of so-called sacred works to achieve salvation, and increased authority given to church leaders. Greek and Oriental ideas strongly influenced the eastern church. This adoption of non-biblical elements helped to create the Roman Catholic Church in the West and the Byzantine or **Eastern Orthodox Church** in the East.

The church in the East became one of the most powerful institutions in the Byzantine Empire. Closely linked to the political framework of the empire, it gradually emerged as the state church. The Byzantine emperor was at the same time the head of the state and the protector of the church and its teachings. This relationship was not found in the West after the fall of Rome. People in the West looked primarily to the bishop of Rome, instead of a king or emperor, for leadership.

East and West also differed over such issues as when to celebrate Easter, whether parish priests should marry, and whether the church should use **icons** (EYE kahnz)—painted images of Christ and the saints, which some thought to be idolatrous. In addition, the leaders of the Byzantine church resented the

The Eastern Orthodox Church

The churches in the eastern Mediterranean that refused to recognize Rome's control over them became known as the Eastern Orthodox. The word *orthodox* comes from two Greek words that together mean "straight (orthos) opinion (doxa)." During the early days of the Orthodox Church the leaders played an active role in the defense of the Trinity and the person of Christ as the Son of God. Later, this church adopted the use of sacraments and taught baptismal regeneration. Although the Orthodox Church continues to claim to teach correct doctrine, Orthodox churches emphasize conformity, ritual, and reverence of icons rather than a personal relationship with Christ.

The Eastern Orthodox Church is made up of various national churches. Today, for example, there is a Russian Orthodox Church, a Greek Orthodox Church, and a Romanian Orthodox Church, among others. In addition, the Orthodox churches do not recognize one man as their leader as the Roman Catholics recognize the pope. Each patriarch exercises authority over his own national church and is equal in position to every other patriarch.

interference of the bishop of Rome in the religious affairs of the East. They refused to acknowledge the bishop of Rome's growing claim that his authority was supreme over all churches (see pp. 144–45).

As a result, bitter rivalry developed between the eastern and western churches. Tensions culminated in 1054 when the pope sent a delegation to Constantinople stating that the pope was assuming authority over the churches in southern Italy that had previously been under the patriarch's authority. When the patriarch refused to accept the pope's actions, the pope's representatives **excommunicated** him (depriving an individual of the sacraments and excluding him from the fellowship of the church). Then, in retaliation, the patriarch excommunicated the pope.

The Empire Under Siege

The Byzantine Empire experienced both success and failure during the period from the sixth to the fifteenth centuries. It enlarged its empire repeatedly, only to see the gains erased by outside forces. During the fourth and fifth centuries, it endured strong barbarian attacks. After Justinian's reign in the sixth century, the empire was besieged on almost every side for several hundred years. From the West came the Lombards, a Germanic tribe that conquered most of Italy. From the North came the Slavs and the Bulgars, who settled in the Balkan Peninsula. Out of the East came the Sassanids, who sought to restore the glory of the Persian Empire. Although often weak and on the brink of collapse, the Byzantines managed to drive out all these foreign invaders.

In the seventh century the Byzantine Empire had to reckon with a new and energetic force—the Arab Muslims. The Muslims, advancing from the Arabian Peninsula, smashed the Byzantine defenses both on land and at sea. Soon they threatened Constantinople itself. But the "city protected by God" (as it was called) withstood the Arab attacks.

Constantinople was aided by its defensible location, its strong fortifications, and a new secret weapon called "Greek fire." Though the Byzantines stopped the Muslim expansion into southeastern Europe, they lost Syria, Palestine, Egypt, and North Africa. The Byzantine Empire at one time encompassed the Mediterranean Sea; by the eighth century its territory had been greatly reduced.

Between 850 and 1050 the Byzantine Empire gradually recovered its former strength and prosperity. No longer did it remain on the defensive; it pushed back the Muslims and reasserted itself as the dominant power in the Mediterranean. This period of military success reached its height under **Basil II** (976–1025). Known as the "Bulgar Slayer," Basil crushed the Bulgars in the Balkan region and added their kingdoms to the empire. The Byzantines not only reclaimed some of the territory they held during Justinian's day but also revived their commercial and cultural interests. Constantinople abounded with the riches of trade, art, and architecture. Merchants and missionaries carried these achievements to other lands; many of these lands still bear the marks of Byzantine culture.

After two centuries of expansion, new obstacles confronted the empire. The growth of commercial rivals—especially the city of Venice, in Italy—challenged Byzantine trade supremacy in the eastern Mediterranean. Competition from Venetian merchants cost the empire sorely needed resources and markets. At the same time, the **Seljuk Turks** emerged as a powerful force in the East. These Turks, originally nomadic tribes from central Asia, had adopted Arab culture and Islam. The important Byzantine territory of Asia Minor fell to these fierce warriors in 1071, when they annihilated the Byzantine army at the Battle of Manzikert (MAN zih kurt). Fearful that Constantinople would fall,

Greek Fire

One reason Constantinople was able to withstand enemy sieges was its secret weapon known as "Greek fire." This weapon, which the Byzantines developed in the seventh century, was an explosive mixture of chemicals possibly including quicklime, sulfur, naphtha, and potassium nitrate. Soldiers squirted it from tubes or launched it in jars from catapults at the enemy. Greek fire ignited spontaneously and burned even under water. This weapon proved to be particularly effective against wooden ships and enabled the Byzantines to control the Mediterranean Sea for many centuries.

Falcon cannons

the desperate Byzantine emperor appealed to the Christians in the West for aid. The West responded by sending several military expeditions, known as the **Crusades**, to free the East—especially the Holy Land—from these Muslim invaders.

One tragic episode occurred in 1204 as an invading army breached the defenses of Constantinople. The invaders captured and looted the city, slaughtering both young and old. Shockingly, these soldiers were not Muslims, but warriors from the West on a "holy" Crusade. Unscrupulous Venetian merchants had enlisted the aid of these Crusaders and used them to destroy Constantinople—Venice's commercial rival. Neither their cause nor their conduct was holy. In fact, they returned to Europe without even attempting to carry out their original mission of freeing the Holy Land. Although Byzantine forces later recaptured Constantinople, the Byzantine Empire never fully recovered from the destruction it suffered.

Cyril and Methodius

For two centuries the empire continued to exist, but it was in a state of steady decline. The empire finally came to an end in 1453, when a new wave of Muslim invaders, the **Ottoman Turks**, blasted through the city's massive walls with falcon cannons, slaughtered its inhabitants, and sacked Constantinople.

Byzantine Civilization Contributions

When the Turks brought an end to the Byzantine Empire, they destroyed the protective barrier that for hundreds of years had shielded the West against the spread of Islam. This protection had given the West time to recover from the long period of chaos that followed the collapse of Rome. In addition, the Byzantine civilization was important in its own right. It was the means by which the classical heritage of Greece and Rome was preserved and transmitted to the West.

While the size of the Byzantine Empire had gradually diminished from its peak under Justinian, the influence of the Byzantine civilization had expanded. The many achievements of the Byzantine society had attracted the less civilized peoples who came into contact with the empire. They marveled at the material wealth that abounded at Constantinople and tried to copy the effective governmental system that the Byzantines had adapted from ancient Rome.

Furthermore, many of the pagan peoples of eastern Europe had embraced Eastern Orthodoxy along with Byzantine culture. Two Byzantine missionaries, the brothers Cyril and Methodius (muh THO dee us), had gone to the Slavic peoples of Russia and southeastern Europe. The Slavic tribes did not have a written language, so Cyril and Methodius developed one for them. Their system, a modification of the Greek alphabet, became the foundation of the Slavic written language.

Byzantine art and architecture demonstrate the wealth and splendor of this once-mighty empire. Byzantine art was primarily intended to glorify God; it adorned the interiors of churches. Craftsmen excelled in wall paintings, carved ivory, illuminated manuscripts (manuscripts decorated with ornate letters or designs in bright colors or precious metals), and marble and metal work. A favorite decorative art—the **mosaic**—graced the walls and ceilings of Byzantine churches. By inlaying tiny pieces of glass or stone in wet cement or plaster, artists could form beautiful patterns and pictures.

Mosaic of Christ from Hagia Sophia

The churches housed some of the best examples of Byzantine art, and they were in themselves the best examples of Byzantine architecture. Byzantine architects demonstrated a mastery of design and engineering skill. They especially excelled in domed structures. The most famous of Byzantine structures is the beautiful Hagia Sophia, sometimes called the Santa Sophia. In size and rich adornment, no other church in the empire could equal it. It became a model of architectural design that was copied in other cities and lands. Still standing today, its great dome reaches a height of 180 feet and has a diameter of 108 feet. Procopius, a sixth-century historian, describes the splendor of the Hagia Sophia as "a spectacle of marvellous beauty, over-whelming to those who see

The Meaning of Icons

A characteristic feature of Eastern Orthodoxy is its use of icons. They occupy prominent places in churches and homes and are held in great reverence by the Orthodox faithful. Scripture does not forbid religious art—as evidenced by the art utilized in the Tabernacle and the Temple—but it does forbid using images to represent God or worshipping images.

Although we frequently speak about looking at a painting, the Orthodox believe that one should not merely look at icons. Instead, the viewer should direct his mind beyond the icon to the heavenly reality it represents. For example, one viewing a picture of the Apostle Peter should not see a painted figure but should see in his mind's eye the real Peter in heaven.

In an effort to make the painted figures appear otherworldly, the artists, who were usually monks, developed several techniques that remained unchanged for many centuries. For example, there are no shadows in icons because the shadows imply something material and earthly. Second, historical scenes that occurred inside a building are often shown outside with the building in the background. In this way, the painters hoped to elevate the event beyond its historical context and give it universal meaning. Third, the figures in icons are portrayed unrealistically with very thin noses, small mouths, and large eyes. This illustrates the fact that the figures supposedly conquered their five senses (their earthly selves) and lived in holiness according to their spiritual nature.

Even the colors used by the icon painters had special meaning. For example, the monks usually portrayed Christ wearing garments of red, blue, and gold. The red symbolized love, and the blue and gold represented truth and heaven. In pictures of the transfiguration, Christ is usually shown wearing white—a symbol of light and holiness.

Notice the icons pictured here. The one above is from the sixteenth century, and the one below is from the twentieth century. Notice that in spite of some obvious differences, both portray the Madonna and child in a similar fashion. (The one on the bottom has a decorative cover.) Unlike Western art with its changing styles, icon painting has for centuries remained basically unchanged.

Top: Mary, Tikhvinskaya Theotokos (Bogoroditsa), *Novgorod School, Mid 16th century. From the Bob Jones University Collection*

Bottom: Mary, Iverskaya Theotokos (Bogoroditsa) *Russian, 20th century. From the Bob Jones University Collection*

it, . . . for it soars to a height to match the sky, and as if surging up amongst the other buildings it stands on high and looks down upon the remainder of the city, adorning it. . . . It exults in an indescribable beauty."

Section Quiz

1. List four titles that were given to the city of Constantinople.
2. What Byzantine emperor sought to restore the greatness of the Roman Empire by extending the boundaries of the Byzantine Empire to their greatest extent?
3. What is the name of the organized church that developed within the Byzantine Empire?
4. What decorative art did Byzantine artists create by using tiny pieces of glass or stone in wet cement or plaster?
5. What is the name of the most famous Byzantine architectural structure?

★ Why did aspects of Byzantine civilization continue to spread even as the Byzantine Empire declined?

II. Early Russia

Beginnings

Looking at a map of the modern world, one cannot help noticing the enormous size of the land of Russia. Covering about one-sixth of the globe, it is the world's largest country. Russia occupies a large portion of two continents—Europe and Asia. Within its borders is a population composed of people of many different racial and linguistic backgrounds. The largest group is the **Slavs,** whose ancestors played a major role in establishing the early Russian state.

No one knows for sure where the Slavs first lived. They moved into eastern Europe as the Germanic tribes there migrated farther westward. Eventually three groups emerged: the West Slavs—the Poles and Czechs—settled in the Danube region; the Yugo-Slavs, or "South Slavs," moved down into the Balkan area; and the East Slavs, the ancestors of the Russians, occupied the territory between the Baltic and Black Seas. Running through the land of the East Slavs is a network of rivers along which they built their village communities. The Slavs participated in the prosperous trade that flourished along these river highways.

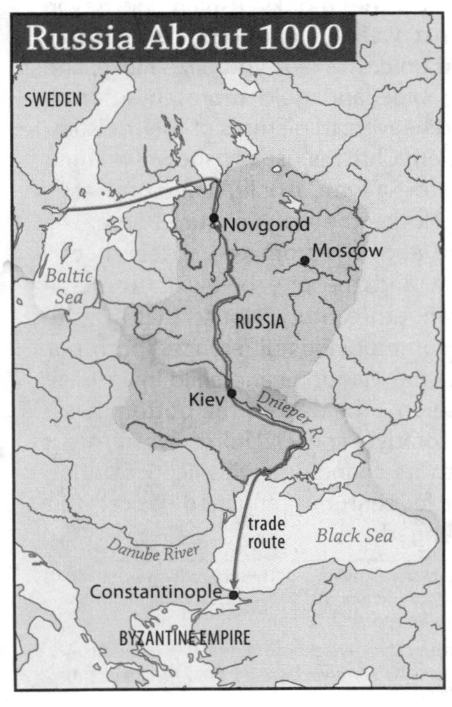

During the eighth and ninth centuries, bands of Swedish Norsemen, known to the Slavs and Byzantines as **Varangians** (vuh RAN jee unz), sailed south from the Baltic Sea using the waterways. Like the Vikings who terrorized western Europe (see p. 137), the Varangians plundered Slavic villages along the rivers. Attracted by the possibilities of opening trade routes with the Byzantine and Muslim civilizations, many Varangian warriors settled along the inland waterways. Slavic settlements often hired Varangian warriors to protect their villages from other raiding tribesmen.

In the city of Novgorod (NAWV guh rawt), according to the one traditional account, the Slavs invited Varangian rule: "Our whole land is great and rich, but there is not order in it. Come to rule and reign over us." Whether by invitation or by force, the Varangian warrior **Rurik** gained control of Novgorod about 862. That year is the traditional date for the beginning of Russian history. Rurik established the first ruling dynasty of Russia. His successors captured and ruled other cities in the region, the most important of these being Kiev (KEE ef). Yet despite their military superiority, the Varangians were greatly outnumbered by the Slavs and were soon absorbed by the populace.

Shortly after Rurik's death, Kiev became the center of the early Russian state. This city was located on the shores of the Dnieper (NEE pur) River, the major route for trade with the Byzantine Empire. For three centuries Kiev held the prominent position in a loose confederation of city-states. Established by Varangian princes, this confederation sought to further the region's common commercial interests and protect important trade routes. The area under Kievan influence became known as Russia, perhaps deriving its name from the Slavic designation of the Norsemen, **Rus**, meaning, "rowers" or "seafarers."

Russian Orthodox Church

Byzantine Cultural Influences

Russian culture bears a strong Byzantine imprint. Because of early commercial contacts, Kiev and Constantinople developed close cultural ties. A significant event in Russian history was the adoption of Eastern Orthodoxy by the Kievan ruler **Vladimir I** in 988. He ordered the destruction of pagan idols and temples and established Orthodox Christianity as the official state religion. By adopting Eastern Orthodoxy rather than Roman Catholicism, Russia cut itself off from the mainstream of Western thought and instead came under the influences of the eastern church and Byzantine culture.

The influence of the Orthodox church upon Russia was great. The Russian language profited from the Slavic alphabet, which the Byzantine missionaries Cyril and Methodius had adapted from the Greek alphabet. The Slavic alphabet enabled the Russians to translate Greek works into their Slavic language. It also prompted the growth of native Russian literature. Russian artists made beautiful icons like those adorning Byzantine churches. The Russians even patterned their cathedrals after Byzantine models. One feature of their cathedrals, however, is uniquely Russian—the "onion-shaped" dome.

Height of Kievan Russia

Kiev reached the zenith of its power and prestige during the reign of Yaroslav (yuh ruh SLAHV) "the Wise" (1036–1054). Yaroslav greatly strengthened the city's position of leadership; Kiev became known as the "Mother of Russian cities." His reign saw the greatest territorial expansion of the early Russian state. He gained international recognition by negotiating marriage alliances between his princely house and the royal families of France, Sweden, Norway, Poland, Hungary, and the Byzantine Empire. He also sponsored the earliest known Russian code of laws, which combined Slavic tribal law and Byzantine law.

Yaroslav desired to make Kiev a rival of Constantinople. In size, wealth, and culture, Kiev became one of the leading cities of its day. It was a prosperous center of commerce—a meeting place of the world's merchants. Yaroslav's patronage of art, education, and the church attracted Byzantine painters, architects, teachers, and priests. With the aid of Byzantines, the Russians constructed their own cathedral of Hagia Sophia. Kiev also boasted schools, libraries, monasteries, cathedrals, and fortifications that Yaroslav built.

After the death of Yaroslav, Kiev lost its prominence among the Russian cities when his heirs fought to determine who would succeed him on the throne. Cities

Vladimir and the Orthodox Church

According to legend, the Russian ruler Vladimir decided that he would establish a monotheistic religion among his people to replace their polytheistic, pagan beliefs. Before he decided what that new religion would be, he investigated what the world had to offer. He summoned representatives of Islam, Judaism, Roman Catholicism, and Eastern Orthodoxy and had each of them explain why his particular religion was best. After listening to the claims of each, Vladimir sent out envoys to observe these religions on a firsthand basis. When they returned, he made his decision.

First of all, Vladimir rejected Islam because the Qur'an forbade the drinking of alcoholic beverages. Second, he rejected Judaism because the Jewish people had been defeated and scattered across the world. Since their God did not seem strong enough to protect them, He could not be counted on to protect the Russian people, thought Vladimir. Third, the king rejected Roman Catholicism because the Catholic churches were dark and damp and the services were dull. Vladimir chose Eastern Orthodoxy.

The reason for his choice was simple. When his envoys returned from Constantinople, they enthusiastically described a service they had attended at the Hagia Sophia. They told him how the whole church seemed to shine as the mosaics reflected the light of the burning candles. They told him of the beautiful music, the clouds of incense, and the gorgeous robes of the patriarch who led the service. Impressed by what he heard, Vladimir adopted Eastern Orthodoxy. The Russian Orthodox Church was established.

that had formerly looked to the Kievan rulers as the Grand Princes of Russia began to assert their independence. New trade routes and commercial centers drew away much of Kiev's wealth and population. Kiev's declining influence suffered a deathblow in the thirteenth century, when the Tartars—fierce Mongolian warriors from central Asia—swept into Russia (see p. 150). They destroyed Kiev in 1240 and ruled Russia until the late 1400s. After the decline of Mongol power, a new center of Russian society—Moscow—arose in the north.

Section Review

1. What ethnic group played a major role in establishing the early Russian state?
2. What city became the center of the early Russian state?
3. What Russian ruler adopted the Eastern Orthodox Church as the official religion of the Russian state?
4. What two Byzantine missionaries developed a written language for the Slavic people of Russia?
5. Under whose leadership did the city of Kiev and the early Russian state reach the height of its power and prestige?

★ According to legend, why did Vladimir choose Eastern Orthodoxy over other religions?

III. The Islamic Civilization

The Land of Arabia

The cradle of Islam was Arabia—a large peninsula that extends south of the Fertile Crescent in the Middle East. This peninsula lies between Asia and Africa, bounded by the Persian Gulf in the East and the Red Sea in the West. In land area, it is about one-third the size of the United States. Much of the land is a barren wilderness of deserts and stony plains. Vegetation is sparse, and agriculture is limited because of the extreme heat and lack of adequate rainfall. This uninviting environment kept most of Arabia in relative isolation until the birth of Islam in the seventh century.

The land of Arabia is also adjacent to the Bible lands. As do the Hebrews, Arabs trace their beginnings back to Abraham: the Hebrews, through his son Isaac; the Arabs, through his son **Ishmael**. Although Ishmael was not the child of God's special promise (Gal. 4:22–23), God blessed him: "I have blessed him, and will make him fruitful, . . . and I will make him a great nation" (Gen. 17:20). Ishmael's descendants dwelt in the Arabian Peninsula and became a numerous people, just as God had foretold.

Arabian Peninsula (brown streaks in the center are sand storms)

Because they had no organized government, the Arab people had little unity before the advent of Islam. Each Arab was loyal to his own tribe, and warfare among the tribes was frequent.

In addition, there were two distinct lifestyles among the people of Arabia. Many of the Arabs traveled through the harsh desert wilderness in independent bands. These nomads, called **Bedouins** (BED oo inz), roamed the desert in search of pastureland and water for their herds of goats, sheep, and camels. Over the centuries the Bedouin way of life has remained relatively unchanged; today they can be seen traveling from oasis to oasis across the desert land.

Not all Arabs were desert nomads, however; some lived a more settled life along the outer rim of the peninsula. They established cities along important trade routes or along the coast, where rainfall was more abundant and the land was more fertile. A few of these cities became important trade centers for camel caravans, which carried goods across the desert to and from other lands. Out of one of these cities arose a leader who united the people of Arabia.

Muhammad's cave in Mt. Hira

The Founding of Islam

Muhammad

Shortly after the death of the Byzantine emperor Justinian in 565, **Muhammad** (moo HAHM id) was born in Arabia. Muhammad (570–632) claimed to be the last and greatest of the prophets of the god **Allah** (AH luh). His teaching became the basis for a new religious movement known as **Islam** (is LAHM), meaning "submission" (to the will of Allah). His followers are known as **Muslims** ("submitters to Allah").

Muhammad, whose name means "highly praised," was born to a poor family in the city of Mecca, in western Arabia. Little is known of his early life except that he became an orphan at the age of six and was reared by his grandfather and uncle. As a young man he entered the employment of Khadijah, a wealthy merchant widow. At the age of twenty-five, he married her. For the first time in his life he enjoyed financial security. He spent much of his leisure time in a cave near Mecca meditating on religion and struggling with the polytheism of his people. During his travels he had encountered many religions, and he borrowed from them to form a new religious movement that would govern every aspect of life.

The Messenger of Allah

Muslim historians record that in his fortieth year, Muhammad received a vision in which the angel Gabriel gave him a divine revelation to "Recite!"

> RECITE in the name of your Lord who created—created man from clots of blood.
>
> Recite! Your Lord is the Most Bountiful One, who by the pen taught man what he did not know. (Sura 96:1)

According to Muslim teaching, these revelations continued throughout Muhammad's lifetime. Initially he feared that these messages might be from Satan. However, Muhammad's wife and a trusted friend convinced him that he was the messenger of God entrusted with a new revelation for man. Muhammad began preaching that there was only one god, Allah, and that he, Muhammad, was Allah's prophet.

The Kaaba in Mecca, 1910. Pilgrims gather around the black stone.

He had little success in gaining converts at first. Muhammad's early followers were family members and close friends. Most of the people of Mecca ridiculed him, viewing his teaching as contrary to their religious beliefs and a threat to the city's commercial interests. Mecca had become a leading trade center, situated at the crossroads of trade routes in western Arabia. It had also developed into a center of religious worship because the **Kaaba** was located at Mecca. This stone building served as a sacred shrine that housed hundreds of idols. People from all over Arabia made pilgrimages to this shrine. Meccan merchants profited from this pagan worship. The principal attraction was the famous Black Stone, possibly a meteorite, set into the wall of the Kaaba. For centuries Arabs had walked around the Kaaba and kissed the Stone as a form of worship. According to Muslim tradition, the angel Gabriel sent the stone to Abraham, who, along with his son Ishmael, built the Kaaba. Rejecting Muhammad's teaching about one god and fearing it would hinder their profitable business, the leaders of Mecca persecuted Muhammad and his followers.

The Flight to Medina

In 622 Muhammad made a historic decision. He and his followers decided to flee Mecca and accept an invitation to move to Medina (mih DEE nuh), a city about two hundred miles to the north. This move is known as the **Hegira** (hih JIE ruh), or "Flight." (It is celebrated as year 1 in the Muslim calendar.) At Medina, Muhammad's following grew rapidly. The Arabs of Medina not only accepted Muhammad as their spiritual leader but made him their political and military leader as well. Once in power, Muhammad the persecuted became Muhammad the persecutor. While in the minority, he had presented his cause peaceably through preaching, but now he advanced it by force and military conquest. With an army of militant Muslim followers, he slaughtered any who opposed him. A bitter struggle with the rival city of Mecca ended in 630 when Muhammad violated a truce and reentered the city of his birth in triumph. He destroyed all the idols of the Kaaba—except the Black Stone—and turned the Kaaba into the center of Islamic worship. Mecca became the "holy city" of this new religious system.

The Teachings of Islam

The Qur'an

The heart of Islam is the **Qur'an** ("recitations"), the sacred book of the Muslims. Muslims believe that the archangel Gabriel revealed the words of Allah to Muhammad through numerous dreams and visions. These revelations formed the basis of his teaching. Many of his followers committed his teachings to memory; others wrote them down on anything they could find. After Muhammad's death, they compiled his teachings into the Qur'an. Composed of 114 chapters, or suras, the Qur'an is the primary authority on Muslim belief and practice. Dedicated Muslims memorize the entire Qur'an, which is about the same length as the New Testament.

The central doctrine taught by the Qur'an is the belief in one god, Allah (al, "the"; Ilah, "god"). According to the Qur'an,

> He is God, besides whom there is no other deity. He knows the unknown and the manifest. He is the Compassionate, the Merciful.
>
> He is God beside whom there is no other deity. He is the Sovereign Lord, the Holy One, the Giver of Peace, the Keeper of Faith; the Guardian, the Mighty One, the All-powerful, the Most High! Exalted be God above their idols! (Sura 59:22–23)

Muslims believe that Allah sent more than one hundred thousand prophets to reveal his will to man. However, Islam reveres Muhammad as the last and greatest of Allah's prophets and the Qur'an as Allah's final revelation, superseding all others.

Islam and Murder

While murder of Muslims (Sura 4:93) (and others, except for a "just cause" Sura 5:32) is forbidden in the Qur'an, killing non-Muslims in battle or following capture and surrender was encouraged, if not commanded, by Muhammad. In Sura 47:6 Muhammad told Muslim soldiers to "strike off" the heads of their enemies on the battlefield. Journals of Muslim conquerors, including Babur and Akbar, in India, recorded the beheading of large numbers of prisoners following conquest. In fact, Muslim forces murdered hundreds of thousands of Hindus by beheading even after they had submitted to Muslim rule.

The moral teaching of the Qur'an serves as a guide for the conduct of its believers. Some passages in the Qur'an encourage Muslims to cultivate humility, duty, kindness, and benevolence. Others condemn idolatry, murder, gambling, drinking of wine, and adultery, although Muslim men are allowed to have up to four wives and may arrange "temporary" marriages. Muslims are taught to fear Allah because, while he may or may not reward good works, he will definitely punish evil in the life to come. The Qur'an gives a description of this "day of judgment":

> He that comes before his Lord laden with sin shall be consigned to Hell, where he shall neither die nor live. But he that comes before Him with true faith, having done good works, shall be exalted to the highest ranks. He shall abide forever in the gardens of Eden, in gardens watered by running streams. Such shall be the recompense of those that keep themselves pure. (Sura 20:74–76)

The Qur'an reflects many ideas that Muhammad drew from Jewish and Christian sources. It mentions several stories and characters from the Old and New Testaments. The Qur'an honors Noah, Abraham, David, and even Jesus as prophets of Allah. Likewise, the Qur'an echoes many concepts found in the Bible. It emphasizes prayer, moral conduct, a coming day of resurrection and judgment, and the existence of heaven (paradise) and hell. Islam also stresses the worship of one god and regards the Bible as a holy book.

But while Muhammad used many biblical terms in his teaching, he distorted biblical truth. Muhammad claimed to worship the same God as the Christians, but the god of the Qur'an is not the God of the Bible. For example, Muhammad rejected the doctrine of the Trinity and denied that Christ is the Son of God (see 1 John 4:2–3). In reference to Christians, the Qur'an says:

> People of the Book, do not transgress the bounds of your religion. Speak nothing but the truth about God. The Messiah, Jesus, son of Mary, was no more than God's apostle. . . . So believe in God and his apostles, and do not say: 'Three' [there is a Trinity]. Forbear, and it shall be better for you. God is but one God. God forbid that He should have a son! (Sura 4:171)

The Five Pillars

The Qur'an teaches about a paradise in which faithful Muslim men will enjoy gardens of delight, rivers of wine, and the company of beautiful women. To have any hope of entering this paradise, a Muslim must perform certain religious duties. The Qur'an teaches Muslims to fear Allah's punishment if these basic religious practices are not observed. These rituals are called the **Five Pillars of Islam**:

1. Shahadah: The shahadah is the thesis of Islam and must be sincerely believed and recited regularly: "There is no God but Allah, and Muhammad is his prophet."
2. Salat: This word means "prayers." Every Muslim must recite prayers up to five times a day while facing Mecca.
3. Zakat: This word means "purification," and it refers to alms (money) that the devout are to give to the poor.

Pilgrims encircling the Kaaba during a Hajj during Ramadan

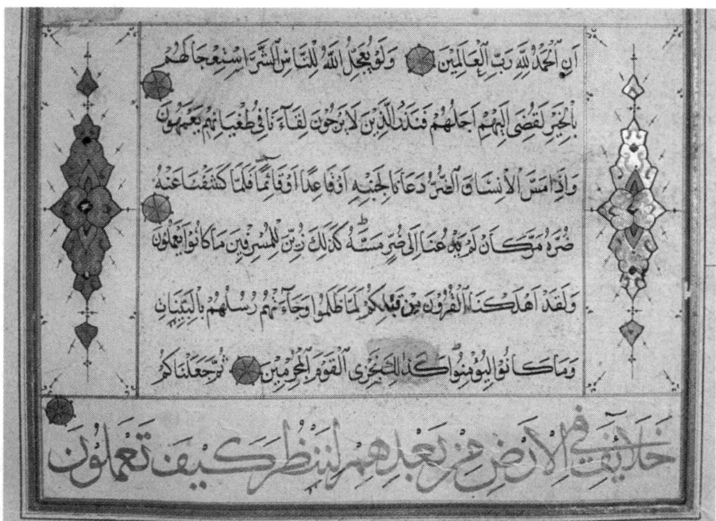

Page from a copy of the Qur'an

4. Sawm: The sawm is a required fast that all Muslims are to observe from sunrise to sunset during the sacred month of Ramadan (ram uh DAHN).

5. Hajj: The hajj is a pilgrimage to Mecca. Every Muslim who is physically and financially able is commanded to make at least one trip to Mecca in his lifetime.

The shahadah expresses a fundamental error of Islam. Muslims believe that the ultimate spokesman for divine truth is Muhammad. The message given to him, preserved in the Qur'an, is supposed to be the final word from heaven. The Bible, however, reserves this high calling for Jesus Christ. He is the Word of God, the ultimate revealer of the Father (John 1:1–3, 18; Heb. 1:1–5). Islam does honor Jesus as a good man and an important prophet, but it vehemently rejects the Bible's teaching that Jesus is God the Son (Matt. 16:13–17).

This rejection has led Islam to many contradictions. We will examine two of them. First, Islam praises Jesus as a prophet of God and accepts some of the books of the Bible, but it rejects the most important biblical claims about Jesus. Many Muslims seek to resolve this conflict by asserting that modern versions of the New Testament are quite different from the New Testament available in Muhammad's time. Other Muslim scholars claim that Christians have misinterpreted the disputed passages. However, there exist today many copies of the New Testament books that were available in Muhammad's day. All of them teach the doctrines that Muslims deny; chiefly, that Jesus is the Son of God.

A second contradiction concerns the implications of Jesus's death on the cross. Islam denies that Jesus came to save people from sin. In fact, the Qur'an even denies that He died (Sura 4:157). Muslims insist that Allah would never allow a great prophet to die such a terrible death. As a result, Islam rejects God's solution for sin with the sacrifice of His Son on the cross. Ignoring this insurmountable contradiction, the Qur'an regularly speaks of Allah as a God of justice who is at the same time a God of mercy and forgiveness. But Allah cannot be just unless he punishes all men for sin. Furthermore, He has no basis to forgive if Jesus never died to pay the penalty for sin.

The Spread of Islam

By the time of his death in 632, Muhammad had united much of Arabia under Islam. But he died without having appointed a successor. This presented a serious problem for Islam and the Arab people. Who should succeed Muhammad as the rightful leader of Islam and the emerging Arab state? The closest friends of Muhammad chose his first four successors from among themselves. These men, who were called **caliphs** (KAY lifs; "successors"), directed the affairs of Islam, exercising spiritual, political, and military authority. The first caliph was **Abu Bakr** (AH-boo BAH-kur) r. 632–34, early convert of Muhammad and father of one of Muhammad's wives. He and the three caliphs who followed him (Umar r. 634–44, Uthman r. 644–56, and Ali r. 656–61) initiated a policy of military conquest that led to the creation of a vast Arab empire founded upon Islam.

With amazing speed, Arab warriors burst forth from their desert homeland, conquering Palestine, Syria, Egypt, Iraq, and Persia. Many factors contributed to this rapid expansion:

Sunni vs. Shia Islam

Initially the key difference between Sunni and Shia Islam was their beliefs on who should succeed Muhammad. Sunnis believed that since Muhammad did not appoint a successor, any worthy Muslim could be appointed to lead Islam. As a result, the caliphate was established. The caliph was a political leader who served as judge, administrator, and general, but he was not the Muslim's spiritual leader.

Shia Muslims believed that Muhammad intended Ali, his son-in-law, to be his successor with authority over political and spiritual matters. Shia Muslims called their leader *imam* rather than *caliph*.

Today, Sunnis use the term *imam* to refer only to the leader of worship in a mosque, while Shiites claim an unbroken succession of imams from Ali to the present. The caliphate was dissolved in 1924 by Turkish leader Mustafa Kemal. However, Sunni Muslims are looking forward to the renewal of the caliphate and believe it will unite Muslims.

1. The Arabs sought an escape from the poverty of the barren Arabian peninsula. Tremendous wealth could be gained through conquest.
2. The Byzantine and Persian (Sassanid) Empires had become weak by the seventh century. Years of constant warfare had left those two rivals exhausted and their territories vulnerable to attack.
3. Islam united the warring Arab tribes around a common cause. The Arabs viewed each conquest as a **jihad** (jih HAHD; "holy war") and they defended the honor of Islam with their swords. Their religious zeal was intensified by the promise that a Muslim's death in battle assured him entrance to paradise.

Umayyad Caliphate (661–750)

In 661 a Muslim general proclaimed himself caliph. He moved the political capital of the empire from Medina to Damascus and established the rule of the **Umayyads** (oo MY yadz). The Umayyads created a hereditary dynasty, ending the practice of selecting the caliph from among the close friends and relatives of Muhammad.

The Umayyads continued Arab expansion. Muslim forces pushed eastward into India, laid siege to Constantinople, and advanced across North Africa. In 711 they crossed the Mediterranean and invaded Spain. They pressed on into southern France until they were stopped by the Franks at the **Battle of Tours** (see p. 132). The year of this battle was 732, one hundred years after the death of Muhammad. Although the Muslim advance into Europe was stopped, the Arabs could boast of an empire that stretched from Spain to India.

The Dome of the Rock was built during the Umayyad dynasty.

First Muslim Setback

The first significant defeat of Muslim forces was inflicted by the Nubians. After conquering Egypt, the Muslims turned south to invade Nubia. The Nubians repulsed the Muslim invasion in 710 and remained free of Muslim control until 1272.

Abbasid Caliphate (750–ca. 1000)

Discontent over Umayyad rule soon mounted. A growing number of non-Arab Muslims were dissatisfied with being treated as second-class citizens by Arab rulers. In addition, many Arab Muslims did not consider the Umayyads the rightful successors of Muhammad. Abbas, a descendant of Muhammad's uncle, overthrew the Umayyad caliph in 750 and founded the **Abbasid** (AB uh sid) caliphate. Under the Abbasids, Arab supremacy within the Muslim empire gradually declined as many non-Arabs were appointed to high government positions. Also, non-Arabs became increasingly influential in Islamic society.

The Abbasid caliphate marks the peak of the Muslim empire. The Muslims controlled more territory than had the ancient Romans. The new capital, Baghdad, became one of the world's leading commercial centers, rivaling Constantinople. In addition, during the Abbasid rule, Islamic culture flourished.

The Turks and the Crusades

The Arabs had been the primary agents in the early spread of Islam. Their military conquests had created the expansive Muslim empire. But during the Abbasid dynasty, the political unity of the Muslim world began to crumble. Disputes over the succession to the caliphate broke out among rival Muslim factions. Soon independent dynasties appeared, each proclaiming its own caliph. Meanwhile, the Seljuk Turks entered the territory of the weakened Abbasids. These fierce and aggressive warriors accepted Islam and led a new wave of Islamic expansion. The Seljuks not only reunited much of the former Arab empire but also took control of Asia Minor, which had been under Byzantine

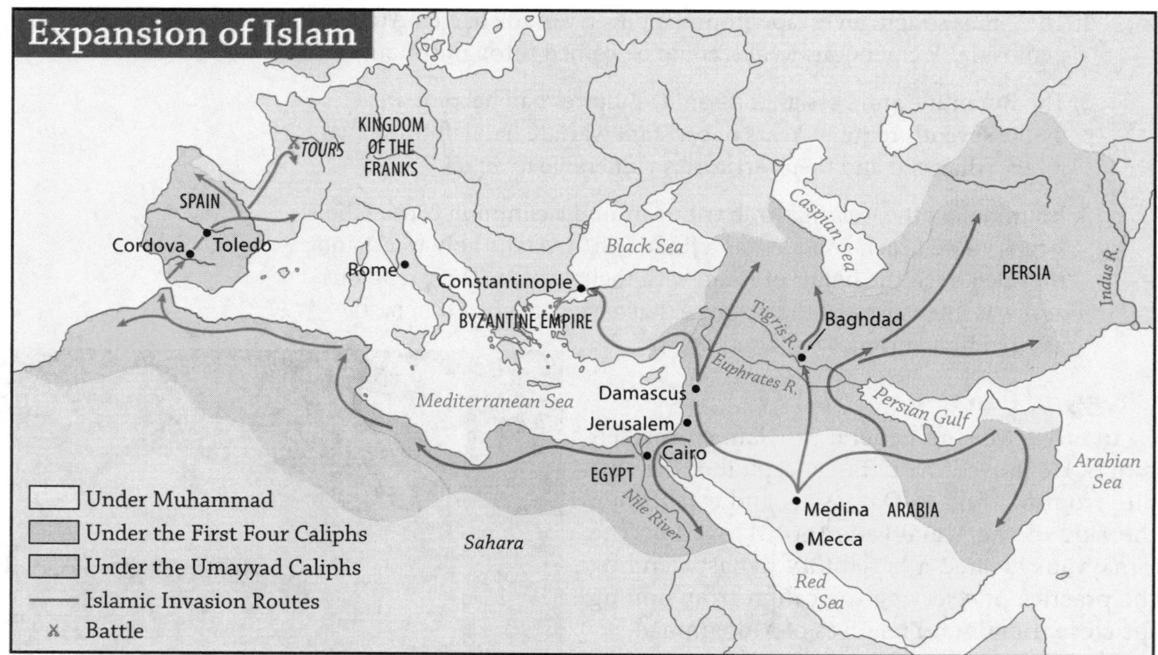

control. Muslim forces destroyed churches and monasteries and attacked Christian pilgrims as they passed through Asia Minor on their way to visit the Holy Land.

The revived aggressiveness of the Muslim empire and reports of the brutal attacks on Christians caused great alarm among the Christian peoples of western Europe. As a result, the West assembled a series of armies to free the birthplace of Christendom from the Muslim Turks (see pp. 167–72). The Crusades did little to remove the Muslims from Palestine, but they did succeed in weakening the power of the Seljuks. In the thirteenth century the Seljuk Empire came to a violent end when the Mongols swept into the Muslim world. At the beginning of the fourteenth century, the Ottoman Turks, former subjects of the Seljuks, restored Turkish rule. Once again Muslim forces built a vast empire. The Ottoman Empire stretched across North Africa, over much of the Middle East, and into southeastern Europe. For a time, the Ottoman navy even controlled the Mediterranean Sea and the Black Sea.

Muslim Culture Contributions

The Arabs built the Muslim empire through conquest. Then they borrowed, embraced, and added to the rich cultural heritage of the peoples with whom they came into contact—the Persians, the Byzantines, the Egyptians, and the Syrians. By blending the many cultural influences within the empire with Islam, the Muslims developed a prosperous civilization.

As previously stated, by the middle of the eighth century, the Muslim empire was no longer predominantly Arab. As a result, Muslim leaders moved the capital from Damascus to Baghdad, and Islam demonstrated a more Persian influence. As the empire continued to expand, so did its trade routes. Now Muslim merchants traveled to China, India, and East Africa, bringing back new products and ideas (such as paper from China and mathematics from India). These products and ideas, as well as the achievements of Muslim culture, later found their way to the West as European merchants opened up trade routes to the Middle East. In addition to trade, these routes also enabled Persian Christians to take the gospel to China.

As the Crusaders came to Muslim lands, they were astounded to find silk, muslin (fine cotton), linen, and damask (cloth woven with silver and gold thread). They admired magnificently woven carpets ("Persian" or "Oriental" rugs), finely tooled leather, delicate filigree jewelry (ornamental work done with fine wire), engraved silver and gold, and exquisite knives and swords. Ships that had carried crusading forces to the Holy Land returned to Europe loaded with these treasures in addition to dates, oranges, lemons, apricots, peaches, and melons, all of which were previously unknown in the West during this period.

An important way the Muslims gained knowledge was to translate manuscripts from other lands into Arabic. They translated the writings of Aristotle, Plato, Galen, Hippocrates, Archimedes, Euclid, Ptolemy, and others. They also translated important works from Persia and India. Many of these manuscripts might have been lost had they not been preserved by Muslim scholars, who built great libraries to house these manuscripts and their Arabic translations.

Medicine

In the field of medicine, the Muslims profited from the Greek writings of Galen and Hippocrates. Muslim doctors put into practical use what they learned from the classics and developed new medical procedures. Two of the most famous Muslim physicians were **al-Rāzi** (AL RAY-zee) and **Ibn Sina** (IB-un SEE-nuh; also known as Avicenna). Both men wrote many medical books in which they recorded their practical experience in identifying and treating various diseases. Al-Rāzi is best remembered for his work with smallpox, and Ibn Sina for his work with tuberculosis.

Muslim doctors developed amazing surgical skills. They performed such delicate operations as removing cancer from the body and cataracts from the eye. The Muslims also built hospitals throughout the empire. Although they did not know about germs, they suspected that dirt led to disease. Therefore, they tried to keep their patients and hospitals as clean as possible. In addition, Muslims had something similar to modern pharmacies that filled prescriptions. Government inspectors supervised these merchants to ensure the purity of the medicines.

Literature

In addition to their religious, scientific, and medical writings, the Muslims produced rich and colorful imagery in both their poetry and their prose. Perhaps the most renowned Muslim poet (also a famed mathematician) was **Omar Khayyam** (OH-mar kie-YAHM). His *Rubaiyat* (roo by YAHT; a poem with verses of four lines) remains quite popular in the West. Like most Muslim poetry it is very picturesque.

> The Moving Finger writes; and, having writ,
> Moves on: nor all your Piety nor Wit
> Shall lure it back to cancel half a Line.
> Nor all your Tears wash out a Word of it.
>
> And that inverted Bowl they call the Sky,
> Whereunder crawling coop'd we live and die,
> Lift not your hands to It for help—for It
> As impotently moves as you or I.

Better known to both young and old is *The Thousand and One Nights* (popularly known as *The Arabian Nights*). Among these fanciful tales gathered from all over the Muslim world are the stories of "Aladdin and His Wonderful Lamp" and "Ali Baba and the Forty Thieves."

Tales of Arabia

The Thousand and One Nights is about a sultan named Shahriyar who each day weds a new bride and then executes her the next morning. One day he marries Scheherazade, a beautiful and intelligent young maiden. That night for Shahriyar's entertainment, she tells him a story but stops at the climax. Eager to hear the conclusion, the sultan decides to wait another day and then execute her. The next night Scheherazade finishes her story but then begins another, stopping again at an exciting part. Shahriyar once more decides to wait so that he can hear the conclusion. This goes on for a thousand and one consecutive nights. At the end of that time, the sultan is so much in love with Scheherazade that he abandons all thought of executing her, and they live happily ever after.

Top: Ottoman certificate of competence in calligraphy
Bottom: Badshahi Mosque in Lahore, Pakistan

Mathematics

The Muslims borrowed much of their basic mathematical knowledge from India. The so-called Arabic numerals are of Hindu origin. So are the decimal system and the concept of zero, which the Muslims popularized. The Muslims studied and improved algebra, which came from India, as well as the geometry and trigonometry of the Greeks.

Art and Architecture

Religion plays an important part in Muslim art. Muhammad is said to have forbidden the representation of men and animals in art. He feared that the people might worship statues or paintings of living things. Therefore, Muslim artists developed decorative designs that are more abstract than representational. The most common patterns found in Muslim art are abstract designs of stems and leaves and geometric figures. Muslim artists also excelled in **calligraphy**, the art of beautiful writing. They adorned the walls of buildings with verses from the Qur'an written in beautiful Arabic script. One of the most honored forms of Islamic art was manuscript illumination; Muslim artists used miniature paintings and decorative colors and ornamentation to illustrate or "illuminate" their books—especially the Qur'an.

In architecture, however, Muslim art reached its highest achievement. The Muslims drew from the architectural styles of Persia and Byzantium but gradually produced their own unique style. The best examples of Muslim architecture are the **mosques** (MAHSKS; places of Muslim worship). Muhammad did not believe Muslims should build elaborate mosques since these buildings were only places of prayer. He said on one occasion as recorded by Ibn Sa'd, "The most unprofitable thing that eateth up the wealth of the believer is building." Nevertheless, his followers spent fortunes on their houses of worship.

The typical features of a mosque are its courtyard, minaret, and dome. In the courtyard is a pool for ceremonial washing before prayer. Either as part of the mosque or adjacent to it is a tall minaret (or tower). From this tower the muezzin (myoo EZ in; "crier") calls the faithful to prayer five times a day. One of the characteristic features of Muslim architecture is the dome, which usually covers the main portion of the mosque. Inside, the walls are generally white and inscribed with quotations from the Qur'an. Some walls, however, are highly decorated with tile and mosaic designs. In one wall of each mosque is a niche that indicates the direction of Mecca, toward which a Muslim prays.

Section Quiz

1. What name is given to the Arab nomads who roam the desert in search of pastureland and water?
2. Who claimed to be the last and greatest of the prophets of Allah?
3. What became the holy city of the Islamic faith? What is the most sacred shrine in that city?
4. What is the name of the holy book of Islam?
5. What is the name for the local Muslim place of worship?

★ How does the Muslim description of Jesus as an honored prophet differ from the Bible's statements about Jesus?

Chapter 6 Review

Making Connections

1–2. How did the reign of Justinian affect the Byzantine Empire? (List two things)

3. How did the Byzantine civilization influence early Russia?
4. How did Islam unite the Arabs?
5. How do Muslims try to resolve the conflict between the Qur'an's claims about Jesus and the Bible's claims about Him?

Developing History Skills

1. If the Arabs are the descendants of Abraham, what is the significance of Genesis 16:10–12 for them?
2. What might have happened if the Franks had lost the Battle of Tours?

Thinking Critically

1. Does the reverence for icons in Orthodox churches violate the command in Exodus 20:4 and Deuteronomy 4:12–24 against making images? Explain your answer.
2. Based on what you have read in this chapter, do Christians and Muslims worship the same God? Explain your answer.

Living in God's World

1. Imagine that you are an emperor who wishes to create just laws for his people. Write a brief law code that deals with some of the areas found in Justinian's law code: protection of property, slavery and freedom, marriage, wills, and commerce. Remember that the Bible provides standards of justice to which all laws ought to conform.
2. Write a brief gospel tract based on a Bible passage such as Matthew 16:13–17.

People, Places, and Things to Know

Byzantine Empire
New Rome
Justinian
Theodora
Nika Revolt
Justinian Code
Hagia Sophia
Eastern Orthodox Church
icons
excommunicated
Basil II
Seljuk Turks
Crusades
Ottoman Turks
mosaic
Slavs
Varangians
Rurik
Rus
Vladimir I
Ishmael
Bedouins
Muhammad
Allah
Islam
Muslims
Kaaba
Hegira
Qur'an
Five Pillars of Islam
caliphs
Abu Bakr
jihad
Umayyads
Battle of Tours
Abbasid
al-Rāzi
Ibn Sina
Omar Khayyam
calligraphy
mosques

7

THE CIVILIZATIONS OF ASIA & AFRICA

I. India
II. China
III. Japan
IV. The Mongol Empire
V. Africa

A section of the Great Wall of China snakes across the Chinese landscape.

The historical books of the Bible center on the nations of Israel, Egypt, Babylon, Persia, Greece, and Rome. However, at the same time that these empires flourished, other equally splendid empires developed in India, China, and Africa. In the centuries following the ministry of the apostles, the gospel also spread to these parts of the world. There is little evidence that Christianity thrived initially in these regions. Recently, however, Christianity has begun to grow in Asia and Africa more quickly than in many other regions of the globe. Therefore, understanding the history of these cultures is important for Christians.

Sunrise in Africa

I. India

India is a land of great diversity. In its **topography** (the physical features of a land), climate, and population, it is a study in contrasts. This triangular subcontinent extends from southern Asia into the Indian Ocean, forming a giant peninsula. Its terrain varies from subtropical rainforest to barren deserts, from low coastal plains to the highest mountain range in the world, the Himalayas. Between the rugged mountain regions in the north and the coastal plains and tropical plateaus of the south lie fertile valleys watered by two great river systems, the Indus and the Ganges. Like the Mesopotamian and Egyptian cultures, the earliest Indian civilization began along riverbanks. The first inhabitants of India probably settled in river valleys along the Indus and Ganges Rivers.

These people must have felt secure from invaders and foreign influences. They were protected by tall mountain ranges in the north and by seas on the east and west. But despite these natural barriers, India did not remain an isolated land. Throughout its history, merchants, foreign invaders, and wandering tribes crossed the mountains along India's northwestern border (through such mountain passes as the Khyber) and settled in the fertile river valleys. As a result, India became a land of many peoples, customs, and languages. From the diverse elements within Indian society, a unique culture developed.

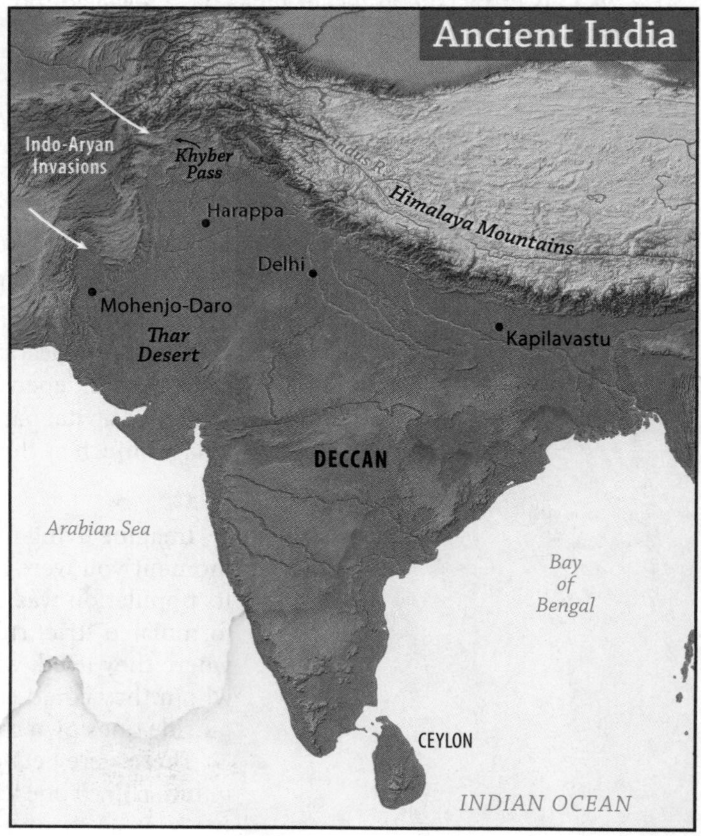

Early Civilization

India derives its name from the Indus River, along whose fertile banks the earliest Indian civilization flourished (ca. 2300 BC). Much of our limited knowledge of this civilization has come from excavations of two of its leading cities: Mohenjo-Daro (moh HEN joh DAH roh) and Harappa (huh RAP uh). These were carefully planned cities with wide, straight streets lined with brick houses. Evidence indicates that these cities had elaborate drainage and sewer systems that were more advanced than those in most modern-day Indian villages. Although a great distance separates India and the Near East, the early inhabitants of India carried on trade with Egypt and Mesopotamia. We know from archaeological evidence that the Indus civilization ended suddenly—perhaps by enemy invasion. It was at this time that a warlike people called the **Aryans** migrated into the Indus Valley.

The Aryans came from central Asia sometime after 1500 BC and subdued the non-Aryan people of northwest India. Many historians believe that the Aryans were

Mohenjo-Daro

When the city of Mohenjo-Daro in the Indus Valley was first built (ca. 2300 BC), the founders carefully planned everything. Wide main streets ran from north to south, and small lanes ran east and west. Houses were built with thick, solid walls to keep the dwellings cool during the long, hot summers. The thick walls also made it possible for buildings to have several stories. The builders used kiln-baked bricks, which were of a higher quality than those dried in the sun. Each house was equipped with a well, and drains took dirty water down the streets and out of the city. In the center of the city were huge public baths, which the men used in religious ceremonies. Also in the center of the town was a huge granary.

All this was suddenly and violently destroyed, possibly by Aryan invaders. From unearthed skeletal remains, archaeologists have learned of the swiftness of Mohenjo-Daro's destruction. The remains of two men who were evidently attempting to hide in a well have been found. A group of people, slowed by a small child, died in the streets. Archaeologists have found the skeletons of another group, who thought they could find safety by crouching down behind a wall. One family grabbed all their possessions and tried to escape, but they were caught and brutally murdered. A young couple tried to hide themselves and their child in a corner of the darkest room in the house, but they too did not escape death. The city's destruction was complete. Never rebuilt, it lay forgotten for many centuries. Excavations of the site in recent times have revealed the grim ending of Mohenjo-Daro.

related to tribes that were invading the Near East, Greece, and Rome at about the same time. The Aryans were herdsmen; they kept large numbers of cows and horses. Although they left behind no cities as the Indus civilization did, they did establish a new language in India—**Sanskrit.**

Our knowledge of the Aryans and their influence on Indian society comes not from archaeology but from a collection of religious literature known as the ***Vedas*** (VAY dus), meaning "knowledge." Preserved in the *Vedas* are early traditions and religious beliefs of the Indians, which were orally passed down from one generation to the next. From Sanskrit literature, we gain insights into the Aryan way of life, which became the basis of Indian culture and tradition. This formative period of Indian history lasted from about 1500 to 500 BC.

Key Features of Indian Society

India has one of the oldest cultures in the modern world. The basic characteristics of Indian society, described in the *Vedas*, have changed little from ancient to modern days.

Joint Family

The family has always been one of the most important social units in India. The extended or **joint family** included the children, grandchildren, wives, and close blood relatives of a common ancestor. The oldest male of the group was the dominant authority over the family. When married, sons did not establish their own homes; instead they remained in their father's or grandfather's household. Each family member had his own duties and obligations. The interests of the family came before those of the individual family members. Parents chose the husbands or wives for their children in order to maintain the family's position and honor in society.

Village Life

Unlike the inhabitants of the Indus civilization, who dwelt in cities, the Aryans settled in small rural villages. Family groups living in a village were governed by a headman or a council of village elders. For the most part, the villages were independent and self-governing. Over the centuries village life has remained a vital part of Indian society. Most people in India today live in small villages much as their ancestors did over two thousand years ago.

Caste

Imagine living in a country in which your status in life was determined the moment you were born. India was, and in some ways still is, such a country. Its population was divided into rigid social groups called **castes**. The Indians formulated strict rules governing the life of the members of each caste group: where they lived, what they did (profession), what they wore, what and with whom they could eat, and whom they could marry. (Marriage was forbidden outside one's own caste.)

There were between two and three thousand different castes and subcastes in India. Each one fell into one of four broad "class" groups. The most important group was the priests, called the *Brahmans*. Next in rank were the rulers and warriors, followed by the merchants and traders. The lowest class group was the *Sudras* (SOO dras)—composed of servants and serfs. Outside the caste system and at the bottom of the Indian social ladder were the outcastes, or "untouchables." They performed the most menial tasks in society. Members of the caste structure avoided the "untouchables"; mere contact with them was thought to bring defilement. While anyone could improve his status within his caste, no one could change castes. Thus with the caste system there was little change in the village and family life of India. This fact explains in part why Indian society remained unchanged for thousands of years.

Religion and the Indian Way of Life

Religion has played a dominant role in shaping Indian culture. From India came two religions that have had a major impact on Asian culture: Hinduism and Buddhism.

Hinduism

Hinduism is ingrained in the Indian way of life. It developed from India's early culture and traditions: social structure, literature, arts, and customs. It has not only preserved the traditional elements of India's past but also served as a unifying influence in India's diverse society. Because Hinduism has no formal statement of doctrine, it was able to absorb into its system of belief a wide variety of gods and religious concepts found among the many peoples of India. (Hindus believe all religions to be equally true and equally false.) To this day, over 80 percent of the people of India are Hindus.

The basic tenets of Hinduism are found in the religious literature of ancient India, namely the *Vedas* and the *Upanishads* (oo PAN uh shadz; philosophical essays elaborating on the teaching of the *Vedas*). Hindus believe that a great god called **Brahman** permeates everything in the universe. The Hindus acknowledge many gods; all deities, however, are considered only manifestations of the eternal, unchanging Brahman. Since Brahman is not a personal being, he is often referred to as the great soul or world soul. The ultimate purpose and goal of every person, according to the *Vedas*, is to reunite his soul with the world soul. This is done through the process of reincarnation, in which a soul passes through many states (or rebirths) before it escapes the physical world and unites with Brahman. This cycle of rebirths is called the wheel of life.

Hindu temple

The Hindu believes that a person's deeds in this life determine his status in the next. If he has lived a good life (that is, if his good works outweigh his bad), then he will move to a higher caste in the next life. The soul of an evil person may be reborn into a lower caste or even into some form of animal life. By observing the religious rituals and ceremonies prescribed by the Hindu priests and by fulfilling the duties and obligations of his caste, a Hindu believes that he (through repeated rebirths) can ultimately gain release from the wheel of life and attain union with the world soul.

Buddha statue

Buddhism

India was also the birthplace of **Buddhism**. The founder of this religion was **Siddhartha Gautama** (sid-DAR-tuh GOU-tuh-muh) (ca. 563–ca. 483 BC), later known as Buddha, the "Enlightened One." At the age of twenty-nine, Gautama became troubled over the misery, poverty, and death that he saw in the world. He became convinced that he should devote all his efforts to find the way of deliverance from suffering. Therefore, he renounced his life of luxury, gave up his princely heritage, left his wife and child, and set out to find peace and true happiness. After spending six frustrating years living as a hermit in self-sacrifice and meditation, Gautama was at the point of despair. Sitting down under a tree, he vowed that he would not move until the truth came to him. According to Gautama, he was pondering the questions of life when he realized the truth and attained enlightenment.

Central to Buddha's teaching are his **Four Noble Truths**: (1) Suffering is part of all existence. (2) Suffering has a cause—selfish desires. As long as man craves pleasure, possessions, and power, he will have sorrow and misery. (3) Suffering can be overcome by destroying selfish desires. (4) If a man follows the Eightfold Path, he will destroy selfish desires and end all suffering. This pattern for living includes correct beliefs, intentions, speech, conduct, livelihood, effort, thoughts, and meditations.

Buddhism is a religion built on works and moral behavior. Buddhists believe that people do not need the help of gods or membership in a higher caste in order to obtain freedom from suffering. Once a man has absolutely freed himself from his selfish cravings, he will no longer be reborn but will enter into *nirvana* (neer VAH nuh), the state of absolute peace and happiness where one loses himself into nothingness.

Both Hindus and Buddhists believe that man can eventually achieve eternal peace (whether in union with the "world soul" or by freeing himself into non-being) by living a good life. The Bible clearly teaches that the final state of all people is either in eternal union with or eternal separation from God, and the only way to have union with God is through Jesus Christ, not merely by living a good life (1 John 5:11–12).

Lack of Political Unity

While many aspects of Indian society have remained the same for centuries, the political history of India has been one of frequent change. Through much of its history, India has been little more than a patchwork of small rival kingdoms. Successive waves of foreign invaders streamed into the Indian subcontinent. The powerful empires established by these invaders provided brief periods of unity and stability for the Indian peoples.

Mauryan Empire

In 326 BC Alexander the Great threatened India. His armies crossed the Indus River and conquered many small kingdoms in India's northwestern region. Alexander intended to advance farther into India, but when his army refused to continue, he had to turn back. According to traditional accounts, he met a young man named Chandragupta Maurya (CHUN-druh-GOOP-tuh MAH-oor-yuh) while in India. As Alexander's empire began to disintegrate after his death, Chandragupta conquered the disorganized and weak kingdoms in the north and created the first strong empire of India—the Mauryan Empire.

The most famous of the Mauryan rulers was Chandragupta's grandson **Asoka.** He extended the Mauryan Empire to include all but the southern tip of India. Sickened by the results of his own bloody conquests, Asoka renounced war and became a convert to Buddhism. He spent much of his reign promoting the Buddhist religion. Asoka is credited with building thousands of Buddhist shrines called stupas (STOO puz). He also had Buddhist teachings inscribed on stone pillars throughout the empire. Many of these stone pillars still stand, providing valuable information concerning Asoka's reign. One of his most far-reaching acts was the sending of Buddhist missionaries abroad. Buddhism soon spread across much of Southeast Asia, where it became a powerful force in other Asian cultures. It did not gain a wide following in India, however. Hindu priests viewed Buddhist teaching as dangerous to the caste system. Fearing that they might lose their prestige and rank in society, they worked against the acceptance of Buddhist beliefs.

Gupta Empire

The first great period of Indian unity was short-lived. Not long after Asoka's death (232 BC), the Mauryan Empire collapsed. The years between the second century BC and the third century AD witnessed new invasions and the rise of small competing kingdoms. However, during this time of turmoil, India did enjoy a profitable trade with Rome and China. Even so, it was not until the fourth century AD, with the rise of the **Gupta** (GOOP tuh) **Empire**, that India entered a new, and perhaps its greatest, era of prosperity and achievement.

One historian has stated that "at the time India was perhaps the happiest and most civilized region of the world." The rulers of the Gupta dynasty reunited northern India under a strong and effective government. Trade flourished and the people prospered materially. India's culture spread throughout Southeast Asia. India's universities attracted students from all over the continent, and its people made great strides in the fields of textiles and ironwork. The Gupta Age was also one of the finest periods of Indian art, architecture, literature, and science.

Gupta literature became renowned for its adventurous and imaginative fables and fairy tales. The foremost Indian poet and dramatist of this period was **Kalidasa** (kah lih DAH suh), whose plays have earned him the title "the Indian Shakespeare." The popularity of various Indian stories soon spread outside India, where many of them found their way into the literature of other lands. (Western authors such as the brothers Grimm and Rudyard Kipling drew upon Indian stories for ideas for their writing.)

This was also an age of advance in mathematics, science, and medicine. Our so-called Arabic numerals originally came from India. Indian mathematicians were among the first to use negative numbers, the decimal, and the zero. Centuries before Isaac Newton, Indian scientists developed their own theories of gravity. Indian astronomers knew that the earth was round and that it rotated on its axis. If in need of medical attention, the people of the Gupta Empire went to free hospitals where Indian physicians performed many surgical procedures.

Ajanta Buddhist monastic caves in India

Spread of the Gospel to India

According to tradition, the apostle Thomas brought the gospel to India. Whether this tradition is accurate or not, travel between the Roman Empire and India was common in the first century. It is likely that early in the church's history Christians did bring the gospel to India. The church historian Eusebius recorded that Origen's teacher, a man named Pantaenus, traveled as a missionary to India. When he arrived he found Christians there already, and they had copies of the Gospel of Matthew. By the fourth century, Christians in Persia had made contact with the Christians in India. The Indians sent their leaders to schools in Persia for training until the Muslims conquered Persia. The scattered communities of Indian Christians were never very large, but they were still in existence when the Portuguese landed in India in the fifteenth century to open trade between India and Europe.

During the sixth century the Gupta Empire collapsed under the repeated attacks of the so-called White Huns (perhaps related to the Huns who plagued the Roman Empire during the fifth century). India again entered a period of political disorder; the country became divided into small warring kingdoms. Waves of foreign invaders again entered the land; but as in the past, Hinduism absorbed the culture of these foreign elements into Indian society. The history of India took a dramatic turn when northern India fell under the domination of Muslims, who brought with them an ideology as all-encompassing as Hinduism.

After years of constant raids, Muslim warriors conquered much of northern India, where they established a Muslim kingdom in 1206 near the city of Delhi. Almost immediately a conflict arose between the Muslim and Hindu elements within Indian society. For example, the Hindus believed in many gods, while the Muslims acknowledged only one. The Hindus followed the rigid caste system, while the Muslims believed in the equality of all men before their god, Allah. Although Muslim control of northern India ended at the close of the fourteenth century, Muslim rulers left India scarred from the brutal execution of vast numbers of Hindus. As a result, the hostilities between Hindus and Muslims in Indian society have continued to the present.

Section Quiz

1. Along the banks of what river did the earliest Indian civilization begin?
2. List the four broad class groups under the Indian caste system.
3. What is the cycle of rebirths (the process of reincarnation) called?
4. Identify the two empires that temporarily brought national unity to India.
5. What famous Indian poet earned the title of "the Indian Shakespeare"?

★ Evaluate India's caste system in light of Bible passages such as Genesis 1:27, Matthew 22:34–40 and Luke 10:25–27, and Isaiah 55:1 and Revelation 22:17.

II. China
The Land

At the heart of eastern Asia is the land of China. In ancient days the Chinese called their land the **Middle Kingdom** because they believed China to be the center of the earth. Today more people live in China than in any other country in the world—close to one-fifth of the world's population. In land size, modern China is slightly smaller than the United States, but China's population is nearly five times greater.

Yangtze River in China

China is one of the world's oldest civilizations. The earliest Chinese lived in the fertile valleys of China's two major river systems: The Huang He (or Yellow) and the Yangtze (YANG see). In this respect, ancient China was similar to other early river-valley civilizations—Mesopotamia, Egypt, and India. But while these other civilizations were conquered by hostile armies, China during its early history remained relatively free from outside influences.

China was isolated from other centers of civilization for many centuries. The vast Pacific Ocean, the tall Himalayan Mountains, and the huge Gobi Desert hemmed in China on all sides. These geographic barriers provided security from most foreign invasions and influences. Because of the relatively small foreign influence on Chinese society, the Chinese developed and maintained a unique and stable culture that remained virtually unchanged from ancient to modern times.

The Importance of the Chinese Family

"The family had functions which in the modern West are commonly assumed by the state. It educated its youth, cared for its unemployed, disciplined its erring members, and supported its aged. In turn, the state held the family accountable for the misdeeds of its members. . . . The individual was of far less importance than the family. The individual member was to make his earnings available to his less fortunate relatives. . . . Marriage was primarily not for the happiness of those who entered into that relationship, but for the purpose of continuing the family line. No sin was greater than that of dying without leaving male issue to revere the memory of one's ancestors."

Kenneth Scott Latourette, A Short History of the Far East, *158.*

Societal Features

Strong Family Ties

The family was and still is the center of life in Chinese society. Chinese families were large, embracing many generations: parents and their children, grandparents and grandchildren, aunts and uncles, nephews and nieces, cousins and in-laws. Ancestors were also included in the Chinese concept of the family. Many Chinese could trace their family history back hundreds of years.

A major responsibility of every Chinese person was to bring honor to his family. One of the worst offenses a person could commit was to dishonor his ancestors by bringing reproach on the family name. The cult of **ancestor worship** became the leading religion in China. Every Chinese house contained an ancestral altar before which the Chinese burned incense to the spirits of their dead. By caring for their family graves and worshiping before these altars, the Chinese hoped to receive blessings and guidance from their ancestral spirits.

Language and Learning

The most noticeable feature of China's spoken language is its tonal quality. By varying the tone of voice on a particular syllable, the Chinese can convey more than one meaning. For example, *ma* may mean "mother," "hemp" (an Asiatic plant), "horse," or "to scold," depending on the pitch of the voice. Communication in China is made difficult by variations in the spoken languages from one region to another. Chinese people from different regions often have trouble understanding each other.

Although the spoken language varies greatly, China does have a common written language. Traditional Chinese writing is not based on a simple alphabet as our English system is; it consists of some sixty-five thousand characters that represent complete ideas, objects, and sounds. For instance, the word for "good" is a combination of the characters for "girl" and "boy." One has to memorize each character in order to be able to read—a fact that makes reading and writing extremely difficult. Over the centuries the vast majority of the Chinese people have been illiterate. Even the most literate Chinese know only about four thousand characters. It is little wonder that those who master the written language have always been given a place of distinction in Chinese society.

good boy girl

China has been called a "scholar's world." In most other civilizations soldiers, priests, or merchants held prominent positions in society. Through much of Chinese history, however, no social group exceeded the influence of scholars. For the would-be scholar, education (consisting mainly of memorizing classical Chinese literature) began at an early age and demanded total dedication of time and energy. The goal of the learned man was a career in government service. Scholarship was the determining factor in obtaining a position, whether it be that of a local magistrate or a high government official. Because there were more scholars than government positions, the Chinese developed civil service examinations to choose the best qualified. Those obtaining the highest test scores received the positions.

Chinese Thought and Life

Two native philosophies greatly influenced Chinese life: Confucianism (kun FYOO shun iz um) and Taoism (TOU iz um). These systems of thought became the heart of China's religious beliefs and practices.

Confucianism

K'ung Futzu (KOONG FOO DZUH) (551–479 BC) is the most honored teacher in Chinese history. The Chinese call him "the Master"; we know him as **Confucius**. Confucius grew up in poverty during a time of social and political unrest in China. Unable to obtain a political office, he devoted his life to

Chinese Characters

When God scattered Noah's descendants throughout the world (Gen. 11:1–9), they carried with them a knowledge of man's earliest history. They knew of Creation, the Fall, and the Flood. Those who migrated to China seem to have preserved some of these truths in their writing system. Since most Chinese characters tell a story, we can break down the more complex characters into simpler ones and discover the meaning of each part.

to forbid

林

wood/tree

示

God

For example, the Chinese character for "to forbid" tells the story of God's command to Adam in Genesis 2:16–17. God planted two special trees in the Garden of Eden: the tree of life and the tree of knowledge of good and evil. God commanded Adam not to eat of the tree of the knowledge of good and evil but gave him permission to eat fruit from any other tree in the garden. It is interesting to note, therefore, that the character "to forbid" is made up of the symbol for "wood" or "tree" (notice that two are indicated) and one of the basic Chinese symbols for God. (This character for God also had the idea of "to command" or "to express.")

The scriptural idea of sacrifice (the killing of a spotless animal) is also found in Chinese writing. The word "to sacrifice" is made up of four major parts: "ox" or "cattle," "sheep," "beautiful" or "unblemished," and "spear" (the weapon by which the animal was killed).

sacrifice

ox/cattle

sheep

beautiful

spear

義

righteous

羊

lamb

me

Closely associated with the idea of sacrifice is the concept of righteousness. The character that means "righteous" or "righteousness" is made up of the symbol for "lamb" and the symbol for "me." Notice that when the two characters are combined to create the word *righteous*(ness), the lamb is placed over the person. In the same manner, Christ, who is the perfect Lamb of God, covers our sins with His blood.

Another interesting study is the character for "boat" or "ship". It is made up of the symbol for "small vessel," the symbol for the number eight, and the symbol that means "person," "population," or "mouth." The largest boat built in antiquity (as far as we know) was the ark. It saved Noah and his family—a total of eight persons.

boat **small vessel** **eight** **person**

The written Chinese language indicates that at some time in the past the Chinese knew God's truth. Although most Chinese people today do not have access to the Scriptures, the written language preserves not only the truth of man's sin but also the wonderful fact of God's saving grace.

teaching. He believed that through proper conduct man could solve the problems of society and live in complete happiness. His disciples recorded and expanded upon his teaching, developing a system of ethics that became a major influence on Chinese culture.

Fundamental to Confucius's teaching was his belief in five basic human relationships: father and son, elder and younger brothers, husband and wife, friend and friend, and ruler and subjects. Confucius believed that maintaining proper relationships in these five areas would bring harmony and order to society. In addition, he placed great confidence in China's past, trusting it as the basis and guide for human behavior. From the ancients he derived the fundamental principle for all human relationships: "What you do not want done to yourself, do not do to others."

The major defect in Confucius's teaching was his neglect of the most important relationship of all—man and God. Only as we fulfill our duties and responsibilities to God are we able to properly relate to our fellow men. God's Word commands us to love God with our whole being and to love our neighbors as much as we love ourselves (Matt. 22:37–39). Only by living in obedience to God is man able to fulfill God's teaching found in Luke 6:31: "As ye would that men should do to you, do ye also to them likewise."

Xingtan Pavilion where Confucius lectured to his disciples

The Sayings of Confucius

The philosophy of Confucius is contained in a collection of his sayings and activities called the *Analects*. Some of what Confucius said is remarkably sound advice. This demonstrates how the image of God in fallen man still enables him to discern a certain amount of wisdom in how to live. However, those who try to live wisely apart from God cannot achieve this goal to the degree that God intended.

- It does not greatly concern me . . . that men do not know me; my great concern is my not knowing them.
- To go beyond is as wrong as to fall short.
- It is moral cowardice to leave undone what one perceives to be right to do.
- Where there is habitual going after gain, there is much ill-will.
- Learn as if never overtaking your object, and yet as if apprehensive of losing it.
- The nobler-minded man . . . will be agreeable even when he disagrees; the small-minded man will agree and be disagreeable.
- Impatience over little things introduces confusion into great schemes.
- The cautious seldom err.
- Faults in a superior man are like eclipses of the sun and moon: when he is guilty of a trespass, men all see it; and when he is himself again, all look up to him.
- When you meet with men of worth, think how you may attain to their level; when you see others of an opposite character, look within and examine yourself.
- They who care not for the morrow will the sooner have their sorrows.
- Learning without thought is a snare; thought without learning is a danger.
- With a meal of coarse rice . . . and water to drink, and my bent arm for a pillow—even thus I find happiness. Riches and honors without righteousness are to me as fleeting clouds.

Taoism

Second in importance to the teaching of Confucius was that of **Lao-tzu** (LOU DZUH) (ca. 604–ca. 531 BC), believed to be the founder of **Taoism.** According to Chinese legend, Lao-tzu taught that *tao* (meaning "the way") was the pervading force in nature. He encouraged men to find peace and happiness by living in harmony with nature. According to Taoist teaching, men can achieve this harmony by ceasing to strive after power, wealth, and learning; instead they should adopt a simple, inactive lifestyle. By being passive and submissive, men can accomplish great things. Taoists illustrated this teaching with the example of water: "There is nothing in the world more soft and weak than water, yet for attacking things that are hard and strong there is nothing that surpasses it. . . . The soft overcomes the hard; the weak overcomes the strong."

Confucianism became the guiding philosophy of China's educational, social, and political systems; Taoism became the basis of mystical, magical, and superstitious elements in Chinese society. In many ways, these two philosophies conflict with one another. Confucianism promotes living an active life and fulfilling one's social obligations. Taoism favors a more passive lifestyle and attempts to free man from the busyness of responsibility. Confucianists strive for improved government, laws, and education, while Taoists minimize external authority and involvement in society.

Dynastic History of China

The Chinese have a passion for history. Their interest in antiquity sparked a great tradition of historical writing, much of which traces the history of China's ruling dynasties (or families). From the periods of dynastic rule, historians have established the major divisions of Chinese history.

The Chinese were able to maintain a strong sense of national unity, but they did experience numerous periods of political upheaval and disorder. Each dynasty went through the same cycle: it began, matured, prospered, and then declined. The unrest that ended one dynasty prepared the way for the founding of a new one. While each dynasty had its own special qualities and left its mark on Chinese culture, the fundamental character of society remained essentially the same throughout Chinese history.

Shang Dynasty

The Shang dynasty, one of the earliest known Chinese dynasties, was established along the Yellow River (called Huang He in Chinese) around 1500 BC. The rulers of this dynasty united much of northern China. Archaeologists have unearthed fine examples of Shang bronze work and marble carvings. Much of our knowledge of Shang culture comes from early Chinese writing inscribed on pieces of animal bones and tortoise shells. To obtain answers about the future from their ancestors, the Chinese wrote questions on bones or shells; then they touched them with a hot metal rod, causing them to crack. By "interpreting" the pattern of the cracks, the Chinese believed they could determine the will of their ancestors.

Zhou Dynasty

Shortly before 1000 BC, the people who lived along the Shang's western border overthrew the Shang rulers. The Zhou dynasty that they established lasted over eight hundred years—longer than any other dynasty in Chinese history. This period is often called the "classical" or "formative" age of Chinese history. Much of China's culture, such as family life, ancestor worship, the writing system, and Confucian and Taoist thought, became firmly established during this time.

The Zhou government was decentralized. While the Zhou rulers retained the ultimate authority, they allowed powerful nobles great freedom in ruling local territories. However, the Zhou rulers became unable to control the nobles, and sporadic fighting broke out among rival states between the fifth and third centuries BC.

Qin Dynasty

Order was restored by Zheng, who took the name **Qin Shi Huang** (r. 247–210 BC). Zheng became the founder of the short-lived but memorable Qin (sometimes spelled Chin) dynasty—the dynasty from which China may have derived its name. Qin Shi Huang (CHIN SHEE HWAHNG), which means "First Emperor of the Qin," was the first to unite the provinces of China under one strong centralized government. He standardized the Chinese weight, measurement, and coinage systems and brought uniformity to China's writing system. Perhaps the most remarkable achievement of the Qin dynasty was the beginning of construction of the Great Wall. The wall was twenty-five to thirty feet high and fifteen feet wide. A road ran along its top, providing for rapid movement of troops and swift communication. A consolidation of existing structures, the Great Wall eventually covered over 1,400 miles of often-rugged terrain. The wall served as a defensive barrier against the invasions of the barbaric Huns (whose descendants later invaded the Roman Empire). Although Qin Shi Huang brought order and protection to China, he did so through harsh and ruthless measures. Soon after his death, the people revolted, ending the Qin dynasty.

Early Christianity in China

History is silent regarding the first Christian missionaries to China. However, there is evidence that a form of Christianity surfaced in China by the 600s. The first Tang emperor had recently established himself. He loved books, and he had built a library with thousands of volumes. When Christian missionaries from Persia arrived with a religion that centered on a holy book, he was very interested, and he asked them to translate the Bible into Chinese.

Later explorers discovered Christian writings in China from this time period. These writings teach that Jesus was born of a virgin, that he died on the cross in the place of sinners, that salvation is by faith and not by works, and that a Christian must love his neighbor and submit to the emperor.

By the 900s the Tang dynasty came to an end. The new Chinese government attacked foreign religions and attempted to eliminate Christianity. In the thirteenth century, with the rise of Mongol rule, Christians from Persia were again able to renew missionary work in China.

Qin Shi Huang

The Tomb and Terra-Cotta Army of Qin Shi Huang

Qin Shi Huang, the first emperor of China, died in 210 BC. His body was entombed in an elaborate mausoleum that had taken workers his entire reign to construct. (Thirty-six years before his death, he drafted nearly a million Chinese laborers for the project.) According to contemporary Chinese historians, the tomb contained a model of his palaces and various government buildings. It also housed a replica of his empire complete with rivers and seas of mercury, which actually flowed by mechanical means.

To protect his grave, the Chinese installed crossbows that would release automatically if an intruder entered the tomb. According to the custom of the day, Shi Huang's son ordered his father's concubines who had not borne him sons to be buried with the emperor. He also ordered that those who had worked on the safety devices in the tomb be buried too. Once the emperor was interred, the Chinese covered the mausoleum with earth and planted trees over it to give the appearance of a hill. Today it is called Mount Li. It stands fifteen stories high in the midst of a plain.

In 1974 a group of Chinese farmers, while digging a well in the Mount Li area, unearthed a subterranean passageway. Inside were huge terra-cotta statues (made of hard, waterproof ceramic clay) of ancient Chinese soldiers. In the years since the discovery, Chinese archaeologists have uncovered about six thousand soldiers—life-size replicas of the men in Qin Shi Huang's army. No two statues are alike. Some are old with wrinkles, and others are young and fair. Some are smiling, and some are serious. In addition to the soldiers, archaeologists found clay horses and chariots. Because the ceiling of the tomb had collapsed and crushed many of the terra-cotta statues, the task of excavating was a difficult one. When the work of the excavators was completed, the Chinese created a museum on the site.

Han Dynasty

The next dynasty to rule China was the Han dynasty, established in 202 BC. This dynasty was so popular that to this day some Chinese call themselves the "sons of Han." The most famous Han ruler was **Wu Ti** (r. 140–87 BC). He drove back the Huns and extended China's territory. To meet the growing need for well-trained government officials, the Han rulers introduced a civil service system in which competitive public examinations determined appointments to government posts. The Han established the **Pax Sinica** ("Chinese Peace") throughout China and much of central Asia. During this period trade routes were opened with the West. Over the "Silk Road"—named for China's chief export—traders brought China into direct contact with the Greek and Roman civilizations. The Han period also marked the entrance of Buddhism into China. It soon became one of China's leading religions.

Description of a Chinese Civil Service Examination

The candidates had to get up in the middle of the night and come to the palace at dawn, bringing their cold meals with them, for they would not be able to leave until the examinations were over. During the examinations they were shut up in cubicles under the supervision of palace guards. There was a rigorous system to prevent bribery or favoritism. . . . While the candidates were let out after the examinations, the judges themselves were shut up within the palace, usually from late January [until] early March, until the papers were properly graded and submitted to the emperor. The candidates were examined first on questions of history or principles of government. There was a second examination on the classics, and finally, after the successful ones had been graded, there was one—under the direct supervision of the emperor—on lyrics, descriptive poetry, and again essays on politics.

Lin Yu-t'ang, The Gay Genius, *38.*

Tang Dynasty

In 220, revolts overthrew the last of the Han rulers. For the next four centuries China suffered from internal wars and barbarian invasions. During this period attempts to establish a lasting central government were unsuccessful. However, in 618 the Tang rulers came to power and restored unity and prosperity to China. The Tang dynasty became a golden age in Chinese history. The Chinese enjoyed a stable government, an expanding empire, increased trade, contact with other civilizations, advances in learning, and magnificent works of art and literature. For example, the Tang era was one of the finest periods of Chinese poetry. The most popular and prolific poet was **Li Po**, who wrote thousands of poems expressing emotional and sentimental themes.

The glory of the Tang lasted about three centuries. As self-seeking rulers began squandering much of the country's wealth, the Tang dynasty lost both prosperity and power. The weakened dynasty collapsed shortly after 900.

Song porcelain

Song Dynasty

Fifty years later a new dynasty—the Song—restored order. Compared to the other dynasties of China's past, however, the Song dynasty was politically weak. Because of China's inability to prevent the northern portions of China from falling under barbarian control, China was divided into the Northern Song (960–1127) and the Southern Song (1127–1279). Despite these problems, the Song dynasty carried on active trade, and the Chinese culture flourished. During this period the Chinese also excelled in painting, printing, and porcelain.

Chinese Culture and the Western World

Only recently has the Western world significantly influenced Chinese society. Over the centuries China resisted the introduction of foreign elements. This distrust of outsiders is the reason the traditional Chinese way of life remained virtually unaffected by the Western ideas and influences for centuries. The contrast between Eastern and Western cultures caused many westerners to view China as a land of mystical enchantment.

While the Chinese generally looked with suspicion upon Western ways and ideas, westerners profited from their contacts with the Chinese. Europe became an open market for many Chinese goods; silk and porcelain were among the most popular. The Chinese appear to have been the first to produce silk. They carefully guarded the secret of the silkworm, whose cocoon provided the silk thread needed to make this beautiful fabric. The Chinese also developed the process for making porcelain, a white, translucent form of pottery that is still known as "china." In Europe, Chinese silk became fashionable, and porcelain was one of the most valued possessions.

The Chinese developed a method called block printing in which they carved raised characters on a block of wood. By inking the block and pressing it on paper, the Chinese were able to print multiple copies. However, the printing of different pages involved the slow process of carving another block of wood. To speed up this process, the Chinese invented movable type—that is, they carved smaller separate blocks for each Chinese character. The blocks could then be rearranged and reused. However, because there were thousands of characters, movable type was not widely used in China, nor was it practical.

Many other products associated with the Western world originated in China. Can you imagine a school classroom without paper or an ink pen? The Chinese were the first to develop paper (as we know it) and one of the first people to use ink. Think what navigation would be like without the Chinese invention of the magnetic compass. Another important Chinese discovery was gunpowder; this substance was first used in the manufacturing of fireworks. The Chinese were remarkably ahead of the West with regard to many discoveries and inventions.

A Western View of China

"Many of [China's] traditional customs are the opposite of those of the Occident [the West] and, accordingly, seem bizarre. In the old China the men wore skirts and long gowns, the women baggy trousers. At banquets what we think of as a dessert came first and rice concluded the meal. Men in greeting one another shook their own hands, not the hands of the other (a much more sanitary proceeding than that of the West, be it said). The place of honor was on the left, not on the right. In meeting on the streets gentlemen removed their spectacles and not their hats. White not black was the color of mourning."

Latourette, 158.

Did Europe Get Moveable Type Printing from China?

Evidence seems to suggest that movable type printing was developed in Europe independently of any connection with China. Unlike the Chinese, who found little use for this invention, European printers found great use for movable type printing, and it played an important role in publishing Bibles and Reformation literature beginning in the 1500s.

Section Quiz

1. What did the ancient Chinese call their land? Why?
2. What social group held the most esteemed position in Chinese society?
3. What is perhaps the most remarkable building achievement that occurred under the Qin dynasty?
4. List five specific contributions that China made to the Western world.

★ Evaluate Qin Shi Huang's rule in China.

III. Japan

Over one hundred miles off the coast of Asia—opposite China, Korea, and Siberia (Russia)—is the island nation of Japan. Japan consists of four main islands and hundreds of lesser ones. If placed alongside the Atlantic coast of the United States, Japan would stretch from Maine to Florida. In land area Japan is about the size of the state of California. Most of this land, however, is mountainous; less than 20 percent of it is suitable for farming. Through much of its history, Japan was more geographically remote than China; for centuries it remained isolated from the mainstream of the world's civilizations. It was not until the late nineteenth century that Japan made its presence felt in the arena of world affairs.

Early History

Although Japan is younger than most Asian civilizations, little is known about its early history. Instead of keeping historical records as the Chinese did, the early Japanese passed down myths and legends, many of which played an influential role in shaping Japanese culture. According to Japanese mythology, the god Izanagi and goddess Izanami, while standing on the rainbow bridge of heaven, dipped a jeweled spear into the ocean. Drops falling from the tip of the spear formed the islands of Japan. The god and goddess descended to live on the islands. Their offspring were the Japanese people.

Our first historical glimpse of ancient Japan finds the land divided by a number of warring clans. In early Japanese society, the clan—a group of families claiming descent from a common ancestor—was the basic unit of social, religious, and political organization. Each clan had its own land, its own god, and its own chieftain. The chieftain served as both political and religious leader. By the fifth century AD, one clan had risen in power and prestige over rival clans. Centered on the island of Honshu (the main Japanese island), the **Yamato clan** extended its authority and forged a unified Japanese state.

The leaders of the Yamato clan used Japanese mythology to secure the loyalty of other clan chieftains. According to legend the first emperor of Japan, **Jimmu Tenno** (tenno, "heavenly prince"), was a direct descendant of the sun goddess. The Yamato clan claimed that its rulers were descendants of Jimmu Tenno; they were, therefore, believed to be divine. From this clan arose the imperial family of Japan. Subsequent Japanese emperors all claimed Jimmu Tenno as their divine ancestor. Unlike China, which has had many ruling families or dynasties, Japan has had but one imperial family in its history. For this reason, the imperial family has served as a symbol of unity and continuity in Japanese society.

Shinto shrine

Supporting the belief in the divine origin of the emperor was Japan's native religion, **Shintoism** (meaning "the way of the gods"). Shintoism was originally a form of nature worship that attributed deity to anything in nature that was awe-inspiring or extraordinary, such as fire, a waterfall, or a high mountain. However, Shintoism also stressed the supremacy of the sun goddess and the divine descent of the emperor. In many respects it became a religion of feeling, inspiring love for one's homeland, loyalty to one's clan, and reverence for one's emperor.

Buddhist temple in Japan

Influence of China

As previously stated, Japan remained in relative isolation during its early history. In the fifth to the eighth centuries, however, the Chinese invaded the Japanese islands. This was not a military invasion by soldiers but a cultural invasion of ideas, learning, and art. China was experiencing the golden age of the Tang dynasty, and the Japanese welcomed the influx of what they considered the superior Chinese culture.

There were two important vehicles that transmitted Chinese culture to Japan. The first was the Chinese writing system, which the Japanese adopted and later adapted to complement their spoken language. For the first time, the Japanese were able to keep written records and produce their own literature. From an understanding of Chinese characters, they were also able to read and study Chinese literature and learn of the life and thought of the Chinese people.

Secondly, Chinese culture flowed into Japan through Buddhism. The Japanese learned much about the Chinese way of life from Buddhist monks who came over from China. For example, the Japanese learned to appreciate Chinese art and architecture from the numerous Buddhist temples built in Japan. Buddhism became firmly established in Japan during the seventh century when a member of the imperial family, **Prince Shotoku**, made Buddhism the favored national religion. He had many Buddhist temples, hospitals, and schools constructed. He also sent many young men to China to study Chinese ways: agriculture, science, architecture, law, government, philosophy, and religion. Japan borrowed not only Chinese writing, literature, and religion but also China's system of weights and measurements, medical practices, calendar, styles of furniture and dress, and methods of building roads and bridges.

In the mid-seventh century, the leaders of Japan sought to weaken the influence of the local clan chieftains and extend the power of the emperor to all of Japan. They modeled their government after the strong centralized bureaucracy of the Tang dynasty. This turnabout in the Japanese political and economic structure became known as the "Great Change" or **Taika** (tie EE kuh) **Reform**. Like the Chinese, the Japanese established civil service examinations, granting government posts to men of ability. A new judicial code and tax system came into existence, and at Nara the Japanese established their first permanent capital, which was copied after the main city of China. (Later the capital was moved to Kyoto, where the Japanese emperors maintained their court until 1868.)

The Taika Reform changed the nature of Japan's political structure from semi-independent clans to a centralized government headed by the emperor, at least in theory. In reality, government authority came to rest in the hands of powerful families who controlled the key posts of government. One such family, the **Fujiwara**, had married their daughters to the sons of the imperial family. When a male child was born, they forced the ruling emperor to abdicate. The Fujiwara elders then ruled Japan as regents of the infant emperor.

The Way of the Warrior

A Japanese warrior learned Bushido almost from birth. One authority on Bushido describes the early training this way: "Does a little [baby] cry for any ache? The mother scolds him in this fashion: 'What will you do when your arm is cut off in battle? What [will you do] when you are called upon to commit *hara-kiri*?' "

Rise of the Samurai

The Fujiwaras enjoyed the wealth and extravagance of the imperial city. However, the luxurious life of the royal court brought corruption and bankruptcy to the government. Disorder followed as the central government was no longer able to provide protection for outlying provinces. Many provincial governors began to rely on strong military clans for protection. Soon power struggles broke out among rival military families. In the twelfth century **Yoritomo**, the leader of the Minamoto clan, became the supreme military leader of Japan when he defeated the only remaining powerful clan. The powerless emperor granted Yoritomo the title of **shogun** ("great general"). Yoritomo created a warrior state, ruled by military rather than civilian officials. Although the line of the imperial family continued, powerful shoguns held the real power over the Japanese government from 1192 to 1868.

With the rise of the office of shogun, the warrior class became the leading class in Japanese society. The Japanese warrior was called **samurai** or bushi. Besides mastering the military skills of horsemanship, fencing, archery, and jujitsu (a form of martial arts), the samurai studied history, literature, and the art of writing. He used these skills in providing protection for his master and lord. An unwritten military code known as the **Bushido** (BOOSH ih doh; "the way of the warrior") governed the conduct of the samurai. It demanded that he live by loyalty, honor, duty, justice, courage, sincerity, and politeness. To avoid the disgrace of capture, atone for deeds of misconduct, or resolve questions regarding his loyalty to his master, a warrior could end his life with honor by committing suicide according to the ceremonial practice of hara-kiri.

Minamoto no Yoritomo

Section Quiz

1. What was the basic social, religious, and political unit in early Japanese society?
2. According to legend, who was the first Japanese emperor? What do the Japanese believe about his ancestry?
3. The culture of what foreign civilization had a profound effect on Japan's history?
4. What was the name of the reform movement that sought to weaken the influence of local clan leaders while strengthening the authority of the emperor and the central government?
5. What were Japanese warriors called? What was the unwritten military code that governed their conduct?

★ How did Shintoism contribute to the power of the state in Japan?

IV. The Mongol Empire

In this chapter and the preceding one, we have examined the major civilizations of Asia and eastern Europe to the thirteenth century. Despite being separated by great distances and diverse cultural backgrounds, the civilizations of India, China, Byzantium, Russia, and the Muslim empire shared a common threat: each land was invaded by fierce warriors coming out of central Asia. Since ancient days, central Asia had been the homeland of many nomadic peoples. Vast grassy plains, known as the steppes, stretch from western China to eastern Europe. This pastureland was a highway along which roving tribes moved as they sought food for their flocks and herds.

One of these roving tribes was known as the Huns. They advanced into China and Europe while the Turks, also a nomadic people, moved into Byzantine and Islamic territories. By the thirteenth century another group, the Mongols, had united the peoples of central Asia. The Mongols spread across the Asian steppes, creating an empire that stretched from China across central Asia to Russia, southward into Byzantine and Muslim territories, and later into the land of India. In less than a century, the Mongols built the largest land empire in history.

Chinggis Khan statue

Building the Mongol Empire

The Mongol people arose in the north of China, in the land known today as Mongolia. Their round felt tents dotted the eastern portion of the Asiatic grasslands. They raised sheep, goats, and horses. They had no government but were divided into small tribes. In approximately 1162, Temujin (TEM yoo jin) was born to the family of a tribal chief. Overcoming many hardships in his youth, Temujin succeeded his father as leader of his tribe at the age of thirteen. He gradually united all the Mongol tribes under his authority and established an empire in the steppes. He became "lord of all the people dwelling in felt tents." In 1206 the Mongols gave him the title "**Chinggis Khan**" (CHENG-gis KAHN), meaning "universal ruler."

Chinggis Khan was one of the greatest conquerors in history. He is said to have believed that he had a divine commission to conquer the world. Having organized the Mongols into a well-disciplined fighting force, he conquered northern China. He then turned his army westward. The Mongols overran central Asia, advanced to the banks of the Indus River, pushed into Persia, and crossed into southern Russia. Returning from his western conquests, Chinggis renewed his campaign against China. His death in 1227, however, prevented him from seeing the whole of China fall under Mongol control.

Much of Chinggis's success lay in the organization and mobility of his army. He skillfully deployed his forces in battle. His army, which he divided into groups of tens, hundreds, and thousands, could strike with great speed. In addition, the Mongols were expert horsemen. Riding into battle on horseback,

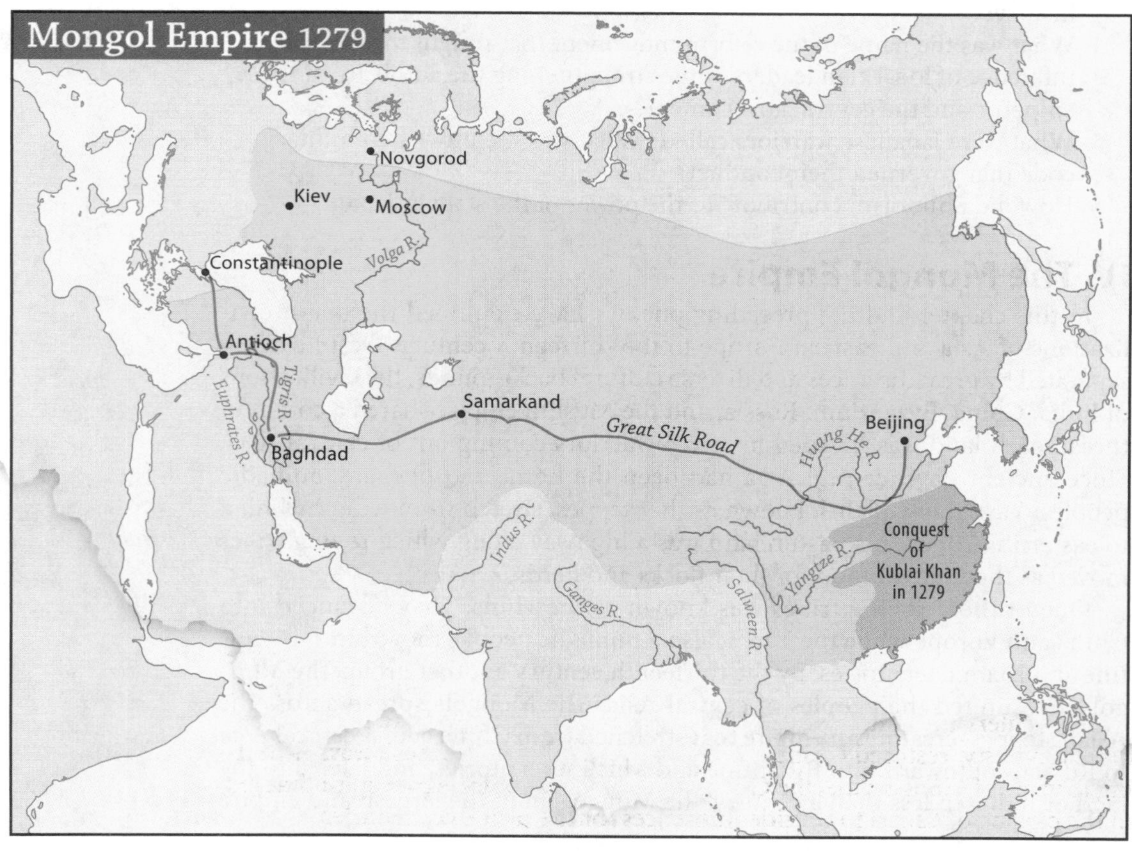

they had a distinct advantage over the armies of other civilizations. (The horse was the most prized Mongol possession.) Much like the ancient Assyrians, the Mongols gained a reputation for terrorizing the peoples they were about to conquer. They often massacred the entire population of a city to teach others the futility of resistance. The Mongol conquests left fear, destruction, and death in their wake.

Mongol expansion did not cease with the death of Chinggis. His sons and grandsons enlarged his empire. Their armies completed the conquest of China, swept farther into Russia, and overran the Muslim states in central and southwestern Asia. They sacked Baghdad, brought an end to the Abbasid dynasty, and broke the power of the Seljuk Turks.

The Mongols chose Chinggis's son to succeed him as the Great Khan, the ruler of the entire Mongol Empire. But the empire eventually became too large for one man to rule effectively. By the time of the fifth ruler, the empire had already begun to fragment into many separate Mongol states, each ruled by a descendant of Chinggis. In the following pages we will examine separately the Mongol states established in China, Russia, central Asia, and India.

The Yuan Dynasty in China (1279–1368)

The Mongol attack came as no surprise to the Chinese. For hundreds of years the Chinese had defended their borders against the attacks of central Asian nomads. But none of the previous invaders had possessed the military strength of the Mongols. Not even the Great Wall could stop their advance. The conquest of China begun by Chinggis was completed by his grandson **Kublai Khan** (KOO-blie KAHN). Kublai was the last of the Great Khans, the heir to the entire Mongol world. After a long campaign, he succeeded in conquering southern China, the stronghold of the ruling Song dynasty (see p. 144).

Kublai Khan

Kublai Khan established the Mongol (or Yuan) dynasty, the first foreign dynasty to rule all of China. He moved the capital to Cambaluc (modern-day Beijing), where he directed the affairs of the Mongol Empire. His primary interest was China. He built highways that facilitated trade and communication between China and the rest of Asia. He invited missionaries, scholars, artists, merchants, and engineers from all over the world to his capital. Kublai employed many of these foreigners as government officials. The most famous European traveler to Mongol China was Marco Polo (see p. 231). Polo lived in China seventeen years. Many of those years he spent in the service of Kublai. He later wrote a glowing account of his travels and of the wonders of Kublai's court. His stories gave most Europeans their first glimpse of the land of China.

With the death of Kublai, the world empire founded by Chinggis Khan came to an end. The Mongols still ruled most of Asia, but no longer could they boast of a unified empire. The empire quickly divided into many independent Mongol kingdoms. The descendants of Kublai continued to rule in China. However, the peace and prosperity that the Yuan dynasty brought to China did not overcome the Chinese resentment of foreign rule. To make matters worse, Mongols had excluded the Chinese from holding positions in the government. As a result, discontent mounted even as the successors of Kublai grew weaker and more decadent. Rebellion eventually broke out, and in 1368 the Chinese drove the Mongol rulers back into Mongolia. A new Chinese dynasty, the Ming ("brilliant") dynasty, restored Chinese rule and reestablished Chinese ways. Reacting to years of Mongol rule, the Chinese adopted an antiforeigner spirit that led to the closing of China to outside influences for the next five centuries.

Statue of Batu Khan

The Golden Horde in Russia

While Kublai was occupied with the conquest of China, another grandson of Chinggis, **Batu Khan**, led the Mongols into Europe. Between 1238 and 1242, the Mongols—or Tartars, as the Europeans called them—crushed the Russian defenses and penetrated Hungary and Poland. Western Europe now lay vulnerable to Mongol attack. But upon hearing of the death of the Great Khan, Batu stopped his advance. He withdrew to the Volga River in Russia, where he consolidated his conquests in central Asia and Russia. His realm, the strongest Mongol state in Western Asia, became known as the "**Golden Horde**." (The word *horde* comes from the Mongol *ordu*, which means "camp.")

For nearly two hundred fifty years, Russia remained under the yoke of the Golden Horde. The Mongols not only exacted tribute from the Russian cities but also gathered recruits for their army from among the Russian people. During the period of Mongol domination, Russian ties with western Europe and the Byzantine Empire weakened as Asian influences grew stronger.

During this period Moscow transformed from an insignificant town to the capital of the budding Russian nation. Many factors aided Moscow's rise. Moscow stood at the center of Russia's inland waterways. Its location was advantageous for both trade and defense. Furthermore, the leaders of Moscow cooperated with the khans of the Golden Horde. They served as the khan's tax collectors. In return, the khans recognized the prince of Moscow as the Grand Prince of Russia. The Russian church also enhanced the prestige of Moscow. When the head of the Orthodox Church moved from Kiev to Moscow, Moscow became the religious center of Russia.

While Moscow grew strong and prosperous, the Golden Horde weakened. By the late fourteenth century, the grand princes openly challenged their Mongol overlords. Under **Ivan III,** who was the Grand Prince from 1462 to 1505, Moscow refused to pay further tribute to the Mongols. By 1480 Moscow had freed itself from the Mongol yoke and had become the political and religious capital of the new state. Ivan extended his control over much of northern Russia. He laid the foundation for an independent Russian state and emerged as its autocratic (ruling with unlimited authority) leader. After the collapse of Constantinople in 1453, many people considered Moscow the "Third Rome."

Later Mongol Empires

Tamerlane's Empire

Bust of Tamerlane

In the late fourteenth century, there arose a central Asian conqueror who attempted to rebuild Chinggis's empire. His name was Timur the Lame; he was known to the Europeans as **Tamerlane**. Tamerlane belonged to a Mongol-Turkish tribe and claimed to have descended from Chinggis Khan.

Having established his power in central Asia, Tamerlane raised an army and began a new wave of Mongol invasions. His army swept over the Muslim lands in southwestern Asia, capturing Baghdad and Damascus and defeating the Ottoman Turks in Asia Minor. His march into southern Russia weakened the Golden Horde and indirectly aided the Russian princes in their struggle to gain freedom from Mongol control. Turning to the East, Tamerlane led his army into India, where in 1398 he reduced the city of Delhi to ruins and slaughtered an estimated one hundred thousand so-called infidels in a single day. He died in 1405 while planning an invasion of China.

Tamerlane was an able, but cruel, conqueror. He left a trail of merciless plundering, destruction, and massacres. His conquests reached from India to Asia Minor. But his empire was much smaller than the earlier Mongol Empire, and it collapsed shortly after his death.

The Mughal Empire in India

India was a frequent target of Mongol attacks. From the time of Chinggis Khan up to the invasion of Tamerlane, Mongol raiders had terrorized the people of northern India. But unlike most Asian lands, India had not fallen under Mongol rule; not until the sixteenth century did the Mongols gain control of India. **Babur**, "The Tiger," a descendant of the two greatest Asian conquerors, Chinggis Khan and Tamerlane, became the leader of the Turkish-Mongol tribes in what today is Afghanistan. With an army of about twelve thousand men, Babur crossed the mountain passes and invaded northern India. After capturing the capital city of Delhi, he slaughtered or enslaved the Hindu inhabitants and established the **Mughal** dynasty in 1526. ("Mughal" is the name given to the Mongols in India.) Later Mughal rulers extended the empire and imposed Islam over all but the southern tip of India.

Under the Mughals, Indian civilization was transformed. While the cruel destruction inflicted by Tamerlane continued, the Mughal rulers eventually established a subjectively enforced law and order that enabled a period of achievement in art and architecture. The most successful Mughal ruler was Babur's grandson **Akbar** (1556–1605). Akbar expanded the empire to include all of northern and central India. In addition to being a skilled military general, Akbar was also an able administrator who reformed Indian government. Yet even Akbar, a so-called secular ruler, approved the slaughter of nearly half a million Hindus and the enslavement of many women and children in the name of Islam.

Mongols and Islam

Initially, the Mongols killed and conquered without regard to a nation's religion. However, over time, Mongol leaders converted to Islam and added jihad to their motives for conquest and brutality. Tamerlane is the first known Mongol leader who clearly sought to carry out jihad and brutally slaughtered Hindus by the hundreds of thousands because of their polytheism. He also killed many Christians in campaigns against India and Armenia by burying them alive, in addition to other brutal forms of execution. Removing all doubt as to his intentions, Tamerlane recorded his goal of slaughtering Hindus and sparing Muslims who also lived in India.

Babur and Akbar continued to carry out jihad against the Hindus of India, resulting in an enormous loss of life.

Andrew G. Bostom, ed., The Legacy of Jihad, *77-78, 459.*

Section Quiz

1. What name is given to the vast grassy plains that stretch from western China to eastern Europe?
2. Who united the Mongol tribes and established a Mongol empire in the steppes? What title was he given?
3. What Mongol ruler conquered China? What was the name of the Mongol dynasty in China?
4. What city rose to prominence during the period of Mongol domination in Russia?
5. What descendant of Chinggis Khan and Tamerlane set up a Mongol dynasty in India? What was the name of this dynasty?

★ Why were the Mongols unable to retain power over conquered nations over time?

African savannah

V. Africa

Although the Mongols spread over Asia and threatened Europe, they left untouched one great land—Africa. The second largest continent, Africa covers over one-fifth of the earth's land surface. It is nearly four times the size of the continental United States. Although much of the continent is a large plateau, its mountains, deserts, grassy flatlands, and jungles give Africa a unique beauty.

We have studied some of Africa's history in earlier chapters. The Egyptians established on the banks of the Nile the earliest recorded civilization in Africa. Carthage built a thriving civilization in North Africa in the days of the Roman Republic, and the Romans later made the area part of their empire. After the collapse of Rome, Muslims swept across North Africa and brought the region under Islamic domination.

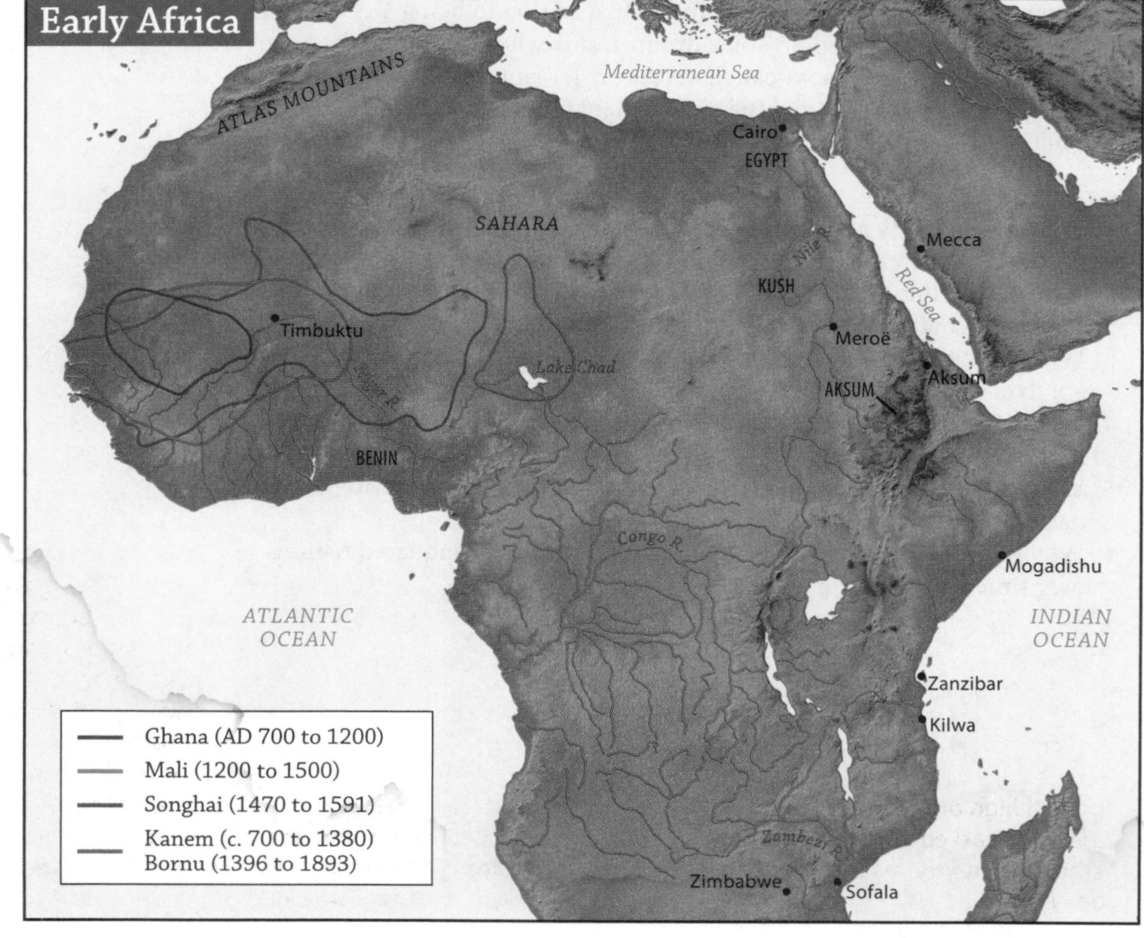

As important as these events are, they involve only a portion of that great continent. The history of the rest of Africa, known as **sub-Saharan Africa** (so named because it is south of the Sahara), is not as well known but is nonetheless important.

Ancient African Civilization

Centuries before Europeans penetrated sub-Saharan Africa, several African empires and kingdoms flourished. In ancient times, two important kingdoms arose in northeast Africa, south of the Egyptian civilization. The earliest was the kingdom of Kush, which centered in what is today northern Sudan. (Ruins of its capital, Meroë, still exist near the modern city of Khartoum.) Originally a province of the Egyptian Empire, Kush (Nubia) grew in power until by 700 BC it had not only overthrown Egyptian rule but also conquered all of Egypt and established its own dynasty of pharaohs. (The Tirhakah of Ethiopia mentioned in 2 Kings 19:9 is one such Kushite ruler, Taharqa.) The Assyrians drove the Kushites out of Egypt in the mid-600s BC, but the Kushite kingdom continued for nearly another thousand years.

Kush eventually fell to a kingdom to its east known as Aksum (or "Axum"). The ruler of Aksum recorded the shattering defeat he inflicted on the Kushites around AD 330:

> I made war on them. . . . They fled without making a stand, and I pursued them . . . killing some and capturing others. . . . I burnt their towns, both those built of bricks and those built of reeds, and my army carried off their food and copper and iron . . . and destroyed the statues in their temples, their granaries, and cotton trees and cast them into the [Nile].
>
> *Robert W. July,* A History of the African People, 2nd ed., 43.

Aksum was unusual among the early African kingdoms in that it embraced a form of Christianity. Later tradition claimed that the rulers of Aksum were descendants of King Solomon and the Queen of Sheba. However, the kingdom's conversion to Christianity was probably the work of a Syrian Christian named **Frumentius**. Aksum's conversion intensified its already extensive trade with the Roman Empire. Later the Muslim invasions in North Africa cut off Aksum from almost all European contact. The civilization nonetheless continued to exist and became the nucleus of the modern state of Ethiopia.

Aksum stele (rectangular stone tower recording an important event)

Frumentius, "Apostle to the Abyssinians"

The conversion of Aksum (sometimes known as "Abyssinia") was the result of the ministry of an unlikely missionary named Frumentius. We have little information about his early years. We know that he was a professing Christian and a Roman citizen, probably from Tyre, who was born around AD 300. While still a young man, he and his brother were traveling abroad with a relative. Pirates attacked their ship, massacring most of the crew and passengers. The pirates spared the brothers, however, and sold them into slavery in Aksum. Frumentius and his brother, like Joseph in Egypt, rose to high positions in government because of their abilities. As treasurer and secretary to the king of Aksum, Frumentius earned the trust of high officials in government. When the king died, the queen asked Frumentius to help administer the government until the young prince was old enough to rule on his own.

While serving the kingdom, Frumentius also promoted his Christian faith. He encouraged Christian merchants from the Roman Empire to hold private services during their visits to Aksum. Under Frumentius's preaching and guidance, the citizens of Aksum also began to convert to Christianity. The young prince whom Frumentius served was probably Ezana, the king who won the great victory over Kush in 330. Ezana seems to have accepted Christianity later in life. Historians note that he did not credit his victory over Kush to pagan gods, as he had done with victories earlier in his reign, but "by the might of the Lord of Heaven Who in heaven and upon earth is mightier than everything which exists." He also praised the "Lord of Heaven, Who . . . to all eternity reigns the Perfect One." Ezana's conversion was perhaps the crowning work of Frumentius, a man since remembered as the "Apostle to the Abyssinians."

Central and Western Africa

During Europe's Middle Ages several important kingdoms arose in central and western Africa. Our knowledge of these civilizations is somewhat sketchy because most of their histories were not written down but were passed on orally. However, oral tradition, archaeology, and some accounts written by non-Africans provide us a general picture of these cultures. In central Africa, for example, the kingdoms of Kanem (ca. 700–1380) and Bornu (1396–1893) thrived on the shores of Lake Chad. These successive kingdoms derived their profits from the camel caravan trade and built strong military forces.

Even more important were the three kingdoms of western Africa—Ghana, Mali, and Songhai, each progressively larger than the previous. All three built prosperous civilizations whose wealth derived from the gold mines within their empires and the camel caravan trade in gold, salt, and other precious items that crossed the Sahara. The Niger (NIE jur) River in particular provided a base for these empires as its waters drew travelers crossing the desert.

Camels were the perfect means of transportation to carry precious cargo across the Sahara.

The kingdom of Ghana rose to prominence first, enjoying its heyday from ca. 700 to 1200. Muslim forces from northern Africa attacked and weakened Ghana in the eleventh century but proved unable to conquer the region. In its place rose the kingdom of Mali, dominating western Africa from 1200 to 1500. The most famous ruler of Mali was **Mansa Musa** (r. 1312–ca. 1337). Since the Mali rulers had converted to Islam, Mansa Musa made a pilgrimage to Mecca in 1324. So splendid was his traveling party that it caught the attention of the non-African world. Musa took with him sixty thousand men and several thousand pounds of gold. He even astonished the Egyptians with his wealth during a stay in Cairo. Musa's capital, Timbuktu, became Africa's most important center of trade. He also encouraged learning in his realm, attracting so many scholars to Timbuktu that it is said books began to rival gold as an item for trade.

In the fifteenth century, the Songhai Empire overthrew the Mali Empire. It extended farther than either Ghana or Mali, stretching to the Atlantic in the west and pressing the kingdom of Bornu on Lake Chad in the east. Its wealth proved more attractive than its power proved fearsome, however. Armed with muzzle-loading guns, invading Moroccan forces brought an end to the Songhai Empire in 1591, and with it, an end to the western African empires.

East African City-States

Arusha, Tanzania, Africa

Along the eastern coast of Africa lay a series of important trading ports, each an independent city-state. These trading ports had existed as early as the days of the Roman Empire, and after the collapse of Rome, they continued to flourish as outlets for gold, iron, ivory, and animal skins to the Arabs and Persians. Prosperous city-states such as Kilwa (in what is today Tanzania) received goods from the tribes and kingdoms in the interior and sold them to Arab sea traders. As a result of this profitable trade, as well as a temperate climate, the seaside city-states grew wealthy and cultured. In the fourteenth century a Muslim visitor wrote, "Kilwa is one of the most beautiful and well-constructed towns in the world." A European visiting in 1500 wrote, "In this land there are rich merchants, and there is much gold and silver and amber and musk and pearls. Those of the land wear clothes of fine cotton and of silk and many fine things."

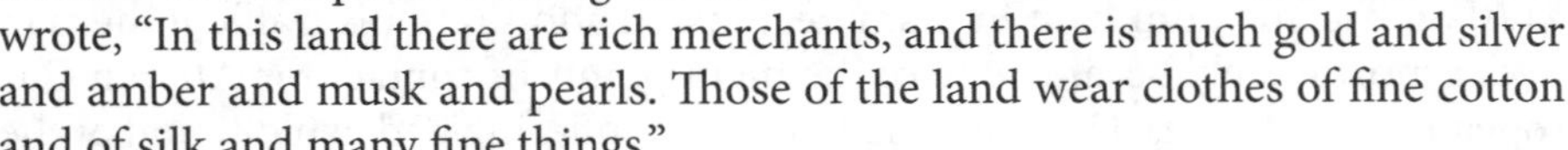

Although they were independent of each other, the city-states shared a common culture, one that was a mixture of Arab, Persian, and African elements. The architecture, for example, was predominantly Arab. The language of the city-states, **Swahili**, was more dominantly native African but contained elements of Arabic, Persian, and Indian. The city-states enjoyed centuries of prosperity, but after 1500 they were conquered by Portuguese forces who attacked the coasts to seize control of trade. The Swahili language has survived, however, and the term *Swahili* is used even today to describe the culture of some eastern Africans.

Benin relief sculpture

Forest Kingdoms

Providing the goods for the eastern city-states to sell were the "forest kingdoms" of the interior of Africa. Records of these kingdoms are even more scarce than those of the central and western empires to the north. The best-known forest kingdoms are those with which Europeans came into contact right after the close of the Middle Ages. Perhaps the most important was the kingdom of Benin in western Africa (today's southern Nigeria). It arose in 1440 and lasted until 1897. In addition to being a center for trade, Benin produced fine statues and relief sculptures in bronze. The metalworking of Benin became one of the highest known artistic accomplishments of early African history.

African Culture

Daily life for most Africans centered less on kingdoms and empires than on smaller social organizations. Many Africans concerned themselves with little more than life as it existed in their villages. The family was foundational. Since **polygamy** (marrying more than one spouse) was common in many tribes, families were large and complex. Several families with a common ancestor formed a clan. A group of two or more clans, in turn, formed a tribe. The tribe was perhaps the most important cultural organization, and a single tribe dominated many African kingdoms.

Religious belief in Africa was diverse. Some regions, such as Aksum, embraced a form of Christianity. Islam claimed a large number of converts, but Islamic visitors from the Middle East often complained that much of the African adherence to their religion was only superficial. Muslim patterns often influenced African kingdoms, however, in structuring their governments, organizing their systems of education, and establishing their currency.

The majority of the people in sub-Saharan Africa held to traditional tribal religions. In general, these traditional religions taught that there was a high god who created the universe and below him were a number of lesser gods and the spirits of dead ancestors. Prayers and sacrifices were offered to these gods to ward off illnesses and increase crop yields.

Most Africans relied on farming or herding to sustain themselves and their families. Trade, however, was the mainstay of the African kingdoms. Gold, salt, ivory, and animal skins were perhaps the most valued products. Beginning late in the Middle Ages, African trade began to change. As Europeans began sailing to African ports, the camel caravan trade became less important. Tragically, a new trade opened with Arabs and later with Europeans—the slave trade. Although slavery had existed in Africa for centuries, demand for slaves increased as Islam became dominant in many regions. In addition, this traffic in human lives unfortunately became one of the main points of contact for African-European relations after 1500, leading to terrible suffering and exploitation of the African people.

Section Review

1. What ancient African civilization conquered the Egyptians for a time?
2. What ancient African civilization converted to Christianity?
3. Name the three western African kingdoms in chronological order. What were the two bases of their wealth?
4. What African kingdom was noteworthy for its fine metalworking in bronze?
5. Name three items that were important goods in African trade.

★ What is the significance of the Swahili language?

Chapter 7 Review

Making Connections

1–3. Describe the significance of family in the nations of India, China, and Africa.

4. Why did China remain largely protected from foreign invasions while India was frequently invaded?
5. How important was the concept of loyalty to the samurai warrior? How might he resolve any question of his loyalty?

Developing History Skills

1. Contrast the levels of trade in India, China, and Africa with western Europe during this period. (You may need to consult Chapter 8 for more information about Western Europe.)

Thinking Critically

1. Evaluate the Hindu teaching of life after death in light of biblical teaching (see Heb. 9:27; Dan. 12:2; 2 Pet. 3:13).
2. How does each of the Eastern religions mentioned in this chapter rely on human works to find happiness in this life and in the life to come?

Living in God's World

1. Pick one of the religions covered in this chapter and explain how an understanding of that religion will affect how you share the gospel with its adherents.

People, Places, and Things to Know

topography
Aryans
Sanskrit
Vedas
joint family
castes
Hinduism
Brahman
Buddhism
Siddhartha Gautama
Four Noble Truths
Asoka
Gupta Empire
Kalidasa
Middle Kingdom
ancestor worship
Confucius
Lao-tzu
Taoism
Qin Shi Huang
Wu Ti
Pax Sinica
Li Po
Yamato clan
Jimmu Tenno
Shintoism
Prince Shotoku
Taika Reform
Fujiwara
Yoritomo
shogun
samurai
Bushido
Chinggis Khan
Kublai Khan
Batu Khan
Golden Horde
Ivan III
Tamerlane
Babur
Mughal
Akbar
sub-Saharan Africa
Frumentius
Mansa Musa
Swahili
polygamy

THE MEDIEVAL WORLD

III

Writers give various titles to the era in Europe lasting from 500 to 1500. You are probably already familiar with names such as the "Dark Ages," the "Medieval Era," and of course the "Middle Ages." (The term *medieval* itself comes from Latin words meaning "middle ages.") The "darkness" of the ages lies more in our ignorance of the period than in its actual character. The era is, however, a "middle" age. The medieval world is a bridge between the ancient world of Greece and Rome and our modern world. Far from being an unhappy blot on the history of man, the Middle Ages are an important stage in the course of history.

590 Gregory I becomes pope

751–887 Carolingian Dynasty

843 Treaty of Verdun

871 Alfred the Great becomes king

919 Henry the Fowler becomes king

1077 Canossa

400 | 500 | 600 | 700 | 800 | 900 | 1000

1122 Concordat of Worms
1152 Frederick I becomes king
1226 Louis IX becomes king
1337–1453 Hundred Years' War
1377–1418 Great Schism
1453 Fall of Constantinople
1492 Ferdinand & Isabella expel Moors
1100
1200
1300
1400
1500

8

THE MAKING OF MEDIEVAL EUROPE

During the Middle Ages, European society was composed primarily of three classes of people: the clergy, the nobility, and the peasants. Each played an important part in shaping European life and culture. Their roles in society have been described simply: the clergy were called to pray; the nobility, to fight; and the peasants, to work. Accordingly, each group represented an institution of medieval Europe—the church, the feudal system, and the manor.

Three classes of people shaped life in medieval Europe: the clergy, nobility, and peasantry.

I. Early Medieval History

At the beginning of the Middle Ages, western Europe faced widespread invasions, social unrest, and political disorder. The kingdoms established by leaders of Germanic tribes were often small and lacked strong central governments. Gradually the **Franks** became the most powerful of the Germanic peoples. They established many independent kingdoms in Gaul (modern-day France). From these Frankish kingdoms arose a new empire that temporarily reunited much of western Europe.

Clovis and the Franks

In 481 **Clovis** became the head of a Frankish tribe in northern Gaul. Through treachery and exceptional military ability, he conquered other Frankish tribes, uniting them into one kingdom. He soon became known as "King of the Franks." Once Clovis pushed the Visigoths out of southern Gaul, his territory included most of the area of present-day France (which takes its name from the Franks).

Important to the history of both western Europe and the Frankish kingdom was Clovis's outward conversion to Christianity. Like the emperor Constantine, Clovis was in danger of being defeated in battle when he cried out to God for help. He vowed to believe in God and be baptized in His name if granted the victory. Emerging victorious in battle, Clovis remained true to his vow. He even required three thousand of his soldiers to be baptized into the church. As a result, Clovis gained the support of the Roman Catholic Church, which found him to be a powerful champion for its cause. Thus began an alliance between the Frankish rulers and the Church of Rome that lasted for centuries. The so-called conversions of Clovis and his men were typical of many medieval conversions made for convenience or by coercion.

The Origin of Names

People have not always had first and last names as we do today. During Bible times, for example, most people had only one name. However, to avoid confusion with another person who had the same name, people often added a second name: for example, Simon the Canaanite (Matt. 10:4) and Alexander the Coppersmith (2 Tim. 4:14). During the Middle Ages this practice of adopting a second name continued. Some names were descriptions of a person's appearance or character, such as "the Pious," "the Fat," or "the Red." (The modern English surnames, or last names, Reid, Reed, and Read mean "Red.") Some names, such as Cook, Miller, Tailor (Taylor), Carpenter, Smith (from blacksmith), and Clark (from clerk), described a person's occupation. Other names described the place near which a person lived: Stone, Hill, Wood, and Ford. Finally, many people took their father's name as their second name. For example, the son of John became Johnson; the son of Henry became O'Henry; the son of Greg became MacGregor. Later, even this naming system became confusing. As a result, it became customary for a son to keep his father's last name, regardless of his own occupation or where he might live. While most modern surnames still have a particular meaning, for the most part they no longer bear any relationship to one's work, the first name of one's father, or one's place of residence.

The Mayors of the Palace

Clovis died in 511, after having established a strong, unified kingdom. In accordance with Frankish custom, the kingdom was divided among his four sons. Their descendants continued to reign over the Franks well into the eighth century. This royal family line was known as the **Merovingian House**, taking its name from an early ancestor of Clovis named Merovech. However, the Merovingian family was plagued by quarrels. The custom of granting a share of the kingdom to each of the king's sons caused brothers to become rivals. Each sought to gain the others' territory, using murder and treachery when necessary. Yet despite the domestic feuds and confusion under the Merovingian kings, Frankish rulers remained in power.

Even so, by the seventh century, they had lost much of their prestige and effectiveness through drunkenness, immoral living, and family strife. They became known as the "**do-nothing kings**." They reigned, but they did not rule. The principal palace official (called the major-domo, the **mayor of the palace**) became the real power behind the throne. Originally, the mayor of the palace supervised only the king's household, but succeeding mayors extended their authority over the financial, military, and administrative functions of government.

Near the end of the seventh century, **Pepin II** became the mayor of one of the stronger Frankish states. He defeated all rival mayors and reunited almost all of the Frankish territories under one rule. The Merovingians still occupied the throne, but they were mere puppets of the mayors. Probably the best remembered of all the mayors of the palace is **Charles Martel**, son of Pepin II. In 732 Charles won his fame by stopping the advance of the Muslims into Europe. He defeated them at the Battle of Tours in western France. This feat earned him the title Martel, or "the Hammer."

Pepin the Short (751–768), like his father Charles Martel, served as mayor of the palace. He possessed all the powers of the king, but he wished to have the title as well. Pepin appealed to the pope, asking him to decide whether he, Pepin, or the "do-nothing" Merovingian king should be the rightful ruler of the Franks. The pope replied that the one who wielded the power should be king. Pepin promptly deposed the king and seized the throne in 752. Two years later the pope traveled to France and sealed the change in ruling families by anointing Pepin "by the grace of God king of the Franks." The Carolingian House—named after its most illustrious member, Charlemagne—now officially ruled the Franks.

In return for his support, the pope asked Pepin to protect him against the **Lombards**. They were a Germanic people who through conquest had moved into northern Italy (a region still known today as Lombardy). In the first half of the eighth century, the Lombards had invaded central Italy and now threatened the city of Rome. Coming to the pope's aid, Pepin defeated the Lombards and gave their lands to the pope. Known as the "**Donation of Pepin**," these lands eventually became the Papal States. The pope, head of the Roman Church, became a ruler involved in European politics. His successors continued to rule as kings over this region for the next one thousand years.

The Empire of Charlemagne

When Pepin died in 768, his sons Carloman and Charles succeeded him as corulers. After only a few years, Carloman died, and Charles became the sole ruler of the Frankish kingdom. Charles was not only the greatest Carolingian king but also one of the outstanding figures of the Middle Ages. His accomplishments won him the title **Charlemagne** (SHAR luh mane), or "Charles the Great."

Charlemagne's Character

According to Einhard, Charlemagne's close friend and biographer, "Charles was large and strong, and of lofty stature, though not disproportionately tall (his height is well known to have been seven times the length of his foot)." Undoubtedly his "lofty stature" did not come from his father, Pepin the Short, but from his mother, who was called *Berte au grand pied*, or "Big-Foot" Bertha.

Charlemagne

Charlemagne possessed many virtues, but he was not without his vices. On one occasion, he is reported to have beheaded several thousand prisoners in cold blood. In addition, his personal life was marred by sin. He had little regard for the sanctity of marriage; he married, divorced, and remarried many times.

Charlemagne's Conquests

The Frankish kingdom reached its peak under Charlemagne's rule (768–814). As his father had done, Charlemagne rescued Rome, which had again been invaded by Lombards. He took for himself the title "King of the Lombards." With this foe subdued, he directed his military campaigns against the Saxons, a Germanic tribe in northern Europe. After thirty years of bitter struggle, he conquered this people also. Near the Danube River in central Europe, he defeated the Avars, a nomadic people similar to the Huns. And in the south, he drove the Spanish Muslims back across the Pyrenees. By the time of his death, Charlemagne had created an empire that stretched over most of western Europe. He laid the foundation for the modern European nations of France, Germany, and Italy.

Charlemagne divided his empire into hundreds of administrative districts, or counties. He appointed counts to supervise each district.

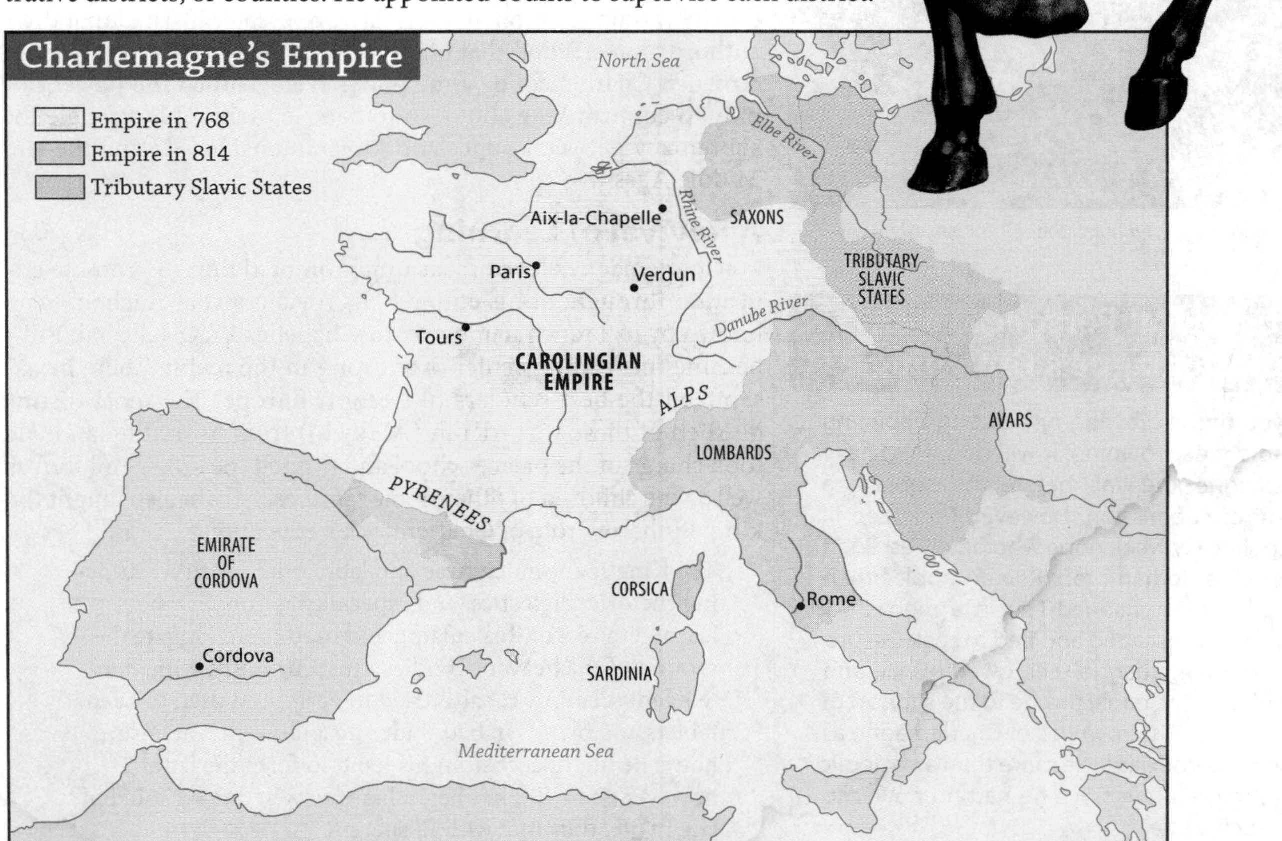

They administered justice, maintained the peace, and raised an army in times of war. To ensure the enforcement of his policies on the local level, Charlemagne created the office of ***missi dominici***, or the king's envoys (messengers). He sent pairs of these messengers into the districts to investigate local conditions and to hear complaints leveled against any of the local officials. These envoys then sent back written reports to Charlemagne.

Because such officials were subject to bribery, Charlemagne chose only men of proven ability and character. Furthermore, he stated that no *missi dominici* could serve in any district in which he held property, nor could two serve together for more than one year.

Throne of Charlemagne, Palatine Chapel, Aachen, Germany

Charlemagne's Crowning

Since the days of the Roman emperors, no one man in the West had ruled as much territory as Charlemagne. Western Europe looked upon him as another Constantine, ruling and protecting both church and state. As a result, while Charlemagne was attending a church service in Rome on Christmas Day, 800, Leo III, a grateful pope, placed a crown on his head and proclaimed him Roman emperor. The assembly present cried out, "To Charles Augustus, crowned by God, the great and pacific [peaceful] emperor of the Romans, life and victory."

Although the title "emperor" did little to increase the actual power of Charlemagne, it did have an important impact upon later medieval history. His empire fell apart after his death, but Charlemagne's crowning had revived the idea of a restored Roman Empire that would again unite the territories of western Europe. This crowning also raised a serious question: whose authority is supreme—the state's or the church's? Though Charlemagne's authority was unquestioned in his day, popes later insisted that their authority superseded that of kings, pointing out that a pope had crowned Charlemagne. Some popes even claimed the power not only to confirm kings but also to depose them. This struggle for supremacy between popes and kings intensified during the late Middle Ages.

Historical Perspective on Charlemagne's Crowning

If you find a drawing or painting depicting Charlemagne's crowning, it will doubtless have Charlemagne kneeling before the pope in a position of submission. However, Pope Leo III was a politically weak pope who barely escaped murder by a Roman mob. Roman nobles then deposed and imprisoned Leo in a monastery, from which he escaped and fled to seek the protection of Charlemagne. Leo owed his life and restoration to the papal throne to the support of Charlemagne. His crowning of Charlemagne as Roman emperor was little more than a symbolic gesture of gratitude since he had no power to confer such a title.

A Revival of Learning

Charlemagne's love of learning prompted him to promote education throughout his empire. His royal court at Aachen, (also known by its French name, Aix-la-Chapelle; AYKS lah shah PEL) became the leading center of learning in the realm. There he assembled the best scholars of western Europe. The most distinguished of these was Alcuin (AL kwin) from York, England. He took charge of the palace school and trained the king's children as well as the children of other noble families. Alcuin also taught the king. Einhard wrote of Charlemagne's education:

> The King spent much time and labor with [Alcuin] studying rhetoric, dialectics, and especially astronomy; he learned to reckon [calculate], and used to investigate the motion of the heavenly bodies most curiously, with an intelligent scrutiny. He also tried to write, and used to keep tablets and blanks in bed under his pillow, that at leisure hours he might accustom his hand to form the letters; however, as he did not begin his efforts in due season, but late in life, they met with ill success.
>
> *Einhard,* The Life of Charlemagne, *trans. Samuel Epes Turner, 54.*

Perhaps it was under Alcuin's influence that Charlemagne developed his deep concern for a better-educated clergy. He encouraged the church to establish schools to upgrade the literacy of the priests and monks. In a letter to church leaders, Charlemagne set forth what has been called the charter of education for the Middle Ages. In it, he said:

> And hence we have begun to fear that, if [the clergy's] skill in writing is so small, so also their power of rightly comprehending the Holy Scriptures may be far less than is befitting; and it is known to all that, if verbal errors are dangerous, errors of interpretation are still more so. We exhort you, therefore, not only not to neglect the study of letters but to apply yourselves thereto with that humble perseverance which is well-pleasing to God, that so you may be able with greater ease and accuracy to search into the mysteries of the Holy Scriptures.
>
> *Donald A. White,* Medieval History: A Sourcebook, *239.*

Aachen Cathedral in Germany; the building was begun by Charlemagne and was the coronation church for thirty German kings.

Charlemagne's educational reforms renewed interest in the Bible and the works of classical writers. For several centuries in western Europe there had been little opportunity for an education; as a result, few people could read or write. During that time many ancient manuscripts were lost or damaged; others were full of copyists' mistakes. One of the most important contributions of Charlemagne's reign was the rediscovery and preservation of these ancient works. In addition, God used the Carolingian scholars to preserve copies of the Bible.

Monasteries became the primary centers for studying, copying, and preserving ancient manuscripts; they were the "printing houses" and libraries of the Middle Ages. Monks undertook the painstaking process of making handwritten copies of earlier works. During this period, they developed a new and beautiful style of handwriting known as the **Carolingian minuscule**. This clean and simple writing style became the model for much of our lowercase writing today. Many manuscripts were "illuminated" with colorful illustrations.

Sample document written in Carolingian miniscule

Disintegration of Charlemagne's Empire

Although the effects of this renewed interest in learning lasted for centuries, Charlemagne's impressive empire deteriorated rapidly. Within a century after his death, the Carolingian Empire had collapsed, torn by civil war and pillaged by foreign invaders.

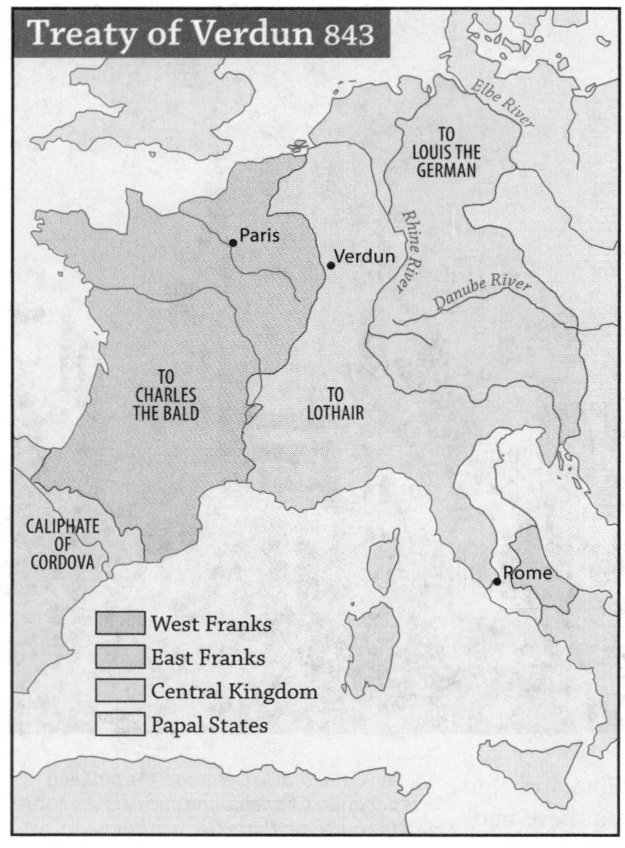

Problems from Within

When Charlemagne died in 814, his empire passed to his only surviving son, Louis the Pious. During Louis's reign, a bitter rivalry broke out among his sons over which portion of the empire each would inherit. Even before Louis's death this rivalry led to war.

After years of fighting, the brothers met at the city of Verdun to settle their differences. In the **Treaty of Verdun** (843), they agreed to split the empire into three separate kingdoms: **Charles the Bald** received West Frankland; **Louis the German**, East Frankland; and the eldest brother, **Lothair**, retained the title of emperor and ruled the land between his brother's kingdoms. (See map to the left.) Notice how closely the modern states of France, Germany, and Italy correspond to these divisions.

When Lothair died, Charles and Louis wasted little time in seizing portions of his kingdom. (Part of this territory is still known today as Lorraine, "Lothair's kingdom.") Political fragmentation characterized the last days of the empire as the Carolingian rulers persisted in their strife. In addition, the successors to Charlemagne's grandsons were weak and incompetent rulers, as is demonstrated by the disrespectful surnames they were given: Louis the Stammerer, Charles the Fat, Louis the Child, and Charles the Simple.

Problems from Without

During the ninth and tenth centuries, the Carolingian Empire offered little resistance to the foreign invaders that beset

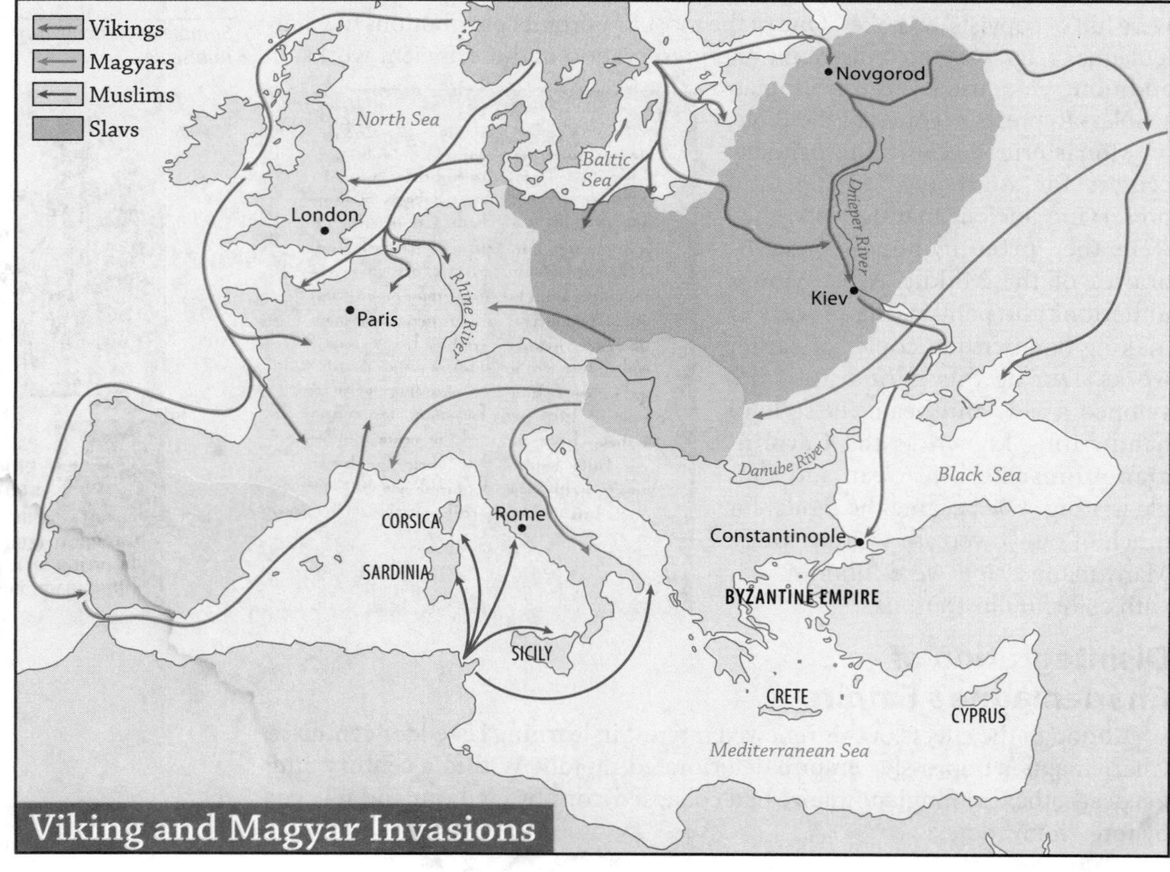

it on every side. From North Africa came Muslim raiders who devastated the Mediterranean coast of Europe and seized many prisoners to be sold into slavery. They captured Sardinia, Corsica, and Sicily and pillaged southern Italy with similar tragic results. From the East came the **Magyars**, a group of Asiatic nomads who later became known as the Hungarians. They swept into the Danube region of southeastern Europe, where they ravaged the eastern borders of the empire.

However, the most feared invaders were the **Vikings**, or Norsemen. These Germanic tribes swooped down from the north out of the lands known today as Norway, Sweden, and Denmark. Fearless warriors, skilled seamen, and daring adventurers, Viking sailors braved the waters of the Atlantic to sail to Iceland, Greenland, and North America. Some sailed down the rivers of Russia, while others sailed along the coastal waters of Europe and into the Mediterranean region, plundering coastal villages and towns. The Vikings struck terror into the hearts of the people of Europe; their swift raids left villages aflame, homes and crops destroyed, and churches and monasteries ransacked. Few in Europe felt safe from the attacks of the dreaded Norsemen. "From the fury of the Northmen, O Lord deliver us" was a prayer offered in churches across western Europe.

Section Quiz

1. What man united the Frankish tribes and became known as "King of the Franks"?
2. What palace official became the real power behind the Frankish throne?
3. At what battle and in what year did Charles Martel defeat the Muslims?
4. Under whose rule did the Frankish empire reach its peak?
5. Name the treaty that split the Carolingian Empire into three parts, and identify the brothers and the portion of the kingdom they received.

★ Evaluate Charlemagne's approach to Christianizing his kingdom.

II. Early Medieval Culture

The Feudal System

Development

As Charlemagne's empire disintegrated, powerful nobles replaced the weak Carolingian kings. There arose a new political system in which local rulers offered the people protection in return for their services. This system, known as **feudalism**, was the form of government prevalent in western Europe from the ninth to the thirteenth centuries. It provided relative order and security until more centralized governments emerged.

Land was the basis of wealth and power during the Feudal Age. Governing power formerly exercised by a central government gradually passed into the hands of landholding nobles, called **lords**. In theory, the king was the supreme lord, holding all the land in the kingdom by right of conquest or inheritance. But when foreign raiders threatened his territory, the king had to rely on the help of powerful nobles. In return for their services (usually military aid), the king granted them the use of landed estates. The land grants became known as **fiefs**, or in Latin, *feudum*, from which our word *feudal* comes.

A fief could be extremely large or very small. The recipient of such an estate became the king's **vassal** (servant). A vassal did not own the land, or fief, but held it as payment for service rendered to the king. Originally, the king granted his vassal the use of a fief for as long as the vassal lived. When the vassal died, the fief reverted to the king. Later, however, many fiefs became hereditary, remaining in the hands of the vassal's eldest son upon payment of a fee. Often a vassal parceled out portions of his fief to gain the services of lesser nobles, who became his vassals, and he, in turn, their lord. Each new vassal could likewise partition his fief and become a lord. This process, called **subinfeudation**, could continue until a fief was too small to subdivide any further.

Painting depicting medieval homage. The vasssal on the left is placing his hands between the lord's hands. The man in the middle is the witness.

Relationships and Obligations

At the heart of feudalism was the relationship that existed between a lord and his vassal. Solemn ceremonies symbolized the agreement entered into by these two nobles. **Homage** was the ceremony by which a man became a vassal and thus eligible for a fief. This ceremony usually took place in the lord's court with many witnesses present. The would-be vassal knelt before the lord and placed his hands between his lord's hands; he then professed himself to be the "lord's man." With a ceremonial kiss, the lord recognized him as his vassal. After performing homage, the vassal took an oath of fealty (fidelity), pledging faithfulness and loyalty to his lord. In turn, the lord handed to the vassal a small stick, lance, or clod of earth. By this symbolic act, known as **investiture**, the lord gave to the vassal the right of use of a fief.

In addition to the grant of a fief, the lord guaranteed his vassal protection and justice. The vassal's primary duty was to provide military service for his lord. He was expected to furnish a specified number of knights (for at least forty days a year) to assist the lord in his battles. Not all of the vassal's responsibilities were military, however. A vassal also agreed to supply financial payments on special occasions, such as when his lord's eldest son became a knight or when the lord's eldest daughter was married. Vassals attended the lord's court to give counsel and to assist in the administration of justice. In addition, the vassal was obligated to pay a ransom if his lord were captured in war. Although a vassal's duties were many and varied, he benefited from this feudal relationship. A fief gave a vassal authority and power; the greater the size of the fief, the greater the vassal's prestige. Often, through subdividing the land, a noble became the lord of many vassals. This increased his dignity, but it also increased his obligations. It often led to conflicting loyalties, as when lords warred against one another.

Bodiam Castle, England

Life of the Nobility

The **castle** was the center of life for the nobility. It was not only the lord's home but also the local jail, the treasury, the armory, the court, and the seat of government. Modern books and films have romanticized daily life in the medieval castle. Yet as impressive as feudal castles may have appeared from a distance, they were often damp, cold, musty, and dark. Tapestries and flowers were used to add warmth and cheer to the otherwise bleak surroundings. Feudal castles had few of the comforts and luxuries that we associate with the elegant, aristocratic palaces of a later day.

Knight on his steed

Castles were built primarily for defensive purposes. The word *castle* comes from the Latin word *castellum,* meaning "fort" or "fortress." At first castles were often just wooden blockhouses set on high mounds surrounded by a stockade and a ditch (moat). It was not until about the tenth century that castles assumed the features that most people think of today: massive stone walls, towering battlements, wide moats, and wooden drawbridges. It was the lord's responsibility to protect the inhabitants of the surrounding countryside. When invaders threatened the land, the local villagers fled into the safe confines of their lord's castle. High atop the castle's battlement, defenders could repel an attack with spears and arrows or by pouring molten metal or dropping large boulders on the heads of attackers.

Also important to the protection of life and property during the Middle Ages was the **knight**. In the early Middle Ages, anyone brave and strong enough could become one. Later, however, knighthood was restricted to the nobility.

The preparation for knighthood was long and hard. At age seven, a boy's initiation formally began. At that time his parents placed him in the care of a knight (often an uncle) for special training. For the next several years, the youth, or **page**, developed both his mind and body. He studied academic subjects such as religion, science, and history. The page also spent time learning to fence (fight with a sword), ride a horse, and hunt with falcons and dogs. In his midteens, the page became a **squire**, the personal servant of a knight. His training became more intense, and his responsibilities increased. The squire cared for the knight's armor, weapons, and horse. He dressed his knight each morning and waited on him, his family, and guests as they ate.

When he was about twenty-one, a squire became eligible for knighthood. Occasionally a man was knighted instantly on the battlefield in recognition of unusual bravery. More often, however, a squire received knighthood in a special religious ceremony. The squire spent the night before the ceremony praying before his armor, which lay on the altar of the church. The ceremony climaxed the next morning when the squire, kneeling before an elder knight or priest, was dubbed, or tapped on the shoulders with the flat side of a sword's blade. The ceremony often ended with a display of the young man's knightly skills.

The knight promised to live by a strict code of behavior, called the "code of chivalry." The word ***chivalry*** comes from the French word for *horseman* (i.e., a knight). It is closely related to the English word *cavalry.* A true knight was expected to be brave in battle, skillful with his weapons, honest, generous, and loyal to his lord. He never attacked an unarmed knight but gave him the opportunity to put on his armor before engaging him in battle. Likewise, it was improper for an entire company of knights to attack a single knight; they were to fight him one at a time.

The Roman Catholic Church gradually influenced the knightly code. According to the twelfth-century philosopher John of Salisbury, knights were

Reenactment of a jousting tournament

to "defend the Church, assail infidelity, venerate the priesthood, protect the poor from injuries, pacify the province, pour out their blood for their brothers, and if need be lay down their lives." The church not only tried to improve the conduct of the knights but also attempted to place limitations on feudal warfare through decrees known as the **Peace of God** and the **Truce of God**. By the Peace of God the church forbade the pillaging of church property and extended protection to all noncombatants in society. The Truce of God sought to limit fighting to specified weekdays by forbidding combat from Wednesday evening to Monday morning. Although often unable to enforce these decrees, the church did strive to improve some of the harsh and brutal conditions of the feudal period.

Even in times of peace, the knight was expected to maintain his skills. He often went hunting and fishing, but his real love was fighting. When peaceful conditions kept him at home, he sometimes kept fit by staging a mock war, called a tournament. The typical tournament included two types of contests: the joust and the melee. Jousting was a competition between two knights on horseback who charged at each other, carrying lances with which each tried to unseat his opponent. The melee was a team competition. At a signal, the two sides rushed at each other on horseback and fought what amounted to a full-scale battle. Often they fought within a fenced area so that the battle would remain compact and thus more intense and exciting to watch. The weapons were usually blunted, but there were still many injuries and even some deaths. One historian states that the tournaments "satisfied the craving of both fighters and spectators for 'red-blooded' excitement in a manner that reminds one of the Roman gladiatorial games, the Spanish bullfight, the rougher aspects of American football, and prize fighting."

Loren C. MacKinney, The Medieval World, *230.*

Section Quiz

1. What was land granted by kings to nobles in return for their service called?
2. What place was the center of life for the nobility?
3. What two stages of preparation did a young man go through to become a knight?
4. Name the strict code that governed knightly behavior.
5. What two types of activities were part of the typical tournaments among knights?

★ What were the positive and negative influences of the Roman Catholic Church on the knightly code?

The Manor

The **manor** was home for the majority of people living in western Europe during the Middle Ages. It was the center of medieval society, a self-contained farming community controlled by a lord and farmed by peasants. The manorial system arose out of the economic and social conditions of the early medieval period since during that time trade decreased, the size and number of towns diminished, and money was rarely used as a medium of exchange. Most Europeans lived on estates, where they labored to provide for their daily needs.

Because of the decline of trade, the manor had to be largely self-sufficient. Each manor usually had its own priest and skilled workers. Craftsmen made such items as furniture, shoes, tools, and woven cloth. The laborers on each manor produced their own food, built their own homes, and made their own clothing. They grew crops and raised cattle, sheep, and pigs; they constructed bridges and roads. About the only items the manor could not provide were salt, iron, and tar, all of which had to be imported unless available locally.

Manors varied from one locality to another. Factors such as climate and soil influenced the quality of life on the manor; the people on one manor might prosper, while those on another might barely eke out a living. Some manors were large estates composed of many villages and thousands of acres of land. Others were simply small villages with only a few hundred acres. Likewise, there was a wide range in the population on the manors, from a dozen families to more than one hundred.

The center of a typical manor was the village, usually located near a stream or at a crossroad. Here peasants lived in clusters of cottages, which were often one- or two-room huts with thatched roofs and walls made of various materials, including dried mud and straw. The peasants enjoyed few comforts or possessions and had meager furnishings. Nearby was a small plot on which a peasant family could plant a vegetable garden and build a stable to house any livestock it might own. It was not uncommon for some of the livestock to be housed inside the cottage.

Two buildings dominated the manor: the lord's residence and the village church. Depending on the size of the manor, the lord's dwelling might be a castle or a simple wooden building known as the manor house. In either case, it was often situated on a high hill or some other defensible site. Usually the village was close by; when enemies attacked, the villagers sought refuge inside the fortified walls of the lord's house. Not far from the manor house stood the village church and the priest's home. The church steeple towered above the manor, directing the villagers' gaze heavenward. The church was not only the place of worship but also the place for village meetings, court sessions, and social gatherings.

Activities were not confined to the village. Villagers obtained building material and firewood from nearby forests and grazed their livestock in the pastures. They fished in streams and ponds and hunted for game in the manor's woodlands. The lord and villagers divided the cultivated fields on the manor.

Artist's conception of a typical medieval village with a blacksmith, a grist mill, and a village oven.

One-sixth to one-third of the arable land was set apart as the lord's **demesne** (dih MAYN)—the land reserved for the lord; the rest was allotted to the villagers. The village peasants often worked together to plow the land, sow the seed, and harvest the crops since no one peasant had enough equipment or oxen to do the job alone. The open fields were divided into long, narrow strips. In each field, a villager farmed one or more of these strips. Often the lord's demesne was not a separate field but rather the most fertile strips in each open field.

During the early Middle Ages, most manors employed a **two-field system** of farming. In this system villagers planted crops on half of the cultivated land, leaving the other half to lie fallow for a year to recover its fertility. The following year, they reversed the procedure.

Later a **three-field system** came into common use, especially in northern Europe. This system established a pattern of rotating planting among three fields. In the spring the peasants planted one field with barley, oats, or beans; in the fall they planted a second field with rye or wheat. The third field remained uncultivated for one year. This rotation of crops increased the long-term productivity of the land as one crop replaced the nutrients that a previous crop had consumed.

The population on even the smallest manors reflected the medieval class structure: clergy, nobility, and peasantry. While throughout the Middle Ages the highest social status belonged to the clergy and the nobility, every person on the manor had specific duties. The parish priest cared for the religious needs of the villagers, while the local lord provided protection and justice. The peasants worked to provide for the physical and nutritional needs of everyone on the manor.

A small percentage of the people on the manor were **freemen**. These were the more privileged peasants who served as manorial officials or skilled laborers, such as blacksmiths, millers, and carpenters. Some freemen owned their own land, but others rented land from the lord of the manor. Freemen did not have the same obligations as the average peasant. For example, freemen were often exempt from laboring in the lord's fields. Furthermore, they had the freedom to leave the manor. Although they had greater privileges, the freemen's living conditions differed little from those of average peasants.

Below: Blacksmith
Bottom: Grist mill
Bottom right: Water wheel used to power the grist mill

The majority of those living on a manor were peasants known as **serfs** (from the Latin *servus*, which means "slave"). The status of the serf was midway between the ancient slave and the medieval freeman. He had the use of a small portion of land and had opportunity to provide for himself and his family. Unlike the freeman, the serf was bound to the land on which he was born and was not free to leave the manor without the lord's permission.

In return for the use of the lord's land and his protection, the serfs owed the lord various services and payments. These services often took the form of labor; serfs were bound to work on the lord's demesne. They plowed his fields, sowed and harvested his crops, gathered his hay, and cared for his livestock. The lord might call on them to build fences, clear woodland, or dig a moat for his castle. Usually the serfs devoted two or three days a week to working for their lord, an obligation known as **week work**.

Artist's conception of a village oven

Serfs also had to pay the lord—usually in produce—for the use of his land and its resources. Serfs gave the lord a portion of their crops, a share of the fish caught in the village stream, cheese in exchange for pasturing their cattle in the lord's fields, and a share of the firewood cut. In addition, the serfs were obligated to use the village mill and bakery owned by the lord. They paid to use these facilities with a portion of their grain and flour.

The only world most peasants ever knew was the manor on which they were born. It was their home—the place of their work, their worship, and their death—just as it had been for their ancestors before them. In fact, a peasant seldom traveled more than twenty miles from the place where he was born.

Each year there were two major holy days (holidays)—Easter and Christmas. Christmas brought a two-week celebration (alluded to in our carol "The Twelve Days of Christmas") and a great banquet at the lord's house. There were also other holidays, such as May Day (in the spring) and Harvest Day (much like our Thanksgiving).

Even with the holidays, life was hard for the peasant on the manor. He worked from sunrise to sunset. Yet despite all his labors, the average peasant barely managed to subsist. He often suffered from poverty and misery. What little income he earned usually went either to the lord in rent and fees or to the church in tithes. Famines also plagued the land, and frequent feudal wars ruined crops and killed livestock. Strenuous labor, filthy living conditions, poor diet, and lack of medical care combined to give the average peasant a short lifespan.

Section Quiz

1. Where did the vast majority of people in Europe during the Middle Ages live?
2. What two buildings dominated the manor?
3. Name the term that described the peasant laborers on the manor.
4. Why did the serfs work for their lord and give him part of the crops they raised?

★ During the Middle Ages, why would peasants willingly become slaves and submit to a lord?

The Medieval Church

Outwardly, things looked bleak for western Europe at the outset of the Middle Ages. Rome had fallen; the order and stability the empire had once provided were gone. Barbarian tribes began to carve out their own kingdoms from the territory once held by the caesars. Monuments of Rome's former grandeur—its aqueducts, amphitheaters, public baths, and roads—were in disrepair. Productivity and trade, as well as education, were on the decline. The lifestyle of the barbarians gradually replaced Greco-Roman culture.

Amidst the confusion and change there remained one stable institution. It represented order and authority and preserved elements of classical culture. This institution became known as the Roman Catholic Church. It served as the heart of medieval society, influencing almost every aspect of life. The Roman Church cared for the poor, sick, and aged and took the leading role in education. (There was little literacy and learning outside of monasteries during the medieval period.) As the church absorbed almost all of the people in western Europe, it amassed great power, prestige, and wealth. Gradually, the church assumed leadership in political as well as religious matters.

To fully understand the Roman Church, one must examine Christianity and its development in the days of the Roman Empire. At that time (and still today) the word *church* had two different meanings. Specifically, it referred to a local assembly of believers. There were many such local churches scattered throughout the Roman world. The word also had a universal meaning, namely, the "body of Christ." In this sense, *church* referred to the spiritual body composed of all true believers everywhere who were united by faith in Christ. Scripture presents Jesus as "the head over all things to the church, which is his body, the fullness of him that filleth all in all" (Eph. 1:22–23). Recognizing the unity of their faith, the early Christians described this church as ***catholic***, a word meaning simply "universal" or "encompassing all."

As mentioned in Chapter 5, a bishop oversaw a collection of local assemblies and answered to an archbishop. Over time the bishop of Rome exercised rule over all western churches. As a result, the universal body of Christ came to be understood as an outward, visible institution that became known as the Catholic Church.

Jerome and the Vulgate

Because most people in the Roman Empire spoke Latin, there was a great need for a Latin translation of the Bible. From the earliest days of the church, many people had attempted to meet that need. By the fourth century there had been so many mistakes in translating and copying the Scripture that most Latin manuscripts were no longer reliable. To correct the problem, the Bishop of Rome asked a scholar named Jerome (340–420) to revise the Latin text. Jerome agreed to do so and worked for over twenty years, revising existing translations of portions of the Bible and making original translations of other portions. The result of his labor is a translation that came to be called the Latin Vulgate—a name which means "common" or "well-known." Although Jerome's work also contained some inaccuracies, the Vulgate became the most widely-used Bible of the Middle Ages. Later it became the official Bible of the Roman Catholic Church.

St. Jerome, *Pietro Paolini, from the Bob Jones University Collection*

Head of the Church

The church and bishop of the city of Rome played key roles in the development of the Roman Church. As discussed earlier (see p. 100), the church had been organized according to the political and geographical divisions of the Roman Empire. The Church of Rome administered one of the five patriarchates, the highest-ranking divisions within the church. (Jerusalem, Antioch, Alexandria, and Constantinople administered the other four.) As previously mentioned, at first the patriarchates were equal in rank and authority; however, the Church of Rome gradually rose to a place of preeminence. Its bishop began to assume sole authority over the church in the West.

There were many reasons for this rise in power and prestige. The bishop of Rome presided over the largest and wealthiest city in the western empire. As the people of the Mediterranean world looked to Rome for political and economic leadership, it was natural for them to look to Rome for spiritual guidance as well. Furthermore, all the other patriarchal

Saints

The word *saint* means "set apart" or "holy." According to the New Testament, every Christian is a saint through the righteousness of Jesus Christ (Rom. 1:7). However, at some point after the time of the apostles, an increasing number of leaders in the developing Roman Church began to apply the term *saint* only to Bible characters or to noteworthy Christians (those who died a martyr's death or were believed to have performed miracles). To honor these people, the medieval church held special services and declared certain days to be sacred in their memory. Many of these days—such as St. Patrick's Day and St. Valentine's Day—are still celebrated today.

The Roman Church taught that the saints are in heaven helping people on earth in times of trouble and interceding on their behalf before the throne of God. Certain saints became known as "patron" saints because they were believed to intercede for a special group of people. People could pray to St. Lucy if they had eye trouble, St. Martha if they needed help with cooking, or St. Valentine if they were in love. Likewise, each occupation had a patron saint; for example, St. Sebastian for athletes, St. Hubert for hunters, and St. Matthew for tax collectors. (The Roman Church continues to designate saints as patrons for modern times: for example, St. Michael is the patron saint of policemen, St. Joseph of Arimathea is the patron saint of funeral directors, and St. Clare—who died in 1253—is the patron saint of television.) Countries, too, had their own special saints: St. George of England, St. Patrick of Ireland, St. Denis of France, and St. Boniface of Germany.

Honored above all other saints was Mary, the mother of Christ. Leaders of the medieval church taught that Mary was the queen of heaven. They instructed the people to call her the Mother of God and pray to her frequently. Many believed that she never sinned and that she remained a virgin forever. Under the teaching of the Roman Catholic Church, Mary became more important in a person's daily life than Christ Himself.

Ukranian art that calls Mary the "mother of God"

bishops were located in the East. With the collapse of the western empire in the fifth century, the Roman bishop became one of the few remaining sources of stability in the West. Under Bishop **Leo I** of Rome, the prestige of the office was further enhanced when, in 452, the barbarian Huns threatened the city of Rome and Leo persuaded their leader Attila to spare the city. Leo was hailed as *papa* or pope ("Father-Protector"). This title had been applied to other bishops in both the East and the West. By the sixth century, however, it referred almost exclusively to the bishop of Rome.

During the fifth and sixth centuries, the bishops of Rome began to translate their prestige into authority over all churches. For the most part they were successful. By the end of the sixth century, the bishop of Rome was generally regarded as the pope, the head of the visible church in the West.

To support their claim of primacy ("first in rank"), the bishops of Rome advanced the **Petrine theory**. This theory, based on Matthew 16:18–19, holds that Christ made Peter the first pope and gave him supreme authority over the church on earth. According to this theory, Peter became the vicar, or substitute, of Christ on earth. As the first bishop of Rome, he transferred his office with all its authority to those who succeeded him.

Perhaps the best representative of the early medieval popes was **Gregory I** (r. 590–604), called "the Great." As bishop of Rome, he greatly expanded the power and authority of his office by defending its supremacy. In fact, Gregory is commonly recognized as the first true pope—a title which he, however, disclaimed. Gregory preferred the title "servant of the servants of God." He was a man of deep devotion and fervent piety who exercised episcopal care over the churches of Gaul, Spain, Britain, Northern Africa, and Italy. Yet Gregory also promoted many unbiblical doctrines that the Roman Catholic Church later officially embraced: the mass, the equal authority of tradition and Scripture, and

Little Horwood Church, Buckinghamshire, England

the sacrament of penance. He also promoted the existence of **purgatory** (a place of temporary punishment where souls bound for heaven must go after death to pay for so-called minor unconfessed sins).

Teaching of the Church

The Middle Ages is often called an "age of faith." Religion dominated society, and nearly every aspect of a person's life was influenced by the Roman Catholic Church. The power of the Roman bishops grew greater than that of monarchs. And the few bright spots of culture that existed at this time were made possible by the church.

As previously mentioned, one significant contribution of the Middle Ages was the continued copying of the Bible in monasteries. Those who could read and had access to manuscripts continued to study the Bible in the Middle Ages. Also, the method of interpreting the Bible improved as the allegorical approach of seeing symbols and pictures of truth in historical passages of the Bible slowly gave way to a more literal approach. But access to Scripture also revealed many practices that had developed over time but could not be found in the Bible. In response, some argued that church tradition had the same authority as the Scriptures. As a result, the doctrine and practice of the Roman Catholic Church became a dangerous mixture of truth and error.

The **Roman sacramental system** developed, in part, from misinterpretations of Scripture texts about baptism and the Lord's Supper. By the second century the idea that baptism regenerates and cleanses from sin gained acceptance. Baptism, and then the other sacraments, became defined as "the visible sign of an invisible grace." The Roman Catholic Church defines a sacrament as a religious act that grants grace (spiritual benefit) based on the recipient's right intentions. Rome teaches that the sacraments are necessary for salvation; they are thus made the core of worship and teaching in the Roman Catholic

Medieval Religious Superstitions

Closely associated with the growing worship of Mary and the veneration of so-called saints was the importance that many in the church attached to relics. A relic is an object associated with a saint, such as a piece of clothing or even a part of the saint himself, such as a bone or a lock of hair. During the Middle Ages, many rulers as well as churches made great efforts to secure relics. The reason for such interest was twofold. First, churches under the influence of Rome taught that mass could not be celebrated unless it was performed upon an altar that contained a relic of a saint. Second, many in the church taught that those who properly viewed and honored the relics would spend less time in purgatory. This teaching helped to promote pilgrimages to shrines housing the relics of saints.

Many of the relics, however, were fakes. Some churches claimed to have Noah's beard, a bit of manna, the bones of Balaam's donkey, and some feathers from the wings of the archangel Michael (to name only a few). In addition, various churches claimed to have relics related to the life of Christ: straw from the manger, some of the wine Jesus made at Cana, drops of sweat from Gethsemane, the crown of thorns, and some of Christ's blood. So many places claimed to have part of the true cross that one sixteenth-century churchman sarcastically remarked that if all the pieces of the "true" cross were gathered together, there would be enough wood to build a ship!

It was such superstition, believing that these relics acted as some sort of good luck charm, that helped to blind the minds of many people during the Middle Ages to the truth of God's Word.

Church. In addition, the church claims the exclusive right to administer the sacraments and to do so only to those in fellowship with the visible church.

By the end of the twelfth century, the Roman Catholic Church recognized **seven sacraments** and taught the following regarding them:

1. Baptism initiates one into the church by washing away original sin.
2. Confirmation brings one into full fellowship with the church and confers on him the Holy Spirit to strengthen his spiritual life.
3. Through penance a church member earns forgiveness for sin committed after baptism. Penance includes contrition (sorrow), confession (to a priest), satisfaction (actions done to make amends for sins), and absolution (forgiveness by a priest of the guilt of sins).
4. The Holy Eucharist (YOO kur ist), or Holy Communion, is both a sacrament and a sacrifice in which the priest sacrifices Christ anew. During this service, known as the **mass**, the priest claims to transform the bread and the wine into the actual body and blood of Christ. This change is known as **transubstantiation**.
5. Matrimony unites a man and a woman as husband and wife.
6. Holy Orders sets an individual apart for the service of the church by ordaining him into the priesthood.
7. Extreme Unction, sometimes called the last rites, gives an anointing or blessing to a seriously ill or dying person. Its purpose is to grant absolution from any remaining sin and to offer spiritual comfort.

Whitby Abbey

Through the sacraments, the Roman Catholic Church wielded great power over the Western world because the church claims that no one can be saved without receiving the sacraments, and they can be administered only by the church. Thus, it maintained that there was no salvation outside the one visible so-called catholic church.

Medieval theologians such as Thomas Aquinas compared the sacramental system in the medieval Roman Church with the sacrifices and symbols of Old Testament Israel. But the New Testament makes clear that the rituals of the Old Testament had no power to save. They simply pointed ahead to Christ Who alone can save. This issue is so important that Paul's letter to the Galatians insists that to attempt to gain salvation by combining Old Testament rituals with faith in Christ was to follow a false gospel. The Reformers would later argue that Paul's argument applied to the sacramental system as well.

Leaders of the Church

There gradually arose a sharp distinction between the common church parishioners and those who entered (through Holy Orders) in the special service of the church. The leaders of the church were called **clergy**; the parishioners were called the **laity**. Only the clergy were members of the church. Thus, in the medieval mind, only the clergy were servants of the church.

Benedict of Nursia

In any organization, people participate for many different reasons. So it was in the medieval Roman Church. Some wore the clerical garb but were not in sympathy with the cause; they joined out of ambition, hoping to gain the wealth, luxury, and power that often accompanied prestigious church offices. Others joined to find a haven from personal or family problems. Though many had poor motives, some men joined the ranks out of a sincere desire to serve God. Thus the medieval church had the dedicated and the indifferent, the giving and the selfish, those who sought eternal rewards and those who desired material gain, those who furthered the cause of Christ and those who hindered it.

The clergy of the Roman Church were organized into different branches of service. One branch was called the **secular clergy** (from *seculum*, Latin for "world"). These men conducted religious services, administered the sacraments to the laity, and supervised the business and property of the church.

The **regular clergy** renounced the things of this world. Some sacrificed their own personal ambitions in order to maintain an active mission of social service. Most retired to a life of solitude and study. They lived in monastic communities under strict regulations. (The word *regular* comes from the Latin *regula*, meaning "rule.")

The most popular system of rules in medieval Europe came from Benedict of Nursia (480–547), often called the "Father of Western Monasticism." Characterized by discipline and order, the **Benedictine Rule** strictly regulated the lives of monks. They engaged in such daily activities as manual labor, study, religious services, and prayer. Monks entering this order took vows of poverty, chastity (celibacy), and obedience to the abbot, the leader of the monastery.

The regular clergy, or monks, played an important role in the growth of the medieval church and in the progress of Western society. Some became missionaries of the medieval church. Two of the most renowned medieval missionaries were English monks: **Patrick** (ca. 387–ca. 460), who took the gospel to Ireland, and **Boniface** (ca. 672–754), who was known as the "Apostle of the Germans." Monks also developed new farming techniques.

Section Quiz

1. List two reasons for the rise of the bishop of Rome to prominence over other bishops.
2. What term describes a religious act (necessary for salvation) that grants spiritual benefit to the one who does it?
3. Which religious act brings one into full fellowship with the Roman Catholic Church and supposedly confers the Holy Spirit to strengthen one's spiritual life?
4. Members of what group were considered members of the Roman Catholic Church?
5. Name the two English monks who were known for their missionary activity.

★ Evaluate the claim that the bishop of Rome has supremacy over all other bishops based on Matthew 16.

Chapter 8 Review

Making Connections

1–3. List three contributions made by monasteries during the Middle Ages.

4. Briefly explain the process of subinfeudation.

Developing History Skills

1. Develop a basic timeline showing the development of the medieval church based on information found in this chapter.
2. Develop a family tree covering four generations of the Carolingian House.

Thinking Critically

1. According to the Roman Catholic Church, how is a person saved? Compare your answer with what the Bible teaches in Titus 3:5 and Ephesians 2:8–9.
2. What does the Roman Catholic Church teach concerning the mass? Compare this with Hebrews 10:10–14.

Living in God's World

1. Imagine that you are a Christian king in medieval Europe. Write a list of laws concerning the practice of religion in your nation.
2. Evaluate the feudal system from a biblical point of view. Describe an economic system for an agrarian culture that is consistent with biblical teaching.

People, Places, and Things to Know

Franks
Clovis
Merovingian House
do-nothing kings
mayor of the palace
Pepin II
Charles Martel
Lombards
Donation of Pepin
Charlemagne
missi dominici
Carolingian minuscule
Treaty of Verdun
Charles
Louis the German
Lothair
Magyars
Vikings
feudalism
lords
fiefs
vassal
subinfeudation
homage
investiture
castle
knight
page
squire
chivalry
Peace of God
Truce of God
manor
demesne
two-field system
three-field system
freemen
serfs
week work
catholic
Leo I
Petrine theory
Gregory I
purgatory
Roman sacramental system
seven sacraments
mass
transubstantiation
clergy
laity
secular clergy
regular clergy
Benedictine Rule
Patrick
Boniface

9

CHURCH AND STATES

I. Reforms in the Church

II. A European Empire

III. Rise of Feudal Monarchies

IV. Rescue of the Holy Land

In this engraving, Holy Roman Emperor Henry IV is humbling himself before Pope Gregory VII.
SEF/Art Resource, NY

The collapse of the Carolingian Empire and the declining influence of the Roman Catholic Church made the ninth century in western Europe a period of widespread political chaos and moral corruption. Reforms beginning in the tenth century, however, strengthened the Church of Rome and led to greater religious and temporal power for the papacy. Able German rulers revived the imperial tradition by establishing the Holy Roman Empire. In England and France feudal kings gradually increased their influence over the noblemen. These changes brought about a struggle for power in Europe. Popes clashed with kings, and kings challenged nobles as each party sought to make its power supreme. Yet in the midst of the struggle, these rivals joined forces in an attempt to rescue the Holy Land from the Muslims. Their efforts, called the Crusades, failed to accomplish their intended goal. They did, however, expose western Europe to the influences that would usher in the modern age.

I. Reforms in the Church

By placing a crown on Charlemagne's head and declaring him emperor, Pope Leo III unintentionally established a precedent. Later popes claimed that this practice demonstrated their superiority over civil rulers. In Charlemagne's day no such claim of supremacy existed. During the political disorder that followed the collapse of Charlemagne's empire, however, the papacy had opportunity to establish its claim of supreme political power. Yet the church's assertion of supremacy came gradually and experienced many setbacks. Corrupt popes and worldly clergy cost the Roman Church much of its prestige and influence. However, the reforms of the eleventh through thirteenth centuries restored much of the church's prestige and elevated the papacy to the height of its power.

Need for Reform

During the ninth century and the early part of the tenth, much of the Roman Church had sunk deep in moral corruption. It amassed great wealth as many churchmen neglected their religious duties for temporal gain. When the political conditions in Europe became more unstable, the church needed protection for its large landholdings. The greatest threat to the church's possessions was the Viking raiders. Churchmen secured protection from these and other enemies by entering into feudal relationships. They became vassals, and their loyalties were divided between the church and feudal lords. Some kings and nobles began to claim the right not only to appoint church officials but also to invest them with their religious authority—a practice known as **lay investiture**.

Soon it became commonplace for lay lords to appoint men with few spiritual qualifications to church offices in return for their political loyalty and financial favors. Unscrupulous men, enticed by the wealth and power of high church office, bought and sold church positions. The condition of the papacy was little better. Inept and immoral men filled the office and brought disgrace upon the church. In addition, striving factions of nobles in Rome struggled over the appointment of popes.

The scandalous conditions in the Roman Church prompted a reform movement. It began in 910 at a monastery in Cluny, France, and spread quickly throughout the church. Members of this movement exposed and sought to remedy abuses within the Roman Church. They introduced measures to forbid simony (the buying and selling of religious goods, which at the time extended to the selling of church

The Church and Large Landholdings

How did the Roman Church become a major landholder in Europe? This accumulation of land occurred gradually as some landholders left their land to the church in their wills. The church then assigned church officials to manage the land for the Roman Church. Over several generations, the Church of Rome acquired vast tracts of land managed by many church officials. These church officials became lords with vassals who swore their allegiance to their lord, who then answered to the pope. This intermingling of secular and sacred responsibilities became the breeding ground for many of the problems that led to the call for reform of the Roman Church.

Church-State Relations

Whose power is greater—the church's or the state's? The medieval world viewed both the church and the state as God's instruments, each possessing God-given authority and definite responsibilities in society. Even so, the powers asserted by one were often in direct conflict with those claimed by the other. Following Constantine's decision to make Christianity an accepted religion in the Roman Empire, the roles of church and state became less distinct and more intertwined.

The Bible tells us that God established both institutions. For this reason, the two should not be in conflict. Both are God's ministering agents for the good of society. The church is to be a bulwark of moral righteousness, striving to bring people to Christ through the preaching of the gospel and instructing governmental leaders in what is just and righteous. The state is to be a safeguard of justice and order, providing protection through its God-given authority. The Christian citizen has an obligation to both.

Sin has thwarted man's attempt to achieve an ideal church-state relationship. In the past some churches have failed to provide moral leadership and have sought political power. Likewise, the state has often overstepped its bounds of authority and has interfered with the church and the home. During the Middle Ages the tension between church and state led to an intense struggle for power. Satan encourages this conflict even today as he attempts to harm God's people and frustrate God's purpose.

Henry's Revenge

While Gregory VII won a fleeting victory at Canossa in 1077, Henry IV had no intention of submitting to the papal claims. Henry spent the next three years defeating rebellious German nobles and consolidating his power. Gregory excommunicated Henry again in 1080. In response, Henry rallied his forces and conquered Rome in 1084. Gregory was deposed, and a new pope was elected. Gregory went into exile and died about a year later.

offices), to free the church from secular control resulting from lay investiture, and to restore the dignity and authority of the papacy.

One of the most influential of the reforming monastic orders was the **Cistercians** (sih STUR shunz). Monks of this order adopted lives of seclusion and strict discipline. They wore rough garments, abstained from meats, and worked hard in the fields. This order was made popular by its most zealous member, **Bernard of Clairvaux** (klare VOH; 1091–1153). A man of deep piety and sincere devotion, Bernard demonstrated by his life the genuineness of his religious convictions. He was an outspoken critic of worldliness in the Roman Church and in society.

Rivalry Between Pope and Emperor

A primary goal of church reform was to rescue the papacy from the state of weakness and corruption into which it had fallen. In 1059, the **College of Cardinals** was created to ensure that churchmen rather than Roman nobles or German kings would choose the popes. After almost two centuries of worthless popes, men of moral strength and able leadership restored dignity to, and increased the power of, the papal office. In fact, the papacy soon became the driving force of the reform movement.

Probably the greatest of the reforming popes was **Gregory VII** (r. 1073–85). As a Benedictine monk, Gregory had been a leading advocate of papal reform. He used his influence as pope to curb other abuses in the church and to strengthen his office. Gregory believed that the Roman Church was superior to the state; therefore, he wanted to free the church from secular control. This meant doing away with lay investiture.

In 1075 Gregory formally prohibited (on pain of excommunication) any layman from appointing a person to church office or investing a person with spiritual authority. The German emperor Henry IV refused to obey, insisting on his right to appoint the bishops in his realm. He declared that Gregory was not pope but a "false monk." In retaliation, Gregory excommunicated him and freed Henry's subjects from their oaths of loyalty. The struggle between the two might have continued, but growing discontent among the German nobles prompted Henry to seek the pope's forgiveness. In the winter of 1077 at Canossa (a castle in northern Italy), the desperate Henry was said to have stood barefoot in the snow for three days, waiting for the pope to speak to him. Gregory had temporarily won a great victory for the papacy.

The struggle over lay investiture did not end with Gregory and Henry. It continued until 1122, at which time the pope and the German emperor reached a compromise. At the city of Worms, they signed an agreement—the Concordat of Worms—that recognized the right of the church to elect its own bishops and abbots and to invest them with spiritual authority. These elections, however, had to be held in the presence of the emperor or his representatives. In addition, the emperor retained the right to invest church officials with secular authority.

New Religious Orders

In the thirteenth century, new religious orders continued the reforms begun by the Cluniac and Cistercian movements. Unlike earlier monastic orders whose members sought seclusion from society, the new Franciscan and Dominican orders emphasized service to one's fellow man. They labored to bring about reform by living and preaching among the people—especially those in the growing towns. Members of these orders were called **friars** ("brothers"). Renouncing worldly possessions, they pledged themselves to lives of poverty. Since the friars begged for their daily sustenance, these orders are sometimes referred to as **mendicant** ("begging") **orders**.

Francis of Assisi (uh SEE see; 1182–1226), the son of a rich merchant, was the founder of the Franciscan order. As a young man he exchanged his wealth for beggar's rags and devoted his life to preaching and ministering to the poor and sick. A contemporary of his, a Spanish nobleman named **Dominic** (1170–1221), founded the Dominican order. Dominic devoted his life to battling heresy. He believed that the best way for the church to combat heresy was to educate its members. Consequently, the Dominican order established a reputation in the field of learning; its members taught

Francis of Assisi and the Manger Scene

Of all the objects associated with Christmas, none is more familiar than the manger scene. Usually included in this portrayal of Christ's birth are figures of Mary, Joseph, shepherds, three wise men, an ox, and a donkey. The baby Jesus lies on a bed of hay in a wooden manger. From the Scriptures we know that there are several misconceptions in this traditional representation. For instance, the wise men did not come with the shepherds to the manger but arrived sometime later (Matt. 2:9–11). Also, Scripture does not tell us how many wise men there were. Nor do we know what animals were present in the stable when Christ was born. Furthermore, Christ was probably laid in a stone manger, not a wooden one.

The man responsible for unintentionally popularizing these misconceptions was Francis of Assisi. To dramatize for the common people the events surrounding the birth of Christ, Francis tried to physically recreate the scene. He built the manger of wood because it was plentiful in his native land. (He had no way of knowing that mangers in Palestine were made of limestone, which was plentiful there.) He had townspeople portray Mary, Joseph, the shepherds, and the wise men. Although the wise men were not actually present at the manger, Francis included them so that he might bring together the events related to the Christ child. Around the manger Francis placed an ox and a donkey, interpreting Isaiah 1:3 as referring to Christ's birth: "The ox knoweth his owner, and the ass his master's crib." At midnight on Christmas Eve 1223, Francis held an outdoor service using this manger scene. He hoped to show the people how Christ came in poverty and how He was born to a life of suffering and death. Because of his popularity and devout life, Francis's manger scene became the model that others copied.

The Basilica of San Francesco, where Francis of Assisi is buried

at Europe's finest universities and supplied the Roman Catholic Church with some of its greatest scholars. Combining their intellectual training with their zeal for fighting heresy, the Dominicans became the leaders of the Inquisition—a church court established to discover and try heretics.

The mendicant orders differed from previous orders by pledging their allegiance to the pope. They championed the cause of the papacy in its clashes with powerful bishops and princes. As was true in previous orders, many Franciscan and Dominican orders abandoned their vows of poverty to gain wealth and sacrificed spiritual power to expand political authority.

Zenith of the Papacy

The years of reform restored the church's prestige, tightened its hold over its members, and broadened its influence on medieval society. Nowhere was this power more evident than in the papacy. For centuries popes had contended that their power exceeded that of kings; the reality of that claim was now established. The battle over lay investiture and the formation of new religious orders had resulted in increased papal authority throughout Europe.

Pope Innocent III
Scala/Art Resource, NY

Innocent III

Papal power and prestige reached its zenith under Pope **Innocent III** (1198–1216). No pope before or after him exercised such extensive authority over both church and state. Innocent likened his authority to the sun, and that of kings, to the moon:

> The Creator of the universe set up two great luminaries [sources of light] in the firmament of heaven; the greater light to rule the day, the lesser light to rule the night. In the same way . . . he appointed two great dignities; the greater to bear rule over souls (these being, as it were, days), the lesser to bear rule over bodies (these being, as it were, nights). These dignities are the [papal] authority and the royal power. Furthermore, the moon derives her light from the sun, and is in truth inferior to the sun in both size and quality, in position as well as effect. In the same way the royal power derives its dignity from the [papal] authority.
>
> *Henry Bettenson, ed.,* Documents of the Christian Church, *157–58.*

College of Cardinals

As the Roman Catholic Church grew in size and power, the popes needed assistance in administering church affairs. Initially gathering together important church leaders from around the city of Rome, the popes gradually organized what is called the College of Cardinals. The word *college* simply means "association" or "society." The term *cardinal* possibly comes from the Latin word *cardo*, which means "hinge." (Just as a hinge is vital to a door, so cardinals are vital to the operation of the church.)

Although the title *cardinal* goes back to the fifth century, it was not until the twelfth century that the college took the form it has today. The cardinals have two major functions: to advise and assist the popes in administering church affairs and, when a pope dies, to elect a new one (who is usually one of their own number). This procedure was designed to protect papal election from political influence.

Just as the pope serves as a kind of king over the Roman Catholic Church, the cardinals serve as the princes. Each cardinal wears a bright red robe and red hat and has the title "Your Most Eminent Lord."

How was Innocent III able to enforce this claim when earlier popes had failed? A large measure of his success is due to the strength of the Roman Catholic Church over which he ruled. By the thirteenth century the Roman Church had matured into a large, wealthy, and powerful organization. By summoning the vast resources of the church that were at his disposal and by taking advantage of its strong influence on society, Innocent established his authority over all of Europe.

Papal Weapons

It was difficult for anyone to resist the ecclesiastical weapons that the popes directed against those who offended the Roman Church. Chief among the weapons in the church's arsenal were the following:

1. *Excommunication*—the punishment of an individual by depriving him of the sacraments and excluding him from the fellowship of the Roman Church. This was an especially powerful weapon in the hands of the pope because churchmen believed that the pope controlled access to heaven and could through excommunication deprive an individual of any hope of eternal salvation.

2. *Interdict*—the suspension of public church services and of the administration of all sacraments (except baptism and extreme unction) in a given location. Popes often used this weapon against disobedient kings. By placing a king's realm under an interdict, the pope hoped that the suspension of spiritual blessings from the church would bring about a public outcry that would force the erring king to submit.

3. *Inquisition*—a special church court commissioned by the pope to stamp out heresy. Heresy, which the Roman Church defined as the holding of beliefs contrary to its teaching, was considered to be the greatest of medieval crimes. Therefore, popes granted inquisitors special powers to seek out and judge alleged heretics. Inquisitors often used torture to make the accused admit to heresy; under such torture, even many innocent people "confessed." Those who would not bend, even under torture, often faced death as punishment. Over time, even those who did confess faced the possibility of death by burning at the stake.

The Inquisition

Started by Pope Gregory IX (r. 1227–41), the Inquisition was an organization of the Roman Catholic Church dedicated to uncovering and punishing heresy (defined as any teaching contrary to the Roman Catholic Church). The inquisitors, often members of the Dominican Order, were frequently well-educated and respected individuals. Nevertheless, they believed (as did the Church of Rome) that it was proper to force people to change their views by subjecting them to physical punishment.

The Inquisition generally operated in a methodical manner. A group of inquisitors would come into a particular town and gather the people together, and then one of them would preach a sermon on the evils of heresy. The preacher urged those who held heretical views to confess them, promising that if they confessed voluntarily, the Inquisition would be lenient with them. After the sermon the inquisitors took up lodging in the town and waited.

Over the next several days, people came to the inquisitors and confessed their heresies. While doing so they often mentioned the names of others who held similar views. After a set period of time, the inquisitors began to call in those who had been accused of heresy by others. An accused person was not required to answer the Inquisition's summons, but if he failed to do so he was presumed guilty and placed under arrest. The accused then had to stand trial before the panel of inquisitors. He could not call any witnesses in his defense; he was not told who had accused him of heresy, and his trial was held in secret. The Inquisition did allow him to have a lawyer, but few attorneys ever agreed to help an accused heretic. The lawyers feared that they too might come under suspicion of heresy. If during the trial the accused person steadfastly maintained his innocence, the inquisitors often used torture to force a confession. For example, they might pull his bones out of joint on the rack or burn various parts of his body with a hot iron. When subjected to such terrible suffering, the prisoner often readily confessed to anything. Once the inquisitors completed their last trial, they again gathered the whole town together. At this meeting one of the inquisitors preached another sermon. Then he read the sentences handed down, beginning with the least severe and ending with the most severe. The punishments varied greatly. Some people had to do penance, some lost their property, and some were sentenced to prison. Those who refused to recant, however, were handed over to the secular authorities to be burned at the stake. After the executions, the inquisitors moved on to another town and repeated the process.

Galileo Before the Holy Office of the Vatican

Robert-Fleury, Joseph Nicholas (1797-1890), Galileo Before the Holy Office of the Vatican. *Oil on canvas, 196 x 308 cm. RF567. Photo: Hervé Lewandowski. Louvre, Paris, France. Réunion des Musées Nationaux/Art Resource, NY*

By the end of the fifteenth century, the Inquisition began to die out; however, Ferdinand and Isabella revived it in Spain. In addition, the success of the Protestant Reformation (see chap. 12) prompted Pope Paul III (1534–49) to give the Inquisition a central organization called the Holy Office. Under this organization, the Inquisition took on a new intensity in several European nations. The Spanish Inquisition proved to be particularly barbaric as it tortured and killed suspected Protestants, Jews, and Muslims. By the early nineteenth century, the Inquisition finally ended its bloody activities in Spain, where it had lingered long after other countries outlawed it.

Section Quiz

1. What was the practice called in which kings and nobles appointed church officials and invested them with religious authority?
2. What pope and emperor had a showdown at Canossa in 1077? Which man initially won?
3. List the two new religious orders whose members begged for their daily sustenance. Identify the founder of each.
4. Under which pope did the papacy reach its zenith?
5. List and define the three major weapons used by the papacy during this period.

☆ Should the medieval church have sought to gain political authority over kings?

II. A European Empire

Since the time of the Tower of Babel, men have often dreamed of a universal empire that would unite all the peoples of the earth under one government. This dream was revived in the tenth century with the founding of the Holy Roman Empire.

Founding of the German Kingdom

After the death of Charlemagne, his grandsons divided the Frankish empire (see p. 164). In East Frankland, the weak descendants of the ruler Louis the German offered little protection against the Magyars—savage horsemen who were terrorizing southeastern Europe. Local tribal leaders called dukes assumed the role of protectors. Each duke ruled like a king in his own territory, called a duchy. After the death of the last Carolingian king, the dukes elected one of their own to lead them against outside attackers.

The German nobles selected the Saxon duke **Henry the Fowler**, the first of the Saxon line of German kings. According to tradition, Henry was called "the Fowler" because the messengers who brought him the news of his election found him enjoying his favorite pastime—hunting game with hawks. As king, Henry I (r. 919–36) forced the other dukes to acknowledge his royal status, but he permitted them to guide the internal affairs of their own territories. His chief concern was to strengthen his own duchy of Saxony so that he could build a strong base for his royal power. He repelled the raids of the Slavs and the Magyars and expanded German territory eastward—a movement that would continue throughout German history.

Henry's son **Otto I** (r. 936–73), often called "the Great," became one of the strongest German kings. Unlike his father, he was not content with the mere title of king but sought to actually assert his royal authority over the other duchies. To aid him in his struggles against rival dukes, he relied on the support of high-ranking church officials, many of whom he had appointed to office. These powerful bishops and abbots served Otto as vassals, giving him their allegiance and supplying soldiers for his army. In addition to his conflict with the nobles, Otto won a great victory over the Magyars. After that defeat, the Magyars no longer menaced German territory. They settled in the lower Danube valley, where they are known today as the Hungarians.

Cathedral of Magdeburg, Germany, where Otto the Great is buried

Establishment of the Holy Roman Empire

Tenth-century Italy was divided into many warring factions. Fearing that a rival duke would seize northern Italy and threaten his monarchy, Otto crossed the Alps, took possession of Lombardy, and proclaimed himself king of Italy. Ten years later, in 962, he crossed the Alps again, this time marching his army into Rome. The pope, who had appealed to him for protection against the Roman nobles, crowned Otto emperor. Like Charlemagne, Otto had come to the pope's rescue and in return had received the emperor's crown. Otto believed that his new role as protector made him superior to the pope, a claim disputed, of course, by the papacy.

The conquests and coronation of Otto revived the memory of the Carolingian and Roman empires. Later German kings considered themselves the successors of Charlemagne and the Roman caesars. Because of its alliance with the Roman Church and its symbolic association with the empire of ancient Rome, the German empire became known as the **Holy Roman**

Holy Roman Empire About 1000

Empire. But as the eighteenth-century French author and philosopher Voltaire observed, it was "neither holy, nor Roman, nor an empire." The empire was built on the union of Germany and Italy and on the alliance of the church and state, neither of which could provide a strong foundation.

Conflict Within the Empire

Conflict of Interest

Although the Holy Roman Empire founded by Otto I became the most powerful state in Europe, it experienced many internal conflicts. The first was a conflict of interest. The German rulers often intervened in Italian affairs. Otto's grandson, Otto III, built a palace in Rome and planned to make Rome the capital of the empire. Concerned for Italy's welfare, the German rulers neglected the affairs of their homeland. This lack of attention gave the German nobles an opportunity to increase their power. The divided interests of the Holy Roman emperors ultimately weakened their authority and hindered efforts to create a unified Italy and a unified Germany.

Conflict with Popes

Another conflict that plagued the empire was the struggle between the emperors and the popes. Beginning with Otto I, the emperors actively intervened in papal affairs. They even began choosing the popes. In addition, they continued the longstanding practice of appointing important church officials within their realm (a situation later to be resolved by the Concordat of Worms in 1122; see p. 180). As the Cluniac reforms spread throughout the Roman Church, the popes began to challenge the emperor's authority, especially in the matter of lay investiture.

Crown of the Holy Roman Empire (962) made for Emperor Otto I (r. 936–73)

Conflict with Nobles

The third and perhaps most damaging conflict within the empire was the one between the German nobles and the Holy Roman emperors. For almost a century while the emperors had been preoccupied with Italian affairs, the German nobles had enjoyed great independence. The situation began to change, however, when a new royal line, the **Salian House** (1024–1125), succeeded the Saxon kings. The Salian kings (including Henry IV) attempted, unsuccessfully, to establish a strong centralized monarchy that would weaken the power of the great nobles. After the death of Henry's son, who had died without an heir, civil war broke out among rival noble families competing for the crown.

The civil wars further weakened the German monarchy and led to the development of feudalism throughout the empire. The large duchies in Italy and Germany broke up into many small states. Powerful nobles became feudal lords, forcing lesser nobles to become their vassals. During this period, several of the strongest nobles firmly established the practice of electing the German monarch. The power of the nobles became supreme in the land.

The Empire Under the Hohenstaufens

In 1152 the German princes hoped to bring an end to the civil wars by choosing as king a member of the Hohenstaufen (HO un SHTOU fun) family, **Frederick I**, also called Barbarossa ("Red Beard"). Frederick (r. 1152–90) sought to restore the glory and stability of what he termed the "holy empire." Like previous German kings, Frederick meddled in Italian affairs. His expeditions brought strong papal opposition. Though most of Frederick's advances into Italy ended in failure, he was successful in forming a marriage alliance between his son and the heiress of the kingdom of Sicily.

The last notable Hohenstaufen ruler was **Frederick II** (r. 1215–50), the grandson of Frederick I. Frederick was heir not only to the German throne but also to the throne of Sicily. The latter kingdom was established by the Normans in the eleventh century and included all of southern Italy. Frederick II grew up in Sicily, where he became acquainted with the Greek and Arab cultures. Later his court would become a leading center of culture. One of the most learned men of his day, he also distinguished himself as a patron of artists and scholars.

As a boy, Frederick became the ward of Pope Innocent III, the most powerful man in Europe. Innocent recognized the threat of having Hohenstaufen possessions encircling the Papal States. Therefore, he secured the German throne for Frederick in return for his promise to give up the throne of Sicily. Shortly after Innocent's death, however, Frederick broke his promise. He devoted almost all his attention to Sicily and Italy, leaving the feudal princes of Germany relatively free from imperial interference. Frederick expanded his Italian holdings and might have united all of Italy under his control had it not been for the resistance of the papacy.

The death of Frederick II in 1250 marked the decline of the Holy Roman Empire. German kings continued to call themselves Holy Roman emperors, but their contact with Italy was minimal. The attempts of the German emperors to unite Germany and Italy ended in failure. Their lack of success marked the beginning of a long period of disunity for the two countries. Not until the late nineteenth century did Italy and Germany become unified national states.

Section Quiz

1. What German king founded the Holy Roman Empire? In what year did this take place?
2. What did the French philosopher Voltaire observe about the Holy Roman Empire?
3. What conflict of interest did many of the German emperors have?
4. From what family did the German princes choose a king in hopes of ending the period of civil war? List two emperors who belonged to this family.

★ Why did the Holy Roman Empire fail to live up to its name?

Alfred the Great

III. Rise of Feudal Monarchies

England

The Anglo-Saxons Settle England

Roman authority over the Celts in Britain came to an end in the early fifth century. After nearly four hundred years of occupation, the Roman legions had to withdraw from the island in order to protect Roman territory on the Continent. Soon afterwards, Germanic tribes from northern Europe, including the **Angles** and the **Saxons**, invaded Britain. They established their own independent kingdoms and transformed "Roman" Britain into England (or "Angle land," meaning the "land of the Angles").

During the ninth century, the Danes (Scandinavian Vikings) began to raid the land. The petty kingdoms of the Angles and Saxons had little success in resisting the Danes—that is, until the time of King **Alfred the Great** (r. 871–899). Alfred, the ruler of the important Saxon kingdom of Wessex, defeated the Danes and pushed them back into northeastern England. He extended his rule over the south of England, laying the foundation for a unified English monarchy.

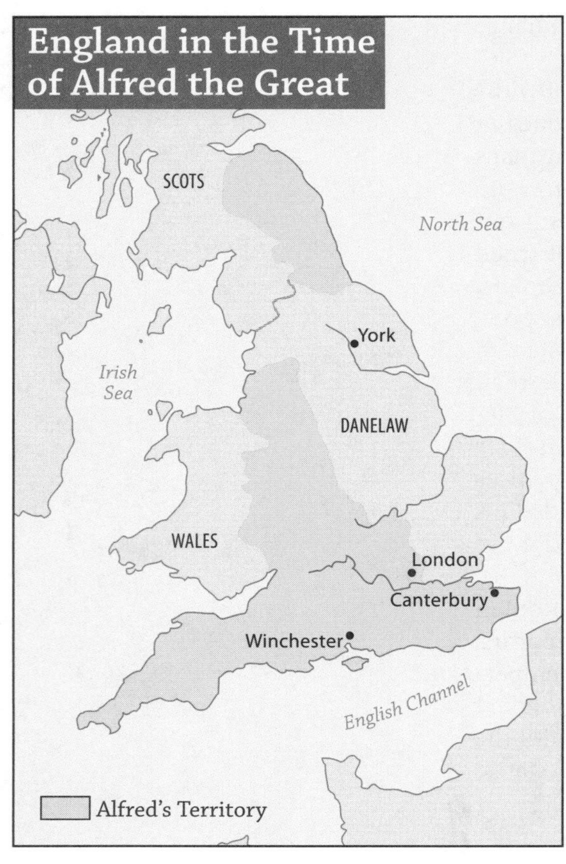

Alfred's success was not confined to the battlefield. He was an able ruler and a patron of learning. He built a navy to repel future Danish invasions—an undertaking that earned him the title "founder of the English navy." He strengthened the Anglo-Saxon practice of local government. His realm was divided into many local districts called **shires** (counties), governed by officials called shire-reeves (from which we get our word *sheriff*). He built churches, founded schools, and invited foreign scholars to his court. During his reign, scholars began to translate important literary works into the common language of the people. In addition, monks began to compile the ***Anglo-Saxon Chronicle***, which traces the history of England from Roman times to Alfred's day. The *Chronicle* was continued after Alfred; monks added current events and revised older passages.

Alfred was a man of strong character. He won the love and respect of his people as well as the admiration of later generations. Unlike many of the men who have been highly praised by historians, Alfred truly deserved the title "the Great." His life demonstrated that true greatness lies not in wealth or worldly fame but in a man's character—not necessarily in what a man does but in what he is.

Less than a century after Alfred's death, the Danes renewed their attacks. England fell to the Danish ruler **Canute**, who made England part of the Danish Empire, which also included Norway. Although Canute ruled England well, his successors were weak. The Anglo-Saxons eventually drove out the Danish rulers and placed **Edward the Confessor** on the throne.

William of Normandy Conquers England

Edward (r. 1042–66) was a descendant of Alfred. He was called "the Confessor" because of his devotion to God. In January of 1066, he died without a direct heir. His cousin William, the French duke of Normandy, claimed the throne, asserting that Edward had promised it to him. The English nobles, however, refused to grant William the crown. Instead they elected **Harold**, the powerful earl of Wessex, king. William refused to be deprived of what he

Britain's Bayeux Tapestry: The Battle of Hastings: Scene 2

thought was rightfully his. Obtaining the blessing of the pope, he raised a large army, crossed the English Channel, and invaded England.

On October 14, 1066, the armies of William, duke of Normandy, and Harold, earl of Wessex, met in the famous **Battle of Hastings**. Much more was at stake than the English throne; the outcome of this battle altered the course of English history. Before the day ended, Harold had been killed and the Anglo-Saxons defeated. William, known as "the Conqueror," established a new line of English kings, the Norman dynasty.

William brought to England the centralized feudalism of Normandy and established himself as feudal lord over the entire country, which, in theory, was now his by right of conquest. He divided his holdings among his military followers, feudal vassals called **tenants-in-chief**. To maintain his power over all the feudal nobles, he required that all who became vassals through subinfeudation also swear allegiance to him as their lord. He also extended his authority over the English church; William—not the pope—appointed the bishops of his realm.

To determine the taxable resources that belonged to him as king, William commissioned a great survey. His royal officials traveled throughout the country gathering detailed information about property holders and their belongings. According to the *Anglo-Saxon Chronicle,* "there was not a single hide or rood [1/4 acre] of land, nor even was there an ox or a cow or a pig left that was not set down in his writings." The findings of the survey were collected in a record known as the ***Domesday Book***.

The Domesday Book

Why was William's census called the *Domesday Book*? Some historians have suggested that the name came from *Domus Dei*, the chapel in which the book was kept in Winchester Cathedral. It has also been suggested that because the book represented the official and final record of a person's holdings, it was compared by the common people to the coming Day of Judgment, or "dooms day," when God will open the Book of Life. Nevertheless, most scholars believe that the word *dome* comes from the Anglo-Saxon word *doom*, which means merely the judgment or decision of the king.

Reforms Strengthen Royal Authority

When William's sons William II and Henry I died without a male heir, the Norman line came to an end. After a period of dispute over rightful succession, the crown passed to the Plantagenet (or Angevin) family, founded by **Henry II** (r. 1154–89), the great-grandson of William the Conqueror. A Frenchman, Henry possessed more wealth and territory outside of England than within. Through inheritance and marriage, he had gained landholdings in France that far surpassed those ruled directly by his feudal lord, the French king. This situation provoked jealous rivalry between the French and English thrones.

Henry II

Henry strengthened royal authority in England by expanding the jurisdiction of the royal courts. Before this time, each lord had his own court for deciding cases concerning his vassals and serfs. Henry established circuit courts with justices who traveled throughout the land hearing cases. During Henry's time, the circuit courts usually heard only cases involving land disputes, but later other cases were handled also.

Before the circuit justices arrived in a shire, a jury composed of men of that district would make a list of **indictments** (accusations) of what crimes had been committed and who the suspected offenders were. (From this practice arose the modern-day grand jury, which decides whether there is sufficient evidence to hold an accused person for trial.) When the justice heard a case, he often relied on information supplied by a smaller jury of men acquainted with the facts of the case. Gradually, it became the accepted practice to have "twelve good and truthful men" serve on this jury, the forerunner of trial juries in America. Unlike their modern counterparts, however, these men gave evidence upon which the justice could render a verdict, instead of being the ones to hear the evidence and give the verdict.

As a result of Henry's judicial reforms, more cases were tried in the royal courts than in the feudal ones. The decisions of Henry's justices provided uniform laws for all of England and thus superseded the local feudal laws. This **common law** not only helped ensure justice but also helped to draw the English people together into a unified nation.

Henry hoped to strengthen his authority over the church by appointing his friend **Thomas à Becket** archbishop of Canterbury, the highest church office in England. Once in office, however, Becket became a bitter opponent of Henry's interference in church matters. The controversy reached a climax when Henry attempted to bring clerics who committed grave crimes to trial in royal, instead of church, courts. Becket resisted. Outraged by his opposition, Henry reportedly exclaimed, "What a pack of fools and cowards I have nourished in my house, that not one of them will avenge me of this turbulent priest!" Four knights, hearing the king's rash words, traveled to Canterbury and murdered the archbishop at his altar. Because of the popular uproar over Becket's death in 1170, the king abandoned his plans to control the clergy. Becket became a martyr and his tomb a popular shrine.

Magna Carta Limits Royal Power

After Henry's death his oldest son **Richard I** (r. 1189–99) became king. Richard, known as "the Lion-Hearted," was an able warrior and an admired crusader. Nevertheless, he contributed little to the English crown. He spent less than six months of his ten-year reign in England. His participation in the Third Crusade (see p. 197) and the defense of his French holdings from the king of France occupied most of his reign. While he was absent from England, his brother John

Trial by Ordeal

One way the Anglo-Saxons attempted to determine the innocence or guilt of a person charged with a crime was trial by ordeal. There were four forms of trial by ordeal.

Trial by cold water. The charged person was taken to a pond, which was blessed by a priest. He was bound hand and foot and thrown into the water. If he floated, he was judged guilty, for the "holy water" had rejected him. If he sank, he was judged innocent, for the water had accepted him. He was then rescued—presumably in time to save his life; if not, his innocence supposedly merited entrance into heaven.

Trial by hot water. A person was forced to plunge his arm into boiling water. A priest would then wrap a bandage around his arm. After three days the bandage was removed. If the arm was blistered, the man was judged guilty; but if it had healed, he was judged innocent. Our saying "in hot water" probably comes from this ordeal.

Trial by hot iron. This ordeal was much like trial by hot water, except in this case a person had to carry a red-hot piece of iron in his hands for a prescribed distance.

Trial by morsel. A person was made to swallow a lump of dough. If he choked, he was judged guilty; if he did not, he was judged innocent.

The people of the Middle Ages falsely believed that God would immediately reveal guilt or innocence through these means. With the rise of the royal courts of Henry II, trial by ordeal in England gradually came to an end. By the time of King John's reign, it had all but disappeared. It then became the practice to determine the guilt or innocence of an accused person by the facts of the case rather than by an ordeal.

and the king of France plotted to overthrow him. His reign provides the setting for the adventures of the legendary English hero Robin Hood.

The death of Richard elevated **John** (r. 1199–1216) to the English throne. John was a competent ruler, but he lacked the strong personal qualities that had won Richard the trust and admiration of the people. John's weak will and cruel, unscrupulous ways brought him nothing but trouble. John's reign was marked by continual conflict with three formidable opponents: the French king, the pope, and the English nobles—all of whom got the better of him. The French king Philip II took advantage of John's weakness and extended his royal control over many of John's French possessions.

In the meantime, John clashed with Pope Innocent III over who would be the next archbishop of Canterbury. When the archbishop of Canterbury died in 1206 and John failed to appoint a new one, the monks at Canterbury decided that they would choose a new archbishop. (This choice was usually made with the approval of the king and the English bishops.) The monks sent the man of their choice to Rome to be confirmed by the pope. When John heard of this, he was outraged and had the bishops choose another man, who was also sent to Rome. When both men arrived in Rome, Innocent III refused to confirm either. Instead he selected a friend of his, an English cardinal named Stephen Langton, to be archbishop. When John refused to allow Stephen into England (he had been out of the country for several years), trouble broke out.

Key Provisions of the Magna Carta

Certain provisions of the Magna Carta transcended the immediate occasion for which they were framed and became the bases of later political concepts.

No Taxation Without Representation. "No scutage [a feudal tax] or aid shall be imposed in our kingdom save by the common council of our kingdom." (clause 12)

Trial by Jury and Due Process of Law. "No freeman shall be taken, or imprisoned, or dispossessed, or outlawed, or banished, or in any way injured, nor will we go upon him, nor send upon him, except by the legal judgment of his peers, or by the law of the land. To no one will we sell, to no one will we deny or delay, right or justice." (clauses 39–40)

Innocent placed England under an interdict and excommunicated the king. Having no allies and threatened by a French invasion, John submitted to the pope, even to the point of becoming the pope's vassal and making England a fief of the papacy. Restored to the pope's graces, John was able to avert Philip's invasion of England. However, he was not able to put down a rebellion of the English barons (nobles).

Magna Carta Memorial at Runnymede

The English barons were dissatisfied with John's reign. They resented his excessive taxes and his disregard for their feudal privileges. In 1215, the infuriated nobles revolted. At Runnymede, a meadow near London, they forced John to set his seal to the **Magna Carta** (Latin for "Great Charter"). Originally intended as a guarantee of feudal rights, the Magna Carta became one of the most important documents in English history. Later Englishmen looked to the Magna Carta as establishing the principle that the king's power is limited: the king is not above the law and can be removed for refusing to obey it.

Parliament Becomes an Important Institution

One of England's most gifted medieval kings was **Edward I** (1272–1307). He attempted to extend English rule over all of Britain—Wales, Scotland, and England. He conquered Wales and made his son Prince of Wales. (Since that time, it has been customary to confer the title "Prince of Wales" on the eldest male heir to the English throne.) Edward's attempts to subdue Scotland, however, met with fierce resistance.

Probably the most important and enduring contribution of Edward's reign was the development of **Parliament**. It had always been the custom of English kings to seek counsel from a group of advisers. The Anglo-Saxon kings had the **witan**, an assembly of the great men of the kingdom. William the Conqueror established the Great Council—also known as the ***curia regis*** (king's council)—a feudal body composed of his chief vassals.

When Edward became king, he enlarged the membership of the Great Council to include representative knights from every shire and representative burgesses (citizens) from every town. The word *parliament* (from a French word meaning "to speak" or "to discuss") came to designate this expanded assembly. The meeting of Parliament during Edward's reign has been called the "Model Parliament" because it had the basic features of later Parliaments.

In the fourteenth century, members of Parliament met in two separate groups: the chief vassals in one, and the knights and burgesses in another. The members of the latter group were called the "Commons" because they represented the community. Their assembly became known as the House of Commons, and that of the chief feudal lords became known as the House of Lords.

Over the centuries Parliament became more and more powerful. Edward had acknowledged that the king could not propose new taxes without the consent of Parliament. Therefore he, as well as his successors, had to summon Parliament regularly in order to obtain needed revenue. The members of Parliament soon discovered that by withholding their approval of new taxes, they could force the king to hear their grievances. This "**power of the purse**," as it came to be called, gradually transformed Parliament from an advisory body into a legislative body. The rise of Parliament served as a check on the king's power and in later centuries helped to convert English government into a limited monarchy.

France

The Capetians and Their Royal House

The kingdom of West Frankland, once the heart of the Carolingian Empire, broke up into many feudal realms soon after the death of Charlemagne in 814.

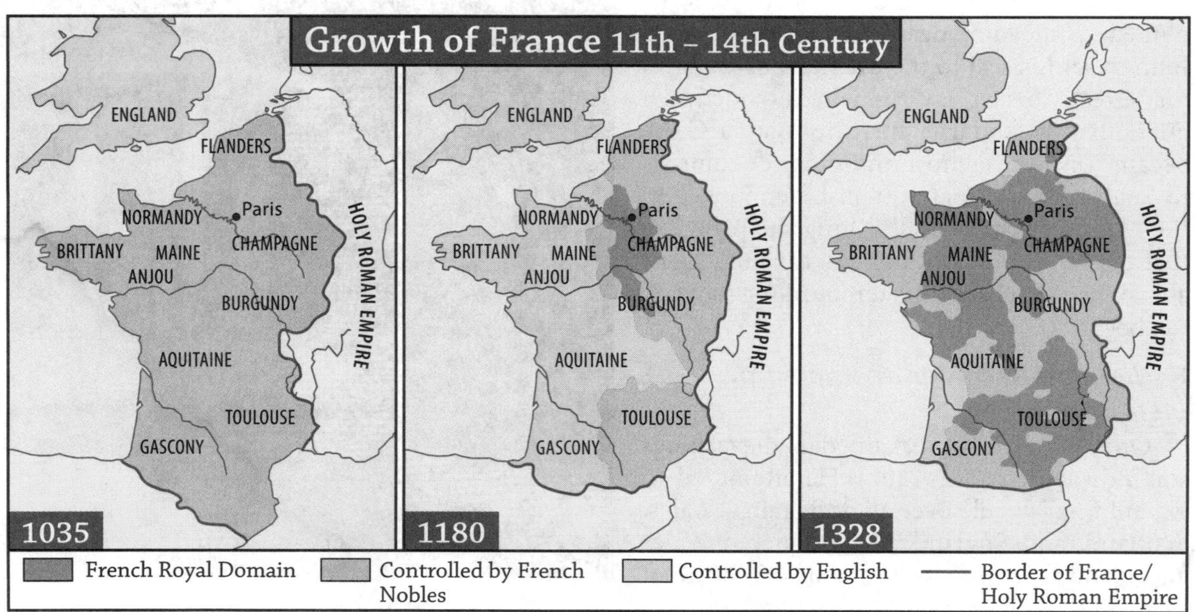

In 987 the great feudal lords chose the count of Paris, **Hugh Capet** (KAY pit; r. 987–96), as their king, thus ending the weak rule of the Carolingian monarchs. Hugh founded a new royal line, the Capetian (kuh PEE shun) House, whose members built a strong feudal monarchy in France.

Many factors helped the Capetian kings to steadily increase their power over the feudal lords. For instance, for more than three hundred years every Capetian king had a son to succeed him. There were therefore no wars of succession to threaten the stability and continuity of royal power. This power gradually increased as the size of the royal domain increased. Capetian rulers enlarged their royal possessions by conquest and through marriage alliances. They also developed an effective system of centralized government, which laid the foundation for the French national state. Furthermore, the Capetians found valuable allies in the Roman Church and townspeople. By tapping the wealth of the towns and the church, the Capetians won financial independence from the great feudal lords.

Philip II and Royal Expansion

Although the early Capetians bore the title of king, they actually ruled only a small area around Paris, known as the **Île-de-France** (EEL duh FRAHNS). Like an island, it was surrounded by feudal lands ruled by the king's vassals. Many of these vassals were powerful lords possessing more land and authority than the French king. (William, duke of Normandy and Henry Plantagenet are noted examples.)

The early Capetian kings were constantly struggling to maintain control of their feudal holdings. Not until the reign of the fifth Capetian king, Louis VI (r. 1108–37), did the French king become master of his royal domain. For the first time the Capetians had a strong and solid base from which they would extend their royal power over the rest of the kingdom. It was **Philip II** "Augustus" (r. 1180–1223), however, who became known as the real founder of France. By enlarging the territory under his rule and by increasing his power over his vassals, he began a period of Capetian predominance.

The chief obstacle to the expansion of royal power in France was the large amount of land held by the English kings. Although the Plantagenets were vassals of the French king, their landholdings in France far exceeded those ruled directly by the French king. Philip II attempted to deprive the English kings Henry II and Richard the Lion-Hearted of their continental holdings but met with little success. He found King John easier to deal with. A controversy broke out between John and one of his French vassals. When John refused to stand trial in Philip's court as the French monarch's vassal, Philip declared John's French lands forfeited. Because John had lost the support of his French vassals and had alienated the English nobles, he lost Normandy, Anjou, Maine, and Touraine to Philip. The French king had broken the power of King John in France and, in doing so, had tripled the size of his own royal domain.

Philip also increased the effectiveness of royal government. He replaced local feudal officials with new royal ones called ***baillis*** (bah YEE), or bailiffs, whom the king appointed and paid. Similar to Henry II's itinerant justices, these bailiffs collected royal taxes, enforced feudal rights, and administered justice, reinforcing the king's authority throughout his realm.

Philip's attempts to increase royal power in France met with one major setback. Shortly after taking a Danish princess as his wife, Philip had his marriage annulled by the French bishops. Pope Innocent III, who seized every opportunity to intervene in the internal affairs of the European states, refused to recognize the annulment. He excommunicated Philip and placed France under an interdict. Forced to back down, Philip took back his Danish wife; but in doing so he had to put away another wife, whom he had married in the meantime.

Louis IX and Royal Dignity

Philip's grandson, King **Louis IX** (r. 1226–70), has been called the ideal medieval king. He combined sincere piety and just rule to build respect and loyalty for the French throne. His character is demonstrated in the instruction he gave to his son and heir:

> Fair son, the first thing I would teach thee is to set thine heart to love God; for unless he love God none can be saved. . . .
>
> If God send thee adversity, receive it in patience, and give thanks to our Saviour, and bethink thee that thou hast deserved it, and that He will make it turn to thine advantage. If he send thee prosperity, then thank Him humbly, so that thou become not worse from pride. . . .
>
> Maintain the good customs of thy realm, and abolish the bad. Be not covetous against thy people; and do not burden them with taxes and imposts save when thou art in great need. . . .
>
> See that thou hast in thy company men, whether religious or lay, who are right worthy, and loyal, and not full of covetousness, and confer with them oft: and fly and eschew the company of the wicked. Hearken willingly to the Word of God and keep it in thine heart. . . .
>
> Give often thanks to God for all the good things He has bestowed upon thee, so that thou be accounted worthy to receive more.
>
> In order to do justice and right to thy subjects, be upright and firm, turning neither to the right hand nor to the left, but always to what is just.
>
> *Sir Frank Marzials,* Memoirs of the Crusades, *321–22.*

Concerned about the welfare of his subjects, Louis IX made peace and justice the primary goals of his reign. He sought to protect the rights of all, regardless of their rank in society. Louis further expanded the jurisdiction of the royal courts over the feudal courts. He also established a permanent royal court at Paris, which served as the supreme court of the land. Fearful that his royal agents (the bailiffs) might infringe the feudal rights of his subjects, he appointed special men to search out abuses in the royal government. He was also the first French king to issue ordinances (i.e., legislation) without first consulting his chief vassals. His efforts at judicial reform earned him the title "the French Justinian."

Louis IX led two crusades against the Muslims in North Africa. Although he was a zealous warrior, both campaigns failed. While on his second crusade, he contracted a disease and died. He is remembered in history as "Saint Louis."

Pope Boniface VIII

Philip IV and Royal Strength

The climax of Capetian rule came during the reign of **Philip IV** (1285–1314). Known as "the Fair" (because of his handsome features), Philip IV further expanded royal power in France. He strengthened the organization and authority of the central government. As the royal government increased in size, the king needed greater revenue. Philip therefore taxed the French people as no French king before him had done.

The need for revenue led Philip to tax the French clergy also. Pope **Boniface VIII** stepped in and decreed that no king could impose a tax on clergy. Philip countered by refusing to allow gold and silver (especially the tithes of the French church) to be exported from France, thus decreasing the papal revenues. In another controversy, Philip defied Boniface's authority despite the threat of being excommunicated or having an interdict placed on his land (see p. 183). Philip succeeded where others had failed in defying the papacy because he had the support of the French people. Their loyalty was gradually shifting away from the Roman Church and the papacy to the state and the French king.

To strengthen popular support for his policies, Philip summoned representatives from the church, the nobility, and the townspeople to meet at Paris. The meetings of these three estates (or classes) became known as the **Estates-General**. The king sought advice from this representative body, but he did not wait for its consent to enforce legislation or raise taxes. Thus the power of the French monarch grew without restraints such as those the English Parliament imposed on the English kings. This trend partly explains why the French government developed into an absolute monarchy while the English government became a limited monarchy.

Section Quiz

1. What man defeated the Danes and laid the foundation for a unified English monarchy?
2. What two men struggled for the English throne in 1066? What was the name of the battle where this issue was settled? Who won?
3. On what document did English nobles force King John to affix his royal seal? In what year did this take place?
4. What ruling family came to power in France following the last of the Carolingian monarchs? List five kings in this section who belonged to this royal family.
5. List the English and the French advisory/representative assemblies that developed during this period and identify each with its respective country.

★ Why were the French rulers able to gain independence from feudal lords, while the English rulers were forced to work with and share power with English feudal lords?

Pope Urban II

IV. Rescue of the Holy Land

For centuries tourists have flocked to see the land where Christianity began. Even in medieval times eager pilgrims from Europe journeyed to the Holy Land. They viewed Jerusalem as the center of the earth and revered the sites associated with the life of Christ as sacred places. Many of these people journeyed to Jerusalem to demonstrate their piety; others hoped to earn forgiveness of sins. Many believed that somehow they could draw nearer to God's presence by visiting the holy places.

The Call

During the eleventh century, the Seljuk Turks advanced into Palestine and seized the holy places of Christendom, making it almost impossible for European pilgrims to travel to the sacred sites. They also invaded Asia Minor and threatened the security of Constantinople. Seeing his land in peril, the Byzantine emperor appealed to Christians in the West for help against the Turks. Pilgrims returning from the Holy Land also called for the recovery of the holy places, describing the terrible atrocities committed by the Muslim Turks against churches, monasteries, and groups of pilgrims.

Crusader castle in modern Syria

In 1095 Pope **Urban II** addressed a council of church leaders and French noblemen at Clermont, France, calling for a holy crusade to free the Holy Land from the Turks: "This royal city [Jerusalem] . . . situated at the center of the earth, is now held captive by the enemies of Christ. . . . She seeks, therefore, and desires to be liberated and ceases not to implore you to come to her aid." He called on the feudal nobles to stop fighting one another and to join instead in fighting the Turks. He urged them to avenge the wrongs done by this "wicked race," to "enter upon the road to the Holy Sepulcher [the tomb where Christ was buried]," and to "wrest that land from the wicked race, and subject it to yourselves."

The response to Urban's moving appeal was overwhelming; those present were said to have enthusiastically answered, "It is the will of God!" Urban is reported to have replied: "Let these words be your war-cry when you unsheathe the sword. You are soldiers of the cross. Wear on your breasts or shoulders the blood-red sign of the cross. Wear it as a token that His help will never fail you, as the pledge of a vow never to be recalled." During the two centuries that followed, many Europeans were obsessed with the winning of the Holy Land. Wandering preachers spread the idea, causing thousands to answer the call. The people were convinced by leaders of the Roman Church that their task was "God's work" and that they were fighting a "holy war." They went forth with the symbol of the cross sewn on their garments. Those marked by a cross were called crusaders, and their military campaigns became known as the **Crusades** (derived from the Latin *crux*, meaning "cross").

The Crusaders: Their Motives

What prompted the crusaders to leave their homes and journey such long distances to fight the Turks? Some had a pious desire to serve Christ, to defend the church, and to rescue the Holy Sepulcher. At the same time there were

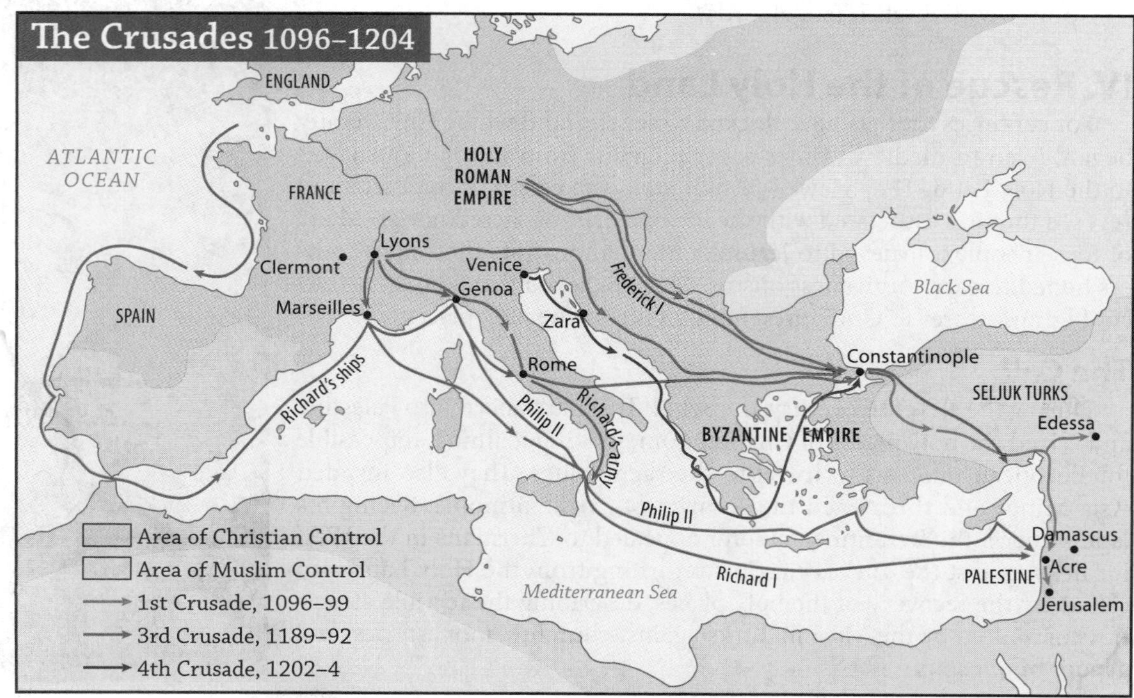

those who desired adventure, seeking an escape from the humdrum life on the manor. Still others hoped to gain fame or fortune. Some knights joined a crusade simply because they could enjoy their favorite pastime—fighting—with the blessing of the Roman Church. Merchants embarked on the Crusades looking for new opportunities for commercial gain.

The Roman Church was a powerful force behind the Crusades. The promise of both earthly and heavenly rewards convinced many to take the crusader's vow. Church leaders guaranteed the protection of the family and property of the crusader while he was away. Criminals and debtors undertaking the so-called holy cause received pardons. In fact, some of the popes proclaimed that participation in the Crusades was a substitute for penance. Hardened sinners were told they could earn forgiveness of sins by joining one of these campaigns. Furthermore, many in the Roman Church assured the crusaders that anyone who died while on a crusade would be granted eternal life. Notice the similarity of this false teaching to that of Islam (see p. 123). Both proclaimed their cause to be a holy war. Both promised paradise to their warriors who fell in battle.

The Campaigns

There were eight major Crusades between 1095 and 1291. Some crusaders traveled alone or in small bands; most, however, joined the large organized expeditions.

The First Crusade

Excitement mounted as the year of departure drew near for the first major expedition (1096–99) to the East. Masses of zealous peasants, eager to reach the Holy City, embarked on the long journey in advance of the main armies. These common people had few supplies and even less fighting experience. Those that survived the perilous journey found themselves no match for the Turks, who slaughtered them.

The crusaders' cause fared much better when the main body of knights reached Palestine. Despite the heat, a shortage of supplies, and dissension among their leaders, the crusaders broke Muslim resistance and succeeded in capturing Jerusalem. After taking the city, they slaughtered its inhabitants. According to an exaggerated eyewitness account, the city was filled with corpses and blood. In the temple area alone, "men rode in blood up to their knees and bridle reins. Indeed," the account continues, "it was a just and splendid judgment of God that this place should be filled with the blood of unbelievers, since it had suffered so long from their blasphemies."

Of all the crusades, the first was the most successful. Besides winning the Holy City, the crusaders established four small feudal kingdoms along the Mediterranean coastline. It was not long, however, before a new Muslim offensive threatened these so-called Crusader states. In response the Second Crusade was launched in 1147. Unlike the first, this second campaign ended in miserable failure, with the Western forces suffering defeat at the hands of the Turks.

Statue of Saladin

The Kings' Crusade

In 1187 the Muslims recaptured Jerusalem under their new leader, **Saladin**. News of Saladin's victory stirred the Europeans to organize the Third Crusade, also known as the Kings' Crusade (1189–92). Three of the most powerful kings in Europe led the crusading armies: Frederick Barbarossa of Germany, Philip Augustus of France, and Richard the Lion-Hearted of England. This Crusade began as the largest of all, but troubles plagued the expedition from the start.

The Children's Crusade

In 1212, Pope Innocent III called for a new Crusade. According to chronicles of the day, the response was unexpected. Those who gathered by the thousands, in towns throughout France and many German states, were children rather than adults. Filled with religious zeal, the children set out for the Holy Land convinced that God wanted to use them to free it from Muslim control.

Accounts describe a young shepherd boy named Stephen from the town of Cloyes, France, who had a vision. He claimed that Christ told him to lead a Crusade of children to the Holy Land. Stephen journeyed to St. Denys just north of Paris, where he encouraged other children to join him. Word spread quickly, and by August thousands of children had gathered. Stephen told them that God had promised that the Mediterranean Sea would open for them so they could walk through on dry land just as the children of Israel had walked through the Red Sea. Following Stephen, they marched toward the sea.

When news of Stephen's vision reached Germany, another young boy, Nicholas, felt that he too was called to lead a Crusade. He attracted a large following in the city of Cologne. (Like St. Denys, Cologne was a pilgrim center.) Of the thousands of children who left with Nicholas, only about a third reached the Mediterranean coast. When the sea did not open, they were sadly disillusioned; too weary to travel home, the surviving children were said to have remained in Italy.

Meanwhile, Stephen's group reached Marseille, a crusader port in southern France. They too discovered that the sea did not open for them. Many returned home, but a few thousand remained, still hoping for a miracle. It was then that two merchants offered the children free passage to the Holy Land. Thinking that this was God's miracle, they accepted. Of the seven ships that set sail, two wrecked on an island during a storm. The other five made their way to the North African coast, where the merchants sold the children into slavery. Following eighteen years of silence, a priest who had accompanied the children and who was himself enslaved, escaped and made his way back to Europe and told of the fate of the children.

Fort St. Jean in Marseille, France; Marseille was a Crusader port in southern France.

Frederick drowned on the way to the Holy Land. In addition, constant strife between Richard and Philip led Philip to return to France with his army shortly after his arrival in the Holy Land. Richard remained and defeated Saladin in many battles, but he did not succeed in taking Jerusalem. Richard and Saladin then agreed to a three-year truce that allowed Western pilgrims free access to the holy places in Jerusalem.

The "Diverted" Crusade

Unlike earlier crusaders who maintained the pretense of a religious undertaking, the participants of the Fourth Crusade (1201–4) soon abandoned the ideals of their predecessors and openly pursued political and economic ends. Venetian merchants agreed to transport the crusaders to the East, but because of miscalculation, the crusaders were unable to pay the transportation fees. In order to pay their way, they agreed to support a Venetian attack on the city of Zara, a rival seaport in the Adriatic. The conquest of this city whetted the crusaders' appetite for plunder and booty and weakened their desire to reach the Holy Land. The Venetians realized this and diverted the crusaders to Constantinople, Venice's chief rival. The wayward warriors never reached the Holy Land and never raised a sword against the Muslims. Instead, they attacked the Byzantines, who had originally requested their help against the Turks. In 1204 Constantinople fell to the crusaders, who pillaged the city (see p. 114).

The Later Crusades

Crusaders continued to journey to the Holy Land throughout the thirteenth century. But their campaigns were no more successful than the earlier ones. The expeditions were poorly organized and lacked strong leadership. Meanwhile, attitudes in Europe were changing. With each failed campaign, the religious zeal and fighting spirit so prevalent in Europe before the Crusades gradually subsided. Soon Europe became occupied with new expeditions. These were dominated by rising nations rather than the Roman Church and were motivated by commercial interests more than religious concerns. The crusader was replaced by the explorer. The motto "take up the cross" was changed to "seek out and discover." And the goal of recovering the Holy Land gave way to finding new commercial routes to the Far East.

The Consequences

For the Middle East

The Seljuk Empire declined and eventually came under the domination of the Ottoman Empire. However, the change of empires did not affect the dominance of Islam in the Middle East. In addition, Muslim traders sold goods at exorbitant prices to Europeans, who had come to place a great value on the spices, fruits, and other commodities brought back to Europe by the crusaders and European merchants. This led to a rush for European nations to find alternate routes to the East in order to bypass the Muslim middlemen.

For Medieval Europe

Although it is impossible to measure the effects of the Crusades on western Europe, there is little doubt that they brought about several profound changes. The following are the most evident:

1. The Crusades weakened the feudal structure of Europe. Feudal nobles, seeking to raise money to go on Crusades, allowed the serfs to buy their freedom. Freed serfs left the manors with hopes of finding new opportunities in the growing towns. With the decline of the feudal structure came the emergence of strong nations ruled by kings. Under the pretext of financing the Crusades,

several European kings gained the power to tax. Taxation provided badly needed revenues, which monarchs used to extend their powers.

2. The Crusades expanded the commercial activity of Europe. The crusaders were amazed at the riches they found in the East. They came to know and desire such luxuries as sugar, spices, fruits, silks, cotton, and glass mirrors (which were obtained by Middle Eastern countries primarily through trade with the Orient). The heightened demand for these goods in Europe led enterprising individuals to import them. The increase in trade prompted the renewal of a money economy (as opposed to a barter system) and the need for banking services. It also motivated Europeans to search for even greater profits by finding new routes to the wealth in the East.

3. The early Crusades strengthened the leadership of the papacy. The popes called for the Crusades and collected taxes or tithes for their financing. They were thus able to extend their powers in both secular and sacred matters. As most of the Crusades failed, however, people became disillusioned and began to disregard the continued calls for new Crusades by the papacy. Respect for the crusading ideals and the papacy continued to diminish as popes called for Crusades to seek out and kill so-called heretics in Europe and battle with unruly German kings.

4. The Crusades opened new horizons to the people of medieval Europe. Contact with the East changed their attitudes and introduced them to other civilizations, such as the Byzantine and Muslim empires. In addition, the Crusades renewed interest in the knowledge of ancient Greece and Rome—knowledge that had been preserved by the civilizations in the East. Furthermore, the Europeans' travel experiences and increased understanding of world geography gave impetus to the later period of exploration.

Section Quiz

1. What pope called for a holy crusade to free the Holy Land from the Turks? In what year did this occur?
2. How many major Crusades were there? Over what span of years did they occur?
3. What is the nickname of the Third Crusade? List the kings (with their countries) who went on this crusade.
4. To where was the Fourth Crusade diverted? Who diverted the Crusade?

★ Did the Crusades ultimately strengthen or weaken the papacy? Defend your answer.

Chapter 9 Review

Making Connections

1. How did Henry II of England and Philip II of France strengthen royal authority in their respective countries?

2–4. Why did Europeans join the Crusades? List three reasons.

Developing History Skills

1. Beginning with one of the consequences of the Crusades, make a list of historical events or developments that proceeded from this consequence.

Thinking Critically

1. Contrast the reigns of John of England and Louis IX of France in light of scriptural passages including Proverbs 16:5–7, 12, 18–19.
2. Was fighting in holy wars like the Crusades a worthy goal for the Christians of that day?

Living in God's World

1. In the Middle Ages, church and state struggled over which would be supreme. In the modern-day West, the church and state have been separated from one another. Evaluate these three options biblically: church over state, state over church, church and state separate.
2. Imagine that you are a feudal lord in the Middle Ages. How should being a Christian affect the way that you act?

People, Places, and Things to Know

lay investiture
Cistercians
Bernard of Clairvaux
College of Cardinals
Gregory VII
friars
mendicant orders
Francis of Assisi
Dominic
Innocent III
Henry the Fowler
Otto I
Holy Roman Empire
Salian House
Frederick I
Frederick II
Angles
Saxons
Alfred the Great
shires
Anglo-Saxon Chronicle
Canute
Edward the Confessor
Harold
Battle of Hastings
tenants-in-chief
Domesday Book
Henry II
indictments
common law
Thomas à Becket
Richard I
John
Magna Carta
Edward I
Parliament
witan
curia regis
power of the purse
Hugh Capet
Île-de-France
Philip II
baillis
Louis IX
Philip IV
Boniface VIII
Estates-General
Urban II
Crusades
Saladin

The Reshaping of Medieval Europe

- I. Revival of Trade
- II. Growth of Towns
- III. Medieval Learning and Art
- IV. Emergence of National States
- V. Decline of the Roman Church

The growth of towns dramatically changed the social structure of medieval Europe.

In the previous chapter, we discussed the religious life of people in the Middle Ages. In this chapter, we will discuss the economic, social, and political developments of the Middle Ages, which reveal the beginnings of modern Western society. All of these aspects are intertwined. During the late medieval period (1200–1500), Europe experienced significant changes. Merchants pursued trade with renewed vigor, towns grew in size and importance, and a new social class emerged. Contact with other cultures sparked interest in learning and the arts, and national states began to appear. At the same time, the feudal and manorial systems weakened, and the Roman Church, once the dominant force in Europe, declined in strength and influence.

Great Hall of Study at the University of Bologna

I. Revival of Trade

During the early Middle Ages, trade activity sharply declined in Europe. Money was in short supply. Travel was often treacherous since roads were poor, and robbers and pirates often threatened merchants on the trade routes. Towns, which were once the heart of economic activity, declined in size. The manors became the new economic centers of medieval Europe. Unlike towns and cities, manors depended less on trade and were virtually self-sufficient. The few items that could not be made or grown on a particular manor could be obtained by barter—exchanging goods for goods. For the most part, trade remained localized and relatively insignificant.

Trade Routes

The reopening of trade routes between western Europe and the East became a major factor in the revival of European commerce. During the early Middle Ages, Byzantine and Muslim merchants had dominated trade in the Mediterranean region. Later, however, enterprising Italian merchants, with their large fleets, began to secure trade rights in the Near East. Soon Italian cities such as Venice, Pisa, and Genoa gained a virtual monopoly on Mediterranean trade.

European commerce expanded as the Italian merchants became middlemen in trade between Europe and the Orient. Once goods from the Far East reached the Mediterranean, Italian merchants transported them to Europe, where they were distributed to European markets. Traders who brought goods from the Orient reached the Mediterranean by three principal routes:

1. The southern route was almost entirely on water. Ships laden with goods from India and China sailed across the Arabian Sea and northward up the Red Sea. The goods were then hauled overland to the Nile River and transported to the Mediterranean.

2. The central route combined land and sea travel. Ships from the Far East carried goods to the Persian Gulf, where caravans transported the merchandise to Baghdad or Damascus. Other traders then brought the goods to port cities along the Mediterranean and Black Seas.

3. The northern route, known as the "Silk Road," was an overland route across central Asia. It connected Beijing and Constantinople.

Italy controlled Mediterranean trade, but Flanders was the marketplace of northern Europe. The region of Flanders (which included parts of present-day Belgium, France, and Holland) lay at the crossroads of northern European trade routes. The Flemish, who were makers of fine cloth, had easy access to the markets of Europe.

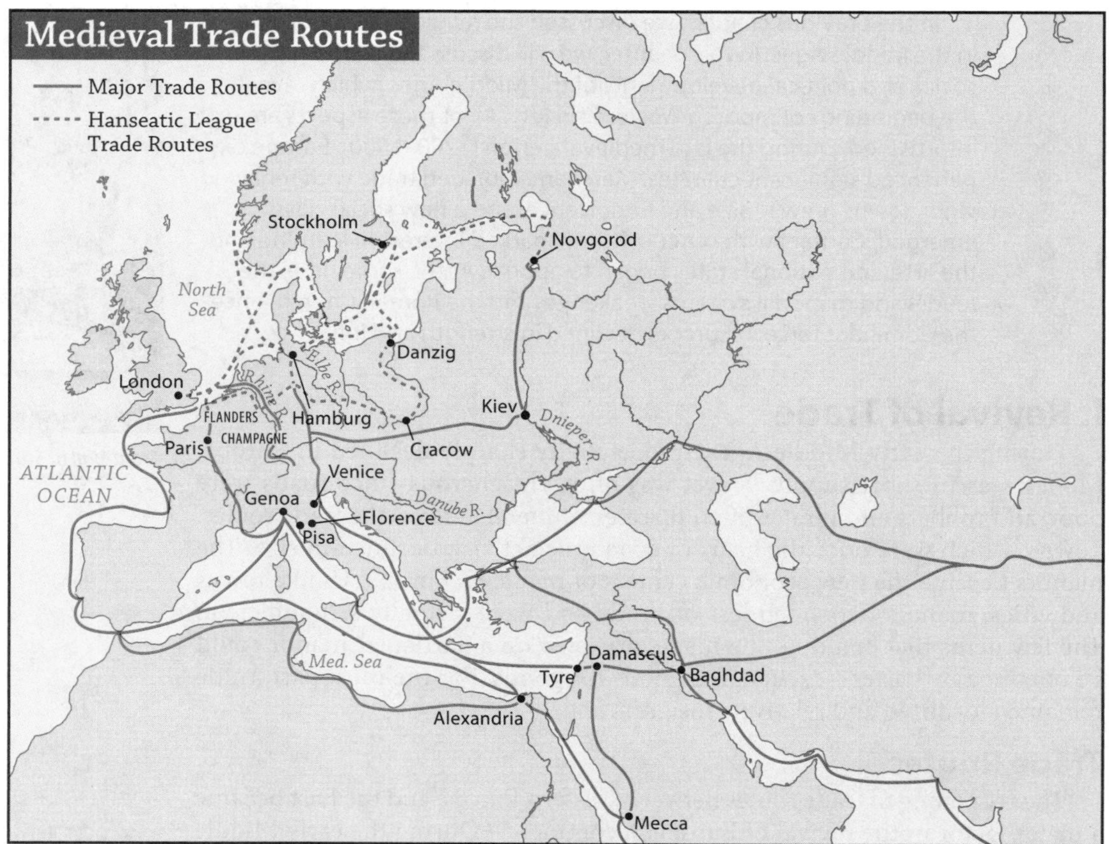

Markets and Fairs

As trade activity increased, so did the need for places where merchants could meet and exchange their goods. On the local level, markets became the primary centers for trade. Once a week traders met along important highways, in church courtyards, or in village squares. The goods sold there benefited both the people on the manor and those in the towns. The market offered incentive for the laboring serfs to produce more because at the market they could sell their surplus produce. Many serfs saved their money, desiring to buy goods or hoping one day to be able to buy their freedom from the manor. The market also offered craftsmen and merchants an opportunity to sell their goods. Thus, these places of trade met the demands of the local population. Townspeople obtained surplus food from the manors, and the people of the manor acquired articles made and sold by local craftsmen and merchants.

Trade fairs operated on a larger scale than local markets and attracted merchants from all over Europe as well as many foreign countries. These fairs were sometimes great regional or international events. Merchants assembled annually, and the fairs could last from several days to several weeks. Because they were held in nearly every part of Europe, fairs were often scheduled in sequence so that merchants could attend one after the other.

Fairs provided a meeting place for East-West trade. Italian middlemen and foreign merchants from Constantinople, Damascus, and Alexandria brought spices, silks, precious gems, cotton, linen, rugs, and dyes from the East. Peddlers and town merchants bought these "luxury" items and distributed them locally. In return, foreign merchants purchased local products such as wool, grain, timber, and fish.

One of the most famous and important of the medieval fairs was held in Champagne, a region in northeastern France. This province became an important trade center for merchants traveling between Flanders and Italy. At almost any time during the year, fairs were being held in the towns of this region, each one lasting about six weeks.

Fairs such as the ones at Champagne were more than just places to exchange goods; they were festive occasions.

> The neighboring lords and their families came to see and to buy and to enjoy the diversions of the fair. The monks from the abbey and the secular clergy mingled with the throng. No doubt many an artisan and many a runaway serf from the neighboring manors was drawn hither by the strange sights and sounds and the gay-colored crowd. Mountebanks [sellers of "medicine"], jugglers, and musicians of every description vied in their efforts to attract the crowd, men with trained monkeys, dogs, or dancing bears, wrestlers, wandering minstrels singing ancient lays, fakers [magicians] without number were there to entertain and astonish the populace. There were gathered as in modern fairs the thief, the pick-pocket, the cutpurse, the thug, the prostitute, beggars. Often the sergeants were hard pressed to maintain order in this heterogeneous mob.
>
> James Thompson, *An Economic and Social History of the Middle Ages*, 602.

Portrait of a merchant
bpk, Berlin / Gemaeldegalerie, Staatliche Museen / Holbein, Hans the Younger / Art Resource, NY

Money and Banking

The barter system in use during the early Middle Ages could not meet the expanding demands of the trade fairs. Therefore, money gained wider use as a means of exchange. This development helped trade and provided a standard of value for the purchase and sale of goods. Feudal lords and commercial towns began minting their own coins. Their values varied greatly, depending on the amount and purity of the metal contained in them. Certain coins of high quality became widely accepted as mediums of exchange. One, for example, was the **florin**, a gold coin minted by the city of Florence.

Because most merchants did not know the value of coins minted outside their own region, **moneychangers** grew in importance at the markets and trade fairs throughout Europe. These men were experienced in judging the approximate value of coins, discovering counterfeit currency, and determining one currency's value in relation to another. Merchants could be assured of the value of a foreign currency that they accepted for their goods. If the merchants then wanted that currency exchanged into their own, moneychangers were also ready to perform that service—for a fee.

Florin coin

Moneychangers did more, however, than just evaluate and exchange money for merchants. They provided many other services that we commonly associate with modern banks. Since they dealt constantly with money, moneychangers went to great lengths to protect their own funds. Realizing this, merchants began entrusting their surplus cash to the moneychangers for safekeeping. Over time, moneychangers also became moneylenders. Kings, nobles, and even popes borrowed from them to finance their activities. For example, a king might borrow money to finance a Crusade to the Holy Land. He risked great danger, however, by carrying large sums on his journey. It was much safer and more convenient to obtain a letter of credit in Europe. (Letters of credit were much like our modern checks.) Once the king reached the Holy Land, he could present the letter of credit to another moneychanger and receive cash in return. It is not surprising to learn that our word *bank* comes from the Italian ***banca***, which means "bench," referring to the table of the moneychangers.

Quentin Metsys, The Moneylender and His Wife, *Museé du Louvre. Paris*

The Medieval Church and Business Practices

There was little economic freedom in Europe throughout much of the medieval period. Most people had little opportunity or incentive to improve their way of life. Feudal lords held virtual monopolies over the economic life on the manors. In addition, some of the teachings of the Roman Church tended to discourage economic activity.

In a day when religion dominated society, it was natural for the church to shape the economic ideas. The Bible teaches, "Lay not up for yourselves treasures upon earth, . . . for where your treasure is, there will your heart be also" (Matt. 6:19, 21). As a result, the church said that a seller must not take advantage of the buyer simply to gain more wealth for himself. Instead, the seller must charge a **just price** for goods sold—a price that included the cost of materials, a fair return for labor expended, and a reasonable profit. If any man received a profit greater than his needs, he was expected to give it to charity.

Furthermore, the Roman Church prohibited usury—the practice of charging interest for the use of lent money. Based on passages from the Mosaic law, usury was considered a sin (Exod. 22:25; Lev. 25:35–37; Deut. 23:19–20). The church assumed that anyone who borrowed money was in great need. Therefore, it was wrong for someone to profit from a loan made to a brother in need. Such a loan should be an act of charity, not a money-making venture. The revival of trade made this teaching obsolete. Merchants borrowed money not because of poverty but for business investment. Soon it became acceptable to charge interest on loans made for investment purposes. Profit made on such loans was considered a fitting reward for the risk taken since loss was an equal possibility.

The revival of trade and changes in business methods brought new opportunities and incentives to much of Europe's population. Sound economic principles made Europe prosperous: the dignity of labor, the legitimacy of profit, freedom of exchange, and individual responsibility for economic matters. More and more people in Europe were gaining financial independence.

Section Quiz

1. Who served as middlemen in trade between Europe and the Orient?
2. What were the primary centers of trade on the local level in Europe? What were the centers of trade for large-scale international trade?
3. Where did we get our word *bank*?
4. What is the term for charging interest for the use of loaned money? What institution condemned this practice during the Middle Ages?

★ Should the medieval church have attempted to influence economic policy? Were the policies advocated by the medieval church wise?

II. Growth of Towns

Towns, like trade, did not entirely disappear in the West during the Middle Ages. Even so, Europe could boast few cities that could compare in size and population to the many bustling cities of the Roman Empire or other parts of the world. Renewed trade, however, stimulated the growth of towns. Towns provided needed markets and were important centers of exchange.

By the eleventh century, forces at work in Europe began to give shape to the forerunners of the modern city. Improved farming methods led to increased agricultural production. Townspeople who wished to devote their full energy to a specific trade or craft could depend on others to produce surplus food. An increased food supply encouraged families to have more children and boosted Europe's population. As Europe's population grew, so did its towns. Some towns revived within the decayed walls of old Roman cities, while others sprang up at locations important to trade: crossroads, bridges, fords, river mouths, and harbors.

Townsmen Gain Basic Freedoms

Merchants and craftsmen, who lived in the growing urban centers, did not fit into the medieval class structure. They were not lords, vassals, or serfs. And their labor contributed little to the agricultural output of the local manor. Nevertheless, nearly every town was initially subject to some feudal lord.

Townsmen with common interests soon banded together to gain freedom from feudal interference and to secure local self-government. They achieved this independence in a variety of ways. Some towns bought privileges from feudal lords who were willing to grant certain liberties in exchange for large sums of money. Other lords bestowed these privileges freely, since a thriving town meant greater revenues from sales taxes and tolls. However, some lords did not want to relinquish control under any circumstances. In such cases, towns might support a king who would grant them freedom in exchange for payment of taxes.

Bellinzona, Switzerland; located between northern Italy and the Alps region, this area was a Roman military fortress. In the twelfth century a city began growing around the fortress that is today the capital city of the Swiss canton Ticino.

The privileges granted to a town by a feudal lord were usually written down in a legal document called a **charter**. This document outlined the rights and freedoms of the townspeople. The more favorable the charter, the greater the number of people attracted to settle in the town. While liberties varied from town to town, most townsmen shared certain basic freedoms:

1. *Free Status*. The most important privilege enjoyed by a townsman was that of being a freeman. No matter what his previous status, a man who lived in a town for a year and a day gained his freedom. A serf, for example, who ran away from his manor and managed to escape capture by living in a town for one year broke all ties with his manor. An old German proverb said, "Town air makes one free."

2. *Exemption from Manorial Obligations*. Town charters usually exempted townsmen from laboring for the lord of the manor. The townsmen as a group, not as individuals, owed service to the lord. This service was usually rendered in the form of a cash payment.

3. *Town Justice*. Townsmen also won the privilege of administering their own justice. Instead of being tried in a feudal court and judged by feudal customs, a townsman was tried in the court of his town and was judged by townspeople and town customs.

4. *Commercial Privileges*. The chief commercial freedom granted to townsmen was the right to buy and sell freely in the town market. The merchants were free from feudal interference and were protected from competition by outside merchants.

Merchants and Craftsmen Establish Guilds

Merchants and craftsmen in growing towns banded together to protect their common commercial interests. They formed organizations called **guilds**, whose primary function was to regulate the business activity of a given town.

Guild halls in Ghent, Belgium

By acting together, town merchants gained greater security, discouraged outside competition, and increased profits. Guilds also provided aid to members in need. They established schools and cared for the poor, widows, and orphans. Powerful guilds helped towns obtain favorable charters and played an important role in town governments.

There were two types of guilds: merchant and craft. The earlier type was the merchant guild. It guarded the trade interests of merchants by giving them a monopoly of a town's trade. The guild restricted outsiders from doing business in town except upon payment of a heavy fee. The guild also fixed prices at which goods could be bought and sold in the town market.

At first each town had only one guild. But as a town's trade grew and became more specialized, each merchant guild divided into many craft guilds. There were guilds for the town's bakers, tanners, shoemakers, butchers, wheelwrights, and other craftsmen. Each craft guild regulated the hours its members worked, the wages earned, and the number of employees hired. Members of a particular guild guaranteed the quality of their products. They punished members who used shoddy materials, dealt dishonestly, or sold goods cheaper than the established price.

Within each craft guild there were three classes of members: apprentices, journeymen, and masters. A young boy began his training as an **apprentice**. He entered the home of a master craftsman and was expected to work hard in return for his food, lodging, and training. It was the master's responsibility to teach the young apprentice not only the skills of the trade but also proper conduct. At the end of his apprenticeship—a period varying from two to seven years—the young man became a **journeyman**, or "day-laborer." He could then seek employment and earn wages as a skilled worker. Usually a journeyman remained at the home of his master and worked at his master's shop.

Every journeyman looked forward to the day when he could become a master himself. This required years of experience, as well as funds to open a shop. To become a **master**, a journeyman had to undergo an oral examination, present an example of his workmanship (called a "master piece"), and take an oath to conduct himself according to the regulations of the guild. Once approved by the other masters of the guild, the new master could open his own shop and take on his own apprentices and journeymen.

Sometimes towns formed associations with other towns to promote and protect their mutual commercial interests. The most famous of these was the **Hanseatic League**, composed of more than seventy German cities in northwestern Europe. The Hanse (German for "guild") sought to organize and control trade in Sweden, Russia, Flanders, and England. Although the Hanse primarily sought commercial privileges, it also became a powerful political force. The Hanse negotiated treaties, maintained its own navy, and even waged war against other countries.

A New Social Class Emerges

In early feudal society, a great social and economic gulf had separated the nobility and the peasants. With the growth of towns during the eleventh and twelfth centuries, however, a new social class arose, commonly referred to as the **middle class**. It was composed of merchants, bankers, craftsmen, and skilled laborers. These were the "men of the town" known as burgesses in England, *bourgeois* in France, and *burgers* in Germany. (The word *burg* means "a walled town.") The members of this new class had freedom and money. They were energetic, independent, mobile, and growing in number and power. Their world was the town market, and their livelihood was trade. The middle class contributed to the decline of feudalism and helped shape modern society.

The Black Death

The plague spread to Europe from Asia, possibly carried by the rats and fleas in merchant ships. During the Middle Ages, however, people did not know the cause of the disease. This uncertainty made the plague even more fearsome. The Black Death seemed uncaused and unstoppable. Members of every social and economic class fell to its onslaught. Most people sought above all to save themselves. One witness of the plague wrote, "One citizen avoided another, hardly any neighbor troubled about others, relatives never or hardly ever visited each other. Moreover, such terror was struck into the hearts of men and women by this calamity, that brother abandoned brother, and the uncle his nephew, and the sister her brother, and very often the wife her husband. What is even worse and nearly incredible is that fathers and mothers refused to see and tend their children, as if they had not been theirs."

The widespread destruction brought out the best and worst in mankind. Some devout men viewed the plague as the judgment of God and turned to Him. They devoted themselves to the treatment of the ill and the easing of suffering wherever possible. Others, however, gave free reign to their lusts. Their philosophy became, "Eat, drink, and be merry; for tomorrow we die."

Boccaccio, Decameron, *trans. Richard Aldington, 4.*

Filling a mass grave at night during the plague in London, ca. 1665. Approximately 100,000 died in London.

Most noblemen considered the middle class a threat to their position in society. Social ranking, formerly determined by birth or landholding, had gradually shifted toward those who possessed the greatest amounts of money and goods. A nobleman's wealth was in his land; a merchant's wealth was his money or goods. While the nobleman usually spent the money he derived from his land, the merchant invested his money, often at great risk, to gain more wealth. Soon many merchants, bankers, and master craftsmen possessed more goods, fine clothes, and comfortable dwellings than the feudal lords.

By challenging the nobility's social position, the middle class also weakened the nobility's political authority. By the twelfth century, most towns had gained some degree of self-government. Although townsmen were able to regulate trade within their own town, they realized that the sectionalism produced by feudalism and the tolls and sales taxes levied by feudal lords hindered widespread trade. As a result, the middle class desired the stable and uniform government a national king could offer rather than the localism of feudal lords. Kings who had previously relied on nobles to supply revenue and soldiers now could draw upon the rich resources of the towns and the middle class, usually in the form of taxes.

Town Life

Medieval towns were small. By the thirteenth century, only a few, such as Paris, Rome, Venice, and Florence, had populations of over fifty thousand. The typical town averaged only about five thousand people. Most towns were enclosed by thick walls for protection. As the population of the town grew, conditions became overcrowded. Old walls had to be torn down and new ones built to create more room. Because land space within walled towns was limited, houses were crowded together along narrow streets. It was not uncommon for houses to be four or five stories high. The upper stories of houses often extended out over the streets.

The streets below were dark, crooked, and filthy. The townspeople tossed their garbage into open gutters lining the roads. According to medieval writers, the stench from some towns could be smelled miles away. Poor sanitation caused disease, and epidemics spread rapidly, carried throughout the town by the pigs, rats, and dogs that roamed the streets.

Although town life was not easy or comfortable, it was often exciting. During the day the streets hummed with the noise of merchants and peddlers selling their wares, of craftsmen plying their trades, and of children playing in the streets. The center of activity was the town square. Here visiting merchants displayed dazzling items from foreign lands. Within the square's large open space, the town's militia drilled, boys played, and actors performed. Lining the square were the town hall, various guild halls, and the towering cathedral.

Narrow street in Seborga, Italy

Section Quiz

1. What factors contributed to the growth of towns in medieval Europe?
2. List four basic freedoms shared by most townspeople.
3. What was the primary function of a guild?
4. What were the three classes of members of craft guilds?
5. What new social class arose with the rise of towns in the eleventh and twelfth centuries? What were the chief occupations of the people of this class?

★ Why do you think the Hanseatic League maintained its own navy and waged war against countries?

III. Medieval Learning and Art

The Middle Ages is often considered a period of ignorance and superstition—a "dark age" for learning. While there was little formal education of the masses throughout much of this period, education never completely died out. Learning continued, primarily under the influence of the Roman Church. The monks constituted the vast majority of the educated. The primary centers of education were the monasteries and cathedrals.

A basic part of medieval education was the liberal arts curriculum, which was divided into two groups of studies: the **trivium**, consisting of grammar (Latin), rhetoric (effective speaking), and logic; and the **quadrivium**, consisting of arithmetic, geometry, astronomy, and music. A medieval bishop and historian described his own education:

> [I was taught] by means of grammar to read, by dialectic [logic] to apprehend the arguments in disputes, by rhetoric to recognize the different meters, by geometry to comprehend the measurement of the earth and of lines, by [astronomy] to contemplate the paths of the heavenly bodies, by arithmetic to understand the parts of numbers, by harmony to fit the modulated voice to the sweet accent of the verse.
>
> *Gregory of Tours,* History of the Franks, *trans. Ernest Brehaut, 248.*

During the twelfth century, a revival of learning began to sweep across Europe. It was brought about by several factors:

1. Political and economic conditions in Europe were improving, producing a climate more favorable for intellectual and cultural pursuits.

2. Europe's contact with the Byzantine and Arab civilizations through the Crusades exposed Europe to ancient documents and new ideas. These cultures transmitted to Europe not only their own knowledge but also the preserved learning of ancient Greece and Rome. New avenues of study opened as Justinian's code of laws, the works of Aristotle, copies of the Bible in Greek, and Greek and Arabic medical writings became available in Europe.
3. As towns grew and the functions of government expanded, there was an increasing need for education. A theological training was no longer sufficient to meet all the needs of law and business. Greater numbers of people—including many from the rising middle class—were seeking to enter the ranks of the educated.

Universities

One of the most important developments during this period was the rise of universities. These new centers of learning gradually replaced most of the old monastery and cathedral schools of the Roman Church. During this period, students had little concern about the town or school in which they studied. They were more interested in the qualifications of their teacher. Students traveled all over Europe to find the best instructor in their subject area. A master teacher attracted many students, who paid him a fee to teach them. As the number of teachers and students grew in a given locality, the students and scholars—like craftsmen—formed educational guilds for privileges and protection. Initially,

University Life

University life has changed significantly over the years. Early universities had no campuses, buildings, laboratories, or athletic facilities. Classes met wherever the teacher could find a place to lecture. All lectures were conducted in Latin. Students sat on the floor, on straw, or on small benches. The privileged few who could afford it took notes on wax tablets or parchment. Most students spent several hours each day memorizing the lectures by repeatedly reciting them. After the invention of the printing press, the cost of books declined to the point that the sons of wealthy parents could afford a textbook or two. Gradually textbooks became more affordable, and less affluent students gained access to them.

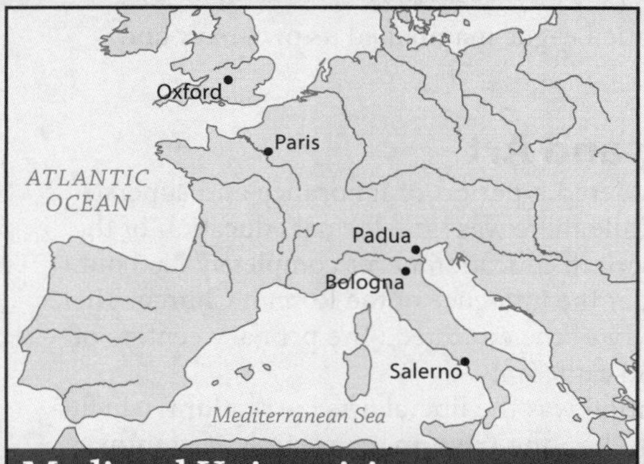

Medieval Universities 12th Century

While the academic setting has changed dramatically over the centuries, some things about university life never change. For example, many students will still write home only when they are in need of money.

The following letter from a medieval student to his parents could well have been written by his modern counterpart: "This is to inform you that I am studying at Oxford with the greatest diligence, but the matter of money stands greatly in the way of my promotion, as it is now two months since I spent the last of what you sent me. The city is expensive and makes many demands; I have to rent lodgings, buy necessaries, and provide for many other things which I cannot now specify. Wherefore I respectfully beg your paternity by the promptings of divine pity that you may assist me, so that I may be able to complete what I have well begun."

In another letter, a father writes to his son who is away at school. The contents of the letter would not seem out of place in modern society: "It is written, 'he also that is slothful in his work is brother to him that is a great waster.' I have recently discovered that you live dissolutely and slothfully, preferring license to restraint and play to work and strumming a guitar while the others are at their studies, whence it happens that you have read but one volume of law while your more industrious companions have read several. Wherefore I have decided to exhort you herewith to repent utterly of your dissolute and careless ways, that you may no longer be called a waster and that your shame may be turned to good repute."

C. H. Haskins, Studies in Medieval Culture, *10, 15.*

any association of people, such as a guild, was called a ***universitas***. But gradually the term came to designate only those people united for the common purpose of education.

Two of the earliest universities were at Bologna in northern Italy and at Paris. Students organized the university at Bologna and formed a guild to ensure that their teachers provided the education for which the students paid and to protect against economic and political abuses by the townspeople. The university at Paris grew out of an old cathedral school and was supervised by a guild of masters or professors. Each school offered training in specialized areas of study. Bologna became a leading center for the study of law. Paris became the center for the study of theology. These schools served as models for other universities.

Rules for Teachers Set Down by Students at Bologna

A professor might not be absent without leave, even a single day, and if he desired to leave town he had to make a deposit to ensure his return. If he failed to secure an audience of five for a regular lecture, he was fined as if absent—a poor lecture indeed which could not secure five hearers! He must begin with the bell and quit within one minute after the next bell. He was not allowed to skip a character in his commentary, or postpone a difficulty to the end of the hour, and he was obliged to cover ground systematically, so much in each specific term of the year.

James W. Thompson and Edgar N. Johnson, An Introduction to Medieval Europe, *730.*

Philosophy and Theology

The schools and universities of twelfth-century Europe provided a home for a new intellectual movement known as **Scholasticism.** Scholasticism finds its roots in Bible study. The scholar began by reading the Bible. He outlined the book he was reading and then reread the book in sections. As he read these sections, the scholar would note the doctrines discussed by those parts of the Bible, and he would write down questions that the Bible brought to mind. He then would think through all the possible answers to the questions he had recorded in an attempt to discern the right answer. After many years, the questions were removed from the commentaries on the Bible text and organized logically in categories, such as God, angels, man, and the sacraments. The Scholastic method raised the question of how knowledge gained by revelation and knowledge gained by reason fit together. In general, Scholastic theologians believed that revelation was most important and that reason served to help Christians understand revelation.

Statue of Anselm

Three of the most significant Scholastic thinkers were Anselm, Peter Abelard (AB uh lard), and Thomas Aquinas (uh KWY nus). In their writings, these men wrestled with the relationship between revelation and reason. The earliest of these was **Anselm** (1033–1109), the archbishop of Canterbury whose view of the relationship between reason and revelation may be summed up by the following statement:

> I do not try, Lord, to attain Your lofty heights, because my understanding is in no way equal to it. But I do desire to understand Your truth a little, that truth that my heart believes and loves. For I do not seek to understand so that I may believe; but I believe so that I may understand. For I believe this also, that "unless I believe, I shall not understand."

Anselm realized that faith in God's revelation is essential to proper understanding. Nevertheless, he did not reject the use of reason. Anselm believed Christians should use reason to better understand God's revelation. He is best remembered for his use of logical arguments to support two major doctrines of the Christian Faith: the existence of God and the satisfaction concept of the atonement (that Christ's death on the cross satisfied God's holiness and justice and redeemed fallen man).

Peter Abelard (1079–1141) advocated the frequent asking of questions as the "first key to wisdom." Abelard, a popular teacher of philosophy and theology at Paris, governed his studies by the following principle: "By doubting we arrive at inquiry (asking critical questions), and through inquiry we perceive the truth." In his most famous work, *Sic et non* ("Yes and No"), Abelard listed 158 questions concerning

Thomas Aquinas

important articles of faith. With each question he presented pro and con statements made by earlier church scholars. He thereby demonstrated that seemingly contradictory views existed. Abelard expected his students to use critical reasoning to harmonize the seemingly contradictory statements of the earlier scholars. When statements could not be harmonized, they were to settle on the view that had the greatest authority supporting it. However, some church leaders viewed his emphasis on reason as dangerous to the teachings of the Roman Church.

Scholasticism reached its height under **Thomas Aquinas** (1225?–74), called "the prince of the Schoolmen." Aquinas faced a new challenge. Until his time reason was used by the Schoolmen to help in formulating theology. But once the philosophy of Aristotle was rediscovered, the Schoolmen wondered if an entire philosophical system, especially a pagan one, could serve as an aid to theology. Some theologians said no, and they rejected Aristotle altogether. Other theologians said yes, and where theology and philosophy disagreed, they said there could be two different truths: something could be true in philosophy and false in theology or true in theology and false in philosophy. Aquinas rejected both of these views. He said that Aristotle's philosophy could be used to help understand theological ideas, but he also said that when the church's teaching and Aristotle disagreed, the church's teaching was right and Aristotle was wrong. Aquinas's book *Summa Theologiae* followed this approach to theology and philosophy.

The Scholastics were the first systematic theologians, and much of the theology they developed was believed by later Roman Catholics as well as Protestants. But the Scholastics also experienced a serious problem. They began by studying the Bible, and then they began studying the questions that their study of the Bible raised, and then they began to study the answers that men gave to those questions. Their study moved further and further away from Scripture, and reason began to take center stage instead of revelation. This departure resulted in a reaction against Scholasticism that eventually bore fruit in the Protestant Reformation.

Roger Bacon and the Future

In a fascinating letter, the thirteenth-century English scientist and philosopher Roger Bacon forecast what he believed would become of the technological achievements of the future. Some of his predictions demonstrate an astonishing foresight.

He predicted, for example, improvements on ships that would "do away with the necessity of rowers, so that great vessels, both in rivers and on the sea, shall be borne about with only a single man to guide them and with greater speed than if they were full of men." The modern reader can easily imagine trains or cars when Bacon describes "carriages [which] can be constructed to move without animals to draw them, and with incredible velocity."

Long before the twentieth century, men dreamed of building flying machines. Bacon was one of these dreamers. His idea, however, was unlike modern airplanes: "Machines for flying can be made in which a man sits and turns an ingenious device by which skillfully contrived wings are made to strike the air in the manner of a flying bird." Bacon's predictions demonstrate that scientific inquiry is not just experimentation and observation. Scientists need a healthy imagination too.

Medieval Science

In medieval times few people devoted much attention to science. Medieval thinkers focused on the world to come and placed little emphasis on the present physical world. In their opinion, faith and reason were the only sure guides to knowledge. Science was merely a secondary source of knowledge, which at best could only confirm truths that theology and philosophy had already established.

Magic and superstition clouded medieval science. Astrologers sought to interpret the future based on the position of the stars, while alchemists attempted to transform common metals into gold. The little scientific knowledge that did exist had been handed down from ancient sources. Churchmen compiled this information into handbooks of knowledge called encyclopedias. Because these compilers did not question the accuracy of their sources or conduct any experiments themselves, they often passed down gross misconceptions and falsehoods.

Chaucer's Pilgrims

Chaucer's *Canterbury Tales,* written in the late fourteenth century, gives a wonderful picture of medieval England. The following two selections are from his descriptions of the twenty-nine pilgrims. Because of the changes in the language over the last six hundred years, the English of Chaucer's day is rather difficult for the modern reader to understand.

A KNYGHT ther was, and that a worthy man,
That fro the tyme that he first bigan
To riden out, he love chivalrie,
Trouthe and honour, fredom and curteisie.

A MARCHANT was ther with a forked berd,
In mottelee, and hye on horse he sat;
Upon his heed a Flaundryssh bever hat,
His bootes clasped faire and fetisly.

The body of scientific knowledge increased during the twelfth and thirteenth centuries as Greek and Muslim works began to circulate in Europe. For the most part European "scientists" were content to accept the findings of the past without verification. Even so, there were some who began to critically reexamine inherited scientific ideas. One of the best known of these new scientific thinkers was the Englishman **Roger Bacon** (c. 1214–94). He was keenly aware of the obstacles facing scientific advancement: "There are four principal stumbling blocks to comprehending truth, which hinder well-nigh every scholar: the example of frail and unworthy authority, long-established custom, the sense of the ignorant crowd, and the hiding of one's own ignorance under the show of wisdom."

Although not the first to conceive of the idea, Bacon advocated observation and experimentation as tests for scientific conclusions. Thanks to Bacon and others, science was beginning to free itself from the shackles of mysticism, superstition, and unreliable authority. Nevertheless, it was not until a later day that scholars grasped the full importance of the scientific method.

Language and Literature

The language of the learned during the Middle Ages was Latin. It was firmly established in the universities and governments throughout Europe and was the official language of the Roman Catholic Church. It was not the spoken language of the common people, however. The common tongue varied from region to region; French, German, Italian, Spanish, and English were among those spoken. By the twelfth century, writers began to use the common spoken language, or **vernacular**, in literature.

Among the earliest forms of vernacular literature were the heroic epics—long narrative poems that celebrated the adventures of legendary heroes. Many of these epics have become national treasures: England's *Beowulf*, France's *Song of Roland*, Germany's *Song of Nibelungs*, and Spain's poem "The Lay of the Cid" about El Cid. Wandering minstrels called **troubadours** popularized the vernacular in lyric poetry. They traveled from

Statue of Dante Alighieri in Florence, Italy

castle to castle singing their songs of love and adventure to noblemen and their ladies. They also popularized stories about knights, chivalry, and love. Probably the best known of these medieval romances are the tales of King Arthur and the Knights of the Round Table.

The two greatest writers of the late medieval period were Dante and Chaucer. **Dante Alighieri** (DAHN-tay ah-lee-GYEH-ree) (1265–1321) was an Italian poet. His *Divine Comedy* ranks as one of the most brilliant works in all literature. In this long poem Dante takes an imaginary journey through hell, purgatory, and paradise. His work reflects the religious beliefs, social order, and political turbulence of the late Middle Ages.

Geoffrey Chaucer (CHAW sur) (c. 1343–1400) was a prominent English poet. His masterpiece, *The Canterbury Tales*, presents a collection of stories told by pilgrims on their way to visit the tomb of Thomas à Becket at Canterbury (see p. 190). Chaucer used his skill as a storyteller and his insight into human behavior to depict English life and customs. By their masterful use of the vernacular in literature, both Dante and Chaucer aided the development of their native languages.

Art and Architecture

The art of the Middle Ages was primarily religious. Since most laymen were illiterate, the church used the visual arts to teach Bible stories. Artists depicted Bible characters and popular "saints" of the church with certain characteristics. These symbols helped the observer identify the painted or sculptured figures. For example, John the Baptist is always shown wearing an animal skin and carrying a staff with a cross on top. The skin illustrates the fact that "John was clothed with camel's hair" (Mark 1:6). The cross symbolizes his message: "Behold the Lamb of God, which taketh away the sin of the world" (John 1:29).

The most prominent form of medieval art was religious architecture. The people of Europe poured much of their wealth and energy into building impressive cathedrals. An eleventh-century French monk described the architectural revival that began about the year 1000:

> There occurred, throughout the world, especially in Italy and Gaul, a rebuilding of church basilicas. Notwithstanding the greater number were already well established and not in the least in need, nevertheless each Christian people strove against the others to erect nobler ones. It was as if the whole earth, having cast off the old . . . were clothing itself everywhere in the white robe of the church.

Pécs Cathedral in Hungary, an example of Romanesque architecture

From 1050 to about 1150 the prevalent architectural style in Europe was **Romanesque** (roh muh NESK), which means "Roman-like." Romanesque builders modified the rectangular Roman basilica (which earlier church architects had copied) and constructed churches in the shape of a Latin cross. Thick walls supported the tremendous weight of stone vaults and ceilings. Other features included rounded arches, heavy columns, and small doors and windows. The interiors of these churches were dark and gloomy.

Beginning about the thirteenth century, architects devised a way to support stone vaults and ceilings by the use of "flying" or external buttresses. These supports made it possible for cathedrals to have higher ceilings, thinner walls, and larger windows and doors. This new style was called **Gothic**.

Cathedral of Notre Dame in Paris, an example of Gothic architecture

In contrast to the dark and heavy elements of the Romanesque, Gothic architecture was light and delicate. The spacious and lofty Gothic cathedrals created an atmosphere of dignity and serenity. Their high towers and pointed arches soared toward heaven, inviting people to turn their thoughts toward God. Another feature of Gothic architecture was stained-glass windows. They added beauty, light, and color to the interior of churches. They also served as a type of "visual Bible." By arranging the glass pieces, artists illustrated biblical stories in vivid colors.

Section Quiz

1. List three factors that aided a revival of learning during the twelfth century.
2. What were two of the earliest universities begun in Europe? How did they differ?
3. What is the name of the intellectual movement characterized by a renewed interest in theology and philosophy? What did the philosophers and theologians of this movement try to harmonize?
4. What clouded the work of medieval science?
5. Who were the two greatest writers of the late Middle Ages? Beside each man's name, identify his native country and the title of his important work.

★ How is the debate over the relation between Aristotle and theology similar to modern controversies between science and theology?

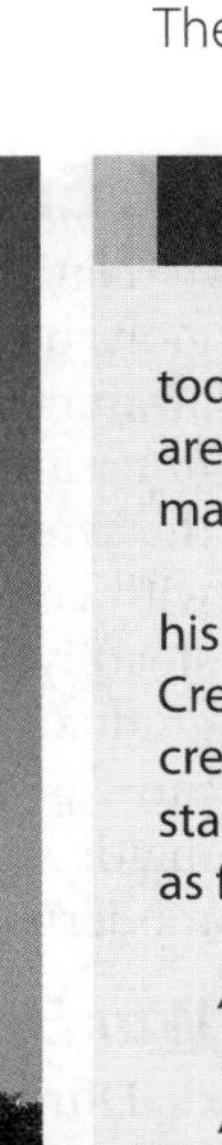

Medieval Hymns

Although most of the hymns we sing today are of more recent origin, there are several medieval hymns that have remained famous to this day.

In 1225 Francis of Assisi wrote his "Canticle of the Sun, and Hymn of Creation"—a poem praising God for His creation. This poem, which has seven stanzas in its English paraphrase, begins as follows:

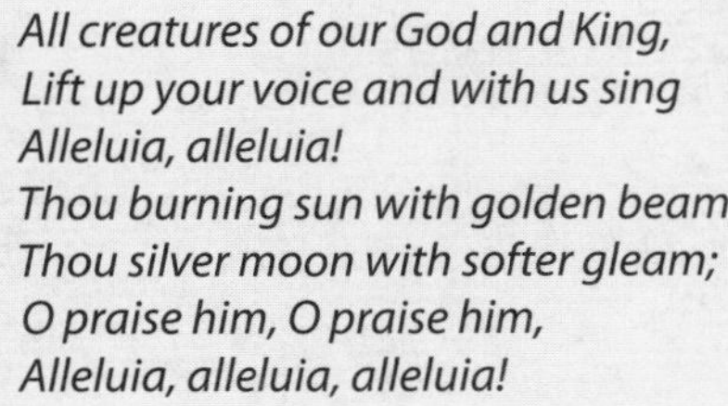

All creatures of our God and King,
Lift up your voice and with us sing
Alleluia, alleluia!
Thou burning sun with golden beam,
Thou silver moon with softer gleam;
O praise him, O praise him,
Alleluia, alleluia, alleluia!

Another much-loved hymn came from the pen of Bernard of Clairvaux, who wrote a seven-part poem that speaks of Christ's body on the cross. The final part speaks of the head of Christ:

O sacred Head, now wounded,
With grief and shame weighed down,
Now scornfully surrounded
With thorns, Thine only crown;
O sacred Head, what glory,
What bliss till now was Thine!
Yet, though despised and gory,
I joy to call Thee mine.

Finally, there is what many regard to be the finest of all medieval hymns—"Jesus, the Very Thought of Thee." Although tradition has ascribed this poem to Bernard, the authorship is uncertain. However, it is a hymn that every Christian should be able to sing from the heart:

Jesus, the very thought of Thee
With sweetness fills the breast.
But sweeter far Thy face to see,
And in Thy presence rest.

Jesus, our only joy be Thou,
As Thou our prize wilt be;
In Thee be all our glory now,
And through eternity.

IV. Emergence of National States

Nation-states developed in the late Middle Ages as people in certain regions became more fully aware of their common traditions and language. This awareness became the foundation of nationalism. Accompanying the growth of nation-states was the rise of national monarchies. The monarchy served as the symbol of national pride. The independent king ruling a group of people with common interests formed the basis of early nation-states. Royal power steadily increased in the fourteenth and fifteenth centuries while feudalism gradually declined. As differences among the various people in Europe became more distinct, boundaries between nation-states began to solidify. By 1500 the major states of Europe were established. The medieval age was passing; the modern age was at hand.

War Between England and France

During the fourteenth and fifteenth centuries, England and France became embroiled in a long struggle known as the **Hundred Years' War**. Intermittent battles and broken truces spanned the years from 1337 to 1453. What began as a conflict between feudal lords ended as a rivalry between two emerging nation-states. The war contributed to the decline of feudalism in England and France while stimulating the growth of national identity in both countries.

Causes

For centuries English and French monarchs had confronted one another over the matter of English holdings in France. Although Philip II had drastically reduced the size of the English possessions, the king of England still held the duchy of Aquitaine. More fuel was added to this flame of discord when the French monarch attempted to take possession of the rich commercial territory of Flanders. This act threatened England's profitable wool trade. War finally erupted after the last Capetian king died without a male heir. The English king, **Edward III**, whose mother was the sister of the three previous French kings, claimed to be the rightful heir to the French throne. But the French nobles were unwilling to give the crown to the long-time rival of the French monarchs. Instead, they chose Philip VI of the house of Valois (vah LWAH) as king.

Conflict

English forces crossed the Channel and won several major victories over the French—at Crécy (kray SEE) in 1346, at Poitiers (pwah TYAY) in 1356, and at Agincourt (AJ in kort) in 1415. Their success was due in large part to new battle tactics and weapons. The English relied on archers armed with **longbows**. Some arrows shot by these powerful weapons could penetrate certain types of armor. The longbow gave English archers greater range and accuracy than their French counterparts, who used the conventional crossbow. Through the strategic deployment of bowmen and knights in battle, the outnumbered English routed the French.

A skilled longbow archer could send an arrow a distance of 270 yards.

The English nonetheless had little to show from their victories over the French. Decades of skirmishes had left them drained of resources. Political unrest at home decreased their zeal for fighting a foreign war. For the French, the war was one of humiliation and destruction. They not only suffered one defeat after another but also saw their countryside pillaged by the English knights.

Even though the English won most of the battles, the French eventually won the war. What turned the tide for the French was a surge of nationalism inspired by a simple peasant girl named **Joan of Arc**. Believing that heavenly voices had directed her to drive the English out of France, she roused the weak French king to action, rallied the dispirited French troops, and accompanied the French army into battle. Although English forces captured Joan and burned her at the stake in 1431, her example stirred the French army to achieve victory over the English.

Henry VII, *ca. 1500, by Michael Sittow; Henry has a red rose in his hand for the house of Lancaster.*

Consequences

The English defeat became a blessing in disguise. No longer did the English kings concentrate their efforts on holding on to their French possessions. Instead they began to build a strong nation-state at home. The war also furthered the cause of nation-making in France. The rivalry over the English presence in France had stirred French nationalism. This bolstered the cause of the French kings as they continued to increase their royal powers.

In England—after a century of fighting on French soil, the English troops returned home only to become involved in a civil war. Two rival families, the houses of York and Lancaster, fought for the English throne. The series of conflicts between these noble families became known as the **Wars of the Roses**. (The emblem of the House of York was a white rose; the emblem of the House of Lancaster, a red rose.) After thirty years of intermittent conflict, the struggle ended when Henry Tudor defeated Richard III at the battle of Bosworth Field. Henry was crowned King **Henry VII** (r. 1485–1509). He founded the powerful Tudor dynasty. During the sixteenth century, the Tudors firmly established the power of the English monarchy and built the English nation into a major European power—a position England held for over four hundred years.

In France—weary of the death and destruction, the Estates-General had, during the war, allowed the French king to levy a royal land tax called a ***taille*** (TAH yuh) with which he could maintain a strong army and thereby defeat the English. The eventual success over the English greatly increased the power of the French king. Unlike the English king, who had to depend on Parliament for funds, the French king could raise money without consent of the Estates-General. There was no check on his growing power.

Reconquista in Spain and Portugal

Nation-states did not develop as quickly in the Iberian Peninsula (see map on p. 220) as they had in England and France. For three centuries, most of the peninsula had remained under Muslim control. In the eleventh century a few small non-Muslim states in the north began a concerted effort to drive out the **Moors** (Spanish Muslims). By the late thirteenth century, warriors of the ***Reconquista*** ("reconquest") had successfully reclaimed the entire peninsula except for the kingdom of Granada.

As European forces drove the Moors out, the small northern states expanded into the reclaimed land. Three principal kingdoms emerged: Portugal, Castile, and Aragon. Like most other European states, these kingdoms experienced struggles between a developing monarchy and feudal nobles. There arose in each kingdom the equivalent to an Estates-General or Parliament—the **Cortes**, a council composed of nobles, clergy, and representatives of the cities. The expulsion of the Moors, together with the support from the growing towns and the decline of feudalism, increased the power of each king above that of his feudal nobles and the Cortes.

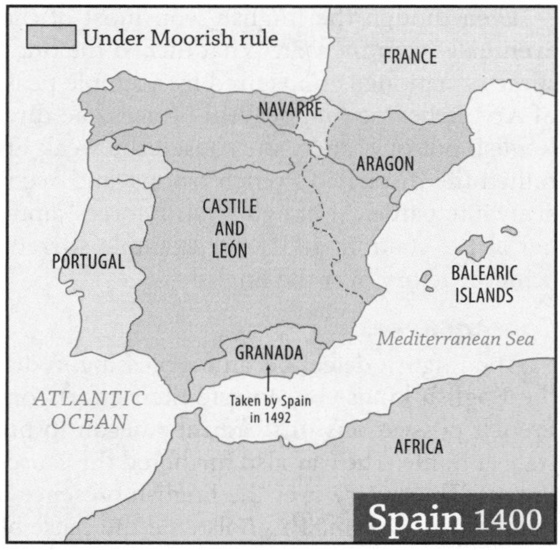

The nation of Spain was created when **Ferdinand**, heir to the throne of Aragon, married **Isabella**, heir to the throne of Castile. (The kingdom of Portugal remained independent.) Ferdinand and Isabella firmly established their royal power in the new nation. They authorized the Spanish Inquisition, a systematic persecution of Muslims and Jews. Inquisitors later directed their attacks against Christians who opposed the Roman Catholic Church. Ferdinand and Isabella completed the Reconquista by driving the Moors out of Granada in **1492**, the same year that Christopher Columbus, under Spanish sponsorship, landed in the New World.

Disunity in Italy and Germany

In contrast to the rising tide of nationalism and strong monarchies elsewhere in Europe, Germany and Italy remained divided into many small regional states. "Germany" and "Italy" were geographic expressions, not unified nations.

The collapse of the Hohenstaufen house in the thirteenth century brought an end to German influence in Italy. Italy was left divided among the kingdom of Naples, the Papal States, and powerful northern cities such as Florence, Venice, Genoa, and Milan. There was little opportunity for national unity while each region struggled to prevent the others from becoming too powerful. Despite its political turmoil and disunity, Italy prospered commercially and later gave birth to the period of cultural achievement known as the Renaissance (see Chapter 11).

During this period, imperial authority declined in Germany and small territorial states emerged. The office of emperor remained, but the real power of government passed into the hands of the great nobles. By the middle of the fourteenth century, a written constitution known as the **Golden Bull** established the **Diet** of the Holy Roman Empire. The Diet was the German equivalent of the English Parliament and the French Estates-General. The most important members of the Diet were the seven electors (three archbishops and four noble princes) who selected the German emperors. The electors generally chose weak men as emperors in order to protect the power of the German nobility. In addition, they passed the imperial crown from one family to another so that no single family would become too powerful. While other lands were striving toward national unity, the German electors sought to avoid it.

Despite the efforts of the German nobles, the **Habsburg** family built a strong base of power among the southern German states. These states became known

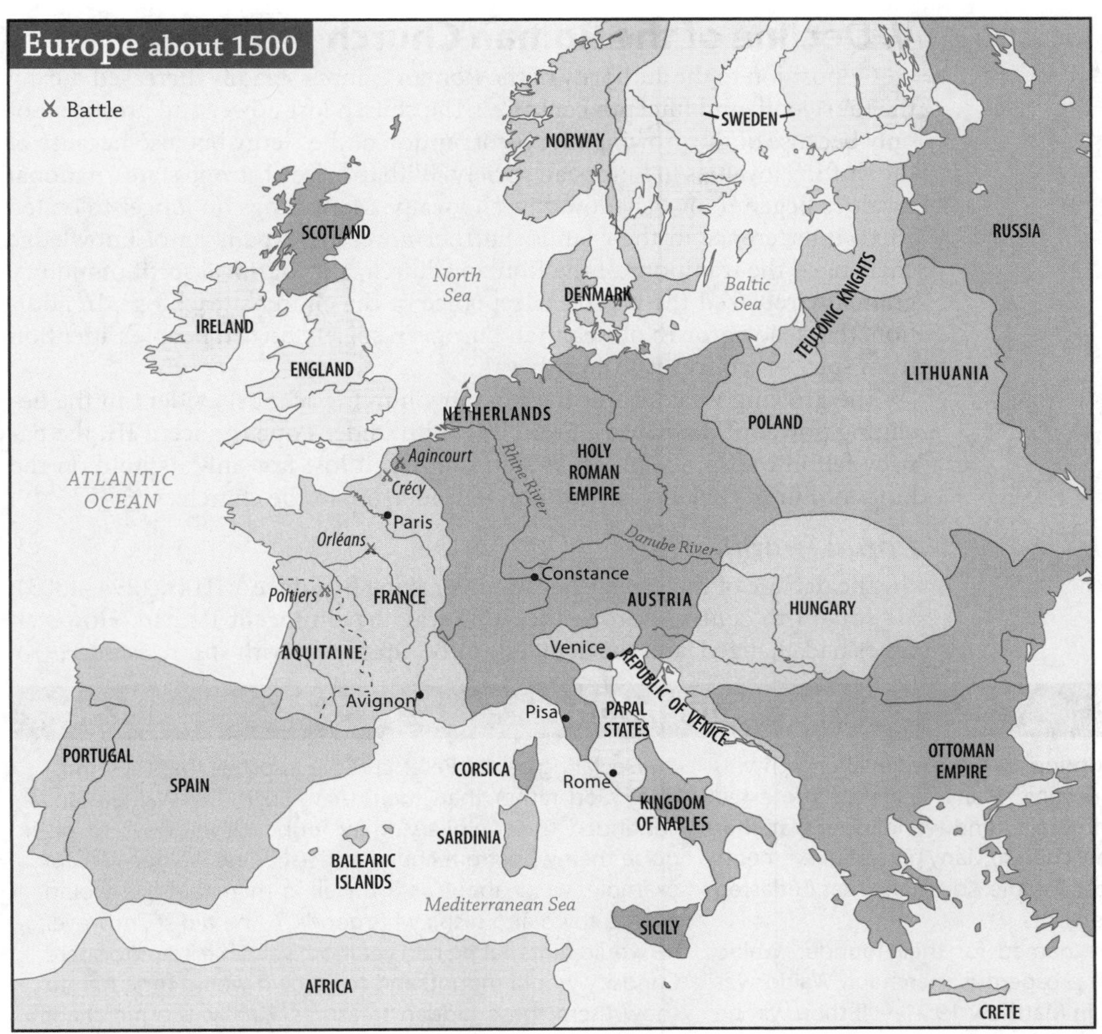

collectively as Austria. (Members of the Habsburg family ruled from the city of Vienna until after World War I.) After 1438 only members of this family were elected to the German throne. Emperor **Maximilian I** (1493–1519) greatly enlarged the Habsburg possessions through marriage. His first marriage brought the rich region of the Low Countries (modern Belgium and Holland) under his rule. His second marriage brought him Milan. He also formed a marriage alliance between his son and the daughter of Ferdinand and Isabella of Spain. In this way Spain, the Low Countries, the Holy Roman Empire, and territory in the New World (the Spanish possessions) came under Habsburg rule.

Section Quiz

1. What two nations fought during the Hundred Years' War? What were the dates for this war?
2. Which side won most of the battles of this war? What side won the war?
3. What people did the Spanish and Portuguese seek to drive out of the Iberian Peninsula? What was this effort called?
4. What was the German constitution called? What assembly did it establish?
5. Following the collapse of the Hohenstaufen house, what family came to occupy the throne of the Holy Roman Empire and ruled it until after World War I?

★ Why were German efforts to avoid national unity unsuccessful?

V. Decline of the Roman Church

Opposition to the authority of the Roman Church steadily increased during the fourteenth and fifteenth centuries. The church lost power and prestige, not only because of the growing moral corruption of the clergy but also because of the shifting loyalties in European society. With the rise of strong states, national loyalties began to overshadow church loyalty. Many kings no longer tolerated papal interference in their lands. Furthermore, the expansion of knowledge challenged the traditions of the Roman Church, and a critical spirit of inquiry gradually replaced the passive acceptance of the church's teachings. In addition, the steady growth of wealth in European society turned people's attention from spiritual concerns to earthly gain.

The growing weakness of the Roman Church was most evident in the declining power of the papacy. From its zenith under Pope Innocent III, the papacy fell into disgrace in less than a century. It lost not only its hold on the kings of Europe but also its position of leadership in the church.

Papal Humiliation

The decline of the papacy began under Pope **Boniface VIII** (r. 1294–1303). He sought to control Europe the same way that Innocent III had. However, times had changed, and the demands of Boniface met with stiff resistance.

The Waldensians

The increasing corruption of the medieval church was not unnoticed by Christians. Many believers protested strongly against the immorality and worldliness that characterized the institutional church. Many protest movements arose and vanished in the Middle Ages. One that outlasted all others was the Waldensians.

The Waldensians are named for their founder, Waldo of Lyons (died 1217). A prosperous merchant, Waldo was moved by Jesus' words in Matthew 19:21—"If thou wilt be perfect, go and sell that thou hast, and give to the poor, and thou shalt have treasure in heaven: and come and follow me." He sold all that he had and gave the proceeds to the poor. Then Waldo, and others who followed him, began living a life of simplicity and poverty, seeking to witness to all men. As he told a papal representative later, "We have decided to live by the words of the Gospel, essentially that of the Sermon on the Mount, and the commandments, that is, to live in poverty without concern for tomorrow."

In the beginning the Waldensians did not differ from other reform movements such as that of Francis of Assisi. The Waldensians, however, remained laymen instead of becoming priests. They went about preaching and began to translate parts of the Bible into the common language. Their preaching and translating drew the opposition of the church hierarchy, who considered them ignorant laymen, and the pope condemned the movement.

Waldo of Lyons

Declaring as did Peter and the apostles that they must "obey God rather than men" (Acts 5:29), the Waldensians continued their ministry. They found clever ways to disguise their work from church officials. One Waldensian, for example, went about as a traveling merchant. He would enter a town and display his goods. As he did so, however, he would hint that he had yet more valuable items to share. Curiosity would mount, and the crowd would urge him to show them these hidden treasures. Finally, the merchant revealed his special "wares"—the "pearl of great price" (Matt. 13:46)—and he would preach to them.

For the next two centuries the Waldensians suffered persecution from Roman Church authorities, but they survived in the mountains of Switzerland, northern Italy, and southeastern France. During the Reformation, the Waldensians joined forces with the Protestants. Persecution intensified during and after the Reformation as Roman Catholic rulers tried to exterminate the Waldensian groups in their domains. As a result, some Waldensians fled to other areas to escape the persecution. One group, for instance, settled in North Carolina in 1893. As protestors against corruption of the Roman Church even before the Reformation, the Waldensians won the praise of English poet John Milton as "them who kept [God's] truth to pure of old / When all our Fathers worship't sticks and Stones."

Trouble began when the French king Philip IV decided to levy a tax on the French clergy. The pope denounced this act, but his words went unheeded. The conflict intensified when Philip arrested a bishop who was accused of violating French law and brought him before a royal court to stand trial. Boniface ordered Philip to release the bishop. When Philip refused, Boniface issued the famous papal **bull** (an official papal document) ***Unam Sanctam*** (1302). In this strong statement of papal supremacy, Boniface asserted that "it is altogether necessary to salvation for every human being to be subject to the Roman pontiff."

Philip, supported by the French people, defied the pope. He accused Boniface of heresy and sought to bring him to trial. Philip's agents, accompanied by a band of soldiers, traveled to the papal residence and took the pope captive. Boniface was severely beaten and nearly died. After three days of captivity Philip's agents freed the feeble pope. He died a few weeks later.

Papal Exile

National awareness and royal power triumphed over the demands of the papacy. A short time after the death of Boniface, Philip pressured the College of Cardinals to elect a Frenchman to the papal office. The new pope moved the papal capital from Rome to Avignon (AH vee nyawn), a city in France. From 1309 to 1377 the popes—all Frenchmen—resided at Avignon. This period is known as the **Babylonian Captivity** of the Church, or the Avignon Exile. Although the popes were not actually held captive, they did remain under the influence of the French kings.

During the Avignon years, the power of the papacy declined even further. The rising tide of nationalism caused the English, Germans, and Italians to resent a French-controlled papacy. In addition, critics of the Roman Church denounced the wealth and corruption that marked the Avignon court. Some of the popes raised new church taxes and sold church offices to maintain their

The papal palace at Avignon

lives of luxury. While the Avignon popes were able administrators of the church bureaucracy, they appeared to show little concern for spiritual matters. Once again calls for reform echoed across Europe.

Papal Schism

Pope Gregory XI (r. 1370–78) returned to Rome in 1377 but died soon after taking up residence in the city. The French-dominated College of Cardinals, threatened by a Roman mob, elected an Italian as pope. Several months later, the cardinals declared the election invalid and elected a new pope, who ruled from Avignon. The Roman Church now had two popes—one in Rome and one in Avignon. Both men claimed to be the rightful pope, and each excommunicated the other. For forty years this **Great Schism** divided the allegiance of the nations of Europe.

In 1409 church leaders met at Pisa to resolve the schism within the Roman Church. The council deposed both popes and appointed a new one. However, the other two refused to relinquish their office, so the church now had three popes. The matter was finally settled at the **Council of Constance** (1414–18). This large gathering of church leaders succeeded in deposing the other claimants to the papal office and secured the election of Martin V as the sole pope. The council healed the schism and restored the papacy to Rome. But because it was unwilling to enact any meaningful reforms, the council failed to stop the growing criticism of the church's doctrine and practice. As a result, the Babylonian Captivity and the Great Schism added more fuel to the smoldering discontent that would soon flame into the Protestant Reformation.

Section Quiz

1. Who issued the papal bull *Unam Sanctam*? What did it assert?
2. To what city was the papacy "exiled"? What is this period called?
3. What church council finally settled the Great Schism?

★ Why was French King Philip IV able to ignore the pope's demands and decrees?

Chapter 10 Review

Making Connections

1. Why was the consistent quality of coinage important?
2. How did moneychangers make traveling less dangerous?
3. What parts of a "just price" are good? What part is flawed?
4. How did guilds protect the consumer?

Developing History Skills

1. Based on the information in this chapter and Bible passages such as 2 Kings 24:15 and Daniel 9:2, briefly recount Judah's captivity and explain why the period of papal exile in Avignon, France was referred to as the Babylonian Captivity of the Church.

Thinking Critically

1. In the *Divine Comedy*, Dante describes a trip to hell and speaks of clergy, popes, and cardinals residing in the fourth ring of hell because of their greed (*Inferno*, Canto VII, lines 46–48). Based on the information in this chapter and other sources, explain why Dante was able to make such statements without fear of punishment by civil authorities or the Roman Church.

Living in God's World

1. If you were a Christian magistrate during the Middle Ages, what regulations would you impose on the town fairs to remove some of the abuses noted in the quotation on page 205?
2. If you were a leader in a church, what Scripture should guide you in the kind of art that is used in church?

People, Places, and Things to Know

florin
moneychangers
banca
just price
charter
guilds
apprentice
journeyman
master
Hanseatic League
middle class
trivium
quadrivium
universitas
Scholasticism
Anselm
Peter Abelard
Thomas Aquinas
Roger Bacon
vernacular
troubadours
Dante Alighieri
Geoffrey Chaucer
Romanesque
Gothic
nation-states
Hundred Years' War
Edward III
longbows
Joan of Arc
War of the Roses
Henry VII
taille
Moors
Reconquista
Cortes
Ferdinand
Isabella
1492
Golden Bull
Diet
Habsburg
Maximilian I
Boniface VIII
bull
Unam Sanctam
Babylonian Captivity
Great Schism
Council of Constance

THE AWAKENING WORLD

IV

"The Awakening World" may seem a strange title for Unit IV. Had the world been asleep before? The word *awakening* here signifies a new expansion of man—geographically, mentally, and, most importantly, spiritually. The Renaissance recaptured the artistic excellence of the ancients and taught men again to use their God-given talent and reason. The explorers revealed the immensity of the world and brought exciting, unknown lands to the attention of Europe. In the midst of these achievements of mind and body, God sent an "expansion" of the soul, the spiritual revival known as the Reformation. Greater than all the beautiful works of the Renaissance artists, more dramatic than all the discoveries of the explorers, more influential than all the kings and wars of the era was a simple sentence penned by the apostle Paul and proclaimed by a former German monk named Martin Luther: "The just shall live by faith."

1309–77 Avignon Papacy

1382 Wycliffe Bible

1414–18 Council of Constance

1492 Columbus sails to the Americas

1493 Line of Demarcation

1300 | 1350 | 1400 | 1450

1517–1648
Reformation
1517
Ninety-Five Theses
1545–63
Council of Trent
1555 Peace
of Augsburg
1588 Spanish Armada
1598 Edict of Nantes
1608 Quebec founded
1500
1550
1600
1650

11

The Renaissance

I. Characteristics of the Renaissance

II. Course of the Renaissance

III. Consequences of the Renaissance

Florence, Italy—birthplace of the Renaissance

A new age was dawning in Europe in the fourteenth century. The Western world was on the threshold of a widespread revival in learning and of a brilliant flowering of the arts. This period of change in Europe from the fourteenth century through the sixteenth century is known as the **Renaissance** (REN uh sahns), a French word meaning "rebirth." The spirit of this age is evident in the confident outburst of a young German: "What a century! What genius! It is sheer joy to be alive. . . . Learning flourishes; men are spiritually quickened." This chapter focuses on the intellectual and artistic developments that constituted this transformation in Western civilization.

Florence, Italy

I. Characteristics of the Renaissance

Contrast with the Middle Ages

The Renaissance man considered the time in which he lived a sharp break from the ignorance and superstition of the Middle Ages. To him the medieval period was merely a backward, unimportant interval between the achievement of classical culture and the glory of his own "modern" age. He failed to realize that the Renaissance was the culmination of gradual changes that had begun during the Middle Ages.

The Renaissance attitude toward life differed sharply from the medieval outlook. The Renaissance man's hearty zest for living was a dramatic departure from the sober, otherworldly concerns of earlier generations, who were consumed with the welfare of their souls and with the work of the church. People during the Middle Ages fixed their thoughts on the future joys of heaven. The dusty past and the troubled present were of little interest or importance. The Renaissance man, on the other hand, gloried in the past and lived with enthusiasm in the present. The future could take care of itself, or so he thought.

Focus on Man

The Renaissance emphasized human individuality, ability, and dignity. In medieval times the group—not the individual—had been all-important (for example, the church, a guild, or a particular social class). During the Renaissance, however, the reverse was true. People praised the wonders of human achievement. They conceived of the ideal man as one with diverse interests and talents.

This renewed focus on man's capacities is called **humanism**. Unlike modern secular humanism, Renaissance humanism did not abandon belief in God. Nevertheless, like every movement that puts undue emphasis on human ability, it led to the false assumption that man is basically good. "There is nothing to be seen more wonderful than man," wrote an Italian humanist. Shakespeare's immortal character Hamlet exclaims, "What a piece of work is man! How noble in reason! How infinite in faculty! in form and moving, How expressive and admirable! in action, How like an angel!"

Created in God's image and given dominion over creation, man does possess a unique position in God's universe. But God's image in man was badly marred by the Fall in the Garden of Eden. Because of Adam's disobedience man is a sinner in need of the Savior.

The godly man acknowledges that God is the source of all wisdom and the giver of all talents and abilities (James 1:17). The psalmist David said to God, "I will praise thee; for I am fearfully and wonderfully made" (Ps. 139:14). He humbly recognized man's true character and the source of man's understanding (Ps. 8:3–6, 9). Because many people in Renaissance society denied man's true nature, much of their culture was devoid of eternal values, biblical ethics, and godly living.

Humanism

Humanism is an overemphasis on human worth and ability, leading man to glorify himself instead of God. There have been many historical expressions of humanism. The Greek humanists, for example, emphasized the uniqueness of man above the animals; they taught that man's reason was the standard of truth. Like the Greeks, most of the Renaissance humanists praised human accomplishment and talent. Although most were church members and acknowledged the existence of God, other Renaissance humanists were primarily interested in classical learning.

Humanists understood the truth that man, created in God's image, is the apex of God's creation. However, because it tends to minimize or reject man's submission to God, humanism inevitably leads people away from God and spiritual concerns. It promotes the false idea that man is good and that he is independent of or superior to God. The secular humanism of the twenty-first century altogether rejects belief in God and worships man as God.

Revival of Learning

The expansion of trade and the growth of town and national governments during the later Middle Ages increased the need for well-educated laymen with professional skills. Merchants, bankers, lawyers, clerks, and diplomats—to name a few—needed a well-rounded education to meet the demands of an increasingly complex society. Renewed business activity also indirectly sparked interest in classical literature. Lawyers needing to draw up business contracts and other legal documents turned to Roman law to see how the ancients had handled such matters. In the process of their research, they discovered the writings of Cicero and other Latin authors. Renewed interest in classical literature prompted men to collect and study these writings.

Soon a new course of study became popular in the West. The humanities, also known as the liberal arts, included the study of history, science, and grammar, as well as classical literature and philosophy. Those who studied the liberal arts were known as **humanists**. Unlike the Scholastics of the Middle Ages, most Renaissance humanists prepared themselves for life in the secular world rather than for service in the Roman Church.

The goal of Renaissance education was to develop well-rounded individuals. Humanists, who considered ignorance the source of evil, looked to education as the remedy for sin. They criticized medieval man for being ignorant and narrow-minded, and they praised men of their own day for their zest for life, wide interests, and quest for knowledge. They scorned the medieval practice of passively accepting ideas without questioning their accuracy. Renaissance man became more critical. He examined established ideas to discern their trustworthiness.

Renaissance humanists greatly admired the classical age of ancient Greece and Rome. They praised the amazing versatility that the ancients had possessed. Cicero received special honor because he was not only a renowned scholar, lawyer, and statesman but also an eloquent orator and master of literary expression. By following the example of the ancients, the humanists believed they could reshape their own age according to classical values. They stimulated a "rebirth" of interest in the literature, art, and philosophy of the classical age.

This fascination with classical culture led to an intense search for ancient manuscripts. Men went to great lengths and spent vast fortunes to obtain classical works. They found many Latin manuscripts in the libraries of monasteries, where they had lain neglected and forgotten for centuries. Although Greek works were rare in the West, many had been preserved in the East by the Byzantine and Muslim civilizations. As the humanists recovered these precious works, they examined them to determine their accuracy and authenticity. Essential to such an investigation, of course, was a thorough knowledge of the classical languages. This need gave rise to the renewed study of Greek and classical Latin during the Renaissance period.

Tower of Palazzo Vecchio, Florence, Italy

Section Quiz

1. What is the name of the period during the fourteenth through the sixteenth centuries in European history in which learning and the arts revived and flourished?
2. Define *humanism*.
3. What new course of study became popular in Europe during the Renaissance? What subjects or disciplines were included in this course of study?
4. What was the goal of Renaissance education?
5. What period of history did the Renaissance humanists admire?

★ Why did Renaissance scholars seek ancient manuscripts? How would the discovery of discrepancies between the Greek and Latin texts of the Bible have helped prepare the way for the Reformation?

Terra-cotta bust of Lorenzo de' Medici

Florentine 15th or 16th Century, probably after a model by Andrea del Verrocchio and Orsino Benintendi. Lorenzo de' Medici. *Samuel H. Kress Collection. Image courtesy of the National Gallery of Art, Washington.*

II. Course of the Renaissance

The Renaissance began in Italy. This land had been the center of the ancient Roman Empire, and even in the fourteenth century, the Italians still thought of themselves as Romans. In their long history Italians had also come into close contact with the Byzantine and Islamic civilizations. Several cities in northern Italy had maintained trade and cultural ties with the East during the Middle Ages. When commerce began to revive throughout Europe during the eleventh and twelfth centuries, the Italian cities rose to prominence. Their control of the Mediterranean trade routes to the East brought them great riches. To display their newly acquired wealth, these cities commissioned talented artists to design buildings, decorate churches, and carve statues for public squares. Affluent bankers and merchants became the sponsors or **patrons** of these artists. No longer were artists dependent solely on the Roman Church for support.

Chapel of the Princes, Florence

Nigetti, Matteo (1560-1649). Cappella dei Principi, S. Lorenzo, Florence, Italy. Scala/Art Resource, NY

Perhaps the most famous of the Renaissance patrons, besides the Roman Church, were the members of the **Medici** (MED uh chee) **family**. The Medici were prominent Italians who had become enormously wealthy through commerce and banking. They used their riches and prominence to gain political control of the city of Florence. The Medici also used their financial resources to promote learning and the arts. They sponsored searches for manuscripts, established a public library (one of the first in Europe), and commissioned great works of painting, sculpture, and architecture. The most notable and most generous patron of the Medici family was **Lorenzo de Medici** (1449–1492), called *Il Magnifico* ("The Magnificent"). During his rule the city of Florence became the most influential city of the Renaissance movement.

Until about 1500 the Renaissance remained primarily an Italian movement. During the sixteenth century, however, enthusiasm for art and learning spread throughout Europe. It was carried abroad, in part, by students who had studied in Italy and merchants who traded with Italian cities. The Renaissance took hold in England, France, Germany, and the Netherlands. At first the people of these lands copied the Italians, but before long they developed their own ideas and styles.

Thought and Literature

Italian Humanist Writers

The city of Florence, home of the powerful Medici, was the birthplace of the Renaissance. This bustling city was the center of Italian commerce. Members of its wealthy class, who sponsored art and learning, made Florence the center of culture in Italy. Most of the writers, painters, sculptors, and architects of the early Renaissance lived in this city.

At the beginning of the fourteenth century, Florentine writers gave expression to the growing secular attitudes. They looked to the literature of ancient Greece and Rome for inspiration. Their study of the classics stirred an increased emphasis on education in Europe.

Petrarch and Laura

Of Laura Petrarch wrote the following:
"He for celestial charms may look in vain
Who has not seen my fair one's radiant eyes,
And felt their glances pleasingly beguile.
How can Love heal his wounds, then wound again,
He only knows who knows how sweet her sighs,
How sweet her [conversation], and how sweet her smile."

The pioneer of Renaissance humanism and one of the most important figures in Italian literature was **Francesco Petrarch** (1304–1374), the son of a Florentine merchant. As a youth he followed his father's wishes and entered law school. But his real love was the classical writings of Greece and Rome. His father did not approve of his spending more time reading these ancient works than studying law. One day he found his son's copies of the classics and threw them into the fire. But then, moved by Petrarch's grief, he managed to snatch two works from the flames.

After his father's death, Petrarch gave up his study of law and devoted his life to classic literature. He searched monastic and church libraries to find ancient manuscripts, which he collected and studied. He composed his own Latin poems, modeling them after classical poetry. These he considered his best works. Later generations, however, remember him best for his vernacular writings. In sonnets (fourteen-line poems) and letters to his friends, he expressed human interest and emotions. Petrarch wrote about nature, his pride in his homeland, and his love for Laura (the woman he idealized). His love of poetry had an immense influence on later writers.

Niccolo Machiavelli

In letters addressed to his heroes of the past—Cicero, Virgil, and Livy—Petrarch placed his own day on an equal plane with the days of ancient Rome. Because Petrarch led the way in reviving interest and study in classical literature, he is known as the Father of Humanism.

Another Italian, **Baldassare Castiglione** (cahs tee LYOH nay; 1478–1529), wrote one of the most famous books on etiquette (social behavior) published during the Renaissance. The topic of good manners was popular at that time. As more people acquired wealth and moved into a higher social class, they were eager to behave in an acceptable manner. In his book *The Courtier*, Castiglione describes the ideal Renaissance gentleman. He presents the courtier or gentleman as a man of character, well-educated, courageous, and courteous. Such a man should demonstrate the nobility of his character whether on the battlefield or in the fashionable places of society. *The Courtier* quickly became a bestseller and was translated into many different languages. It set the standard for courtly behavior all over Europe.

One of the most influential Renaissance writers was the Florentine public official and political thinker **Niccolo Machiavelli** (mah kyah VEL ee; 1469–1527). From 1489 to 1512 Machiavelli worked as a diplomat for the Florentine Republic. During these years he was able to observe firsthand various political developments in Europe.

Rules for Proper Conduct

Besides *The Courtier*, other books of etiquette circulated in Europe during the Renaissance. *The Book of Manners*, written by Giovanni della Casa (1503–1556), is typical of such publications. These excerpts typify the author's advice.

> A man should never boast of his birth, his honors, or his wealth, and still less of his brains.
>
> It is not a polite habit . . . to carry your toothpick either in your mouth, like a bird making its nest, or behind your ear.
>
> You should also take care, as far as you can, not to spit at mealtimes, but if you must spit, then do so in a decent manner.
>
> Refrain as far as possible from making noises which grate upon the ear, such as grinding or sucking your teeth.
>
> Anyone whose legs are too thin, or exceptionally fat, or perhaps crooked, should not wear vivid or parti-colored hose, in order not to attract attention to his defects.
>
> A man must . . . not be content to do things well, but must also aim to do them gracefully.

The unrest and division in Machiavelli's native land deeply disturbed him. Italy at this time was divided into a number of competing, warring states, with mercenary soldiers being used to fight their battles. Even the papacy became involved in these petty conflicts. Popes often acted like secular rulers as they sought to expand the boundaries of the Papal States. The kings of France and Spain added to the political and economic turmoil by fighting a series of wars over Italian territory.

Machiavelli wrote several important and influential works on government. The most important and controversial of these is an essay titled *The Prince*. In this work Machiavelli reflects on the political conditions of his day and tells readers that the successful ruler must do what is expedient and not be governed by principles of right and wrong. Such a man uses force when necessary since "it is much safer to be feared than loved." Later rulers took his advice to cast aside virtue and embraced this wicked system as an ideal political philosophy.

What Did Machiavelli Really Think?

Perhaps a better source of Machiavelli's own political views is his *Discourses on the First Ten Books of Livy*. In this work he examined the politics of ancient Rome and derived lessons for rulers of his day. Favoring a republican form of government, he wrote, "When there is combined under the same constitution a prince, a nobility, and the power of the people, then these three powers will watch and keep each other reciprocally in check."

Northern Humanist Writers

While the Italian Renaissance initially influenced the Renaissance in northern Europe, the emphasis of northern humanists differed from that of their Italian counterparts. The northern humanists generally had a greater interest in religious matters than the Italian humanists. These religious concerns often led to a greater emphasis on church reform in the North. Accordingly, several northern humanists gave more attention to Christian than to classical sources. They placed the study of the Hebrew Old Testament and the Greek New Testament above the writings of Cicero, Virgil, and other ancients.

Perhaps the most honored and influential scholar of the Renaissance was **Erasmus** of Rotterdam (1466–1536). As a young man he entered a monastery, but his stay was brief. Soon he began to travel throughout Europe and obtained

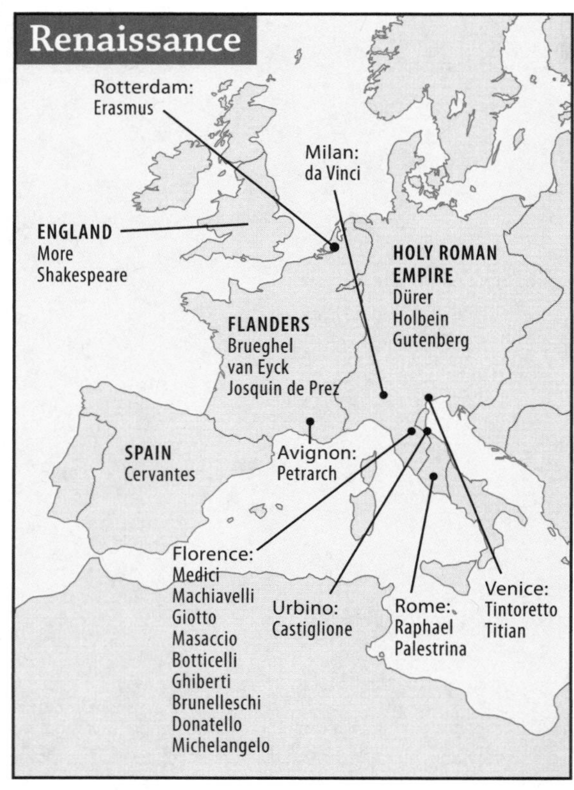

Scripture in the Vernacular

In the preface of his Greek New Testament, Erasmus explains to readers his position on translating Scripture:

> I strongly dissent from those who are unwilling to have the Scriptures translated into the vernacular and read by the ignorant, as if Christ taught so complicated a doctrine that it can hardly be understood even by a handful of theologians. . . . It is perhaps reasonable to conceal the mysteries of kings, but Christ seeks to divulge his mysteries as much as possible. I should like to have even the most humble women read the [Gospels] and the Epistles of St. Paul. . . . Would that the plowboy recited something from them at his plowshare, that the weaver sang from them at his shuttle, and that the traveler whiled away the tedium of his journey with their tales.

The Renaissance: Maker of Modern Man, *National Geographic Society, 300.*

an education in Latin and Greek. Erasmus quickly distinguished himself as the foremost scholar of Europe and became widely acclaimed as the Prince of Humanists. In his most famous work, *In Praise of Folly*, Erasmus uses satire to point out the evils and follies of Renaissance society.

Erasmus became a leading advocate of church reform and was an outspoken critic of monasticism, the ignorance and worldliness of many of the clergy, and the Roman Church's empty ritualism. Yet he refused to break with the Roman Catholic Church.

Erasmus capitalized on his skill in biblical languages and became the first to publish a Greek New Testament in 1516. Martin Luther used Erasmus's Greek New Testament to make a German translation of the New Testament. Many others, including the translators of the King James Version, also used Erasmus's text as the basis for translating the New Testament into the common languages of the people.

A close friend of Erasmus was the English humanist Sir **Thomas More** (1478–1535). More devoted much of his life to the service of his country. His interest in social and political matters prompted him to write a book setting

A selection of Hans Holbein's illustrations for Erasmus's In Praise of Folly

Gutenberg

A resourceful German named Johannes Gutenberg helped to change the course of history. He is recognized as the man who developed movable-type printing in Europe. The Chinese had developed movable-type printing in the eleventh century, but there is no evidence that Europeans were aware of this accomplishment. Gutenberg's goal was to print the Bible, and around 1456 he printed the Bible that was later named after him.

The advent of movable-type printing is a milestone in the history of the Western world. The cost of books dropped steadily because copyists no longer had to produce the books by hand. In addition, mass production continued to bring down the price of printed works. The printing press also paved the way for the rapid spread of ideas, including humanist works of the Renaissance and Protestant works of the Reformation.

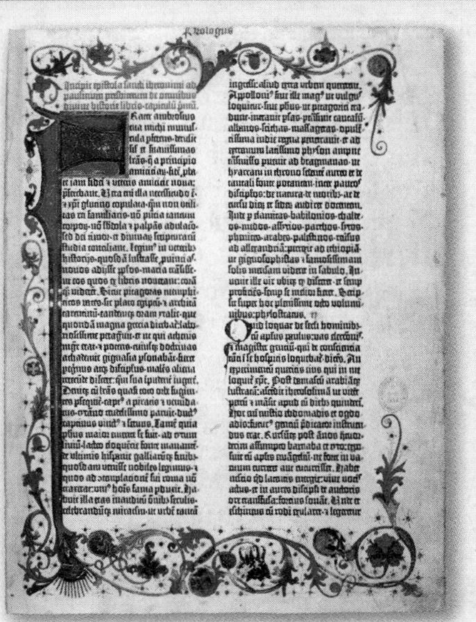

forth his views on the ideal government. This work, entitled *Utopia* (meaning "nowhere"), is the story of an imaginary state built on Christian principles and Plato's philosophy. More believed that if men would govern themselves by a sense of community and brotherly love, they could achieve political, social, and economic equality. According to More, the three deadliest sins of the English community were laziness, greed, and pride. In Utopia, all men would be compelled to work. Thus everyone would have economic security, eliminating all laziness and greed. All pride would be centered in the state.

The foremost Spanish writer of the late Renaissance was **Miguel de Cervantes** (sur VAN tez; 1547–1616). His novel *Don Quixote* (DAHN kee-HO-tay) is one of the most enduring works in all of literature. It satirizes chivalry and the chivalric literature that was popular in Cervantes's day. The main character, Don Quixote, imagining himself to be a knight, puts on a suit of armor, mounts an old horse, and gallops around the Spanish countryside seeking to right the world's wrongs. In doing so, he makes a fool of himself. Accompanying Don Quixote on his many adventures is his faithful squire Sancho Panza, whom Cervantes presents as a more practical, down-to-earth person. Through this work Cervantes pokes fun at outdated medieval ideas while presenting a vivid picture of life in sixteenth-century Spain.

Renaissance literature reached its peak in the works of **William Shakespeare** (1564–1616), who is generally considered the greatest playwright of all time and the finest poet in the English language. Shakespeare, the son of a prosperous trader, was born and reared in Stratford-upon-Avon, a small town northwest of London. As a young man he went to London, where he became a successful actor and playwright. His fame spread during his early career after he published two long narrative poems. Shakespeare gained financial success as a leader and a stockholder in a prominent London theatrical group called the Lord Chamberlain's Men, later known as the King's Men. He purchased stock in two playhouses, the more famous of which was the Globe Theatre, where most of his plays were performed.

Shakespeare's lifework includes 154 sonnets and at least thirty-seven plays. His dramatic works are classified into histories, comedies, and tragedies. The tragedies, including *Hamlet*, *Othello*, *King Lear*, and *Macbeth*, are generally

More's Ill-fated Public Service

More entered the service of Henry VIII (the king of England) because, as he said, "If better men did not go into politics, worse ones would." Although he served Henry well, More was beheaded for treason when he refused to take an oath recognizing Henry as head of the church in England. Despite the corruption in the Renaissance papacy, More still believed in the pope's supremacy in the Roman Church. Therefore, he chose to die rather than violate his conscience.

Shakespeare and National Pride

In his historical play *Richard II*, Shakespeare penned these words:

This royal throne of kings, this sceptred isle,
This earth of majesty, this seat of Mars,
This other Eden, demi-paradise,
This fortress built by Nature for herself
Against the infection and the hand of war,
This happy breed of men, this little world,
This precious stone set in the silver sea,
Which serves it in the office of a wall,
Or as a moat defensive to a house,
Against the envy of less happier lands;
This blessed plot, this earth, this realm, this England.

recognized as his greatest works. Fourteen of his plays are set in Italy. This delighted English audiences, because in true Renaissance spirit they looked to Italy as the birthplace of learning. Several of Shakespeare's plays reflect the surge of national pride in England.

Shakespeare left an indelible imprint on Western culture through his writings. Shakespeare's poems and plays have been the object of careful study by scholars in every generation since his death. His literary genius enriched the English language and influenced its development. Many of the phrases and expressions that he coined are part of everyday speech in modern society.

Section Quiz

1. In addition to the Roman Church, what family became the most famous patron (sponsor) of Renaissance learning and art? Who was the most noted patron of this family?
2. Who is called the Father of Humanism because he led the way in reviving interest and study in classical literature?
3. What work of Erasmus did later reformers and Bible translators use?
4. What contribution did Johannes Gutenberg make to European history?
5. What Englishman is generally considered the greatest playwright of all time?

✯ In *The Prince*, what was Machiavelli subtly denying or disregarding?

The Visual Arts

From a biblical perspective, Renaissance art was superior to medieval art because it recognized the goodness of God's creation. Renaissance artists rightly presented man as the greatest of God's creatures in a good creation rather than directing all attention to an otherworldly realm. Sadly, Renaissance humanism exalted man to a position independent of God instead of arriving at a biblical balance.

Renaissance artists drew their inspiration and ideas from the classical world. They broke with the artistic traditions of the Middle Ages in the following ways:

1. Renaissance art emphasized the present physical world. Medieval art had emphasized the spiritual realm and the life to come.
2. Secular patrons often supported the Renaissance artists. During the Middle Ages, the Church of Rome had almost exclusively patronized the artists.
3. Most Renaissance artists were extremely proud of their work and wanted their names known and their works praised. Medieval artists, on the other hand, had worked primarily for the glory of God and the church and usually did not gain any personal recognition.
4. Renaissance artists gave a realistic, three-dimensional aspect to their works. Medieval art was flat and two-dimensional.

5. Most Renaissance portrait painters frequently painted kings, merchants, and other important secular individuals. Medieval painters usually portrayed church leaders, biblical characters, or saints of the Roman Church.

6. Painting and sculpture were the most popular media during the Renaissance. The glory of medieval art was its architecture.

Early Italian Painters

Giotto di Bondone (JAWT-toh DEE bone-DOH-nay; c. 1267–1337) is the most famous painter of the early Italian Renaissance. He is often called the Father of Renaissance Painting. He opened a new era of art in the Western world. Up until his time, figures in paintings were stiff and flat; medieval artists painted expressionless people and set them against a plain gold background. This practice created an impression of calm serenity—a heavenly atmosphere. Giotto, however, sought to make painting more natural. His figures were more realistic and exhibited human feelings. He also tried to add a three-dimensional look to his paintings by making greater use of backgrounds.

Lorenzetti Ambrogio, Annunciation *(1344)*

Giotto is most famous for his **frescoes** (paintings on wet plaster) on the walls of the town church at Padua. Although he tried to make his painting as realistic as possible, he never fully mastered the technique of perspective—portraying a three-dimensional appearance on a flat surface.

Florentine artists of the fifteenth century achieved greater realism in their paintings by creating works that gave a sense of life, action, depth, and feeling. Early in the century **Masaccio** (mah SOT choh; 1401–28) added new techniques to painting. By means of shading (contrasting light and dark), he created a three-dimensional effect in his paintings. This technique enabled him to portray human figures with a realism that had been missing in the works of previous painters.

In the late fifteenth century, **Sandro Botticelli** (bot ih CHEL ee; c. 1444–1510) added another dimension to Renaissance art: movement. He depicted forms with bold lines and gave clarity and a sense of activity to his characters. With their flowing hair and wispy garments, his painted figures seemed

Below, left: Botticelli's The Adoration of the Magi *(1475)*
Below: Botticelli placed himself in the painting

Savonarola: Preacher of Righteousness

A generation before the Reformation, a Dominican friar named Girolamo Savonarola (1452–1498) sought to bring moral reform to the city of Florence and to the Roman Church. He opposed the corrupt rule of the Medici family and severely criticized Pope Alexander VI, a man notorious for his immoral lifestyle. Savonarola warned the Florentines of a coming day of judgment and called on them to repent of their wicked ways. At the height of his popularity, crowds of ten to twelve thousand people flocked to hear his sermons. He soon became the leading religious figure in the city.

As a result of his preaching, the secular culture that dominated the city began to change. For example, people built great bonfires into which they threw playing cards, gambling dice, immoral books and pictures, and objects of luxury. Not everyone, however, enthusiastically accepted the reforms that Savonarola had begun. Alexander VI sought to silence him and prohibited him from preaching, but Savonarola continued to boldly denounce the wickedness of his day. Alexander then tried to buy his silence by offering to make him a cardinal, but Savonarola refused. The pope finally excommunicated him, but Savonarola ignored his action.

However, the people of Florence were intimidated by the pope's action, and they abandoned the friar. City officials arrested Savonarola, after which he was tortured, tried, and condemned to die by hanging. The crowds that had once gathered to hear him preach now gathered to watch him die. Authorities hanged Savonarola, burned his body, and cast his ashes into the Arno River. (His ashes were scattered so that no one could preserve them as a relic.)

Many of Savonarola's contemporaries considered him a failure. The city had cast aside his reforms and had consented to his execution. God, however, does not measure success or failure on the basis of popular approval. He rewards His servants who are faithful—even unto death.

Statue of Savonarola

to move and sway. Botticelli's early paintings reflected the humanistic spirit prevalent in the Medici court. He painted pagan themes of classical mythology. But when the Medici family was expelled from Florence, Botticelli came under the influence of the preaching of the monk **Girolamo Savonarola.** He became one of Savonarola's converts, and his painting, as a result, took on a more religious and moral outlook.

High Renaissance Painters

The artistic achievement of the Italian Renaissance culminated in the early sixteenth century. During this period, known as the High Renaissance, the center of culture shifted from Florence to Rome, and the papacy became the major patron of Italian artists. High Renaissance artists mastered the painting techniques that the Italian artists of the fifteenth century had pioneered. The most famous High Renaissance painters are Leonardo da Vinci, Raphael, and Michelangelo.

Raphael

Leonardo da Vinci (duh VIN-chee; 1452–1519) is probably the best example of the so-called Renaissance man. He displayed interests in a wide range of fields. Da Vinci was an accomplished sculptor, architect, painter, and musician. He also studied anatomy, botany, geology, astronomy, engineering, and mathematics.

As a young man da Vinci received training in painting and sculpture at Florence. Distinguishing himself as a painter, he was admitted into the Florentine painter's guild. But he believed that the restrictions of the guild stifled his creative talents. Da Vinci was eager to explore new ideas; the city of Florence, he thought, was too dependent on the classical age. Therefore, in 1482 he sought a position in Milan under the sponsorship of the duke of Milan.

While in Milan da Vinci painted his famous mural *The Last Supper* on a wall in a monastery. The painting illustrates his mastery of perspective and exemplifies the Renaissance love for balance. He vividly depicts the intense feelings

In da Vinci's Humble Opinion

In a letter Leonardo da Vinci wrote to a prospective patron, he proudly listed his qualifications:

> And in short, according to the variety of cases, I can contrive various and endless means of offence and defense [that is, weaponry]. . . . In time of peace I believe I can give perfect satisfaction and to the equal of any other in architecture and the composition of buildings, public and private; and in guiding water from one place to another. . . . I can carry out sculpture in marble, bronze, or clay, and also I can do in painting whatever may be done, as well as any other, be he whom he may.
>
> *E. G. Holt,* Literary Sources of Art History, *170.*

of the disciples when Christ announced that one of them would betray Him. Although the painting quickly began to deteriorate and has been repeatedly restored, it remains one of the most famous religious paintings of all time. Perhaps da Vinci's most famous work is the *Mona Lisa.*

Raphael, Madonna del Granduca, *c.1505.*

Raffaello Sanzio (1483–1520), better known as **Raphael** (RAF ee el), completed an enormous number of paintings and frescoes in his short lifetime. His interest in painting undoubtedly began at home because his father was a painter. As a young man Raphael studied the works of the masters in order to perfect his own technique. He soon became one of the most beloved painters of his time.

Raphael is famous for his paintings of sweet-faced Madonnas in which he idealized motherhood. He sought to express the peace and quiet joy of life rather than its anguish and strain. He is also known for the magnificent frescoes that decorate the papal residence in Rome. *The School of Athens* is an excellent example of his work; it displays balance, harmony, and perspective. In this painting he creates a spacious setting in which are gathered the great philosophers and scientists of the classical world.

Michelangelo Buonarroti (my-kul-AN-juh-lo bwawn-uh-RAW-tee; 1475–1564) is one of the most famous artists in all of history. His contemporaries praised his artistic masterpieces. As a young boy he exhibited unusual skill in sculpting. It is said that he learned how to handle a chisel and hammer before he could read and write. When he told his father that he wanted to study painting and sculpture, his father was furious. His father believed manual labor was beneath the dignity of the family. However, when Michelangelo displayed little

Michelangelo, Creation of the Sun, Moon and Plants, *from the Sistine Chapel in the Vatican*

The Sistine Chapel; ceiling frescos after restoration. The creation of sun, moon, and plants. Michelangelo Buonarroti (1475-1564). Sistine Chapel, Vatican Palace, Vatican State. Erich Lessing/Art Resource, NY

interest or ability in school, his father apprenticed him to a leading Florentine artist. While an apprentice, the talented youth caught the eye of Lorenzo de Medici, who took Michelangelo into his household as his adopted son.

In 1508 Pope Julius II commissioned Michelangelo to paint the ceiling of the **Sistine Chapel** in the Vatican (the papal residence in Rome). Protesting that he was a sculptor and not a painter, Michelangelo began the mammoth project reluctantly. After four years of working on scaffolds nearly seventy feet above the floor, he finished painting the 5,800-square-foot ceiling. The original plan had called for only twelve figures; however, when Michelangelo finished the project, he had painted over three hundred figures, most of which were ten to eighteen feet tall. This magnificent fresco depicts the stories of Creation, the Fall, the Flood, and the redemption of man as prophesied by the Old Testament prophets. Nearly a quarter of a century later, Michaelangelo painted the front wall of the chapel with his conception of the Last Judgment. This painting is filled with violent, frenzied action portraying a dynamic Christ calling the saved to heaven and condemning the lost to hell.

Venetian Painters

During the late Renaissance the city of Venice became a leading center of culture. It is located on a cluster of islands at the northern end of the Adriatic Sea. Numerous canals dissect the city; these serve as streets along which gondolas, or flat-bottomed boats, transport people about the city. Its merchant fleet once made it the strongest sea power in the Mediterranean region. Venetian merchants controlled the important trade routes to the East. The economic prosperity the city enjoyed encouraged cultural activity. Wealthy merchants built grand palaces and commissioned artists to adorn the city with great works of art. The beautiful, wealthy, and proud city of Venice became known as the Queen of the Adriatic.

The people of Venice, however, were wicked and materialistic. They eagerly sought after luxury, pleasure, and prestige. Each year the city staged elaborate pageants; beneath all the glitter and pomp was a city sunk deep in moral decay.

Even the art of Venice mirrored its materialism. It attested to the Venetian love for money, precious gems, rich clothing, decoration, and festive occasions. Artists painted wealthy merchants, proud city officials, and beautiful women. These paintings, filled with radiant color and light, reflect the city's secular and sensuous spirit.

The Pilgrims of Emmaus *(1530) by Titian*

Tiziano Vecelli (c. 1488–1576), known as **Titian** (TISH un), was the leading figure of the Venetian school of painting. He ranks with Michelangelo as one of the foremost painters of the Renaissance. A prolific painter known for his rich use of color, Titian is especially remembered for his portraits. His works contain a freshness, warmth, and vitality missing in the serene Renaissance portraits of southern Italy. He captured on canvas the personality of his subject, not just the physical appearance. His fame spread throughout Europe. He painted pictures for the Holy Roman emperor and the kings of Spain and France, becoming one of the few Renaissance painters to grow wealthy through his work.

Albrecht Dürer, Knight, Death, and Devil, *National Gallery of Art, Washington, D.C.*

Tintoretto (1518–1594) was the last of the great sixteenth-century Venetian painters. He was born Jacopo Robusti but is known by his nickname Tintoretto (Italian for "little dyer") because his father was a dyer by profession. In his paintings he sought to combine the bright colors of Titian and the masterful drawing of Michelangelo. His works exhibit a dramatic excitement full of tension and action.

Northern European Artists

The German painter **Albrecht Dürer** (DOOR ur; 1471–1528) was sometimes called the Leonardo of the North. Like da Vinci, he was accomplished in many different fields: writing, designing, engraving, and painting. He had a high regard for Italian art and was the first northern artist to travel to Italy for the express purpose of studying art. His paintings illustrate his love for both classical and religious themes. He also had a keen interest in nature, an interest reflected by his amazingly accurate watercolors of floral scenes. Although Dürer is a celebrated painter, he is best remembered for his woodcarvings and engravings, which were used to illustrate printed books. He is the first artist to sign even his most insignificant drawings. His "signature" consisted of a capital *A* straddling a capital *D*.

Another celebrated German painter was **Hans Holbein** (HOHL bine) the Younger (c. 1497–1543). He is considered the finest portrait painter of the Northern Renaissance. He traveled throughout Europe working in many countries—especially

Pieter Brueghel's The Peasant Wedding

England. Holbein became the official court painter of Henry VIII, the king of England. He not only painted the portrait of Henry, his wives, and his son but also designed Henry's clothes, jewelry, and tableware. This German master also painted the portraits of leading figures of the Northern Renaissance, such as Erasmus and Sir Thomas More.

One of the founders and an outstanding representative of the Flemish school of painters was **Jan van Eyck** (van IKE; c. 1380–1441). In his early career he illustrated manuscripts, which required careful attention to minute details. Van Eyck's concern for detail carried over to his large paintings. He was one of the first to use oil paints, a medium that allowed him to achieve greater realism in his painting.

During the fifteenth century, Flemish painters created a distinctive style of art known for its realism, landscapes, and scenes of contemporary life. In the sixteenth century **Pieter Brueghel** (BROY gul; c. 1525–69) helped develop and perfect this style. He is best remembered for his **genre painting**, a type of painting that depicts scenes of everyday life. These works show the peasants in their daily activities: farming in the fields, hunting in the woods, and dancing in the village square. When Brueghel painted biblical events, he depicted them as though they took place in Flanders.

Ghiberti's North Doors with twenty-eight panels depicting scenes from the New Testament

North Doors: New Testament scenes, Four Apostles and Fathers of the Church. Ghiberti, Lorenzo (1370-1455). Baptistery, Florence, Italy. Scala/Art Resource, NY

Architects and Sculptors

Both architects and sculptors were influenced by the spirit of humanism. They greatly admired the art of the classical world. Renaissance architecture and sculpture, like painting, also reflected the new secular concerns of the Renaissance Age. In the medieval period the primary function of architecture had been to glorify God through the building of magnificent cathedrals. During the Renaissance, however, architects also designed and built spacious palaces and comfortable villas for powerful princes and wealthy merchants. Similarly, sculpture, which had been used during the Middle Ages to decorate churches, now graced town squares and homes of the wealthy.

Around 1401 the leading men of Florence held a contest to select an artist to design a set of bronze doors for one of the entrances to the baptistery of Florence. Among the many artists who entered the competition were **Lorenzo Ghiberti** (gee BEHR tee; 1378–1455) and **Filippo Brunelleschi** (broo nuh LES kee; 1377–1446). According to the contest rules, each participant had to present a sculptured relief depicting the story of the sacrifice of Isaac. Ghiberti's work was judged the best.

For the next two decades Ghiberti worked on the doors. The finished doors contained twenty-eight

The Florence Cathedral, showing Brunelleschi's dome on the right

panels depicting New Testament stories. The city later commissioned him to do a second set of doors. This time he chose to depict stories from the Old Testament. According to Michelangelo, Ghiberti designed the ten panels on these doors "so fine that they might fittingly stand at the Gates of Paradise." Ghiberti himself said, "Of all my work it is the most remarkable I have done, and it was finished with skill, correct proportion, and understanding."

Disgusted with losing the competition to design the doors of the baptistery in Florence, Brunelleschi turned from sculpture to architecture. He traveled to Rome where he studied Roman monuments. He later returned to Florence and defeated Ghiberti in a competition to design and construct a dome for the cathedral of Florence. Not since the days of ancient Rome had anyone in the West constructed such a magnificent and lofty dome. Brunelleschi's dome became the crowning glory of the Florence cathedral. Most of the domes designed during the Renaissance conformed to his model.

Brunelleschi looking up to his cathedral dome

Donatello (c. 1386–1466) was the leading sculptor of the early Renaissance. He was born in Florence and as a young boy served as an assistant to Ghiberti. He later accompanied Brunelleschi to Rome, where both studied classical statues. Although strongly influenced by these classical works, Donatello gave to his sculptures a new realism and expression. He mastered the art of sculpting freestanding statues. One of his most revolutionary works was his statue of David, whom he depicted as a young Florentine shepherd boy. Donatello also cast the first full-scale equestrian statue (man on horseback) since Roman times. His realistic, freestanding statues later inspired the most outstanding sculptor of the Renaissance—Michelangelo.

Michelangelo was a man of many talents. He was a noted painter, sculptor, architect, engineer, and poet. While in his early twenties, he completed one of his most famous masterpieces, the *Pietà* (pyay TAH; an Italian term meaning "pity" or "compassion"). It depicts the virgin Mary mourning over the crucified Christ. When the work was unveiled, one viewer exclaimed, "This cannot be the work of some unknown artist. It must be the work of our master in Milan."

Michelangelo's Pietà

Discrepancies of the *Pietà*

In sculpting the *Pietà*, Michelangelo went beyond usual artistic methods of portraying subjects realistically because he wanted to express what he considered to be the ideal. The sculpture contains a number of contradictions. For example, Michelangelo portrays Christ after the Crucifixion without any disfigurement; in fact, the figure of Christ is a model of physical perfection. Another interesting feature is that Mary is presented as a young girl—one too young to be the mother of Christ. Michelangelo created this distortion of historical fact in order to emphasize the purity of Mary. Furthermore, though the figure of Christ is life-size, Mary is larger than life. It is estimated that if she were to stand, she would be eight to nine feet tall. When questioned about these discrepancies, Michelangelo said, "The hands execute, but the eye judges." To the admiring eye these distortions are not readily apparent.

Hearing this, Michelangelo returned later that night and carved into the ribbon across Mary's chest, "Michelangelo Buonarroti, Florentine, made this."

Another famous work by Michelangelo is his marble statue of David. Like many Renaissance artists, Michelangelo glorified the human body. His David, standing eighteen feet high, is the embodiment of Michelangelo's vision of a perfect specimen of young manhood.

Music

The most prominent type of musical composition during the early Middle Ages was known as **plainsong**, or Gregorian chant. Sung to Latin words, these simple, single-lined melodies became the official music of the medieval church. Most medieval music was mystical and spiritual in nature; its purpose was not to appeal to the senses and emotions of its listeners but to their spirits. Medieval music attempted to remove the listener from the cares of the world.

Renaissance music was more secular. Like the visual arts, it did not remain under the exclusive patronage of the Roman Church. With the advent of the printing press, copies of music became more available. Both the number of musicians and the popular interest in music increased. Music moved into the palaces of the nobles and the homes of the middle class. Even ordinary people could purchase printed song books. "How-to-do-it" books instructed would-be musicians in how to play a musical instrument. The lute became the most popular instrument of the day. This instrument, which resembles a pear-shaped guitar, was widely used to accompany singers.

Josquin des Prez

One of the leading figures in music during the early Renaissance was the Flemish composer **Josquin des Prez** (duh PREH; c. 1450–1521). His life and music mark the transition between medieval and modern times. His contemporaries hailed him as one of the foremost composers of the day. Martin Luther said of him, "He is the master of notes; they do as he bids; as for the other composers, they have to do as the notes will."

With a simple and charming style, des Prez composed both sacred and secular works. He is best remembered for his masses (music sung during the mass service), hymns, and more than one hundred motets—unaccompanied Latin songs that combined different melodies and words with a plainsong melody. Less serious were his **chansons**, lighthearted songs that set secular lyric poems to music.

A lute

Palestrina

The most famous composer of church music during the Renaissance was the Italian composer Giovanni Pierluigi (c. 1526–1594). He is better known as **Palestrina**, taking his name from the town of his birth. As a boy he sang in his town's church choir; later he served as the organist and choirmaster of the Palestrina Cathedral. Palestrina was the master of **polyphonic** music (consisting of many melodies), which he composed for choirs to sing without accompaniment.

During his lifetime, Palestrina composed more than nine hundred musical pieces. He also revised many of the old Gregorian chants. By the sixteenth century, church music had become so complicated that it was difficult to understand what the choir was singing. Commissioned by the papacy, Palestrina simplified much of the Roman Church's official music. In his own day he was hailed as the Prince of Music.

Section Quiz

1. During the High Renaissance, what city became the cultural center of Italy?
2. List the three most famous painters of the High Renaissance period; beside each, give the title of one of their masterpieces.
3. What beautiful, wealthy city, called the Queen of the Adriatic, became the center of culture during the late Renaissance? Identify two leading painters from this city.
4. Identify a Northern Renaissance artist for each of the following characteristics: portrait painting, genre painting, woodcarvings and engravings, and detailed realism through oil painting.
5. Who was the most famous composer of church music during the Renaissance? What type of music did he master?

★ Did Renaissance music tend to be sacred or secular? Explain your answer.

III. Consequences of the Renaissance

The Renaissance and the Reformation that followed it are in many respects exact opposites. The Renaissance was a secular age; men placed confidence in human ability and gloried in human achievement. Artists and scholars, who looked to classical Greece and Rome for inspiration and authority, helped stir a great revival in learning and the arts. The Reformation was a religious age; men placed confidence in God and gloried in God's salvation. Men of God, who looked to the Bible as the sole authority, helped stir a great spiritual revival.

Despite these differences, it would be wrong to assume that there was no connection between the Renaissance and the Reformation. Every period of history is preparatory to the age that follows. In God's providence, the age of the Renaissance prepared western Europe for the coming age of the Reformation (which we will discuss in the next chapter).

Positive

The Renaissance provided the tools that shaped the Reformation movement. In this sense the Renaissance made the Reformation possible.

First, the Renaissance provoked a spirit of inquiry. People no longer meekly accepted the authority of the Roman Church. Instead they critically evaluated its teachings for themselves. This analytical spirit encouraged some to examine the Scriptures to see which teachings were scriptural and which needed to be discarded.

Second, it revived interest in the literature and languages of antiquity. In their search for classical sources, Renaissance humanists recovered many Christian sources—manuscripts of the Old and New Testaments. The discovery of these manuscripts led to a renewed interest in the biblical languages (Greek and Hebrew) and in the study of the Bible itself.

Third, it developed movable-type printing. The new publishing industry made possible the mass production of written material. The printed page would be instrumental in spreading the ideas of the reformers throughout Europe.

Fourth, it made education more widely available to the middle class. More people were now able to read what was being printed.

Fifth, it stressed the importance of the individual, thus restoring the proper emphasis on individual responsibility—the obligation each man has to God and to his fellow man.

Negative

First, the Renaissance's secular emphasis helped weaken moral restraints and thereby made the need for reform more readily apparent. The Roman Church, which should have been the example of moral righteousness, was caught up in worldliness and wickedness as many church leaders lived openly in luxury and immorality.

Second, the humanists, who sought to imitate the best of the classical world, often embraced its evils. The revival of classical literature and art carried with it the danger of a revival of heathenism in religion and morality.

Third, the worship of classical forms often led to the worship of classical ideas. Some humanists and artists combined culture with Christian faith and devoted their genius to the cause of truth and virtue, but the majority effectively worshiped the gods of Greece and Rome rather than the God of the Bible.

Fourth, as educational opportunities improved, many embraced the error that ignorance is a source of evil and that education would solve man's spiritual problems.

Fifth, many who embraced the Renaissance supported the lie that man is, by nature, good and capable of achievement apart from God.

Chapter 11 Review

Making Connections

1–3. Contrast the attitudes of the Renaissance man and the medieval man toward life. (List three.)

4–5. Contrast Renaissance and medieval art. (List two.)

Developing History Skills

1. Assess the influences of previous and current empires on Italy, as well as other advantages that resulted in this peninsula becoming the home of the early Renaissance.
2. Drawing on information from previous chapters, defend or dispute the following statement: "Every period of history is preparatory to the age that follows."

Thinking Critically

1. Defend from the Bible the shift of Renaissance paintings from an otherworldly emphasis to a focus on the goodness of creation. (Considering the opening and closing chapters of the Bible may be helpful).
2. Why did the Renaissance in northern Europe tend to differ from the Renaissance in Italy?

Living in God's World

1. Imagine you are a Renaissance author, painter, or composer. You meet a friar one day while traveling from one city to another. He tells you that if you really want to serve God you must take holy orders. How would you respond?
2. In the medieval worldview, past generations were considered better than present and future generations. People believed that God had created a good and perfect world that was running down over time. In the Renaissance worldview, the present generation had surpassed previous generations in knowledge and skill, and future generations were likely to excel even further. Briefly analyze these ideas from a biblical worldview.

People, Places, and Things to Know

Renaissance
humanism
humanists
patrons
Medici family
Lorenzo de Medici
Francesco Petrarch
Baldassare Castiglione
Niccolo Machiavelli
Erasmus
Thomas More
Miguel de Cervantes
William Shakespeare
Giotto di Bondone
frescoes
Masaccio
Sandro Botticelli
Girolamo Savonarola
Leonardo da Vinci
Raphael
Michelangelo
Sistine Chapel
Titian
Tintoretto
Albrecht Dürer
Hans Holbein
Jan van Eyck
Pieter Brueghel
genre painting
Lorenzo Ghiberti
Filippo Brunelleschi
Donatello
plainsong
Josquin des Prez
chansons
Palestrina
polyphonic

12

The Reformation

I. Forerunners

II. Beginning

III. Spread

IV. Counter-Reformation

Wall of the Reformers Monument, Geneva, Switzerland

On November 10, 1483, in the mining town of Eisleben located in the heart of Germany, a son was born to Hans and Margaretta Luther. Before this boy reached the age of ten, European explorers had sailed to the southern tip of Africa and had landed in the New World. The age of exploration and discovery had begun. Meanwhile, the Renaissance was flourishing in Italy and was beginning to spread to northern Europe. Throughout Europe a spirit of nationalism was stirring. Men busied themselves with religious activity, but there was little true godliness.

This was the age the young Martin Luther grew up in. This son of German peasants became one of the leading figures of the sixteenth century. Through God's leading he initiated the Protestant Reformation and was an outspoken leader during its early years. This religious movement began during the early sixteenth century as a protest against the corruption in the Roman Catholic Church. Luther and the other Protestant reformers soon realized that the corruption of the Roman Catholic Church resulted from false doctrines that had developed during the Middle Ages. Reform of corrupt practices would need to go hand-in-hand with doctrinal reform. People needed to recognize the Bible as the sole authority for Christian life and belief. In addition, they needed to understand that salvation was through Christ and His work alone and not through the sacraments of the Roman Church. From this return to biblical Christianity, many Protestant denominations developed.

I. Forerunners

The spiritual awakening that swept across Europe during the sixteenth century was the culmination of centuries of activity. For many generations men had attempted to curb the abuses in the church. Most reforming efforts, however, were directed only against its most visible evils. Many had failed to recognize the need for doctrinal purity and genuine moral reform. Attempting to stir inward reform, godly reformers attacked the church's corrupt teaching as well as its corrupt practices. These brave men held to the Bible as the sole authority for the Christian faith. Asserting that Christ was the only Head of the church, they rejected the authority of the pope. God used these godly men to prepare the way for the later reformers of the Reformation Era.

John Wycliffe

One of the strongest voices of protest against the wickedness in the Roman Church came from the Englishman **John Wycliffe** (WIK lif; c. 1328–84). Wycliffe was a fearless preacher, a distinguished scholar, and a patriotic leader. Long associated with the University of Oxford, he earned fame as a teacher, lecturer, and theologian. Nevertheless, it is for his work as a religious reformer that he is best remembered. Because many of his convictions and teachings were later embraced by the sixteenth-century reformers, he has been called the "Morning Star of the Reformation."

John Wycliffe

From his study of the Bible, Wycliffe became convinced that the church as it came to be dominated by Roman Catholicism had strayed from its original purity both in doctrine and practice. Through sermons, lectures, and writings, he opposed the temporal power and wealth of the Roman Church. Wycliffe sought to purge the church of its corrupt clergy. He denounced monastic orders, criticized the practice of confessing sins to a priest, and rejected the doctrine of transubstantiation (see p. 175). He, as well as other Englishmen of his day, resented the claims of the papacy upon the church in England. But

The English People Reading Wycliffe's Bible *(detail) oil on canvas by George Clausen, 1927. WOA 2603 ©Palace of Westminster Collection*

Wycliffe went a step further than his countrymen when he proclaimed the papacy to be an institution "full of poison." He preached Christ as the only Head of the church. The pope, he said, "is not the head, life or root except perchance of evildoers in the church." He called the pope "the antichrist" and "the leader of the army of the devil."

Wycliffe upheld the Bible as the supreme authority for all believers, clergy as well as laity. He believed that every Christian should study the Bible and that God's Word is the only source of spiritual truth and the only accurate presentation of the way of salvation. Wycliffe contended that a knowledge of Scripture would expose the error in the practice and teaching of the Roman Catholic Church and would start true reform. For this reason, he initiated the translation of the Bible from Latin into English so that more people could discover the truths found in Scripture. This first complete English translation of the Bible—known as the Wycliffe Bible—was finished in 1382. Wycliffe also trained men, mostly laymen, to preach the gospel. By twos, these servants of the Lord, barefoot and clad in coarse garments, went out with staffs in hand (a symbol of their pastoral office) to live and preach among the people.

John Huss

Wycliffe's reforming efforts met with stiff opposition. Church leaders sought to suppress his teaching, which they condemned as heretical. In 1384 Wycliffe died from a stroke, but his death did not end the persecution. For more than a century after his death, the church attempted to eradicate his teaching and followers in England. Many of his followers, known as **Lollards**, were imprisoned, tortured, and burned at the stake. However, the flame of truth could not be extinguished.

John Huss

Wycliffe's views soon spread to the Continent (mainland Europe), where they influenced the Bohemian reformer **John Huss** (c. 1369–1415). From the city of Prague, Huss challenged the Bohemian people to oppose the worldliness in the church. Huss, who taught and defended many of Wycliffe's beliefs, was accused by church leaders of spreading heresy. Though excommunicated, he remained steadfast in his beliefs and continued to be a popular preacher.

In 1414 church leaders met in the city of Constance to settle the pressing disputes over the papal schism (see p. 224) and church reform. Sigismund, the Holy Roman emperor, wishing to settle the question of heresy in Bohemia, summoned Huss to the **Council of Constance**, giving him a promise of imperial protection. Huss traveled to Constance expecting to have an opportunity to defend his teaching from the Word of God. But soon after his arrival, church leaders had him imprisoned and placed on trial for teaching heresy. When the officials could not show from God's Word that he was in error, Huss refused to renounce his beliefs. In spite of the emperor's promise of protection, the council condemned him to die at the stake.

The day of execution came, and Huss was led to the stake. Moments before the fire was kindled, he was asked to **recant** (renounce his beliefs) and thereby save his life. He responded, "I shall die with joy today in the faith of the gospel which I have preached." Although the flames ended his earthly life, his influence remained strong, and the work for reform continued. His Bohemian brethren, stirred by his death, vigorously adhered to his teaching despite increased persecution by the Roman Church.

The same council that condemned Huss to death also reexamined the writings of Wycliffe. The Roman Church formally condemned Wycliffe as a heretic on 260 different counts and ordered his writings to be burned. His enemies at the council also ordered his body to be dug up and burned—an act that supposedly signified his condemnation to hell. More than a decade passed, however, before this order was carried out. In 1428, forty-four years after his death, Wycliffe's bones were dug up and burned. His ashes were thrown into a nearby stream.

The Roman Church seemingly triumphed over Wycliffe and Huss. Both men had called attention to the deplorable condition of the church; neither, however, had been able to initiate any widespread or lasting reform. In the providence of God, the time was not yet ripe. The task of breaking the grip of the Roman Church was left for a later generation. Nevertheless, these "reformers before the Reformation" faithfully stood for truth and boldly opposed the errors of Roman Catholicism. In doing so, they prepared the way for the Protestant Reformation.

Chaucer and the Clergy

In *The Canterbury Tales* Geoffrey Chaucer, a contemporary of John Wycliffe, ridicules the clergy of his day. His descriptions of a monk and a friar display the popular contempt for the selfish desires and worldly interests of many members of the clergy. In contrast to these examples of religious hypocrisy, Chaucer presents the tale of a town parson who is materially poor but rich in true godliness.

A good man was there of religion,
And a poor PARSON OF A TOWN,
But rich he was of holy thought and work.
He was also a learned man, a clerk,
That Christ's gospel truly would preach;
His parisshens devoutly would he teach.

This noble ensample to his sheep he gave,
That first he wrought, and afterward he
taught.
Out of the gospel he the words caught,
And this figure he added eke thereto,
That if gold rust, what shall iron do?
For if a priest be foul, on whom we trust,
No wonder is a lewed [ordinary] man to
rust.

To drawen folk to heaven by fairness,
By good ensample, this was his business.
But it were any person obstinate,
What so he were, of high or low estate,
Him would he snybben sharply for the
nonys.
A better priest I trowe that nowhere none is.
He waited after no pomp and reverence,
He maked him a spiced conscience,
But Christ's lore and his apostles twelve
He taught, but first he followed it himself.

Section Quiz

1. What Englishman's protest against the Roman Church prior to the Reformation period earned him the title "Morning Star of the Reformation"?
2. What did this "pre-reformer" uphold as the supreme authority for all believers? What great work did he do in order to expose the corruption of the Roman Church to the English people?
3. What English author presented contrasting views of the clergy of his day—the hypocrisy of a wealthy, worldly monk with the godliness of a poor town parson? What was the title of his work?
4. What city is associated with the life and ministry of John Huss?
5. What council condemned Huss to be burned at the stake? What other man did this council condemn as a heretic?

★ How did those who preceded the Reformation pave the way for it? Provide two examples.

Martin Luther

II. Beginning

The name **Martin Luther** is inseparably linked to the Reformation period. His courageous stand against the Roman Catholic Church sparked the religious awakening known as the Protestant Reformation.

Luther's Early Life

Strict discipline characterized Martin Luther's early training both at home and at school. At the age of eighteen, he entered the University of Erfurt, where he became acquainted with both Scholastic and classical studies. It was also at the university that he saw a complete Bible for the first time.

After graduation Luther planned to obey the wishes of his father and prepare for a legal career. But these plans, as well as the course of his life, changed suddenly during the summer of 1505. While returning to Erfurt after a visit with his parents, Luther was caught outside in a violent thunderstorm. When a lightning bolt struck nearby, Luther, thinking himself near death, cried out in terror, "Saint Anne, help me! I will become a monk." To the shock of his parents and friends, Luther remained true to his vow. Soon after returning to Erfurt, he entered an Augustinian monastery.

Luther spent his days in the monastery zealously performing good works, which he hoped would earn him his salvation. In 1507 he was ordained a priest. A few years later he was made professor of Bible at the newly formed university at Wittenberg and became a pastor of the town church. Though a respected monk, pastor, and teacher, he was filled with doubt and despair over his own salvation. How could he, a sinner, stand before a just and holy God? His good works offered no relief from his burden of guilt and sin. Through his study of Scripture, however, Luther soon discovered that no amount of good works could justify a sinner before God; justification was by faith alone. Luther later described his spiritual awakening:

> Night and day I pondered until I saw the connection between the justice of God and the statement that "the just shall live by faith" [Rom. 1:17]. Then I grasped that the justice of God is that righteousness by which through grace and sheer mercy God justifies us through faith. Thereupon I felt myself to be reborn and to have gone through open doors into paradise. The whole of Scripture took on a new meaning, and whereas before the "justice of God" had filled me with hate, now it became to me inexpressibly sweet in greater love. This passage of Paul became to me a gate to heaven.
>
> *Roland H. Bainton,* Here I Stand: A Life of Martin Luther, *49–50.*

This doctrine transformed Luther's life, and to the day of his death, it was the heart of his preaching. ***Sola fide*** (justification by faith alone) became the rallying cry of the Reformation movement.

Saint Anne?

While the Bible is silent about the name of the mother of Mary, the mother of Jesus, Catholic tradition maintains that Anne was Mary's mother. By Luther's day she was regarded as the patron saint of miners. Since Luther's father had become wealthy as a miner, Luther would have learned to reverence this so-called saint. When he thought he might die in the sudden storm, Luther instinctively called out to the saint with whom he was most familiar, Saint Anne.

Controversy

In 1514 Pope **Leo X** (1513–21) launched a campaign to complete the rebuilding of St. Peter's Basilica in Rome. Because of the lavish spending of the Renaissance popes, the papal treasury had been drained of funds. In order to raise the needed money, Leo sent out agents to sell **indulgences**, certificates which, according to Catholicism, granted pardon from the punishment of certain sins. In 1517 one of these agents, a Dominican friar named **Johann Tetzel**, began selling indulgences near Luther's parish at Wittenberg. People flocked to see Tetzel, believing they could purchase forgiveness for sins. He told them that by buying an indulgence a person could free a relative from suffering in purgatory. He is said to have preached, "As soon as a coin in the coffer rings, the soul from purgatory springs." Martin Luther had concluded that salvation was God's free gift and detested the exploitation of his people in the name of religion. From his pulpit he preached against the abuses accompanying the sale of indulgences.

Pope Leo X and Two Cardinals, *by Raphael*

Leo X's issuance of indulgences was nothing new for the Roman Church. For centuries, popes had granted certificates of pardon. It was the position of the Roman Church that although Christ died to save men from hell, they still had to do penance or suffer in purgatory as punishment for their individual sins. The popes maintained that they had the power to suspend these punishments for specific individuals. This practice rested in the theory that the saints did more good works than necessary to get themselves into heaven. Their so-called excess works, along with the merits of Christ's perfect life, were to be collected in a type of spiritual bank, known as the **treasury of saints**. According to this theory, the pope served as treasurer and could dispense these extra good works. At first, popes granted indulgences only to people who performed some special work, such as giving money to charity or fighting on a crusade. However, by the time of the Renaissance, popes often sold indulgences to raise money for church projects. This is one of the abuses that drove Luther to produce his Ninety-Five Theses, or questions for Rome to answer.

Johann Tetzel

While Tetzel's methods were scandalous, his cash boxes overflowed with money for Leo's building program. However, some sincere church members questioned the practice of selling indulgences. They wondered why the pope, if he were truly the keeper of the treasury of saints, did not give these merits out freely to all, or why, if he could pardon one soul from purgatory, he did not pardon everyone. Luther raised these same questions. He had been dismayed to find that some members of his congregation who had purchased indulgences were unwilling to change their wicked ways. Concern for the spiritual well-being of his parishioners prompted Luther's protests. His opposition to the sale of indulgences ultimately shook all of western Christendom.

Luther's Break with Rome

The Ninety-Five Theses

On October 31, 1517, Luther posted a list of grievances that later became known as his **Ninety-Five Theses**. Luther's document challenged the sale of indulgences, and he wrote these talking points in Latin for a scholarly debate. Little did he realize he would stir up a great controversy. Almost overnight Luther's document became a symbol of defiance against the corruption and hypocrisy of Rome. By questioning indulgences, Luther inadvertently—but providentially—challenged the whole system of Roman Catholicism.

Within weeks, copies of his Ninety-Five Theses, printed in German, circulated widely in Germany and received a sympathetic response among

Luther's Trip to Rome

In the fall of 1510, while still a monk, Luther traveled to Rome on business for the Augustinian order. He had eagerly anticipated the trip; in Rome there would be many opportunities to visit sacred shrines and venerate relics of the saints. Luther considered Rome a holy city—a place where he could draw closer to God.

What he found, however, deeply disturbed him. Renaissance Rome was a city given over to wickedness. Even church leaders indulged in sins of every kind. Prostitution and other forms of sexual immorality flourished. Greed and ambition controlled the actions of both clergy and laity. During his visit Luther encountered stories of how Pope Alexander VI (1492–1503) had used treachery and murder to accomplish his purposes.

As a reformer, Luther used his experiences in Rome and other cities to illustrate the corruption of the Roman Catholic Church. On one occasion in 1537, Luther told a group of friends, "I wouldn't have missed being in Rome for a great deal of money. I wouldn't have believed it if I hadn't seen it for myself. For so great and shameless is the godlessness and wickedness there that neither God nor man, neither sin nor disgrace are taken seriously. All godly persons who've been there testify of this, and this is the witness of all the ungodly who have returned from Italy worse than they had been before."

Martin Luther, Table Talk, *ed. and trans. Theodore G. Tappert,* Luther's Works, *vol. 54, 237.*

St. Peter's Basilica today

Wittenburg Castle Church, where Luther pastored

the people. Many Germans were disgusted with indulgence salesmen such as Tetzel; others looked for an occasion to stop the flow of German money into the papal coffer at Rome. Indulgence sales soon dropped off sharply—angering Tetzel and other church officials. They denounced Luther as a heretic and urged leaders of the Roman Church to take action against him. At first Pope Leo X refused to get involved in what he considered a minor quarrel among monks. But when funds from parts of Germany stopped flowing into the papal treasury, the pope reacted.

The Leipzig Debate

Opponents of Luther, thinking him to be nothing more than an ignorant and misguided monk, sought to engage him in debates in order to show him the error of his ways. But Luther, armed by years of diligent study of the Scriptures and guided by the Spirit of God, proved to be more than their match. The climax of this confrontation occurred in the debate at Leipzig (LIPE sig) during the summer of 1519. Here Luther met the formidable scholar **Johann Eck**, a champion of Catholicism. The debate occurred over three weeks, and centered on the question of authority in the church. Luther asserted that the pope had human rather than divine authority and that he could err just as any other man. The great reformer insisted that Scripture was the only reliable authority. Eck charged that Luther was holding views similar to those of John Huss, whom the Council of Constance had condemned as a heretic a century earlier. In response Luther maintained that not all of Huss's teachings were heretical—a position that led him to the conclusion that even church councils might err.

The Leipzig debate only widened the breach between Luther and Rome. Luther had entered the debate believing himself to be a good Roman Catholic; in his view all he had done was to call attention to a few corrupt practices that other sincere Catholics had found equally offensive. But because he renounced the authority of popes and councils, he was driven to the Scriptures for guidance. He soon became even more firmly convinced that the Bible alone is the sole authority for the Christian faith.

In the months that followed, Luther wrote a series of pamphlets intended to rouse the German people to action. He wanted them to take a stand against the corrupt Roman system. Because the papacy failed to take the initiative, he called on civil rulers to reform the church. He attacked the sacramental system of the church, stating that it distorted the true meaning of salvation. He maintained that every believer was a priest and that each had the freedom to approach God personally through faith (Eph. 2:18; 1 Pet. 2:9).

Johann Eck

The Road to Worms

The pope was unable to take serious action against Luther. One reason for this was that Luther was the subject of one of the most respected and powerful territorial princes in all of Germany, Frederick the Wise, Elector of Saxony. Frederick opposed the idea of having any of his subjects stand trial outside of Germany—especially if that trial were to take place in Italy.

Charles V

In June of 1520, the pope finally heeded the counsel of his advisers. He issued a papal bull that condemned Luther for advancing heretical doctrines and gave him sixty days to recant. If Luther did not submit, he would be excommunicated. At a public gathering near the city gate of Wittenberg, Luther responded to the pope's ultimatum; he ceremoniously tossed the papal bull into a bonfire. By this act he sealed his separation from Rome. As expected, a few weeks later he was formally excommunicated from the Roman Church.

The newly crowned German emperor, **Charles V**, sensing Luther's strong public support, refused to condemn him without a hearing. In the spring of 1521 he summoned Luther to the city of Worms to appear before the German Diet. The emperor gave Luther the promise of imperial protection to and from Worms, but Luther's friends reminded him of what had happened to John Huss in a similar situation. Despite their warnings, Luther proceeded to Worms to defend the truth before the imperial Diet.

On the afternoon of April 17, 1521, Luther stood before the emperor, princes, and bishops of the Holy Roman Empire at the **Diet of Worms**. He was given no chance to defend his teaching. Instead he was simply asked whether a number of books lying on a table in front of him were his writings and whether he would recant the heresy contained in them. To the first question Luther answered yes; to the second, he asked for time to consider his answer. The next day the questions were again put to him, and he was asked to give a clear and simple reply. With firmness of conviction, he gave his memorable declaration:

> Unless I am convicted of error by the testimony of Scripture or (since I put no trust in the unsupported authority of pope or of councils, since it is plain that they have often erred and often contradicted themselves) by clear reason I stand convicted by the Scriptures to which I have appealed, and my conscience is taken captive by God's word, I cannot and will not recant anything, for it is neither safe nor right to act against the conscience. Here I stand. I can do no other. God help me! Amen.

Luther left the city. The emperor soon afterwards issued an edict declaring Luther an outlaw of the empire. He banned Luther's writings, forbade anyone to give him aid, and demanded that he be seized and turned over to the authorities. If captured, Luther was to suffer the fate of a condemned heretic—death. God, however, was not through with this man. Luther lived for twenty-five years under the imperial edict and died a natural death in 1546. During these years the truth of God's Word, which he so boldly defended, took root in the hearts and lives of men and women all over Europe.

Wartburg Castle, Germany, where Luther translated the New Testament from Greek into German

Progress in Germany

Continuation of Luther's Work

Despite the Edict of Worms, the doctrines of the Reformation continued to spread rapidly. They were proclaimed from pulpits, heralded from street corners, and circulated in printed pamphlets. Perhaps the greatest help to the reforming cause in Germany was Luther's translation of the New Testament (and later the whole Bible) into German. This work, based on Erasmus's Greek New Testament, created widespread enthusiasm for the Bible among all classes of German people. The power and beauty of its expression helped to create a standard German language for all Germany.

Melanchthon

Luther's work did not end with his translation of the Bible. In order to make the principles of the Reformation so clear that even a child could understand them, he wrote his *Shorter Catechism*. In question-and-answer form, this catechism gives instruction in the fundamental doctrines of Scripture. Luther also used music as a means of teaching the gospel. He urged the people to sing doctrinal hymns at home, work, and church. His own hymn, "A Mighty Fortress Is Our God," called the "victory hymn of the Reformation," is one of the best-known and most-loved hymns of the Christian church.

As the followers of Luther's teaching increased in number, it soon became necessary to frame an official statement of Lutheran beliefs. In 1530 **Philipp Melanchthon**, Luther's close friend and coworker, drew up the **Augsburg Confession**, which clearly sets forth the chief doctrines for which Luther and his followers contended. This document became the doctrinal standard for the Lutheran Church and has remained that denomination's most highly respected statement of faith.

Preoccupation of Charles V

One reason for the rapid spread of Lutheran doctrine was Charles V's preoccupation with the political affairs of Europe. Charles, the crowned ruler of the Holy Roman Empire, was also the ruler by inheritance of the Habsburg possessions of Spain, Sicily, Naples, the Netherlands, and Austria, plus territory in the New World. His vast holdings gave him great power but many problems as well. He was constantly defending the borders of his far-flung possessions, putting down revolts, and repelling invasions.

Between the years 1522 and 1546, Charles fought several wars with his chief rival, **Francis I**, the king of France. The French king was particularly concerned that his country was encircled by Charles's possessions. Meanwhile, Charles was faced with another threat. The Ottoman Turks, led by **Suleiman** (r. 1520–66), invaded the eastern portion of the Holy Roman Empire. By the early 1540s Charles had halted the Turkish advance and had signed a truce with the French king. He could now turn his attention to the religious situation in the German states. But over twenty years had elapsed since the Diet of Worms. Lutheranism was firmly established.

In 1546, the year of Luther's death, Charles began his attack on the German Protestants. For nearly nine years his imperial and pro-Catholic forces waged war against the anti-imperial and Protestant forces of German princes. In 1555 a compromise settlement was finally reached in the **Peace of Augsburg**. It allowed each prince the right to choose whether his territory would be Lutheran or Roman Catholic. The people within a given territory had to either accept the choice of their prince or move elsewhere. The peace only postponed the religious and political problems in Germany; in 1618 war would break out once again.

The Term Protestant

The term *Protestant* dates back to the early days of the Reformation. In 1529 representatives of the German states gathered in the city of Speyer to discuss the religious situation in Germany. At that meeting the Roman Catholic majority attempted to halt the progress of the Reformation, hoping to eventually suppress it altogether. They passed an edict which, among other things, required the Lutheran princes to guarantee the religious liberty of Roman Catholics living under their rule. At the same time, however, Roman Catholic princes could deny religious liberty to Lutherans living in their territories. The Lutheran princes opposed the entire edict, stating that they would "protest and testify publicly before God" that they would agree with "nothing contrary to His Word." It is from their courageous protest that the word *Protestant* comes. Today the term refers to anyone who holds to the biblical teachings of the Reformation in opposition to Roman Catholicism.

Section Quiz

1. What pope launched a fundraising drive to rebuild St. Peter's Basilica? What did his agents sell in order to raise the needed money?
2. What document did Luther prepare in October 1517 for academic debate about indulgences?
3. At the Leipzig debate, Eck charged that Luther was holding views similar to what earlier reformer? What conclusion did Luther reach as a result of this debate?
4. To what city was Luther summoned to appear before the princes, bishops, and emperor of the Holy Roman Empire? Who was the emperor who presided over the assembly?
5. What settlement ended the civil war that broke out among the Catholic and Protestant princes of Germany? What compromise was reached by this settlement?

★ Evaluate the positive and negative aspects of the Peace of Augsburg.

III. Spread

The Protestant Reformation was not confined to the land of Germany. Nor was Luther its only leader. God raised up reformers in many lands who protested the abuses of Roman Catholicism and sought to restore biblical Christianity. Though the reformers often differed on matters of biblical interpretation, they were in agreement with the key doctrines of the Reformation movement: "Scripture alone, faith alone, grace alone!"

Switzerland

Switzerland was one of the first places outside Germany to feel the influence of the Protestant Reformation. The Swiss Confederation began in 1291 when three cantons (or states) banded together for their mutual defense. By the time of the Reformation, the number of cantons had grown to thirteen. Switzerland enjoyed a remarkable degree of independence even though in theory it was still part of the Holy Roman Empire.

Zwingli

Zwingli in Zurich

An early leader of the Swiss Reformation was **Ulrich Zwingli** (ZWING lee). He was born in 1484 in a small village in the northern German-speaking region of Switzerland. He studied at several leading universities, where he developed a keen interest in the classics. His training acquainted him with Erasmus, under whose influence he began to study the Bible. As a young man, Zwingli was ordained a Roman Catholic priest. Early in his ministry, however, he realized that there was corruption in the Roman Church. He soon became an outspoken critic of its abusive practices. In 1519 Zwingli became the priest of the largest church in Zurich, one of the leading towns in the Swiss Confederation.

While in Zurich, Zwingli was exposed to Luther's writings and through them he came to understand that salvation comes only by the grace of God through faith. With the support of the Zurich city council, Zwingli began to make significant changes in his church. These changes aroused Roman Catholic opposition, but Zwingli ably defended his position in several public debates. For one such occasion, he drew up his *Sixty-Seven Conclusions*. These articles, similar in style to Luther's Ninety-Five Theses, set forth Zwingli's belief in the Bible as the sole rule of faith. He rejected Roman Catholic teaching concerning the mass, celibacy of priests, purgatory, and the primacy of the pope. He declared that Christ is the only way to salvation—that He alone is the eternal High Priest, the only mediator between God and man.

Although Zwingli had received a great amount of enlightenment through reading Luther's writings, he disagreed with Luther's view of the Lord's Supper. In an effort to create a united Protestant front and to settle their doctrinal differences, Zwingli and Luther met at Marburg, Germany, in October of 1529. Both men were in general agreement on the doctrines of the Trinity, the person of Jesus Christ, the work of the Holy Spirit, justification by faith, original sin, and baptism. However, at this meeting Zwingli maintained that the Lord's Supper is only a symbolic remembrance of Christ's death. Luther, on the other hand, believed that in the Lord's Supper, Christ is literally present *in*, *with*, and *under* the elements of bread and wine. (This view is commonly referred to as *consubstantiation*.) Neither reformer would change his mind, and so after three days of discussion, the conference ended without resolving the issue.

Zwingli did not live long after this meeting. Civil war broke out in Switzerland between the cantons that embraced Protestantism and those that remained Roman Catholic. In 1531 Zurich went to war against some neighboring Catholic districts. Zwingli accompanied the troops as a chaplain and was killed at the Battle of Kappel as he sought to aid a wounded soldier. Others carried on Zwingli's reforms in Zurich. Some of his followers joined the ranks of the Lutherans, while others merged with the followers of another famous reformer, John Calvin.

The Anabaptists

Although Zwingli and his followers dominated the religious and political life of Zurich, there were those who were not satisfied with the pace or restraint of his reforms. Some of them met together in 1525 and organized their own congregation, calling themselves the Swiss Brethren. Among other things, these men opposed the practice of infant baptism in favor of **believer's baptism**. As a result, those who joined their ranks and had been baptized as infants were rebaptized. For this reason their enemies called them **Anabaptists** (from

Artist's rendering of Anabaptist Dirk Williams stopping to rescue his pursuer who had fallen through the ice. Williams was then captured, tortured, and burned at the stake.

a Greek word that means "baptize again"). The Swiss Brethren did not call themselves "rebaptizers" because they did not find support for infant baptism in Scripture. When the city council tried to force the Swiss Brethren in Zurich to present their children for infant baptism, they refused to comply. As the number of Anabaptists continued to increase, officials responded with persecution. Some of the leaders were imprisoned, others were compelled to flee the city, and one was martyred by drowning.

Other groups that opposed infant baptism continued to spring up in Europe. These varied religious bodies were grouped together under the common title "Anabaptist" even though on many issues they were in sharp disagreement. Some so-called Anabaptists had revolutionary ideas or advocated heresy and twisted Scripture to support their false doctrines. However, most wanted nothing more than to be left in peace to worship God freely and to study His Word. Nevertheless, because of the wrongdoing of a few, all who were labeled Anabaptists were persecuted, and many suffered martyrdom.

In spite of their geographic isolation, most Anabaptists held certain beliefs in common. For instance, in addition to believer's baptism, they believed that only true believers should be members in the local church. This was considered a radical position since all the inhabitants of a particular community in most areas of Europe were automatically church members regardless of their spiritual condition. Second, most Anabaptists believed in the separation of church and state—that is, they rejected state interference in their affairs. In addition, many of them believed it was wrong for Christians to hold political office. (This seemed logical to them since those in political office were often their persecutors.) Third, many Anabaptists believed that a Christian should not take up arms against anyone, even in time of war. This belief is called pacifism.

Most of the groups labeled as Anabaptists either disappeared or merged with the Mennonites. This group of Brethren was labeled, by their enemies, after their founder, Menno Simons. In the seventeenth century, a Mennonite named Jacob Amman split from the Mennonites over matters of discipline, and his followers became known as the Amish. Both groups have continued to the present day.

Calvin at Geneva

John Calvin became one of the most famous and influential magisterial Protestant reformers after Martin Luther. Born in 1509 in northwestern France, he studied both law and theology at the universities of Orléans, Bourges, and Paris. The Reformation was in full swing during his student days: Luther's ideas were undoubtedly being discussed at the French universities. From his later writings, it is evident that Calvin diligently searched the Scriptures during these years to determine the validity of Reformation doctrine. Sometime around 1533 Calvin was converted and joined the Protestant movement.

John Calvin

His Theology—About a year after Calvin's conversion, the king of France intensified his persecution of French Protestants. Calvin fled his native land and sought refuge in the Swiss city of Basel, where he finished one of the most significant and influential books on theology ever written. ***The Institutes of the Christian Religion***, published in 1536 when Calvin was just twenty-six, sets forth Christian doctrine in a systematic outline.

At the heart of Calvin's system of theology was his strong belief in the sovereignty of God. Calvin believed that God predestines all things according to His own will. Everything God does is for His glory, although finite man does not understand God's ways.

His Years at Geneva—In 1536, while returning from a visit to France, Calvin stopped for the night at the beautiful city of Geneva in the French-speaking part of Switzerland. He intended to spend only one night there, but God had other plans. The Protestants of Geneva asked Calvin to stay and become their pastor and teacher. Though hesitant at first, he finally agreed, taking up the work of the Reformation that others had already begun in the city.

Calvin applied his teaching concerning God's sovereignty to everyday life in Geneva. He sought to build a Christian community based on the Word of God. Taking the Bible, especially the Old Testament, as his law book, Calvin encouraged city leaders to conform local statutes to scriptural teaching. He stressed the independence of church and state, but he believed that both were subject to the rule of God. Calvin asserted, as did many in this era, that the duty of the state was to promote piety, punish evildoers, and assist the church by providing an atmosphere that would encourage godliness in the lives of church members. The Geneva city council adopted his teaching and issued orders forbidding dancing, drunkenness, and gambling and requiring everyone to attend church services.

Calvin wanted all the citizens to subscribe to a confession of faith. He also wanted the church to have freedom to deny the Lord's Supper to those who would not confess the Christian faith as the Genevan pastors had outlined it in their confession. However, the city council insisted that it had the right to determine who could partake of the Lord's Supper and whether or not unleavened bread should be used—not the church. When Calvin would not budge on these issues, he was ordered to leave the city. Calvin traveled to Strasbourg and became the pastor of a group of French refugees. During the next three years, the alliance of Calvin's political opponents in Geneva unraveled. In addition, church attendance dwindled, and the Roman Church pressured the Genevan church to return to Catholicism—prompting the city to beg Calvin to return and become their spiritual leader once again. In 1541 Calvin reluctantly returned and remained in Geneva until his death in 1564.

Under Calvin's leadership, the city of Geneva became a leading center of the Protestant Reformation. Calvin's influence, however, reached far beyond Geneva. During his lifetime, many Protestants who had fled Catholic persecution in other countries came to Geneva for protection. Others came to study Calvin's theology. As they returned to their native lands, they passed Calvin's ideas on to others. Many Protestant churches adopted Calvin's system of theology, calling themselves the Reformed churches. This name is still widely used today.

Cathedral of St. Peter, Geneva, Switzerland

England

Cries for reform had echoed in England since the days of John Wycliffe. His persecuted followers, the Lollards, opposed papal tyranny and preached the authority of the Word of God. During the sixteenth century, efforts for reform intensified in England as Luther's writings were widely circulated and read. The English Reformation, which did not have a dominant leader like Luther or Calvin, was influenced by two important factors.

The first factor was *the publication of English translations of the Bible*. The importance of the Word of God in bringing about spiritual revival in Europe cannot be overemphasized. The Bible itself instructs us that "faith cometh by hearing, and hearing by the word of God" (Rom. 10:17). During the late fifteenth and early sixteenth centuries, the Bible was translated and printed in the native languages of almost every European country. In England a number of versions of the Bible were published and distributed. These were translated from the ancient tongues into the common language of the English people. A readable, understandable Bible helped increase the knowledge of God's Word and helped show the English people (as it did people in other lands) the extra-biblical teaching of the Roman Catholic Church.

The second factor was *the involvement of the English rulers*. The English Reformation began as a political movement under the direction of the English crown. During the sixteenth century, members of the **Tudor family** occupied the throne. There were five Tudor rulers in all: Henry VII, the founder of this royal line; his son Henry VIII; and Henry VIII's three children—Edward VI, Mary I, and Elizabeth I. Under most of the Tudors, England broke with the papacy, and the claim of papal authority over the church in England was rejected. Most of the English people supported the crown. They were filled with national pride and resented the claims of a foreign pope on their land. At first the majority of Englishmen remained in the Roman Church. However, a growing number became increasingly dissatisfied with Rome and embraced Protestantism. Political motives gradually gave way to spiritual concerns as the truth of God's Word found acceptance in the hearts of an increasing number of English people.

Henry VIII

King Edward VI of England (1537-1553).

Coblitz, Louis (1814-1863). Oil on canvas. Chateaux de Versailles et de Trianon, Versailles, France. Réunion des Musées Nationaux/Art Resource, NY

The Break with Rome Under Henry VIII

King **Henry VIII** (r. 1509–47) was on the throne of England when the Protestant Reformation began in Germany. He branded Martin Luther a heretic and wrote a book attacking Luther's teaching. The pope promptly proclaimed Henry "Defender of the Faith." Nevertheless, Henry later broke with Rome also, though not for the same reasons that motivated Luther. Henry wanted to divorce his wife Catherine of Aragon, the daughter of Ferdinand and Isabella of Spain. Catherine had been married to Henry's older brother, who had died soon after the wedding. Contrary to church doctrine, the pope permitted Henry to marry Catherine. Because she had borne him no sons to continue the Tudor line, Henry claimed that he had sinned and that God was punishing him (see Lev. 20:21).

The pope, not wishing to offend Catherine's nephew, the powerful emperor Charles V, refused to grant Henry the divorce. Therefore, Henry decided to take matters into his own hands. He appointed a new archbishop of Canterbury, **Thomas Cranmer**, who declared Henry's marriage to Catherine invalid and legalized his new marriage to Anne Boleyn. In 1534, Henry had Parliament pass the Act of Supremacy, which made the king the "supreme head" of the church in England. This act completed the break between England and the papacy. It also placed the English church under the direct control of the state. Even so, during Henry's day, the English church remained true to Roman teaching and practice.

Protestant Gains Under Edward VI

When Henry VIII died in 1547, his son **Edward VI** succeeded him to the throne. Edward, a frail boy, was only nine years old when he became king. He was strongly influenced by his advisers, who were sympathetic to the Protestant Reformation. As a result, sweeping changes were made in the English church. Parliamentary acts legalized the marriage of clergymen, abolished many Catholic ceremonies, and required church services to be in English rather than in Latin. In addition, the clergy were required to use the *Book of Common Prayer* in their churches. This prayer book was drawn up by Cranmer, who had become a leading voice of Protestantism in England. It contains Bible readings and prayers for special occasions and prescribes orders of worship for various church services.

The statement of faith known as the *Forty-Two Articles* reveals the extent of Protestant gains during Edward's reign. Formulated by Cranmer and issued by Edward, it became the official creed of the English church. The document sets forth the major Protestant doctrines of justification by faith alone and the sole authority of the Bible. It renounces transubstantiation and recognizes only two sacraments—baptism and the Lord's Supper.

Catholic Reaction Under Mary I

The sickly Edward died of tuberculosis at the age of sixteen (1553). His half sister Mary succeeded him to the throne. **Mary I**, the daughter of Henry VIII by Catherine of Aragon, was a devout Roman Catholic. She sought to restore Roman Catholicism to England by compelling Parliament to repeal the religious laws passed during Edward's reign. She removed from office thousands of clergymen who had Protestant sympathies or who had married.

As political and religious opposition mounted against Mary's pro-Catholic policies, she revived laws against heresy and began to persecute the Protestants. Hundreds of Englishmen fled to Germany and Switzerland. Many of those who remained in England were imprisoned; some became martyrs at the stake. Two famous victims of Mary's persecution were bishops Hugh Latimer and Nicholas Ridley. They were condemned to be burned at the stake. As the fire was lit, Latimer reportedly said to Ridley, "We shall this day light such a candle, by God's grace, in England, as I trust shall never be put out." Mary next turned her fury on Thomas Cranmer, the man who had declared her mother's marriage invalid. Charged with heresy, imprisoned, interrogated, and facing death, Cranmer weakened. He signed statements renouncing his Protestant beliefs and acknowledging the authority of the pope over the church in England. Yet Mary and the papal representatives sentenced Cranmer to die at the stake. On the day of his execution he publicly condemned his previous weakness and boldly reaffirmed his Protestant convictions. As the flames came up about him, Cranmer thrust the hand that had signed the recantations into the fire so that "this unworthy hand" was consumed first.

Mary I

Elizabeth I

Persecution continued until Mary's death in 1558. During her five-year reign, Mary ordered the execution of nearly three hundred leaders—earning her the nickname "Bloody Mary." However, her actions only strengthened English Protestantism and increased anti-Catholic sentiment.

Break with Rome Confirmed Under Elizabeth

When Mary I died, her half sister **Elizabeth I** (1558–1603) became queen. Her forty-five-year reign marks one of the greatest periods in English history. Elizabeth never married, but she was so devoted to her country that it has been said she was married to the throne of England. A strong and determined woman, she ruled England effectively during a crucial period of its history. During her long reign she was a symbol of stability and strength. The English people affectionately called her "Good Queen Bess."

The Church of England—Though reared a Protestant, Elizabeth favored a compromise solution to England's religious problems. She restored Protestantism to England; yet she tried to avoid alienating the English Roman Catholics. Like her father, she had Parliament pass an Act of Supremacy (1559), which rejected papal authority. This act affirmed the queen's position over the Church of England; however, it

History of the English Bible

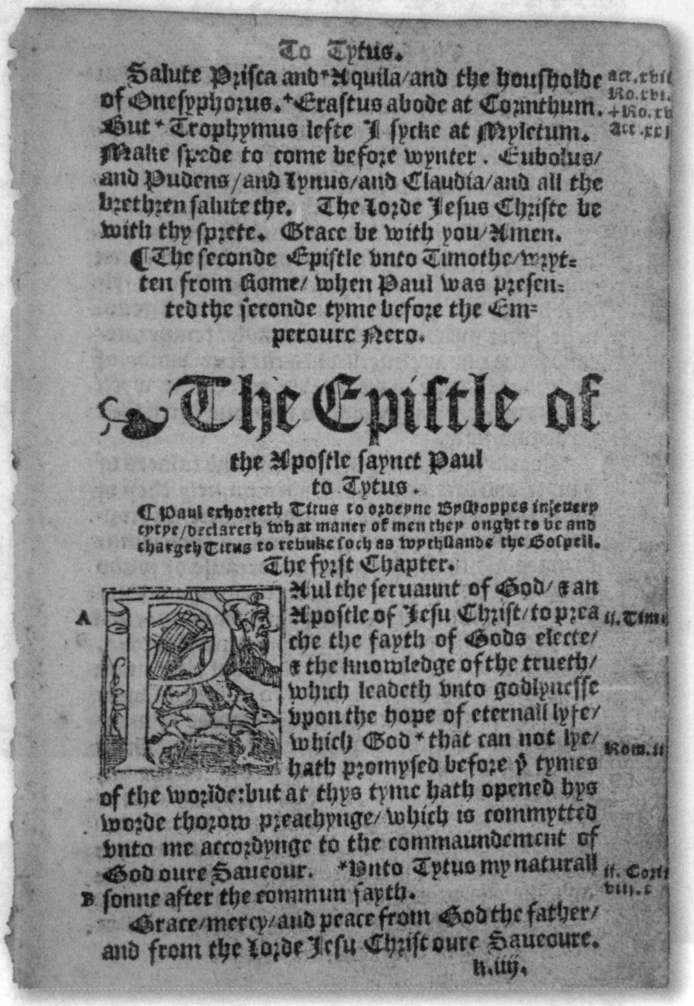

To Tytus.

Salute Prisca and *Aquila/and the housholde of Onesyphorus. *Erastus abode at Corinthum. But *Trophymus lefte I syke at Myletum. Make spede to come before wynter. Eubolus/ and Pudens/and Lynus/and Claudia/and all the brethren salute the. The Lorde Iesus Christe be with thy sprete. Grace be with you/Amen.

¶ The seconde Epistle vnto Timothe/wrytten from Rome/ when Paul was presented the seconde tyme before the Emperoure Nero.

The Epistle of the Apostle saynct Paul to Tytus.

¶ Paul exhorteth Titus to ordeyne Byshoppes in euery cytye/declareth what maner of men they ought to be and chargeth Titus to rebuke soch as withstande the Gospell.

The fyrst Chapter.

Paul the seruaunt of God/ & an Apostle of Iesu Christ/to preache the fayth of Gods electe/ & the knowledge of the trueth/ which leadeth vnto godlynesse vpon the hope of eternall lyfe/ which God *that can not lye/ hath promysed before ye tymes of the worlde: but at thys tyme hath opened hys worde thorow preachynge/ which is commytted vnto me accordynge to the commaundement of God oure Saueour. *Vnto Tytus my naturall sonne after the commun fayth. Grace/mercy/and peace from God the father/ and from the Lorde Iesu Christ oure Saueoure.

K.iiij.

The history of the English Bible begins with John Wycliffe, who believed that everyone should have the opportunity to read God's Word. In 1382 he and his followers produced the first complete English translation of the Scripture—a translation made from the Latin Vulgate. (Wycliffe knew no Hebrew or Greek.) Although the common people wanted to know what the Bible had to say, the clergy strongly opposed Wycliffe's work. The archbishop of Canterbury called Wycliffe "the very herald and child of anti-Christ, who crowned his wickedness by translating the Scripture into the mother tongue." Nevertheless, the religious and political authorities could not destroy God's Word. Wycliffe's translation survived, and some of its wording even found its way into the King James Version. For example, the phrase "strait is the gate, and narrow is the way" (Matt. 7:14) and the words "beam" and "mote" (Matt. 7:3) come from Wycliffe's translation.

William Tyndale (1492–1536), an able Hebrew and Greek scholar, produced the first English Bible translated directly from the ancient biblical languages. Forced to flee his native England, Tyndale went to Germany, where his New Testament was published in 1525. The authorities in England, however, made every effort to seize or purchase these New Testaments as they were smuggled into the country. On one occasion, a London merchant who was Tyndale's friend sold numerous copies at a high price to the bishop of London. Although the bishop had the copies destroyed, Tyndale used the money he received from the sale to finance a better printing of the

First page of Titus from a Tyndale New Testament

changed her title from "Supreme *Head*" to "Supreme *Governor*" in order to be less offensive to Roman Catholics. Under Elizabeth, Cranmer's *Forty-Two Articles* were revised to become the *Thirty-Nine Articles*—another Protestant statement of faith.

The attempt by Elizabeth to settle England's religious problems through compromise is known as the **Elizabethan Settlement**. It laid the foundation for the Church of England, also known as the **Anglican Church**. This institution became the established state church of England and took as its creed the *Thirty-Nine Articles*. While the Anglican Church embraced Protestant doctrines, it did not alter its church government, nor did it abolish certain established rituals that were not expressly forbidden in Scripture. The Anglican Church retained such things as clerical vestments (robes) and candles on the communion table.

War with Spain—England's shift toward Protestantism did not go unopposed by Roman Catholics outside of England. England's most formidable Catholic opponent was King Philip of Spain. **Philip II** (1556–98) was the son of the Habsburg emperor Charles V. When Charles abdicated in 1556, Philip became the ruler of the Habsburg territories in Spain, the Netherlands, and the New World. One of the strongest defenders of the Roman Catholic Church, he worked hard to stamp out Protestantism. He attempted to prevent the spread of the Reformation in his realm by turning the Spanish Inquisition against the Protestants. As leader of the strongest Catholic country in the world, Philip

New Testament! He also managed to publish part of the Old Testament, but before he could translate and publish all of it, he was captured in Belgium. Condemned as a heretic, he was strangled and then burned at the stake.

Tyndale died, but his work was not in vain. Others used what he had done to produce new translations. A year before Tyndale died, Miles Coverdale (1488–1569) published a translation of the entire Bible. Since he did not know Greek or Hebrew, he relied heavily on Luther's German translation, the Latin Vulgate, and Tyndale's work. Two years later one of Tyndale's friends, John Rogers, produced the so-called Matthew's Bible. (He published it under the pseudonym of Thomas Matthew.) This was not really a new translation because Rogers simply combined parts of Coverdale's work with sections of the Old Testament that Tyndale had translated but never published. In 1539 Coverdale himself revised Matthew's Bible. When it was published it measured 16 ½ by 11 inches and received the name *Great Bible* because of its size. This was the first version of the English Bible specifically authorized to be read publicly in the churches. For almost thirty years it was the only version that could be used legally in England.

Bible translation work did not cease, however. During the reign of Mary I, some of the most important Protestant leaders fled to Geneva to escape death. While there, these men produced a Bible in 1560 that contained, in their words, "most profitable annotations upon all the hard places." Known as the Geneva Bible, this was the first English version to have numbered verses. This version also used italics to indicate words that were not actually found in the Greek and Hebrew manuscripts. Within a short time, the Geneva Bible became very popular, especially among the Puritans.

In an effort to weaken the popularity of this unauthorized version, the Church of England commissioned a new translation. It came out in 1568 and became known as the Bishop's Bible. In spite of its official status, it never gained wide acceptance. The culmination of all this early translation work occurred at the beginning of the seventeenth century. King James I authorized a group of about fifty scholars to produce a new revision of the Bible. Following the king's orders, these men used the Bishop's Bible as their guide and consulted other English translations and certain Hebrew, Greek, and Latin manuscripts—especially the Greek New Testament that had been edited by Erasmus.

To make their work more efficient and to guard against errors, the translators divided themselves into six committees. Each committee was assigned a particular task. For example, one group translated Genesis through 2 Kings. Once a particular committee completed a portion of its work, it would send it to the others for evaluation and revision.

In 1611 the scholars delivered their work to the king's printer for publication. The King James Version was a masterpiece, but at first many people resented it. For example, the Pilgrims dogmatically rejected it. They had grown to love the familiar phraseology of the older English versions and did not want to change. But with the passage of time, this beautiful translation won the hearts of people all over the English-speaking world.

sought to bring Protestant England back into the fold of the Roman Catholic Church.

Shortly before becoming king, Philip had married Mary I, the Roman Catholic queen of England. A child born of that union would no doubt have been reared a Roman Catholic and would have been by right the next ruler of England and Spain. But in God's providence Mary died childless, and her Protestant sister Elizabeth became queen. Philip sought to marry Elizabeth. But while he was wooing her, Elizabeth was secretly working against Spain. She encouraged her sea captains (men such as Francis Drake) to plunder Spanish ships returning with treasure from the New World. She also aided the Dutch in their revolt against the Spanish ruler.

Because Elizabeth opposed Philip's political and religious involvement in various parts of Europe, he began plotting her overthrow. He conspired to have Elizabeth killed and have her cousin Mary Stuart—the former queen of Scotland—crowned queen of England. The plot was discovered, however, and Elizabeth had Mary put in prison and later executed.

Exasperated and angry, Philip decided to invade England. He amassed a great fleet of 130 ships which was to sail to the Netherlands, pick up a large Spanish army, and transport the invasion force to England. In 1588 this fleet, called by some the "Invincible Armada," set sail from Spain with the pope's blessing. However, the large, unwieldly Spanish galleons were no match for the smaller, more maneuverable English ships, some of which were commanded

Conflict between the English fleet and the Spanish Armada

by the daring Sir **Francis Drake**. The battered Spanish fleet turned north only to be overtaken by fierce storms that wrecked many Spanish vessels along the coast of Scotland and Ireland. The "Invincible Armada" limped back to Spain with only about half of the number of ships it had set out with.

The defeat of the **Spanish Armada** had a significant impact on world history. First, it preserved England from both Spanish and Roman Catholic domination. Second, it accelerated the decline of Spain, which during the period of exploration had been one of the richest and strongest European countries. The battle weakened Spanish sea power and as a result weakened Spain's position in the New World. Finally, it established England as a sea power at the very time English colonial expansion was under way. The way was opened for English Protestants, instead of Spanish Catholics, to settle in North America.

English Protestants acknowledged God's help in their victory. They had no doubt that the "Protestant wind" that had wrecked the Spanish fleet came from God, for "the Lord hath his way in the whirlwind and in the storm, and the clouds are the dust of his feet" (Nah. 1:3). They could agree with 2 Chronicles 16:9—a verse that applies to both individuals and nations: "The eyes of the Lord run to and fro throughout the whole earth, to shew himself strong in behalf of them whose heart is perfect toward him."

The Puritans—Though Protestantism had triumphed in England, not all Protestants were in agreement with the Church of England. Many believed that the Anglican Church retained too many of the "trappings of popery." They wished to "purify" the church of those practices that reminded them of Roman Catholicism. Thus originated their nickname—the **Puritans**. Other Englishmen saw no hope of bringing about change in the English Church. Those who removed themselves from the church were therefore known as **Separatists**. Englishmen with Catholic leanings were not satisfied with the Church of England either. They hoped to bring the Church of England back in line with Roman Catholicism.

Neither the Protestants nor the Catholics were satisfied with Elizabeth's solution to England's religious problems. As a result, England experienced widespread political and religious agitation during the seventeenth century.

Scotland

John Knox's house, Edinburgh, Scotland

John Knox (1505–72) became the leader of the Protestant Reformation in Scotland. In 1547 he was taken prisoner by the French; he served for nineteen months as a galley slave on a French ship. When released, he went to England, where he became a noted preacher during the reign of Edward VI. When Mary I came to the throne, he fled to Geneva, where he was greatly influenced by John Calvin.

He returned to Scotland in 1559. Through fiery preaching, he attacked the evils of Roman Catholicism. It was said of him, "Others lop off branches, but this man strikes at the root." Under his leadership Scotland rejected Catholicism and became a Protestant nation. The Scottish parliament rejected papal authority, abolished the mass, and adopted for the Scottish Church a Calvinistic statement of faith drawn up by Knox. They established the Presbyterian Church in Scotland.

The Reformation in Scotland flourished even though Scotland had a Catholic queen, Mary Stuart (r. 1542–87). Mary was less than a week old when her father, King James V, died and she was proclaimed queen of Scotland. She grew up in France, however, the homeland of her mother, while her mother acted as her regent in Scotland. In 1561 the young queen returned to Scotland only to find that her Catholic and French upbringing alienated the nationalistic Scottish Protestants.

Her downfall came when she was implicated in plotting her husband's death. To make matters worse, she married her husband's suspected murderer. Forced to abdicate, she fled to England, leaving behind her infant son James VI, the next king of Scotland. When Elizabeth I died in 1601, James VI was invited to assume the English throne; he was crowned King James I of England.

Nursery Rhymes

According to many traditional accounts, some of the most familiar Mother Goose rhymes were written during the Reformation era. Childhood verses such as "Jack and Jill," "Little Boy Blue," and "Little Jack Horner" were probably penned during this period. Since it was not safe at this time to be openly critical of government or church officials, rhymes were a convenient way of poking fun at those in authority. For example, "Little Miss Muffet" satirizes the relationship between John Knox and Mary Stuart.

Little Miss Muffet
Sat on a tuffet,
Eating her curds and whey;
There came a big spider,
And sat down beside her,
And frightened Miss Muffet away.

Miss Muffet is Mary Stuart, who at the age of eighteen sat down as queen upon the throne of Scotland. At first Mary enjoyed herself, but before long the reformer John Knox "sat down beside her." Knox publicly condemned her scandalous behavior and her Roman Catholic beliefs. In addition, he had several discussions with her. Political problems finally forced Mary to flee Scotland and take refuge in England with her cousin, Queen Elizabeth. In the popular mind, however, it was John Knox who had frightened the young queen away.

John Knox

Another familiar nursery rhyme is "Three Blind Mice":

Three blind mice, see how they run!
They all ran after the farmer's wife,
Who cut off their tails with a carving knife,
Did you ever see such a sight in your life,
As three blind mice?

In this rhyme "the farmer's wife" is Mary I, the Roman Catholic queen of Tudor England. The "three blind mice" are the churchmen Cranmer, Ridley, and Latimer, who opposed Mary's reinstatement of Roman Catholicism in England. In response to their efforts, Mary "cut off their tails"—she had the men arrested and executed.

William the Silent

The Netherlands

The Netherlands (including at that time the modern-day countries of the Netherlands and Belgium) was one of the many territories ruled by Charles V. When Charles abdicated, this territory came under the control of his son, Philip II. Because Philip was both Spanish and Catholic, many of his subjects disliked him. Not long after he became king, Protestant unrest in the Netherlands prompted him to send troops to put down the trouble. His troops severely persecuted the Protestants there, causing them to break out in armed revolt in 1568. The Protestants fought bravely under their leader William of Orange, also called **William the Silent**, and for a time even many of the Roman Catholics living in the southern part of the Netherlands turned against Spanish rule.

The war dragged on for years, but the Netherlands, aided by the English, managed to hold off the Spanish troops. In 1581 the Protestant areas of the Netherlands declared their independence from Spain. The Roman Catholic area (modern Belgium) remained under Spanish control. William was murdered a few years later. However, the Dutch Protestants continued their struggle and won a truce with Spain in the early seventeenth century.

France

The writings of Luther flowed into France, arousing widespread interest in the Reformation. The works of John Calvin also had a strong influence there. By the middle of the sixteenth century, there were over two thousand Protestant congregations in France, and perhaps as many as one-half of the nobility had become Protestants. Despite these gains, France remained a thoroughly Catholic country. The government, fearful of the growing political and religious power of Protestantism, fiercely persecuted the **Huguenots** (French Protestants).

One of the most shocking incidents occurred in 1572. Catherine de Medici, the mother of the French king and the real power behind the throne, instigated a massacre of the Huguenots in Paris. Catherine planned this attack and lured many Huguenot leaders to Paris under the guise of attending a marriage that would end the conflict. Early on the morning of August 27 (St. Bartholomew's Day), bands of Roman Catholics began roving the city, breaking into homes and murdering the unsuspecting and unarmed Protestants. Coordinated massacres occurred throughout France.

St. Bartholomew's Day Massacre

François Dubois, Le Massacre de la Saint-Barthélemy, *vers 1572-1584, Huile sur bois, 94 x 154 cm, Photo: J.-C. Ducret Musée cantonal des Beaux-Arts de Lausanne*

By the time the massacre had ended, an estimated twenty thousand Huguenots had been murdered. Although many people condemned the **St. Bartholomew's Day Massacre**, Philip II of Spain praised it, stating that it was "of such value and prudence and of such service, glory, and honor to God and universal benefit to all Christendom that to hear of it was for me the best and most cheerful news which at present could come to me." Even the pope ordered a special celebration in Rome.

The massacre, needless to say, increased the tension between the French Roman Catholics and the Protestants, whose differences had already led to war. Conflict broke out once again, this time over the question of who would rule France. The Valois family, which had ruled France since the fourteenth century, was dying out. Two other families were seeking the throne. The Guise family was Roman Catholic and traced its line back to Charlemagne. The other family, the **Bourbon**, was Huguenot and traced its ancestry back to Louis IX.

Henry of Navarre, the head of the Bourbon family and the leader of the Huguenots, emerged victorious in the struggle for the throne. He declared himself to be Henry IV (r. 1589–1610), the king of France. However, there was one serious problem. The majority of Frenchmen were Roman Catholic and would not allow a Protestant to become king. To please the people and secure the throne he had so eagerly sought, Henry IV became a Roman Catholic. He supposedly remarked, "Paris is well worth a mass." Although Henry IV deserted his Huguenot followers, he did grant them a certain amount of religious toleration in the famous **Edict of Nantes** (1598). However, as we shall see in Chapter 14, this period of toleration was brief.

Henry IV, King of France and Navarra (1553-1610) in armour

Oil on canvas. Louvre, Paris, France. Réunion des Musées Nationaux/Art Resource, NY

Section Quiz

1. What city and country are associated with the ministry of the reformer Ulrich Zwingli?
2. List three beliefs that most of the early Anabaptists held.
3. What influential work on theology did John Calvin write? What city associated with his ministry became a leading center of the Protestant Reformation?
4. Following England's break with the Roman Catholic Church, what became the state church?
5. Who was the fiery Scottish preacher who advanced the cause of the Reformation in Scotland? What Protestant church became the state church in Scotland?

★ How did Henry IV provide temporary relief for the Huguenots?

IV. The Counter Reformation

In the early stages of the Reformation it seemed as if the Roman Catholic Church was fading because of the efforts of the reformers. Northern Europe as well as many areas of eastern Europe had rejected the Roman Church. A strong Protestant movement was under way in France. There were even small Protestant groups in such Catholic strongholds as Spain and Italy. In an effort to prevent further losses to the Protestants, the Roman Catholic Church promoted reforms of its own. In the late Middle Ages, as criticism against corruption in the church mounted, Catholics attempted to correct the problem. However, it was not until the sixteenth century, when large numbers left the Roman Church, that its leaders became seriously concerned about the need for reform.

The Catholic Reformation is often called the **Counter Reformation**. (The word *counter* means "to oppose.") The Protestant leaders had directed their efforts primarily against false doctrine. Most Catholic reformers, on the other hand, attempted to clean up the church by correcting some of the outward moral problems. They failed to see that the root of their problems was doctrinal error.

Ignatius Loyola

St. Ignatius State. Montanes, Juan Martinez (1568-1649). University Chapel, Seville, Spain. Foto Marburg/Art Resource, NY

Jesuits

The Society of Jesus, or the **Jesuits**, became instrumental in promoting the Counter Reformation. This new religious order was founded by the Spanish soldier Ignatius Loyola (loy OH luh; 1491?–1556). While recovering from a battle injury, Loyola underwent a religious experience in which he determined to devote his life to the Roman Church. In 1540 the Jesuit order officially came into existence. Unlike those in other religious orders, the Jesuits took a special vow of absolute obedience to the pope.

From its beginnings the purpose of the Jesuit order was to suppress heresy and to promote Roman Catholic education. The Jesuits realized the importance of careful training. Those who wanted to become members of the organization had to undergo a two-year period of probation. During that time the prospective member studied the *Spiritual Exercises* written by Loyola and learned to be completely submissive to those in authority. "We ought always to be ready to believe that what seems to us white is black if the hierarchical Church so defines it," Loyola once said. If the two-year probation period ended successfully, an individual became a member of the Jesuits. He usually continued his studies, sometimes spending a total of fifteen years in preparation for his work.

The Jesuits used every means available to promote their own order and to turn people back to the Roman Church. They believed it was proper to do wrong in order to accomplish something good. For example, some Jesuits taught that it was acceptable to murder someone—even a ruler—if that death furthered Catholic purposes. They exercised great influence in schools and governments, attacking Protestantism and spreading the Counter Reformation wherever they went. Many Jesuits were also zealous missionaries. Francis Xavier (1506–52) became the best-known Jesuit missionary. He served in India, China, and Japan.

Inquisition

To stop the spread of Protestantism, Pope Paul III (r. 1534–49) reorganized the Inquisition that brought terror and death to Protestants and Jews in countries where Roman Catholicism was dominant. As in previous centuries, the Inquisition operated on the assumption that anyone accused of heresy was guilty until proved innocent. After being arrested, often at night, the accused would stand before an inquisitor. Without knowing what charges had been brought against him or who had brought them, the accused person would be asked to confess his wrong. If mild methods of persuasion failed to produce a confession, the inquisitors often used torture. Many, whether or not they had confessed, were turned over to secular authorities to be burned at the stake. The family of the accused often suffered as well, through arrest or loss of property.

Index of Prohibited Books

When Gutenberg introduced movable-type printing in Europe, the price of books and pamphlets dropped sharply. Previously only the rich could afford books, but by the sixteenth century many people could purchase printed material. Printed copies of the Bible and books written by the reformers circulated throughout Europe. Realizing the impact that the printed page was having on the spread of the Reformation, the Roman Church tried to regulate what its members read. In 1559 the Roman Catholic Church established the ***Index of Prohibited Books,*** which condemned, among other things, forty-eight allegedly heretical editions or versions of the Bible. Only those books that received an ecclesiastical license had official church approval. Even today, books officially sanctioned by the Roman Church contain inside the front cover the Latin words *imprimatur* ("let it be printed") and *nihil obstat* ("nothing hinders").

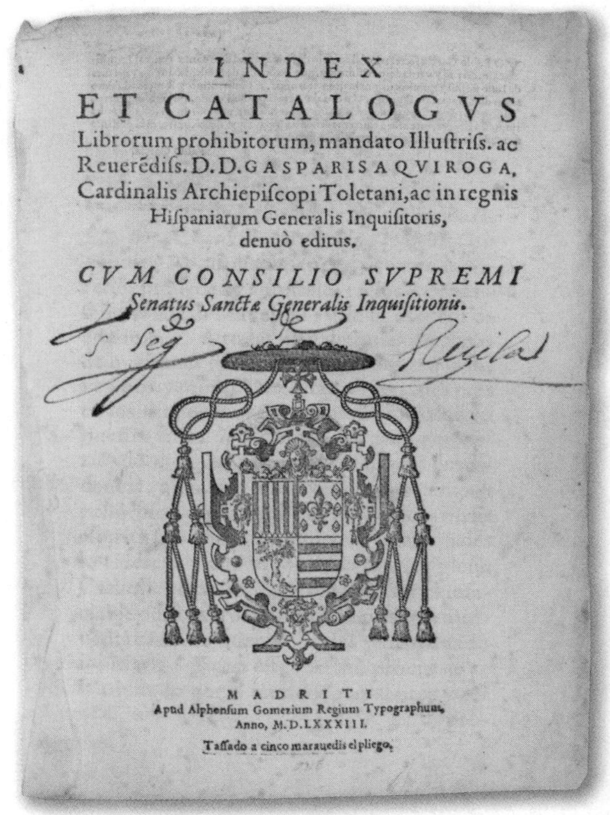
INDEX
ET CATALOGVS
Librorum prohibitorum, mandato Illuſtriſs. ac Reuerēdiſs. D. D. GASPARIS A QVIROGA, Cardinalis Archiepiſcopi Toletani, ac in regnis Hiſpaniarum Generalis Inquiſitoris, denuò editus.

CVM CONSILIO SVPREMI Senatus Sanctæ Generalis Inquiſitionis.

MADRITI
Apud Alphenſum Gomezium Regium Typographum,
Anno, M.D.LXXXIII.
Taſſado a cinco marauedis el pliego.

Title page of Index of Prohibited Books

Council of Trent

Twenty-five years after the beginning of the Protestant Reformation, Pope Paul III called a church council to discuss doctrinal questions and to propose needed reform. Charles V, the Holy Roman emperor, had demanded such a council because the religious division in Germany was increasing. He wanted to end the division and to restore unity to his land. Fearful of what a general church council might do, Pope Paul III structured it in such a way that the pope's representatives, as well as the other Italian delegates, controlled the proceedings. The outcome was predetermined. In 1545 the council held its first meeting in Trent, a city of northern Italy. Church leaders did not meet on a continuous basis but gathered for an extended period of time on three separate occasions. In 1563 the **Council of Trent** held its last session.

The Council of Trent is significant for two major reasons. The council explicitly condemned many of the biblical principles that Protestantism is based on. Most importantly, it rejected the doctrines of justification by faith alone and the sole authority of the Scripture. This sealed the break between Protestant and Roman Catholic churches. Also the council set forth a complete doctrinal position of the Roman Church and made its position binding for all Roman Catholics. The Roman Church tolerated no deviation from the decrees of the council.

Section Quiz

1. What was the name for the Catholic Reformation that sought to stop the spread of the Protestant movement?
2. What new religious order was formed to suppress heresy and promote Roman Catholic education? Who was the founder of this order?
3. What court of the Roman Church focused its attention on finding and punishing those accused of holding Protestant beliefs?
4. What did the Roman Church issue to regulate what its members could read?
5. At what council did the Roman Church set forth its doctrinal position? Which pope called for this council?

★ What impact did the Council of Trent have on the Roman Church?

Chapter 12 Review

Making Connections

1–3. For what teachings did the Roman Church condemn Wycliffe and Huss as heretics? (List three concepts they taught or opposed.)

4–5. How did the Roman Church respond to the Protestant Reformation? (List two aspects of the Counter Reformation.)

Developing History Skills

1. How did the Tudors respond to the Reformation? (List the rulers and briefly describe each ruler's response.) What were the long-term consequences for England?
2. How did France respond to the Reformation? What were the long-term consequences for France?

Thinking Critically

1. Acknowledging our limited understanding of the mind of God in these matters, speculate why John Huss died a martyr's death while Martin Luther lived a full life and died a natural death.
2. What role did the Bible play in the Reformation?

Living in God's World

1. Identify areas of Christianity today that have become corrupted and provide a biblical response in a brief paragraph.
2. At the heart of the Reformation is the doctrine of justification. Research this biblical topic and write a brief paragraph explaining the doctrine of justification by faith alone. Note possible misunderstandings that people might have and clarify them.

People, Places, and Things to Know

John Wycliffe
Lollards
John Huss
Council of Constance
recant
Martin Luther
sola fide
Leo X
Johann Tetzel
indulgences
treasury of saints
Ninety-Five Theses
Johann Eck
Charles V
Diet of Worms
Philipp Melanchthon
Augsburg Confession
Francis I
Suleiman
Peace of Augsburg
Ulrich Zwingli
believer's baptism
Anabaptists
The Institutes of the Christian Religion
Tudor family
Henry VIII
Thomas Cranmer
Edward VI
Mary I
Elizabeth I
Elizabethan Settlement
Anglican Church
Philip II
Francis Drake
Spanish Armada
Puritans
Separatists
John Knox
William the Silent
Huguenots
St. Bartholomew's Day Massacre
Bourbon family
Henry of Navarre
Edict of Nantes
Counter Reformation
Jesuits
Index of Prohibited Books
Council of Trent

13

EXPLORATION AND DISCOVERY

I. Preparation for Discovery

II. Process of Discovery

III. Parallel to Discovery: The Commercial Revolution

Replica of Henry Hudson's ship, the Half Moon

The two hundred years from 1450 to 1650 marked the great age of European exploration and discovery. Men crossed uncharted waters, braved violent storms, and suffered starvation and disease as they sailed to distant parts of the globe. What prompted these explorers to face untold perils? Most desired wealth; some sought adventure and fame; others sought to spread the gospel to heathen lands. But whether motivated by greed, pride, or compassion, these explorers opened the continents of North and South America, the coast of Africa, and part of Asia to European trade and colonization.

I. Preparation for Discovery

Several developments in Europe gave rise to this Age of Exploration. The Crusades awakened interest in lands beyond Europe's borders. Travelers such as **Marco Polo** stirred the popular imagination with tales of strange customs and unbelievable riches in the Far East. The Renaissance provided western Europe with the means, namely navigational equipment and finances, to reach the Orient. In the endeavor to reach the East, Europeans discovered the New World.

Motives for Exploration

Search for New Trade Routes

Spurred by the Crusades and the stories of Marco Polo and others, Europeans reopened trade routes with the East. They imported numerous luxury items from China, India, and the Spice Islands (located north of Australia). Merchants traded for precious gems, silk, and expensive porcelain (china). Spices, such as cloves and cinnamon, were in great demand. Europeans used them to flavor and preserve food and as ingredients in drugs and perfumes.

All these items came across Asia to Europe by way of the Middle East. But there were many problems for traders along this long route. Much of the terrain was rugged and difficult to cross. In addition, Muslim rulers charged trading caravans for the privilege of passing through their territory; taxes and tolls drove up the prices of the products. Furthermore, the Italians held a monopoly on Oriental trade. Merchants from Genoa controlled the northern routes that came overland from Asia, and merchants from Venice controlled the southern routes that ran along the coast of India, up the Persian Gulf, and across the desert to Palestine. (See map on p. 204.) Not only were Italians draining gold from the rest of Europe, but they were also keeping traders from other European countries from sharing in the profits.

In the 1400s these problems became more acute when the Ottoman Turks seized power in the Middle East. These recent converts to Islam attacked caravans and destroyed trading posts. The Europeans, who still craved Eastern luxuries, needed to find a new route to the Orient. Some wondered if it might be possible to get to the East entirely by sea, avoiding the Turks, the Italian traders, and all the tolls and taxes. The quest began in earnest in the late fifteenth century. Early European adventurers

Marco Polo and the Awakening of Curiosity

Marco Polo was only seventeen when he set off on a journey that would revolutionize the world. He was accompanying his father, Nicoló, and his uncle Matteo, both Venetian traders, on their second voyage to the little-known kingdom of Cathay (China). The year was 1271.

For four years the three men traveled eastward, finally reaching the city of Cambaluc (Beijing), the capital of Cathay. Young Marco Polo quickly became a favorite of the ruler, Kublai Khan. He learned the languages of the court and by the age of twenty-three became the Khan's adviser. The Polos lived in Cathay for seventeen years, traveling and seeing sights that few Europeans ever dreamed of. In 1292 they began the long journey home. When they arrived in Venice, their old friends did not recognize them; most at first refused to believe their stories, but the travelers convinced them by producing a wealth of gems that they had received in Cathay.

Three years after his return to Italy, Marco was captured while fighting in a local war and jailed in Genoa. To pass the time, he recounted his adventures to a fellow prisoner, who recorded them in what was soon to become a very popular book: *The Book of Sir Marco Polo Concerning the Kingdoms and Marvels of the East*. The work was far more accurate than the few other books about Cathay that were available in Europe at that time. Its readers were astonished by the tales of a strange black rock (coal) that the Mongols burned. They thrilled to the description of fantastic riches in gold, spices, and many other luxuries. They wondered about the islands of "Cipango" (Japan) that Polo described. More importantly, they learned of the great sea (the Pacific) that lay beyond Asia.

Nearly two centuries after Polo, a man from Genoa read this book and wondered if the ocean to the west—the Atlantic—might be the same one that Polo saw. This man's name was Christopher Columbus.

sailed south and east around Africa, others sailed west across the Atlantic, and some even tried to find a Northwest Passage through Arctic ice.

Quest for Gold

For many years there had been stories circulating in Europe that there was gold—lots of gold—somewhere in Africa. Europeans, however, knew very little about this huge continent. While the northern coast was well known to travelers, few Europeans had traveled south into the heart of the continent. Occasionally African traders arrived in Mediterranean ports, bringing gold from the interior, but no European knew exactly where this gold came from. Not surprisingly, many wanted to find it. Explorers were willing to take great risks to obtain wealth but often suffered great losses instead.

Desire for Adventure and Glory

While some explorers craved great riches, others sought the thrill of adventure and the praise of men. The Renaissance, which encouraged a spirit of curiosity and emphasized individual achievement, may have played a part in these desires. Men risked their lives, sailing through unknown waters and traveling to distant lands. Through their daring adventures, they hoped to achieve worldly fame. While several explorers did become famous for their exploits, many others died in the quest for glory.

Religious Concerns

Though overlooked or neglected by some historians, religious concern also motivated many explorers. The crusading spirit was alive in Europe because the Muslim threat was still very real. Even as late as the fifteenth century, the Moors still controlled the southern portion of the Iberian Peninsula. After the fall of Constantinople to the Ottoman Turks in 1453, Europeans feared a full-scale Muslim invasion of eastern Europe. European rulers searched for ways to stop further Muslim victories.

There were rumors of a king in Africa named **Prester John**, supposedly a wealthy and powerful Christian who wanted to help the Europeans fight the Muslims. During the fifteenth century, explorers sailed along the west coast of

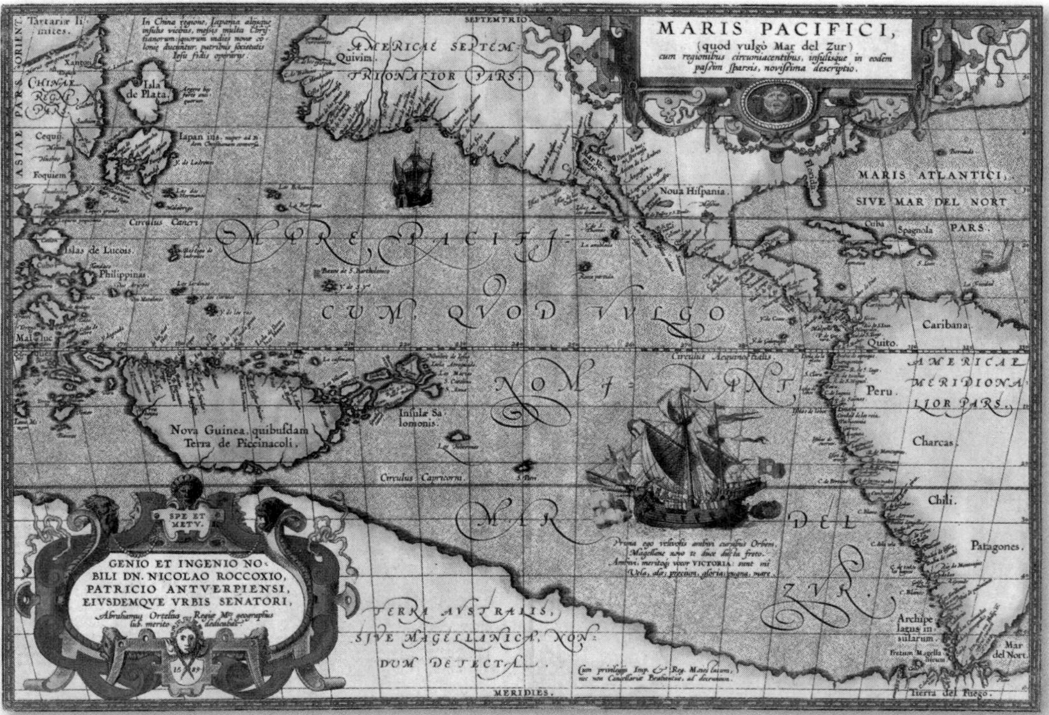

A map published in 1589

Africa searching for Prester John's kingdom. They hoped to enlist his help; by attacking from both the north and south, their combined forces could defeat the Muslims. However, Prester John was not to be found.

Not all of Europe's religious zeal was directed against the Muslims. Some explorers sought to spread the gospel to people of other cultures. However, most of the early explorers were Roman Catholics who won converts to the Roman Church rather than to Christ.

Competition Among European Nations

Exploration was also sparked by the commercial rivalry among the nations of Europe. As Italian merchants brought precious gems, spices, and silks from the East, Europeans were filled with great excitement—but also with great envy. Non-Italian merchants wanted to profit from the Oriental trade, and kings wanted to increase their own countries' wealth and power. As the explorers traveled to unknown regions, they claimed their discoveries for the country for which they sailed. The European countries were eager to start trade with the people of newly discovered lands. Nations established trade settlements and encouraged colonization in order to protect their commercial interests. Little thought was given to those who already lived in these regions.

Tools for Exploration

Navigational Aids

Three things became very important to explorers: accurate maps to guide them to their destination, a compass to tell them what direction they were actually going in, and some kind of "locator" instrument to tell them their position. On a trackless and featureless ocean, they needed accurate and trustworthy instruments.

Maps—Maps of the known world became much more accurate in the fifteenth century as Italian mapmakers updated sailing charts based on the reports of traders and fishermen. These maps were fairly reliable guides for sailing in the Mediterranean Sea or along the European coast, but they were of little help to the explorers, who sailed in uncharted waters. As explorers returned from their voyages, they updated their maps to include their discoveries. With the invention of printing, these updated maps were widely distributed, encouraging further exploration.

Instruments—The **compass** greatly aided sailors in navigation and mapmaking. Invented by the Chinese, the early compass was a magnetized needle floating in a bowl of water on a piece of reed or cork. In the late 1300s, Europeans mounted the compass on a stiff card marked with the cardinal points (north, south, east, and west). This small improvement made a great difference to sailors, who could now use the instrument easily on a moving ship. The compass became an invaluable tool; it helped sailors determine direction and follow a definite course.

Sailors also relied on more complicated instruments to determine their position on an unmarked ocean. The three most common instruments—the astrolabe, the quadrant, and the cross-staff—measured the angle between the sun or a star (usually the North Star) and the horizon. From this information the sailor could determine his **latitude**, or distance from the equator. With any one of these instruments, the captain of a ship, even though out of sight of land, could compute his position with a limited degree of accuracy. The instruments did have two major drawbacks,

Navigational instruments

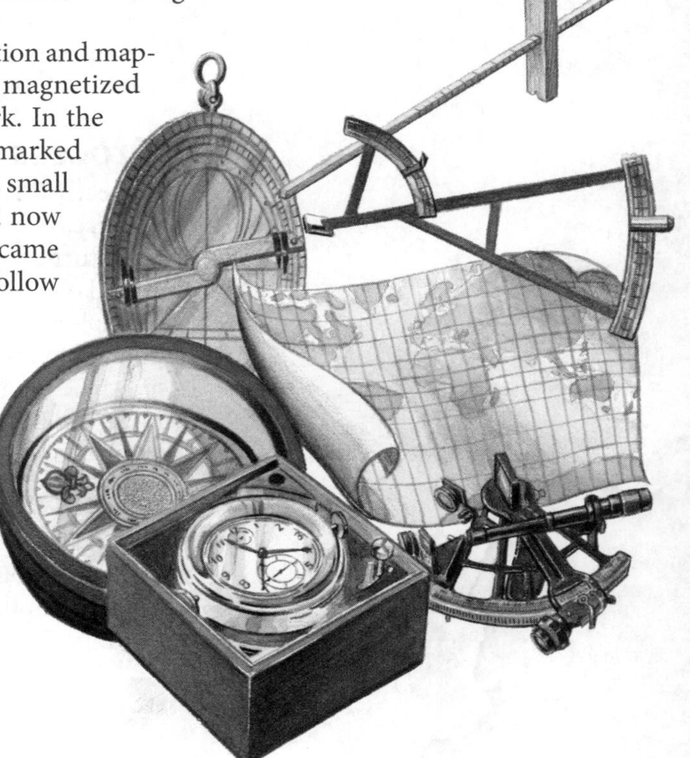

however. They were useless in cloudy weather, and they were not very accurate when used on the rolling deck of a ship.

Seagoing Vessels

Around 1400 Europeans began to build ships to sail long distances over wide and sometimes stormy seas. Early ships used to cross the Mediterranean Sea had made great use of oars. However, an oar-powered ship would need such a large crew to travel the ocean that it could not carry enough supplies to feed the crew. Oceangoing vessels, therefore, needed to use sails. However, of the two types of sails in use, triangular and square, neither was satisfactory for a long ocean voyage.

The Arabs used triangular sails, which made their boats easily maneuverable, even when the wind changed directions. This kind of sail, however, could power only a relatively small craft. Such vessels would not be big enough to carry the needed supplies and then return with enough spices to make a trip profitable.

Northern sailors, such as the Vikings, used square sails, which could power a larger ship and required a smaller crew. They could carry enough supplies and had room for a large quantity of spices. However, these ships were not very maneuverable.

The solution came in the middle of the fifteenth century with the development of a versatile ship called a **caravel**. This light, fast vessel was popular with the early explorers. It had several masts on which were mounted large square sails to provide power and smaller triangular sails to provide maneuverability. The caravel's high sides and its broad and deep construction made it suitable for ocean travel.

Section Quiz

1. List five motives that prompted European explorers to "seek out and discover."
2. What man's account of his travels awakened European curiosity in the Orient? In what Asian land did he spend seventeen years?
3. What three things were of great importance to the early explorers?
4. What light, fast vessel was popular with the early explorers of the late fifteenth century?

★ Why were early maps of limited help as explorers ventured farther in search of new lands and new trade routes?

II. Process of Discovery

The early European explorers were pioneers. They set sail across vast, unexplored oceans with uncertain prospects of ever returning home. While some never returned, others brought back the exciting news of their discoveries. They told of new routes to the Orient, of great riches to be gained, of new lands to be explored, and of people who needed to be evangelized. Europe eagerly responded to the challenge. Merchants, soldiers, settlers, and missionaries followed the explorers. Through trade along the African coast and in Asia and through colonization in the New World, Europe rapidly extended its influence to many regions of the world.

Portugal and Spain

Portugal and Spain were the leading nations of the Age of Exploration. Several factors accounted for their early success. Shipping had long been a principal industry in these lands; Portugal and Spain were bounded by the waters of the Atlantic Ocean and the Mediterranean Sea. Because the Italians had gained a monopoly on trade in the Mediterranean, sailors from the Iberian Peninsula turned southward to the coast of Africa and westward across the Atlantic in search of new trade routes to the East. Furthermore, the experienced Portuguese and Spanish sailors were greatly aided by the navigational and mapmaking skills they had learned from the Moors. One of the strong motivating forces behind their drive for discovery was the crusading spirit, which was still very much alive in the peninsula. (The last Muslim stronghold in the Iberian Peninsula was not conquered until 1492.) Many Portuguese and Spanish sailors initially set sail to spread Roman Catholicism and battle Muslims.

Above left: Prince Henry the Navigator
Above: Statue of Bartolomeu Dias
Below: Vasco da Gama

Portugal Rounds Africa

Prince Henry (1394–1460), called "The Navigator," was largely responsible for Portugal's early success in exploration. Although he never went on an expedition, he has been called "the greatest figure in the history of exploration." As a youth, he was fascinated with the great land of Africa to the south. How big was it? Where was the source of the gold that came out of its interior? Where was Prester John's kingdom? These questions led Prince Henry to start a school of navigation on the coast of Portugal. It was not a *school* in our sense of the word; it was more like a *storehouse* of knowledge about navigation. He attracted to his palace geographers, astronomers, mapmakers, and sea captains. Under his sponsorship, these men improved navigational instruments, drew up more accurate maps, and developed the caravel. Henry sent sailors out to explore the coast of Africa and to bring back all the information they could find. On each voyage, Henry's sailors went farther south along Africa's coast. They had not yet reached the equator when he died in 1460, but his accomplishments laid the foundation for the achievements of two other men who would finish the job that he had begun.

In 1487, nearly thirty years after Prince Henry's death, the king of Portugal sent **Bartolomeu Dias** down the coast of Africa to find a sea route to India. As he neared the southern tip of the continent, a fierce storm blew his ships out of sight of land for thirteen days. When he finally sighted land again, he noticed that the sun rose on the ship's right instead of its left; he was therefore heading north. He rightly concluded that he had rounded the tip of Africa during the storm and that indeed there might be an all-water route to the Orient. When his men refused to go any farther, he turned around and headed back to Portugal. As he rounded the tip of Africa again, he sighted a huge rocky cape, which he named "The Cape of Storms." The king later changed its name to "The Cape of Good Hope" because he hoped that Dias had finally found a direct water route to India.

Ten years after Dias's discovery, the king of Portugal selected **Vasco da Gama** to lead an expedition around the Cape of Good Hope to India. In 1497, with a fleet of four ships, da Gama set sail from Lisbon, Portugal. He did not follow the African coast all the way to the Cape of Good Hope as Dias had done. Instead, he made a great westward sweep to gain more favorable winds and currents. At one point he was actually closer to South America than to Africa. He stayed out of sight

The Cape of Good Hope

of land for fourteen weeks before reaching the tip of Africa. (In future centuries, wind-driven vessels would follow this route pioneered by da Gama.)

Nearly a year after leaving Portugal, da Gama arrived in India. He was the first European to reach the great subcontinent by sailing around Africa. He told those who met him, "We have come to seek Christians and spices." But he found Muslim merchants living there who controlled trade in the region and opposed his efforts to trade with the Indians. Despite much opposition, he was able to trade for spices—enough to pay for the voyage sixty times over!

The Portuguese swiftly took advantage of da Gama's discovery of the ocean route to India. They soon not only controlled this water route but also broke the Muslim trade monopoly in the Indian Ocean. The Muslim fleet was no match for the heavy artillery on the Portuguese ships. It was not long before ships loaded with spices were a familiar sight in Portuguese ports.

Spain Sails Westward

When Dias returned from his voyage around the Cape of Good Hope, an Italian named **Christopher Columbus** heard his report: India could be reached by sailing around the tip of Africa. But Columbus, who had studied the writings of the ancient geographer Ptolemy and the traveler Marco Polo, believed that he could reach Japan and China by sailing west—that Japan was perhaps as close as three hundred miles from Portugal. For many years he tried without success to persuade the king of Portugal to finance his voyage westward. But the king's advisers declared the undertaking to be impossible. In Spain Columbus was finally able to secure support for his voyage from King Ferdinand and Queen Isabella. In August of 1492 he set sail from Spain with three ships: the *Niña*, the *Pinta*, and the *Santa Maria*.

Relief statue of Columbus and Queen Isabella

Columbus wrote that he believed he was commissioned by God to spread the gospel in distant lands. He was confident that his voyage would be a success. His men, however, did not share his optimism. After weeks of being out of sight of land, they demanded that the ships turn back. Columbus was able to persuade them to continue for two or three more days. Two days later, on the morning of

October 12, he sighted land and named it San Salvador ("Holy Savior"). Columbus thought that he was near the East Indies; actually, he was in the Bahamas. He sailed south to Cuba, which he thought was Marco Polo's Cathay, and to Hispaniola, which he identified as Cipango (Japan).

In three later voyages Columbus explored further in the Caribbean and landed on the South American continent in what is now Venezuela. He never found the great riches he was looking for, and he continued to believe that he had reached Asia. Although Columbus was mistaken as to where his voyages had taken him, his discovery was nonetheless of great importance. He opened up a "New World" that attracted European exploration and colonization for centuries following. Sadly, Columbus unintentionally also prepared the way for an Indian slave trade.

Columbus was not the first to discover the New World, however. The Vikings made the voyage from Europe in the tenth and eleventh centuries. A few historians even think that the ancient Phoenicians landed in South America before the time of Christ. But in God's plan, the lands of the New World remained virtually unknown to Europe until the sixteenth century—a time when Europeans were also rediscovering the truth of God's Word. During the seventeenth century, the New World, especially North America, became a haven for Christians and others who fled from political and religious persecution in Europe.

Landing of Christopher Columbus

As a result of Columbus's discoveries, Spain began to compete with Portugal for trade rights and new territory. To avoid disputes with Portugal, Spain asked Pope Alexander VI to divide the world between the two countries. In 1493 he issued a bull that drew a **Line of Demarcation** running north and south down the middle of the Atlantic Ocean. (See map on p. 283.) Portugal, he said, could claim lands to the east of the line, while Spain could claim those to the west. After negotiations between Spain and Portugal, it was agreed the following year to move the line farther to the west.

This agreement between Spain and Portugal had several important results.

1. It encouraged Portugal to colonize in Africa and the East Indies, which were east of the line.
2. It gave Spain the right to nearly all of the New World with one exception—the line cut across Brazil, giving that land to the Portuguese, who later explored and settled there. That is why even today the language of Brazil is Portuguese, while the rest of South America speaks Spanish.
3. It cut Spain off from going east around Africa to get to India and China. To remain competitive, Spain had to find a westward route. It was not long before the Spanish found a sailor who would do it.

The Naming of America

When Columbus landed on an island in the Caribbean in 1492, he mistakenly assumed that he had succeeded in reaching Asia. Upon his return, most Europeans believed his reports, but when later expeditions failed to bring back any riches, doubts began to arise. An Italian merchant named Amerigo Vespucci sailed west to settle the uncertainty. What he found was not a water route to the Orient but a new continent. He was the first European to reach and explore the landmass that now bears his name—South America.

Hearing of Amerigo Vespucci's discovery, a German mapmaker named Martin Waldseemüller began to sell maps of the new continent. Proposing that the land be named after its discoverer, he referred to it as "America." The name was accepted, and before long people applied it to the large landmass to the north of the Spanish possessions as well. They called it "North America."

In September of 1519 **Ferdinand Magellan** set out with a fleet of five ships to do what Columbus had failed to accomplish. By this time he knew that Columbus had found not the Orient but an intervening landmass. He thought that he could sail around its southern end and then get to the Spice Islands through Spanish territory. He sailed from Spain to the coast of South America, where he spent the winter. There he saw natives who were so large that he named them Patagonians ("Big Feet"). He then sailed around the southern tip of South America through what we now call the Strait of Magellan. There one of his five ships deserted, and he lost a second in a severe storm. When he finally reached the ocean to the west, he appreciated its calmness so much that he named it *Pacific* ("peaceful").

As the three ships sailed westward across the Pacific, they ran out of supplies, and many sailors starved to death. Finally they reached the Philippines, but Magellan was killed when he tried to help a local ruler in a tribal war. Magellan's crew continued and reached the Spice Islands, where they took on a large cargo of spices. With only one ship left, they sailed around Africa and back to Spain. The ship returned with only eighteen of the more than two hundred men who had started the trip. This three-year-long, tragic voyage, the first **circumnavigation** of the earth, has been called "the greatest single

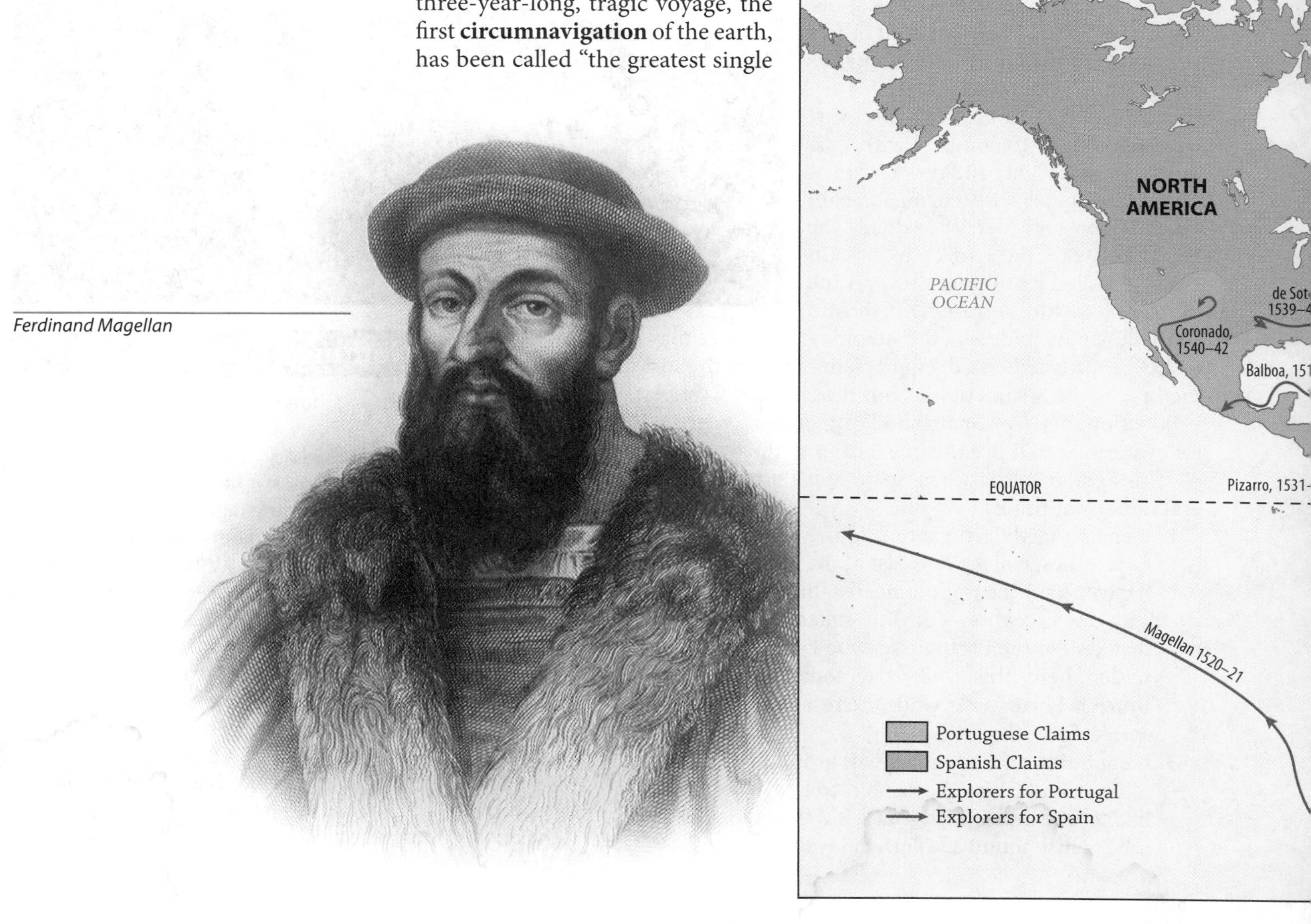

Ferdinand Magellan

human achievement on sea." It demonstrated that one great body of water covered the earth. Magellan's voyage also made it clear to Europeans that the discoveries of Columbus were not as near to Asia as Columbus had hoped.

Section Quiz

1. What two European nations led the way during the Age of Exploration?
2. What member of the Portuguese ruling family greatly aided the Age of Exploration? What nickname did he earn?
3. Da Gama's discovery led to the Portuguese establishment of an all-water route to what land?
4. For whom are North and South America named?
5. Who settled the trade disputes between Spain and Portugal by dividing the world between the two countries? What was the dividing line called?

★ How did Henry's interest in navigation promote European exploration?

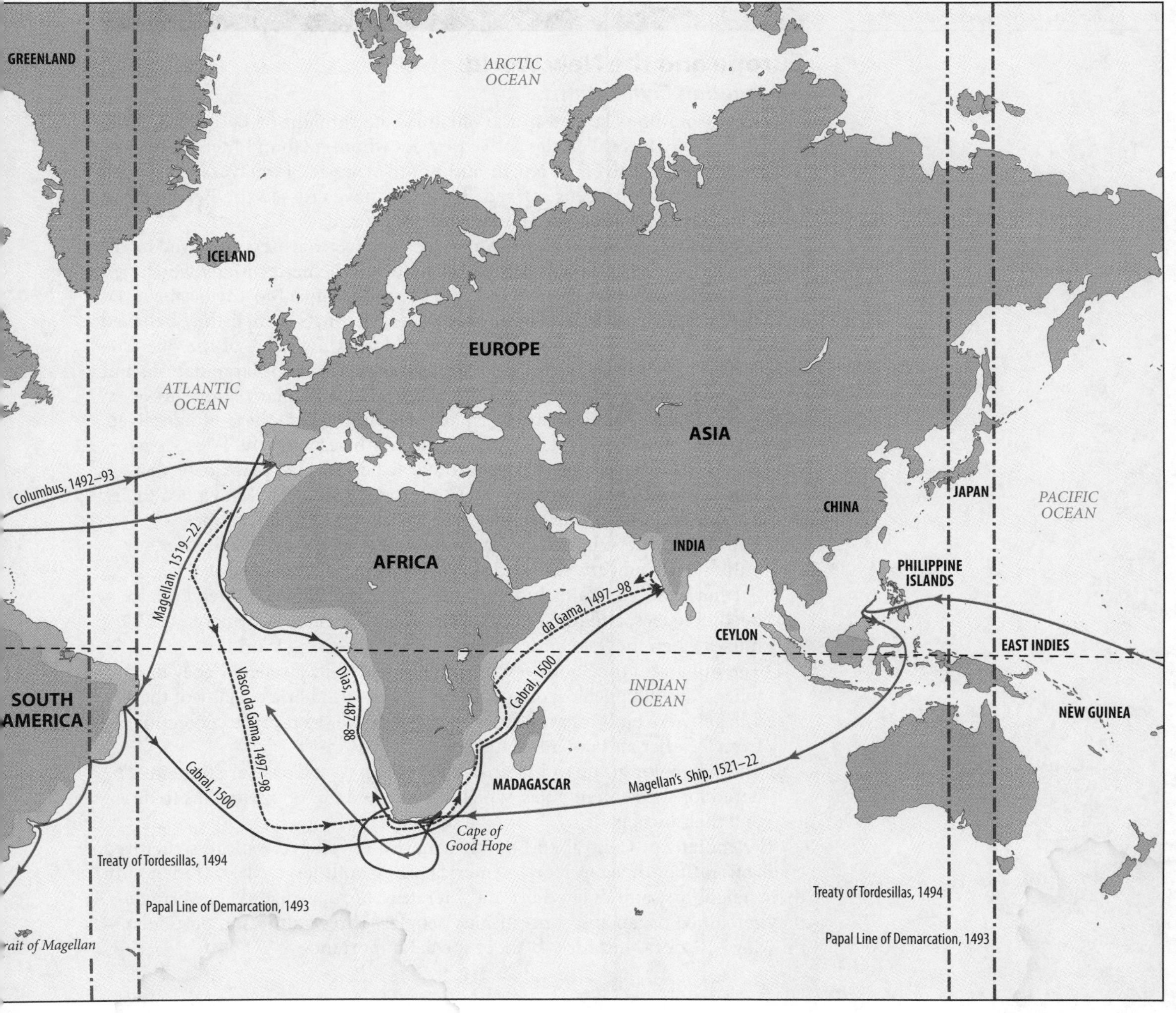

Mesa Verde in southwest Colorado; ruins of the ancient dwellings of the Ancestral Puebloans

Europe and the New World

Amerindian Civilizations

When Columbus landed in the Bahamas, he thought he had reached the East Indies. He thus called the native peoples whom he found there "Indians." These peoples had lived in North and South America for several thousand years before the Europeans arrived. They may have crossed the Bering Strait between Asia and Alaska and then moved southward.

Of the Indian groups in North America, some were farmers and lived in villages; others, because they were hunters, followed the herds. Many worshiped nature: the sun, the moon, the wind, and the mountains. Most tribes believed in a "Great Spirit" as well as a number of lesser spirits, which they believed watched over them. For many years they had no knowledge of the one true God. The North American Indians did not normally form large nations but lived in small groups or tribes. All the tribes in a particular region, however, had many similarities. There are five main regions in which these Indians lived: the Northeast, the Southeast, the Plains, the Southwest, and the West Coast.

1. The Northeastern Indians, unlike other tribes, formed a five-tribe confederation led by the Iroquois (IHR uh KWOY). They are known for their use of wampum, or shell money, and for their birch-bark canoes.
2. The Southeastern Indians were most famous as "mound builders"; they built burial and ceremonial mounds, many of which still exist.
3. Farther west, the Plains Indians roamed the grasslands, hunted buffalo, lived in tepees, and fought often with other tribes. They began to use horses when the Spaniards brought them to the New World.
4. The Indians of the Southwest are often called "cliff dwellers." They built villages, called pueblos, out of adobe, or sun-dried brick. Many of these villages were built into the sides of cliffs in order to provide protection from weather and potential attackers.
5. The last major group of Indians, those of the West Coast, are remembered for their totem poles, which they carved out of tree trunks to depict their local gods.

The Indians of Central and South America developed a more structured civilization than those in North America. They built large cities, traded with their neighbors, and created art and literature of high quality. Nevertheless, they remained pagan and superstitious peoples. Three cultures in particular—the Mayas, Aztecs, and Incas—are of special importance.

Mayan ruins in Yucatán Mexico; Mayapan (banner of the Mayas) was the last great Mayan capital.

The **Mayan** civilization, which flourished from the fourth century through the tenth century, was noted for its artistic and intellectual achievements. Like that of the ancient Greeks, the Mayan civilization was not a unified nation but consisted of many city-states located in the Yucatán (YOO kuh TAN) Peninsula in southeastern Mexico. They built great pyramids, temples, altars, and paved highways. The Mayas developed hieroglyphics and studied astronomy with as much dedication as the ancient Egyptians. They computed the length of a year almost exactly (to 365¼ days), built astronomical observatories, and developed a system of mathematics that even included the concept of zero as a placeholder. The Mayas also worshipped many false gods, including a feathered serpent. During the ninth and tenth centuries, the Mayan civilization declined, and the people abandoned their centers of culture. When the Spanish arrived, the remaining Mayans fiercly resisted Spanish conquest, but they eventually succumbed to Spanish domination.

The **Aztecs** established their civilization after the decline of the Mayan civilization. About 1345 they built the city of Tenochtitlán (tay NAWCH tee TLAHN) on an island in the middle of a lake in central Mexico. This walled city, connected by several long bridges to the mainland, had a huge pyramid temple as well as several other beautiful temples. Describing the network of canals throughout the city, one of the first Europeans to see the city called Tenochtitlán "the Venice of the New World."

The Aztecs were fighters, and they required every able-bodied Aztec man to serve in the army. With an aggressive and well-trained force, they conquered more than five million people and collected tribute from them all. The army often took prisoners of war to sacrifice to their gods. Sometimes Aztec priests even ate the flesh of their human sacrifices. The Aztecs proved to be better fighters than governors, however, and never developed a real empire.

The **Inca** Empire, which reached its zenith between 1380 and 1570, flourished along the western coast of South America where Peru is today. Inca families lived in tightly organized communes in which several families shared

The ruined city of Machu Picchu (meaning "old peak") in the Andes Mountains of modern Peru is one of the best preserved treasures of Inca culture. Located nearly eight thousand feet above sea level, Machu Picchu was apparently unknown to the Spanish and was discovered by an American explorer in 1911.

possessions. Most Incas were farmers, raising maize (corn), potatoes, and cotton. All of the communes were closely controlled by the ruler—"the Inca"—whom the people worshiped as a god.

Unlike the Mayas and the Aztecs, the Incas ruled a genuine empire. They not only conquered neighboring peoples but also took over their lands and exercised absolute rule over them. Upon conquest, the Incas abolished human sacrifice and cannibalism. They also planned Incan cities carefully and connected them with well-constructed roads. Describing the road between Cuzco, the Inca capital, and Quito, one Spanish conqueror said, "The roads constructed by the Romans in Spain . . . are not to be compared to it." The roads even crossed deep canyons on a type of suspension bridge that was strong enough to support heavy use. Along these roads the Incas set up a courier system that could deliver messages over distances of more than one hundred fifty miles per day.

Spanish Exploration

The early Spanish explorers who came to the New World found that the Indian tribes could be easily conquered. Spain, which claimed rights to this land, sent **conquistadors** ("conquerors") to search for riches, to convert the Indians to Catholicism, and to establish Spanish authority. By using their firearms and horses, which the terrified Indians had never seen, small bands of Spanish soldiers were able to subdue entire Indian tribes and empires.

But the conquistadors were often cruel to the Indians they had come to "convert." Many of these men used the same ruthless methods to gain both riches and "converts." They apparently saw no conflict in their quest for both. However, their desire for wealth and fame often overshadowed their religious zeal, making their religious efforts a poor reflection of the gospel.

The first notable conquistador was **Vasco Núñez de Balboa**. He came to the New World in search of adventure but soon found himself working on a farm on the island of Hispaniola. Dissatisfied and heavily in debt, he stowed away aboard a ship bound for the mainland, where a new colony was to be established. Balboa joined the colony as a soldier, but by plotting against those in charge, he was able to win control of it. Under his leadership the colony moved to a site on the coast of Panama.

Vasco de Balboa

Balboa knew that complaints had been lodged against him before the king of Spain. The only way to gain royal favor, he concluded, would be to find gold or make some striking discovery. Balboa heard rumors of a great ocean to the west and of a people wealthy with gold. In 1513, with a force of some two hundred men, he began cutting his way westward across what is today Panama, making his way through the heavy jungle of the isthmus (a narrow strip of land connecting two larger landmasses). After three weeks Balboa and his men neared the western coast. Wanting to be the first European to see the new ocean, Balboa ordered his men to wait while he walked to the crest of a small mountain. There he saw a great body of water, which he named the "South Sea"; Magellan renamed it "Pacific" seven years later.

Balboa sent word of his discovery back to Spain, hoping to receive a royal commendation. However, in the meantime authorities arrested him on false charges made by a jealous rival and beheaded him.

In 1519 **Hernando Cortés**, called "the greatest of the conquistadors," landed on the shore of Mexico. After sinking his ships so that none of his soldiers would desert, he moved his army inland toward the Aztec capital. When the Aztec king, **Montezuma**, heard of their approach, he thought that Cortés might be the returning god Quetzalcoatl (ket SAHL koh AH t'l), or at least his representative. (The Aztecs' chief god, Quetzalcoatl, was supposed to return to them someday from across the sea.) Instead of fighting Cortés, Montezuma welcomed him with gifts of gold and jewels, which only intensified the Spaniard's greed. Cortés himself had said, "We Spaniards suffer from a disease that only gold can cure."

Above: Hernando Cortés
Below: Cortés and Montezuma at a Mexican temple

The Requirement

Before the conquistadors made war on the Indians, they were required to read to the Indians a document issued by the king of Spain. The statement, known as the *requerimento*, informed the Indians that the eternal God gave the pope in Rome the authority over all men. Pope Alexander VI in turn had given Spain authority over the New World. This document invited the Indians to embrace the Roman Catholic religion and to become loyal subjects under Spanish rule. If they refused, the document warned that "with the help of God, we [the Spanish] shall powerfully enter into your country and shall make war against you in all ways and manners that we can, and shall subject you to the yoke and obedience of the Church and of Their Highnesses. We shall take you and your wives and your children, and shall make slaves of them, and as such shall sell and dispose of them as Their Highnesses may command. And we shall take your goods, and shall do you all the mischief and damage that we can, as to vassals who do not obey and refuse to receive their Lord and resist and contradict him." The *requerimento* effectively gave legal justification to those Spaniards who enslaved or massacred Indians who would not submit. To make matters worse, conquistadors often read the Spanish document to the Indians without a translator to enable the Indians to understand the demands made upon them. At other times conquistadors read the document when no Indians were present to hear it or after they had already imprisoned the Indians. While the ruler of Spain did abolish use of the *requerimento* in 1556, brutal treatment of Indians by Spanish forces continued.

This painting of Las Casas by Constatine Brumidi is hanging in the Senate wing of the Capitol.

After a time of uneasy peace, war broke out. The Spanish guns took their toll as the Spaniards massacred hundreds of Aztecs. Montezuma was stoned to death by his own people as a traitor. In 1521, after a four-month siege, Cortés finally defeated the Aztecs and destroyed the city. On its ruins he began to build what is now Mexico City. This city later became one of the capitals of New Spain. One of the several **viceroys**, or "assistant kings," appointed by the Spanish king, lived there.

Cortés and his men were not satisfied with their successes. Some soldiers headed north, still lusting for gold. Others fought over their newly acquired treasures. Cortés finally returned to Spain in 1541 and died six years later, a discouraged and frustrated man.

Francisco Pizarro (pih ZAHR oh) was probably the cruelest of all the conquistadors. He came to the New World for one reason: to find gold. He accompanied Balboa in his march across the Isthmus of Panama. After Balboa's execution, he decided to find the people to the south—the Incas—who were rumored to be very wealthy. In 1531 he and his men set out for Peru. After landing by ship on the coast, they marched through jungles for six months, plundering villages as they went. Raiding the Inca empire, they captured **Atahualpa** (AH tah WAHL pah), the Inca ruler, and held him for ransom. Atahualpa promised to fill a room with gold and silver to buy his release. After receiving the promised ransom of gold and silver, Pizarro broke his promise and executed Atahualpa. With only a handful of men, he completed the conquest of the great Inca Empire.

Two years later Pizarro founded the city of Lima, which is today the capital of Peru. Soon afterwards, other Spaniards, as greedy as Pizarro and jealous of his gold, attacked and killed him in his home. Pizarro had found more gold in the New World than anyone else, but greed—his own greed and that of others—prevented anyone from enjoying it. Like Pizarro, most other conquistadors died violently, fighting to keep the gold which they thought would help them enjoy life.

Not all Spaniards who came to the New World were after gold. In 1502 **Bartolomé de las Casas** (1474–1566), a Roman Catholic friar, arrived in the Americas as a missionary to the Indians. Deeply distressed over the cruelty of his countrymen, he wrote several works decrying the abuse of the Indians in the New World. He described, for example, the death of one Indian chief who was being burned at the stake. A priest told him to become a Christian so he could go to heaven. The man refused, saying that he did not want to go to any place where there were Christians. Unfortunately, the Indians, like many people today, were turned away from the gospel by the lives of people who falsely claimed to be Christians.

Las Casas devoted his life to improving the plight of the Indians in the New World. In 1542 he helped pass the "New Laws," which protected the Indians from being made slaves. Previously, the Spanish had forced the natives to work on plantations where they were overworked and mistreated. These new laws forbade this practice. Las Casas also opposed the common Roman Catholic practice of giving people the choice of converting to Catholicism and being allowed to live as slaves or rejecting the Roman Church and being killed. No man, he said, could be converted by force; real conversion comes only to those who are persuaded gently.

Spanish exploration was not confined to Latin America. Rumors of "a land of gold" to the north enticed other explorers to the regions of what is now the United States. In 1539 **Hernando de Soto**, who served with Pizarro in Peru, landed near Tampa Bay, Florida, in search of "golden" cities. In his exploration of the southeastern United States, he discovered the great Mississippi River. Though he did not find gold, his expedition led the way for further exploration of the North American continent.

Another explorer of the lands to the north was **Francisco Vásquez de Coronado** (KOR uh NAH doh). He set out from Mexico in 1540 to find the "Seven Cities of Cibola," which were reportedly rich in gold. He led his expedition into what is now New Mexico and Arizona and then on through what is now Kansas and Texas. Some of his men went westward and discovered the Grand Canyon.

Neither de Soto nor Coronado realized the value of the lands they explored. Since they found no gold, they concluded it to be a waste of time to explore further. Because of these two expeditions, the Spaniards decided to concentrate their efforts on the land they already held, leaving most of North America open for other European nations to explore.

French, Dutch, and English Exploration

When the pope gave Spain and Portugal rights to all newly discovered lands in 1493, the other nations of Europe objected. King Francis I of France commented sarcastically, "I should like to see Adam's will, wherein he divided the earth between Spain and Portugal." After Magellan's voyage, most Europeans realized that the land to the west was not Asia, but a new world; and the French, Dutch, and English sought to claim some of it for themselves.

French Explorers—The first great French explorer in the New World was **Jacques Cartier** (kar TYAY), who made three voyages to what is now eastern Canada. In 1534 he sailed to Newfoundland and Labrador, which was so desolate that he remarked, "I am rather inclined to believe that this is the land God gave to Cain."

On his second voyage (1535) he sailed up the St. Lawrence River to an Iroquois Indian village. The view from a nearby mountain was so impressive that Cartier named the site "Mount Royal" (in French, "Montreal"). Today one of the largest cities in Canada stands there. Like many other explorers of his day, Cartier was certain that there existed a water route—the so-called Northwest Passage—which would take him to the Pacific Ocean and from there to the Orient, but he was unsuccessful in finding it.

The Legend of El Dorado

Many early explorers came to the New World with one thing in mind: gold. The story that excited them more than any other was the legend of El Dorado. According to American Indian folklore, El Dorado ("the gilded one") was the name of both a wealthy ruler and his fabulous city. This land supposedly possessed untold amounts of gold dust—so much, in fact, that each morning its ruler sprinkled his body with gold dust and each evening washed it off in a lake. It was said that his people threw golden statues and jewelry into the lake as offerings to their gods and that gold was so plentiful that gold dust clung to the roots of plants when they were pulled up.

Explorers hunted all over northern South America in search of this magnificent ruler and his country. Many men lost their lives in this land of rugged mountains and fierce Indian tribes. No one ever found El Dorado, of course, for it did not exist except in legend. Years later American poet Edgar Allan Poe wrote a somber poem about the search for El Dorado. In his poem an explorer, wearied by years of vain searching, "met a pilgrim shadow" and asked "Where can it be—/ This land of Eldorado?" The shadow grimly answered:

"Over the mountains
Of the moon,
Down the valley of the shadow,
Ride, boldly ride,"
The shadow replied—
"If you seek for Eldorado!"

Life at Sea

Life at sea was full of hardships during the Age of Exploration. In return for their hard labor, sailors were paid very little and were fed the worst sorts of food imaginable. Since many ships remained at sea for long periods of time, the sailors often had to live for months on a dreary diet of biscuits (hardtack), salt beef, salt fish, and beer. The salted meat was tough, usually stank, and often had maggots in it. The biscuits were usually of poor quality. Some sailors jokingly refused to eat those biscuits that were not infested with maggots, stating that they did not want to eat something that even the maggots had refused. All ships carried barrels of water, but within a short time the water became stagnant and undrinkable. It became discolored, gave off a terrible odor, and was full of tiny organisms. Unfortunately, the only thing on board that did not spoil was the liquor.

One disease that plagued sailors and brought death to many was a vitamin-C deficiency called scurvy. It caused the gums to become swollen and bloody (loosening the teeth in the process) and caused the limbs to become swollen and discolored. Although no one knew about vitamin C at the time, various sea captains stumbled upon a cure for scurvy, finding that fresh fruit and vegetables stopped it. Since fresh produce could not be carried on long sea voyages, the British navy made it compulsory in 1798 for their ships to carry lime juice. Because of this practice, British sailors acquired the nickname "limeys."

Some seventy years after Cartier, **Samuel de Champlain** (sham PLANE), called the "Father of New France," explored and colonized the area around the St. Lawrence River. In 1608 he founded the city of Quebec. He worked closely with the local Indians, who led him to two of the Great Lakes (Ontario and Huron) and to what we now call Lake Champlain. Like Cartier, he was looking for a route west to China.

A replica of Henry Hudson's ship, Half Moon

Another noted French explorer was the Jesuit missionary **Jacques Marquette** (mar KET). In 1673 he and a friend, **Louis Joliet** (JOH lee ET), explored the Mississippi River. They paddled canoes downstream to a point in southern Arkansas before turning back. In 1682 Sieur de La Salle (luh SAL) traveled to the mouth of the Mississippi River and claimed the entire Mississippi Valley for France. He called it "Louisiana" in honor of King Louis XIV of France.

Dutch Explorers—The most famous explorer for the Netherlands was the Englishman **Henry Hudson**, whom the Dutch hired to find a shorter route to the East. He explored the northeastern coast of America in his ship the *Half Moon*. In 1609 he entered the Hudson River, thinking it might be the Northwest Passage. He continued upriver to where Albany, New York, now stands. His exploration gave the Dutch a claim to the region. In 1621 the Dutch founded the city of New Amsterdam, which is today New York City.

English Explorers—The English began exploring the New World soon after Columbus's first voyage. They hired an Italian sailor named **John Cabot** to lead the first English expedition to North America. After a six-week voyage across the Atlantic, Cabot dropped anchor off the coast of Canada. The first European after the Vikings to set foot on the North American mainland, he returned to England and was rewarded by King Henry VII. In 1498 Cabot made a second voyage to the New World, this time accompanied by his son Sebastian. They explored the northern coast of North America. Though they did not find gold or spices, they found rich fisheries off the Newfoundland coast. The two expeditions to the New World were the basis for England's claim on America. The Cabots paved the way for the founding of English colonies on the North American continent a century later.

Like the Spanish, the English also looked for gold. But they went about obtaining it much differently. For the most part, the English did not engage in the extreme cruelty to the Indians that was typical of the Spaniards. The English brought their families and sought to develop the land, not exploit it. Their first permanent settlement was **Jamestown**, founded in 1607 near the mouth of Chesapeake Bay. Under the leadership of Captain **John Smith**, the settlers built a village and began to explore the land. In 1608 much of the village burned down, and the few remaining settlers had almost given up when a new governor, Lord de la Warr, arrived. The influx of new settlers and fresh supplies gave new life to the struggling colony.

Statue of John Smith

Courtesy of the APVA Preservation Virginia

This English settlement, the first of many in the New World, was the beginning of what would later become the United States of America. Most of the freedoms that Americans have enjoyed—freedom of religion, freedom of speech, and many others—resulted from the influence of Protestant settlers who traveled to North America during the seventeenth century.

Europe and the Orient

The West Reaches the East

Europe's exploration efforts were not limited to the New World; its main interests were on the other side of the world in the Orient. Spain was largely excluded from this area by treaty with Portugal (although Spain did colonize the Philippines). Portugal, the Netherlands, and England, however, traded and colonized extensively in the East.

The Portuguese—Soon after da Gama returned from his historic voyage, the Portuguese, under the leadership of **Pedro Cabral**, established a trading post in India. From this small beginning they were able to establish numerous trading posts throughout the Indian Ocean. Their fully armed ships gave them an insurmountable advantage over Muslim and native traders in the region.

In 1506 **Affonso de Albuquerque** (AL buh KUR kee) was named the viceroy of Portuguese holdings in the East. He discouraged cruelty to the natives and led his men in setting up trading posts and plantations along the trade routes to support and protect Portuguese traders. Under his leadership the Portuguese began to build a vast commercial empire. They captured and controlled the entrances to the Persian Gulf and the Red Sea. Shortly after Albuquerque's death they pushed farther eastward. By 1520 they had taken Ceylon (present-day Sri Lanka) and the town of Banten on the island of Java. The latter controlled one of the two water entrances to the Far East. Since the Portuguese already controlled the other entrance at the straits of Malacca, they were in an excellent position to dominate all the sea trade between Europe and Asia. In 1542 they began trading with Japan, and in 1557 they founded the colony of Macao on the Chinese mainland.

However, the Portuguese "eastern empire" had some fatal weaknesses. It was spread out too widely for the little country of Portugal to administer and defend effectively. Furthermore, since many sailors died at sea, Portugal's manpower was drained to a critical point. (About one voyage in seven ended in disaster.)

Mount Semeru in Java

Finally, the cruelty of the traders—despite Albuquerque's reforms—caused the Asians to hate them. With the lack of cooperation essential for successful trading, Portuguese commercial interests were hampered. When other European nations began to compete for business in the East, the Asians granted it to them.

The Dutch—The Dutch were not a wealthy people in the sixteenth century, but they were experienced sailors. When prices soared under the Portuguese monopoly, the Dutch decided to go directly to the source for their Asian goods. In 1596 they settled on Java and Sumatra and expelled the Portuguese from the key city of Banten. They later captured the main Spice Islands and founded the city of Batavia, which became a key port and trading post in the East Indies. They soon became the only nation that Japan would trade with. They also began trading with Formosa (modern Taiwan) and seized the island of Ceylon. By the middle of the seventeenth century, Dutch control extended from Persia to Japan.

In order to provide fresh water, vegetables, and meat for ships making the long voyage around Africa to the Indies, the Dutch in 1652 established a settlement at the Cape of Good Hope at what is now Cape Town, South Africa. The mild climate of the cape attracted many settlers; before long it became a sizable colony.

The English—When England defeated the Spanish Armada in 1588, the English realized that they had enough sea power to carry on a busy trade with the East. In 1591, almost a century after da Gama, English merchant-seamen made a trading voyage to India. Although they started late, the English far surpassed the Portuguese in long-range influence in the Orient. They followed the Dutch into the East Indies, trading alongside them for several years. Soon, however, they turned their main attention to India. England seized control of the Persian Gulf and opened trade on both the east and west coasts of India. This was the beginning of England's influence in India—an influence that continued into the twentieth century.

Francis Xavier

The East Responds to the West

China and Japan resented Western intervention in their affairs. The same satisfied attitude that had kept them from exploring other lands for most of their history also kept them from welcoming traders to their lands. They had been secure in their traditions, and they did not take kindly to European sailors who attempted to claim their properties for unknown kings and their souls for Roman popes. The Portuguese, who were the first to come to the East, were especially tactless and cruel, and by 1550 there had already been several bloody battles between Chinese and Portuguese soldiers. The people of China resisted the European way of life as well as Christianity. They wanted to be left alone. The Chinese did allow the Portuguese to colonize the port city of Macao, but for this privilege the Portuguese had to pay $30,000 per year in tribute. Except for isolated instances, there was no direct trade between China and the European countries for many years.

Japan at first was more friendly to the Europeans than China was. The Japanese welcomed **Francis Xavier**, the famous Jesuit missionary. Later, however, the government, influenced by Buddhism, expelled the foreign missionaries who had followed Xavier to Japan. Those who stayed were severely persecuted. More trouble broke out in 1639 when the Japanese shogun learned that Portuguese trading ships were smuggling in Catholic missionaries disguised as merchants. Furious, he commanded that any Portuguese who came to Japan be killed on sight. Some traders who did not think the shogun was serious learned otherwise and paid with their lives. The Japanese did allow a few Dutch ships to trade in their ports, but for the most part, Japan, like China, remained closed to European travelers.

Section Quiz

1. List the five major regions in North America where groups of Indian tribes lived.
2. What were the three major native Indian cultures of Central and South America?
3. After crossing the Isthmus of Panama, Balboa saw what body of water? What did he call it? Who gave it its present name?
4. List the country for which each of the following explorers sailed and claimed territory in the New World: Jacques Cartier, Samuel de Champlain, Henry Hudson, and John Cabot.
5. List the Oriental possessions gained by each of the following countries during the Age of Exploration: Portugal, the Netherlands, and England.

★ Why were European missionaries forbidden in China and Japan?

III. Parallel to Discovery: The Commercial Revolution

During the fifteenth and sixteenth centuries, Europe underwent many political, social, religious, and aesthetic changes. There were also many economic changes. Ownership of land was no longer considered the basis of wealth. Money became the medium of exchange in trade. As new sources of gold and spices were discovered in distant lands and used as a medium of exchange, wealth became redefined. Soon after the earliest explorers had returned home,

Spanish gold doubloons and pieces of eight salvaged from a 1715 wreck; the pieces of eight are cut from an eight-ounce piece of molten silver and stamped with the shield of Philip V of Spain and the cross

commercial ventures were organized to establish trade ties with newly found peoples across the seas. Soon, great wealth began to flow into Europe from around the world. Europe's business thinking and practice changed. These changes became known as the **Commercial Revolution**.

Mercantilism: Nations Acquiring Wealth

The dominant economic system practiced during the Age of Exploration is called **mercantilism**. Mercantilists believed that the newly found wealth should benefit the mother country. A nation's strength and greatness was believed to rest upon the amount of gold and silver it possessed. For this reason, the goal of nations governed by mercantilism became obtaining as much precious metal as possible. To achieve this goal, nations acquired colonies, sought to become self-sufficient, and worked to maintain a favorable balance of trade by exporting more than they imported.

Under mercantilism, colonies existed to supply the mother country with raw materials and to provide markets where goods from the mother country could be sold. To prevent competition, the colonies were not allowed to produce anything that the mother country produced. Nor were the colonies allowed to trade with any other country. Mexico, for example, had to buy everything it needed from Spain, and whatever it produced had to be sold to Spain. Likewise, it was not allowed to trade directly with other Spanish colonies; for Mexican products to reach Peru, for example, they had to be shipped across the ocean to Spain and then back again to Peru. As a result of mercantilism, the mother countries became wealthy.

Under this system the government regulated a nation's economic activity, creating national monopolies that deterred competition. More often than not, the interests of the government superseded the interests and welfare of the people—especially those in the colonies—and the colonies usually suffered.

Mercantilists did not view trade as a "two-way street" benefiting both buyer and seller. They thought of it only in terms of the seller, who obtained gold and silver for his product. This one-sided foreign trade, in which goods went out of a country and gold and silver came in, was a detriment to a country's agriculture and industry. The goods and crops a nation produced were deemed important only if they could be traded abroad for gold and silver. Once gold and silver were obtained by a mercantilist country, the wealth was seldom used to benefit the people. Instead, these precious metals were hoarded in royal treasuries.

Capitalism: Individuals Advancing Wealth

The opportunity for acquiring great wealth also became open to individuals. During this period another economic system—**capitalism**—developed alongside mercantilism. Unlike mercantilism, the goal of capitalism was not simply to acquire wealth but to advance wealth. Enterprising individuals used what money they had to make more money. They invested their wealth, often at great risk, in hopes of making a profit.

Many of the early capitalists were bankers. They made money by buying and selling bills of exchange, by safeguarding money for others, and by exchanging money. They often invested their own resources in business ventures, such as financing trade voyages. But sea travel at this time was perilous: it was not uncommon for the stormy seas to send ships to the bottom of the ocean or for pirates to seize a ship's cargo. Such disasters could bring financial ruin to an individual. To spread the risk, men organized **companies** in which they pooled their resources; they shared the gains as well as the losses.

From this practice arose the **joint-stock company**. People invested money in such companies, and in return they were issued stock certificates showing the amount of money they invested. The invested money became part of the company's **capital**, or supply of money. The company then used this capital to finance a business venture. If the company made a profit, the stockholders received payment in the form of **dividends**.

There were many joint-stock companies during the Age of Exploration. Three are especially important. The English East India Company, founded in 1600 with only a small amount of capital, began trading primarily in India. It

The East Indiaman Worley (1795)

Creator: Robert Salmon, National Maritime Museum, London

was astonishingly successful. Profits for the years 1609–13, for example, averaged almost 300 percent each year (that is, investors received back every year dividends three times their original investment). The Dutch East India Company, founded in 1602, traded in the East Indies (such as Java and Sumatra). It too made great profits, paying dividends of 18 percent each year for many years. The French Company of New France traded in Canada, mainly for furs. These companies did more than just trade, however. They also set up bases, or settlements, to make their work more permanent.

Another method of getting people to help finance an enterprise was to post in a public place a prospectus—details of a proposed business venture. People wrote their names below the prospectus, stating that they would help share the cost of the enterprise. If it was a success, they would share in the profits; if it was a failure, they agreed to sustain the loss. It is from this practice that we get the word **underwriter**, which today we use to describe an insurance company. One of the earliest insurance companies was Lloyds of London. It was founded in 1688 by a group of men who underwrote voyages to the New World.

Section Quiz

1. What are the changes in Europe's business thinking and practice during the fifteenth and sixteenth centuries called?
2. What was the dominant economic policy of most European nations during the Age of Exploration?
3. What was the purpose of colonies under this economic policy?
4. The use of wealth to make more wealth defines what economic policy?

★ Which economic policy (mercantilism or capitalism) provided the greatest long-term benefits for a country? Why?

Chapter 13 Review

Making Connections

1–2. How did the Renaissance (Ch. 11) influence the Age of Discovery? (List two ways.)

3–5. Distinguish the economic policies of mercantilism and capitalism. (List three distinctions for each.)

Developing History Skills

1. What were the long-term results of Portuguese and British colonization?
2. What effect did the defeat of the Spanish Armada in 1588 have on the early history of the English colonies in North America?

Thinking Critically

1. Evaluate the motives of many of the explorers in light of 1 Timothy 6:9–10.
2. If a Christian ruler had to choose between adopting a mercantilist approach or a capitalist approach, which should he choose? Why?

Living in God's World

1. Recently historians have emphasized that Europeans were wrong to force the native peoples to submit to them and to adopt European cultures. Some have even declared that Christian missions is wrong. They claim that missions is simply another way of replacing a native culture with a Western culture. Respond to this claim.
2. Choose a land explored by the Europeans and research its religious beliefs. Did the country have a form of Christianity in which the people already believed? Did it have a form of morality by which people lived? If so, explain what they believed from a Christian perspective.

People, Places, and Things to Know

Marco Polo
Prester John
compass
latitude
caravel
Prince Henry
Bartolomeu Dias
Vasco da Gama
Christopher Columbus
Line of Demarcation
Ferdinand Magellan
circumnavigation
Mayan
Aztecs
Inca
conquistadors
Vasco Núñez de Balboa
Hernando Cortés
Montezuma
Francisco Pizarro
viceroys
Atahualpa
Bartolomé de las Casas
Hernando de Soto
Franciso Vásquez de Coronado
Jacques Cartier
Samuel de Champlain
Jacques Marquette
Louis Joliet
Henry Hudson
John Cabot
Jamestown
John Smith
Pedro Cabral
Affonso de Albuquerque
Francis Xavier
Commercial Revolution
mercantilism
capitalism
companies
joint-stock company
capital
dividends
underwriter

THE ENLIGHTENED WORLD

V

Europeans living from 1600 to 1800 believed that they were living in an "enlightened" age. During that period, improving political and economic conditions hastened the decline of feudalism and eroded the power of the nobility. Consequently, strong absolutist monarchs were able to grasp political power. At the same time, that period—known as the Age of Reason—saw outstanding scientific and artistic accomplishments. Men expanded on the concepts of individual dignity and responsibility to which the Renaissance and Reformation had given expression. Philosophers popularized the concept that "all men are created equal." In harmony with this "enlightened" attitude, people began to challenge the absolutist ways of kings in search of individual freedom. The spirit of liberty and equality gave rise to the American War for Independence and the French Revolution.

1618–48 Thirty Years' War

1649 Execution of Charles I

1660 Restoration

1688 Glorious Revolution

1720–42 Great Awakening

1600 · 1650 · 1700

1756–63 Seven Years' War

1763 Treaty of Paris ending the Seven Years' War

1775–83 American War for Independence

1799–1815 Napoleonic Era

1799 Directory founded by Napoleon

1802 Napoleon named First Consul for Life

1804 Napoleon crowned Emperor

1805 Napoleon victorious at Austerlitz

1750 | 1800 | 1850

14

PURSUIT OF POWER IN EUROPE

Portrait of Louis XIV

Most Europeans living in the seventeenth and eighteenth centuries accepted the fact that God had established governments. In their day, the governments of Europe were controlled by monarchs. Though these monarchs emphasized their right to power, they often failed to properly exercise the responsibility of power, choosing instead to satisfy their own pleasures and increase their personal power. Monarchs also sought to increase their power and prestige by seizing additional territory—a practice that usually led to war. To prevent stronger rulers from taking their land, kings formed diplomatic alliances to maintain a balance of power in Europe. Thus, they hoped to ensure that no single nation became strong enough to dominate the entire continent of Europe.

Charles II's Long Walk (3.1 miles) at Windsor Castle in England was inspired by a similar path at Louis XIV's palace at Versailles.

I. Power of Kings: Absolute or Restrained

During the Middle Ages, royal power in Europe remained limited for several reasons. Popes struggled with kings over the question of whose authority was greater. Strong feudal nobles competed with kings for power within a territory. But with the papacy's decline in power and the passing of feudalism, royal power began to increase.

During the seventeenth and eighteenth centuries, European rulers worked to make their political power **absolute** (unlimited and unrestrained). They sought to increase their royal authority by (1) increasing their control over their nation's finances, religion, and nobility; (2) increasing the size of the standing army and/or developing a strong navy; (3) increasing the size of the government bureaucracy and making it an instrument of their royal will; and (4) increasing the size of their territory—through war if necessary. They justified the extension of their power on religious grounds. They asserted that God had established their authority; therefore, they ruled by "**divine right**." This right, they said, gave them absolute authority: they were not bound by any manmade laws but were responsible only to God for their actions.

Absolutist rule was accepted by most Europeans, who believed that a strong ruler was the best way to ensure security, order, and prosperity. Nevertheless, some people recognized the danger of an unrestrained increase in royal power. In some nations, representative assemblies that had developed alongside growing monarchies championed the opposition to absolute royal power. However, with the exception of the English Parliament, these assemblies had little success in restraining royal control. Most absolutist kings were able to crush any opposition to their authority.

Absolutism Triumphs in France

France became the leading absolutist nation in Europe during the seventeenth century. Two chief advisers to the French throne, Cardinals Richelieu and Mazarin, secured much of the power wielded by French kings. For several decades, Richelieu and then Mazarin guided both French policy and French kings. They increased their personal power by strengthening royal power in France and French power in Europe. Their efforts encouraged the growth of absolutism in France, and King Louis XIV became the ultimate beneficiary

Religious Defense of Absolutism

A staunch defender of political absolutism was the French Catholic Bishop Bossuet (baw SWAY), whom King Louis XIV chose to tutor his son. He wrote the following:

> The royal power is absolute. With the aim of making this truth hateful and insufferable, many writers have tried to confound absolute government with arbitrary government. But no two things could be more unlike. . . . The prince need render an account of his acts to no one. . . . Without this absolute authority the king could neither do good nor repress evil. . . . God is infinite, God is all. The prince, as prince, is not regarded as a private person: he is a public personage, all the state is in him; the will of the people is included in his.

But Bossuet also warned kings:

> Kings, although their power comes from on high, . . . should not regard themselves as masters of that power to use it at their pleasure. . . . They must employ it with fear and self-restraint, as a thing coming from God and of which God will demand an account. . . . Kings should tremble then as they use the power God has granted them; and let them think how horrible is the sacrilege if they use for evil a power which comes from God.

James Harvey Robinson and Charles A. Beard, Readings in Modern European History, *1:6-7.*

Cardinal Richelieu

of Richelieu and Mazarin's labors. For more than seventy years, he ruled France with unparalleled pomp and power, becoming the leading absolutist ruler of Europe.

Growth of Absolutism: Richelieu and Mazarin

Bourbon king **Henry IV** helped lay the foundation for absolutism in France. After his victory in the French civil wars (see p. 269), Henry worked to strengthen royal power. He reduced the privileges of the nobility and increased government control of the economy. However, he was assassinated by a Catholic extremist in 1610, and his nine-year-old son, Louis XIII (r. 1610–43), came to the throne. During the years of Louis's youth, his mother, Marie de Medici, ruled France. But in 1624 the Duc de Richelieu (RISH uh LOO)—better known as **Cardinal Richelieu**—became Louis XIII's chief minister.

Richelieu set about to strengthen the power of the king by destroying the Huguenots, whom he viewed as a danger to the state. He also wanted to weaken the great nobles and prevent them from regaining their lost power. Richelieu sought to accomplish the first of his policies by putting extraordinary burdens on the Huguenots. For example, he forced them to house French soldiers but exempted Roman Catholics from such obligations. Richelieu ordered Huguenot children to be taken from their homes and to be reared by Roman Catholics. He also sent spies to Huguenot churches to listen for any criticism of the government. Critics were either arrested or heavily fined.

Richelieu made progress toward accomplishing his second objective—weakening the nobility—by removing nobles from positions of authority in local government. He replaced them with officials directly responsible to the king. In addition, Richelieu destroyed many of the castles of the nobility. He imprisoned those who defied him and executed those he considered to be a threat.

To increase the prestige and power of France, Richelieu brought France into the **Thirty Years' War** (1618–48), the last great religious war fought in Europe. It began in Bohemia, the proud land of John Huss, when Protestant Bohemian nobles revolted against the newly crowned Catholic emperor, who had revoked their religious freedoms. The emperor sent his troops into the country and ruthlessly crushed all Protestant resistance. Before long, the war had spread to other parts of the Holy Roman Empire; Protestantism seemed to be on the verge of collapse.

Gustavus Adolphus (gus-TAY-vus uh-DAHL-fuss; r. 1611–32), king of Sweden, rescued the Protestant cause. With a small band of troops, Gustavus landed in northern Germany, recruited additional soldiers, and marched against the emperor's pro-Catholic, pro-imperial forces. Gustavus won several important victories but then was killed in battle. Soon after his death, France entered the war—on the side of the Protestants.

Although France was a Roman Catholic country, Richelieu feared what would happen if the Holy Roman emperor solidified his power by subduing all his Protestant opponents. France would then be surrounded by two strong Habsburg powers—Spain and the Holy Roman Empire. For this reason, Richelieu joined the Protestant cause in 1635, making the war more a political than a religious conflict.

After several more years of fighting, the war finally ended in 1648 with a Protestant-French victory. The peace treaties, collectively known as the Peace of Westphalia, contained several important provisions. (1) The treaties recognized the independence of the Protestant provinces of the Netherlands and the Swiss confederacy. (2) The treaties recognized more than three hundred independent German states and reaffirmed the principle that each prince would determine the religion of his territory. For all practical purposes, this resulted in a more politically fragmented Germany. France emerged as the strongest nation on the continent of Europe.

Richelieu died in 1642. King Louis XIII died only five months later, and the crown of France passed to Louis's five-year-old son, **Louis XIV** (r. 1643–1715). During Louis XIV's youth, the government was controlled by a new chief minister, **Jules Mazarin**. Mazarin maintained the absolutist policies of his predecessor, Richelieu. Shortly after the wily Cardinal Mazarin and the young king came to power, Mazarin imposed new taxes, and France began to experience unrest. Those who opposed the growing power of the crown participated in a series of riots, civil wars, and antigovernment plots. These upheavals, known as the **Frondes**, forced Louis XIV to leave Paris for a time, but they were unsuccessful in destroying French absolutism and ended in 1653. They were the last serious attempt to limit the power of the king until the outbreak of the French Revolution in 1789. (See Chapter 16.)

Cardinal Mazarin. 1641.

Oil on canvas. Mignard, Pierre (1612-1695). Réunion des Musées Nationaux/Art Resource, NY

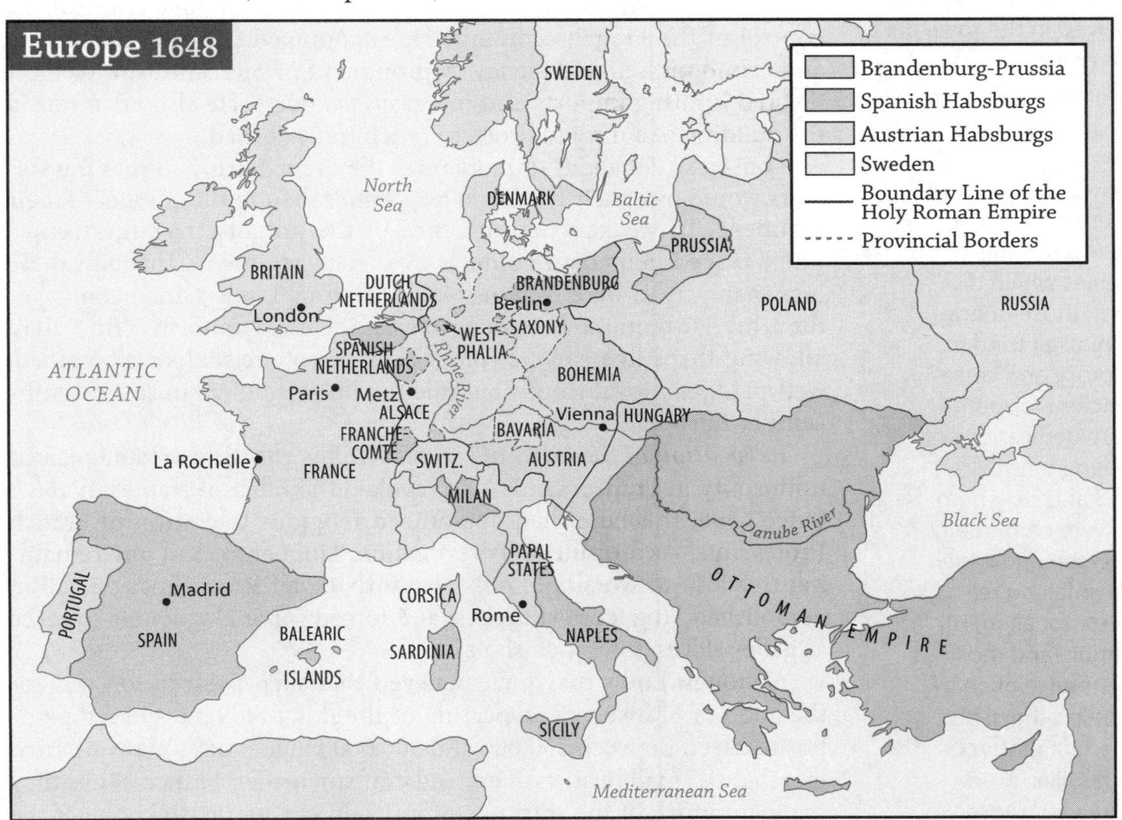

Epitome of Absolutism: Louis XIV

When Mazarin died in 1661, Louis XIV decided against appointing a replacement. Instead, Louis became his own chief minister. He told his advisers, "You will assist me with your counsels when I ask for them." Louis believed in "one king, one law, and one faith." These three were wrapped up in the person of the king and his power over the state. Although he may never have said, "*L' état, c'est moi*" ("I am the state"), these words reflect Louis's view of himself. From 1661 until his death in 1715, Louis dominated European affairs to such an extent that historians sometimes call these years "the Age of Louis XIV."

The palace of Versailles

Financial and Military Policies—One of the first things Louis did after the death of Mazarin was to set French finances in order. The French government was close to bankruptcy because it was spending money faster than it took it in. To remedy this dangerous situation, Louis appointed **Jean-Baptiste Colbert** (kohl BEHR; 1619–83) as his minister of finance. Colbert brought temporary fiscal order to France by tighter government control of the French economy. He encouraged commercial activity and economic self-sufficiency. A proponent of mercantilism, Colbert favored limiting imports and increasing exports. He also encouraged the building of a navy to protect French trade abroad.

Louis also set about to reorganize the French army so that the soldiers would owe their loyalty to him rather than to the colonel of their regiment. To weaken the influence of the nobility over the troops, Louis placed lieutenant colonels over each regiment. Through these lieutenants, who were responsible to the king, Louis gained control of the army. He required his troops to wear identical uniforms rather than allowing them to wear the colors of their colonels. His well-trained, well-paid, and loyal troops became the finest soldiers in seventeenth-century Europe.

Revocation of the Edict of Nantes—In his efforts to create religious uniformity in France, Louis XIV revoked the Edict of Nantes in 1685. Since 1598, this edict had guaranteed religious toleration of French Protestants. As a result of its revocation, Huguenots lost any remaining freedom to worship. Louis also forbade all Protestant education, demolished Huguenot churches, and forced some Huguenots to serve as galley slaves on French ships.

Although Louis may have believed that such persecution was for the good of France, his revocation of the Edict of Nantes had the opposite effect. Between 250,000 and 500,000 Huguenots—many of them merchants, small businessmen, and craftsmen—left France. Since they made up much of the spiritual, moral, and economic backbone of the country, their departure had a devastating effect on the French nation. The nations in which the Huguenots settled benefited from their spiritual fervor and productive skills. Some of these lands were rivals of France; thus, Louis unintentionally strengthened his enemies.

Life at Versailles—Louis XIV took the sun as the symbol of his reign. As the "Sun King," he considered himself the center of European life, with everyone else "revolving" around him. Louis was a proud man who loved to glorify himself and his own accomplishments. He loved luxury and the attention of the people of his court.

Louis XIV's Vanity

A nobleman who lived in the royal palace described Louis's vanity:

> [It was] without limit or restraint; it colored everything and convinced him that no one even approached him in military talents, in plans and enterprises, in government. Hence those pictures and inscriptions in the gallery at Versailles which disgust every foreigner; those opera prologues that he himself tried to sing; that flood of prose and verse in his praise for which his appetite was insatiable; those dedications of statues copied from pagan sculpture, and the insipid and sickening compliments that were continually offered to him in person and which he swallowed with unfailing relish; hence his distaste for all merit, intelligence, education, and most of all, for all independence of character and sentiment in others; his mistakes of judgment in matters of importance; his familiarity and favor reserved entirely for those to whom he felt himself superior in acquirements and ability; and, above everything else, a jealousy of his authority which determined and took precedence of every other sort of justice, reason, and consideration whatever.

James Harvey Robinson and Charles A. Beard, Readings in Modern European History, *1:10.*

To show his power and splendor, Louis had a great palace built about twelve miles southwest of Paris. When completed, the palace of **Versailles** (vehr SYE) was an awesome sight. Around the palace were elaborate formal gardens. The building itself was nearly a half mile long and contained hundreds of grandly decorated rooms. Dazzling works of art adorned the palace's interior. To maintain the building's symmetrical appearance, Louis refused to allow chimneys to be seen from the front of the palace, even though their shortness meant smoky rooms. Elegance and grandeur were important, not utility.

Louis used his palace to impress his subjects. He also used it to keep the nobility subservient to him. He required nobles to live at Versailles for at least part of each year. While they were there, Louis kept them so busy that they did not have time to plot against him. There were plays, balls, and frivolous activities that kept their minds distracted from the affairs of state.

From the time Louis rose in the morning until he went to bed at night, the nobility flocked around him. They vied with one another for the privilege of performing some small task, such as handing him his shirt in the morning or bringing him a cup of hot chocolate at night. Everything in Louis's life became a pompous ritual designed to make the king the absolute center of attention.

In spite of all its grandeur, Versailles was the center for all that was base and immoral. Adultery and homosexuality were openly embraced. Gambling was commonplace. Every sort of vice could be found in the king's palace.

Foreign Policy—To expand French territory and increase his influence in Europe, Louis XIV engaged in a number of wars. He tried to extend French borders to what he said were their natural boundaries: the Rhine, the Alps, and the Pyrenees. Although he did gain some territory, these wars brought much harm to France. Their cost, in addition to Louis's extensive building programs, brought France to the edge of bankruptcy. On his deathbed, Louis said to his heir, "Try to remain at peace with your neighbors. I have loved war too much. Do not copy me in that, or in my overspending."

Royal chapel in the palace of Versailles

Louis died in 1715. He reigned longer than any other European king. Louis had outlived both his son and grandson, who were heirs to the throne. His great-grandson **Louis XV** (r. 1715–74), who was five years old when Louis XIV died, succeeded him to the throne. During the early years of the young king's reign, capable regents kept France out of war and rebuilt its economy. But Louis XV, following the example of Louis XIV, later involved France in disastrous and humiliating wars, which once again drained the royal treasury. This bankruptcy played a decisive role in the eventual overthrow of the French monarchy.

Section Quiz

1. What right did rulers of this period claim that gave them absolute power and placed them above man-made laws?
2. What two chief advisors to the French kings Louis XIII and Louis XIV helped strengthen the power of France and the French monarchy?
3. What was the last great religious war fought in Europe? On what side did France enter the war?
4. What French king's reign became the model of absolutism throughout Europe? What was the name of his new palace?
5. What did the French king revoke in 1685? What group was persecuted as a result?

★ How was French support for Protestants during the Thirty Years' War inconsistent with French treatment of Protestants in France?

Absolutism Spreads in Europe

French absolutism influenced other European monarchs, who gradually embraced not only absolutism but also France's language, fashions, and morals. Three territories in particular came under the rule of absolutist monarchs: Brandenburg-Prussia, Austria, and Russia. Following the example of Louis XIV, known as the "Grand Monarch," the rulers of these territories increased their personal and national power.

Absolutism in Brandenburg-Prussia

After the Thirty Years' War, Germany remained a fragmented land made up of hundreds of small, weak states. One of these, Brandenburg-Prussia, gradually obtained enough power and territory to become the strongest of the German states. Brandenburg-Prussia (later simply called Prussia) was an unlikely candidate to become a major European power. Prussia's soil was poor, its economic resources were few, and its territories were scattered. Prussia had no natural frontiers such as mountains or rivers to provide protection. Yet it did have energetic and capable rulers (called electors) who used any means necessary to increase their power and the size of their territory. These rulers built a large standing army and established an efficient bureaucracy. They also gained the cooperation of the Prussian nobility, called **Junkers** (*Y*OONG kurz), who worked closely with the electors in governing the country and serving as officers in the Prussian army.

The first important Prussian ruler, **Frederick William** (r. 1640–88), was called "the Great Elector" because he became the most powerful of the German princes who elected the emperor. He forged Prussia's scattered territories into a unified state. Frederick William's chief source of power was the standing Prussian army, which numbered about thirty thousand men. He increased taxes to support such a large army; in fact, Prussians paid twice as much in taxes as French citizens did during this period. The army became a chief instrument by which Prussian rulers obtained and demonstrated their absolute power. During the next two centuries, militarism played a major role in creating and shaping a German national state.

Under Frederick William's successor, **Frederick I** (r. 1688–1713), the army continued to grow. Frederick I, however, was more interested in the arts than in warfare. He sought to imitate Louis XIV in as many ways as possible. Frederick had a new palace built for himself and beautified Berlin, the capital of Prussia, with many new public buildings.

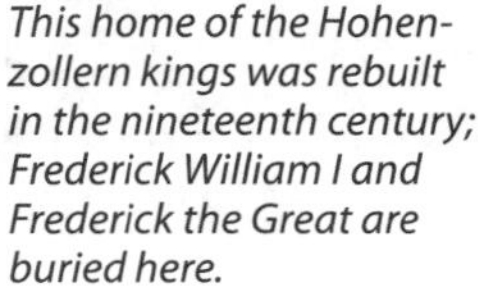
This home of the Hohenzollern kings was rebuilt in the nineteenth century; Frederick William I and Frederick the Great are buried here.

Although Frederick I did little to increase the actual power of Prussia, he did increase Prussia's prestige among the other German states. After the War of the Spanish Succession (see p. 316), Frederick acquired for his successors the title of "King in Prussia." (The title "King *of* Prussia" would have been unacceptable to the Holy Roman emperor, who officially ruled all the German states.) This royal title helped to enhance the Prussian rulers' prestige among the nations of Europe.

Building upon the foundation of his predecessors, **Frederick William I** (r. 1713–40) firmly established Prussian absolutism. He was a violent-tempered man who believed in discipline and routine. He not only reduced court luxury and created a strong centralized bureaucracy but also demanded absolute obedience from all citizens. "Salvation belongs to the Lord," he said. "Everything else is my business."

Frederick William I spent most of his time building up Prussia's military forces. During his reign, the army grew to 83,000 men. It was a highly trained and battle-ready force, but Frederick William was not eager for war. He had spent so much money and energy on the military that he could not bear to see his men killed in battle. At the end of his life, Frederick William had built one of the five largest armies in Europe, despite the fact that Prussia did not rank in even the top ten in population. "Prussia," said one of his contemporaries, "is not a state with an army but an army with a state."

Frederick II

Although Frederick William I loved military life, his son **Frederick II** (r. 1740–86) seemed to have no interest in the army. As a young man, Frederick II loved to compose music, play the flute, write French poetry, and follow French fashions. His father opposed such pursuits, and the two quarreled constantly. Though Frederick II never abandoned his interest in culture, he did become one of Prussia's greatest military heroes. He became known as Frederick "the Great," the greatest soldier of his day. During his reign, he tripled the size of the Prussian state. Frederick also strengthened Prussia's economy by establishing a silk industry and by stabilizing grain prices. He enacted a wide variety of political and social reforms. For example, he abolished the torture of prisoners and granted religious freedom to Roman Catholics and Jews. Yet despite these and other reforms, Frederick remained firmly dedicated to the principle of absolutism.

By Frederick II's day, Prussia was a strong rival to the Habsburg rulers of Austria. The **Hohenzollern** (HO uhn ZAHL urn) rulers built Prussia into a first-class European power. This provided an advantage for Prussia as it competed with Austria for control of the many German states. Eventually, Prussia won the struggle, and the Hohenzollern rulers united the German states into one country during the nineteenth century.

Absolutism in Austria

By the beginning of the eighteenth century, the **Habsburg** rulers of Austria not only controlled a large amount of territory but also held the title of Holy Roman emperor. Although this title gave them no additional power, it did give them an added measure of prestige.

Despite these advantages, Habsburg rulers were unable to create a strong absolutist state. Many obstacles hindered them. (1) The Roman Catholic Church and the nobility held great power and opposed any limitation of their traditional rights. (2) Austria was surrounded by aggressive neighbors (particularly France and later Prussia) who desired to seize Habsburg territories that bordered on their own. Since the Austrian rulers needed the support of the nobles to defend the country, the rulers dared not upset them by increasing their own royal power. (3) The Habsburgs ruled so many different nationalities

Joseph II (1741-1790), Emperor Holy Roman Empire
Contemporary of the French Revolution, which he foresaw in his letters to his sister Marie-Antoinette, Queen of France. Canvas. Hickel, Joseph (1736-1807). Heeresgeschichtliches Museum, Vienna, Austria. Erich Lessing/Art Resource, NY

Peter I the Great (1672-1725) 1838
(Oil on canvas) (see also 144528) by Hippolyte Dearoche (Paul) (1797-1856) Hamburger Kunsthalle, Hamburg, Germany/The Bridgeman Art Library

that it was almost impossible to create a strong, unified government. The Hungarians especially resented Austrian control and did not willingly cooperate with their Habsburg rulers.

During the eighteenth century, the emperor **Joseph II** (r. 1765–90) made a strong effort to create an absolutist state in Austria. He began his reign as coruler with his mother, Maria Theresa (r. 1740–80). During the years of joint rule, Maria Theresa made gradual and careful changes. After her death, Joseph II embarked on a bolder course of action, directing his efforts against the power of the nobility and the Roman Catholic Church. He forced both groups to pay higher taxes, while reducing the tax burden on the peasants. At the same time, he made the government more centralized by weakening local authority.

Many of Joseph's actions were directed specifically against the Roman Church. For example, he dissolved hundreds of monasteries, allowing to remain only those that performed what he termed a useful service, such as teaching or ministering to the sick. He altered the church's organization and in 1781 granted religious freedom to non-Catholics. Since many of Joseph's changes were both sudden and drastic, few of them continued after his death. In fact, the nobility and the Roman Catholic Church regained many of their former privileges and reasserted their authority. Absolutism was never as strong in Austria as it was in many other European nations.

Absolutism in Russia

Soon after Russia gained its independence from the Mongols (see Ch. 7), **Ivan IV** (r. 1533–84), called Ivan "the Terrible," became the ruler. He expanded Russian territory and built the beautiful St. Basil's Cathedral in Moscow. A cruel tyrant, Ivan had many of the Russian nobility murdered. In a fit of rage, he even murdered his own son. Ivan also oppressively taxed his people, treating them like slaves of the state. To glorify himself and his position, Ivan took the title of **czar**, a term that comes from the word *Caesar*.

After Ivan's death, Russia underwent a period of upheaval. Rival groups fought for control of the government, while bands of peasants roamed across Russia, killing and plundering. This turmoil finally ended in 1613, when the **Romanov** family came to the throne. (This dynasty ruled Russia until it was overthrown by the revolution of 1917.) **Peter I** (r. 1682–1725), one of the early Romanovs, did much to continue Russia's transformation into an absolutist state.

When Peter became czar, Russia was out of step with the rest of Europe. It was isolated and backward; Russia's economy was weak, and its government was disorganized. He determined that if Russia were to become a great power, it would have to adopt Western ways. Therefore, in 1697 Peter traveled in western Europe and learned all that he could. He visited Holland, France, and England, and when Peter returned to Russia to put down a revolution, he brought back more than seven hundred western Europeans. Many of them were shipbuilders, mathematicians, and engineers.

With this outside help, Peter began a westernization and modernization program in Russia. The Russians, with the help of these Western experts, worked to improve the Russian economy; they encouraged production of consumer goods such as paper products and textiles. They also began building a navy and a new capital, which they called St. Petersburg.

Peter tried to force Western ways upon his people. He outlawed long beards and oriental costumes such as long robes on men. In 1699, Peter introduced the Western calendar, which ended the Russian tradition of celebrating New Year's Day on the first of September (a date the Russians believed marked the first day of creation). However, many Russians resented these changes.

In addition to his westernization program, Peter had another major goal: to expand Russian territory and acquire warm-water ports. In the **Great Northern War** (1700–1721) the Russians defeated Sweden and won additional territory along the Baltic Sea. Because of this victory, the Russians gave Peter the title "the Great."

Peter strengthened his absolute powers in Russia by seizing greater control of the Russian Orthodox Church. When the head of the church (the patriarch) died, Peter did not allow anyone to fill the vacancy. Instead, he created the Holy Synod, which governed the church like a board of directors. Peter and his successors controlled the Synod, ensuring that the Orthodox Church remained in line with the policies of the czar.

Portrait of Empress Catherine II of Russia

She wears a robe of silver silk and ermine coat. Around her neck the order of Saint Andrew with cross. Anonymous, 18th century. Portraitgalerie, Schloss Ambras, Innsbruck, Austria. Erich Lessing/Art Resource NY

After the death of Peter (d. 1725), absolutism resumed in Russia under Empress **Catherine II** (r. 1762–96), who also came to be called "the Great." Catherine II was a hardworking and very capable ruler, but she was openly immoral and was driven by uncontrolled ambition. For example, shortly after her marriage to Peter III she gained the trust of those in power and had him murdered. Like Peter I, she sought to increase the authority of the monarchy. She allowed the nobles to retain their privileged positions as long as they served the state. In 1766, Catherine gave the nobles the right to exile rebellious peasants to Siberia. This harsh treatment produced several violent uprisings during her reign, and her government savagely suppressed them. Discontent continued to mount until the twentieth century, when the Russian people finally overthrew the tyranny of the czars. Tragically, the Russian people simply exchanged one form of repression for another (see Chapter 20).

Catherine seemed to be an enlightened reformer. She encouraged education and corresponded with some of the notable scholars of her day. However, though she supported certain social reforms, she was an absolutist monarch at heart. Catherine demonstrated this motivation by being the first Russian monarch to formally institute government censorship. She also weakened the Russian Orthodox Church by transferring church property to the government. In addition, Catherine forced Russians to westernize, following the example of Peter the Great.

In foreign affairs, Catherine continued Russia's expansion program, particularly at the expense of the Poles and the Turks. One of her major territorial goals was to secure additional seaports. During Catherine's reign, the Russians seized some territory on the north shore of the Black Sea from the Turks. The goal of later Russian czars to control the Black Sea and compete in Mediterranean trade became an important issue in international diplomacy.

Section Quiz

1. What three countries followed the example of France and came under absolutist rule?
2. By what name were the nobility who aided the Prussian rulers known?
3. What Austrian ruler sought to create an absolutist state by attacking the church and nobility?
4. How did Peter the Great propose to get Russia in step with the rest of Europe?
5. Give the name of the ruling family in each of the following countries: Prussia, Austria, and Russia.

★ Why did Russia seek to control territory along the Black Sea?

Absolutism Defeated in England

Unlike the other countries we have discussed so far, England did not become an absolutist state. English kings had to contend with Parliament, which over the centuries had gradually increased its power and which refused to surrender its hard-won rights. Of special significance was its right to grant or deny a king's request for additional revenue.

During the sixteenth century, the Tudors worked with Parliament to gain their desired goals. They relied on skillful politicians to advise them, and they remained sensitive to public opinion. As a result, they were able to control parliamentary legislation. During the last years of Queen Elizabeth's reign, however, tension began to grow between Elizabeth and Parliament. At issue was whether the crown or Parliament should have the ultimate responsibility for directing government policy.

The King James Version

A group that came to be known as the Puritans presented James a petition expressing their desire to see the Church of England purified from "popish" ceremonies. Since James had been trained by Presbyterians in Scotland, they hoped he would be sympathetic to their requests. James was not a Presbyterian at heart, however, and ignored all but one of their requests. In response to their petition, he appointed a group of 47 scholars to make a new English translation of the Bible that was completed in 1611. Initially, many Christians were satisfied with the existing English translations and hesitated to use this new one. To lend royal authority to the new work, it was called the Authorized Version, although today it is commonly referred to as the King James Version.

Since Elizabeth was the last surviving member of the Tudor dynasty, she made sure to name a successor. Her choice was King James VI of Scotland, the son of Mary Stuart. Although Elizabeth had ordered Mary to be beheaded for treason (see p. 265), her selection of the Stuart family to take the throne of England was not surprising. James was Elizabeth's cousin and her closest living relative. Parliament, therefore, invited James to become the king of England after Elizabeth's death. When James (r. 1603–25) became the king of England, he took the title **James I** because England had never had a king by that name.

James I

James made very clear from the beginning of his reign that he expected everyone to conform to the Anglican Church. On one occasion, he told the Puritans that if they did not cooperate, he would "harry them out of the land." True to his threat, James harassed those who refused to compromise their religious convictions. However, a small group of Separatists escaped James's persecution. Known as the Pilgrims, they sailed to the New World in search of a land where they could practice their religious beliefs without government opposition.

Not all of James's problems were religious. In addition to a scandalous private life, he spent government money extravagantly and relied on personal favorites rather than veteran politicians to give him political advice. James believed he was king by "divine right"—a fact that Parliament did not dispute. But Parliament did question the extent of his authority and was angered by the highhanded manner in which he governed the kingdom.

Since James had financial problems, he was forced to call Parliament into session and ask for additional funds. But each time Parliament met, it debated James's foreign and domestic policies. This so infuriated him that he dismissed the House of Commons time after time. "That which concerns the mystery of the King's power is not lawful to be disputed," James had said. The only thing that his hasty actions accomplished, however, was to unite his opponents against him.

James's son, **Charles I** (r. 1625–49), inherited his father's views. Charles's policies intensified the tension between the king and Parliament. During his reign, the persecution of the Puritans became more severe, causing thousands of them to leave the country and sail to the American colonies.

Like his father, Charles wanted to be an absolute ruler but did not have the army or the bureaucracy to enforce his will. When he convened Parliament, many of its members proved to be quite uncooperative. They demanded that the king recognize their rights to free speech and freedom from arrest. Charles responded to their request by dismissing them. Later, he reconvened Parliament, but when they repeated their demands, he dismissed them once again.

In need of funds, Charles was forced to recall Parliament a third time. Angry with the king, members of Parliament drew up a document called the **Petition of Right** (1628). Among other things, it stated that the king did not have the right to make people pay taxes without Parliamentary consent and that Parliament would not tolerate arbitrary imprisonment of any subjects. They informed Charles that if he refused to sign the document, they would not grant him any additional funds. Charles signed the petition, but when Parliament made further demands, he dismissed them once again. From 1629 to 1640 he sought to govern England without calling Parliament into session by using every means possible to raise money apart from Parliament. Charles sold knighthoods, forced various individuals to loan him funds, and established high taxes on shipping. In the process, however, he succeeded in alienating merchants and landowners.

Charles I

In spite of everything Charles tried to do, he had to recall Parliament when Scotland rebelled against him. His agents had tried to force the Scottish church to use the Anglican prayer book, and the Scots responded by raising an army to defend their religious liberties. In a very weak position, Charles was ready to make concessions to Parliament. He was forced by financial necessity to sign various acts that greatly strengthened Parliament's power. These acts guaranteed (1) that Parliament would meet every three years, even without royal permission; (2) that Parliament could not be dissolved without its own consent; and (3) that no taxes were legal except those passed by Parliament. In addition, Parliament abolished those royal courts that had become tools of Charles's absolutist policy.

In the following months, the Puritans in Parliament also demanded an end to episcopal church government and criticized the formalism of the Anglican prayer book. At the same time, Parliament extended its political power by placing the military under its control. Realizing that his power was slipping away, Charles decided to act.

In January 1642, he marched into the House of Commons with four hundred armed men. Charles demanded that five of his harshest critics be arrested. These men, however, could not be found. They had escaped from the chamber only minutes before. Charles's rash behavior in this regard only further antagonized Parliament.

Each side began gathering an army, and before the year was over, war had broken out. The Puritans, the lesser gentry, and the merchants supported Parliament's cause. Their opponents called them **Roundheads** because most of them had short hair. Most members of the nobility as well as the Anglicans supported the king. The Roundheads called them **Cavaliers**—a reference to the Spanish soldiers, the *cavaliero*, who had killed many Protestants in Europe.

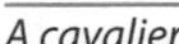

A cavalier

Initially, the king's forces were victorious. But when Parliament reorganized its army and removed incompetent leaders, the New Model

Oliver Cromwell

Army, as it was called, gained the upper hand. Under the able leadership of **Oliver Cromwell** (1599–1658), the Roundheads defeated Charles at the Battle of Naseby (1645). This defeat proved to be the deathblow to the Royalist cause, and Charles surrendered eleven months later.

The victory of Parliament's forces did not bring an immediate end to England's problems. The leaders of Parliament and the commanders of the army disagreed over how the new government should be run. Not all who had opposed the king wanted to destroy the monarchy; many simply wanted to limit the king's power. Leaders of the parliamentary army, however, envisioned a republic where every man would have equal opportunities and privileges. They saw nothing wrong with replacing England's longstanding political traditions to attain that end.

When the conservatives (those who wanted only to curb Charles's power) in Parliament realized that the war had gone further than they had intended, they tried to dissolve the army. The army, however, refused to disband. Its forces occupied London and expelled several conservatives from the House of Commons. In 1648, the conservatives who remained in Parliament made an alliance with Charles, who had just escaped from captivity and was willing to make several concessions to regain his throne. However, Cromwell's army easily put down all resistance. Cromwell's forces recaptured Charles and expelled some 140 conservative members from the House of Commons, leaving a governing body of less than one hundred men. (At the beginning of the civil war, the House of Commons had more than five hundred members.) The remaining members, together known as the Rump Parliament, set up a special court that tried and condemned the king for treason. On January 30, 1649, officials beheaded Charles I.

The next eleven years (1649–60) were a time of experimentation in new forms of government in England. Cromwell, the leader of the army, had no program for governing the country. Consequently, he ruled by trial and error. At first, he and the "Rump" jointly governed England, but problems soon arose. Cromwell found, just as Charles I had before him, that it was very difficult to rule with an independent-minded Parliament. So Cromwell dissolved Parliament and ruled without it until his death in 1658.

Charles II

Taking the title Lord Protector, Cromwell established what is called the **Protectorate**. He ruled in accordance with a written constitution, the *Instrument of Government*. Although his rule was sometimes arbitrary, he was a man of deep religious conviction who tried to do what he thought was best for the people. Nevertheless, the Protectorate came to an end soon after Cromwell's death. His son Richard succeeded him as Lord Protector, but he did not have the same forceful personality or leadership ability that his father had. In addition, most Englishmen were dissatisfied with the country's political condition. They wanted the Stuart monarchs to return to the throne.

Sensing the sentiment of the people, Richard allowed the Parliament that Charles I had called in 1640 to reconvene. The members in turn asked Charles's son to take the throne. He accepted their offer, and in 1660 England had a new king—**Charles II** (r. 1660–85).

The reestablishment of the Stuart monarchy is called the **Restoration**. In reality, the old monarchy was not restored because Parliament retained much of the power it had won earlier. In 1679, for example, Parliament again passed the

Studies in Adversity: John Milton and John Bunyan

John Milton (1608–74) and John Bunyan (1628–88) are towering figures of seventeenth-century English literature. Each overcame great adversity to write works of literature that have endured for hundreds of years.

Milton is one of the greatest English poets. Keenly aware of the political and religious issues of his day, he spent much of his early career writing tracts and pamphlets. He supported the Puritan cause and argued against the corrupt clergy of the Church of England. During Cromwell's Protectorate, he served as Latin secretary to the Council of State. In this position, he had opportunity to use his literary skills to defend the Puritan government.

Milton's official duties, however, were soon overshadowed by personal tragedies. In 1651, his infant son died. A year later, his wife died, leaving him responsible for the care of three young children. Throughout this period, his eyesight steadily weakened; by 1652 he was completely blind. Milton nevertheless continued in his government post and in the writing of poetry. He remarried in 1656, but this wife died also. He lost his position in government in 1660 when the English monarchy was restored under Charles II.

A man of immense scholarship and energy, Milton then devoted himself wholly to his writing. His greatest work, the epic *Paradise Lost*, was published in 1667. This powerful poem recounts the Creation, the rebellion of Satan, and the Fall of man in the Garden of Eden. The mature Milton, whose life had been one of painful struggles, was not bitter against his Maker. His trust in God is evident in his statement of purpose in the opening lines of *Paradise Lost*: to "assert Eternal Providence, / And justify the ways of God to man."

Unlike Milton, John Bunyan was a preacher of humble origin and little formal education. During the English Civil War, he had served briefly as a soldier in Cromwell's army, taking part in skirmishes with Royalist forces. After leaving the military, he married and settled down as a tinker (one who repairs metal utensils) in the small village of Bedford. Soon thereafter, Bunyan was converted to Christianity. He joined a little Baptist church and began studying the Scriptures. Eventually, he became pastor of the tiny congregation.

In 1660, he was arrested by government officials. Because he refused to stop preaching, Bunyan was put behind bars. His wife and four children were forced to take care of themselves. (One daughter was blind, and another child died at birth shortly after Bunyan was jailed.) His imprisonment lasted nearly twelve years. During that time, he began to write. By the time he was freed from jail in 1672, his masterpiece, *The Pilgrim's Progress*, was almost complete. Largely autobiographical, this simple but exciting narrative relates the journey of a man named Christian from the City of Destruction to the Celestial City. Translated into more languages than any other book except the Bible, it has encouraged and guided readers for centuries.

Top: Milton
Bottom: Bunyan

Habeas Corpus Act (first passed under Charles I), which made it illegal for the government to arbitrarily hold someone in jail. By obtaining a writ of habeas corpus, a prisoner could force the government to officially charge him with a crime or release him. This act meant that English monarchs could no longer imprison a person simply for being critical of their policies. Juries could issue verdicts without fear of being imprisoned for rendering unpopular decisions, and the press could openly criticize royal policy.

Although his power was limited, Charles II did his best to remain financially independent of Parliament. He received monetary grants from Louis XIV in return for promises to support the objectives of French foreign policy. Charles also told Louis that he would publicly declare himself a Roman Catholic. But despite his promises, Charles did very little that really helped France, and he did not profess Roman Catholicism until he was on his deathbed.

Whigs and Tories

As the English Parliament grew in power and influence, factions developed within its ranks. These competing groups became the forerunners of Britain's first political parties—Whigs and Tories.

Following the Restoration, Parliament became sharply divided over the policies of Charles II. Some members disliked the favoritism he showed toward the Roman Catholics and France. Others were opposed to the idea of having the throne pass to the Roman Catholic James, duke of York. The leader of this opposition, the earl of Shaftesbury, realized that if he could influence a majority of votes in Parliament he could control the government and the king. His group became known as the Country Party.

Another group consisted of those who considered the person of the king and his rightful heir to be sacred. Led by the king himself, this group became known as the Court Party. It came into open conflict with the Country Party when Charles did not produce a legitimate son. Those opposing the succession of James introduced a bill into Parliament excluding him from the throne.

The fight over this bill became intense, with the Court Party defeating its passage. In the debates, each side called the other side names. Those against James were called "Whigs"—a name applied to Scottish robbers who killed their victims before plundering them. Those supporting James were called "Tories"—a name applied to Irish rebels. Soon the opposing parties adopted these nicknames as their official titles.

Once the matter of Protestant succession to the throne had been settled by an act of Parliament, the two parties shifted their attention to other issues. The divisions between them were never as sharp again. The Tory Party continued to favor the king and the Anglican Church and to oppose great change in the status quo. The Whigs were now willing to support the king, but they favored a policy of religious toleration and were eager to see certain changes made in government policy. Although the Whig Party faded away, the Tory Party has continued to the present.

Since Charles II had no legitimate children, he was succeeded by his brother **James II** (r. 1685–88). James was an ardent Roman Catholic and a firm believer in absolutism. In spite of his tactless actions, Parliament decided to tolerate him since he was old and his only heirs were two Protestant daughters. But the political picture changed dramatically in 1688, when James's second wife, a Roman Catholic, gave birth to a son. Members of Parliament feared that absolutism would be reestablished and England would be forced back into the fold of Rome.

In June 1688, leaders of Parliament invited William of Orange (the leader of Protestant Netherlands and husband of James's daughter Mary) to come to England and take the throne. William accepted the invitation and landed in England with a small Dutch army. Many Englishmen rallied to support him. When James tried to send his troops against William, he found that even his officers had deserted to the other side. Having no other recourse, James fled to France with his wife and son.

The House of Commons declared that "King James II, having endeavored to subvert the constitution of the kingdom by breaking the original contract between king and people, and by the advice of Jesuits and other wicked persons having violated the fundamental laws, and having withdrawn himself out of the kingdom, has abdicated the government, and that the throne is vacant." The House

English Bill of Rights

The English struggle for rights and liberties goes all the way back to 1215 when King John signed the Magna Carta at Runnymede. The Bill of Rights (1689) is a landmark of English constitutional history. It marked the first time that the demands on the monarch were made on behalf of a representative assembly. Among the ancient rights and liberties declared in the Bill of Rights are the following:

- That the pretended power of suspending of laws or the execution of laws by regal authority without consent of Parliament is illegal.
- That it is the right of the subjects to petition the king, and all commitments and prosecutions for such petitioning are illegal.
- That the raising or keeping a standing army within the kingdom in time of peace unless it be with consent of Parliament is against law.
- That the subjects which are Protestants may have arms for their defence suitable to their conditions and as allowed by law.
- That election of members of Parliament ought to be free.
- That the freedom of speech and debates or proceedings in Parliament ought not to be impeached or questioned in any court or place out of Parliament.
- That excessive bail ought not to be required, nor excessive fines imposed, nor cruel and unusual punishments inflicted.

William III (left) and Mary II (right)

Portrait of Queen Mary II,
Sir Godfrey Kneller,
From the Bob Jones University Collection

added that "it hath been found by experience to be inconsistent with the safety and welfare of this Protestant kingdom to be governed by a popish prince."

England had undergone a "bloodless" or **Glorious Revolution** when Parliament dethroned James II. Parliament then invited **William and Mary** to become joint rulers of England. Their reign marked the only time in English history that the country had corulers.

However, before Parliament officially granted the throne to William and Mary, it drew up a set of conditions that had to be met. Those conditions were embodied in a document called the **Bill of Rights** (1689), which limited royal power, established certain civil liberties, and forbade future kings or queens from being Roman Catholics. William and Mary accepted Parliament's conditions and were crowned William III (r. 1689–1702) and Mary II (r. 1689–94).

In 1701, Parliament passed the **Act of Settlement**, which had far-reaching consequences for the English crown. By this act, Parliament established its right to grant the throne to whomever it wished. The concept of kings ruling by "divine right" had passed away. England had become a nation ruled by constitutional law—that is, law established by tradition and acts of Parliament.

After the reign of Mary's sister, Queen Anne (r. 1702–14), the throne passed to a German, George of Hanover (a descendant of James I). Because the new king, who took the title of George I (r. 1714–27), could not speak English, he had to rely on others to carry out many of the responsibilities of government. During his reign and the reign of his successor, George II (r. 1727–60), the cabinet system of government developed in England.

Cabinet government first began during the reign of Charles II, who often called his closest advisors to his office—called a "cabinet"—to discuss matters of state. George I, who had little interest in political matters, did not attend cabinet meetings. He left the affairs of government in the hands of his chief minister, Robert Walpole, whom historians consider to be the first prime minister of England. Executive powers gradually shifted from the king to the chief ministers of the king's cabinet. Later, the prime minister and the cabinet, who were originally responsible only to the king, became accountable to Parliament.

Portrait of Sir Robert Walpole (1676-1745) Earl of Orford, 1743

(Oil on canvas) by John Theodore Heins (1732-71) ©Norwich Castle Museum and Art Gallery/The Bridgeman Art Library

Section Quiz

1. What body in England competed with the monarchy for authority? What special privilege did that body hold over the monarchy?
2. What family succeeded the Tudors to the throne of England? What member of this family succeeded Queen Elizabeth to the throne?
3. What English king was beheaded during the English Civil War? Who was the leader of the Roundheads, the parliamentary forces?
4. Who came to the English throne as a result of a "bloodless" revolution?
5. What English document placed limits on royal power, guaranteed fundamental liberties of the English people, and prohibited future English monarchs from being Roman Catholic?

★ Why was England able to reject royal absolutism?

II. Balance of Power

To increase their power on the Continent, some European monarchs used their armies to seize the territories of weaker nations. Each ruler watched his neighbors closely, ensuring that they did not become too strong. Nations formed alliances in an effort to preserve the **balance of power**, thereby hoping to ensure that no one nation would dominate the other countries of Europe. When they felt it was necessary, they went to war to maintain this balance. Because war often demonstrated new strengths and weaknesses in nations, many shifts in diplomatic alliances resulted. Countries that had previously been enemies often became friends, and nations that were once allied squared off against each other. Despite the many changes in alliances during the eighteenth century, Prussia remained the constant foe of Austria, and England was always aligned against France. The three major wars of this period demonstrated the workings of this system of alliances.

War of the Spanish Succession (1702–1713)

In 1700, the Habsburg king of Spain died, leaving no direct heir to the Spanish throne. In his will he granted the throne to his young grandnephew Philip, who was also the grandson of Louis XIV of France. Louis, seeing an opportunity to make political and territorial gains, claimed the Spanish throne for Philip. Other nations in Europe—especially England and the Netherlands—feared what the union of France and Spain might bring. They formed the **Grand Alliance** to block Louis's actions.

The armies of the Grand Alliance won many victories on the European continent. At Blenheim in 1704, they almost wiped out the French force. In 1705, England captured Gibraltar, a post on the southern tip of Spain. The English also fought the French in North America in what was called Queen Anne's War.

The war ended in 1713 with the signing of a series of agreements called the **Treaty of Utrecht**, which included the following provisions:

1. Philip was allowed to retain the throne of Spain as long as the crowns of France and Spain were not united.
2. Spain had to surrender its possessions in the Netherlands and in the Mediterranean area to Austria.
3. Britain won various Canadian territories from France: Newfoundland, Nova Scotia, and the Hudson Bay territory. In addition, Britain kept the strategic Mediterranean port of Gibraltar. (During the war, England and Scotland were united into a single kingdom called Great Britain. From that time, it has been proper to speak of Britain rather than England.)

War of the Austrian Succession (1740–48)

"Because a Monarch robbed a neighbor he had promised to defend, red men scalped each other by the Great Lakes of America, while black men fought on the [Indian] coast of Coromandel." Thus did British historian Thomas Macaulay describe the War of the Austrian Succession—a conflict that spread to three continents.

Maria Theresa

In 1713, the emperor of Austria, Charles VI, drew up a document called the **Pragmatic Sanction**. It was designed to prevent Austria's neighbors from taking advantage of his daughter, **Maria Theresa**, once she came to the Austrian throne. The rulers who signed the document agreed to respect the territorial boundaries of Austria, allowing Maria Theresa to rule in peace.

One ruler who had no intention of honoring the agreement that his father had signed was Frederick II of Prussia. He desired the rich mining area of Silesia, which belonged to Austria, and decided to seize it. In August 1740, after Maria Theresa had been empress for only two months, Frederick invaded the province. By the following year, Prussia had firmly established its hold on Silesia and had signed a peace treaty with Austria.

The situation in Europe became more complicated when France entered the war against Austria, hoping to gain territory at Austria's expense. Spain also entered the war to retrieve the Italian lands it had lost to Austria in 1713. Britain entered the war on the side of Austria to neutralize French power and Prussia's threat to George II's Hanoverian domains.

The war was not confined to the European continent, however. It spread to North America, where the British defeated the French, and to India, where the French defeated the British. Weary of war, the nations of Europe finally decided to end the conflict and signed the **Treaty of Aix-la-Chapelle** in 1748. This treaty did not settle the differences among the nations; it merely ended the fighting temporarily. Except for Silesia, which Frederick was allowed to keep, the treaty restored the ***status quo ante bellum*** (how things were before the war).

William Pitt

The Battle of the Plains of Abraham, the climax of the British victory over France in the Seven Years' War (known in North America as the French and Indian War)

Seven Years' War (1756–63)

In 1754, fighting (called the French and Indian War) broke out between France and Britain in the New World. At the same time, Frederick II decided to take some more of Austria's territory. He assumed that France would not interfere, because France and Austria had been bitter enemies for centuries. Neither did he fear British reprisals since he had just signed a defensive alliance with Britain in January 1756. But Frederick miscalculated. France unexpectedly reversed its foreign policy. Fearing the growing threat of Prussia's might, France put aside its old antagonism for the Austrian Habsburgs and joined Austria to stop Prussian expansion. This radical change in alliances, called the **Diplomatic Revolution**, set the stage for the **Seven Years' War**.

Soon after the fighting broke out, the British statesman **William Pitt** the Elder devised a system for winning the war. His strategy called for supplying Prussia financial aid and using that nation to keep French troops preoccupied in Europe. Meanwhile, Britain would attempt to destroy French sea power, making it easier to defeat the French in North America and India.

Britain had tremendous success with its part of the plan. In North America, it had more than forty thousand regular and colonial troops. By the end of the war, these troops had seized many French forts and had captured the key French city of Quebec. In India, British forces under the leadership of Robert Clive defeated the French and the Indian princes who had allied with them.

On the continent of Europe, however, Prussia ran into difficulties. Open hostilities began when Frederick II invaded the neighboring kingdom of Saxony. He soon found himself surrounded by enemies. Russia, Sweden, most of

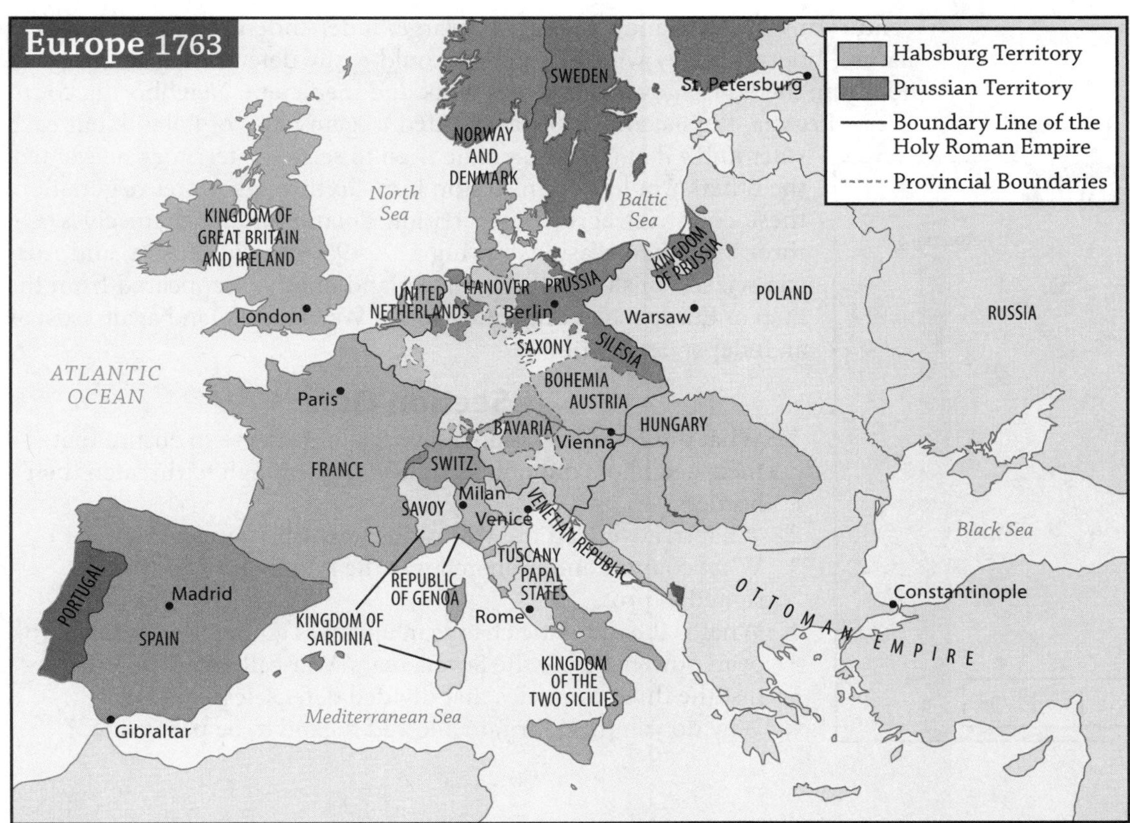

the German states, and Spain had joined France and Austria in opposing Prussia. At first, Frederick's superior army and his brilliant leadership kept his enemies at bay. But his opponents outnumbered him, and although he won battles, he despaired of ever winning the war. In addition, when George III became the new British monarch in 1760, he cut off all subsidies to Prussia. By the end of that year, the Russian army had burned Berlin, and all seemed lost. Frederick and Prussia, nevertheless, survived the conflict because Russia dropped out of the war. In 1762, a new czar who greatly admired Frederick II came to the throne. He withdrew his troops from Prussian territory and signed an agreement with Frederick. Unable to continue without Russian support, Frederick's other opponents withdrew from the conflict one by one. The Treaty of Hubertusburg (1763) brought the war to a close on the continent of Europe and allowed Frederick to maintain his hold on Silesia.

In that same year, France, Britain, and Spain signed the **Treaty of Paris**. This settlement had a number of important consequences.

1. France lost all territory on the mainland of North America. Britain acquired all of Canada and French territory east of the Mississippi.
2. France lost most of its commercial holdings in India. The Battle of Plassey (p. 431) paved the way for the British East India Company to eventually take over all of India.
3. Spain lost Florida to Great Britain but received New Orleans and Louisiana from France in return.

As a result of the Seven Years' War, England became not only the leading European power but also a world power.

The Partition of Poland

The balance of power was not always maintained by war; sometimes diplomatic negotiations proved to be more effective. One such case in the eighteenth century involved Poland, which was a large, independent nation that lacked natural boundaries by which its people could easily defend their territory. In addition, the Polish government was weak and inefficient. Neighboring countries—Prussia, Russia, and Austria—plotted to gain parts of Poland, but each ruler knew that the moment he tried to seize the territory he wanted, the others would step in to stop him. So through secret negotiation, these countries agreed to partition Poland among themselves. On three separate occasions during 1772–95, Prussia, Russia, and Austria seized Polish territory until Poland finally disappeared from the map of Europe. Not until after World War I did Poland again exist as an independent nation.

Section Quiz

1. What did European monarchs seek to preserve to ensure that their neighbors did not become strong enough to threaten their borders?
2. What treaty ended the War of the Spanish Succession?
3. What country and monarch was the Pragmatic Sanction designed to protect?
4. What is the dramatic change in alliances among the major European powers before the Seven Years' War called?
5. List the three countries that divided defenseless Poland.

★ Why do you think Britain allowed Poland to be partitioned?

Chapter 14 Review

Making Connections

1–2. How did Cardinal Richelieu strengthen the power of the French king? (Give two ways.)
3–4. How did Peter I and Catherine II strengthen their authority at the expense of the Russian Orthodox Church?
5. Why did the English people restore the monarchy following the death of Cromwell?

Developing History Skills

1. Evaluate the historical significance for France of the Revocation of the Edict of Nantes.
2. Summarize the historical significance of Britain's victory in the Seven Years' War and its impact on other countries in the eighteenth century.

Thinking Critically

1. Assess the rule of Louis XIV in light of Proverbs 16:12.
2. Compare the excerpts from the English Bill of Rights mentioned on page 314 with the first ten amendments to the U.S. Constitution and note similarities. (You can find a copy of the Constitution in *American Republic* or *United States History* or on the Internet.)

Living in God's World

1. Aristotle lists three forms of government: monarchy, aristocracy, and constitutional (rule by the many under a constitution) along with their perversions: tyranny, oligarchy, and democracy. Of these three forms he says monarchy is the best and constitutional government the worst, but of the perversions he says democracy is the least evil and tyranny the most. Do Aristotle's observations align with Scripture? Explain.
2. If you were the tutor for one of the young absolute monarchs mentioned in this chapter, what form of government would you advocate as the best? Base your answer on Scripture and on your answer to the previous question.

People, Places, and Things to Know

absolute
divine right
Bourbon
Henry IV
Cardinal Richelieu
Thirty Years' War
Gustavus Adolphus
Louis XIV
Jules Mazarin
Frondes
Jean-Baptiste Colbert
Versailles
Louis XV
Junkers
Frederick William
Frederick I
Frederick William I
Frederick II
Hohenzollern
Habsburg
Joseph II
Ivan IV
czar
Romanov
Peter I
Great Northern War
Catherine II
Puritans
James I
Charles I
Petition of Right
Roundheads
Cavaliers
Oliver Cromwell
Protectorate
Charles II
Restoration
Habeas Corpus Act
James II
Glorious Revolution
William and Mary
Bill of Rights
Act of Settlement
cabinet government
balance of power
Grand Alliance
Treaty of Utrecht
Pragmatic Sanction
Maria Theresa
Treaty of Aix-la-Chapelle
status quo ante bellum
Diplomatic Revolution
Seven Years' War
William Pitt
Treaty of Paris

15

AGE OF REASON

I. Scientific Discoveries
II. Intellectual Attitudes
III. Spiritual Awakening
IV. Artistic Reflection

Galileo and Vivani

When God created man in His image, He gave him (among other things) the gift of reason. Because of sin, however, man's understanding is darkened, and he is filled with spiritual blindness (Eph. 4:18). Only by the entrance of God's Word into the heart can a person receive light and understanding (Ps. 119:130). During the seventeenth and eighteenth centuries (known as the **Age of Reason**) some individuals used reason under the authority of Scripture to expose errors in theology and philosophy while defending biblical truth. But for many, this era marked a shift from the use of reason as a help to understand God's Word and His world to reason as the supreme authority by which everything, including God's Word, must be tested. In this chapter we will examine the effects of these two attitudes on science, philosophy, religion, and the arts.

Voltaire was noted for his sharp criticisms of organized religion and typified the thinking of many during the Age of Reason.

I. Scientific Discoveries

During the Middle Ages, most Europeans relied on two principal authorities for their understanding of the universe: ancient philosophers and church tradition. The tendency was to passively accept the validity of what the ancient philosophers or the Roman Church taught, rather than seek to uncover new knowledge about God's world. However, there were some who advocated experimentation and observation rather than merely reading old philosophers. As a result, some medieval scientists made careful annotations and conducted experiments that led to the development of new technologies, including the magnetic compass, mechanical clocks, and lenses. These scientific advances prepared the way for the greater scientific discoveries that would follow.

The intellectual atmosphere in Europe continued to develop during the sixteenth century. The Renaissance had rekindled a desire for learning, and the Reformation had reasserted the Bible as the trustworthy authority for man's understanding. Thoughtful individuals had discovered errors in church tradition and in the writings of ancient philosophers. Realizing they could no longer accept blindly what the Roman Church had to say about the Bible, these individuals searched out the truths of God's Word for themselves. Similarly, since they could no longer depend on what ancient philosophers taught about God's universe, scientists sought out the laws of nature for themselves. In coming years some men would seek to pit science and reason against Scripture, but others would find in science a means of glorifying God: they would examine the handiwork of His creation and find practical knowledge to help their fellow man.

The Scientific Method

Scientists use the **scientific method** when seeking answers to their questions about the physical world. This method is a pattern of thinking that uses the following steps:

1. Recognize the inadequacy of existing knowledge to explain a given question.
2. Perform observations in an attempt to find possible answers.
3. Seek to find a pattern in the observations on which to base conclusions or theories.
4. Choose the most appropriate hypothesis to explain the observations.
5. Test the hypothesis by further observation and experimentation.

Through this method of inquiry, scientists are able to gain a better understanding of the orderly function of God's universe. However, although science is a useful tool in obtaining knowledge, it has limitations. Science can explain *how* something happens, but it cannot explain *why* it occurs that way. Nor can it make moral judgments. Science is limited to what people observe about the physical world; it cannot, for example, deal with the origin of the universe.

In addition, scientific inquiry is limited by man's finite abilities; humans are fallible. Scientists are limited in their observations and may reach wrong conclusions. Furthermore, a scientist's presuppositions will influence how he interprets the evidence and may even determine what questions he is willing to explore. Because scientific knowledge is constantly expanding, scientific "facts" are often later proved incorrect. This has happened often since the late Reformation period, as scientists began to dispel many ancient and medieval superstitions.

The Scientific Tools

New tools helped seventeenth-century scientists in their investigation of the physical world. Astronomers developed telescopes, which allowed them to study the movement of stars and planets. With microscopes scientists could see bacteria and other organisms not visible to the naked eye. The thermometer and the barometer presented new opportunities for a closer study of weather. These and other inventions gave scientists access to a wealth of new and more accurate data.

Galileo's telescope

With the expansion of scientific knowledge, scientists needed a more precise way to express their theories about their observations. Mathematics soon became the language of science. Calculus, analytical geometry, logarithms, and the slide rule enhanced scientific investigation and made possible further scientific discoveries.

The Scientific Revolution

From the Renaissance to the eighteenth century, scientific inquiry and achievement advanced so rapidly that historians often speak of a scientific revolution. This "revolution" greatly increased man's knowledge of the physical universe. Old myths and legends were discarded as men discovered the principles that God established to govern His creation.

Copernicus

Astronomy

Astronomy, the study of celestial bodies, is an ancient science. The Magi of Matthew 2:1–12 might have been astronomers. Until the sixteenth century, astronomers usually relied on the theories of the ancient Greek geographer Ptolemy. He taught that the entire universe revolves around the earth—a theory known as the geocentric, or "earth-centered," theory. The changes that came with the scientific revolution transformed astronomy, radically altering it as a science.

The Polish astronomer Nicolaus **Copernicus** (kuh PUR nih kus; 1473–1543) questioned Ptolemy's theory of the universe. Copernicus, who did not have a telescope to study the heavens, used instruments such as the astrolabe to measure the position of stars and planets in the skies. He found that the movements of heavenly bodies would be difficult to explain if the earth were the center of the universe. Therefore, he concluded that the sun is the center and that the earth and other planets orbit around it. This view is called the **heliocentric**

Comets

Until well into the sixteenth century, most people had a superstitious fear of comets. In fact, from ancient times people viewed them as evil omens. Even as late as 1556, Thomas Digges, an English mathematician and astronomer, wrote, "Comets signify corruption of the stars. They are signs of earthquakes, of wars, of changing of kingdoms, great dearth of corn, yea, a common death of man and beast."

Since disastrous events sometimes coincided with the appearance of a comet, such superstitions persisted. The Roman emperor Vespasian believed that a comet seen in AD 79 was an evil sign, but he supposedly remarked, "This hairy star does not concern me; it menaces the king of the Parthians [Rome's enemy], for he is hairy and I am bald." Yet it was Vespasian who died in AD 79, and in that same year an eruption of Mount Vesuvius buried the cities of Pompeii and Herculaneum. Thus, the course of events reinforced some people's fear.

In 1066, another comet appeared in the sky, greatly alarming the English Saxons. They had just experienced the death of their king, Edward the Confessor, and wondered what else the year had in store for them. In October, the Saxons were defeated at the Battle of Hastings, and King Harold was killed. William of Normandy went on to become the new ruler of England.

The comet that had appeared in 1066 was the same one that Englishman Edmund Halley viewed in 1682. Halley's observation and study indicated that the comet moved around the sun in an elliptical orbit. He further calculated that it appeared regularly, approximately every seventy-five years. When the comet appeared again in 1758 as Halley had predicted, astronomers appropriately named it Halley's Comet. It reappeared in 1835, 1910, and 1986; its next appearance should be in 2061.

(sun-centered) **theory**. The Roman Catholic Church, which had officially embraced the old geocentric approach, opposed the publication of Copernicus's findings. Those who accepted the heliocentric theory risked being persecuted as heretics by the Roman Church.

The noted German astronomer **Johannes Kepler** (1571–1630), a Lutheran, did not fear the threats of the Roman Church. Although he agreed with Copernicus that the earth revolves around the sun, he disagreed with him on the nature of the orbit. Copernicus had taught that the orbits of the planets are circular. Kepler, however, found that the orbits are elliptical (oval-shaped). A devout Christian, Kepler prayed that God would keep his investigations free from personal bias: "I ask God to make my spirit strong so that I direct my glance at the pure truth, from whichever side it should be presented, and do not let myself be misled, as so often happens today, by the admiration or contempt of persons or sides."

Galileo

The best-known astronomer in history is probably the Italian **Galileo Galilei** (GAL-uh-LAY-oh GAL-uh-LAY-ee; 1564–1642). Galileo made important contributions to other scientific fields as well—notably physics. As a young man, he observed a lamp swinging in the Pisa cathedral. As he watched, he wondered if there was a regular rhythm to the swing. After repeated experiments with pendulums, he found that though he increased the size of the arc, the pendulum still swung in rhythm; therefore, he suggested the use of the pendulum to measure time. The results of his work can be seen today in timepieces such as the grandfather clock.

Galileo improved on a Dutch invention, the telescope, and used it in his own work. He confirmed the heliocentric theory and agreed with Kepler that the planets move in elliptical orbits. When Galileo published his findings, however, he also came into conflict with the Roman Catholic Church, which tried him for heresy. He was told that unless he retracted his contention that the earth moved, he would be excommunicated. Kneeling before the Inquisitors, he publicly retracted, but according to legend, as he rose from his knees he muttered, "But it does move!"

Isaac Newton

The same year that Galileo died, **Isaac Newton** (1642–1727) was born in England. Like Galileo, he was an astronomer who also contributed to several other fields, such as physics and mathematics. For example, he demonstrated with a prism that "white light" is actually composed of many different colors. With his invention of the reflecting telescope and his development of calculus, Newton was able to make more accurate observations and to apply mathematics to the study of the universe.

We remember Newton best for his discovery of the laws of gravity. According to a story related by the French philosopher Voltaire, Newton once observed an apple falling from a tree. Intrigued, he wondered why objects fall. From his observation and experimentation, he formulated his famous theory of gravitation. He explained not only why objects fall to the ground but also how planets are held in their orbits by the pull of gravity. Newton expressed these ideas in his greatest work, *Principia*, published in 1687. His contributions won him the esteem of his day; English poet Alexander Pope praised his achievements: "Nature and nature's Laws lay hid in Night: / God said, 'Let Newton be!' and all was light."

Medicine

While astronomy led the way for scientific development in the Age of Reason, there were many important discoveries in other fields. The study of medicine, which involved the practical application of these discoveries, was greatly affected by the scientific revolution.

In 1543, **Andreas Vesalius** (vuh SAY lee us; 1514–1564) of Flanders published his great treatise on human anatomy, *On the Fabric of the Human Body*. He gained information for this monumental work from the dissection of cadavers (corpses). By examining the actual structure of the human body, Vesalius disproved many ridiculous ancient theories, such as the idea that the heart contained a bone. With a clearer understanding of how the human body functions, doctors were better able to treat illness and disease. For his contribution to science, Vesalius has been called the Father of Anatomy.

Swiss-born P. A. T. Bombast Von Hohenheim (1493–1541) made the first clinical study of disease and established the use of chemicals in the treatment of illness. He became better known by his self-given name, **Paracelsus** (PEHR uh SEL sus), which means "better than Celsus," a famous Roman physician. Paracelsus suggested that since the human body is chemical in nature, chemicals should be used to treat disease. Although not all of his prescriptions were safe or effective, he advanced the science of medicine.

Left: Vesalius
Right: William Harvey

The Englishman **William Harvey** (1578–1657), called the Father of Experimental Biology, also prepared the way for modern medicine. He carefully studied the heart and circulation of the blood. Ancient theory held that both the heart and the liver prepared different kinds of blood, which were sent to the different parts of the body to be consumed. Harvey discovered that the heart alone acts as a pump, pushing blood through the arteries and the veins; thus, blood is not "consumed" but constantly circulated.

Another Englishman, **Edward Jenner** (1749–1823), developed the smallpox vaccination. His work in his field is a model of the scientific method. First, he observed that milkmaids who contracted the disease cowpox did not contract smallpox, a dreaded disease that kills or horribly disfigures its victims. Jenner speculated that if a person were inoculated with the fluid from a cowpox sore, he would then be immune to smallpox. He tested his theory by inoculating a boy with cowpox, from which the child contracted only a mild case. Later, he inoculated the same boy with smallpox. The child did not contract that disease. Jenner called his method of inoculation against disease "vaccination" after the Latin word *vaccinia*, meaning "cowpox." Today, because of Jenner's work, smallpox has been nearly wiped out.

Edward Jenner practicing his method of vaccinating against smallpox

Collection of the University of Michigan Health System, Gift of Pfizer Inc. UMHS.23

Chemistry

The modern concepts of chemistry developed out of the medieval so-called science of alchemy. Despite some abuses, alchemists handed down a legacy of lab techniques and functional equipment with which to conduct experiments. The alchemists' approach to experimentation also laid the foundation for the modern scientific method. In their day, Newton, Boyle, and Francis Bacon would have been considered alchemists. However, these men and many others made significant scientific contributions.

Irishman **Robert Boyle** (1627–91) was the first to publish the law of inverse gas pressure. Boyle found that increasing pressure on a gas reduces its volume whereas decreasing the pressure causes the volume to expand. Scientists call this principle Boyle's law. In addition to studying chemistry, Boyle, who was a dedicated Christian, diligently studied the Bible. He lectured in defense of Christianity and sought to refute those he termed "notorious infidels." He even left money in his will so that these lectures could be continued after his death.

English Unitarian minister and chemist **Joseph Priestley** (1733–1804) discovered several important chemical substances: ammonia, oxygen, nitrous oxide (better known as "laughing gas"), hydrochloric acid, and carbon dioxide, among others. Modern carbonated beverages owe their existence to his work with carbon dioxide. Priestley, who was influenced by his friend Benjamin Franklin, also performed experiments with electricity.

Left: Robert Boyle
Right: Joseph Priestley

Lavoisier in his laboratory
Collection of the University of Michigan Health System, Gift of Pfizer Inc. UMHS.19

The Father of Modern Chemistry was Frenchman **Antoine Laurent Lavoisier** (luh VWAH zee ay; 1743–94). He used logical rather than fanciful terminology for chemicals. For example, he named one substance *hydrogen* ("water former") because it forms water vapor when mixed with air. Lavoisier also formulated the law of conservation of matter, which states that matter cannot be created or destroyed; it only changes form.

Contributions in Other Scientific Fields

Many other scientists contributed to the scientific revolution. Anton van Leeuwenhoek (LAY vun h*ook*; 1632–1723) of the Netherlands greatly improved the microscope by making lenses that could magnify up to 160 times. With such lenses he discovered the existence of microbes and bacteria. Gerhardus Mercator (mur KAY tur; 1512–94) from Flanders devised a way to map the earth on a flat surface. Today the Mercator projection, as it is called, is still a standard pattern for mapmaking.

Section Quiz

1. What were the two principal authorities for truth during the Middle Ages?
2. List three new instruments that aided scientific investigation of the physical world.
3. What Polish astronomer challenged the theory of an earth-centered universe? What is his view called?
4. What contribution did Edward Jenner make to the field of medicine?
5. Who is the Father of Modern Chemistry?

★ How did alchemy contribute to the development of modern chemistry?

II. Intellectual Attitudes

Scientific discoveries prompted philosophers to apply the scientific method to both their study of man and their search for truth. In doing so, they placed such a strong emphasis on the power of human reason that this period of history is known as the Age of Reason. It culminated in an eighteenth-century intellectual movement called the **Enlightenment**.

Philosophers of the Enlightenment looked to human reason as the solution for all of life's problems. They praised reason for making possible the achievements of science and providing new approaches to learning. Reason, they believed, was the gateway to human progress. No longer was reason considered just a method of gaining knowledge; these philosophers believed it was the only sure source of knowledge and truth—an attitude known as **rationalism**.

Sir Francis Bacon

Forerunners of the Enlightenment

Approaches to Learning

New approaches to learning aided the expansion of knowledge during the seventeenth century. Two methods of reasoning—the inductive and the deductive—assisted scientists in their investigation of the physical world and aided philosophers in their quest to understand that world.

Inductive Reasoning—One of the leading advocates of the inductive method of reasoning was English philosopher Sir **Francis Bacon** (1561–1626). In his important work *Novum Organum*, he criticized the manner in which many ancient and medieval philosophers arrived at their conclusions about the natural world. Their hasty generalizations, he asserted, created great obstacles for later generations. Believing that people must get rid of all false ideas before they can arrive at truth, Bacon questioned all existing knowledge. He advocated the use of careful observation and experimentation before arriving at general conclusions. Scientists, he asserted, should form tentative conclusions and then gather more information to verify their results. Such reasoning—from specific cases to a general conclusion—is called the **inductive method**.

Bacon believed that man, using this rational approach, could discover and understand truth. Likewise, he could dispel superstition and error. Many of Bacon's contemporaries, however, objected to his insistence that all knowledge should be questioned. They considered his method an assault on religion. Bacon answered this charge: "If the matter be truly considered, natural philosophy is, after the word of God, at once the surest medicine against superstition and the most approved nourishment for faith; and therefore she is rightly given to religion as her most faithful handmaid, since the one displays the will of God, the other is his power." Sadly, less than a century later, people exalted reason as the highest authority, placing it above faith in God and His Word.

Descartes

Deductive Reasoning—Another method of gaining knowledge was advanced by the French philosopher and mathematician **René Descartes** (day KART; 1596–1650). He feared that people could be deceived by their senses and that observation and experimentation were therefore unreliable. While Bacon let observation and experience guide his reason, Descartes relied on reason aided by the methods of mathematics. Like Bacon, however, Descartes believed that every false idea and prejudice had to be discarded before one could arrive at truth. This led him to doubt everything. The first step in his system of thought was to find some truth or idea that could not be doubted. No one, he believed, could doubt that man is a thinking being, capable of understanding truth. Thus he began his quest for truth with the premise, "I doubt, therefore I think; I think, therefore I am." On this premise he built his system of thought. He taught that by starting with such a simple premise, through careful logic, people could arrive at another, more complex truth. This system is called the **deductive method** of reasoning.

Explanations of Reality

Inductive and deductive reasoning were vital elements of the scientific method, helping scientists to understand the natural world. But could these same reasoning processes be applied to the study of man and society? Through reason, could man comprehend the spiritual realm? And what was the relationship between the physical and spiritual worlds? Philosophers of the seventeenth century sought answers to these questions.

From a man-centered perspective, Descartes constructed a system of philosophy known as **dualism** (*dual* meaning "two"). According to Descartes, there are two types of reality: mind (the spiritual world) and matter (the physical world). While Descartes admitted that there are certain spiritual truths (such as the existence of God) that reason cannot discover, he taught that people can discover truths about the physical world only by using reason. In fact, Descartes emphasized reason so strongly that he stated, "We should never allow ourselves to be persuaded of anything except by the evidence of our reason."

Pantheism and the Word of God

The Bible teaches that God is everywhere (Ps. 139:7–10; Jer. 23:24), but it also teaches that God is distinct from His creation (Col. 1:17; 3:1–2). However, pantheists do not recognize God as a personal being. Instead, they think of Him as an abstract system of truths. As a result, pantheists reject, among many truths revealed in God's Word, the biblical concept of God as a heavenly Father.

Spinoza

Baruch Spinoza (1632-1677). Anonymous, 17th century. Jewish philosopher. His "Tractatus theologico-politico" defends freedom of thought and tolerance. Herzogliche Bibliothek, Wolfenbuettel, Germany. Erich Lessing/Art Resource, NY

Another philosopher who emphasized the importance of reason was **Baruch Spinoza** (spih NO zah; 1632–77). Spinoza was one of the first Bible interpreters to demand that reason judge whether Scripture passages are true or not. He also taught that the Bible was a historical book without relevance to the present. Instead of the biblical distinction between God and His creation, Spinoza taught that everything in the universe, whether spiritual or physical, is all part of one great substance called "god." This view is called **pantheism**.

Another influential philosophy of the seventeenth century was empiricism. Empiricism—the idea that all knowledge comes through experience—was the philosophy of Englishman **John Locke** (1632–1704). Locke rejected the idea that God has implanted certain truths within each person from birth. Instead, he maintained that the mind of a baby is like a blank tablet on which the experiences of life are written. Thus Locke argued that given the right experiences and education, a child would grow into the right kind of person. He rejected the doctrine of original sin, choosing to believe that humans are basically good. Locke agreed that divine revelation is vital but denied that it could contradict man's reason.

The questions that these philosophers were raising were not new. They had been discussed by philosophers and theologians throughout the Middle Ages. The difference was that these philosophers now believed that their own reason or their own sense experience carried more authority than Scripture.

Above: John Locke
Below: Montesquieu

Spokesmen of the Enlightenment

The scientific discoveries and philosophic ideas of the seventeenth century gave rise to a spirit of optimism in the eighteenth century as men looked to their own reason as the hope for the future. The eighteenth-century French writers and social critics known as the *philosophes* (FIL uh SOFS) became the most prominent spokesmen of the so-called enlightened attitude. These men were more than mere thinkers; they were social reformers. They openly challenged established values and institutions in hope of conforming society to their ideas. They contended that certain religious beliefs restricted a person's freedom to think and express himself. They championed a secular society, religious toleration, freedom of speech, and the natural rights of all people. The *philosophes* mistakenly believed that man could solve society's problems and that progress and perfectibility were attainable for both society and man.

Locke

Political reform became one of the chief concerns of the eighteenth-century *philosophes*. Many of the French writers were influenced by the political ideas of the seventeenth-century English philosopher John Locke. Locke advanced the idea that people possess certain natural and unalienable rights—rights that cannot be transferred or surrendered. In his *Two Treatises of Government*, he stated that the basis of government is the consent of the governed. People enter into a social contract with government; if government violates the people's trust, the people have a right to change their government.

Montesquieu

Locke's ideas, which were advanced as a justification of the Glorious Revolution in England, inspired the *philosophes*. Among those influenced by his rational defense of natural rights and his promotion of the idea that men could change their government was the Frenchman Baron de **Montesquieu** (MAHN tes kyoo; 1689–1755). He believed that England symbolized political freedom. The liberty of the English, he concluded, resulted from the separation of the three powers of government: the executive, the legislative, and the judicial. Montesquieu's political theory had a great impact on the framers of the Constitution of the United States.

Voltaire

The leading figure of the Enlightenment was François-Marie Arouet, better known as **Voltaire** (vawl TEHR; 1694–1778). He used his clever wit to criticize other people. As a young man, Voltaire was thrown into prison for insulting a French noble. Later he was banished from France. He went to England, where he became an admirer of the ideas of Isaac Newton and John Locke. The atmosphere of intellectual freedom that he found in English society made a strong impression on him.

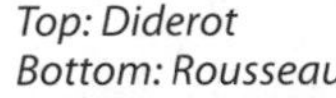

Top: Diderot
Bottom: Rousseau

Voltaire became an outspoken critic of the abuses in society, especially political and religious intolerance. As a result, he learned to hate organized religion and advocated a religion ruled by human reason. Voltaire was also a popular champion of freedom of the press. His cutting wit made him a favorite in many aristocratic and scholarly circles. However, Voltaire's scathing attacks on the arbitrary rule of kings and nobles resulted in his being forced to flee country after country.

Diderot and the Encyclopédie

The chief instrument for spreading the ideas of the philosophes was the French *Encyclopédie*. Like its modern counterparts, the *Encyclopédie* included articles on almost every conceivable subject. This multivolume work was edited by **Denis Diderot** (DEE duh ROH; 1713–84). He wrote several hundred articles himself, but more than two hundred other writers also contributed to the work. The articles expressed the Enlightenment philosophy, often in its most radical form. The French government and the Roman Church officially opposed the publication because it undermined their authority.

Rousseau

Another philosophe who contributed to the *Encyclopédie* was **Jean-Jacques Rousseau** (roo SOH; 1712–78). Although he was a friend to the other philosophes, Rousseau was out of step with most of them because he favored emotion and sentiment above reason. He has often been called the Father of Romanticism. Rousseau's slogan "back to nature" also set the pattern of thought for the first half of the nineteenth century, which was called the Romantic Age (see chapter 17).

Rousseau also became an influential political writer. He believed people are born free and should be able to do whatever they want to do. Rousseau also believed in the basic goodness of humanity. Personal liberty and order in society, he contended, would come as people freely obey the laws of society. In his work *The Social Contract*, he maintained that government should be built on and should carry out the "general will" of the people. By "general will" Rousseau meant majority rule. Unlike most political thinkers of his day, he favored a democracy rather than a representative government or an absolute monarchy. Rousseau's political ideas influenced leaders of the nineteenth-century political movements that advocated popular participation in government.

The Religion of the Enlightenment

Many scientists and philosophers of the Enlightenment put their faith in reason instead of in God's revelation, the Bible. Though they did not deny the existence of God, they refused to accept orthodox Christianity because it did not conform to their new ideas. They rejected the supernatural, ridiculing both the miraclulous and prophetic elements in Scripture. They also denied the fact that humans are born in sin, believing instead that they are basically good. Reason was their standard of truth: it was their guide to understanding the universe and the proper way to worship God. This new religion was called **deism**.

Deists viewed the universe as a machine. God was its First Cause, or Grand Architect. He designed the universe as a self-sustaining mechanism and established the natural laws by which it operates. Deists asserted that once God had finished Creation, He no longer intervened in human affairs. To the deist, God was merely an impersonal being, much like a clockmaker who, having made a clock and wound its spring, sat back and let it run.

Deists had little use for a personal God or His salvation. They asserted that the truths of religion could be discovered naturally. They believed that a virtuous life guided by human reason would be rewarded in the life to come. Despite these boastful claims, deism was built on mere human wisdom. The Bible warns against such error in 1 Corinthians 2:5, 14, and 16.

Section Quiz

1. What English philosopher was one of the leading advocates of the inductive method of reasoning?
2. What name is given to the idea that everything in the universe is part of one substance called "god"? Who was the leading advocate of that philosophy?
3. What were the most prominent spokesmen of the "enlightened" attitude called? What country were they from?
4. What aspect of English government did the French philosopher Montesquieu credit as aiding political liberty?
5. What aspects of biblical Christianity did some Enlightenment philosophers and scientists reject? What became the new religion of the Age of Reason?

★ Why do deists reject miracles?

III. Spiritual Awakening

Not everyone living in the Age of Reason trusted in human wisdom as the only way to find truth. Many people realized that although science could improve man's standard of living, it could not improve man; neither could man through his own wisdom understand the things of God. Genuine enlightenment came as men discovered the truth of God's Word and submitted to it.

This spiritual enlightenment produced several revivals that changed the lives of men and women and altered the moral climate of the countries where these revivals occurred. As a result, Christian groups in parts of Europe and the American colonies rejected the false premise that a purely intellectual knowledge of Christ or simply belonging to a church resulted in salvation. Instead, they proclaimed that true repentance of sin and faith in Christ alone made one a child of God. These believers emphasized that Christians should live holy lives in conformity to God's Word while also seeking earnestly to bring others to salvation.

Pietism in Germany

In the seventeenth century, a movement known as **Pietism** arose in Germany. (The word *pietism* originated in 1689 as a term of ridicule for those who gathered for Bible study.) By the middle of the century, the Lutheran Church had fallen into spiritual decay. The clergy, often poorly trained and sometimes unconverted, neglected the spiritual needs of their people. Their dull, lifeless sermons produced no change in the unconcerned attitudes of many church members.

In the midst of this spiritual decline, a Lutheran minister in Frankfurt named **Philipp Spener** (SHPAY nur; 1635–1705) became burdened for his congregation. Realizing that those who had experienced personal conversion needed close Christian fellowship, Spener organized special meetings in his home for Bible study and prayer. In addition, he published his famous work *Pia Desideria* ("Pious Wishes"), in which he outlined the failures of the church and issued a call for spiritual renewal. Though many church officials attacked his ideas, concerned Christians throughout Germany followed his example and organized themselves into groups known as *collegia pietatis* ("assemblies of piety").

As the movement continued to grow, **August Francke** (FRAHNG keh; 1663–1727), a professor at the University of Halle, became a leader in the training of Pietist pastors and missionaries. Through his efforts, student lay preachers carried the gospel throughout Germany, and mission works were established in the American colonies and India. In addition to his teaching responsibilities, Francke helped establish and supervise an orphanage, elementary and secondary schools, and a Bible-printing organization. In all, he established twenty-one different types of educational institutions that emphasized godliness and Christian wisdom. Though persecuted by various civil and religious authorities, he temporarily turned Halle into the most influential center of German Pietism.

Count **Nikolaus von Zinzendorf** (TSIN tsen DORF; 1700–1760) also studied under Francke at Halle. Later, Zinzendorf left the Lutheran Church and became the leader of the Moravians. This group, which began in Bohemia and Moravia during the time of John Huss, had almost died out by the eighteenth century. In 1722, however, a small group of Bohemian refugees settled on Zinzendorf's estate and established a religious community which they called Herrnhut ("Lord's Lodge"). From this humble beginning, the movement grew as zealous Moravian missionaries traveled around the world, not only preaching the gospel but also seeking to unite all Christians. It was through the Moravians that John Wesley came to a personal assurance of salvation.

Count Nikolaus von Zinzendorf

Nicholaus Ludwig Count von Zinzendorf with the Daily Watchwords, 1761 (oil on panel) by Swiss School (18th century) Private Collection/The Bridgeman Art Library

The Moravians became one of the first Protestant movements to stress missions. When there were no more than three hundred occupants of Herrnhut, the Moravians began to send out missionaries. As their group increased, they continued to send up to one quarter of their members out as missionaries to North America (to the Indians), the Caribbean islands, Greenland, and as far as Australia.

The Pietists did much good work for the Lord, but they also had a significant weakness. They elevated personal experience over sound doctrine as found in Scripture. At first they simply assumed sound doctrine, but the next generation emphasized experience without teaching doctrine. The third generation then followed the spirit of the age in looking to their own experience and reason as authorities since Scriptural doctrinal authority had been minimized. This led to the confusing situation of many liberals who very piously expressed their love for Christ and God but at the same time denied key beliefs of the Christian faith.

Revival in England

By the eighteenth century, interest in spiritual matters had almost disappeared in England. Throughout the country, most Anglican clergy sought personal comfort and ease and seemed interested primarily in secular pursuits. Smaller denominations also became complacent. As a result, few pastors preached salvation by grace through faith, and moral corruption seemed to worsen with every passing year. Nevertheless, during the eighteenth century a mighty spiritual awakening shook England as God blessed the preaching of faithful men.

John Wesley

John Wesley

Probably the best known of these preachers is **John Wesley** (1703–91). During his lifetime, he traveled about 250,000 miles on horseback and preached around 42,000 sermons. Ordained as an Anglican minister in 1728, Wesley returned to Oxford University as a student and joined a club that his brother Charles had helped to establish. Although many of this "Holy Club" were unconverted at the time, they tried to live righteous lives. They met often for mutual encouragement. Many students mocked their methodical lifestyle and often referred to them derisively as "Methodists"—a term that Wesley's converts later gladly accepted.

Conversion—In 1735 Wesley sailed to the American colony of Georgia to be a missionary to the Indians and to serve as pastor in the town of Savannah. During the voyage and then later in Savannah, however, Wesley came into contact with some Moravians, who impressed upon him his own spiritual need. Though he had tried to live a good life, he realized that something was lacking. Wesley records in his journal that soon after he arrived in Georgia, the head of the Moravian settlement there spoke to him:

Susanna Wesley (1669-1742)

Susanna Ann Wesley was born in London on January 20, 1669. Although her father was a Nonconformist minister, Susanna later joined the Anglican Church. Samuel Wesley, whom she married in 1689, was also reared in the home of a Nonconformist minister. Later, however, he too joined the established church and became an Anglican minister.

For almost forty years, Samuel and Susanna served the rural parish of Epworth in Lincolnshire. Samuel devoted his time to scholarly pursuits while Susanna managed the household and reared the children. (She had nineteen children, nine of whom died in childhood.) Although she carefully budgeted the family's meager income, the Wesleys were always poor and often in debt. Furthermore, their house burned down twice and had to be rebuilt.

Since poverty prevented her sons from attending school until they were about twelve years old (there were no schools for girls), Susanna taught all of her children at home. As soon as a child could talk, she taught him to pray and to memorize Scripture. Realizing that her busy schedule made it difficult to spend sufficient time with each child individually, Susanna set aside a special time in the evenings for each of them. After he had left home, John Wesley wrote to his mother that he would give anything to be able to spend Thursday evenings (his special time) with her again.

Though Susanna Wesley never achieved earthly wealth or fame, she reared two sons who by God's grace brought revival to eighteenth-century England. She said of her life, "I am content to fill a little space if God be glorified." The space she filled as a dedicated Christian mother was certainly glorifying to God.

"Do you know Jesus Christ?" I paused, and said, "I know He is the Saviour of the world." "True," replied he; "but do you know He has saved you?" I answered, "I hope He has died to save me." He only added, "Do you know yourself?" I said, "I do." But I fear they were vain words.

Because of conflicts with some of the colonists, his ministry in America soon failed. As he returned to England, he wrote in his journal, "I went to convert the Indians; but O! who shall convert me?" Back in London, he contacted some Moravians, and on May 24, 1738, "went very unwillingly" to one of their meetings on Aldersgate Street

where one was reading Luther's preface to the Epistle to the Romans. About a quarter before nine, while he was describing the change which God works in the heart through faith in Christ, I felt my heart strangely warmed. I felt I did trust in Christ, Christ alone, for salvation; and an assurance was given me that He had taken away my sins, even mine, and saved me from the law of sin and death.

Ministry—After his conversion, Wesley began to travel throughout the British Isles, preaching as often as four times a day. He once wrote, "I look on all the world as my parish." Since most Anglican churches soon closed their doors to him, he began to preach to large crowds in the open air and saw many conversions. Opposition to his preaching increased, however, and on numerous occasions he faced stone-throwing mobs, hostile clergymen, and unsympathetic civil officials. Yet his ministry never faltered. He rose daily at 4:00 a.m. and usually preached his first sermon of the day at 5:00 a.m. On one occasion when he was seventy, he spoke to thirty-thousand people, and all heard him clearly. At eighty, he still traveled four to five thousand miles a year to meet his preaching responsibilities.

Although Wesley did not intend to leave the Anglican Church, he is considered the founder of the Methodist Church. He originally planned for the Methodist societies, which his converts had organized, to remain within the church like the *collegia pietatis* in Germany had remained within the Lutheran Church. The Anglican hierarchy, however, refused to ordain Wesley's lay preachers. Ultimately, the Methodist societies were forced out of the Anglican Church. When Wesley died, the Methodists had 630 lay preachers and about 175,000 members.

George Whitefield

The work of Wesley and others like him had a tremendous impact on Britain. Spiritual revival broke the apathetic attitudes among professing Christians and led to domestic reform and foreign missions. The revival also improved the moral condition of England—helping to restrain the type of social upheaval that soon engulfed France (see Chapter 16). In addition, the spiritual awakening stimulated an interest in Christian education, led to the establishment of the first Sunday schools, and encouraged the production of good Christian literature and music.

George Whitefield

One of John Wesley's contemporaries was a dynamic evangelist named **George Whitefield** (WHIT feeld; 1714–70). The son of a tavern keeper, Whitefield had played a leading role at Oxford, along with Charles Wesley, in founding the group that became known as the Methodists. Whitefield was converted in 1735 and was ordained an Anglican minister the following year. Whitefield also traveled constantly and preached the gospel wherever he went. When he and the Wesleys were excluded from preaching in Anglican churches, Whitefield encouraged the Wesleys to follow his example and preach wherever people tended to gather. He not only preached throughout Britain with great results but also crossed the Atlantic seven times on preaching tours in the American colonies. Whitefield was used of God to play a substantial role in the Great Awakening in America.

Awakening in the American Colonies

During the first half of the seventeenth century, many Puritans fled England and settled in the American colonies. For several years, the spiritual zeal of these colonists remained strong, but by the end of the seventeenth century their descendants were no longer fervent for the Lord. During the eighteenth century, George Whitefield summarized the condition of the American churches this way: "I am verily persuaded, the generality of preachers talk of an unknown, unfelt Christ. And the reason why congregations have been so dead, is because dead men preach to them."

Jonathan Edwards

During 1740–42, as the Methodist revival progressed in the British Isles, America experienced the climax of a tremendous spiritual harvest known as the **Great Awakening**. Through the preaching of Whitefield and other traveling evangelists, thousands of people heard the message of salvation. The real key to the long-term spiritual success of the Great Awakening, however, lay with local pastors who ministered faithfully to the needs of their own congregations.

One such pastor, whose name is inseparably linked with the Great Awakening, is **Jonathan Edwards** (1703–58). A brilliant young man who graduated from Yale at the age of seventeen, Edwards used his considerable talents to further the cause of Christ. In 1729 he succeeded his grandfather as pastor of the Congregational Church in Northampton, Massachusetts. Through his sermons and books, he advocated the need for personal conversion. He was a diligent lifelong student, often studying thirteen hours a day and writing works of great theological and philosophical depth.

Probably the most famous sermon Edwards ever preached was "Sinners in the Hands of an Angry God," delivered in 1741 at Enfield, Connecticut. Basing his sermon on the phrase "their foot shall slide in due time" (Deut. 32:35), Edwards warned his unrepentant hearers that only God's mercy kept them from instantly plunging into hell:

> O sinner! consider the fearful danger you are in. . . . Are there not many here who have lived long in the world, and are not to this day born again? . . . Therefore, let every one that is out of Christ now awake and fly from the wrath to come.

As Edwards preached, the Spirit of God brought such conviction on the congregation that people began to cry out, "What shall I do to be saved?" Many people began to weep. In fact, the noise became so loud that Edwards had to stop preaching several times and urge the people to be quiet that he might continue his sermon. As a result of that sermon, many of the unsaved in Enfield came to salvation.

This incident is only one example of the spiritual awakening that swept through the American colonies. Although many political and social benefits derived from the Great Awakening, the most significant results were spiritual. A large number of the colonists were converted. For example, in New England alone, which had a population of 300,000, between 25,000 and 50,000 people were converted, and 150 new churches were established. Christians became concerned about mission work and made renewed efforts to reach

Foundations for Modern Hymnody

From the Reformation until the eighteenth century, English Protestants did not use hymns in their church services. Instead, they sang rhymed settings of the Psalms, believing that church music should be drawn directly from Scripture. Many of these psalm settings, however, were poorly written and hard to sing. Determined to improve the music in his own congregation, a minister named Isaac Watts (1674–1748) began to write hymns. Although at first many Protestants of all denominations rejected this "innovation," Watts persevered in his efforts. He is known today as the Father of English Hymnody.

Watts believed that hymns should be doctrinally sound and easily understood. Sometimes he paraphrased a psalm; for example, "O God, Our Help in Ages Past" is based on Psalm 90, and "From All that Dwell Below the Skies" is based on Psalm 117. On other occasions, he composed hymns that were based upon a particular scriptural theme, such as "When I Survey the Wondrous Cross." In everything he wrote, Watts tried to direct the worshipers' attention to Christ.

Churchgoers in the early eighteenth century did not have hymnals; therefore, the pastor or someone else had to read the lines of the psalm or hymn aloud. After each line was read, the congregation would sing it, and then the reader would proceed to the next line. Therefore, Watts ensured that each line of his hymns made sense when read by itself.

Joy to the world! the Lord is come;
Let earth receive her King;
Let every heart prepare him room,
And heaven and nature sing.

Although Watts laid the foundation for English hymnody, Charles Wesley (1707–88) popularized hymn singing in England. Like his brother John, Charles traveled as an evangelist, but his health forced him to retire early. He settled down to a pastoral ministry and continued to write hymns; by the time he died, he had written more than six thousand.

Charles Wesley is considered the greatest English hymn writer. With his hymns, he sang the Methodist revival into the hearts of the people and helped strengthen them in Christian doctrine. Whereas Watts's hymns are formal and reserved (reflecting the age in which he lived), Wesley's are filled with emotion. For example, Watts wrote,

Come, sound his praise abroad
And hymns of glory sing;
Jehovah is the sovereign God,
The universal King.

Wesley, on the other hand, penned the following words on the first anniversary of his conversion:

O for a thousand tongues to sing
My dear Redeemer's praise,
The glories of my God and King,
The triumphs of His grace!

Wesley wrote hymns to fit every occasion, including Christmas hymns ("Hark! the Herald Angels Sing"), Easter hymns ("Christ the Lord is Ris'n Today"), and communion hymns. He also wrote hymns of praise, comfort, and contemplation. In all of his compositions, however, he emphasized primarily the theme of love. For example, "Jesus, Lover of My Soul" and "Love Divine, All Loves Excelling" proclaim the love of Christ. Many of Wesley's hymns also highlight the themes of grace, light, and joy.

the American Indians with the gospel. In addition, several groups established schools for the training of Christian ministers. The Presbyterians, for example, established the College of New Jersey, which later became Princeton University. In spite of several denominational splits, the revival also helped to draw together Christians of various denominations in a bond of fellowship and cooperation in winning the lost. This Great Awakening was the first of several revivals that were to come to America over the next two centuries.

Section Quiz

1. List three major Pietist leaders in Germany.
2. Name two men who founded the Methodists.
3. Who is known as the Father of English Hymnody?
4. Who is considered the greatest English hymn writer?
5. What was the name of the spiritual revival in America that climaxed in the 1740s?

★ How could Pietism lead to rationalism? How can truly pious people avoid following the same dangerous path?

El Greco, St. Martin and the Beggar, *National Gallery of Art, Washington, D.C.*

IV. Artistic Reflection

Between the Renaissance and the Enlightenment, Europe underwent great social, political, religious, and intellectual changes. These changes produced tension and restlessness among the people of Europe. But with the coming of the Enlightenment, doubt and uncertainty gave way to an emphasis on order and restraint. The values, attitudes, and concerns of these historical periods are reflected in their architecture, painting, music, and literature.

The Baroque Age in Art

The doubts and contradictions of the sixteenth century and the new ideas and discoveries of the seventeenth century found expression in two styles of art: mannerism and baroque. These styles illustrate different aspects or moods of the troubled and changing times.

Mannerism was the artistic style that was prevalent throughout much of the sixteenth century. It reflected the political and religious tension of the Reformation era. Unlike Renaissance artists, mannerist artists did not strive for realism and balance. Instead, their works are filled with distortions and exaggerations: colors are often unnatural or clashing, and the human form is often distorted. An outstanding painter in this style was **El Greco** (1541–1614), a Greek who settled in Spain. His figures have elongated bodies and limbs. He often created a mystical atmosphere with dramatic and sharply contrasting colors.

The art of the seventeenth century captured the mood of the time and is as varied as the personalities of the artists who created it. This new style was called **baroque**, a term probably originating from a Portuguese word meaning "an irregularly shaped pearl." The term, originally used in a negative sense, refers to the period in art history that stretches from 1600 to about 1750. (Nineteenth-century art critics regarded the art of the seventeenth century as theatrical, deformed, and too ornamental.)

The baroque style is grand, dynamic, heroic, active, swirling, sensual, and emotional. It engages the complete attention of the viewer. It includes everything from the ornate façades (fronts) of buildings to beautiful fountains; from gigantic canvases that seem to reach out and include the viewer, to arrogant portraits; and from dazzling church domes to lofty, painted ceilings that seem to reveal views of paradise. The baroque style originated primarily as an architectural style and soon spread to painting, sculpture, and music.

Bernini sculpture

Bernini

One of the most famous architects of the seventeenth century was the Italian **Giovanni Bernini** (behr NEE nee; 1598–1680). He designed beautiful fountains for Roman plazas and the expansive colonnades outside St. Peter's Basilica. He was also an accomplished sculptor and painter. His sculptures captured subjects in motion: their hair flowing, their muscles rippling, and their robes billowing.

Rubens

While Bernini popularized the baroque style in architecture and sculpture, a Flemish artist, **Peter Paul Rubens** (1577–1640), popularized the baroque style in painting. As a young man, he traveled to Italy and studied the works of

Rise of the Rococo Style

During the eighteenth century the grand baroque style of Rubens gave way to a delicate style known as rococo, a French term that means "a pebble." (It refers to the small, shell-like ornaments that characterize rococo decoration.) Rococo is essentially a French style and was used most often in interior decoration. (It later spread to several German states and Austria.) The rococo style exchanges the power and grandeur of the baroque for refined elegance; it is delicate and feminine. Whereas the baroque style "shouts" at the beholder, the rococo style "whispers."

the master painters of the High Renaissance. Later, he traveled throughout Europe as a diplomat. His ability as a painter, however, did not go unnoticed. He received so many requests for his works that he was forced to employ other artists to help him meet the demand. These assistants worked under his direction to complete parts of his paintings; he applied the finishing touches. His canvases are dramatic and often contain rich landscapes and robust figures.

Above: Rubens painting
Below: Rembrandt painting

Rembrandt

No discussion of baroque painting is complete without mention of **Rembrandt van Rijn** (REM-brant VAN RINE; 1606–69), perhaps the greatest Dutch painter of all time. His paintings are usually filled with gold tones and warm browns. By contrasting light and dark (a technique known as chiaroscuro), he created subtle moods on canvas. His portraits reveal a psychological insight into human nature; he portrays many of his subjects in deep contemplation.

Rembrandt grew up in a Protestant country and was introduced to the Bible by his mother, whom he often painted with her Bible. The themes of many of his paintings were inspired by biblical stories. Early in his career, he looked to the Bible only as a source for ideas. In his later religious works, however, he attempted to give a visual interpretation of Scripture. He sought to convey a message rather than simply please the eye of some patron.

Monticello, an example of neoclassical architecture

The Neoclassical Period in Art

In contrast to the emotionalism of baroque art, much of the art of the eighteenth century was orderly, formal, calm, and balanced. It expressed the conviction of the Enlightenment that the universe is a rational and orderly system. Since the universe runs according to fixed laws, eighteenth-century man reasoned that art should also conform to certain restrictions. Artists of this period, like Renaissance artists, imitated the classical ideals of ancient Greece and Rome. Thus developed the new artistic style of the **neoclassical** (or "new classic") period. Interest in classical art was further heightened by the discovery of the ancient cities of Pompeii and Herculaneum (see p. 89).

The Baroque Age in Music

Like baroque art, baroque music expresses the vigor of the seventeenth and early eighteenth centuries. Many of the adjectives that describe baroque art (see p. 338) apply to baroque music, which broke with past tradition, initiating a radical departure from the music of the fifteenth and sixteenth centuries.

1. Baroque composers gradually turned from **polyphony** (music in which several melody lines of equal importance are intertwined) to **homophony** (music with one basic melody line and several supporting harmony parts—much like a hymn).
2. Although some of the greatest composers still wrote primarily for the church, the trend was toward secular music commissioned by royalty and the aristocracy.
3. New types of musical compositions were developed during the baroque era, including the opera, the ballet, and the oratorio.
4. Instrumental music became more important during this period, giving rise to the development of the orchestra. Also during this age, craftsmen perfected the techniques of organ building and violin making.
5. Before the baroque era, vocalists often sang *a cappella* (without accompaniment). During the baroque period, instrumentalists usually accompanied vocal numbers.
6. Since many of the earliest baroque composers were Italian, Italian musical markings (which are still used today) became the standard markings for music throughout Europe. For example, *adagio* tells the performer to play slowly whereas *forte* tells him to play loudly.

Monteverdi
Ashmolean Museum, University of Oxford

Monteverdi

One of the leading composers of Italian baroque music was **Claudio Monteverdi** (MAHN tuh VEHR dee; 1567–1643). He is especially famous for his operas. He wrote his first opera, *Orfeo*, in 1607. In that work, as in his other operas, he skillfully combined text, music, scenery, and dances into a unified masterpiece. Partially through his influence, opera became a popular form of entertainment. Opera houses were built in many Italian cities, and for a small charge almost anyone could enjoy this new musical form.

Handel

One of the most famous "English" opera composers was a German immigrant to England named **George Frederick Handel** (1685–1759). He spent his early years as a composer of Italian-style operas. Later he turned to composing oratorios—musical compositions for solo singers, chorus, and orchestra that tell a sacred story without the dramatic action employed in operas. In all, Handel wrote about twenty oratorios, of which the best-known and best-loved is *Messiah*.

He wrote *Messiah* in 1741 for a charity concert in Dublin, Ireland, and finished the oratorio's more than fifty numbers in only twenty-four days. He wove majestic passages of Scripture with beautifully composed choruses and arias (melodic sections sung by solo voices). The central theme of the oratorio is Jesus Christ, the Messiah, the fulfillment of God's plan of Redemption. Among the best-loved numbers from *Messiah* are the aria "I Know That My Redeemer Liveth" and the "Hallelujah" chorus. The popularity of *Messiah* has endured, and it remains one of the most frequently performed oratorios.

Handel

J. S. Bach

Another great baroque composer was **Johann Sebastian Bach** (1685–1750). Bach came from a musical family that lived in a predominantly Lutheran section of Germany. In fact, young Martin Luther had lived in the same area around two hundred years before; Luther's music and theology had a strong influence on the Bach family. Most of Bach's musical career was spent in performing, conducting, and composing music for the Lutheran Church. Bach's own personal faith and knowledge of the Scriptures shine in his religious music.

Bach was a prolific composer. While serving as music director in the city of Leipzig, for example, he was expected to produce a new cantata for the worship service each Sunday. (Bach's cantatas were twenty- to thirty-minute compositions based on a scriptural text and performed by choirs, soloists, and instrumentalists.) He wrote more than two hundred cantatas and several oratorios, as well as organ, chamber, and orchestral music.

Bach did not travel widely, and his work was not as well known or appreciated as that of some other composers of the age. A local butcher was reported to have used copies of his music to wrap meat. Later generations, however,

J. S. Bach

To the Glory of God

Johann Sebastian Bach was a man of strong Christian faith who dedicated his talents to God. While playing the organ (which he called his pulpit) and while composing, he sought to create music that would strengthen and uplift the listener spiritually. He knew the Scriptures well, and at his death his library contained more than eighty books on theological or devotional subjects.

On the manuscripts containing his sacred compositions, Bach often wrote two sets of initials. On the first page of a manuscript he usually wrote the letters J.J. which stood for Jesu Juva ("Jesus help"), and on the last page he usually wrote S.D.G—Soli Deo Gloria ("to the glory of God alone").

Although he composed most of his music for use in church, Bach believed that all of his musical efforts should be for God's glory. On one occasion he put together a small book to teach music to his oldest son. On the title page he wrote the initials I.N.J.—In Nomine Jesu ("in the name of Jesus"). Bach believed that all activities—even those that seemed to be secular—should be done in the name of Jesus Christ.

have recognized the greatness of Bach's musical style. One of his most famous compositions is the *Passion According to St. Matthew*, an oratorio that he wrote for Good Friday, April 15, 1729. In that work Bach used Matthew's Gospel to tell the story of Christ's Crucifixion.

The Classical Age in Music

The classical age in music covers the period from 1750 to the early 1800s. Classical music turned from the elaborate style of J. S. Bach to an elegant style that showed precision, clarity of composition, and emotional restraint. The main types of compositions—sonatas, concertos, string quartets, and symphonies—reflected the order and balance of the Enlightenment. This music became a popular pastime among the aristocracy and the rich middle class. In addition, a new instrument, the piano, became a favorite, and many wealthy people even had one in their homes.

Haydn

The man who played a major role in setting the style for classical music was the Austrian composer **Franz Joseph Haydn** (HYE dun; 1732–1809). During his lifetime, he wrote a large amount of music, including 104 symphonies, 83 string quartets, more than 50 piano sonatas, several operas, and 2 oratorios. He set the style for symphonic composition, using large orchestration and dividing the work into four movements. Although he was not the first to compose a symphony, he has been called the Father of the Symphony. His musical works influenced other composers, including two of his most famous pupils—Mozart and Beethoven.

Above: Wolfgang Amadeus Mozart
Below: Molière

Mozart

Wolfgang Amadeus Mozart (1756–91) was a musical genius. He learned to play the harpsichord at the age of four and composed pieces at the age of five. When he was six years old, Mozart traveled with his father on a three-year European tour during which he played before princes and monarchs of Europe, winning their hearts. It was said that he could listen to a piece of music once and later reproduce it from memory. On one occasion, a member of his father's string quartet was absent. With no difficulty, the young Mozart filled in as second violin. The visitors present were astonished at his ability, to which he replied, "Surely you don't have to study and practice to play second violin, do you?"

Mozart was a versatile composer and excelled in many different types of musical compositions. Many of his twenty-two operas are still performed today; especially popular are *The Marriage of Figaro*, *Don Giovanni*, and *The Magic Flute*. He also composed forty symphonies, instrumental music, and chamber music. His works for piano helped to popularize that new instrument. Despite the early fame he won as a child prodigy, Mozart died in poverty at the age of thirty-five and was buried in an unmarked grave.

The other great composer of this period was Ludwig van Beethoven (1770–1827). His early works reflect the classical style. But he was caught up in the momentous events of the early nineteenth century, and his later compositions reflect the trend toward what would be called romanticism. (See Chapter 17.)

Literature in the Age of Reason

As was true for art and music, the literature of the Age of Reason was characterized by an imitation of the classical works of ancient Greece and Rome. Writers established definite rules, based on classical models, which they tried to follow to express themselves reasonably and clearly. This was the age of neoclassical literature.

One of the most famous French writers of the seventeenth century was playwright **Molière** (maw LYEHR; 1622–73). He is best remembered for his comedies, in which he pokes fun at the hypocrisy and vices in society.

The Age of Reason was an age of satire. The foremost poetic satirist was Englishman **Alexander Pope** (1688–1744). In his biting and witty satires, he exposed the follies of his day. For example, he wrote,

> Of all the causes which conspire to blind
> Man's erring judgment, and misguide the mind,
> What the weak head with strongest bias rules,
> Is pride, the never-failing vice of fools.

Pope was one of the most quoted poets of his age. Even today, many of his phrases are familiar, such as "To err is human, to forgive divine" and "A little learning is a dangerous thing." Though a brilliant writer, Pope was steeped in the humanistic philosophy of the Enlightenment. He wrote, "Know then thyself, presume not God to scan; The proper study of mankind is man."

Another popular English satirist was **Jonathan Swift** (1667–1745). As Pope was a master of verse, Swift was a master of prose. His greatest work, *Gulliver's Travels*, recounts the exciting but strange adventures of a man named Gulliver. Although it has become a favorite children's story, Swift intended the book as a satire on human behavior. He wondered how people with the capacity of reason could be so complacent and inhumane? Swift mistakenly believed that society's problems resulted from man's failure to use his capacity of reason.

Left: Daniel Defoe
Right: Edward Gibbon

Prose writing gained in popularity during this period. The works of two writers in particular helped lead to the development of the modern novel. *Robinson Crusoe* by **Daniel Defoe** and *Pamela* by Samuel Richardson are considered forerunners of this literary form.

Another English writer, **Edward Gibbon** (1737–94), wrote perhaps the most famous historical book of the eighteenth century—the six-volume *Decline and Fall of the Roman Empire*, in which he traced the history of Rome from the reign of Augustus to its eventual overthrow by barbarian tribes. As a lover of classical culture and a critic of Christianity, Gibbon blamed not only the barbarian tribes but also the Christians for Rome's decline. He claimed that Christianity reawakened the fighting spirit of the Romans and caused religious controversy, which brought about internal disorder within the empire.

Section Quiz

1. What artistic age spanning from 1600 to 1750 is characterized by its grand, heroic, sensual, and emotional style?
2. Who was one of the most famous architects of the seventeenth century? What did he design?
3. List two characteristics of the rococo style.
4. Who is the most famous composer of oratorios of this period? What is his best-known and best-loved oratorio?
5. Who wrote *Robinson Crusoe*? Of what literary form was this book a forerunner?

☆ Would Edward Gibbon be an objective source of information about Christianity in the Roman Empire? Why or why not?

Chapter 15 Review

Making Connections

1–2. Distinguish between inductive and deductive reasoning.

3–5. How did the Wesley/Whitefield revivals positively impact Britain and the American colonies? (List three.)

Developing History Skills

1. Evaluate the spiritual impact of the tiny Moravian movement on many areas of the world.
2. Summarize the political ideas of the Enlightenment that influenced the formation of government in the United States following the War for Independence. Include the source of each idea.

Thinking Critically

1. Assess the accuracy of the following statement, "Science is a trustworthy method for gaining knowledge."
2. Hymns, such as those written by Watts or Wesley, play what role in a church service?

Living in God's World

1. How should you as a Christian respond to someone who puts his own reason or his own experience in the place of final judge of what is true and false?
2. Pick a biblical doctrine (look at a basic theology book), do some reading and Bible study about it, and pray about the doctrine. Thank God for it (be specific). Confess any sins that you have done related to it. Make requests to God based on that doctrine. Then write a brief paragraph describing how meditating on a doctrine has affected your relationship with God.

People, Places, and Things to Know

Age of Reason
scientific method
Copernicus
heliocentric theory
Johannes Kepler
Galileo Galilei
Isaac Newton
Andreas Vesalius
Paracelsus
William Harvey
Edward Jenner
Robert Boyle
Joseph Priestley
Antoine Laurent Lavoisier
Enlightenment
rationalism
Francis Bacon
inductive method
René Descartes
deductive method
dualism
Baruch Spinoza
pantheism
John Locke
Montesquieu
Voltaire
Jean-Jacques Rousseau
deism
Pietism
Nikolaus von Zinzendorf
John Wesley
George Whitefield
Great Awakening
Jonathan Edwards
mannerism
El Greco
baroque
Giovanni Bernini
Peter Paul Rubens
Rembrandt van Rijn
neoclassical
polyphony
homophony
Claudio Monteverdi
George Frederick Handel
Johann Sebastian Bach
Franz Joseph Haydn
Wolfgang Amadeus Mozart
Molière
Alexander Pope
Jonathan Swift
Daniel Defoe
Edward Gibbon

16

Attempts at Liberty

Napoleon

People have yearned for true freedom ever since Adam's sin brought bondage to the whole human race. At the time of the Reformation, the Protestant reformers reasserted that true liberty is found only in Jesus Christ. These reformers realized that people did not have to be bound by the traditions of Roman Catholicism. Jesus Christ, by His death on the cross, has secured spiritual liberty for mankind—that is, freedom from the penalty and power of sin.

During the Enlightenment, men asserted that God had provided political liberty as well. Thomas Jefferson stated, "The God who gave us life gave us liberty at the same time." Enlightenment philosophers claimed that man was endowed with certain "natural rights," the most cherished being the rights to life, liberty, and personal property. But in the eighteenth century, few people enjoyed these rights; ecclesiastical and political absolutism was the order of the day. The desire for personal and political liberty, however, prompted a series of revolutions.

This chapter contrasts two eighteenth-century revolutions: the American and the French. Unlike modern revolutions, the so-called American Revolution was a conservative movement tempered by the Protestant background of the colonists. Americans attempted to preserve time-honored traditions of religious and political liberty. The event, therefore, is described more accurately as the War for Independence. The French Revolution, on the other hand, became radical. The French sought to overthrow the power of a corrupt monarchy, aristocracy, and church. Like many later revolutions, the French Revolution did not establish liberty but led to social upheaval and dictatorship.

I. American Struggle to Preserve Liberty

Colonial Liberties

Unlike the French and Spanish settlements in the New World, English settlements were formed by individuals and groups seeking freedom. These people sought to escape oppression, poverty, and absolutist governments. Some people, of course, sought adventure; others sought wealth. Most of the early settlers, however, came to the New World seeking a haven from religious persecution in Europe. At great personal cost, they left their homelands for a wilderness where they hoped to begin a new life—a life grounded in religious and political liberty.

In 1620, a group of English Separatists called **Pilgrims** set sail for America. They sought a land where they would be free to worship God without government opposition. Though they had been granted permission to settle in the Virginia Colony, navigational errors and storms forced them north to Massachusetts. There they settled and founded the Plymouth Colony. From the outset, the Pilgrim leaders realized the need for discipline to maintain order among themselves because they knew that unrestrained liberty leads to anarchy. While still aboard the *Mayflower*, they drafted a temporary agreement called the **Mayflower Compact**, establishing civil authority for the Plymouth Colony.

A replica of the Mayflower, *the ship that brought the Pilgrims to North America*

> Having undertaken, for the glory of God, and advancement of the Christian faith, and honor of our king and country, a voyage to plant the first colony in the northern parts of Virginia, [we] do by these presents [witnesses] solemnly and mutually in the presence of God, and of one another, covenant and combine ourselves together into a civil body politic, for our better ordering and

preservation and furtherance of the ends aforesaid; and by virtue hereof to enact, constitute, and frame such just and equal laws, ordinances, acts, constitutions, and offices, from time to time, as shall be thought most meet and convenient for the general good of the colony, unto which we promised all due submission and obedience.

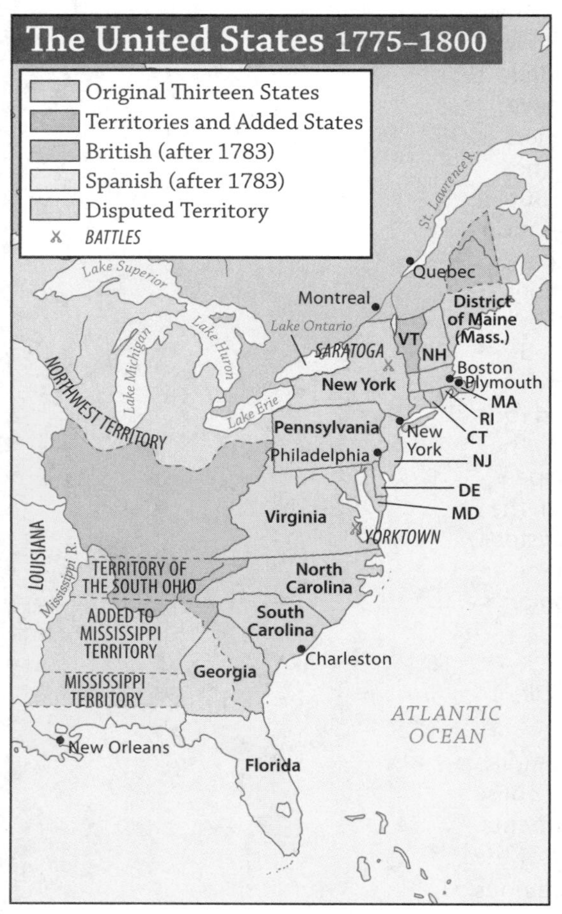

Ten years after the Pilgrims landed at Plymouth, a steady migration of Puritans crossed the Atlantic. They, too, longed for a land where they could freely practice their religion. In 1630, under the leadership of Governor John Winthrop, more than one thousand Puritan men and women settled in New England—most in Boston. Like the Pilgrims, these Puritans believed that they had been sent on a divine mission. They sought to establish an ideal state based on biblical principles. The purpose of government, they believed, was to promote piety and restrain evildoers. The state was to assist (not interfere with) the church in molding godly character in the community. But their ideal society eventually failed as later Puritan generations professed, but did not possess, the religious convictions of their parents and grandparents. Nevertheless, Puritan morality and theology had a great impact on the culture of the American colonies.

In addition to the Pilgrims and Puritans, other Englishmen settled along the North American coastline. They were joined by Irish, Scottish, German, Dutch, and French settlers. As the number of colonies grew, so did their differences. Distinctions developed—the natural result of the wide variety of geographic and climatic conditions within the colonies. Each section—from the New England colonies to the middle colonies and down to the southern colonies—developed its own lifestyle and trade pattern; each had a unique appeal for immigrants of different religious and vocational backgrounds.

Even with their diversity, many American colonists shared a common European background and a Protestant heritage. In spite of the colonies' different types of organization, their forms of government were remarkably similar. That similarity often resulted from a common respect for English law and a desire for local self-government.

British Restrictions

Until 1763, English colonists living in America under the authority of the British crown and Parliament enjoyed great freedom and prosperity. But after a series of wars on the European continent (see Chapter 14), the direction of Britain's policy toward its colonies changed. Britain was faced with the development of a worldwide empire that was neither planned nor organized. Furthermore, it was nearly bankrupt because of the cost of the French and Indian War. Britain therefore looked to its colonies to "pay their own way" by making financial contributions to the mother country in exchange for the benefits Britain provided.

Between 1763 and 1774, Parliament passed a series of new laws placing restrictions on colonial trade. The colonists raised their voices in protest while remaining loyal to both king and country. They recognized that Britain provided a bulwark of defense against French and Spanish designs on the West and unfriendly Indians on their frontiers. Furthermore, their objections were not related to the amount of taxes they had to pay because they paid very little in comparison to their English relatives. So what was the cause of their protest? After enjoying nearly 150 years of noninterference, the American colonists resented the new parliamentary measures as an invasion of their internal affairs. They believed that Parliament had overstepped its authority and had violated

Forcing Colonists to House British Troops

To punish the people of Massachusetts for the Boston Tea Party, the British government forced the colonists to quarter (house) British troops in their homes. This was a violation of the English Bill of Rights, which complained about the king "raising and keeping a standing army within this kingdom in time of peace, without consent of Parliament, and quartering of soldiers contrary to law." Thus, the British government was placing an intolerable burden on the colonists in Massachusetts that the British people themselves had refused to endure.

the colonial charters. These charters specified that all powers of taxation rested with the colonial assemblies, not with the houses of Parliament. Thus the issue was not the amount of the taxes but who should levy and collect taxes. "No taxation without representation" became a popular rallying cry in the colonies.

In December 1773, colonial opposition to parliamentary acts escalated to action. Under the cover of night, a group of colonials dressed as Indians dumped a shipload of tea into Boston Harbor to protest a new tax on tea. In response to the "Boston Tea Party," Parliament closed the port of that vital colonial city to all shipping. Other laws reduced colonial liberties in Massachusetts. Martial law was imposed, and the colonists were forced to house and financially support the British troops sent to enforce the unwanted edicts of **George III** and Parliament. The colonials viewed such acts as intolerable.

Another act that alarmed the colonists was the Quebec Act. Parliament extended special privileges to the territory of Quebec, a former French colony, by granting favored status to Roman Catholicism and reinstating French law. The colonists perceived this act as a dangerous precedent that could pose a threat to their religious and political freedom.

The American colonists protested these acts and expected to see these new laws repealed since previously Parliament had backed down after firm colonial resistance. But now the louder the colonial protest grew, the more British troops arrived to enforce the decrees of the king and Parliament. A growing number of colonists viewed armed resistance as the only option to defend their homes from the British troops sent to oppress them. They began to stockpile munitions in the event that such resistance proved necessary. When the British learned of one such stockpile, they sent troops to destroy it. Along the way, these troops encountered colonial militiamen, and two skirmishes ensued at Lexington and Concord near Boston in April 1775. Thus began a war that neither side had planned or desired.

Concord Bridge, where the first shots of the American War for Independence were fired

American Independence

Attitude Toward War

When it became necessary for the colonists to resist the British invasion, they did so reluctantly, reservedly, but purposefully. They did not seek a rebellion or a war. Nevertheless, they believed that their English rights had been violated, and many refused to bow to parliamentary pressure, despite the threat of military force. But not all colonists favored armed resistance against Britain. Though they disliked British interference in colonial matters, these colonists remained loyal subjects.

Reenactment of the fighting between the colonists and the British

The Christians in the colonies were also divided in their views of resistance. Many believed that they should be loyal to their elected representatives in the colonial legislatures. Therefore, when their elected representatives called for opposition to the edicts of Parliament and king, those Christians were able to support the colonial cause in good conscience. Other Christians, however, believed that their first loyalty lay with the British government in London. When war began, many of them sided with Britain.

Before fighting broke out, few colonists had thoughts of separating from Britain. But as fighting continued, the mood among the colonists gradually changed. Their cause became a struggle to preserve their freedom and to secure independence from Britain. This spirit was clearly stated on July 4, 1776, in the **Declaration of Independence**. That document, written primarily by Thomas Jefferson and adopted by the Continental Congress, declared firmly,

> That these United Colonies are, and of Right ought to be, Free and Independent States; that they are Absolved from all Allegiance to the British Crown, and that all political connection between them and the State of Great Britain, is and ought to be totally dissolved; and that as Free and Independent States, they have full power to levy War, conclude Peace, contract Alliances, establish Commerce, and to do all other Acts and things which Independent States may of right do.

Course of the War

The fighting, which broke out more than a year before the signing of the Declaration of Independence, dragged on for seven years. During the early years of the conflict, it seemed as though Britain would crush American resistance. The small and poorly-equipped American army suffered great hardships and often had to retreat from the more numerous British forces. The American cause, however, was strengthened by the determined leadership of General **George Washington**. Also, the American soldiers were fighting for their homes and freedom. These proved to be strong personal motivations that the British troops, many of whom were German mercenaries, could not match.

The turning point in the war came in October 1777, when the American forces won a major victory over the British at Saratoga, New York. After hearing of that victory, France openly declared its support for the American cause and provided the colonies with badly needed aid. (Later, Spain and the Netherlands also entered the war against Britain.) At Yorktown, Virginia, in 1781, the combined French and American forces forced the British army commanded by Lord Cornwallis to surrender. When news of the surrender reached London, the British government, which was involved in a struggle with the French, Dutch, and Spanish around the world, was willing to bring the war to an end.

Emanuel Leutze, Washington Crossing the Delaware, *Metropolitan Museum of Art, New York*

After two years of negotiations, the **Treaty of Paris** (1783) was signed. The British made many concessions to the Americans—many more than they could have anticipated. Most important, though, they officially acknowledged the independence of the American colonies. The Americans had won their war for independence. Theirs was the first significant revolution of the era; it was also the only one on such a large scale that was successful. Its success was due in large part to its conservative nature, rather than a rebellious nature. Its protest was not against government as such but against too much government and a government that had violated its own rules. The colonists did not fight an offensive war; they simply defended their homeland and fought to preserve the freedoms they had enjoyed for more than a century.

Constitutional Republic

After the war, the American colonists had their independence, but they lacked a strong national government. At first, they organized themselves as independent states in a weak confederation. Under the Articles of Confederation, however, the states had so much power that the central government was ineffective. In 1787, delegates from the various states met to amend the Articles. Instead, they adopted a new constitution.

After carefully examining the strengths and weaknesses of governments throughout history, the delegates to the Constitutional Convention chose a republican form of government modeled after the Roman Republic. They divided the powers of government among three branches: executive, legislative, and judicial. To ensure that no one branch became too powerful, they gave each branch specific functions and specific checks on the other branches.

To remedy the problems they experienced under the Articles, the convention established the principle of **federalism**, delegating specified powers to the national government and reserving all other powers for the state governments or the people. They sought to give the central government sufficient power to function on behalf of the mutual interests of the states. At the same time, they left to the states the freedom to act in matters affecting their individual interests.

Independence Hall, Philadelphia

The framers of the Constitution stressed such concepts as **popular sovereignty** (government based on the consent of the governed) and the "natural rights" of all men. In this regard, they reflected the influence of the Enlightenment. But while Enlightenment philosophy taught that man was essentially good, the constitutional fathers had a healthy fear of human nature and the power of government. Their Protestant-Puritan heritage taught them that man could not be trusted.

Although the new Constitution placed checks and balances on the federal government, it contained no specific guarantees that government would protect the personal and religious liberties for which the Americans had fought so valiantly. Many leaders refused to support ratification of the new Constitution unless such provisions were added. Therefore, the constitutional leaders promised that among the first acts of the new Congress would be the introduction of several amendments to the Constitution. The first ten amendments, called the **Bill of Rights**, clearly defined these liberties and placed restraints on governmental interference. The most cherished personal liberties were listed in the first amendment:

> Congress shall make no law respecting an establishment of religion, or prohibiting the free exercise thereof; or abridging the freedom of speech or of the press; or the right of the people peaceably to assemble and to petition the government for redress of grievances.

The Constitution, formally adopted in 1789, established a new nation—the United States of America. Under this constitution, American citizens enjoyed greater freedom and prosperity than any other people on earth. From the days of their early settlement, through their difficult years of war, in the framing of their government, and in the developing of their new nation, many Americans looked to God for guidance, deliverance, and strength.

Section Quiz

1. In spite of the diversity of American colonists, what is one characteristic they had in common?
2. Following the Seven Years' War, what did England expect from its colonies in exchange for the benefits England provided?
3. What was at the root of the colonial protest against the actions of Parliament?
4. What battle fought in October 1777 was the turning point in the War for Independence? What European country openly supported the American cause as a result of this victory?
5. What word describes the aspect of government that delegates specific powers to the national government and reserves all other powers for the state and/or local governments?

★ Why were the American colonies able to defeat the strongest power in Europe?

II. French Destruction of the Old Regime

During most of the eighteenth century, France was the cultural center of Europe. European monarchs imitated the French absolutist government; they fashioned their royal courts after Versailles. French fashion, art, and learning became the envy of Europe. France had one of the largest populations and one of the most active trade economies in Europe. But beneath the surface of this seeming prosperity were roots of unrest and turmoil. French *philosophes* had espoused the ideas of personal rights and liberties. However, under the authority of an absolute monarch and the domination of the Roman Church, few

Frenchmen enjoyed such freedom. "When the righteous are in authority," Solomon wrote, "the people rejoice: but when the wicked beareth rule, the people mourn" (Prov. 29:2).

The Enlightenment had raised expectations of reform in French government and society. The American War for Independence gave hope to Frenchmen who desired the same freedoms for themselves. Yet the French political and social order remained the same. In addition, extravagant government spending and oppressive taxation brought the country to the brink of economic collapse. Such were the conditions in France on the eve of the French Revolution.

Reasons for Discontent

Of the many factors that contributed to the French Revolution, none by itself was sufficient motivation for revolt. But when linked together, they stirred widespread discontent with the **Old Regime** (the name given to the political and social order in France before the French Revolution). Revolution was only a short step away.

Social Inequality

As late as 1789, French society was still organized according to the old feudal class divisions of estates. The inequality of social privileges and taxation, which were determined by one's social class, caused deep-seated resentment among the underprivileged.

The **First Estate** consisted of the clergy of the Roman Catholic Church. (Since the revocation of the Edict of Nantes in 1685, the Roman Catholic Church had been the only recognized church in France.) The church had great wealth: it controlled vast land estates and was exempt from taxation. It used part of that wealth to provide education and to care for the sick and needy; yet many of the upper clergy (such as the bishops) considered the church's wealth to be their own. The wealthy clergy made up part of the aristocratic group that often advised the king in state matters. However, the lower clergy (the parish priests) were poor or, in some cases, destitute.

The nobility made up the **Second Estate**. They, too, were a privileged class. Nobles were exempt from many of the taxes levied by the French king. They also held some of the highest positions in government and society. In addition, the nobility owned vast estates, amounting to an estimated 40 percent of the land in France. Most of the nobles, however, were not interested in improving their land but were concerned only with exploiting it. Many nobles lived extravagantly at Versailles and paid agents to extract as much as they could from the impoverished tenants who lived on their estates. Because nobles could lose their titles for participating in trade, they sought to increase their income by assuming the best and most financially rewarding posts in the army, church, and legal professions. Many of the nobles who took such posts did not do any of the work that their positions demanded; they let others do the work while they drew the income.

Population of France in 1789

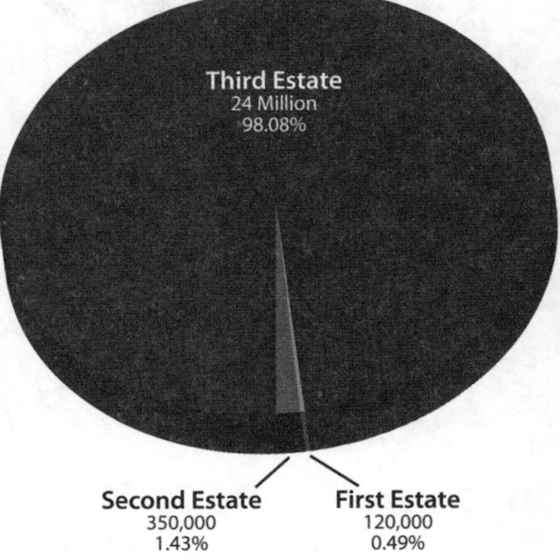

The **Third Estate** was by far the largest class, comprising 98 percent of the French population. Of the three estates, this class had the greatest social and economic diversity among its members. It was subdivided into three groups. At the top were the lawyers, doctors, bankers, and wealthy businessmen. Below them came the workers in the cities and towns. At the bottom of the social structure were the peasants, who comprised about 80 percent of the population. Although some of the peasants owned their land, the majority were extremely poor, working as tenants on the large estates of the wealthy elite. Although their wages were low and they generally had few material possessions, the peasants bore the heaviest tax burden. In addition, the peasants suffered under lingering feudal obligations. They were required to do the following:

1. Pay an annual fee to the noble who owned the land on which they lived and worked.
2. Pay a fee to the former owner when the land changed hands.
3. Pay an annual fee for the use of mills, ovens, and winepresses, even if they did not use them.
4. Perform the *corvée*—a system of forced labor. During the Middle Ages, the peasants had performed the *corvée* for their feudal lord. In eighteenth-century France, the peasants worked for the government, building and maintaining roads and canals.
5. Respect the nobles' hunting privileges. From ancient times, the nobles had been allowed unlimited freedom to hunt, unhindered by property rights. Peasants, however, were forbidden to kill rabbits, crows, or foxes even if these animals ruined their crops.

Political Inefficiency

Louis XVI at the age of twenty in 1775

Neither King Louis XV (r. 1715–74) nor King **Louis XVI** (r. 1774–92) had the character or inclination to rule France in the absolute fashion of Louis XIV. They were indifferent to the affairs of government. They had little sense of responsibility, being more interested in the frivolous pleasures of life at Versailles. When they did turn their attention to matters of state, they often followed the capricious advice of their mistresses or fell prey to the intriguing schemes of the nobles in their court. Local rulers still imposed old feudal obligations, increasing their power while further restricting the freedom of the French people. The central government, which should have been a unifying force, was thus incompetent and inefficient.

The different social groups, hoping to take advantage of this confused situation, were eager to assume political power. The nobles thought that Louis XIV had unlawfully deprived their ancestors of their positions of authority. The middle class, well versed in Enlightenment thinking, wanted political power equal to their economic wealth. The lower classes resented their unfair burden of oppressive taxation in addition to numerous outdated feudal obligations.

Economic Irresponsibility

Unbalanced Tax System—As previously mentioned, the French system of taxation was grossly out of balance. The privileged classes were exempt from most taxation. Those who had the least—the peasants—bore the greatest part of the tax burden. The peasants resented not only the unequal assessment of tax obligations but also the wasteful manner in which the tax money was used.

The most common and important taxes levied by the French government were the *taille*, the *capitation*, and the *vingtième*. The *taille*, originally levied for military purposes, was a tax on real and personal property; the *capitation*, or poll tax, was a tax on each person; and the *vingtième* was an income tax. Some of the nobles, clergy, and wealthy middle class either purchased or were granted exemptions from many of these taxes. Others, because of their privileged status, evaded their tax responsibilities altogether. Their failure to share the tax burden not only increased the financial strain on the peasants but also reduced the income the government received and thus contributed to the national debt.

Virtual Bankruptcy—Despite levying heavy taxes, the French government continued to sink deeper into debt. The successors of King Louis XIV continued to wage war and spend extravagantly. Louis XV plunged France into the Seven Years' War, which cost France most of its colonies and overseas trade. Louis XVI, who had no sympathy for the American colonists' cause, nevertheless aided the Americans in hopes of weakening Britain. In addition, both monarchs continued to spend money from the public treasury for their personal luxuries at Versailles.

To reduce the national debt, the French government levied more taxes, debased the French currency, and borrowed more money from private banks. But these steps only increased the financial problems. To make matters worse, no one knew exactly how much money the government actually needed to pay its bills since France did not have a budget. Finally, in 1787, the private banks refused to extend any more credit to the French government. This financial crisis paved the way for the outbreak of the revolution.

Beginning of the Revolution

Calling of the Estates-General

From the beginning of Louis XVI's reign, able finance ministers had tried to solve France's economic problems. They told Louis that no money remained in the treasury and urged him to tax those who were paying no taxes. Louis, however, was a weak king who did not wish to offend anyone. Therefore, when the economic proposals of his finance ministers proved to be highly unpopular with the nobility, Louis dismissed his ministers. The nobles accused Louis of mismanagement and said that only the Estates-General could change the tax laws. That representative body, however, had not met since 1614. Desperate to find a solution to France's economic problems, Louis sent out a decree instructing the people to choose representatives for a meeting at Versailles in May 1789. He told the people to give their deputies lists of grievances (called ***cahiers***) that they wanted the king to consider. Little did he realize what trouble he had invited.

The Opening of the Estates General at Versailles, May 5, 1789.

Helman, Isidore S.H. (1743-1809). Bibliotheque Nationale, Paris, France. Erich Lessing/Art Resource, NY

In towns and villages across France, the people met to choose deputies to represent them at Versailles. Excitement ran high at the meetings of the Third Estate. Led by the educated middle class, the people drew up their *cahiers*. Their lists of grievances were similar from province to province; most called for a written constitution, equal taxation, equal justice, and the destruction of the remnants of feudalism. The First and Second Estates chose deputies too. For the most part, their *cahiers* contained ideas different from those of the Third Estate. They did, however, call for a constitution that would stop the king from infringing on their rights and privileges.

Convening of the Estates-General

The deputies made their way to Versailles in late April 1789. They arrived armed with their *cahiers*, fully expecting the king to listen carefully to their complaints and to right the wrongs so readily apparent in French society. The deputies of the Third Estate, however, were soon disillusioned. At the formal reception given by the king, he kept them waiting for hours. Unlike the richly attired nobles and clergy, they had to dress in black, keep their hats off, and enter the hall through a side door. When they were finally presented to the king, Louis XVI stood in silence as they filed by.

The opening meeting on May 5 was also a disappointment. Louis XVI, instead of assuring the deputies that he would be interested in their ideas for reform, was noncommittal. His only instructions were that they should meet as estates and vote as estates—each estate receiving one vote.

The deputies of the Third Estate objected. They wanted each delegate's vote to be counted separately, regardless of his estate. They would thus have the majority vote because the deputies of the Third Estate outnumbered those of the First Estate 578 to 291; the Second Estate had only 270 deputies. They realized that if each estate received only one vote, their reforms had little chance of passing. The First and Second Estates were not interested in the grievances of the Third Estate; thus, the Third Estate could be outvoted two to one.

The Tennis Court Oath

The National Assembly, considering that it has been summoned to establish the constitution of the kingdom, to effect the regeneration of public order, and to maintain the true principles of monarchy; that nothing can prevent it from continuing its deliberations in whatever place it may be forced to establish itself; and, finally that wheresoever its members are assembled, there is the National Assembly; Decree that all members of this assembly shall immediately take a solemn oath not to separate, and to reassemble wherever circumstances require, until the constitution of the kingdom is established and consolidated upon firm foundations.

John H. Stewart, A Documentary Survey of the French Revolution, *88.*

Forming of the National Assembly

The disagreement over voting continued until June 17, when the delegates of the Third Estate proclaimed themselves the National Assembly. Since they were sent by the people, they claimed to speak for the people. These delegates asserted the principle of popular sovereignty and denounced the unfair social order of France. They invited the members of the other two estates to join them, and a few did.

On June 20, when the members of the Third Estate arrived at their assembly room, they found the doors locked. Undaunted, the deputies gathered in the nearby royal indoor tennis court. There they adopted the famous **Tennis Court Oath**, declaring that they would not disband until a written constitution was established.

Three days later, at a joint meeting of the Estates-General, Louis again stated his opposition to a meeting of the three estates as a group unless it was for the purpose of raising taxes. While he made some reforming concessions, he insisted that the "old distinction" between the estates be maintained. He then dismissed the deputies and left. Most of the members of the First and Second Estates left with him, but the deputies of the Third Estate remained. By then, they were defiant.

Tennis Court Oath, June 20, 1789

The Oath of the Jeu de Paume, when the Three Estates refused to disband upon royal orders. June 29, 1789. Musée de la Ville de Paris, Musée Carnavalet, Paris, France. Erich Lessing/Art Resource, NY

The Storming of the Bastille, July 14, 1789, *by an unknown artist, depicts the arrest of the governor of the prison.*

When the king's messenger returned to tell them to go home, one of their leaders said, "Go and tell those who sent you that we are here by the will of the people and that we will go only if we are driven at the point of the bayonet!" When this message was conveyed to the king, he responded, "Well, let them stay."

On June 27, Louis ordered the First and Second Estates to join the National Assembly, which now called itself the National Constituent Assembly. The Assembly immediately set about to draw up a constitution. For a while it looked as if the king had surrendered to the Third Estate. However, he had not. On the advice of some members of his court, he ordered troops to Versailles and Paris, supposedly for protection. What he actually had in mind was to close down the Assembly. This double-mindedness was typical of Louis. He did not hesitate to change his mind to keep the peace or avoid offending someone. Like the "double minded man" of James 1:8, Louis was foolishly indecisive.

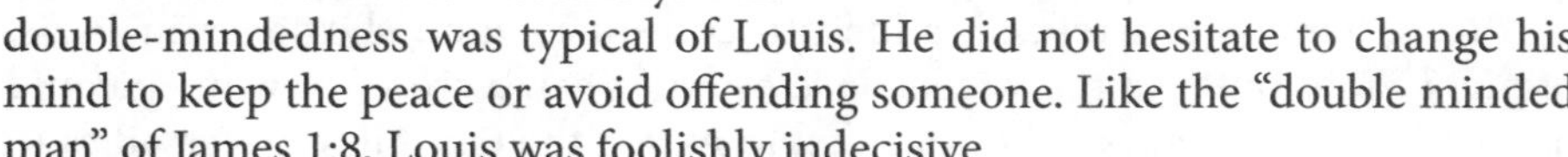

Storming of the Bastille

On July 12, Paris became the scene of rioting and looting by angry mobs. Angered by both high prices for bread and rumors that Louis's troops intended to murder them, the Parisians began searching for weapons to defend themselves. The disturbance lasted well into the next day, when the mob heard that arms were stored at the Hôtel des Invalides (a hospital for soldiers) and the Bastille (a royal prison for political prisoners). On the morning of July 14, 1789, part of the mob stormed the Invalides; others laid siege to and captured the Bastille. When the gates to the Bastille were opened, the mob stormed in and murdered the governor of the prison and his men.

The storming of the Bastille was the action of a frenzied mob. Yet it came to symbolize the downfall of the Old Regime. When Louis heard of the incident, he said, "This is a revolt." His aide replied, "No, Sire. This is a revolution!"

Phases of the Revolution

Destruction of the Old Regime

The storming of the Bastille intensified uprisings throughout the French countryside. Peasants unleashed their frustration by plundering the homes of the nobility and destroying the feudal records that obligated them to service. In hope of stemming fear and halting the increasing violence, the National Constituent Assembly passed legislation that made sweeping changes in French society, bringing the Old Regime to an end. From 1789 to 1791 the Assembly passed more than two thousand laws. One of the first steps it took was to abolish feudalism. Many of the nobles in the Assembly, frightened by the peasant uprisings, renounced their feudal rights and privileges.

Most prominent among the Assembly's early actions was the adoption of the **Declaration of the Rights of Man** on August 27, 1789. This declaration derived its ideas partly from the English Bill of Rights; partly from the ideas of

Montesquieu, Locke, and Rousseau; and partly from the American Declaration of Independence. In the Declaration of the Rights of Man, the Assembly listed what it considered to be the natural rights of all people and the rights that they possessed as citizens.

> Men are born and remain free and equal in rights. Social distinctions can be based only on public utility.
>
> The aim of every political association is the preservation of the natural and imprescriptible rights of man [rights that cannot be taken away]. These rights are liberty, property, security, and resistance to oppression. . . .
>
> Liberty consists in the power to do anything that does not injure others. . . .
>
> Law is the expression of the general will. All citizens have the right to take part personally or by their representatives in its formation. It must be the same for all, whether it protects or punishes. . . .
>
> Every individual [is] presumed innocent until he has been proved guilty.
>
> No one should be disturbed because of his opinions, even in religion.

Louis, however, refused to give his consent to the recent legislation passed by the Assembly. His refusal, added to continued food shortages in Paris, brought mobs out into the streets once more. When a crowd of women could not get bread at a bakery, they decided to march the ten miles to Versailles to protest their plight. Their number swelled to several thousand. En route, they were joined by many French soldiers. On reaching Versailles, they burst into the meeting of the Assembly and demanded bread. Getting little satisfaction there, a group of the marchers broke into the royal palace the next day and murdered two of the king's guards. They insisted that the royal family accompany them back to Paris. The king gave in, and he and his family traveled back to Paris. A few days later, the delegates of the Assembly moved to Paris as well.

In response to this latest uprising, Louis gave his approval to the decrees of the Assembly. But the problem that had ignited the Revolution—France's bankruptcy—had not been solved. In fact, it had become worse. The people refused to pay the king's tax collectors, and the Assembly had not devised any new system of tax collection. Finally, the Assembly came up with a solution. Since the Roman Catholic Church possessed great quantities of land, the Assembly confiscated it. The Assembly then issued paper money, called *assignats*, which was backed by the value of that land. They used these *assignats* to pay off the debts of the government.

In addition to seizing the Roman Church's lands, the Assembly passed the **Civil Constitution of the Clergy** (July 1790). This bill placed the church under state control, provided for the election of all the clergy by the people, and required the clergy to take an oath of loyalty to the state. When the pope condemned the constitution, many clergy refused to take the oath. As a result, two groups of Roman Catholic clergy arose in France: juring clergy (those who took the oath) and nonjuring clergy (those who did not take the oath). In many areas of France, the people would not recognize the juring clergy. Thus, while the Assembly had weakened the influence of the Roman Catholic Church in France, it had antagonized many of the French Roman Catholics, creating yet another problem.

Overthrow of the Monarchy

Although 1790 was a rather peaceful year by revolutionary standards, 1791 proved to be another turbulent year. The king, seeing his powers being taken away and fearing for his life, tried to escape from France. Once out of the country, he hoped to enlist the aid of foreign monarchs and restore his power in France. He and his family disguised themselves and slipped out of the palace on the night of June 20, 1791. Their carriage was almost to the border when they were recognized by a postmaster. They were captured and escorted back to Paris by an armed guard.

In September, the National Constituent Assembly completed the constitution over which it had labored for two years. The document restructured the French government. The king's power, formerly absolute, was now limited by a constitution. The constitution also guaranteed equal taxes, ended special privileges, created a balanced system of justice, and established a new governing body called the Legislative Assembly. Louis was compelled to agree to this constitution, and he issued a proclamation calling on all Frenchmen to support it.

Problems of the Legislative Assembly—In October 1791, the Legislative Assembly convened for the first time. Its newly elected members had no experience in governing France. In addition, the body was divided into several factions. One group of legislators wanted to maintain the limited monarchy as established by the constitution. Because they were satisfied with the accomplishments of the revolution and sought no further changes, they were known as the conservatives. Another group wished to rid France of the monarchy completely and to establish a republic in its place. These radicals advocated sweeping changes in the government. The third group, the moderates, sided with the conservatives on some issues and with the radicals on others.

Few Frenchmen supported the new government. The king and some of the nobility and clergy hoped to restore the Old Regime. Other Frenchmen, however, believed that the Revolution had not gone far enough. They wanted even more reforms. Some of them wanted to abolish the monarchy. The **Jacobins** advocated the most radical changes. (They took their name from an empty Jacobin convent that they used for meetings.) Although the Jacobins gathered followers from all over France, the group in Paris became the most influential. Its most prominent leaders were **Jean-Paul Marat** (mah RAH), **George-Jacques Danton**, and **Maximilien de Robespierre** (ROHBZ pee EHR).

The Death of Marat *by Jacques-Louis David*

To achieve their radical goals, the Jacobins often stirred up mobs in the cities, especially in Paris. Jacobin rabble-rousers appealed to Paris workers known as the *sans-culottes*—literally, "without breeches." (Unlike the men of the upper and middle classes, the men of these lower classes did not wear fashionable knee breeches but full-length trousers.) The Jacobins believed that the new constitution favored only the middle class. They wanted a greater share of French wealth for themselves and more power in the French government.

War with Austria and Prussia—In April 1792, the Legislative Assembly, backed by the king, declared war on Austria. (From this time until the final defeat of Napoleon in 1815, there was almost constant war in Europe.) Each political faction within France had a different reason for wanting war. The king, for example, hoped that Austria would defeat the Assembly's forces and come to his rescue.

Right, Left, and Center

Three terms used today to describe various political philosophies originated, surprisingly, from the seating arrangement in the French National Assembly. When that legislative body first convened, a group called the Girondins sat on the speaker's right. The conservatives of their day, the Girondins were satisfied with the Constitution of 1791 and wished to see it preserved. The Jacobins, on the other hand, wanted the king removed and a republic introduced. Those who espoused that liberal philosophy sat on the speaker's left. The moderates, who wanted some (but not radical) changes, were seated between the Girondins and the Jacobins. From this arrangement, we derive our terms *right* for conservatives, *left* for liberals, and *center* for moderates.

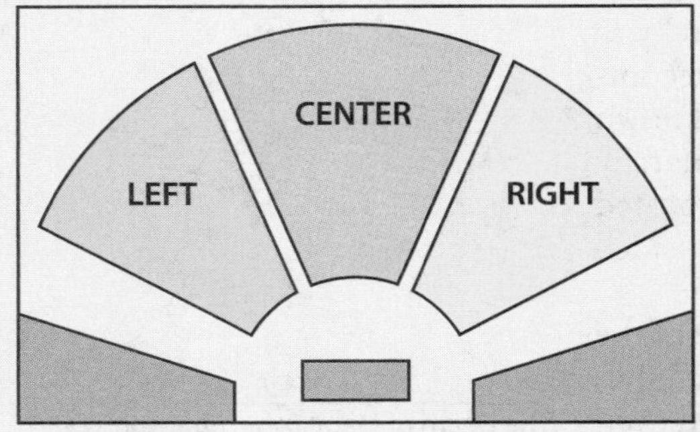

The Assembly hoped that a quick defeat of Austria would gain the French people's support for their government. The Jacobins, however, did not want war; they feared that a French victory would end their hopes of seizing power. Therefore, Marat and Danton deliberately sabotaged the war effort by delaying requests for army supplies.

Things did not go well for France early in the war. Prussia soon joined with Austria. The Austrian and Prussian armies, under the leadership of the Duke of Brunswick, invaded France. In July 1792, the Duke issued the **Brunswick Manifesto**, calling on the French people to rally behind their king and protect him from the leaders of the Revolution. He threatened to punish those who harmed the king and promised that he would restore Louis XVI to authority when Paris was captured.

Execution of the King—The Brunswick Manifesto, along with early military defeats, made the people of Paris distrustful of Louis. On August 10, 1792, a mob under the leadership of Danton invaded the palace and murdered the king's Swiss guards. (Louis temporarily found refuge with the Assembly.) The mob demanded that the Legislative Assembly call for another convention to write a new constitution for France. Facing tremendous pressure from the radicals, the Assembly called for elections to a new body that was to be called the National Convention.

In August and September, while new deputies were being chosen, Danton became the virtual dictator of France. During this time, many supporters of the monarchy met violent deaths by the radical mobs. In September, widespread massacres took place. Mobs emptied the prisons of nobles and nonjuring clergy who were suspected of working against the Revolution—mercilessly slaughtering them.

On September 22, the newly elected National Convention abolished the monarchy and proclaimed 1792 to be Year One of the French Republic. The new government, faced with internal disorder and foreign invasion, took action against Louis XVI. Tried and found guilty of treason, the king was sentenced to death. On January 21, 1793, Louis XVI, who had once been called "Good King Louis," was taken by coach to a square in the middle of Paris, where he was led to the guillotine. He was allowed a few last words: "I die innocent," he said; "I pardon those who have occasioned my death." As drums rolled, the blade did its work, and the head of the former king was held up for the crowd to see. The people threw their hats into the air and shouted, "*Vive la nation*!" ("Long live the nation!")

The beheading of Louis XVI

The Reign of Terror

The French Revolution now took an even more destructive and bloody turn. The rebellion and violence in French society were not without their consequences—national suffering was sure to follow.

The Committee of Public Safety—Faced with unrest at home and a critical situation on

The Guillotine

During a debate in the National Assembly about the equality of all Frenchmen, a man named Dr. Joseph Guillotin rose to express his views on capital punishment. Under the Old Regime, he said, nobles received special treatment. When the situation called for their execution, they were decapitated by ax or sword, whereas the common man suffered execution by hanging or burning at the stake. If all Frenchmen were equal, Dr. Guillotin pointed out, all of the condemned should be given a humane means of execution. The Assembly agreed and appointed Dr. Antoine Louis to develop an instrument of execution. After much research and experimentation on sheep and cadavers, he developed the guillotine, which was named for Dr. Guillotin. (The guillotine was not a new instrument. It had been used in Scotland, Germany, and Italy; Dr. Louis just developed a new, streamlined model.) In March 1792 the National Assembly adopted the guillotine as the official instrument of execution in France. In later years of the Revolution, thousands of "equal" Frenchmen mounted the scaffolds to be "shaved by the national barber."

Model of guillotine

Photo: Bulloz. Musée de la Ville de Paris, Musée Carnavalet, Paris, France. Réunion des Musées Nationaux/Art Resource, NY

the battlefront, the National Convention appointed twelve men to take over the everyday affairs of government, particularly the war. With Robespierre as their leader, these men made up the **Committee of Public Safety**. They set about to create a new order in France.

This Committee gave the Revolutionary Tribunal orders to suppress opposition to the Revolution. Anyone suspected of being an "enemy of the people" was arrested. Most suspects, regardless of whether they were guilty, were hastily tried and executed—some were drowned, others were shot, and many more were guillotined. An estimated twenty to forty thousand people died at the hands of the Tribunal. Surprisingly, the largest percentage of those executed were peasants or *sans-culottes*. The slogan of the Revolution—"Liberty, Equality, and Fraternity (brotherhood)"—had become virtually meaningless.

The Committee responded to the looming threat of foreign invaders by mobilizing the entire nation into a unified effort to defeat its enemies. In August 1793 the Committee issued a decree of ***levée en masse***, stating that "the young men shall go to battle; the married men shall forge arms and transport provisions; the women shall make tents and clothes, and shall serve in the hospitals; the children shall turn old linen into lint; the old men shall [go] to the public places to stimulate the courage of the warriors and preach the unity of the Republic and the hatred of kings." This was one of the first instances of a nation calling on all of its citizens to take an active part in the war effort.

The citizen army won a series of victories over the forces of the European **coalition** (a temporary alliance of nations), which was determined to prevent the revolution from spreading throughout Europe. News of the victories reduced the tension back in Paris. Danton and others no longer felt that the Reign of Terror was necessary. Danton appealed to Robespierre to stop the bloodshed, but Robespierre had him arrested as a traitor and then guillotined. Members of the Convention became alarmed when Robespierre stood in the assembly and declared that many traitors were still in their own ranks. "These must be weeded out," he said, "to save the Republic." Fearful for their own lives and weary of the Reign of Terror, the Convention had Robespierre and his followers arrested and sent to the guillotine. Like so many other revolutions, the French Revolution illustrates the saying that "a revolution devours its own." Proverbs 11:5 states, "The wicked shall fall by his own wickedness."

The End of the National Convention—In 1795, a new constitution was enacted, bringing an end to the Convention and establishing the **Directory**. This new government provided for a two-chamber legislature: the Council of Five Hundred and the Council of Ancients. The executive branch was a group of

A British cartoon from 1798 portrays the French Revolution as a devouring monster who, having ravaged the Continent, is attempting to take Britain as well.

five men called the Directors, who were to be nominated by the Council of Five Hundred and elected by the Council of Ancients.

The Directory inherited many problems. Constant warfare had brought France once more to the edge of bankruptcy. Internal unrest was threatening to cause another revolution. As before, various groups worked to overthrow the new government to gain their selfish ends. Although Prussia had made peace with France in 1795, France still faced the threat of Austrian and British forces. The Directory placed the hopes of the defense of France in the hands of a young general named Napoleon Bonaparte.

Napoleon

Section Quiz

1. What name was given to the political and social order in France before the French Revolution?
2. Who bore the greatest tax burden under the French system of taxation?
3. What is the name for the list of grievances that the delegates took to the convening of the Estates-General?
4. List one of the most common grievances listed by the delegates of the Third Estate.
5. What action of the Parisian mob is considered the beginning of the French Revolution?

★ Why did the phrase "Liberty, Equality, and Fraternity" become an empty promise to the average French citizen during the Revolution?

III. The Napoleonic Era

Few individuals have so influenced and dominated the continent of Europe as did **Napoleon Bonaparte** (1769–1821). So strongly did he make his presence felt in Europe that the period from 1796 to 1815 is often called "the Napoleonic Era."

Napoleon was born on the island of Corsica. He attended a military academy in France, and he spent many hours during his early career in the army studying military strategy. He served in the revolutionary army and later distinguished himself when he suppressed a Paris riot in 1795, helping to pave the way for the establishment of the Directory. As a result, the Directors of the new government chose him to lead the French forces against the Austrians. Instead of directly attacking Austria, however, Napoleon launched a campaign in northern Italy, which was under Austrian domination. Fighting by what his opponents called "new rules"—marching at night, fighting on Sundays, and fighting in the rain—he won victory after victory. He exacted a heavy toll on his defeated foes, allowing his poorly equipped soldiers to take booty. In 1797, Austria made peace with France, and Napoleon returned to Paris a hero.

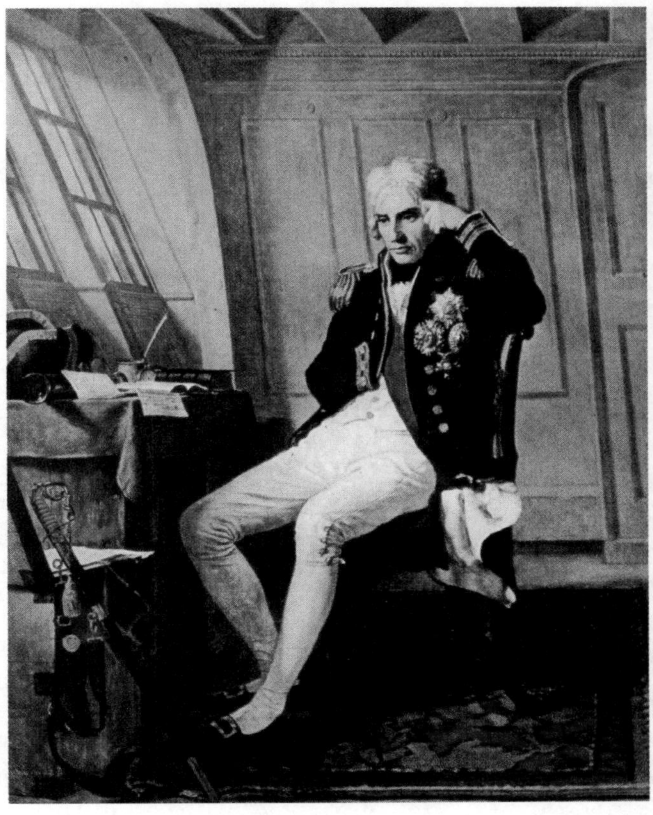
Lord Nelson

Members of the Directory were jealous and fearful of Napoleon's popularity. To get him out of Paris, they directed him to invade England. Rejecting this idea, he decided instead to attack Egypt to cut off Britain's trade with the Near East. In 1798, he invaded Egypt with an army of some thirty-five thousand men. After some early victories by Napoleon, the British fleet under the command of **Lord Nelson** destroyed the French fleet anchored at Alexandria. The British then blockaded Napoleon and his troops in Egypt, cutting them off from needed supplies. In this desperate situation, Napoleon received word that a new European coalition composed of Britain, Russia, Austria, and the Ottoman Turks had been formed to renew the war against France. Leaving his army in Egypt, Napoleon made his way back to France.

Overthrow of the Directory

Napoleon landed in southern France, where crowds welcomed him as a new caesar returning in triumph. (They did not know of his defeats or of the fate of his army in Egypt.) Declaring that he had come to save France, he triumphantly made his way to Paris. Once there, he and his supporters staged a successful ***coup d'état*** (KOO day TAH), a sudden and illegal seizure of power. By the end of 1799, a new government, called the Consulate, was formed under yet another constitution. When Napoleon submitted the constitution to the people for confirmation in a vote called a plebiscite, they overwhelmingly approved. The constitution established a three-man Consulate modeled after the Roman government. The real power, however, was concentrated in the First Consul, Napoleon.

Promising peace and the restoration of internal order, Napoleon first worked to establish peace with France's external foes. After long negotiations, France signed peace treaties with Austria (1800) and Britain (1802).

Meanwhile, Napoleon initiated many domestic reforms. He began public works programs (constructing roads, bridges, and canals); founded the Bank of France, which standardized the monetary system. Napoleon also set up an equitable tax system, which helped to stabilize the national debt. He also established a system of public education supervised by an agency called the University of France. Perhaps his most famous accomplishment was the codification of French laws, later to be named the **Code Napoleon**. Napoleon appointed a commission to systematize the various laws that came out of the Revolution. This code established the civil, criminal, and commercial laws of France, many of which still exist today.

Since most Frenchmen remained loyal Roman Catholics, Napoleon realized that he could increase his popularity and influence by restoring certain privileges to the Roman Catholic Church. Therefore, in 1801 he reached an accord with the pope that returned certain lands to the church, allowed seminaries to operate, and permitted church services to be held openly. In addition, the agreement specified that the state would nominate the bishops and pay the salaries of all the clergy. Although Napoleon appeared to restore the role of the Roman Church in France, he undermined this agreement with other laws that were hostile to the church.

Creation of Napoleon's Empire

Napoleon's Crowning

After seizing the French government in 1799, Napoleon worked to increase his personal power. In 1802, he held a plebiscite in which the people overwhelmingly agreed to make him First Consul for life. Then, in 1804, the Senate proclaimed Napoleon the emperor of France. In a spectacular ceremony in Notre Dame Cathedral on December 2, 1804, Napoleon took the imperial crown from the hands of the pope and placed it on his own head. Napoleon's assumption of imperial power officially brought the Republic to an end. France, which had begun the Revolution with the weak rule of an absolute king, now had an ambitious emperor who ruled with absolute power.

Napoleon's Conquests

Napoleon's unbridled ambition would not be satisfied until he became master of all Europe. His chief obstacle, however, was Great Britain. Napoleon began planning an invasion of Britain, but his plans were thwarted by a decisive naval battle in 1805. The British fleet, under the leadership of Admiral Lord Nelson, encountered the French fleet off the Cape of Trafalgar on the southern coast of Spain. Nelson was killed in the ensuing battle, but his fleet ensured Britain's control of the seas by soundly defeating the French.

Abandoning his English invasion, Napoleon launched an all-out campaign against British allies on the Continent. Austria, Russia, and Sweden had joined with Great Britain in 1805 to form the Third Coalition against France. Although outnumbered, Napoleon's army crushed the combined armies of Austria and Russia at Austerlitz. Then, in 1806, Napoleon dissolved the Holy Roman Empire and set up the Confederation of the Rhine, composed of western German states under Napoleon's protection. When Prussia entered the war against France, its armies were likewise defeated.

The Battle of Trafalgar

© National Maritime Museum, Greenwich, UK

Austerlitz—Napoleon's Greatest Triumph

Napoleon Bonaparte was the greatest military commander of his day. He consistently defeated opponent after opponent for almost twenty years. Napoleon's method was to move with speed and flexibility, keeping his forces spread out for easy movement yet close enough to join quickly for battle. Napoleon believed that by concentrating on a single weak point in the enemy's position, he could defeat his opponent. Above all, he planned his campaigns in a daring manner that confused and frustrated his opponents. No battle illustrates Napoleon's military genius more clearly than the Battle of Austerlitz.

In 1805, the French faced the combined armies of Austria and Russia, called the Allies. Napoleon responded by suddenly invading Austria with seventy thousand French troops. He surrounded and captured thirty thousand stunned Austrian troops at Ulm and then turned northward to face the Russians and remaining Austrians. He decided to bait a trap for them. First, Napoleon selected a site near the town of Austerlitz for the battle. Then he made his army appear smaller by sending twenty thousand men one day's march behind him. He ordered his main forces to fall back slowly, luring the Allies forward to the chosen battlefield. Finally, he tempted the Allies to attack the right end of his line by crowding his troops at the foot of a plateau and exposing his line of retreat to the enemy.

Czar Alexander I arrived in the Allied camp and took command of the forces. Seeing the apparently weak French position, he assumed that Napoleon had blundered and ordered an attack. On December 2, the Russian and Austrian forces rolled forward. They planned to swing around the southern end of the French line, cut off Napoleon's retreat, and then crush the French emperor's force—which was exactly what Bonaparte expected them to do.

Napoleon was ready. He had already called back the twenty thousand men he had hidden. As the Allies moved forward, the French retreated from the heights. Meanwhile, an early morning fog covered the movements of the other French forces as they prepared a surprise blow. When the Allies were halfway down the slope chasing the "retreating" French, Napoleon sent his other forces forward in a sharp counterattack. Surprised and confused, the Allies began to give way. The center of the Allied line broke, and the French swept south, "rolling up" the enemy's line and driving them back. Thousands of panicking Russian troops had to flee across frozen lakes whose icy surfaces cracked and broke under their weight. By the end of the day, thousands of prisoners had fallen into French hands, and the Allied armies fell back in disorganized retreat.

The Battle of Austerlitz, December 2, 1805 (detail). Painted 1810.

Chateaux de Versailles et de Trianon, Versailles, France. Erich Lessing/Art Resource, NY

By 1808, Napoleon had truly become the master of the mainland of Europe, and his personal power was at its height. Nevertheless, Great Britain still controlled the seas. Thus, Napoleon could not directly attack the British Isles. Instead, he devised a plan of attack that became known as the **Continental System**. Using his superior land forces, Napoleon attempted to close Europe's ports to British ships. He hoped that such a blockade of British trade would cause the British economy to collapse.

Napoleon's Downfall

As Napoleon's armies swept through Europe, many Europeans initially welcomed the French troops as liberators who had come to free them from the oppression of their absolute rulers. They soon found, however, that Napoleon had merely replaced one form of oppression with another. In many European countries, Napoleon replaced the national rulers with his relatives and demanded that these subject lands furnish him with soldiers and supplies. Napoleon also looted many lands of their national art treasures, which he took back to France. Overall, he showed little concern for their national feelings or interests.

Nationalistic pride soon began to stir across Europe, and people began to seek freedom from French domination. Furthermore, they resisted the Continental System because even though it was aimed at destroying the British economy, they too were suffering from the loss of British trade.

Conflict broke out in the Iberian Peninsula when Portugal violated the blockade against British trade and Spain revolted against the rule of Napoleon's brother. French troops were sent to crush the uprisings, but they met with fierce resistance from small bands of Spanish troops who attacked the French garrisons and then retreated into the hills. These attacks were called ***guerrillas*** (Spanish for "little wars"). In addition, British troops soon landed in Portugal and began a campaign that eventually drove the French out of the peninsula.

Disaster in Russia

The Portuguese were not the only ones who refused to cooperate with the Continental System. In 1810, Russia broke with the system too. When Czar Alexander I refused to suppress British trade, Napoleon declared war on Russia. He amassed a huge army, called the Grand Army, totaling about six hundred thousand men (including many non-French soldiers), and in 1812 invaded Russia.

Napoleon planned to engage the Russians in one decisive battle near their western border. But when the Russians realized that their forces were outnumbered, they slowly retreated, drawing the Grand Army deeper and deeper into Russia. As the Russian army retreated, they burned everything that might be of

value to the enemy and left nothing. (This strategy is called the **scorched-earth policy**.)

Napoleon continued to press on, hoping that if he could capture Moscow, the czar would come to terms. He won several battles along the way, but he could not destroy the Russian army, which kept retreating. Finally, in September 1812, his army reached Moscow. When Napoleon entered the city, he found it abandoned. That night fire swept through the city, destroying most of it. Napoleon remained in Moscow more than a month, thinking that the czar might still surrender. Winter was approaching, however, and Napoleon knew that his troops were clad only in summer uniforms and did not have enough supplies to spend the winter in Moscow. Frustrated, he finally ordered retreat.

Napoleon's Retreat (oil on canvas) by Robert Alexander Hillingford (1825-1904)

Private Collection/Photo © Bonhams, London, UK/The Bridgeman Art Library

As the Grand Army made its way back across the Russian plains, the bitter cold and snow of the Russian winter set in. The Russians, like packs of wolves, picked off the stragglers one by one. At the Berezina River, they burned the bridges, further delaying the French retreat until new bridges could be built. Some Frenchmen tried to swim across the river but froze to death. Napoleon abandoned his army there and sped on to Paris to maintain control of the government before the people heard the dreadful news. In the end, fewer than one hundred thousand of his soldiers returned safely from Russia.

Defeat and Exile

The following year, Napoleon once more persuaded the French people to raise an army to defend his empire against a new coalition of European powers. In a long campaign in 1813, Napoleon's forces were finally defeated at Leipzig, Germany, in what was later called the Battle of Nations. After a series of negotiations, the European Coalition forced Napoleon to abdicate. They allowed him to go to the small island of Elba just off the western coast of Italy. They granted him the title "Emperor of the Isle of Elba," and he agreed to spend the rest of his life on the island.

Battle of Waterloo

Left: Duke of Wellington
Right: Defeated Napoleon in exile

Meanwhile, the European powers met in Vienna to try to restore order to Europe. But in February 1815, while the Congress of Vienna was meeting, word reached them that Napoleon had escaped from Elba and was making his way to Paris. He entered Paris in triumph and once again raised an army to go against the armies of Britain and Prussia. On June 8, 1815, the armies clashed on the plains of Waterloo in what is today Belgium. The allied forces, under the leadership of the British **Duke of Wellington**, won a decisive victory. Napoleon was banished to St. Helena, a little island in the middle of the South Atlantic, where he lived out his days under guard. He died on May 5, 1821, and was buried on the island. In 1840, his body was moved to Paris. Napoleon had said in 1804, "Death is nothing; but to live defeated and inglorious is to die daily." How he must have "died" during those six years on St. Helena!

Section Quiz

1. What is the period of European history from 1796 to 1815 often called?
2. What event officially brought an end to the French Republic? In what year did it occur?
3. What battle illustrates the military genius of Napoleon and is often called his greatest triumph?
4. What country did Napoleon invade in 1812? What policy did that country practice to impede the French invasion?
5. In what battle was Napoleon defeated for the final time? Who led the allied forces?

✯ Why did Napoleon's Continental System fail?

Chapter 16 Review

Making Connections

1–2. Why did Europeans settle in the American colonies? (List two reasons.)

3. Why were those citizens in France who were least able to pay taxes burdened with the most taxes?
4. What factors combined to bring France to the point of revolution? (List two.)
5. Why were French leaders unable to prevent a revolution?

Developing History Skills

1. Summarize the course of the American War for Independence and its potential impact on the United States for the next two centuries. (You may want to look at Chapters 20 and 22 to help develop your answer.)
2. Summarize the course of the French Revolution and its potential impact on the nation for the next two centuries. (You may want to look at Chapters 17 and 21 to help develop your answer.)

Thinking Critically

1. Compare and contrast the American and French Revolutions.
2. Evaluate Napoleon's rule of France. Provide both positive and negative aspects of his rule.

Living in God's World

1. Imagine you are a member of the legislature of France at the time of the French Revolution. Which statements from the Declaration of the Rights of Man would you, as a Christian, need to dissent from? Why?

People, Places, and Things to Know

Pilgrims
Mayflower Compact
George III
Declaration of Independence
George Washington
Treaty of Paris
federalism
popular sovereignty
Bill of Rights
Old Regime
First Estate
Second Estate
Third Estate
Louis XVI
cahiers
Tennis Court Oath
Declaration of the Rights of Man
Civil Constitution of the Clergy
Jacobins
Jean-Paul Marat
George-Jacques Danton
Maximilien de Robespierre
Brunswick Manifesto
Committee of Public Safety
levée en masse
coalition
Directory
Napoleon Bonaparte
Lord Nelson
coup d'état
Code Napoleon
Continental System
guerrillas
scorched-earth policy
Duke of Wellington

VI THE EUROPEAN WORLD

Except for Australia, Europe is the smallest continent in the world. But in cultural, economic, and political influence, Europe ranked second to none in the nineteenth century. Nearly every important nineteenth-century movement in art, politics, and every other field originated in Europe. The Industrial Revolution made Europe the unquestioned economic and military leader of the era. Europe flexed its newfound muscles too. Colonialism in Asia and Africa expanded as producers sought new sources for raw materials and markets for their goods. Europe's Christian heritage, derived from the work of the reformers and men such as Wesley, also spread throughout the world as missionaries carried the gospel to "the uttermost part of the earth." The nineteenth century was indeed the "European century."

1814–15
Congress of Vienna

1832
Reform Bill

1775 | 1800 | 1825

1864–71
Austro-Prussian War
1866–71
Unification of Germany
1856–60
Second
Opium War
1870–71
Franco-Prussian War
1899–1902
Boer War
1850
1875
1900
1925

17

Reaction and Revolution

I. Search for Stability
II. Triumph of Nationalism
III. Protest of Romanticism

France's tricolor flag, adopted during the French Revolution, became a symbol of revolutionary ideas not only in France but also all across Europe.

The spirit of revolution did not cease with the defeat of Napoleon. From 1815 to 1848, violent uprisings continued to break out on the streets of Paris and spread like a virus all over Europe, causing one European statesman to remark, "When France sneezes, all Europe catches cold." The "cold" to which he referred was the desire for freedom that was being stirred by liberalism and nationalism, the longing for independence and local autonomy.

Conservative elements, however, opposed these forces of change. The reactionary rulers of Europe sought to repress reform and restore the social and political order present in Europe before 1789. But their task was not easy. Rulers tried to suppress revolts with their armies; for the most part, they were successful in the early part of the nineteenth century. But they could not stamp out revolutionary ideas. Such ideas found expression in virtually every aspect of European culture—especially in the literature, art, and music of the romantic movement. As a result, the second half of the nineteenth century saw the forces of liberalism and nationalism triumphing over the forces of conservatism.

Top: Portrait of Alexander I of Russia
Bottom: Portrait of Talleyrand

I. Search for Stability

Napoleon had produced a new Europe. His conquests had shattered existing national boundaries and had overthrown ruling families. His military campaigns had unleashed nationalism and liberalism all across Europe. But with his downfall in 1814, Europe was ready for peace; there had been almost continuous fighting for twenty-five years. The victorious nations of the Grand Alliance—Britain, Austria, Prussia, and Russia—were now faced with restoring order and stability in Europe. They decided to convene a congress of European leaders to draw up a settlement.

Congress of Vienna: Restoration of the Old Order

In September 1814, the leading statesmen of Europe gathered in Vienna, Austria. Many European rulers were present, and hundreds of diplomats and their wives from nearly every European country crowded into the city. The **Congress of Vienna** was a glittering social occasion. When the delegates were not involved in the difficult negotiations, they and their wives spent much time at lavish parties, festive balls, and musical performances.

The delegates did not meet in large formal sessions. Most of the negotiations were conducted in small, informal, and often secret gatherings dominated by the spokesmen for the great powers: **Lord Castlereagh** (KASS ul RAY), the foreign minister of Britain; Czar **Alexander I** of Russia; and **Prince Klemens von Metternich**, the Austrian minister of foreign affairs.

Metternich (1773–1859) was the leading figure at the congress. He was a **reactionary** who wished to reverse the trends begun by the French Revolution and restore Europe to its pre-Revolution conditions. So strong was his influence over the congress and later European politics that the period from 1815 to 1848 is called the "Age of Metternich."

Another important figure at Vienna was **Charles Maurice de Talleyrand** (1754–1838). Talleyrand, the representative of defeated France, was a shrewd and opportunistic politician. He had been a delegate to the Estates-General in 1789, a prominent figure in the National Assembly, and later foreign minister under the Directory and Napoleon. He attended the congress as the new foreign minister of the French king Louis XVIII, the restored Bourbon monarch. Talleyrand took advantage of the disagreement among the great powers at the congress to secure a favorable settlement for France.

Delegates to the Congress of Vienna; Talleyrand is seated on the right with his arm resting on the table. Metternich, in white breeches, is standing on the left.

Redrawing the Map of Europe

Many Europeans hoped that the Vienna peace settlement would support some of the rights and freedoms championed by the French Revolution. But the leading diplomats at Vienna were more concerned about restoring order to Europe. They sought to reestablish political stability, maintain the balance of power among the leading European nations, and respond to the revolutionary ideas spread by France.

Safeguards Against France—In dealing with defeated France, the congress was fairly lenient. Members feared that harsh punishment would only infuriate the French and thus hinder any chances of working out a lasting peace in Europe. The congress did, however, strip France of its conquests, reducing its territory to its 1792 borders. In addition, France had to pay indemnities—compensation to other nations for war damages.

Although the members of the congress agreed to this moderate settlement, they still feared the French. To prevent any further acts of French aggression, they sought to encircle France with a buffer of strong powers. They united the Austrian Netherlands (Belgium) with the Dutch Netherlands to form a protective barrier to the north. To the east, they gave Prussia territory along the Rhine River and retained the Confederation of German States established by Napoleon. On France's southern border, they enlarged the Kingdom of Sardinia. (See map on p. 375.)

Restoration of Legitimate Rulers—During his conquests, Napoleon had deposed many European rulers, placing his relatives on their thrones. The congress removed these rulers and, where possible, restored those whom Napoleon had unseated. In France, for example, the monarchy was reestablished, and Louis XVIII was invited to assume the throne of his brother Louis XVI. (Louis XVI's young son, considered "Louis XVII" even though he did not rule, died in prison during the French Revolution.)

Grants of Compensation—The victors of the Napoleonic Wars and those nations that lost territory in the encirclement of France were compensated with additional territory. In return for giving up its holdings in the Netherlands, Austria received territory in northern Italy. Sweden allowed Russia to keep Finland and received Norway in return. (Norway was taken from Denmark, which had sided with Napoleon.) Although Great Britain did not receive any

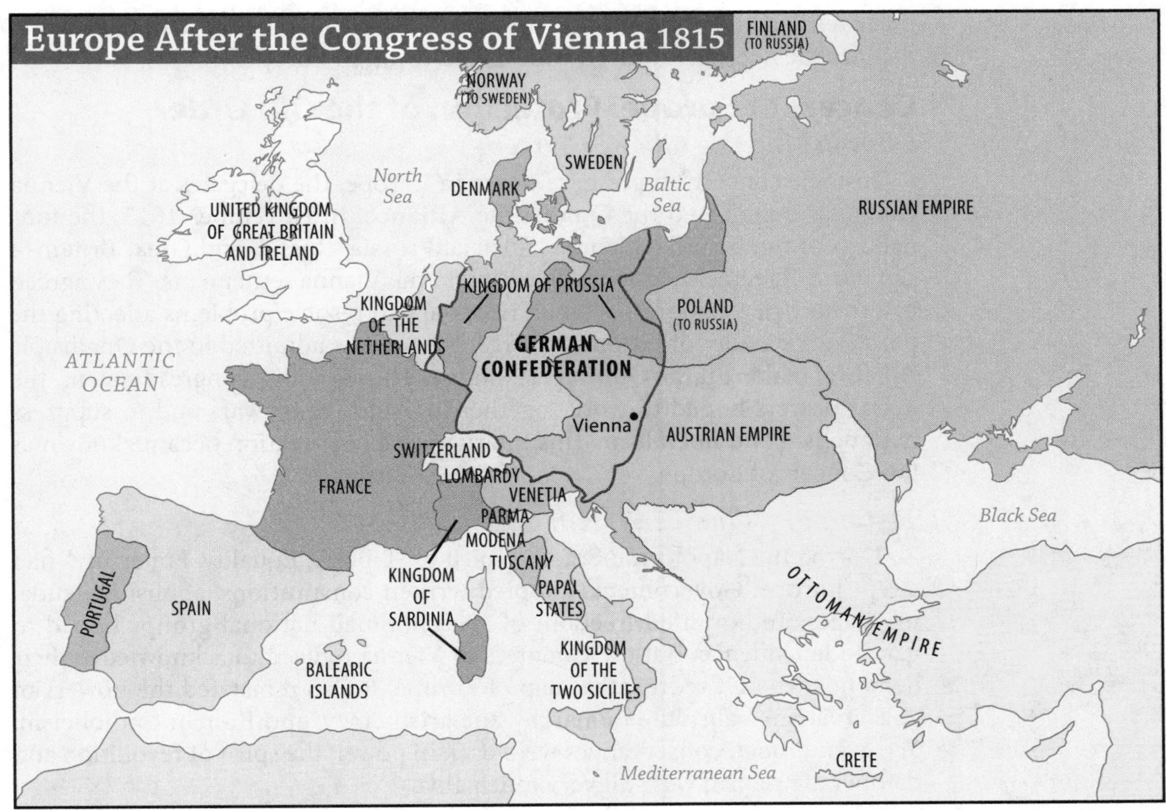

territory on the Continent, it retained control of some French and Dutch colonies seized during recent wars.

Balance of Power—Another chief concern of the Congress of Vienna was to maintain the balance of power in Europe. The delegates wanted to prevent any nation from becoming so strong that it could threaten the security of Europe as France had done. This concern was increased by jealous rivalries among the major European powers. Metternich, for example, was especially fearful of the growing power of Prussia, which threatened Austria's domination over the German Confederation. In addition, the ambition of Czar Alexander I, who claimed all of Poland for Russia, caused further alarm. Talleyrand urged Castlereagh and Metternich to take action, and France, Austria, and Britain signed a treaty pledging to use force if necessary to prevent Prussia or Russia from gaining more power. As a result, both Russia and Prussia backed down from many of their demands.

Final Settlement at Vienna

The congress was close to reaching a final peace settlement in March 1815 when news reached Vienna that Napoleon had left the island of Elba and was on his way to Paris. The leaders of the Grand Alliance decided to unite their armies and once and for all rid Europe of Napoleon. In June, the allied forces, commanded by the Duke of Wellington, defeated Napoleon's army at Waterloo (in present-day Belgium). In the same month, the delegates of the congress put the finishing touches on the peace settlement.

Although the Congress of Vienna had settled the matters of encirclement, legitimacy, compensation, and balance of power, its delegates made few concessions to the causes of nationalism and liberalism. They redrew the map of Europe with little regard for the interests of various national groups. Though the major powers consented to cooperate to prevent a major war, an explosive precedent had been established in Europe. Soon the forces of nationalism and democratic liberalism stirred widespread revolt in Europe.

Concert of Europe: Protection of the Old Order

Establishing the Alliance System

In their concern to preserve peace in Europe, the delegates at the Vienna Congress established the **Quadruple Alliance**. In November 1815, the four nations of the Grand Alliance—Austria, Prussia, Russia, and Great Britain—signed an agreement designed to maintain the Vienna settlements. They agreed to convene new congresses when necessary to resolve problems affecting the peace and stability of Europe. In 1818, France was admitted to the Quadruple Alliance, making it the Quintuple Alliance. Through this "congress system" the major powers hoped to work together to avoid major wars and to suppress nationalism and liberalism. This international cooperation became known as the Concert of Europe.

Testing the Alliance System

During the Napoleonic Era, the spirit of "Liberty, Equality, Fraternity" had swept Europe. Governments adopted written constitutions, abolished feudal privileges, and granted freedom of speech. Small national groups hoped to gain independence. But the Congress of Vienna refused to acknowledge their demands when it redrew the map of Europe. It also reinstated the powers of conservatism—absolute monarchy, the aristocracy, and Roman Catholicism. Yet, even though conservatives were back in power, the spirit of revolution and democratic reform was still very much alive.

Suppressed Revolts in Spain and Italy—Following the defeat of Napoleon, the European leaders reinstated Ferdinand VII as king of Spain. Ignoring the liberal constitution adopted during the revolutionary period—limiting the power of the monarchy and guaranteeing basic freedoms for the people—Ferdinand reintroduced repressive measures to the country. He revived the Inquisition and punished those who spoke out for reform. In 1820 the Spanish people demanded that the king restore the constitution. Ferdinand, having lost the support of the Spanish army, gave in to their demands. The success of the Spanish revolt encouraged a similar uprising in Italy, where the people in the Kingdom of the Two Sicilies forced the king to grant a constitution.

Word of the revolts spread alarm among the rulers of Europe. Metternich feared that one revolution would lead to another and that soon all of Europe would be caught up in the revolutionary fervor. He called for a meeting of the Concert of Europe. At a congress in 1820, the Quintuple Alliance decided to send Austrian troops into Italy to suppress the revolution and restore the king's authority. Two years later, it sent French troops into Spain to crush the revolt. In both instances, the forces of the Quintuple Alliance briefly succeeded at suppressing the will of the people.

Weakness of the Congress System—When the alliance representatives met to settle the uprising in Spain, they also discussed the problem of the Spanish colonies in the New World. Several of the colonies in Latin America had revolted during the Napoleonic Era. By the early 1820s, they had won their independence. Such success, in the eyes of Europe's leaders, set a bad example for Europe. One ardent supporter of monarchical government wrote, "If the New World ever becomes entirely Republican, the monarchies of the Old World will perish!" The congress decided to send troops to help restore the colonies to the Spanish monarchy.

Not every member of the Quintuple Alliance, however, agreed with the plans for intervention in Latin America. Since the Congress of Vienna, Britain had

become disenchanted with the congress system and more sympathetic to liberal reforms. It had not cooperated with the congress in suppressing the Spanish revolt. Now Britain strenuously objected to plans to restore the colonies to the Spanish monarchy. The colonies' independence had broken the Spanish trade monopoly in Latin America. As a result, Britain enjoyed a flourishing trade with that region. Britain threatened to use its navy to stop any European intervention in the New World.

In addition to British objections, U.S. president James Monroe, in a speech to the U.S. Congress, warned the European nations that any attempt to establish or reestablish colonies in the Western Hemisphere would be considered an "unfriendly" act of aggression. Although the United States did not have the power to enforce the **Monroe Doctrine** (1823), the British navy was able to block any attempt on the part of European alliance.

Weaknesses now appeared in the congress system. The Concert of Europe was successful only when it did not infringe on the special interests of one of the major powers. Today, as then, national interests supersede international cooperation. The defection of Britain signaled the decline of the congress system. Although Austria, Prussia, Russia, and France continued to suppress uprisings in Europe, their efforts became considerably less effective.

Success of the Greek Revolt—In 1821, the Greeks rebelled against the Ottoman Empire. During the early years of the struggle, European rulers basically ignored the revolt. It did not immediately affect their national interests. But news of Turkish massacres of the Greek people began to stir the sympathies of Europeans. The Greek struggle captured the imagination of European artists and writers, and it became the subject of many of their works. When the brutal methods of Turkish oppression seemed to doom the cause of Greek freedom, Britain, Russia, and France came to the Greeks' aid. They defeated the Turkish forces and in 1829 secured the Treaty of Adrianople, which recognized Greek independence. The Greek revolt was another example of the weakness of the congress system. In this incident, the major powers of Europe supported the cause of revolution that they opposed at home.

Section Quiz

1. List the four major powers of the Grand Alliance that defeated Napoleon.
2. In what city did representatives of the victorious nations gather to decide how to restore the order and stability of Europe? Who was the leading figure at this congress?
3. The cooperation among the member nations of Europe to avoid wars and to suppress nationalism and liberalism was known as what?
4. Name the two countries where the alliance suppressed uprisings in the 1820s. What country did members of the alliance system assist in its revolt during the 1820s?

★ Why were the Concert of Europe and the congress system doomed to fail?

New Phases of Revolution: Rebellion Against the Old Order

Two leading forces stirring discontent with the old order during the first half of the nineteenth century were liberalism and nationalism. **Liberalism** stressed individual rights such as life, liberty, and property, and personal freedoms such as religion, speech, and the press. Liberals advocated democratic reforms such as written constitutions that guaranteed rights and freedoms and limited the power of autocratic rulers. They promoted parliamentary government and an increased public participation in government.

The middle class were the primary supporters of these liberal goals. They wanted a voice in government equal to their economic influence in society. Joining with the middle class to advance the liberal cause were the masses of urban factory workers and peasants. They, however, often differed with the upper middle class concerning the goals and extent of reform. Instead of the gradual, moderate changes advocated by the middle class, the lower classes often desired more immediate, sweeping changes. They hoped to gain a voice in government to improve their social and economic standing in society.

Closely associated with the cause of personal liberty was the cause of national liberty. A strong spirit of **nationalism** stirred the ambitions of small and large groups alike to seek their independence or to defend their ethnic interests. The cause of nationalism also promoted a strong drive for unification in both the Italian and German states.

Despite the resistance of conservative leaders to political change in Europe, discontent with the old order continued to grow, leading to new revolts. In the early 1830s and again in 1848, a series of revolutions broke out on the Continent. In both instances, the revolutionary fires sparked first in France and soon spread throughout Europe. Although the congress system was no longer effective in dealing with these outbreaks, individual rulers following Metternich's example actively sought to suppress liberalism and nationalism within their borders.

Revolts of the 1830s

When **Louis XVIII** (r. 1814–24) ascended the throne of France following the defeat of Napoleon, he accepted many of the reforms that had come out of the French Revolution. He granted a constitution that guaranteed freedom of the press and religion, ensured equality before the law for all Frenchmen, and set up a legislature similar to the British Parliament. But toward the end of his reign, Louis XVIII began to suppress these liberal trends. He muzzled the press, introduced a secret police, and raised property qualifications that determined voter eligibility. By the time of his death in 1824, France once again was beginning to simmer with discontent.

Louis Philippe

But it was the reactionary policies of the new king, **Charles X** (r. 1824–30), that brought things to a boiling point. Charles believed in the divine right of kings and sought to restore not only absolute rule but also the privileges of the Roman Church and the nobility. In July 1830, the people of Paris rose in rebellion in what is called the **July Revolution**. They raised barricades in the streets and resisted attempts by government soldiers to end the revolt. After three days of fighting, Charles fled to England. The French produced a more liberal constitution and chose the Duke of Orléans, **Louis Philippe** (r. 1830–48), to serve as their king. Initially popular with the French people, Louis was hailed as the "citizen king." Many of the participants in the revolution, however, soon became disillusioned because Louis Philippe catered to the interests of the upper middle class.

News of the July Revolution soon ignited a series of revolts throughout Europe. One of the nations whose smoldering discontent burst into the flame of revolution was Belgium. That tiny state had been given to the Dutch Netherlands by the Congress of Vienna. But the Belgians were dissatisfied; many cultural differences separated them from the Dutch people. Whereas the Belgians were Roman Catholics, the Dutch were predominantly Protestants. The Belgians were farmers and textile workers; the Dutch were bankers and traders. The Belgians spoke Flemish; Dutch was the official language of the schools, the government, and the courts.

When news of the July Revolution reached the city of Brussels, rioting erupted. Belgian nationalists declared their independence and drew up a liberal constitution. The leading European nations, facing unrest at home, were not able to come to the aid of the Dutch government. Leaders of these countries, however, met at a congress in London and signed the **Treaty of London**, which recognized the independence of Belgium. It also declared Belgium to be a perpetually neutral state. Thus, the balance of power would be maintained, and Belgium would be protected from foreign aggression.

Stirrings of nationalism and liberalism caused revolts to erupt in many central European states, but the rulers of Austria, Prussia, and Russia zealously suppressed any disruption of the *status quo*. Austrian and Prussian troops put down small uprisings in the Italian and German states. In Poland, when nationalist leaders tried to break free from Russian control, Czar Nicholas I sent the Russian army to brutally crush the rebellion.

Revolts of 1848

The revolts of the 1830s were suppressed, but resentment remained within the lower classes. They were bitter against the rich middle class, who often excluded them from the moderate gains the upper middle class had received during earlier revolts. Poor harvests and rising unemployment also increased the discontent among the peasants and city workers. In 1848, barricades went up across Europe as revolution once more rocked the continent.

As before, the revolutionary fires began in Paris. In February 1848, unemployed workers and disgruntled students gathered in the French capital. They protested Louis Philippe's policies, which favored the interests of wealthy businessmen. When Louis refused to listen to their demands for reform, rioting erupted. Barricades blocked the streets of Paris as mobs prepared to meet government troops. But when the National Guard joined the side of the workers, Louis Philippe fled to England.

Siege of the Pantheon, *24th June 1848*

The revolutionary leaders proclaimed the establishment of the Second French Republic and set up a temporary government to restore order in Paris and draw up a new constitution for France. At the urging of radical leaders, the government established "national workshops," a social program meant to provide food, shelter, medical care, and jobs for the growing number of unemployed workers. But instead of providing useful jobs, the workshops became a public-relief program, one of the earliest modern examples of socialistic (government-financed) programs.

Napoleon III

The new French constitution established universal manhood suffrage (all men could vote). When elections were held for a new legislature, the voters sent a fairly conservative assembly to Paris. The message was clear—the rural portions of France did not agree with the more radical ideas of the city workers and students. They objected to being taxed to support the unemployed in Paris when they were themselves facing famine. Thus, the newly elected conservative majority abolished the workshops. In reaction, unemployed workers sought to overthrow the government. For three days in June, Paris was the site of a bloody battle. During those "June Days," thousands of Frenchmen lost their lives as the army restored order to the city.

In December, elections were held for the presidency of the Second Republic. Perhaps because of recent violent uprisings, the French people voted for a man whose name symbolized authority. **Louis Napoleon**, the nephew of Napoleon Bonaparte, won by an overwhelming majority. Seeming to champion the rights of the common people, he increased his power over the government. In 1852, he staged a *coup d'état*, proclaiming himself

Emperor Napoleon III of the Second French Empire. (Napoleon Bonaparte's son, who died in 1832, was considered Napoleon II.) Once again, French attempts to achieve democratic reforms through revolution led to widespread violence and to the establishment of a dictatorship.

Metternich's prediction about France again proved true: the infection of revolution spread. Despite Metternich's precautions, revolts spread throughout the Austrian Empire in 1848. For example, strong nationalistic uprisings occurred in Hungary and Bohemia. Venice and Milan also declared their independence from Habsburg control. Demonstrations by university students and workers in Vienna finally forced Metternich to resign.

Austrian emperor Ferdinand I readily gave in to the revolutionary demands. He granted a liberal constitution, abolished serfdom, and promised self-rule for the Hungarians. But as the summer wore on, differences among the revolutionaries gave reactionary forces an opportunity to put down the revolution. Reactionary leaders forced Ferdinand to abdicate in favor of his nephew, **Franz Josef I** (1848–1916). The young emperor renounced the concessions of his predecessor and, with the backing of the army, crushed the nationalist revolts throughout the Austrian Empire.

Although the Napoleonic Wars had exposed the Russian people to the revolutionary battle cry of "Liberty, Equality, Fraternity," peasants in Russia still suffered under the burden of serfdom that bound them to the land. Likewise, the many national groups within Russia's borders still yearned for independence. However, democratic and nationalistic reforms made little progress in Russia.

Czar **Nicholas I** sought to head off uprisings by instituting a policy of "Autocracy, Orthodoxy, and Nationalism." This domestic program called for increasing the czar's control over the state, recognizing only the Russian Orthodox Church, and uniting the diverse national groups within Nicholas's territory around the culture and traditions of Russia—a policy called **Russification**. Nicholas, as well as later Russian czars, suppressed domestic problems instead of trying to find workable and equitable solutions. Although Russia did not experience revolution in the 1830s and 1848, it suffered from devastating social upheaval in the early twentieth century.

The Napoleonic Era also had awakened liberalism and nationalism among the Italian and German states. They sought freedom from repressive rulers, worked for democratic constitutions, and longed for national unification. However, in these states, as in most of Europe, the bright prospects of concessions won soon dimmed. Conservative monarchs temporarily regained the support of the army and crushed the uprisings. Nevertheless, the force of nationalism would triumph later in the century.

Failure of the Revolts

The period following the Napoleonic Wars remained turbulent, with discontent, uprisings, and bloodshed becoming commonplace. Most who took part in the revolts of the 1830s and 1848 shared the common desire of advancing the causes of liberalism and nationalism. However, the revolts that swept across Europe shared something else—most ended in failure.

Discontentment led to violent protests and uprisings, often winning concessions from weakened and frightened rulers. Nevertheless, these gains soon were threatened as the revolutionaries quarreled among themselves. Conflicting goals and backgrounds divided the forces that had previously joined in opposition to the government. Taking advantage of the disagreement and disunity among revolutionary factions, government forces were often able to rally and suppress the revolts.

Underlying this period of turmoil was the failure of governments and their citizens to fulfill their God-ordained civic responsibilities. Government should promote righteousness in a land, and righteousness includes not only right moral conduct but also justice, equity, and liberty. However, many European rulers chose to oppress their subjects rather than show mercy. Citizens needed to respect the authorities that God placed over them while continuing to work for reform. The citizens who sought to throw off all restraints were also wrong in light of the fact that a Christian view of liberty involves obedience and self-control.

Section Quiz

1. From what country were the revolutionary fires of the 1830s and 1848 first ignited?
2. What country gained its independence from the Netherlands through the revolts of the 1830s?
3. Following the violence of the "June Days," whom did the people of France elect as president of the Second French Republic?
4. Name the young Austrian ruler who renounced the concessions of his predecessor and crushed nationalistic revolts throughout his empire.
5. What policy did Czar Nicholas I institute in Russia to strengthen his control over the state?

★ Briefly evaluate the reign of Nicholas I in light of Proverbs 28:16.

II. Triumph of Nationalism

By 1850, the spirit of conservatism and international cooperation established by the Congress of Vienna had waned, and the spirit of liberalism and nationalism had intensified. During the second half of the century, the mood of European politics gradually changed. The years of revolution had dispelled the zeal of romantic idealism; in its place arose a hardened realism. Like Machiavelli's *Prince*, European politicians and diplomats adopted a politics of necessity known as ***realpolitik*** ("the politics of reality"), in which they used whatever means necessary—including force—to advance their national goals. Although most of Europe escaped widespread war during the nineteenth century, the spirit of nationalism resulted in several smaller wars among the major powers.

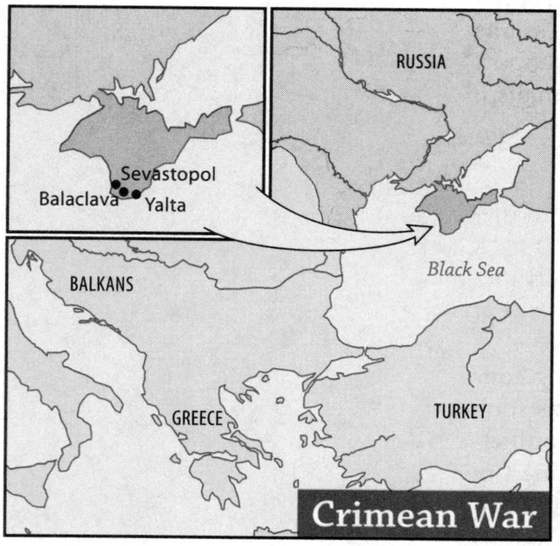

Crimean War

Crimean War

The first major international conflict after the defeat of Napoleon was the **Crimean War** (1854–56). It pitted Britain, France, and the Kingdom of Sardinia against Russia, which was pursuing expansion in the Near East. For centuries, the Ottoman Empire had controlled this region. But by the nineteenth century, the Turks were no longer a mighty power. Weak and corrupt government and strong nationalistic feeling among Europeans under Turkish control signaled doom for the Ottoman Empire. Referring to that empire, Czar Nicholas remarked, "We have on our hands a sick man, a very sick man, who can die suddenly." Nicholas tried to hasten that death by provoking a war with the Turks. He hoped to expand Russia's borders all the way to the Mediterranean.

In 1853, Nicholas demanded that the Orthodox Church in the Ottoman Empire be placed under Russian "protection." When the Turks refused, fighting broke out. Russian victories within the first months of fighting created concern elsewhere in Europe. Britain feared that a Russian victory would upset the balance of power and threaten its access to the Mediterranean. France entered the war primarily because Napoleon III wanted

Pioneers of Military Medicine

Florence Nightingale (1820–1910) established the modern nursing profession through her efforts to help sick and wounded British soldiers during the Crimean War. Newspaper reports detailing the appalling conditions in the Crimea shocked the British public; many people demanded that something be done to alleviate the suffering. The British government responded by recruiting thirty-eight nurses, many of whom had little or no training, to accompany the well-trained Florence Nightingale to the Crimea.

When this small band of nurses arrived, they found that the "hospital" was a filthy and damp former army barracks. The wounded soldiers—wrapped in bloody, vermin-covered blankets—died by the hundreds from their wounds and disease. Florence began her work. At first, she had few supplies, but through donations from Britain she was able to purchase many necessities. Florence believed in efficient organization and hard work, and before long her efforts began to save lives.

Strain and overwork, however, ruined her health, and after returning from the Crimea a national heroine, she rarely ventured out into public again. During the American Civil War, however, Florence advised the United States on how to set up military hospitals. Having received many honors in her lifetime, Florence Nightingale in 1907 became the first woman to receive the British Order of Merit.

Top: Florence Nightingale
Bottom: Mary Seacole

Mary Seacole (1805–81) became another pioneer of military medicine. When the Crimean War began, Seacole sought to serve as a nurse but was rejected because of her gender and ethnicity (Jamaican). Even Florence Nightingale refused to accept her offer to serve. Still determined to go to the Crimea, she used her own money to get there and set up the British Hotel. From there, Seacole helped many soldiers from Britain, France, Italy, and even Russia. Overcoming Nightingale's continued refusal to support her work, Seacole saved many lives and won the appreciation of the soldiers. She was the first woman allowed in Sevastopol after its surrender. For her efforts, Seacole was awarded the British Crimean Medal, the French Legion of Honor, and the Turkish Order of the Medjidie. After the war, she returned to Britain financially devastated and in poor health. British newspapers published her story, inspiring the British public to repay her wartime expenses and relieve her financial plight.

to do something glorious to enhance his prestige. Count Cavour, the prime minister of the Italian kingdom of Sardinia, sided with Britain and France in hopes of gaining their support for the cause of Italian unification.

For two years, the war continued on the Crimean Peninsula. Both sides were hampered by poor organization, supply difficulties, disease, and inept leadership. The war ended soon after the Russian fortress of Sevastopol surrendered. At Paris in 1856, the nations that took part in the war met to discuss the peace settlement. Besides losing territory, Russia agreed to abandon its claim as "protector" of the Orthodox Church within the Ottoman Empire. It also agreed not to build any forts along the Black Sea or to station any warships in those waters. The major nations also promised to keep the Ottoman Empire from being destroyed, thereby preserving the balance of power.

Nationalism in Italy and Germany

The Crimean War illustrated the failure of the congress system. Selfish national interests divided the congress members, leading to war instead of peace. As James 4:1 states, conflicts—both individual and national—occur because of selfish lusts. But while nationalism decreased international cooperation, it also increased the drive for unification in both Italy and Germany.

Unification of Italy 1859–70

Italian Unification

By the mid-nineteenth century, Italy was still what Metternich contemptuously called a "geographic expression." The Italian peninsula remained politically divided; small kingdoms competed with one another, and foreign powers controlled large sections of the country. Nevertheless, the spirit of nationalism was on the rise, fueled by a movement called ***Risorgimento*** ("resurgence"). In 1832, **Giuseppe Mazzini** (maht TSEE nee; 1805–72) started a patriotic society called Young Italy, determining to fight, if necessary, for Italian unification.

The man primarily responsible for unifying Italy was Count **Camillo di Cavour** (1810–61), the prime minister of the Kingdom of Sardinia. Cavour was a wily diplomat who used whatever means necessary to promote Italian unification. When the Crimean War broke out in 1854, Cavour joined Britain and France in sending troops to fight Russia. He had no quarrel with the Russians but hoped that the peace negotiations following the war would give him the opportunity to enlist support for his cause of unification. Cavour knew he would need an ally to wrest the provinces of Lombardy and Venetia from Austrian control. He found his ally in Napoleon III of France, who was seeking to win both territory and military glory.

Napoleon III secretly agreed to help Sardinia gain the Austrian-controlled provinces of Lombardy and Venetia. In return, Cavour promised to cede him the provinces of Nice and Savoy. In 1859, Cavour provoked the Austrians into declaring war on Sardinia. As the Franco-Sardinian armies successfully drove the Austrian troops out of Lombardy, revolts broke out across northern Italy. Rulers of small Italian states were overthrown as Italians joined Cavour's efforts for unification. Fearful of a strong, unified Italy, Napoleon III made a separate peace with Austria. Despite this infuriating setback, Cavour had made considerable progress in unifying most of northern Italy to the Kingdom of Sardinia.

Meanwhile in southern Italy, a follower of Mazzini, **Giuseppe Garibaldi** (GAR uh BAWL dee; 1807–82), rose to prominence. Strongly patriotic and bent on unifying Italy, Garibaldi gathered a band of loyal followers called "Red

Left: Count Camillo di Cavour
Right: Giuseppe Garibaldi

Shirts" and invaded the island of Sicily in 1860. Having conquered it, Garibaldi's forces landed on the Italian mainland and took Naples. Garibaldi next planned to march on Rome and take possession of the Papal States.

At that point, Cavour quickly intervened, fearing that an attack on Rome would draw the French into the conflict on the pope's side. (Since the days of Charlemagne, French troops had guarded the papal city.) Rushing southward with Sardinian troops, Cavour persuaded Garibaldi to hand over his conquests to **Victor Emmanuel II**, the king of Sardinia. On March 17, 1861, just a few months before Cavour's death, an Italian parliament officially proclaimed the establishment of the Kingdom of Italy with Victor Emmanuel II as the first king. With the exception of Venetia and Rome, Italian unification had been accomplished. By 1870, these last two territories were added to the Italian kingdom while the French were engaged in the Franco-Prussian War. In 1871 the city of Rome became the capital of the nation of Italy.

Victor Emmanuel II

Portrait of Vittorio Emanuele II of Italy (1820-1878). Anonymous, 19th century. Museo Civico Fattori, Livorno, Italy. Scala/Art Resource, NY

Otto von Bismarck

German Unification

Despite the failure of the revolts of 1848, the cause of German unification continued to advance. But it was in the economic, not the political, realm that great strides were made initially. Under the leadership of Prussia, the German states established a trade union called the **Zollverein**. The favorable results of this economic cooperation lent support to the movement for political unification.

The architect of political unification in Germany was Count **Otto von Bismarck** (1815–98), a loyal Prussian who was both crafty and opportunistic. Bismarck was not a romantic idealist but was devoted to the practice of *realpolitik*. He believed that the most practical way to achieve his goals was through the hard-nosed policy of "blood and iron," not through idealistic speeches. In 1862, King Wilhelm I made Bismarck the chancellor of Prussia. Bismarck immediately began seeking opportunities to promote German unification under Prussian domination.

War with Denmark and Austria—Bismarck's first opportunity came in 1864, when he deliberately involved Prussia in a dispute with the king of Denmark over the small territories of Schleswig and Holstein. The king of Denmark wanted to incorporate these territories into his kingdom, but Bismarck

protested, claiming them as German territories. Posing as the protector of the German people, he persuaded Austria to join Prussia in a war against Denmark. The brief war ended in a Danish defeat. Following the Danish surrender, Austria and Prussia divided the spoils: Austria took control of Holstein, while Prussia administered Schleswig.

Next, Bismarck sought for a way to discredit Austria and to strengthen Prussia's influence in German affairs. He sought to isolate Austria from other European nations and then use the superior might of the Prussian army to assert Prussian domination. Through skillful diplomacy, Bismarck persuaded both Russia and France to remain neutral in the event of war between Prussia and Austria. He then enlisted the aid of the Italians in a war against Austria, promising Venetia in return for their support. Though Bismarck was now prepared for war, he did not want to be seen as the aggressor. So he stirred up trouble in Holstein, angering the Austrians to such a degree that they declared war first.

The **Austro-Prussian War**, also known as the Seven Weeks' War, erupted in 1866. The Prussians quickly gained the victory and forced the Austrians to agree to the Prussian peace proposal. Prussia acquired both Holstein and additional German territory. Furthermore, Austria agreed to end the German Confederation established by the Congress of Vienna. In its place, a Prussia-dominated North German Confederation was established.

The Industrial Revolution Comes to War

The unification of Germany was accomplished by not only the diplomacy of Bismarck but also the overwhelming success of the Prussian army under Field Marshal Helmuth von Moltke (1800–1891). Moltke's army achieved a series of astonishing triumphs by applying the new technology of the Industrial Revolution to the art of war. Moltke, a tight-lipped Prussian known as the Great Silent One, was not a bold, dashing leader like Alexander the Great or Napoleon. His greatest skill was in efficient organization. A thorough and superior planner, Moltke won quick and decisive victories.

Helmuth von Moltke

Moltke and his staff took advantage of Prussia's growing industrial power. For example, he used the nation's many railway lines to move and organize his troops. In both the Austro-Prussian and Franco-Prussian Wars, Prussia's speed in mobilization gave it an advantage over its opponent. The railroad had become a weapon of war.

The Prussians improved weaponry too. Other countries used muzzle-loading rifles, which required a soldier to stand up and go through several steps to load it. The Prussian army adopted a breech-loading rifle, which could be loaded simply by inserting a cartridge into a chamber near the trigger. A soldier could load while kneeling or even lying down, and he could fire much more quickly. In the Austro-Prussian War, the Prussian guns could fire six shots for every one shot by the Austrian weapons. The Prussians also used steel breech-loading cannons instead of the bronze muzzleloaders that most other nations used. By World War I, Germany had the finest artillery in Europe.

Moltke made full use of the telegraph, an obvious improvement over carrying messages by horse. The Prussians also realized the importance of the growth in population that accompanied the Industrial Revolution. Unlike other countries, Prussia required nearly every male in the country to undergo military training. In wartime, Prussia was able to raise a larger army than any of its opponents—even though the enemy might have a larger population.

The success of Moltke's army persuaded the rest of Europe to follow his example. In a few years, the armies of Europe were more evenly matched, and decisive victories like those of Prussia became harder to achieve. The end result of these "improvements" was the long, drawn-out, and bloody conflict known as World War I. Unintentionally, Moltke's success also destroyed the myth of war as a glorious, noble, and exciting adventure. As one historian wrote, "Moltke killed war by making it so serious, so dull, and so deadly."

The Franco-Prussian War—With Austria now out of the way, Bismarck began working to bring the southern German states under Prussian control. To accomplish this goal, he sought an opportunity to provoke a war with France. Such a war, he believed, would stir up such nationalistic feeling among the German states that it would be relatively easy to persuade them to join with Prussia. In France, an increasingly ill Napoleon III allowed himself to be pushed into war by a prowar party. They wanted to diminish Prussian power before it became too strong for France to handle.

The immediate cause for the **Franco-Prussian War** (1870–71) was the throne of Spain. A liberal revolution had overthrown the corrupt Spanish monarchy in 1868, and the new provisional government invited Leopold, a Hohenzollern prince, to become king. The French opposed such a plan because the Hohenzollern family also ruled Prussia. If Leopold became king of Spain, France would be encircled by the Hohenzollerns. Amid the furor and cries of the French for war, Leopold withdrew his candidacy.

Yet the French were not satisfied. The French ambassador met with the Prussian king, Wilhelm I, who was vacationing at Ems in the Rhineland. He demanded that Wilhelm promise in writing that no Hohenzollern would ever sit on the Spanish throne. Wilhelm refused and sent Bismarck a dispatch (report) of his discussions, granting him permission to publish it in the newspapers. Bismarck did publish the dispatch, but not before he changed the wording slightly to make it seem as if Wilhelm and the ambassador had insulted each other. This "Ems dispatch" so angered the French that they declared war on the equally infuriated Prussians.

As Bismarck had hoped, the southern German states joined with Prussia in the war effort. The Germans invaded Alsace and Lorraine (French provinces) and in less than two months had trapped Napoleon III at the fortress of Sedan. There, Napoleon III and his army of 83,000 men were forced to surrender. On hearing of the surrender, mobs in Paris declared an end to the Second French Empire and established a republic, vowing to continue the war. But the Germans advanced to the outskirts of Paris, and the French cause became hopeless. On January 28, 1871, Paris surrendered after a 132-day siege. Ten days earlier, in the Versailles Palace outside Paris, Kaiser Wilhelm I had been proclaimed emperor of the German Reich (empire), fulfilling Bismarck's plans for unification.

Reforms in Austria and Russia

The Dual Monarchy

The Austrian Habsburgs ruled over a varied and increasingly restless group of nationalities. Of these nationalities, the Hungarians created the most problems for the Austrian government. In 1848, under the leadership of Louis Kossuth (KAH sooth), they had staged an unsuccessful revolt. Later, after the Prussian victory over Austria in the Austro-Prussian War (1866), the Hungarians again demanded self-government. But this time the Austrians were in no position to reject their demands. They made the Hungarians equal partners within the empire. Both countries remained under the Habsburg monarchy and cooperated in matters of finance, foreign affairs, and defense. However, each had its own constitution, official language, flag, and parliament. The Austrian Empire now became the Austro-Hungarian Empire, or **Dual Monarchy**, ruled by Franz Josef I.

Russia Under Alexander II

When Nicholas I died in 1855, his son **Alexander II** (r. 1855–81) became the Russian czar. He recognized that his father's policy of "Autocracy,

Alexander II

Orthodoxy, and Nationalism" had caused widespread discontent. It had also weakened Russia's position as a major European power, resulting in Russia's defeat during the Crimean War. Consequently, Alexander implemented several social reforms.

The most important one came in 1861, when he abolished serfdom, giving the serfs personal freedom and the right to buy land. Radicals pressed for more extensive reforms, but Alexander rejected many of their demands. In 1881, revolutionaries used explosives to assassinate Alexander. When his son Alexander III (r. 1881–94) became czar, he returned to the harsh policies of Nicholas I.

Section Quiz

1. What three European nations fought on the side of the Turks against Russia in the Crimean War?
2. Who was the prime minister of Sardinia primarily responsible for the unification of Italy?
3. Who was the Prussian politician primarily responsible for the unification of Germany? Against what three European nations did he take Prussia to war to achieve his goal?
4. As a result of Austria's military defeat, what nationality within the Austrian Empire was able to achieve self-government?
5. What was Czar Alexander II's most important social reform?

★ What did revolutionaries accomplish by assassinating Alexander II?

III. Protest of Romanticism

The powerful feelings unleashed by the political revolutions of the late eighteenth and early nineteenth centuries resulted in **romanticism**. This cultural movement gave literary and artistic expression to the concepts of "Liberty, Equality, Fraternity." Romanticism also became a reaction against (1) the restraint of the Age of Reason, (2) the violence of the French Revolution, (3) the repression following the Napoleonic Wars, and (4) the often harsh working conditions caused by the rapid growth of the Industrial Revolution.

Dangers of Going to the Extreme

In reacting against rationalism and restraint, romantics tended to go to extremes in the opposite direction, becoming rebels against all forms of rules. Many romantics made their feelings the standard—if it felt good, it must be good. Although emotions are part of the natural makeup of man, people should not be ruled by their emotions. In addition, many romantics exchanged the mind-centered humanism of the Enlightenment for a heart-centered humanism. The Bible, however, warns us in Jeremiah 17:9 about the deceitfulness of our hearts.

In contrast to the Age of Reason, the Romantic Age turned from rationalism to idealism, from the intellectual to the emotional. Romantics emphasized originality above imitation, nationalism above internationalism, and self-fulfillment above the common good. Their attitude shifted from optimism to uncertainty, from contentment to desire.

Romanticism in Literature

The works of romantic writers exhibited a variety of themes, the most popular of which were longing for distant lands or the distant past, fascination with the supernatural and the mysterious, and glorification of the "noble savage." They also emphasized nature, love of freedom, and pride in one's nation. Most of these themes were not new; writers had expressed them in previous centuries but without protests against the status quo. During what we call the Romantic Age, however, scores of well-known writers from many countries contributed to this movement of protest. We will examine a representative sample of them as we look at the themes of romanticism.

Longing for Distant Lands and the Distant Past

Sir Walter Scott (1771–1832) is one of the most famous romantic novelists. As a boy, he loved to visit the ruins of castles and monasteries that dotted the countryside of his native Scotland. Some romantics were enthralled with the beauty of nature, but Scott could not look on a scene without wondering about the people who had lived there or the events that had taken place there in the past. His novels reflect this fascination. Many of his stories are set in Scotland and England during the Middle Ages. One of his most popular novels is *Ivanhoe*, which he set during the reign of the English king Richard the Lion-hearted.

A leading French romantic who was influenced by Scott was **Victor Hugo** (1802–85). He wrote one of the most widely read romantic novels, *The Hunchback of Notre Dame*, a story that takes place in medieval Paris and centers on the Cathedral of Notre Dame. It tells a tale of mystery, suspense, and love.

The poetry of the Englishman **Samuel Taylor Coleridge** (1772–1834) reflects the romantics' interest in faraway places. The exotic stanzas of his poem "Kubla Khan" describe the palace of the thirteenth-century Mongol ruler of China. Another of his poems, "Rime of the Ancient Mariner," relates the fantastic voyage of an old seaman.

From left to right: Sir Walter Scott, Samuel Taylor Coleridge, Johann Wolfgang von Goethe

Fascination with the Supernatural and Mysterious

Early in the nineteenth century, two brothers, **Jakob** and **Wilhelm Grimm**, compiled a two-volume collection of German fairy tales. These tales, drawn primarily from German folklore, include such favorites as "Hansel and Gretel," "Cinderella," and "Little Red Riding Hood." All of them contain elements of the mysterious and supernatural. The supernatural is also reflected in the plays of the German author **Johann Wolfgang von Goethe** (GUR tuh; 1749–1832). His play *Faust* is based on an old folktale about a man who sold his soul to the Devil in return for twenty-four years of youth.

Edgar Allan Poe

The poems and short stories of the American writer **Edgar Allan Poe** (1809–49) illustrate the mysterious. To enhance the effect of his writing, he emphasized one major emotion in each work. For example, his poem "The Raven" conveys a feeling of melancholy, whereas his short story "The Fall of the House of Usher" is filled with terror. Today, Poe is considered the Father of Modern Mystery and Detective Fiction.

Glorification of the Noble Savage

The romantic concept of the noble savage began during the Enlightenment. Many of the *philosophes*, especially Jean Jacques Rousseau, assumed that civilization had corrupted man. Rousseau believed that man is at his best when living in a primitive environment apart from civilization. He held up the American Indian as the best example of the primitive yet uncorrupted noble savage. The romantics readily accepted these ideas and made them a part of their philosophy.

The novels of the American writer **James Fenimore Cooper** (1789–1851) reflect the concept of the noble savage. In a series of five novels known as the Leatherstocking Tales, Cooper recounts the exploits of an American frontiersman (Natty Bumppo) and his Indian companion. These characters live far from civilization and experience a life of freedom close to nature. Of all the novels in this series, the best-known is *The Last of the Mohicans*.

Emphasis on Nature

Closely associated with the concept of the noble savage was the romantic emphasis on nature. Like the *philosophes*, the romantics denied original sin, believing that man was innately good. To them, society and education had corrupted man. They taught that man could have his goodness restored by contemplating nature. One romantic writer who promoted this philosophy was **William Wordsworth** (1770–1850). He expressed his deep love for nature through poetry, which he described as "the spontaneous overflow of powerful feelings."

Left: James Fenimore Cooper
Right: William Wordsworth

Love of Freedom

Another characteristic of the romantics was their rebellion against the constraints of society. Many of them sought to live a life free from all restraints. The English romantic poet **George Gordon, Lord Byron** (1788–1824), was such a man. He indulged in immoral living and soon became enslaved to his own passions. Yet his so-called free lifestyle was not free from sin or its consequences. As a result, his life was filled with personal tragedy and sorrow.

Byron not only wrote about freedom but also actively supported the cause of freedom during his short lifetime. He tried to help the Italians in their fight for unification. He later went to Greece to aid the Greeks in their struggle for independence from the Turks. He died there of a fever in 1824.

Like Byron, the English poet **Percy Bysshe Shelley** (1792–1822) sought to throw off all restraints. Opposing what he called "religious, political, and domestic oppression," Shelley advocated "the sacred cause of freedom." The "oppression" that he so strongly condemned included the Christian faith, the rule of government, and traditional customs and ideas. Several of his poems, particularly "Queen Mab," reflect his destructive attitudes.

Lord Byron in Albanian dress

Pride of Nationalism

The theme of nationalism runs throughout romantic literature and is particularly evident in the writing of the greatest Russian poet, **Aleksandr Pushkin** (1799–1837). His influence on Russian literature is similar to that of Shakespeare on English literature and Dante on Italian literature. Pushkin is considered to be the founder of modern Russian literature.

Many of his works are based on Russian folklore and history. In them Pushkin expresses the romantic longing for freedom. A rebel by nature, he supported the Decembrist Revolt in Russia (1825). Frequently sent into exile, Pushkin was later pardoned by Czar Nicholas I.

Romanticism in Music

Some composers of this period drew heavily on the conventions that had developed to that point, whereas others were eager to push the accepted rules of regularity, balance, and restraint that had defined previous music by such composers as Haydn and Mozart. As works by such innovators became popular, certain traits came to distinguish the music of this era from that which had come before. For instance, as in romantic literature and art, romantic music sought to stir the emotions of its audience.

During the romantic age, popular interest in music increased as new musical instruments such as the accordion, harmonium (reed organ), and piano improved in construction and became more accessible to the general public. Music lovers attended solo recitals by such popular performers as pianist Liszt and singer Jenny Lind, as well as the performances of national and city orchestras. The London Philharmonic Orchestra was formed in 1813 and the New York Philharmonic in 1842.

Nationalism exerted a major influence on romantic music. Many European countries could boast of a national composer: Poland had Chopin, Hungary had Liszt, Bohemia had Smetana, Russia had Tchaikovsky, and Italy had Verdi. These composers often used national folk songs and popular dance tunes in their compositions. Many romantic composers are still well known, and their music is still greatly enjoyed.

The man who bridged the gap between classical and romantic music was **Ludwig van Beethoven** (1770–1827). Although born in Bonn, Germany, Beethoven spent most of his life in Vienna. His early music reflected the classical influence of his teacher, Franz Josef Haydn. Later, however, his music became more dramatic and explosive, blending classical and romantic elements. Beethoven increased the size of the orchestra and added two new instruments: the trombone and the piccolo. He also helped establish the piano as a popular instrument. In his late twenties, he began to lose his hearing; by his fiftieth birthday, he was completely deaf. In spite of this handicap, he continued to compose for the rest of his life.

Left: Ludwig van Beethoven
Right: Franz Liszt

Composers of Piano Music

The Polish composer **Frédéric Chopin** (sho PAN; 1810–49) has been called the "poet of the piano." In 1830, he left his beloved homeland on a concert tour of Europe. He never returned, for in the same year the Russians suppressed the Polish revolt for independence. Chopin refused to return and be subject to such repressive rule. Yet in spite of his self-imposed exile, his love for Poland did not diminish. His musical compositions express his deep affection for his homeland. He drew many of his melodies from Polish folk dances. Later, during World War II, radio stations in Nazi-occupied Poland played Chopin's music as a secret signal to the Polish underground that a coded message would follow. Today, he is still considered the national composer of Poland and his works a symbol of Polish nationalism.

Much of the piano music of **Franz Liszt** (1811–86) was inspired by his native land, Hungary. The best known of his compositions are his Hungarian Rhapsodies. While he was recognized as a composer, Liszt was also hailed as the most accomplished pianist of his time. He transcribed many orchestral works for the piano, and his dazzling virtuosity drew large crowds to his concerts.

Composers of Orchestral Music

The orchestral works of the Russian composer **Peter Ilich Tchaikovsky** (chy KAWF skee; 1840–93) include symphonies, ballets, and overtures. Of his ballets, *The Nutcracker* is particularly beautiful. His *1812 Overture*, written to mark the anniversary of Napoleon's defeat in Russia, is vibrant with Russian melodies. Its glorious finale features thundering cannons and pealing bells.

Like Tchaikovsky, the German composer **Johannes Brahms** (1833–97) produced brilliant orchestral works. Besides composing chamber music and symphonies, Brahms also wrote more than three hundred songs. Though his compositions are romantic, he often drew on musical forms that were also popular during the baroque and classical periods.

Richard Wagner

Composers of Opera

During the nineteenth century, Italians longed for a unified nation free from foreign control. The operas of **Giuseppe Verdi** (1813–1901) stirred this dream. Verdi incorporated into his operas the theme of good triumphing over evil. Often, when the villain in the opera was defeated, the audience cheered, seeing in this action the destruction of Austria, which controlled much of northern Italy. Even Verdi's name became associated with the resurgence of Italian nationalism, because it suggested "*V*ictor *E*mmanuel *R*e (king) *d'I*talia." (Victor Emmanuel was the man who the Italians hoped would become the ruler of a unified Italy.)

The operas of **Richard Wagner** (1813–83) also had a nationalistic, though not a revolutionary, flavor. Wagner based much of his work on ancient Germanic myths, seeking to unite the Germans around a common culture. He expanded the function of the orchestra and wrote vocal parts that demanded singers with very powerful voices. One characteristic of Wagner's musical dramas is his use of short melodies, called motifs, which recur often throughout the composition and each of which represents a particular character, action, or idea.

Romanticism in Art

Like their literary counterparts, romantic artists appealed to the senses and feelings of the beholder. Their use of bright colors was intended to elicit an emotional response. Their subjects were often scenes of local landscapes or faraway places. They chose themes from national legends and folklore and the medieval past. Their works demonstrate an appreciation for nature and a deep sensitivity to the feelings of the common man.

Most French painters of this period continued in the neoclassical style. The most famous neoclassical painter was **Jacques-Louis David** (dah VEED; 1748–1825), whose works demonstrate the neoclassical interest in themes from classical Greece and Rome. The painter **Eugène Delacroix** (duh lah KRWAH; 1798–1863), called "the Great Romantic," broke with the neoclassicism of David.

Delacroix's paintings are filled with bold colors and portray exciting or violent scenes. One of his most popular works is *Liberty Leading the People*, in which he depicts liberty as a Roman goddess carrying the red, white, and blue flag of the Revolution as she leads the mobs of Paris over the bodies of their fallen comrades.

In contrast to the wild, exciting canvases of Delacroix, the painting of Englishman **John Constable** (1776–1837) illustrates another aspect of romanticism—love for nature. Constable is most famous for his landscape paintings. He made frequent use of green, breaking with the ideas of artists who believed that landscapes should be painted in browns.

Throughout most of his career, however, Constable was overshadowed by another English artist, **J. M. W. Turner** (1775–1851), whose watercolor and oil paintings of landscapes and seascapes were greatly admired and eagerly bought. He frequently painted with yellows and oranges, causing one Italian to remark, "The English sell us mustard to eat, and their painters paint with it." As Turner matured, his technique changed—his later work foreshadowed the impressionistic style. (See p. 417.)

Section Quiz

1. What is the name of the cultural movement that gave literary and artistic expression to the concepts of "Liberty, Equality, Fraternity"?
2. List one of the prominent themes prevalent in the works of romantic writers.
3. What man bridged the gap between classical and romantic music?
4. Romantic musicians often expressed their affection for their homeland through their musical compositions. Identify the national backgrounds of each of the following musicians: Chopin, Liszt, Tchaikovsky, Verdi, Wagner.
5. Love for nature was illustrated through the paintings of which two romantic artists?

★ Why did Polish radio stations play Chopin's works prior to sending a coded message to the Polish underground during World War II?

Chapter 17 Review

Making Connections

1–2. Why did the Vienna peace settlement fail to accomplish its goals? (List two reasons.)

3–5. List three goals of liberalism. Which level of European society sought moderate forms of these goals?

Developing History Skills

1–2. What significant events in this chapter led to the unification of Italy? of Germany?

Thinking Critically

1. Should national interests come before international cooperation? Explain your answer.
2. Evaluate the romantic attitude toward freedom in light of God's instruction to Adam in Genesis 2:16–17.

Living in God's World

1. During the late nineteenth century, an anti-revolutionary party was started by Christians in the Netherlands as an alternative to both the Conservative and Liberal Parties. Imagine that you are a newspaper editor for the *De Standaard*, the party newspaper. Write a brief article explaining why the Anti-Revolutionary Party would disagree with both liberals and conservatives. Explain why the name Anti-Revolutionary was chosen for the party.

People, Places, and Things to Know

Congress of Vienna
Lord Castlereagh
Alexander I
Prince Klemens von Metternich
reactionary
Charles Maurice de Talleyrand
Quadruple Alliance
Monroe Doctrine
liberalism
nationalism
Louis XVIII
Charles X
July Revolution
Louis Philippe
Treaty of London
Louis Napoleon
Franz Josef I
Nicholas I
Russification
realpolitik
Crimean War
Risorgimento
Giuseppe Mazzini
Camillo di Cavour
Giuseppe Garibaldi
Victor Emmanuel II
Zollverein
Otto von Bismarck
Austro-Prussian War
Franco-Prussian War
Dual Monarchy
Alexander II
romanticism
Sir Walter Scott
Victor Hugo
Samuel Taylor Coleridge
Jakob and Wilhelm Grimm
Johann Wolfgang von Goethe
Edgar Allan Poe
James Fenimore Cooper
William Wordsworth
George Gordon, Lord Byron
Percy Bysshe Shelley
Aleksandr Pushkin
Ludwig van Beethoven
Frédéric Chopin
Franz Liszt
Peter Ilich Tchaikovsky
Johannes Brahms
Giuseppe Verdi
Richard Wagner
Jacques Louis David
Eugène Delacroix
John Constable
J. M. W. Turner

18

INDUSTRIAL REVOLUTION & EUROPEAN SOCIETY

I. The Industrial Revolution

II. Responses to the Industrial Revolution

III. Changing Outlooks in European Society

Houses of Parliament, London

"It was the best of times, it was the worst of times, it was the age of wisdom, it was the age of foolishness, it was the epoch of belief, it was the epoch of incredulity. . . ."

These opening lines of Charles Dickens's *A Tale of Two Cities* aptly describe European society in the second half of the nineteenth century. In the eyes of many Europeans, this period was the "best of times." Nationalism and democratic liberalism brought about great changes. In addition, the Industrial Revolution dramatically transformed European society. The advances in industrial development gave rise to a belief in progress that affected both intellectual and religious attitudes. Many people believed that both man and society were getting better and better. Yet, for many Europeans, this period was the "worst of times." Crowded slums and miserable working conditions caused many urban workers to despair. To them, it was apparent that the evils of society had not been remedied.

The situation became worse as many intellectual and religious leaders began to question the authority of God's Word. This gradual shift away from God and Scripture produced a secular humanism that replaced belief in God with faith in human potential. However, many skeptics ultimately turned to Christianity when they found secular humanism to be an empty promise. Some even became Christianity's strongest defenders.

This chapter traces the development of the Industrial Revolution and examines its impact on European society. We will devote special attention to Great Britain, where the Industrial Revolution began. We will also look at both the response of European society to the dramatic changes caused by industrial development and the changing outlooks and values that transformed European society.

I. The Industrial Revolution

Shortly before the French Revolution, Great Britain began to experience some sweeping changes of its own. Unlike the French Revolution, which was sudden and violent, the **Industrial Revolution** occurred gradually over several decades. Powered machines began to replace hand tools, and the modern factory system came into existence. These technological developments were revolutionary, not because of the speed with which they occurred but because of their tremendous impact on society.

Beginnings of Industrialism

During the eighteenth century, conditions in British society were favorable for industrial development. Three important factors combined to make the Industrial Age possible:

1. *An adequate food supply*. The Industrial Revolution was preceded by a revolution in agriculture. New machines and better methods of farming led to an increased food supply that was sufficient to meet the demands of the growing urban population.
2. *A large and mobile labor force*. As a result of the increased efficiency and productivity in agriculture, fewer people were needed to produce the food. The unemployed farm workers moved to the centers of industrial development and formed the labor force of industry.

3. *Expansion of trade.* Throughout the eighteenth century, foreign trade became an increasingly vital part of the British economy. This trade expanded as the number of British colonial possessions increased. The newly acquired colonies not only supplied raw materials for British industry but also provided a growing market for British products.

In addition to these factors, Britain's social and political climate provided a favorable setting for industrial development. Because of Britain's geographic isolation from the Continent, it escaped the destruction of the Napoleonic Wars. While other nations experienced revolution in the nineteenth century, British society remained relatively stable and peaceful. Reforms came gradually through parliamentary measures rather than by violent uprisings. Furthermore, the British government encouraged industrial development by issuing patents for new inventions and removing many regulations that had previously hindered economic growth. Likewise, taxes were not excessive, and interest rates were low. These conditions encouraged businessmen to invest in new business ventures.

Charles Townshend

Agricultural Revolution

Jethro Tull and **Charles Townshend** are important figures in the history of agriculture. In the eighteenth century, Tull invented a seed "drill," or planter, that enabled farmers to plant more efficiently, increase crop yields, and end the wasteful scattering of seed. Later, Townshend developed a new system of crop rotation. Instead of leaving a field fallow for a year, he planted clover and turnips in the field. These crops returned needed minerals that other crops removed from the soil. In addition, the yield of turnips and clover could be used to feed farm animals. Townshend also used fertilizer in connection with his system and found that an increased crop yield resulted.

Robert Bakewell used selective breeding to produce larger and healthier farm animals. Since more feed was available (thanks to Townshend's system of growing turnips and clover), farmers no longer had to slaughter most of their animals in the winter. They now had the means to feed them until spring. Because of the work of Bakewell and others, today we have such well-known breeds as Hereford cattle and Berkshire hogs.

Another factor that influenced agricultural production was the enclosure movement. In the past, small farmers had benefited from using certain open fields as common pasture. In the eighteenth century, however, Parliament made it much easier for wealthy landowners to incorporate these common grazing lands into their own estates and form large farms. The small farmer, unable to survive on what little land he owned, often had to sell his land. In order to live, these farmers and their families had no choice but to move to the cities to find work. In spite of all the hardships and upheaval, the enclosure movement made British agriculture more efficient and profitable. Also, this painful transition ultimately provided workers to fill positions in Britain's growing industries.

The Textile Industry

The Industrial Revolution made its real breakthrough in the cotton industry. In the eighteenth century, cotton manufacturing was new to Britain and faced a strong challenge from the established wool industry. The manufacturers of woolen goods enjoyed government support and even persuaded Parliament to pass laws that were designed to hinder domestic cotton production. But with the invention of new machines, cotton production soon exceeded that of the wool industry.

Improvements in the textile industry began in 1733, when **John Kay** invented a "flying shuttle," which made it possible for a weaver to work faster and to weave cloth of greater width. One weaver, however, now needed four spinners to keep him supplied with thread. In 1769, **James Hargreaves** solved this problem with the invention of the spinning jenny. (The word *jenny* may be derived from *gin*, a regional term for *engine*.) That machine could spin up to eight threads at a time. But the thread it spun was coarser and weaker than the thread the old spinning wheel spun. It did not take long, however, for someone to find a solution to that problem too. That same year, **Richard Arkwright** invented a spinning frame that not only produced thread superior to the spinning jenny but also was powered by water. Because his spinning frames were too large for home use, he built special factories for them. For this contribution to the textile industry, Arkwright is often called the Father of the Industrial Revolution.

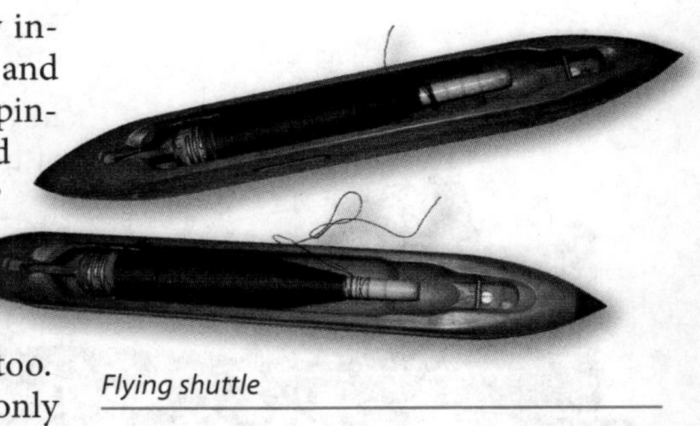

Flying shuttle

Other improvements began to come to the cotton industry in quick succession. For example, in 1779 **Samuel Crompton** invented an even larger spinning machine called the spinning mule. His machine, operated by one person, could spin a thousand threads at a time. Six years later, both spinning and weaving machines were converted to steam power. The only remaining bottleneck in the production process was the harvesting of cotton, which involved a slow process by which cotton seeds had to be separated by hand from the cotton fiber. Before long, the demand for cotton exceeded the supply. But in 1793 the American inventor **Eli Whitney** devised a simple cotton gin with which one man could do the work of fifty pickers. Now spinning, weaving, and preparing raw cotton could keep pace with one another. As a result, the manufacture of cotton goods proceeded at a frantic pace.

Early spinning frame

Why the Demand for Cotton?

You might wonder why so much effort went into turning cotton into thread and why the demand for cotton quickly exceeded the supply prior to Eli Whitney's invention. Two important reasons are cost and versatility. Cloth woven from cotton thread was less expensive than cloth made from wool. Manufacturers then turned the less expensive cotton cloth into inexpensive clothing. In a society where wages were low but where everyone needed clothing and the other items produced from cotton, this was vitally important. With the introduction of cotton, even the working poor could save up and buy a new shirt, a pair of socks, or some slacks, rather than continue to mend the more expensive woolen material. In addition, cotton was versatile. It was used to manufacture denim, underwear, bed sheets, and even fire hoses. While fire hoses are no longer manufactured from cotton, cotton remains the most widely used natural fiber for cloth today.

The Factory System

In the earliest stages of the Industrial Revolution, there were no factories in the modern sense of the word. Workers lived in rural areas. They labored at home, using their own hand tools. For the most part, they were able to set their own work schedules and determine how much they wanted to produce. But the size and expense of the new industrial machinery made it impossible for this domestic system to continue.

The factory system brought the workers, raw materials, and machinery under one roof. Factories were usually located near transportation routes, sources of water power, or natural resources. As the factory system replaced the domestic system, four significant changes took place for the worker. (1) The worker often moved to an urban environment to be near the factory. (2) He no longer owned his own tools but used those provided by the factory owner. (3) He no longer controlled the number of hours he worked per day or the pace at which he worked. (4) He now more often performed his work away from his family. Although these changes were a necessary part of industrialism, they created problems for both workers and society.

Early spinning mule

Development of Industrialism

During the last half of the nineteenth century, industrialism spread throughout much of western Europe. Britain remained the leader, but Germany became a fierce competitor. Although several European countries built factories and railroads, Russia, eastern Europe, and southern Europe remained economically backward and poverty stricken. The pace of industrial growth in the United States, Japan, and some regions of Canada also increased. In South America, Africa, and most of Asia, however, modernization and industrialization were a long way off. In the latter areas, traditional economic patterns continued relatively unchanged by the new economic developments in Europe.

Bessemer process

1. Bessemer furnace in upright position

2. molten iron being poured into furnace

3. furnace returned to upright position after which air is pumped in from the bottom to stir the molten iron and remove impurities

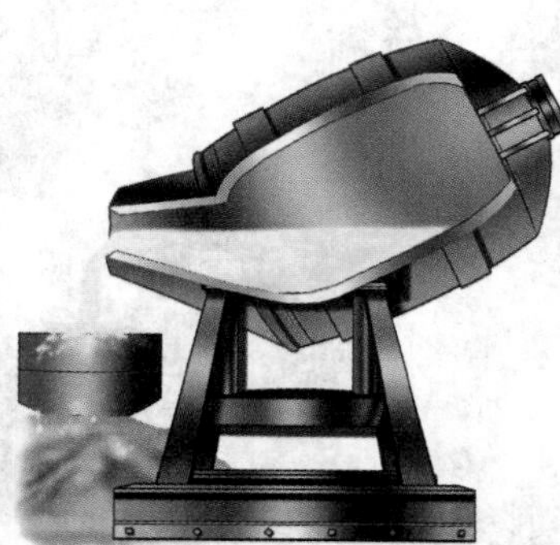

4. purified iron being poured from the furnace to the next step in preparing molten iron

Iron and Steel Production

One of Britain's most abundant natural resources was iron ore. During the early stages of the Industrial Revolution, however, the production of cast-iron objects remained very costly. Before the Industrial Revolution, charcoal (a wood by-product) had been used in the smelting of the ore. Charcoal, however, was becoming increasingly scarce, so ironmakers began to use coke (a coal by-product) in the smelting process. Britain had large coal deposits, and coke became a cheap fuel. In 1784, **Henry Cort** invented a process by which iron ore was "puddled" (stirred) in the furnace to rid it of impurities. He also developed a method of rolling and hammering the iron to produce a versatile product called wrought iron.

Not until 1856 was an inexpensive and efficient steel-making process devised. The man responsible for developing it was Sir **Henry Bessemer**, who found that shooting a jet of air into molten iron would help rid it of more impurities. Then, by adding carbon and other metals, he developed steel. With this process, steel production increased dramatically. For example, Britain, Germany, France, and Belgium produced 125,000 tons of steel in 1860; in 1913 they produced more than 32 million tons. For this reason, the first stage of the Industrial Revolution has been called the "age of iron," the later stage the "age of steel."

New Sources of Power

Many of the early factories were near rivers, streams, or lakes so that they could use water power to run their machinery. Discoveries of new sources of power made the modern factory system possible. In 1769, a Scotsman named **James Watt** designed the first practical and efficient steam engine by improving the design of an earlier model to provide enough power to run heavy machinery. Steam power made it possible for factories to be strategically located near markets or sources of raw materials instead of near a source of water power.

By the late nineteenth century, new energy sources began to replace the steam engine. Through the invention of the electric dynamo (a machine that turned mechanical energy into electrical energy), many factories converted to electrical power. By 1914, half of all the power used in British and German industries was supplied by electricity. Oil provided another energy source. The beginning of oil production followed the drilling of the world's first commercial oil well near Titusville, Pennsylvania, in 1859. Although the oil initially was used primarily to produce kerosene for lamps, the development of the internal combustion engine in 1885 provided new uses for petroleum products.

George Stephenson and the Blücher locomotive

Transportation

Improvements in transportation aided the progress of the Industrial Revolution. Between 1754 and 1788, British roads were greatly improved under a system of turnpike trusts. In a turnpike trust, a group of men financed the building of a road and then charged a toll to those traveling on it. By 1788, Britain had eighteen thousand miles of roads, many of which were built using a method devised by **John McAdam**. Constructed with tightly packed crushed rocks, macadamized roads provided a smoother and more durable surface. Travel by stagecoach became faster than ever before.

The construction of canals made it easier to transport heavy or bulky industrial goods. Canals also shortened the routes and lowered the cost of transportation. England had dug its first canal by 1757, and by 1850 five thousand miles of canals crisscrossed the nation, joining major rivers.

In addition to building roads and canals, Britain took the lead in constructing railroads. The early rail lines were rather short, usually running from coal mines or stone quarries to a nearby port. The first "trains" moved to their destination with the help of gravity and horse power. In 1804 **Richard Trevithick** built a steam-powered locomotive, and ten years later the locomotive of George Stephenson pulled a train of cars for the first time.

As industry grew in the nineteenth century, the need for transportation increased as well. To meet this need, railroad building intensified. For example, in 1860 only about 30,000 miles of railroad existed in the entire world, but by 1890 the United States, Britain, and Germany had a combined total of 213,000 miles of railroad.

Robert Fulton and the Clermont *steamboat*

About the same time that Trevithick put a steam engine on wheels, American **Robert Fulton** put a steam engine in a ship. Although not the first person to do this, he was the first to operate a steamboat as a commercial success. By the middle of the century, iron steamships

Left: Henry Ford and the Model T on the assembly line
Right: The Wright brothers and their airplane

were crossing the Atlantic Ocean in less than ten days, although at first those ships still carried sails because few people trusted the new steam engines.

The steamships and railroads met transportation needs in the nineteenth century; however, two developments at the beginning of the next century pointed the way to the future. In 1903, two brothers, **Orville** and **Wilbur Wright**, made the first successful airplane flight at Kitty Hawk, North Carolina. In 1908, **Henry Ford** began production of his famous Model T automobile.

Mass Production

In addition to the scores of inventions that improved industrial output, new production techniques helped manufacturers produce more goods at a cheaper price. Between 1870 and 1914, industrial production in Europe and North America more than tripled. Several new manufacturing methods made this tremendous growth possible.

1. **Automation**—In the early stages of industrialism, new machines helped workers perform their functions more quickly and efficiently. As the years progressed, other machines were invented to run the first machines. One result of this increased automation was that workers in many factories spent their time ensuring that machines functioned properly rather than directly making the products themselves.

2. **Interchangeable parts**—The expanding role of machines in industrial production gave rise to interchangeable parts. Whereas handcrafted items varied, machine-produced items were all the same. Previously, if some part of a product was damaged, the whole product had to be replaced or a new part custom-made. But with interchangeable parts, a product could be repaired easily and cheaply by replacing the broken piece with an identical piece.

3. **Division of labor**—In the past, skilled craftsmen worked on their products from start to finish. During the last part of the nineteenth century, this procedure changed. A number of workers divided the manufacturing process into several simple procedures, each worker performing a separate function.

4. **Assembly line**—Another method devised to speed up production was the assembly line. Workers stationed along a conveyor belt each assembled

a different specific part of a product. The item then moved down the line, where other workers assembled different parts. Henry Ford's automobile plant became one of the first industries to use this new procedure. By 1913, Ford workers were able to assemble a complete car in only ninety-three minutes.

Thomas Edison and his new phonograph in 1877

Science and Industry

As scientists made new discoveries, factory owners eagerly sought to apply the new knowledge to their particular areas of manufacturing. In the field of chemistry, for example, scientists discovered how to make synthetic products such as dyes and fertilizers. Inventors designed new products that aided not only industry but society as a whole. One of the most famous of the nineteenth-century inventors was Thomas Alva Edison, an American genius whose 1,093 patented inventions included the light bulb, the phonograph, and the motion picture projector.

Business Finance

When historians speak of industrial expansion before 1860, they refer to the increase in the number of small business partnerships. After 1860, large corporations began to replace the small businesses that found it difficult to meet the high cost of machinery, factories, and workers' wages. As corporations became more common, banks and other financial institutions became more important. These institutions not only helped to organize and finance new corporations but also controlled many of them.

Consequences of Industrialism

British society changed dramatically during the age of industrialism. Some of the changes were for the good and others for the bad. This age saw sharp contrasts of prosperity and poverty, opportunity and oppression, morality and immorality, and hope and despair.

Living and Working Conditions

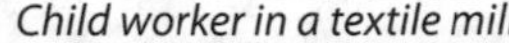

Child worker in a textile mill

In the early stages of the Industrial Revolution, living and working conditions were wretched. The cities were ill equipped to meet the needs of the great number of rural unemployed who flocked to the industrial centers. Housing sprang up quickly to meet the heavy demand—so quickly that little thought was given to the comfort and health of the occupants. As a result, many families shared one-room dwellings. Crowded slums soon appeared in almost every factory town, and people were forced to live in the midst of disease and filth.

The working day in most factories was exhausting, and working conditions were often dangerous. It was not uncommon for men, women, and even children to work fourteen to sixteen hours a day. Mill owners, in order to maximize their profits, often took advantage of their workers. One owner who employed children told parliamentary investigators that during busy times of the year, he expected the children to work from 3:00 a.m. to 10:00 p.m. (They regularly worked from 6:00 a.m. to 8:30 p.m.) Conditions in the mines and factories in which they worked were appalling. Coal mines, for example, were poorly ventilated, and factory machinery had few, if any, safety features. If a worker suffered serious injury on the job, the employer could simply hire another worker to fill his place.

Child mine worker

Increased Population and Productivity

Many positive contributions also came from the Industrial Age. People were better nourished, enjoyed a higher standard of living, and had a longer lifespan than people of the previous century. It is estimated that the population of Europe increased from 190 million in 1800 to 460 million in 1900. The growth in population was especially noticeable in the cities. Before 1840, England had only two cities with more than 100,000 people. But by 1910, forty-eight English cities had more than 100,000 residents.

An increase in the food supply and industrial production accompanied the increase in population. Greater efficiency and productivity reduced the prices of many goods. As a result, people in the nineteenth century had a greater abundance of material possessions than did those of any previous century.

Evaluation of the Industrial Age

Some people today see nothing but evil in the Industrial Revolution. They condemn capitalism, which made the industrial growth possible, for producing the terrible living and working conditions. They blame the free enterprise system for allowing a few people to get rich while many others remained poor. But this view overlooks the fact that conditions in the rural areas were often no better than those in the crowded cities. Farm workers had to work long hours and under many adverse conditions as did the factory workers. Also, one must remember that industrialism provided jobs for the increasing number of unemployed farm workers. To say that no one was concerned about the conditions in which the workers lived and worked is a distortion. The moral and social conscience of the Victorian Age initiated many reforms.

On the other hand, some people tend to gloss over the problems that developed during the growth of industrialism. Although the Industrial Revolution created new opportunities and provided a greater abundance for more people, it also provided opportunity for many to demonstrate the extent of their fallen nature. Some who were blessed with wealth used it to help the less fortunate, but others used their wealth to satisfy selfish desires, even if it meant taking advantage of workers. A growing emphasis on material goods and a decline in spiritual concern became another consequence of the Industrial Revolution. People tend to forget God when they enjoy prosperity and seek material gain.

We must remember that problems—both individual and collective—are the result of sin. In the Industrial Age, as in any other time, greed and cruelty as well as discontentment and immorality resulted in human suffering.

Section Quiz

1. In what country did the Industrial Revolution begin? In what industry did the Industrial Age make its real breakthrough?
2. List two inventions that aided the development of the textile industry. Identify the inventor of each.
3. What is the name of the system in which workers labored at home, using their own tools and determining how much they wanted to work and produce?
4. Name two new methods of transportation that aided the progress of the Industrial Revolution.
5. List the four new production methods that helped manufacturers produce more at cheaper prices.

★ Why did the issuing of patents by the British government encourage the development of the Industrial Revolution?

II. Responses to the Industrial Revolution

Response of Government

Great Britain was the leader not only in industrial production but also in attempts to remedy the social and political problems resulting from the rapid industrial expansion. During the 1830s and 1840s, the British Parliament passed the first significant social reforms. The members of Parliament who sponsored this legislation attempted to correct the abuses of industry and the accompanying problems in society. However, they failed to realize that, over time, increased government involvement in many areas could eventually lead to government control of industry and a decline in individual freedom.

Except for a few isolated incidents, Great Britain avoided the violent uprisings that shook the European continent during the first half of the nineteenth century. The British prevented revolution by bringing about change through parliamentary reform. During this century, Parliament passed many political reform bills that broadened the electorate and enabled a greater percentage of people to have a voice in government.

Social Reform

Among the earliest pieces of social legislation passed by Parliament were acts intended to curb abuses in the factories. Parliament enacted several bills to restrict the long hours and harsh conditions under which many women and children had to work. In 1833, it passed the first effective Factory Act to limit child labor. According to this law, no child under nine years of age was to work in a textile mill. Children from nine to thirteen years old could work but no more than eight hours a day. In addition, they were to receive at least three hours of schooling daily. Those between the ages of thirteen and eighteen could work no more than twelve hours a day. To enforce the law, Parliament appointed inspectors to ensure that the mill owners obeyed it.

Other reforms soon followed the Factory Act of 1833. The Poor Law of 1834 placed the national government in charge of relief measures for those who were too old or too sick to work. The Mines Act (1842) barred from the coal mines all females as well as all males under ten years old. In a further effort to regulate working hours, Parliament passed the Ten Hour Bill in 1847, which limited women and children in any industry to a ten-hour day.

William Wilberforce: "No Common Christian"

In 1785, five years after he entered Parliament, William Wilberforce (1759–1833) underwent a conversion, what he later called "the great change." In his efforts to turn from his previously worldly lifestyle, he considered abandoning politics altogether. However, he heeded the advice of Anglican pastor John Newton to stay in Parliament. Newton said, "It is hoped and believed that the Lord has raised you up for the good of His church and for the good of the nation."

Wilberforce became a serious and fervent Christian. His pastor wrote, "He is no common Christian; his knowledge of divine things and his experience of the power of the Gospel are very extraordinary." Nor was he the kind of politician who makes a religious profession to sway voters but makes worldly wisdom his political philosophy. Wilberforce said, "A man who acts from the principles I profess reflects that he is to give an account of his political conduct at the Judgment seat of Christ."

Although he supported many worthy causes, Wilberforce pressed none so hard or so consistently as the abolishing of the British slave trade. He declared on one occasion, "If it please God to honor me so far, may I be the instrument of stopping such a course of wickedness and cruelty as never before disgraced a Christian country." He faced tremendous opposition to his efforts. The slave trade was profitable, and the planters in Britain's Caribbean possessions predicted economic disaster if it were abolished. The economic arguments swayed many politicians who were concerned about financial prosperity—and their own reelection. Several times Wilberforce presented to the House of Commons a motion to abolish the slave trade. Sometimes he lost by wide margins, at other times by narrow ones. However, even when he managed to get his bill through the House of Commons, the House of Lords rejected it.

During these discouraging times, other Christians sought to encourage him. For example, John Wesley, shortly before his death, wrote to Wilberforce, "Unless God has raised you up for this very thing, you will be worn out by the opposition of men and devils. But if God be for you, who can be against you."

Finally, in 1807, Wilberforce succeeded in guiding an abolition bill through both houses of Parliament. The slave trade was abolished. But Wilberforce was not finished. Although the trade was illegal, slavery continued to exist in British territory. The fight to abolish slavery, however, took more years than Wilberforce had left. Ill health forced him to retire from Parliament in 1825 and leave the battle to others. A few weeks after Wilberforce's death in 1833, the House of Commons voted to abolish slavery.

While others praised him for his humanitarian activities, Wilberforce remained painfully aware of his human failings and frailties, saying, "The genuine Christian . . . humbles himself in the dust and acknowledges that he is not worthy of the least of all God's mercies."

Some social reforms grew out of the humanitarian efforts of individuals. One prominent example was the antislavery movement led by **William Wilberforce**. Motivated by his Christian faith and a sincere compassion for his fellow man, Wilberforce campaigned against the slave trade. His efforts were rewarded when in 1807 Parliament passed a law abolishing the slave trade in British territory. Another act in 1833 began the process of freeing all slaves in the British Empire.

Economic Reform

In 1846, Parliament repealed the **Corn Laws**, which had placed a high tariff on imported grain. Such tariffs limited foreign competition and allowed British landowners to sell their grain at higher prices. The repeal of these laws not only brought down the price of grain (thereby relieving a great financial burden on workers, who had been forced to pay high prices) but also signaled a shift toward free trade in British economic policy.

Political Reform

Reform Bills—At the outset of the nineteenth century, the aristocrats and wealthy landowners controlled Parliament. Property qualifications prevented most of the British people from voting in parliamentary elections. In addition, voting districts (called boroughs) had not changed for almost 150 years. Thus, the landholding class retained control of Parliament, denying equal representation to residents of the growing industrial centers. Members of the middle class, therefore, demanded change. By 1830, they persuaded the House of Commons to pass a reform bill, but the House of Lords vetoed it. When the king threatened to create new lords to ensure that there would be a majority to pass the bill, the House of Lords backed down, and the **Reform Bill of 1832** became law.

Women's Rights Movement

The women's rights movement spanned more than one hundred years as women struggled to gain the right to own property and vote. Although the movement for "universal suffrage" (right to vote) began with the Chartist movement in the late 1700s, women were excluded from that movement. However, women continued to push for suffrage, and the issue received positive attention in some 1865 election speeches in Britain. In 1867 the first petition for women's suffrage was introduced to Parliament. Supporters introduced similar petitions every year thereafter with increasing support, but they failed to pass, due in part to the opposition of political leaders, including William Gladstone.

In 1881, leaders on the Isle of Man (located in the Irish Sea between Ireland and Great Britain) gave women property owners the right to vote. Later, women who lived on the island but did not own land also gained this right. Encouraged by this progress, women increased their efforts. Some groups applied pressure directly on elected officials and campaigned against the opponents of women's suffrage. Other women took more radical steps by violating laws and getting sentenced to jail. A few women prisoners even went on hunger strikes, drawing further attention to women's suffrage.

During World War I, activity for suffrage ceased, but women resumed their efforts after the war. Their persistence resulted in women winning the right to vote in the United States in 1920 and in Great Britain in 1928.

The Reform Bill lowered property qualifications for voting, increasing the electorate by an estimated 50 percent. It also reorganized the voting districts, giving representation to middle-class citizens in the new industrial cities. Merchants, bankers, and factory owners now had a voice in government. But the Reform Bill had not extended the voting privilege to the average man. As a result, dissatisfied workers supported a new movement called **Chartism**. The Chartists advocated universal manhood suffrage, the secret ballot, equal electoral districts, pay for members of Parliament, no property qualifications for

The Grandmother of Europe

Queen Victoria (1837–1901) has become the symbol of nineteenth-century Britain. Her reign of sixty-three and a half years was the longest in British history. Her moral standards and political ideas exemplified the attitudes of many Britons.

In 1840, Victoria married Albert, a German prince of strong character. During their twenty-one years of marriage, Victoria and Albert did much to restore respect for the British monarchy. They not only reduced court expenditures but also set an example of moral uprightness. The relationship between the queen and the prince was happy. When Albert died of typhoid fever in 1861, Victoria was heartbroken. For the next thirty-nine years, she lived in relative seclusion, doing everything in her power to perpetuate the memory of her beloved Albert.

Because many of her nine children and thirty-four grandchildren married into other royal families, Victoria has been called the grandmother of Europe. One of her grandsons was Kaiser Wilhelm II of Germany, and one of her granddaughters was the wife of Nicholas II, the last Russian czar. Other children and grandchildren married into the royal lines of Sweden, Norway, Spain, and Romania. Three monarchs during World War I—Kaiser Wilhelm II, Alexandra (the wife of Nicholas II), and King George V of Britain—were cousins.

members of Parliament, and annual elections to Parliament. The Chartists presented several petitions, but each time Parliament refused to act. Although the Chartist movement failed, all of its demands—except annual elections to Parliament—eventually became law in Britain.

In 1867, Parliament passed a second major reform bill, which again reduced property qualifications for voting. This bill nearly doubled the electorate and shifted additional political power to Britain's industrial centers.

Disraeli and Gladstone—Reforms continued throughout the rest of the century as two dominant political figures, **Benjamin Disraeli** (diz RAY lee; 1804–81) and **William Gladstone** (1809–98), alternated as prime minister of the British Parliament. Benjamin Disraeli began his political career as a liberal but later became the leader of the Tory, or Conservative, Party. Through his efforts, Parliament passed the Reform Bill of 1867. While he was prime minister, Parliament passed several bills related to public health and housing. But Disraeli was primarily involved in foreign affairs. Perhaps his greatest success occurred when he, on behalf of the British government, bought 44 percent of the shares in the Suez Canal from the ruler of Egypt, thereby enhancing British dominance in the Mediterranean region and greatly aiding British trade.

Disraeli's political opponent was William Gladstone, the leader of the new Liberal Party. Gladstone, the son of a wealthy Scottish businessman, was a man of strong character. As a statesman, he placed his moral convictions above political expediency and earned the respect of both friends and enemies. As a man of strong religious faith, he diligently studied the Scriptures and regularly gathered his family for prayer. He also wrote several works on theology. Undoubtedly, his religious beliefs shaped his political outlook and made him a man of compassion toward those less fortunate than himself.

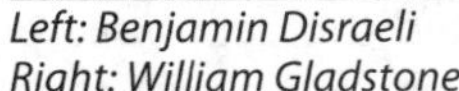

Left: Benjamin Disraeli
Right: William Gladstone

During his four terms as prime minister (1868–74, 1880–85, 1886, and 1892–94), Gladstone emphasized domestic reforms that established a single national court system, instituted voting by secret ballot, and in 1884 extended suffrage to rural communities. Gladstone also supported several education bills, believing that better education would promote wiser voting.

One particularly pressing problem during Gladstone's ministry was the matter of British rule of Ireland. Under James I (1603–25), Protestants had begun settling in Northern Ireland. The rest of the island was primarily Roman Catholic. Southern, Catholic Ireland became increasingly restless under British rule and began demanding home rule. "My mission is to pacify Ireland," Gladstone had said as he took office for the first time. But despite diligent effort, he never achieved his goal. The "Irish Question" would not be easily settled.

The Parliament Bill of 1911—The capstone of Britain's political development came in 1911 with the passage of the **Parliament Bill**. After much heated debate and political maneuvering, the House of Commons managed to wrest some power away from the House of Lords and assert itself as the supreme governing body in Britain. As a result of this bill, the House of Lords could only temporarily delay legislation passed by the House of Commons, not veto it as before. Also, in 1911 the House of Commons approved a salary for its members, making it financially possible for poorer citizens to become members of Parliament.

As Britain's government came to represent more of the people, the attitude toward the role of government began to change. Many people began to expect the government to be directly involved in establishing and funding various social programs. Britain began to develop into a welfare state (a state in which the government assumes the responsibility for the material and social well-being of every individual). Within a few years, Parliament passed bills providing for unemployment insurance, health protection, workman's compensation, and old-age pensions. In addition, it placed secondary education under state control. The result was greater government control and reduced individual freedom.

Ideas of the Socialists

Man has responsibilities to both God and society. Christ makes clear that man's first responsibility is to God and his second is to his fellow man: "Thou shalt love the Lord thy God with all thy heart, and with all thy soul, and with all thy mind. This is the first and great commandment. And the second is like unto it, Thou shalt love thy neighbour as thyself" (Matt. 22:37–39). But too often ungodly man has rejected his obligation to God and sought by his own efforts to correct the ills of society.

Many people during the nineteenth century, believing that man is basically good, sought to remedy the evils around them by changing society. Those who accept this error assume the perfectibility of man and society and reject the fact that *sin* is the root of all social evils. The false teaching regarding man's basic goodness found its clearest expression in socialism.

Wealth of Nations

One of the most influential books on political economics is Adam Smith's *Wealth of Nations*. Published in 1776, it attacked mercantilism, the prevailing economic system of most European nations during the eighteenth century. Smith defined national wealth not by how much gold or silver a nation possesses, but by how many goods it can produce and sell. In other words, wealth depends on productivity.

Smith proposed a policy of free trade among nations. A nation, he believed, should manufacture what it can best and most efficiently produce. What other goods it needs it should purchase from other countries. If each nation were driven by self-interest, all countries would do their best to produce superior products that other nations would want to buy. With increased demand, production would improve, and everyone would benefit.

Smith attacked the economic policies of the British government in his day as restrictive of free trade. He advocated a hands-off policy known as laissez faire, in which government does not interfere in business and trade but provides a favorable climate for business activity. Smith believed that the proper role of government, apart from maintaining law and order, is limited to providing an adequate education system, road system, and defense.

Most people today assume that **socialism** is only an economic term. It is defined as government ownership of the means of production and the distribution of goods for the presumed welfare of society. This definition is correct to a point, but socialism, like any other philosophy, is a worldview and therefore affects *every* area of life. For example, since socialism emphasizes the group rather than the individual, many socialists advocate an international government to replace independent national states. In addition, socialism rejects individual responsibility, limits individual choice, and replaces individual initiative with collectivism (rule by the group).

Four major types of socialism developed in the nineteenth century. Although each form sought to achieve the perfect society through different means, all were built on the same set of false ideas: (1) man is by nature good—it is society that has corrupted him; and (2) if society can be improved, then man will be improved, and all injustice will cease.

Utopian Socialism

Utopian socialism was a direct result of the French Enlightenment. Like many of the eighteenth-century *philosophes*, the utopian socialists believed that if the inequities in society could be abolished, man's natural goodness could be perfected. These socialists believed that the profit motive of capitalism was the basic source of evil and that it stimulated greed and hatred.

Because they assumed that one's environment produced social evil, the utopians believed that proper surroundings and a good education would solve all problems. To test these ideas, several men in Europe and America formed socialist communities that they hoped would set the example for sweeping changes in society. **Robert Owen** (1771–1858), a textile manufacturer, established one such community for his workers at his textile mill in Scotland. He later established an agricultural community at New Harmony, Indiana. But both of his "utopias" failed after only a short time—people were not as unselfish and reasonable as he and others assumed.

Marxism

Another form of socialism was advanced by **Karl Marx** (1818–83), the son of a prominent German lawyer. Marx abandoned the study of law to study philosophy and history. At the age of twenty-three, he received a doctor of philosophy degree, but no German university would hire him because of his radical political views. The Prussian government forced him to flee to Paris, where he met **Friedrich Engels** (1820–95) and other utopian socialists during the early Communist movement in France. During that time, Paris was the center of revolutionary gatherings and Communist leadership. In 1846, the Communists met in Brussels and asked Marx and Engels to draw up a manifesto expressing the views and aims of communism. The two men became lifelong friends, and they produced the *Communist Manifesto*, which appeared during the revolutionary year 1848. The premise of their book is that the "history of all hitherto existing societies [was] the history of class struggles." The goal of history, according to Marx and Engels, is for the workers to unite in opposition to capitalism, smash the superstructure of society, and establish themselves as rulers, creating the "dictatorship of the proletariat."

From Paris, Marx went to England, where he spent the last thirty-three years of his life and wrote his most famous work, *Das Kapital*. In it, he explains in detail his socialist ideas. Marx thought the utopian socialists (a term that he and Engels coined) were impractical; he considered them idle dreamers. He believed that his ideas, which he called "scientific socialism," were based on provable economic principles. Yet his views were actually anything but scientific.

Top: Karl Marx
Bottom: Friedrich Engels

Marx believed that economic forces determined the course of history. To him, every social, political, or religious movement sprang from a desire by one group of people to take economic advantage of another group. According to that view of history, even the Protestant Reformation was not primarily a religious movement; religion was simply a veil that obscured the real economic issues. Marx also believed that history would naturally progress toward perfection. During this process, conflicts between various social, political, or religious movements would be inevitable. Each conflict, however, would somehow be resolved successfully, enabling man to "progress" to a higher stage of development. These conflicts are an essential feature of history, Marx said, and they will continue until man finally reaches the perfect society—a society in which everyone is equal and gladly shares the fruit of his labor with others. That perfect condition is what Marx called *communism*.

According to Marx, all of history had been dominated by class struggle and, from earliest times, the oppressed had fought their oppressors. For example, during the Roman Republic, the plebeians struggled against the patricians; during the Middle Ages, the serfs struggled against their lords; and during Marx's time, the **proletariat** (workers) struggled against the **bourgeoisie** (middle-class property owners, capitalists, and industrialists or factory owners). Marx believed that under communism such struggles would cease since all class distinctions would be eliminated.

Marx taught that one of the ways industrialists exploited (took advantage of) the workers was by paying them less than they deserved. According to Marx, the workers created wealth, and the value of a product was the amount of labor it took to produce it. Yet the wages that the workers received were always less than the value of the products they produced. Therefore, according to Marx, the capitalists were robbing the workers and living unjustly off the labor of others. However, Marx ignored the fact that the capitalists invested great funds in building the factories and buying machines and raw materials, without which industrial goods could not be produced.

How would communism end such so-called injustices and achieve the perfect society? Marx said that the answer lay in revolution. He believed that communist revolutions were a necessary and inevitable part of communist development and that they would begin in industrialized nations, which had a large, class-conscious proletariat. The proletariat would overthrow the capitalist bourgeoisie and establish their own rule, called the "dictatorship of the proletariat."

Once in power, the proletariat would begin to systematically eliminate anything that opposed the ideals of communism, such as private ownership of property and private business. In addition, they would destroy Christianity since, according to Marx, religion was "the opiate of the people," a "drug" that the ruling class used to keep the workers in subjection. Once the last remnant of capitalism had been erased, the dictatorship of the proletariat would disappear because it would then be unnecessary. Thus, Marx believed, man would become a perfect being in a perfect society and would no longer need a state to govern him. (Marxism is the form of socialism that most Communist countries—including China, Cuba, North Korea, Vietnam, and the nations of the former Soviet Union—have pursued.)

Fabian Socialism

British socialists who sought to achieve a socialist society without revolution called themselves **Fabians**. They took their name from Quintus Fabius Maximus, a cautious Roman general who tried to wear down his opponent Hannibal gradually instead of engaging him in open battle. The Fabian socialists believed that the best way to destroy capitalism was to gradually undermine it rather than to seek its sudden overthrow. The Fabians and similar groups throughout Europe and America worked to bring about gradual change by urging the passage of welfare legislation.

Christian Socialism

Most of the so-called Christian socialists were theological liberals who believed that Christianity and capitalism were incompatible. They believed that unregenerate society could and should live according to the Sermon on the Mount (Matt. 5–7). They sought to establish an earthly millennium in which peace and justice would reign. Because many people opposed socialism in any form, the Christian socialists tried to portray it positively. They said that socialism is nothing more than "the embodiment of Christianity in our industrial system." In fact, according to an early Christian socialist paper, "Christianity and Socialism are almost interchangeable terms." Such men, although claiming to be Christian, failed to see that the very basis of socialism, the perfectibility of man by man, is contrary to the teaching of Scripture.

Concern of Christians

Following the admonition of the apostle Paul, who said, "As we have therefore opportunity, let us do good unto all men, especially unto them who are of the household of faith" (Gal. 6:10), Christians were among the first to respond to the needs and problems of an industrialized society. They were not simply social reformers hoping to improve living conditions, help the poor, and reduce crime; they realized that sin lies at the root of all social ills. As William

Spiritual Impact on the Industrial Age

During the Industrial Age, England benefited from the ministry of one of the greatest preachers since Wesley—Charles Haddon Spurgeon (1834–92). Born in the home of a minister, Spurgeon had a godly upbringing and was converted at the age of fifteen. In 1854, he became pastor of the New Park Street Chapel, a Baptist church in London. His congregation grew so large that the church had to construct a new building. During the interim, Spurgeon used various buildings to house his congregation. In 1857, he even preached in the Crystal Palace to a crowd of more than twenty-three thousand. Completed in 1861, the London Metropolitan Tabernacle seated five thousand people and soon had to offer additional services to make it possible for everyone to hear Spurgeon preach. His earnest delivery, wonderful oratory, and searching style earned him the title "the Prince of Preachers."

In addition to preaching, Spurgeon oversaw numerous other ministries. He operated a college for preachers, an orphanage, and a tract society for the sale and free distribution of books and pamphlets. Spurgeon also published a magazine, *The Sword and the Trowel*, and wrote several works, the most famous of which is *The Treasury of David*, his commentary on the book of Psalms.

Near the end of his life, Spurgeon became concerned about the growth of theological liberalism within the Baptist denomination. Using *The Sword and the Trowel*, he began publishing articles attacking the "downgrading" of Scripture by those who denied its inerrancy and authority. Called the "Downgrade Controversy," this conflict led Spurgeon to withdraw from the Baptist Union (an organization of English Baptist churches). Many members of the Union refused to withdraw and instead attacked and rebuked Spurgeon for his stand, voting overwhelmingly to condemn him.

Spurgeon's importance today lies not in the size of his ministry, the number of converts he won to Christ, or even his unmatched eloquence. Spurgeon is remembered, in large part, because of his refusal to sacrifice principle for popularity. Many other popular ministers of the era (who are now little remembered) preached on sentimental or moralistic topics. Spurgeon, however, nourished his congregation with sound teaching regardless of the controversy it might arouse. To the end of his life, Spurgeon refused to yield to opposition—remaining obedient to the Word of God.

Booth, the founder of the Salvation Army, said, "My only hope for the permanent deliverance of mankind from misery, either in this world or the next, is the regeneration or remaking of the individual by the power of the Holy Ghost through Jesus Christ."

Top: George Mueller
Middle: William Booth
Bottom: Dwight L. Moody

One of the earliest movements founded to minister to the laboring classes in British cities was the Sunday school during the late eighteenth century. Founder **Robert Raikes** sought to reach the poor, illiterate, working-class children, and he used the Sunday schools to teach the children about Jesus in addition to reading and writing. Over time, many churches made Sunday school a part of their regular ministry, not only to reach underprivileged children for Christ but also to provide further instruction in God's Word for the members of the church. Since most of the Sunday school teachers were laymen, Bible institutes were founded to train laymen to be more effective Christian workers. Concerned Christians also established homes for juvenile delinquents and orphans. Perhaps the best-known orphanages were founded by **George Mueller** in Bristol, England.

In 1844, twenty-two-year-old George Williams established in London the Young Men's Christian Association, commonly called the **YMCA**. The purpose of the organization was to minister to young men who worked in the city and win them to Christ. Although the primary purpose of the YMCA was spiritual, Williams also emphasized educational, social, and athletic development. The YMCA soon became a worldwide organization. Before long, other people established a women's organization, the YWCA. Sadly, these organizations no longer have the spiritual concern of their founders.

As previously mentioned, **William Booth** (1829–1912) founded the Salvation Army, another ministry with worldwide impact. Booth began working in the London slums in 1865, preaching the gospel and seeking to meet the physical needs of those around him. Throughout his ministry, Booth tried to counteract the apathy of some Christians toward the plight of the poor. He wrote, "Why all this apparatus of temples and meeting-houses to save men from perdition in a world which is to come, while never a helping hand is stretched out to save them from the inferno of their present life?" Booth believed that an unconverted individual needed to see that Christians had a genuine concern for him, just as Christ showed compassion for people during His earthly ministry by healing them and feeding them.

The outpouring of Christian charity during the nineteenth century was due in large part to great revivals that swept across Great Britain and the United States. In the eighteenth century, the Wesleyan revivals prompted the first surge of Christian activity; in the nineteenth century, the revivals of **Dwight L. Moody** (1837–99) and other evangelists brought about a second surge. Moody and his partner, Ira Sankey (1840–1908), believed that conditions in society would improve only when those who lived in that society experienced true conversion. Beginning in 1873, Moody and Sankey held evangelistic campaigns in the large industrial cities of Britain and America, bringing thousands of people to Christ. Many of their converts went on to win others to the Savior, and some devoted themselves to various Christian ministries designed to bring those in the inner cities to Christ.

How many thousands or even millions of souls were snatched from eternal hell through the efforts of Raikes, Mueller, Williams, Booth, Moody, and others will never be known in this life. Although their methods were inventive and unique, their message was the same: "Believe on the Lord Jesus Christ, and thou shalt be saved" (Acts 16:31).

Section Quiz

1. List two of the six goals of the Chartist movement.
2. Name the two dominant prime ministers of Britain during the latter part of the nineteenth century. Give the political party of each.
3. Define *welfare state.*
4. What force did Karl Marx believe determined the course of history? In what famous work did he explain his socialist ideas?

★ Contrast the priorities of Disraeli's and Gladstone's terms as prime minister.

III. Changing Outlooks in European Society

Faith in Scientific Progress

During the second half of the nineteenth century, Europe experienced a rapid expansion in scientific knowledge and technology. Practical inventions provided material comforts that previous generations had not known. The telegraph and telephone, for example, made rapid communication possible. Improved methods of transportation made travel easier. Better nutrition and methods of diagnosing and treating disease increased the average lifespan. Greater industrial output raised the material standard of living for most western Europeans. To many people, science became the source of hope for the future. They believed that mankind could achieve anything if given the opportunity. The impact of science on this age greatly influenced man's perception of himself and the world.

Evolutionary Outlook

Most scientists during the Age of Reason viewed the world of nature much like a machine that operates according to fixed, unchanging laws. To them, the order reflected by nature demonstrated the existence of God and His creative power. But in the second half of the nineteenth century, scientists began to view man and nature as the products of an evolutionary process. The man who laid the basis for the modern theories of biological evolution was **Charles Darwin** (1809–82).

Charles Darwin

In his famous work *On the Origin of Species* (1859), Darwin tried to prove that organisms developed from simple to complex structures through natural causes. According to Darwin, no species is fixed and changeless; rather, it is shaped gradually by its environment over countless ages. Those creatures best able to adapt to their environment survive; those with inferior characteristics perish. This theory is called the "survival of the fittest." However, Scripture says that God made each different animal group to reproduce "after his kind" (Gen. 1:24). Hence, the Bible does not allow for one kind of organism to evolve into another.

In 1871, Darwin published a book titled *The Descent of Man*, which was even more shocking than his previous work. In this book, Darwin applied his evolutionary theory to humans. Darwin observed that man resembles other creatures. Instead of recognizing the hand of a common Creator, he taught that man developed from animals. His theory opposed the biblical doctrine of the special, direct creation of man by God. Scripture declares that God directly created man (Gen. 1:26–27; 2:7).

Revolution in the Physical Sciences

During the 1800s and early 1900s, significant developments in the physical sciences greatly expanded man's understanding of matter and energy, the components of the physical universe. Scientists of this period discovered that matter was made up of distinct units called chemical elements. An English Quaker named **John Dalton** (1766–1844) proposed that each chemical element was composed of particles called atoms, and these were distinct from the atoms of any other element. His ideas helped to explain the distinct characteristics of various substances. Today he is recognized as the formulator of the atomic theory.

Later scientists sought to identify and classify the chemical elements. Knowing that certain elements shared similar characteristics, the Russian chemist **Dmitri Mendeleev** (MEN duh LAY uf; 1834–1907) organized the chemical elements in a chart according to their atomic masses. His system of classification, with columns of elements having shared characteristics, was the basis for the modern periodic table.

Top: Marie Curie
Bottom: Albert Einstein

As scientists continued to investigate, they found more characteristics that distinguished the chemical elements as unique particles. Aiding them in their discoveries was the x-ray tube. German physicist **Wilhelm Roentgen** (RENT gun; 1845–1923) accidentally discovered x-rays while working with vacuum tubes. He called them *x-rays* because he did not fully understand the energies he had discovered. Using x-rays, a young British scientist named Henry Moseley (1887–1915) was able to determine the number of protons in the atoms of an element. On the basis of this information, Moseley and others reordered the periodic table by atomic number (number of protons) rather than atomic mass (Mendeleev's arrangement).

The discovery of radioactive matter added new elements to the chart. The husband-and-wife team of **Pierre** (1859–1906) and **Marie** (1867–1934) **Curie** found two new elements in a type of uranium ore called pitchblende. Those radioactive elements naturally broke down into simpler elements, indicating that all atoms, and thus all matter, are composed of even smaller particles. Such an idea was advanced by British physicist **Ernest Rutherford** (1871–1937). He stated that the atom is composed of at least two distinct parts—a positively charged nucleus surrounded by negatively charged electrons. Danish physicist Niels Bohr (1885–1962) built on Rutherford's theory. Bohr's model of the atom shows a nucleus surrounded by electrons that move in orbits much like planets revolving around the sun. Electrons were assigned to distinct energy levels, but they could move from one level to another by gaining or releasing energy.

The work of perhaps the greatest scientific thinker of the twentieth century, **Albert Einstein** (INE STINE; 1879–1955), showed the relationship between matter and energy, which he demonstrated through the equation $E = mc^2$ (energy equals mass times the speed of light squared). Another of his contributions to science was his theory of relativity. Scientists in the past believed that measurements of time, mass, and length did not vary. According to Einstein's theory, however, moving objects increase in mass as they decrease in length. The amount of increase or decrease depends on the speed of the object.

Impact of Science on Society

The advances in science caused many people to look on science as the means of progress. People began to apply scientific theories of the physical world to the study of man and society.

"Scientific" became a new standard by which society's institutions and values were measured. To many people, science became a religion. They rejected the authority of God's Word for the authority of scientific theory. Often, something done in the name of science was judged true and worthy regardless of whether evidence existed to support it. For example, many people praised Darwin's theory of evolution as scientific while dismissing the biblical account of Creation as mythical. In rejecting the Genesis record, they also rejected their responsibility to God as their Creator. Others incorrectly applied scientific theory to society. Modern philosophers, for example, embraced Einstein's theory of relativity as the guide for the study of ethics (questions of right and wrong). They claimed that since all things in the universe are relative, moral principles are relative too; moral principles simply evolved as man evolved. Through such belief and teaching, sinful people demonstrated their rebellion against God and His Word.

Challenges to Christianity

Although the nineteenth century was a time of great revivals and missionary activity, the Christian church, as we have seen, was besieged by many foes. Even many religious leaders embraced the false religion of science. They rejected the authority of Scripture as the inspired and inerrant (free from error) Word of God. Instead, they tried to "scientifically" discern what portions of God's Word are true and what portions are false. Basing their theories on the evolutionary ideas of Darwin, these men claimed that Judaism and Christianity slowly developed out of ancient Near Eastern civilization. They rejected the fact that God revealed His truth directly to "holy men of God" (2 Pet. 1:21). Many liberal theologians claimed that Moses did not write the first five books of the Bible. They also rejected the miracles mentioned in the Bible, inventing their own natural explanations for those supernatural events. Likewise, because theological liberals rejected the possibility of prophecy, they claimed the Old Testament writers actually wrote down their "prophecies" after the events had happened.

The purpose and mission of the church also came under attack. Those who promoted the social gospel believed that the major purpose of Christianity was to change society and that by changing society individuals would be made better. They rejected the New Testament teaching that the only gospel is the story of the death, burial, and Resurrection of Jesus Christ (1 Cor. 15:1–4). Instead, they preached a gospel of social improvement. The apostle Paul warned against such in Galatians 1:7–8.

The work of Christ was also challenged by a growing materialism and secularization of society. Many people began to concentrate on the things of this world and neglect spiritual things. The number of church members, especially in Europe, remained high, but the number of people who actually attended church declined significantly. In addition, a small but increasing number of people began to leave the church. Weakened by the worldly members who remained, the Christian church as an institution lost much of its influence on the lives of Europeans.

Common to all of the foes of Christianity was a spirit of humanism—the exaltation of man above God. Modern humanists accepted the evolutionary theories and the social gospel, which taught that man was neither created by nor responsible to God. Instead, man was responsible to himself and to society. They did not believe in heaven and hell but rather believed that whatever fulfillment man was going to receive would come through his efforts in this life.

In the late nineteenth century, humanists were a small minority, consisting primarily of unbelieving religious leaders, liberal theologians, and godless intellectuals. But the secularization of society and the spread of this humanistic spirit increased rapidly—permeating all areas of society during the twentieth century.

However, many people during the Victorian era did not undergo a crisis of faith. Faithful believers continued to believe the Bible and demonstrate Christ's redeeming power in their daily lives. Others, including secularists, eventually found their lives to be without meaning and experienced a crisis of doubt. Many former skeptics found Christ and became faithful believers in later years.

New Trends in the Arts

Realism

By the 1850s, a new form of artistic expression known as **realism** had become widespread in Europe. Realists had a growing awareness of the world around them. They rejected both the idealist emotion of romanticism and its fascination with exotic themes and faraway places. Realists believed that life should be portrayed as it really was. Although they did not abandon emotion, they sought to express feelings that touched their everyday lives. They were conscious of the social problems around them and sought with "scientific" objectivity to represent reality. They tended, however, to highlight the darker side of European society: poverty, injustice, and immorality.

One of the earliest realist writers was English novelist **Charles Dickens** (1812–70). Dickens was a social critic who attacked injustice in society through his vivid portrayals of such places as industrial slums and debtors' prisons. In his famous novel *Hard Times*, he depicted the living conditions in industrial cities with the following description of the imaginary city of Coketown:

> It was a town of red brick, or brick that would have been red if the smoke and ashes had allowed it; but as matters stood it was a town of unnatural red and black like the painted face of a savage. It was a town of machinery and tall chimneys, out of which interminable serpents of smoke trailed themselves for ever and ever, and never got uncoiled. It had a black canal in it, and a river that ran purple with ill-smelling dye, and vast piles of buildings full of windows where there was a rattling and a trembling all day long.

Above: Charles Dickens
Below: Gustave Courbet, Beach in Normandy, *National Gallery of Art, Washington, D.C.*

Other writers wrote about man's struggles in this life. British novelist and poet **Thomas Hardy** (1840–1928) portrayed man as engaged in a hopeless struggle against impersonal forces beyond his control. American **Samuel Clemens**, better known by his pen name Mark Twain (1835–1910), viewed life as Hardy did; unlike Hardy, however, he used humor to convey his ideas. The famous Russian novelist **Leo Tolstoy** (1828–1910) realistically described life in Russia during the Napoleonic Wars.

In reaction to the romantic artists, who tended to paint faraway places, realist painters concentrated on observable, commonplace subjects. They tried to portray life as they saw it, not as they imagined it to be. According to Gustave Courbet (koor BEH; 1819–77), a famous realist painter, "an abstract object, invisible or nonexistent, does not belong to the domain of painting." "Show me an angel," he said, "and I'll paint one." Instead of painting angels, he and his fellow realists painted such works as *The Stone Breakers* and *The Third Class Carriage*.

Impressionism

Near the end of the nineteenth century, French artists created a new style of painting known as **impressionism**. The impressionists turned away from photographic realism in their painting and instead made light and color their chief concerns. The impressionists did not outline their figures clearly but used short, choppy brush strokes to capture the vibrating nature of light. To the impressionists, light was all important; what the light revealed did not matter. The most famous of the French impressionists were **Auguste Renoir** (ren WAHR; 1841–1919) and **Claude Monet** (moh NAY; 1840–1926).

Another Frenchman, **Auguste Rodin** (roh DAN; 1840–1917), was one of the foremost sculptors of the nineteenth century. It is difficult, however, to place him within a particular style. His subject matter was romantic, but his technique was often impressionistic. Like the impressionistic painters, Rodin did not make his art photographically exact. As a result, many of his works are not finely polished and have an "unfinished" look. Perhaps his best known sculpture is *The Thinker*.

Still another Frenchman, **Claude Debussy** (DEB yoo SEE, 1862–1918), was largely responsible for the impressionistic style in music. Debussy used unique chord structures in an attempt to express musically what the impressionistic painters were portraying visually—the shimmering effects of light. As a result, he only vaguely outlined the melody and harmony in his works. The impressionistic movement that Debussy championed, however, quickly died out as composers searched for new forms of musical expression.

Left: Young Girls at the Piano *by Renoir*
Right: Woman with a Parasol *by Monet*

Still Life *by Cézanne*

Postimpressionism

Not all artists agreed that color and light should be the ultimate objects of painting. **Paul Cézanne** (say ZAN; 1839–1906), a Frenchman, and **Vincent van Gogh** (van GOH; 1853–90), a Dutchman, believed that impressionism rejected too many traditional artistic concepts and advocated a style that became known as postimpressionism. Among other things, Cézanne and Van Gogh tried to emphasize universal themes and to outline the figures more clearly in their paintings.

For example, Cézanne believed that the artist could reduce everything in nature to basic geometric shapes. He urged his fellow artists to "treat nature in terms of the cylinder, and the sphere and the cone" to make the outlines of various objects more clear. This geometric emphasis in his art made Cézanne a forerunner of cubism (see p. 486). Van Gogh, on the other hand, often distorted the figures in his paintings in an effort to portray the intense emotions he felt toward his subjects. For this reason, he was a forerunner of expressionism (see p. 486).

Section Quiz

1. What man laid the foundation for the modern theories of biological evolution? In what book did he set forth his theory of survival of the fittest?
2. Identify the contribution to science of each of the following men: Dalton, Mendeleev, Roentgen, Bohr, and Einstein.
3. What did advocates of the social gospel movement believe was the major purpose of Christianity?
4. What was the new form of artistic expression in the latter half of the nineteenth century that sought to portray life as it really was?
5. Identify the occupation and artistic style of each of the following men: Dickens, Courbet, Renoir, Debussy, and Van Gogh.

★ Contrast the artistic works in this chapter with those in chapter 15.

Chapter 18 Review

Making Connections

1–2. How did mass production benefit society? (List two ways.)

3–4. How did science contribute to the development of the Industrial Revolution? (List two examples.)

5. How did Parliament respond to demands for increased representation?

Developing History Skills

1. Evaluate Dickens's statement in the opening lines of *A Tale of Two Cities* and substantiate your evaluation with examples from nineteenth-century Britain.
2. Why did the Industrial Revolution begin in Britain rather than in a country in continental Europe?

Thinking Critically

1. Is socialism harmful to society? Why or why not?
2. What impact did Christianity have on Britain during the nineteenth century? Support your answer.

Living in God's World

1. Since humans and society are fallen, and there is no hope of a perfect society until the return of Christ, should Christians concern themselves with correcting social ills on an individual level?
2. Timothy Larsen's book *Crisis of Doubt* challenges the standard narrative about religion in the Victorian era, which implies that most intellectuals of that period abandoned their Christian faith. Larsen's research shows that many of the leading skeptics reconverted to Christianity. How is Larsen a model for Christian historians?

People, Places, and Things to Know

Industrial Revolution
Jethro Tull
Charles Townshend
Robert Bakewell
John Kay
James Hargreaves
Richard Arkwright
Samuel Crompton
Eli Whitney
Henry Cort
Henry Bessemer
James Watt
John McAdam
Richard Trevithick
Robert Fulton
Orville and Wilbur Wright
Henry Ford
William Wilberforce
Corn Laws
Reform Bill of 1832
Chartism
Benjamin Disraeli
William Gladstone
Parliament Bill (of 1911)
socialism
Robert Owen
Karl Marx
Friedrich Engels
proletariat
bourgeoisie
Fabians
Robert Raikes
George Mueller
YMCA
William Booth
Dwight L. Moody
Charles Darwin
John Dalton
Dmitri Mendeleev
Wilhelm Roentgen
Pierre and Marie Curie
Ernest Rutherford
Albert Einstein
realism
Charles Dickens
Thomas Hardy
Samuel Clemens
Leo Tolstoy
impressionism
Auguste Renoir
Claude Monet
Auguste Rodin
Claude Debussy
Paul Cézanne
Vincent van Gogh

19

EUROPE EXPANDS OVERSEAS

I. Extension of European Culture

II. Extension of European Power

The early explorers who traveled around the world opened the door to a great flood of European migration. During the seventeenth and eighteenth centuries, thousands of Europeans crossed the oceans in search of fortune, adventure, or religious freedom in these new lands of opportunity. Though they left their homelands, they did not leave behind their European heritage or culture. They established new settlements that were like "little Europes" overseas. Despite strong cultural and economic ties to Europe, many of these settlements gained political independence in the late eighteenth and early nineteenth centuries and began developing as new nations.

The period of European expansion was renewed during the nineteenth century. Industrialized nations sought new overseas territories as sources of raw materials for their factories and as markets for their industrial goods. Later in the century, nationalistic pride prompted other countries to seek to build overseas empires to symbolize their power and glory. As a result, European nations competed for control of much of the world—especially Africa and Asia. This new scramble for territory came to be known as imperialism.

Although imperialism was an economic and political movement, Christians used it as an opportunity for missionary outreach. The nineteenth century was the greatest period of missionary activity since the first three centuries of the Christian era. Godly men and women dedicated their lives to carrying out the Great Commission: "Go ye into all the world, and preach the gospel to every creature" (Mark 16:15). Although some secular historians claim that the missions movement was merely a form of colonialism, missionaries often served as a check on the abuses of colonial powers.

I. Extension of European Culture

After the Age of Exploration, European civilization was carried to all parts of the globe as Europeans settled in the newly discovered regions of the world. For the most part, the early settlers went to isolated lands—the Americas, Australia, New Zealand, and South Africa. Overcoming the dangers and obstacles of frontier life, transplanted Europeans built thriving colonies. As these colonies grew and prospered, they attracted more European immigrants. At the same time, they became more and more independent of their homelands.

In Chapter 16, we traced the American struggle for independence. Since the United States was considered a model for developing colonies, let us begin by examining the growth of this young nation. The sections that follow will survey the settlement, development, and independence of the British colonies of Canada, Australia, New Zealand, and South Africa and the Spanish colonies in Latin America.

Growth of the United States Following Independence

Geographic and Political Expansion

In the years following independence, the American nation rapidly expanded westward. From the very outset of American nationhood, pioneers pushed westward across the Allegheny and Appalachian Mountains, laying claim to vast tracts of land. In 1803 President Thomas Jefferson purchased more than 800,000 square miles of French territory west of the Mississippi River from Napoleon for $15 million. Known as the **Louisiana Purchase**, this land almost doubled the size of the United States. Much of the territory that makes up the southwestern portion of the United States today was acquired after a war with Mexico (1846–48). In 1849 the discovery of gold in California prompted a great rush to the far West. Thus—through settlement, purchase, and war—the United States expanded its borders from the Atlantic to the Pacific. Additional territory was added in 1867 when the United States purchased Alaska from the Russians. By the end of the century, the U.S. government also controlled Hawaii, Cuba, Puerto Rico, and the Philippines.

Paralleling the expansion of American territory was an expansion in the number of people who had the right to vote and to hold office. Early in the nation's history, laws restricted widespread participation in government. But westward expansion encouraged a more democratic spirit. Frontier conditions broke down social and economic barriers. Men were judged by their character and ability rather than by their social class or financial status. As a result, many of the western states were among the first to adopt universal manhood suffrage. Gradually, other states adopted this democratic practice. Similarly, Americans living in the territories were given the opportunity to be represented in the U.S. government. New states were allowed to join the union on an equal basis with the thirteen original states.

Sectional Differences

Despite the early growth and prosperity of the United States, rival sectional loyalties, especially between the North and the South, divided the young nation. Each section had a different way of life, different values, and different interests. Northern society was a mix of farming areas and urban centers built around industry. Southern society was predominantly rural and revolved around various cash crops. Industrialists in the North wanted high tariffs on imported goods to protect industry from more cheaply produced foreign goods. Many in the South, on the other hand, did not want to pay more for manufactured goods

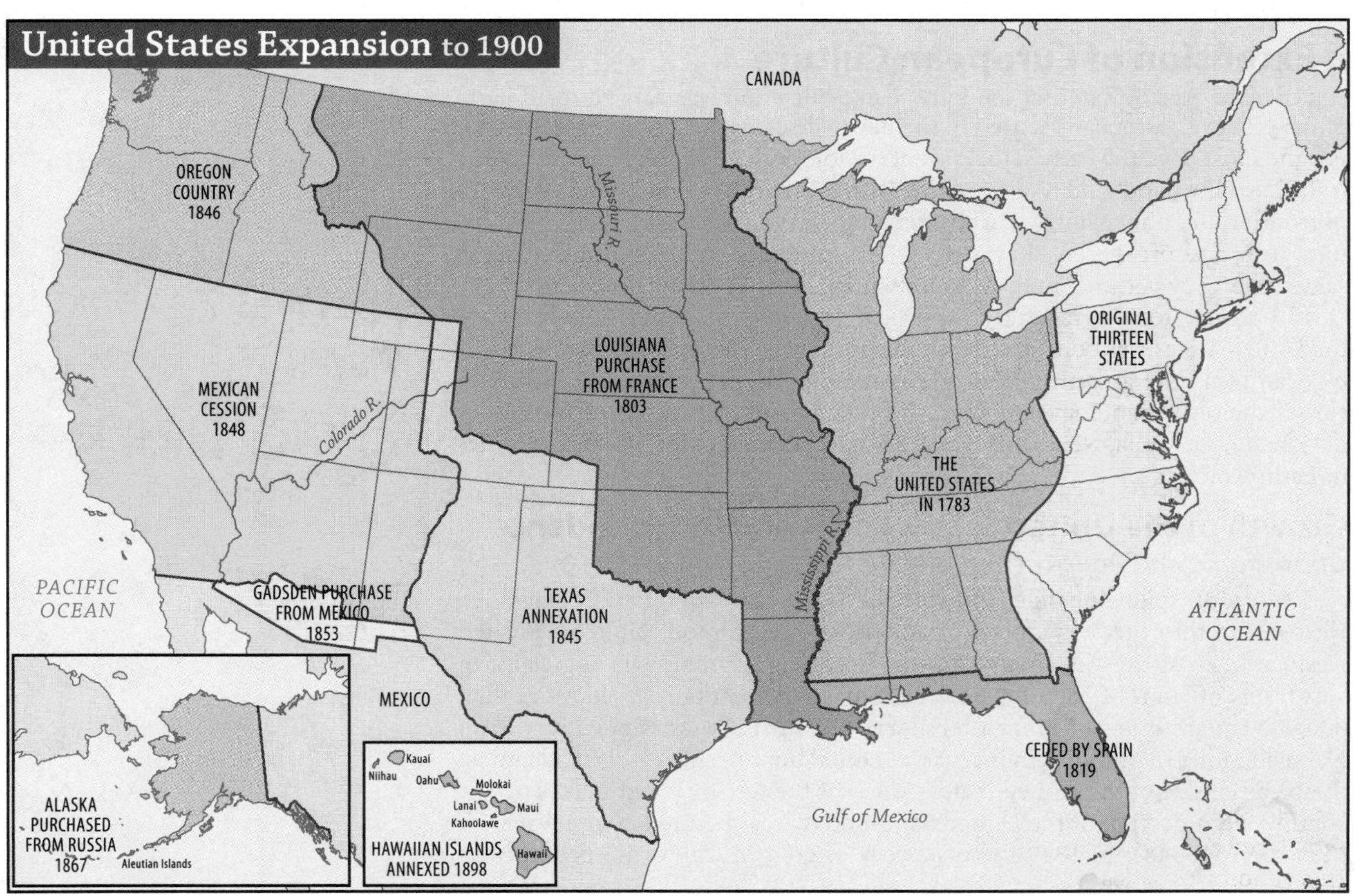

just to help a select group in the North. They preferred to buy less expensive goods from Great Britain. Finally, most northern states discontinued the use of slave labor, whereas large landowners in the southern states counted on its continuation.

As pressing issues came before the U.S. Congress, it became clear that sectional interests overshadowed national unity. Given the different interests and concerns, united action on national issues was possible only through political compromise. Crucial to the interests of both sides was the expanding influence of the West. As western territories asked for admission into the Union, Congress debated over whether they should enter as slave states or as free states. The argument over states' rights and slavery came to a boiling point after the election of Abraham Lincoln in 1860. Eleven southern states responded to Lincoln's victory by seceding from the Union. The bloody war that followed (1861–65) ended with the defeat of the Southern forces and the preservation of the Union.

Growth in Industry and Population

Following the Civil War, the nation entered a period of rapid industrial expansion. A number of factors made this growth possible: the hardworking American spirit, an abundance of raw materials, new inventions, and the expansion of the railroads. This prosperity resulted primarily from God's blessing and provision as demonstrated by several spiritual revivals in America during the nineteenth century.

A growing population provided industry with a large labor force. During the nineteenth century, the population of the United States rose from four million in 1790 to ninety-nine million in 1910. More than one-third of that increase came from immigrants who each year entered this land of opportunity by the thousands. From 1821 to 1910, about thirty-four million immigrants from all over Europe came to the United States. Many of them remained in the cities, providing the backbone of America's rapidly developing industries.

Isolation in Foreign Affairs

The United States was not always as involved in world affairs as it is today. Since the presidency of George Washington, the government had maintained a policy of neutrality and isolation from European politics. Americans were more interested in national security and trade than in "entangling alliances." In a message to Congress in 1823, President James Monroe enunciated what has come to be called the **Monroe Doctrine**. He told Europe that North and South America, "by the free and independent condition which they have assumed and maintain, are henceforth not to be considered as subjects for future colonization by any European powers." Monroe went on to say that the United States would regard "any attempt" by Europe to extend its control "to any portion of this hemisphere as dangerous to our peace and safety." In return, Monroe promised that the United States would not interfere in European affairs.

Although the United States avoided making foreign alliances, it could not remain isolated from world affairs. The first challenge to its isolation came as American merchants and businessmen expanded their foreign trade and investments. To protect and help Americans in their overseas business ventures, the U.S. government signed trade agreements with several European nations. Later in the century, the United States competed with European nations for trade opportunities in new markets such as China and Japan.

Another challenge came from the French emperor Napoleon III, who was eager to build an empire in the New World. He sent French troops into Mexico and placed an Austrian archduke named **Maximilian** in charge of the country. This action was a clear infringement of the Monroe Doctrine, but the United

Top: The U.S.S. Maine *sunk in Havana harbor*
Bottom: The U.S.S. Maine *on the afternoon of February 15, 1898. That night a mysterious explosion sank it and sparked war between the United States and Spain.*

States was embroiled in the Civil War and took no immediate action. When the war was over, however, an American army gathered on the Mexican border and forced Napoleon III to withdraw his troops. Mexican forces captured and executed Maximilian in 1867.

Late in the nineteenth century, additional problems in Latin America drew the United States out of its isolationist position. During the 1890s, reports of Spain's mistreatment of its colony of Cuba roused American sympathy for Cuban independence. In 1898, the U.S.S. *Maine* was sent to Havana Harbor to protect American interests during a series of uprisings in Cuba. On February 15, the battleship exploded, killing 260 American sailors. Though mystery surrounded the explosion, Spain was blamed. The U.S. Congress declared war, and troops were sent to Cuba. After brief fighting, the Spanish forces on the island surrendered. As part of the treaty ending the Spanish-American War, Spain ceded to the United States the territories of Guam, Puerto Rico, and the Philippines.

Further problems arose when some Latin American countries that had borrowed funds from European banks would not or could not repay their loans. In response, European governments threatened to intervene in those countries if necessary to force them to meet their obligations. American president Theodore Roosevelt, however, refused to permit European intervention in Latin America, even for legitimate reasons. Instead, Roosevelt proclaimed what is known as the **Roosevelt Corollary** to the Monroe Doctrine. In case of wrongdoing on the part of any Latin American state, the United States claimed the right to intervene in that country and set its affairs in order.

By World War I, the United States had moved away from its longstanding policy of isolation. But not until after World War II did the United States become heavily involved in world politics.

British Colonies Granted Independence

At the outset of the nineteenth century, Spain lost most of its colonial possessions. During this same period, Great Britain was acquiring new territory and, by the end of the nineteenth century, could boast that the sun never set on its empire. British emigrants transplanted British culture into many lands, including Canada, Australia, New Zealand, and South Africa. The British carried with them their tradition of self-government. As the colonies developed, Britain allowed them greater self-government—it had learned from its experience with the American colonies. As a result, the British colonies eventually gained independence without experiencing widespread revolts.

Canada

Unlike other British possessions, Canada was originally a French colony. From the beginning of European settlement in North America, relations between the French Canadians and the British colonists were unfriendly. The national rivalry between Great Britain and France in Europe often spilled over into the colonies, bringing war and unrest. When the Seven Years' War (known in North America as the French and Indian War) came to an end in 1763 (see Chapter 14), Britain emerged victorious. As part of the peace settlement, France ceded Canada to Great Britain.

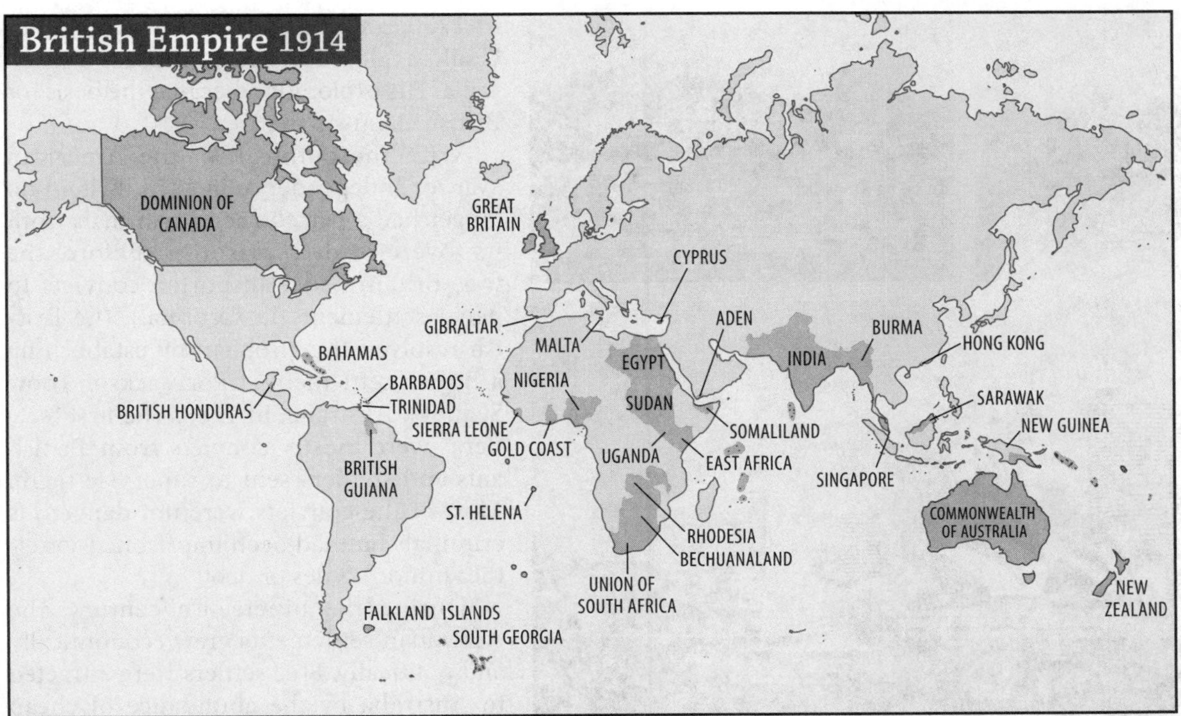

To ensure French Canadian loyalty to British rule, the British Parliament passed the **Quebec Act** in 1774. This legislation permitted the French Canadians to retain their language, law, and customs and to freely practice their Roman Catholic religion. Although the act alarmed the predominantly Protestant American colonies, its concessions temporarily pacified the French Canadians.

During the American War for Independence, thousands of British Loyalists fled to Canada. The French Canadians felt threatened by the growing British population. At the same time, the British colonists did not want to live under the long-established French customs and law. To end the friction, the British Parliament divided Canada into two provinces: Upper Canada (now Ontario), where most of the Loyalists lived, and Lower Canada (now Quebec), where most of the French lived. Each province was granted its own governor, legislative council, and elected assembly. Nevertheless, discontent continued.

The British government sent a new governor general, Lord Durham, to Canada to study problems in the colonies. He recommended that Britain grant Canada self-government in domestic matters while retaining control over foreign affairs. At the same time, he called for a united Canada. Parliament adopted the latter recommendation and combined Lower and Upper Canada by an Act of Union in 1840. In 1867, the government was reorganized again by the **British North America Act**, which created the Dominion of Canada, a federation of four provinces—Quebec, Ontario, Nova Scotia, and New Brunswick. (It also provided for new territories to be added to the union.) Canada remained a part of the British Empire, but it had a much greater degree of self-government than before.

Australia and New Zealand

Australia is an island continent located in the South Pacific. It is nearly as large as the continental United States. Despite its size, it remained virtually unknown before the seventeenth century. Dutch explorers discovered it in the early 1600s, but they did not establish a colony there. More than a century later

Three views of Sydney, Australia: two of the original settlement and one of the modern city

in 1770, an Englishman, Captain **James Cook**, explored the eastern coast of Australia. His exploration became the basis for British claims to the area.

With the outbreak of the American War for Independence in 1775, Britain no longer had a place to send criminals from its overcrowded prisons. (Before the war, Britain had transported convicts to penal settlements in Georgia.) The British resolved this problem by establishing a British settlement at Port Jackson (now Sydney), Australia, in 1788. The first "settlers" were mostly convicts from British jails and soldiers sent to supervise them. Most of the convicts were not dangerous criminals but had been imprisoned for either minor crimes or debt.

During the nineteenth century, the Australian settlements grew economically and politically. Free settlers were attracted to Australia by the abundance of cheap land and the discovery of gold. By the end of the century, Australia became a world producer of wool and meat. In 1901, the independent Australian colonies, with the approval of the British Parliament, united into a federal union, forming the Commonwealth of Australia.

The islands of New Zealand located about one thousand miles southeast of Australia, were first sighted by the Dutch. Captain Cook later made five visits to the islands, exploring them extensively and mapping their coastlines. Among the first European settlers in New Zealand were escaped convicts from the penal colonies in Australia and seamen who had deserted their ships. In addition, the islands were inhabited by native New Zealanders, the **Maoris**. In 1907, New Zealand became a self-governing dominion in the British Empire.

South Africa

The Dutch were the first Europeans to settle South Africa. In 1652, they established the Cape Colony on the southern tip of Africa. During the Napoleonic Wars, Britain seized the colony and encouraged British people to settle at the Cape. The Dutch colonists, called **Boers** (Dutch for "farmers"), resented British rule. Beginning in 1836, hundreds of them began a migration, called the **Great Trek**, northward into the interior, where they founded the republics of the Transvaal and the Orange Free State. In the 1850s, Britain granted these republics their independence.

For several decades, the Boers lived in relative isolation from the British settlers along the coast. But in 1867 diamonds were discovered in the Orange Free State, and in 1886 gold was discovered in the Transvaal. Before long, thousands of miners—mostly British—poured into the region. Growing tension between the Boers and the British led to the **Boer War** (1899–1902). The British won the war and extended their control over those two republics. They were lenient with the Boers, however, providing them with financial help to recover from the war and allowing them to use their own language in schools and courts. In 1910, the British colonies at the Cape and the old Boer republics combined to form the Union of South Africa, joining the British Empire as a dominion.

Latin America Gains Independence

Latin America covers almost eight million square miles and is larger than the United States and Canada combined. It stretches from the northern border of Mexico to the tip of South America. These lands were the home of the major Amerindian civilizations—the Maya, the Aztec, and the Inca (see Chapter 13). But by 1500 the Spanish and the Portuguese had claimed most of this vast region. Because of the strong influence of Spanish and Portuguese customs and languages, which derived from the "Latin" culture of ancient Rome, this region is known as Latin America.

Struggle for Independence

Unlike the English colonies in North America, which experienced a large measure of self-government, the Latin American colonies were tightly controlled by Spain and Portugal. Officials appointed by the crown directed colonial affairs. In the Spanish possessions, most of these civil officials were ***peninsulares***, Spaniards born and reared in Spain. They controlled the government and economic wealth of the colonies. Often, they used their positions selfishly to amass personal fortunes with which they returned to Spain to live lives of ease. Their arrogant attitude angered the ***criollos*** (Spaniards born in the New World). There was also dissatisfaction among the rest of the people—Indians, ***mestizos*** (those of mixed Spanish and Indian blood), and blacks—who were held in low esteem and used by the other two groups to achieve their own ends.

Over the years, growing discontent with the economic restrictions and political corruption of Spanish rule gave rise to independence movements. These movements found support among many of the educated people in Latin America, who were influenced by the works of Locke, Rousseau, and Voltaire. They were also encouraged by the example of the American War for Independence. As a result, isolated uprisings broke out. But not until the early nineteenth century did widespread revolution sweep across Latin America.

The Napoleonic Wars in Europe stirred these revolts. Napoleon removed the Spanish king and placed his brother Joseph Bonaparte on the Spanish throne. However, the colonists, though dissatisfied with Spanish rule, would not tolerate French rule. Two men, **Simón Bolívar** (boh LEE vahr; 1783–1830) and **José de San Martín** (*SAHN* mahr TEEN; 1778–1850), dreamed of a Spanish South America free from outside control. They raised troops to fight "wars of liberation." Bolívar, called "the Liberator," led the struggle for freedom in the north. His troops crushed the Spanish forces and secured the independence of Gran Colombia (comprising what are now the countries of Colombia, Venezuela, Panama, and Ecuador). To the south, San Martín, backed by Argentina (which had already gained its independence), led an army over the Andes Mountains and freed first Chile and then Peru from Spanish domination.

Simón Bolívar

The Portuguese colony of Brazil experienced a more peaceful transition to independence. In 1807, French troops invaded Portugal, forcing the royal family to flee to Brazil. From his new capital in Rio de Janeiro, the king ruled the Portuguese empire. Brazil prospered during that period as trade and industry flourished. In 1821, the king returned to Portugal, leaving behind his son **Dom Pedro** as his regent. But when the Portuguese legislature attempted to reduce Brazil to its former colonial status, Dom Pedro declared Brazil independent and became the emperor of Brazil. Under his rule and that of

José de San Martín

his son Dom Pedro II, Brazil became a thriving nation. But eventually, growing sectional differences in the large country and discontent among Brazil's military leaders forced Dom Pedro II to abdicate. In 1889, Brazil was proclaimed a republic. In the years that followed, however, the military dominated the government.

The birth of liberty in Latin American nations that gained independence from Spain tended to follow a pattern. After gaining independence, the nation's new leaders fought among themselves until military leaders (***caudillos***) stepped in with armed gangs, seized power, and established dictatorships.

Mexico is an example of this pattern. Self-government in Mexico came slowly, although it had been promised in the election of Porfirio Diaz in 1876. He had campaigned as a champion of a free, constitutional democracy. Once elected, he restored order, increased investments by foreign businesses, and led Mexico to become the most prosperous Latin American nation.

Latin America After Independence

Although elected under a constitution, Diaz eventually consolidated his power and became a dictator, ruling for more than thirty years. Gradually, the peasants came to view Diaz and his appointees as self-serving autocrats and puppets of foreign businesses. During Diaz's rule, Indians were reduced to virtual slavery, the Roman Church amassed great wealth, and foreign investors exploited Mexico. This foreign exploitation often led to a hatred of foreigners.

Resistance to the Diaz regime began as localized rebellions against the regional administrators. The critics of Diaz consolidated under the leadership of Francisco Madero, who denounced violent revolution and ran against Diaz in the presidential election. Diaz had Madero and ten thousand of his supporters jailed, ensuring his own victory in the election. Madero challenged the results in court, but the judges, all Diaz appointees, ruled against him.

In response to Diaz's schemes, the people revolted in 1910. The uprising succeeded, and Madero was elected president. As often happens in revolutions, however, Madero's own supporters disputed among themselves, split into several armed factions, and revolted against him. Madero was assassinated. Order was not fully restored until after World War I.

Problems of Self-government

From the time of independence through the rest of the nineteenth century, the new Latin American nations often suffered from common problems. However, the following generalizations did not equally apply to every Latin American country.

Political instability—After gaining their independence, most Latin American countries followed the example of the United States and established republics. Unlike the United States, however, they had little previous experience in self-rule. As previously mentioned, ambitious military leaders often seized power. They ruled as dictators, satisfying their own desires at the expense of their countries. As a result, Latin American countries experienced frequent changes in government as one military dictator was overthrown and another took his place.

Monopoly of land and wealth by a few—From early colonial days, Latin America was dominated by a wealthy, powerful upper class. Though a small minority, this social class owned most of the land, controlled the wealth, and manipulated the government in many Latin American countries. The vast majority of the people remained poor and had little voice in the everyday workings of the government. Without a large middle class to provide stability, Latin American countries suffered from the effects of political favoritism and class conflict.

Powerful influence of the Roman Church—As the Spanish and Portuguese came to the New World, they firmly established Roman Catholicism in Latin America. This religious system became a dominant influence on Latin American culture. The Roman Church gained control of large amounts of land in addition to controlling the educational system. As a result, church leaders often influenced the political process to benefit the Roman Catholic Church.

Ethnic disunity—In addition to blacks, Indians, and inhabitants of European descent, a large number of Latin Americans were of mixed ancestry. Hatred, jealousy, and conflicts of interest often existed among the ethnic groups.

Conflict among Latin American countries—Unlike the United States, the Latin American colonies did not form one nation after gaining their independence. Soon after the wars of liberation, the Latin American people divided into a number of small countries rather than several larger ones. This fragmentation led to several border wars among the nations.

Economic weakness—During the nineteenth century, Latin America had virtually no industry. (Foreign investment from the United States and Europe accounted for what little industry there was.) In most Latin American countries, the economy was built around only a few products, such as bananas, coffee, rubber, or wood. A poor growing season or a struggling world market could bring economic disaster to these countries.

European and U.S. involvement—Political and economic problems within the Latin American countries prompted European nations to interfere in their domestic affairs. The Europeans wanted to protect their foreign investments and to ensure that loans made to these countries would be repaid. Such European involvement in Latin America worried the United States. Because the United States opposed European intervention, it assumed a greater responsibility for policing Latin American affairs. But with the increased dominance of the United States in the Western Hemisphere came a growing resentment of the United States on the part of the Latin American countries.

Section Quiz

1. List four possessions outside North America that the United States controlled by the end of the nineteenth century.
2. What man's exploration was the basis for the English claim on Australia? What was unusual about the first "settlers" there?
3. What were Dutch colonists in South Africa called? What people did they fight for control of the mineral resources found in Transvaal and the Orange Free State?
4. Define *peninsulares*, *criollos*, and *mestizos*.
5. Who were the two major leaders of South America's struggle for independence?

★ Why were Latin American countries often unable to establish stable governments?

II. Extension of European Power

The quest for colonies in the sixteenth and seventeenth centuries was motivated primarily by the economic policy of mercantilism. (See Chapter 13.) European countries looked upon their colonial possessions as a source of wealth. But by the late eighteenth century, European countries found it financially draining to maintain and protect their colonies, many of which were now seeking independence. Likewise, a free trade policy was slowly replacing the one-sided trade of mercantilism. Revolts in Europe during the early nineteenth century further diminished the interest in overseas colonies.

However, between 1870 and 1914, the race for overseas possessions revived. Many European nations competed in a new form of empire-building known as **imperialism**, the dominance and power asserted by one nation over less-powerful nations. During the late nineteenth century, European nations eagerly sought to impose their spheres of influence over most of the world. Empire-building became increasingly important to the foreign policy of many European nations, resulting in fierce rivalries that would eventually contribute to World War I.

Reasons for Imperialism

The motives behind imperialism were diverse. In fact, the motives of any particular nation may have differed from one overseas possession to another or from one time to another.

1. The expansion of industrialism in the late nineteenth century increased the demand for raw materials and new markets. Industrialized nations did not want to depend on other nations for their industrial supplies. They sought to control areas of the world that would meet their industrial needs and provide an outlet for manufactured goods. Unfortunately, the European powers often acted without regard for the rights and desires of the native populations.

2. Imperialism was also motivated by the intense nationalism that characterized Europe from 1870 to 1914. An overseas empire brought national honor and prestige. In addition to the ongoing rivalry between Britain and France, imperialism provided the newly formed nations of Germany and Italy the opportunity to display their growing national strength. European nations were quick to seize control of strategic locations to establish military bases and protect their worldwide interests.

3. "Humanitarianism" became an often-used excuse for imperialism. The British poet Rudyard Kipling expressed this popular nineteenth-century sentiment as he urged his contemporaries to "take up the white man's burden." It is difficult to overstate the racist attitude of Europeans who viewed their society as superior to the civilizations of Asia and Africa. Those who embraced this view assumed it was their responsibility to share the benefits of Western culture—education, medical care, industry, and technology. In truth, some Europeans did launch sincere efforts to improve education, abolish slavery, and stamp out disease and famine in colonial territories. Also, many people did profit from Western aid. However, the native populations found the superior attitude of many Europeans to be offensive. Furthermore, too often humanitarian concerns by the Europeans became nothing more than an excuse to exploit the wealth of these dominated countries.

4. While not a dominant motivation behind Europe's worldwide expansion, the dramatic spread of Christian missions accompanied this expansion. Despite opposition from some imperialist powers, the nineteenth century became the "great century" of missionary activity. As European countries built overseas empires, Christians became acquainted with the spiritual needs of people in distant lands. Even though in many countries Western political and economic control opened the doors for missionary activity, Christian missionaries were not motivated by a desire to exploit or subject foreign peoples. They desired to tell the good news of the Savior who died for the sins of the world. In some parts of Africa, the arrival of missionaries *preceded* the coming of traders and government officials. David Livingstone opened the interior of Africa as he preached Christ in thousands of villages. Livingstone and others also reported the terrible abuses of African slavery and pressed for its abolition. As a result of what the missionaries witnessed, and in their desire to help those who were oppressed, the missionaries often found themselves at odds with imperialists.

Imperialism in the East

Asia

When Europeans sailed to the New World, they found sparsely populated lands. Thus, they were initially able to transplant European culture into these lands with little opposition. But the situation in Asia was different. That densely populated continent was the home of strong and ancient cultures. Although the industrial and military might of Western nations successfully forced open many Asian lands to Western trade, attempts to establish Western culture met with determined resistance.

India

After Vasco da Gama discovered an all-water route to India, European nations set up trading posts along the Indian coast. By the eighteenth century, French and British trade companies had established thriving bases in India. But early in the 1700s, the security of those bases was threatened by the collapse of the Mughal Empire (see p. 149), which left India once again divided into small rival states. The British and French used this political unrest for their economic advantage. They extended their control in India by making alliances with local rulers or by outright conquest of territory.

The strong British-French rivalry that dominated European affairs during the eighteenth century extended to India. During the Seven Years' War (1756–63), an Indian ruler who sided with the French attacked the British settlement at Calcutta. In the **Battle of Plassey** (1757), British forces led by **Robert Clive** defeated the Indian ruler. Three years later, Clive defeated the French as well. The victories made the British East India Company the dominant authority in India; no individual Indian state was strong enough to challenge its power.

For the next hundred years, the British East India Company governed much of India. The British government supervised the company's affairs but did not exercise any direct rule over the country. Because the East India Company was primarily a commercial organization, financial considerations played an important role in determining its political policies. For example, the company tried to keep William Carey and other missionaries from preaching the gospel in India. They believed that such preaching might cause unrest among the Hindu and Muslim populations and thus hurt their business interests. Yet the expansion of the company's authority and the growing efforts by the British

William Carey in India

Young **William Carey** (1761–1834) gave little indication of the great things God was going to accomplish through his life. As a student, he liked history, science, and mathematics, but he had little interest in the Bible. As a boy, he mastered Latin, then Greek, and later Hebrew. As a young man, he taught himself French and Dutch. It might have seemed odd that Carey, a cobbler's apprentice, had such a talent for learning languages. Time would show that God was preparing him for his future work in India. Around the age of eighteen, Carey trusted Christ and began to identify with Nonconformists. Later he was immersed and became an active member of a Baptist congregation.

Since his youth, Carey had been interested in foreign lands. Next to his workbench he had a crude, hand-drawn map of the world on which he wrote geographic and religious facts about each country. When he tried to get others interested in sending missionaries to those countries, however, they told him that the injunction "Go ye into all the world, and preach the gospel" was given only to the apostles. Later, at a meeting of Baptist ministers, Carey made his plea for missions: "Expect great things from God; attempt great things for God." As a result of Carey's sermon, others joined him in establishing the Baptist Missionary Society. Carey, the first appointed missionary, took his family to India in 1794.

When the Careys landed in India they faced many hardships. But William Carey was well established in his faith, competent in linguistics, and firmly resolved to do God's will. He quickly went about establishing the work under two principles: (1) the missionary must be a companion to and an equal with the native peoples, and (2) the missionary must, as soon as possible, become self-supporting. While on the mission field, Carey worked as both an indigo planter and a horticulturist. He established his first church by preaching to plantation workers. He also worked on translating the Bible into the native Bengali languages.

To master the various Indian dialects, Carey set about learning Sanskrit. He translated the Bible into Bengali in 1798. He went on to translate the Bible into twenty Indian dialects and supervised its translation into twenty more. In 1798, a printer joined Carey in his work. Together, they set up a printing press and produced the first Bible and tracts in the Indian dialects.

Carey never returned to England. Once he settled in India, he devoted his life to bringing the gospel to the Indian people. Because of his pioneering accomplishments in mission work, he became known as the Father of Modern Missions. Yet once when someone was talking about his remarkable accomplishments, Carey replied, "Do not talk about Dr. Carey's this or Dr. Carey's that. Talk about Dr. Carey's Savior." He lived by the verse "He must increase, but I must decrease" (John 3:30).

The Sepoy Mutiny

to impose Western ways on Indian society led to the very unrest the British had feared.

In 1857, *sepoys*, the native Indian troops employed by the East India Company, revolted. The immediate cause of the **Sepoy Mutiny** was the introduction of new rifle cartridges. The cartridges—the ends of which had to be bitten off—were greased with sheep fat to keep the powder dry. Rumors spread that the grease used was cow and pig fat. (The Hindus consider the cow sacred, and the Muslims consider the pig unclean.) Although the revolt symbolized the nation's dissatisfaction with Western rule, the sepoys received little support from the majority of the Indian people. British troops were called in, and after several months of bloody fighting, the mutiny was brutally suppressed.

As a result of the mutiny, the British government assumed control of Indian political affairs. It appointed a viceroy to govern India, and in 1877 Prime Minister Disraeli conferred the title Empress of India on Queen Victoria. The British government also assumed the responsibility of providing for the welfare of the Indian people. They improved sanitation and medical care, built roads and railroads, and constructed factories (in areas most beneficial to the

British). They also established new schools that imposed Western thought and culture. But as many young Indians studied the political ideas of the eighteenth century, they became even more desirous of self-government. A movement for self-rule began to build by the end of the nineteenth century.

China

Despite China's vast territory and its large population, the Chinese were not able to withstand European imperialism during the nineteenth century. Under the **Manchu dynasty**, which had ruled China since 1644, all Chinese ports except Canton were closed to foreign merchants. However, by the nineteenth century, internal problems had crippled Manchu leadership. Western nations took advantage of China's growing weakness and demanded greater trade privileges.

Chinese attempts to restrict foreign trade led to war between China and Great Britain. For years, Chinese rulers had done little to stop British traders from smuggling opium (a dangerous drug) into China in return for tea and silks. When Chinese officials finally sought to stop this drug trade, British merchants objected. Tension over the opium trade and all foreign trade sparked the **Opium Wars**, in which British forces were used to preserve the profitable but destructive opium trade. In 1842, the British forced China to sign the Treaty of Nanking, which opened four more trade ports and gave Britain the island of Hong Kong. A second war (1856–60) further weakened China, as French and British forces joined to win additional trade concessions.

Although China never officially lost its independence, other nations heavily influenced its policies and forced it to bend to their will. By the end of the century, many Western countries had secured treaties forcing China to open

J. Hudson Taylor in China

J. Hudson Taylor (1832–1905) was a man who set himself to do God's will and would not allow anything to stop him. At the age of five, after hearing his father talk about the need of taking the gospel to China, he declared that "one day he would go to that country." In 1849, at the age of seventeen, he dedicated himself to the Lord's service. That was when he knew that God was calling him to China. After earning a medical degree, he set sail for China in 1853.

In those days, missionaries were allowed to labor only in the coastal regions of China, near the treaty ports. Soon after he landed, however, Taylor became deeply burdened for the people living inland. During the next seven years, he made many trips inland. With each visit, his burden increased for the millions who had not heard the gospel. In 1860, poor health forced him to return to England. Yet his concern for the Chinese did not diminish. While in England, he revised the Chinese New Testament.

Five years went by, but his health did not improve. It seemed that he would never be able to return to China. But one weekend in the summer of 1865, while resting in Dover, he prayed that God would send twenty-four skilled and willing workers to the inland areas of China. After he prayed, he experienced a calmness of heart and body. When he returned to London, his wife remarked that Dover seemed to have been good for him. He told her of his request and about the renewed strength that the Lord had given him. Two days later, with less than £10, he opened a bank account in the name of the China Inland Mission, an organization dedicated to enlisting people and funds for missionary work in China. On May 26, 1866, Taylor, his family, and twenty-four others set sail for China.

Missionary work in inland China was difficult. The Chinese were reluctant to welcome the missionaries even though Taylor and the others adopted Chinese dress. But Taylor's faith was unwavering. He knew that he was doing God's work and that God would protect and prosper the work. God did exactly that. New areas in China opened up, and more missionaries joined in the task of reaching the Chinese for Christ. Taylor, who had once asked the Lord for twenty-four colaborers, now prayed for one thousand; God answered his request.

China Inland Mission missionaries killed during the Boxer Rebellion

its ports to their trade. Two demands found in many of those treaties especially angered the Chinese: the right of Western nations to station their warships in China's waters and the right of Westerners to **extraterritoriality**. The principle of extraterritoriality stated that Westerners who broke Chinese law had the right to be tried in their own national courts rather than in Chinese courts.

Particularly embarrassing to China was its loss to Japan in the **Sino-Japanese War** (1894–95). China had always thought of Japan as an inferior nation. After this humiliating defeat, Western nations increased their demands for more trade concessions, and China had little choice but to grant them.

Angered by Western actions, some Chinese organized secret societies, pledging to rid China of Western influences. In 1899, following orders from the Empress Dowager, members of these societies began to terrorize both Westerners and Chinese Christians. Throughout the country, rebels destroyed railroads and bridges and murdered Western diplomats, missionaries, and merchants. This uprising, known as the **Boxer Rebellion** (named after a leading society called the "Righteous and Harmonious Fists"), became so serious that European, Japanese, and American troops finally intervened. The rebellion failed, but it contributed to the collapse of the Manchu dynasty.

Top: Commander Matthew Perry
Bottom: Artist's conception of Perry's second fleet

Japan

Japan entered the nineteenth century with a feudal society dominated by the warrior class. Shoguns of the **Tokugawa** family ruled Japan as they had done since the beginning of the seventeenth century. Like China's rulers, Japan's rulers intended to exclude all Western influence and to maintain the country's traditions. But in July 1853 **Matthew Perry**, a U.S. naval commander, sailed into Edo Bay (later called Tokyo Bay) with a small fleet of ships. His mission was to persuade the Japanese to allow trade between the United States and Japan. After presenting the American request, Perry sailed away, telling the Japanese that he would return later for their answer. In February 1854 Perry returned with even more warships. The shogun realized Japan's weak position and reluctantly agreed to open trade. Both nations signed the **Treaty of Kanagawa**, the first treaty Japan ever signed with a Western nation.

The period of Japan's isolation had ended. But how were the Japanese going to respond to Western influences? Would they resist like the Chinese, or would they adopt some Western ways? It took a civil war to settle the issue. The struggle overthrew the shogun and restored the Japanese emperor to his position of authority. The emperor, who adopted the name Meiji (MAY jee; "enlightened rule") for his reign, declared, "The uncivilized customs of former years shall be abandoned."

During the **Meiji Period** (1867–1912), Japan's leaders transformed the nation from a feudal society to a major industrial power. Japanese commissions were sent to Western nations to study their governments, industries, schools, and militaries. The Japanese copied what they considered to be the best methods and institutions. Within a relatively short time, Japan became the first industrial nation of Asia, and the Japanese government adopted a Western constitution. It also established new educational and judicial systems and reorganized the military forces according to Western models.

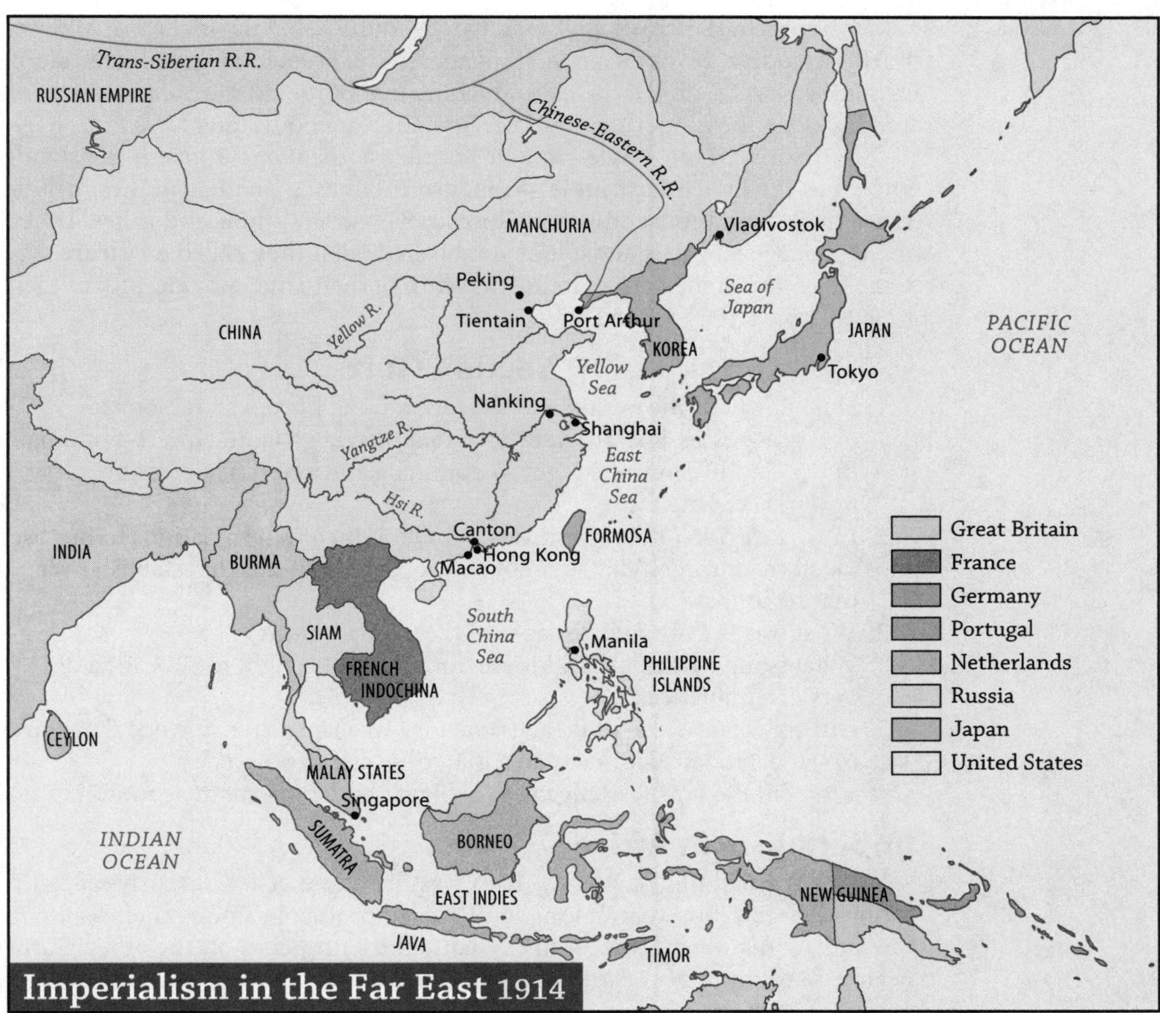

Imperialism in the Far East 1914

By adopting some Western ways, Japan was able to resist Western imperialism. Its new industrial and military might enabled it to compete with Western nations for territory and influence in Asia. Japanese expansionism eventually led to war with China (1894–95), a conflict that exposed the weakness of the Chinese state. Later, in the **Russo-Japanese War** (1904–5), Japan stunned the Western powers by defeating the supposedly mightier Russians on both sea and land (see p. 473). The tiny island nation, by routing its much larger opponents, demonstrated that it was becoming a world power. During the first half of the twentieth century, Japan continued its expansionist policies. Its aggression would contribute to the outbreak of World War II.

Southeast Asia

Southeast Asia includes the territory east of India and south of China, as well as many of the islands in the Pacific and Indian Oceans. Before the nineteenth century, several parts of Southeast Asia had come under European control. But during the nineteenth century the Europeans seized virtually the entire area. The only major territory that remained independent was Siam (today called Thailand), which became a buffer state between British and French possessions. (See map on this page.)

One of the most valuable British possessions was Ceylon (modern Sri Lanka), an island taken from the Dutch in the eighteenth century. Rubber trees and tea grew well there, and the island was also a source of lead and sapphires.

Other important British possessions in Southeast Asia included Malaya, Burma (modern Myanmar), and Singapore. The French had one large colony in Southeast Asia, an area called Indochina that bordered the South China Sea and included the modern nations of Vietnam, Cambodia, and Laos.

The major Dutch possession in Southeast Asia was a group of islands known as the Dutch East Indies—modern Indonesia. The East Indies include more than three thousand islands spread over several thousand miles. When the Dutch seized the islands, they established what they called a **culture system**. They forced the natives to use one-fifth of their land and one-fifth of their time to grow crops for the Dutch.

Section Quiz

1. During what time period was the race among European nations for overseas possessions revived? What name was given to empire-building in which one country sought to dominate and assert its power over less powerful countries?
2. In what region of the world was it difficult for Western nations to impose Western culture? What form of control were they able to establish over that region?
3. What was the immediate cause of the Sepoy Mutiny?
4. What is the name of the Chinese uprising that sought to rid China of Western influences?
5. During what period of Japanese history was Japan transformed from an isolated, feudalistic society to a major industrial power?

★ Why did the Japanese engage in civil war to determine their future?

Imperialism in Africa

As we learned in Chapter 7, Africa was the home of several thriving civilizations before 1500. African kingdoms traded profitably among themselves on the one hand and with the Arabs, Asians, and Europeans on the other. European expansion, however, reduced the African people from trading partners to subjects. Imperialism in Africa became an uneven mixture of exploitation, racism, and humanitarian impulses. The result was a transformed Africa.

African Slave Trade

European exploration of the African coast and the discovery of the New World indirectly prompted the rise of the West African slave trade. In 1441, Portugal became the first European nation to engage in this trade by bringing a small group of Africans to Europe. Yet until the opening of the New World in the sixteenth century, few Europeans owned slaves. They were first used on a large scale after the Spanish arrived in Latin America. The Spaniards enslaved the native Indians, forcing them to work in the mines or on large plantations. The Indians, however, were vulnerable to the new diseases that the Europeans brought. As a result, many of them died. To replenish the labor supply, the Spaniards began importing slaves from Africa. By the eighteenth century, black slavery was common in the New World, and traders from many European nations participated in it.

The slave trade proved to be very profitable and therefore expanded rapidly. The heaviest European trading occurred from 1700 to 1850, during which time approximately 80 percent of all slaves brought to the New World arrived. From the early sixteenth century to about 1870, when the Western slave trade ended, traders had transported up to 9.5 million African slaves, most of whom came from western Africa, to the Americas and Europe.

The European slave traders did not usually capture the slaves. Instead, they bought them from Muslim slave traders and African tribes on the coast. Often,

Muslim Slave Trade

Centuries before Europeans became involved in the dreadful practice of the slave trade, Muslim slave traders seized and transported vast numbers of Africans from North and East Africa to the Arabian Peninsula and the Middle East. Most of those taken into slavery were women and children; African males were routinely slaughtered. Slave traders sold the African women and children to men throughout the Muslim world. Muslim slave trading continued long after Western nations discontinued the practice and survives in some African nations to this day.

David Livingstone and Mary Slessor in Africa

On his fifty-ninth birthday, **David Livingstone** wrote in his journal, "My Jesus, my King, my Life, my All; I again dedicate my whole self to Thee. Accept me, and grant me, O gracious Father, that ere this year is gone I may finish my task." He penned those words two years before his death. He had dedicated his life to reaching Africa for Christ. In his last days, he was often too sick to walk; yet, borne on the shoulders of faithful Africans, he continued to go to villages where the gospel had never been preached.

Finally, on May 1, 1873, his task on earth was ended. While on his knees in prayer, he went to be with his Lord.

Livingstone's body was transported to the coast and sent back to England. His heart, however, was left behind in Africa, buried by natives at the foot of a mvula tree. Today, his earthly remains lie near the central nave in Westminster Abbey in London. The black slab that marks his resting place reads in part,

Brought by faithful hands
Over land and sea,
Here rests
DAVID LIVINGSTONE
Missionary, Traveler, Philanthropist
Born March 18, 1813
At Blantyre, Lanarkshire
Died May 1, 1873,
At Chitambo's Village, Llala

The slab also bears his favorite missionary text: "Other sheep I have, which are not of this fold: them also I must bring, and they shall hear my voice" (John 10:16).

Livingstone's life affected many; his death affected one woman in particular. **Mary Slessor** (1848–1915) was a petite Scottish girl with brilliant blue eyes and curly red hair. She was born into a poor family; her father was a drunkard, but she had a godly mother. At the age of eleven, Mary went to work at a spinning mill. She worked twelve hours a day, six days a week to help with the family's finances. In her heart, however, she dreamed of going to Africa as a missionary. When she heard the news of David Livingstone's death, she asked her mother if she could offer herself for missionary service. Her mother gave her permission. Learning of the heathen customs and poor living conditions in Calabar, West Africa, Mary believed that was the place God would have her labor.

In September 1876, she sailed for Calabar. She began her work with youthful impatience, wanting to see immediate results. But she was reminded to wait patiently on God. Among the many heathen practices that she found among the people, perhaps the most appalling was the custom of killing newborn twins. The natives believed that twins were the children of demons. Mary was able to rescue some of these children, whom she raised as her own. As the years went by, the children became teachers and missionaries to their own people.

After spending a few years at the mission station on the coast, Mary felt the call of God to go upriver to witness to several cannibal tribes. At first, the mission was opposed to the idea, but finally they allowed her to go. Taking her children with her, she settled in one of the cannibal villages. She clearly showed her love for the people; she tended their sick and cared for their unwanted. They returned her love by giving her the honored title of Ma ("mother"). Later, they came to consider her as their queen. When Calabar was taken over by the British government in 1889, she was made vice-consul for the interior of the Niger Coast Protectorate. She was responsible for establishing law and order among the native people. Nonetheless, she remained true to her primary task of winning people to the Lord. She faithfully gave out God's Word, trusting that it would enlighten their hearts. When she moved to another area some fifteen years later, she left behind a thriving Christian community.

After thirty-nine years of self-sacrificing service, her frail body could take no more; she went to be with her Lord on January 13, 1915. What was the secret to her successful labor for the Lord? In her own words, "I have no idea how and why God has carried me over so many hard places, and made these hordes submit to me . . . except in answer to prayer at home for me. It is all beyond my comprehension. The only way I can explain it is on the ground that I have been prayed for more than most. Pray on—power lies that way."

victorious African chiefs sold the prisoners they captured during tribal warfare. As the demand for slaves increased, some groups even launched raids on unsuspecting villages, capturing the inhabitants and selling them into bondage.

Before purchasing a boatload of slaves, the European slave trader had his surgeon examine the captives to determine their physical condition. He then selected only the slaves who seemed to be in good physical condition; weak or sickly slaves would reduce his profits. He wanted slaves who could withstand the inhumane conditions during the voyage across the Atlantic and still bring a good price at the end. After paying for the slaves with guns, gunpowder, liquor, tobacco, trinkets, cloth, iron, or copper, the trader had the slaves branded with a red-hot iron. The brand ensured that the slaves he purchased would not be confused with those purchased by others.

Not all of the slaves put on ships lived to see the New World. About one-fourth of all those who left Africa died during the long voyage across the Atlantic. Crowded conditions onboard allowed disease to spread rapidly. Other Africans chose to jump into the sea when allowed on deck rather than submit to a life of slavery. Lack of exercise and contaminated food and water supplies also contributed to illness and death.

Opening up the Interior

Before the nineteenth century, few Europeans had ever traveled to the interior of Africa. It was an unknown land, often called the "Dark Continent." Among the first European explorers to travel inland was David Livingstone (1813–73). He had planned to be a medical missionary to China but was prevented by the outbreak of the Opium War. Livingstone went to Africa instead, motivated by reports from people who had seen the "smoke of a thousand villages" in the interior, where the gospel had never been heard.

Enduring great physical hardship, Livingstone journeyed into the African interior. He was devoted to opening Africa to the gospel and in the process ending the slave trade. While on one of his lengthy expeditions, he remained away from civilization for so long that people wondered if he was still alive. As part of a publicity campaign, a New York newspaper hired British explorer **Henry Stanley** to find Livingstone. In 1871, Stanley found him at Lake Tanganyika and casually greeted him: "Dr. Livingstone, I presume." Livingstone continued to travel and preach in his beloved Africa until he died there two years later.

Word of Livingstone's endeavors created great enthusiasm among would-be missionaries in Britain and the United States. Unfortunately, his journeys and those of other explorers also opened the door for European trade and imperialism in the areas he had explored.

Artist's rendering of Cecil Rhodes

The Partitioning of Africa

Before 1880, Europe controlled only about 10 percent of the African continent. From 1880 to 1914, however, the race for territory in Africa became so intense that by World War I only Ethiopia and Liberia remained independent.

Britain was interested in the entire continent of Africa. In the north, it secured a controlling interest in the newly built Suez Canal (1869). To protect this lifeline of British trade with India and the Far East, the British government assumed control of the Egyptian economy and government.

In southern Africa, British imperialism was directed by **Cecil John Rhodes** (1853–1902), called "the empire-builder." As a young man, Rhodes went to southern Africa and made a fortune in diamonds. He became a firm supporter of British imperialism, working tirelessly to advance British (and his own) interests in Africa. He dreamed of an uninterrupted line of British territory stretching from Egypt in northern Africa to the Cape Colony in southern

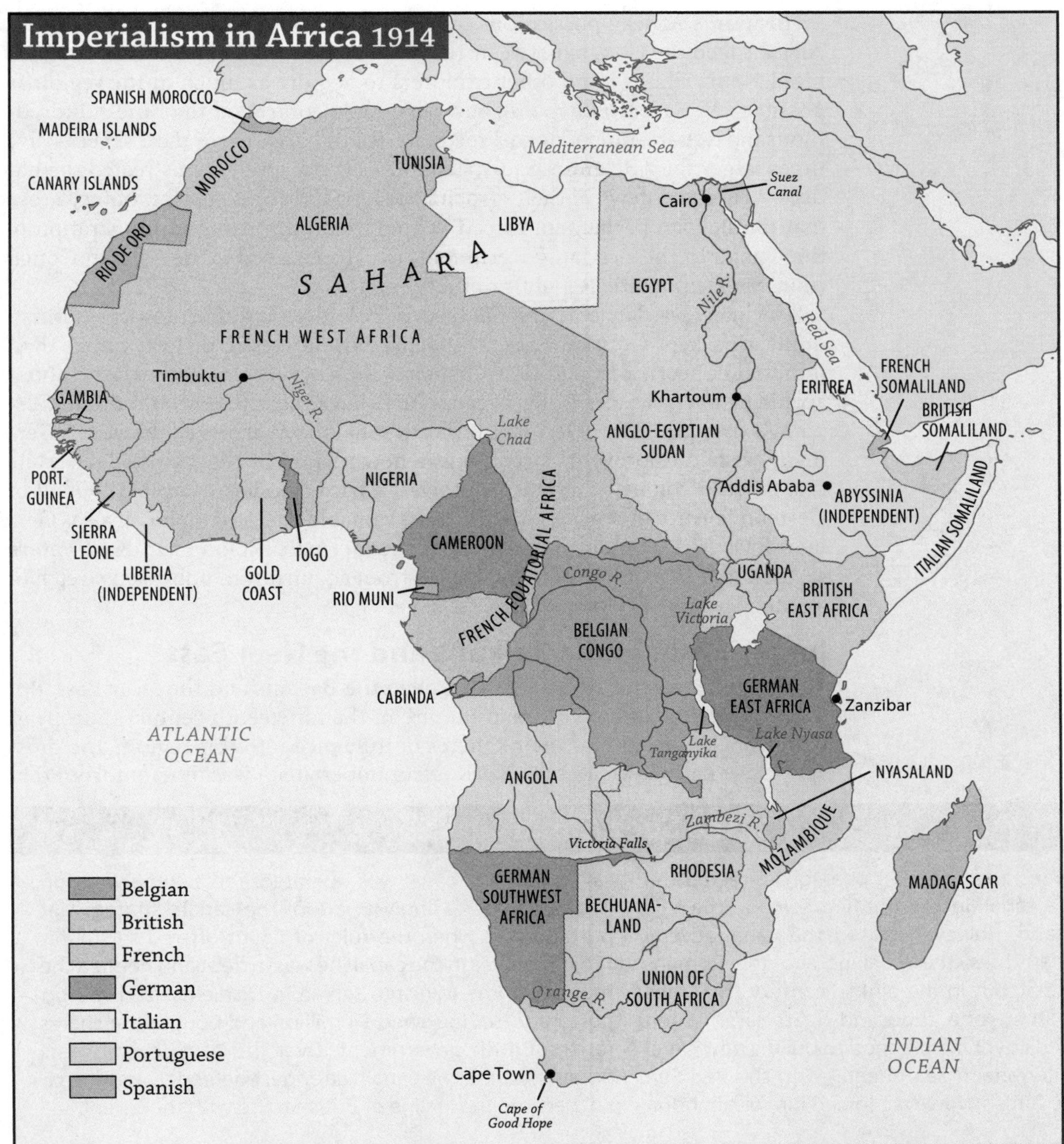

Africa. Although his goal of British control "from Cape to Cairo" was only partially realized, he helped Britain acquire additional territory in Africa, including Rhodesia (modern Zambia and Zimbabwe), which was named after him. His name lives on in Britain's Rhodes scholarships, which provide funds for students from the British Commonwealth, South Africa, and the United States to study at Oxford University.

While Britain seized African territory in the southern and northeastern parts of the continent, France subjugated most of the northern and much of western Africa. In 1830, France slowly began to build its African empire by invading Algeria. The following year, Louis Philippe established an elite army group that would figure prominently in the history of French imperialism—the famous **Foreign Legion**. By the end of the century, France had extended its holdings to include most of West Africa, building the largest land empire in Africa (though it was mostly desert).

Belgium's African possessions consisted of one large mass of land in central Africa called the Congo. Between 1878 and 1884, King **Leopold II** of Belgium hired Henry Stanley and other explorers to acquire as much of the region as possible. As a result, Leopold soon personally controlled the nine-hundred-thousand-square-mile Congo Free State, a land area more than seventy-five times larger than Belgium. Sadly, Leopold's agents severely mistreated the natives. When the news of their atrocities reached Europe, such an outcry arose that the Belgian parliament forced Leopold II to turn over administration of the Congo to the Belgian government, which renamed it the Belgian Congo (modern Democratic Republic of the Congo).

Germany was late entering the race for colonies. The effort toward German unification kept German attention focused on domestic matters rather than imperial concerns. In addition, Bismarck was never very enthusiastic about acquiring overseas territories because he believed that they would dilute Germany's strength. After German unification had been achieved, however, Germany wished to prove its strength as a new nation. In the 1880s, it seized its first African colony—German Southwest Africa (modern Namibia). Of all of Germany's African possessions, the most valuable one geographically was German East Africa (modern Tanzania). The German explorer Dr. **Karl Peters** secured this area, preventing the British from acquiring an unbroken stretch of territory from the Cape to Cairo.

Imperialism in the Balkans and the Near East

For centuries the Turks had controlled the Balkans and the Near East. But with the decline of the Ottoman Empire in the nineteenth century, European nations began to extend their spheres of influence into this region. The most aggressive nation was Russia, but Russian imperialism was different from that

The Suez Canal

In ancient times, the Egyptian pharaohs directed the construction of a canal linking the Red Sea and the Nile River. Drifting sand, however, closed the canal several times. In later centuries, the Persians and the Romans reopened the canal, but in the eighth century the Arabs closed it. More than one thousand years later, when Napoleon invaded Egypt, he planned to build a new canal to link the Mediterranean Sea directly with the Red Sea. His defeat by the British, however, forced him to abandon this idea.

But interest in the canal did not die. A Frenchman named Ferdinand de Lesseps (1805–94) secured permission from the Egyptian ruler and organized an international company to finance and build the waterway. Under de Lesseps's direction, the company sold 400,000 shares of stock and began construction in 1859. Costs were much higher than anticipated, but the hundred-mile-long canal was opened in 1869.

At first, Great Britain opposed the project, thinking that the canal would threaten Britain's trade with Asia. Britain refused to purchase any of the original shares of stock and thus had no say in how the canal was operated. Yet, as time went on, it became increasingly aware of the canal's strategic importance. So when the ruler of Egypt offered to sell his 176,602 shares in the canal (he was in debt and needed the money), Prime Minister Benjamin Disraeli seized the opportunity. He borrowed £4 million and bought the shares for the British government. Over the next several years, Britain became the canal's strongest defender, and the canal became the lifeline of British trade with the Orient.

of other European nations. For example, whereas Britain and France sought territory overseas in Africa and Asia, Russia sought to gain additional territory simply by expanding its borders.

One of Russia's major territorial objectives was to control the straits leading from the Black Sea to the Mediterranean. But Russian expansion in the Balkans threatened to upset the balance of power in Europe. Such concerns had led to the Crimean War in 1854–56. In 1877 Russia renewed its efforts to extend its influence into this region by initiating a war with the Turks. After suffering disastrous defeats, the Turks surrendered and signed the Treaty of San Stefano. The war strengthened Russia's position in the Balkans while virtually pushing the Ottomans out of Europe. But, once again, the European nations stepped in. At the Congress of Berlin (1878), they forced Russia to return some of the territories it had won from the Turks.

Russia continued its expansionistic designs, however. It made a concerted effort to push southward through Afghanistan and Persia toward the Persian Gulf. The British feared that such expansion would imperil both their prize possessions of India and the Suez Canal, which was their lifeline to India and the East. The rivalry between the two nations was temporarily settled in 1907 by the **Anglo-Russian Entente**. This agreement divided Persia (Iran) into three zones: the British dominated the southern zone, the Russians dominated the northern zone, and the middle zone remained neutral. In Afghanistan, the Russians recognized British influence and agreed not to interfere in Afghanistan's internal affairs.

Finally, Russia tried to expand eastward into Manchuria in hopes of establishing a warm-water seaport. Russia seized Port Arthur in 1897 and began work on the Chinese Eastern Railroad in Manchuria in 1898. Russian troops seized all of Manchuria in 1900 during the Boxer Rebellion. Russia lost this region, however, in the Russo-Japanese War in 1905.

Results of Imperialism

Negative Results

The military and industrial might of European nations enabled them to exploit the people and resources in their overseas empires. Too often, territorial officials and foreign merchants amassed personal fortunes at the expense of the native populations. Some Europeans even abused the native peoples. When dividing African territory, for example, imperial powers often ignored ancient tribal boundaries. This led to strife as tribes were arbitrarily grouped together or divided and ruled by different European countries.

While the Europeans improved the infrastructure of the conquered nations, the improvements were designed for the benefit of the Europeans rather than the native populations. As a result, rural areas and other regions considered less important were neglected. This created a large gulf between urban and rural areas that would linger long after the Europeans had left. Later, many of these countries would have to bear the cost of providing a more effective infrastructure even as they suffered from a large drain of capital because the Europeans took much of the country's wealth back to Europe.

It also became common for the Europeans to train and arm a professional army in some of these countries to protect against attacks by other European powers. While this seemed to be a practical matter at the time, it became a source of instability later when these colonies gained their independence. Dictators could easily step in and use the army to subjugate the people.

Even with the best of intentions, European imperialism delayed the natural development of these subject countries. For example, several African countries were developing into modern states when European forces invaded and subjugated them. European interference set African development back several generations.

Positive Results

Although many aspects of imperialism were negative, some good things occurred as well. For example, some of the imperial nations instituted democratic governments and bureaucracies to administer them. The Europeans also established modern judicial systems that have proven to be successful.

The most significant benefit to the native populations, however, was the missionary outreach. God used imperialism, a selfish and materialistic movement, to open foreign land's to the gospel. Christians in Great Britain, in particular, responded to the unique opportunities that imperialism afforded to send forth missionaries. By 1900, 5,901 missionaries were from Great Britain, one-third of the total number of missionaries then ministering around the world.

Along with spreading the news of salvation, the missionaries started schools and colleges, taught the people trades, opened orphanages, began hospitals and medical clinics, and helped eliminate life-threatening customs. Some missionaries developed written languages for the people and translated the Bible into the native tongues, enabling the people to read God's Word and other important documents.

Many missionaries also became advocates for the native peoples. As they lived among the people and understood the harmful effects of European oppression, they spoke out in opposition to the poor treatment that the people were subjected to.

Section Quiz

1. Which famous explorer opened the interior of Africa to the gospel message?
2. What canal did Britain secure control of to protect its trade with India and the Far East?
3. What man directed Britain's imperialistic efforts in southern Africa, becoming known as the "empire-builder"? What was his goal for British imperialism in Africa?
4. What European king personally controlled an area in Africa seventy-five times the size of his own country? What was that area called?
5. What congress of European nations in 1878 forced Russia to give up territorial gains in the Balkan region?

✯ Why did Russia not seek territory overseas as many other European countries did?

Chapter 19 Review

Making Connections

1–2. What motives prompted European nations to establish overseas empires? (List two.)

3–5. Provide three examples of Christians taking advantage of imperialism to spread or demonstrate the gospel.

Developing History Skills

1. Contrast the independence movements among the British and Spanish colonies.
2. Summarize the long-term consequences of Perry's visits to Japan.

Thinking Critically

1. Justify or condemn the practice of imperialism. Support your answer.

Living in God's World

1. Imagine that you are a missionary working among a people in Central Africa. Write a letter to the British governor defending the people to whom you minister against imperialist confiscation of their land and forced relocation.
2. Imagine that you are a British leader during the early nineteenth century. Craft a policy for how the British government should relate to foreign peoples that its subjects trade with.

People, Places, and Things to Know

Louisiana Purchase
Monroe Doctrine
Maximilian
Roosevelt Corollary
Quebec Act
British North America Act
James Cook
Maoris
Boers
Great Trek
Boer War
peninsulares
criollos
mestizos
Simón Bolívar
José de San Martín
Dom Pedro
caudillos
imperialism
Battle of Plassey
Robert Clive
William Carey
Sepoy Mutiny
Manchu dynasty
Opium Wars
J. Hudson Taylor
extraterritoriality
Sino-Japanese War
Boxer Rebellion
Tokugawa
Matthew Perry
Treaty of Kanagawa
Meiji Period
Russo-Japanese War
culture system
David Livingstone
Mary Slessor
Henry Stanley
Cecil John Rhodes
Foreign Legion
Leopold II
Karl Peters
Anglo-Russian Entente

THE MODERN WORLD

The bright promise of the nineteenth century collapsed in the disasters of the twentieth and twenty-first centuries. Two global wars destroyed the myth that mankind is ever-progressing and improving. The totalitarian dictatorships of the Communists, Fascists, and Nazis mocked the earlier cries of "liberty and justice for all." At times the democratic nations seemed weak and tired. After World War II, the world lived for nearly fifty years in an uneasy balance between two great nuclear superpowers and their allies. Then the tragic realities of terrorism were added to the dangers of totalitarianism. The order of the nineteenth century was far removed from the relativism and chaos of the twentieth and twenty-first centuries. Rarely has an age so aptly illustrated Paul's statement to Timothy: "In the last days perilous times shall come" (2 Tim. 3:1).

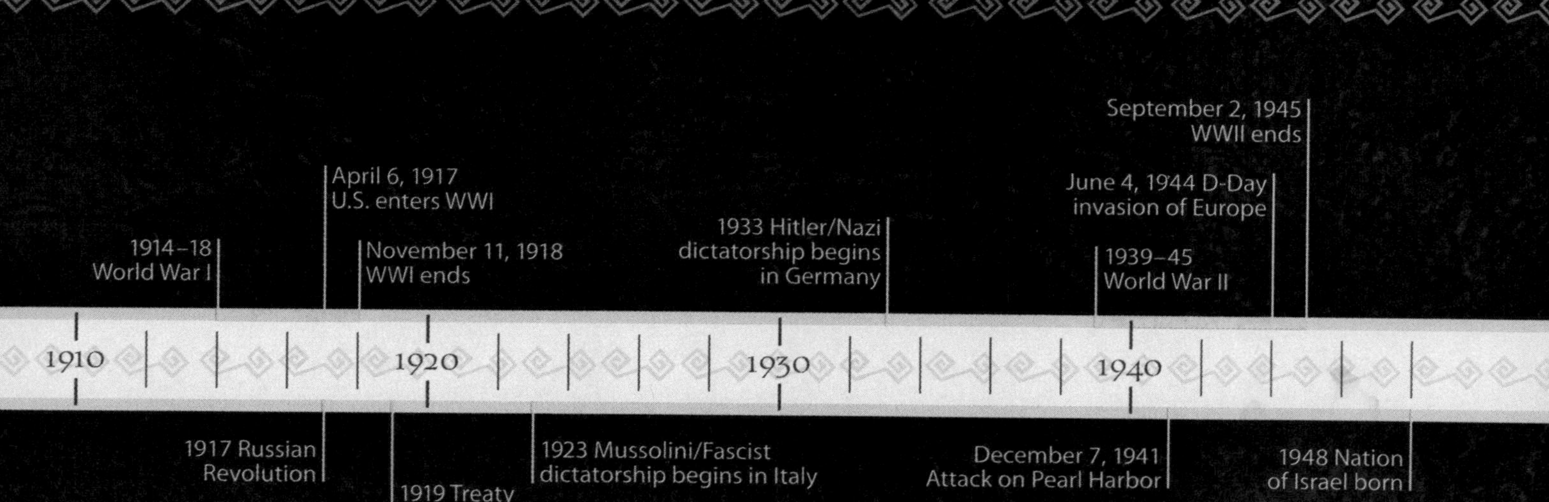

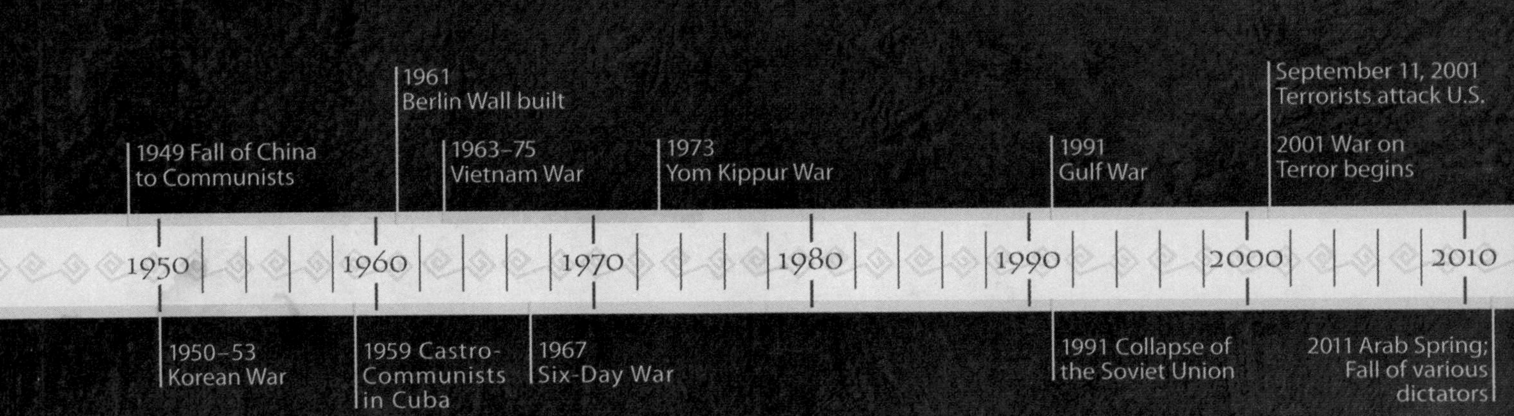
1961
Berlin Wall built
1949 Fall of China
to Communists
1963–75
Vietnam War
1973
Yom Kippur War
1991
Gulf War
September 11, 2001
Terrorists attack U.S.
2001 War on
Terror begins
1950
1960
1970
1980
1990
2000
2010
1950–53
Korean War
1959 Castro-
Communists
in Cuba
1967
Six-Day War
1991 Collapse of
the Soviet Union
2011 Arab Spring;
Fall of various
dictators

20

The Great War

I. Promise and Peril

II. The Pressing Conflict

III. The Pursuit of Peace

A British Mark IV tank carrying soldiers into combat

A psychologist in the early twentieth century taught his patients to say, "Every day in every way, I'm getting better and better." Many people in the late nineteenth and early twentieth centuries thought the same of the world. The future seemed bright and full of promise. Some people even thought that man was on the verge of bringing in the millennial reign of Christ. Much of the earth appeared to be experiencing peace and prosperity, and many influential people thought that it was the result of mankind's power, intelligence, and innate goodness. But alongside man's pride in his own accomplishments lay the reality of his sinfulness. In 1914 a terrible war shattered the dreams of the optimists. Tension and discord confronted hope and enthusiasm. Peril replaced promise as nations rushed headlong into the catastrophe called "The Great War," now known as World War I.

I. Promise and Peril

Reasons for Hope

Winston Churchill, a leading statesman of the twentieth century, described the nineteenth century as a time when the "accumulation of health and wealth had been practically unchecked." The rise of industrialism made possible a higher standard of living for more people than ever before. Science seemed to be eradicating disease; efforts at peace and international cooperation increased as the century continued. Because of this apparent progress, most people were optimistic about the future.

International Cooperation

The late nineteenth century saw the rise of organizations to promote international cooperation. In 1864 Jean Henri Dunant, a Frenchman who believed that "all men are brothers," founded the Red Cross. This international organization seeks to help those who suffer from natural disaster or war. International cooperation also improved as communications improved. In 1868 the International Telegraph Union was founded, followed by the Universal Postal Union in 1875. In addition, many countries standardized their systems of weights and measures. In 1889 the Pan-American Union was established to promote trade and peace among the countries in the Western Hemisphere. In 1896, in a symbolic gesture of cooperation, a number of countries revived the Greek Olympic games.

International Efforts at Peace

Following the failure of the Concert of Europe (see p. 376), various individuals and organizations tried to maintain world peace. One individual who became famous for his promotion of international peace was the wealthy Swedish chemist **Alfred Nobel** (1833–96). In his will he established the Nobel Peace Prize to recognize men and women whose accomplishments furthered the cause of peace. Nobel had gained his fortune by inventing dynamite. Misgivings about his invention's great destructive potential prompted him to set aside funds for the cause of peace.

Nobel was not alone in his efforts; another philanthropist was **Andrew Carnegie** (1835–1919), an American steel manufacturer. Carnegie donated funds to build the Peace Palace at The Hague (the seat of government in the Netherlands). He intended that The Hague be a place where international disputes could be settled through peaceful means. Ironically, the Palace

Andrew Carnegie

The Peace Palace at the Hague

was completed just as World War I began. By 1910 about 160 peace organizations were in existence; between 1800 and 1914, 250 international disputes had been arbitrated (settled by a third party).

Reasons for Fear

Neither scientific progress nor attempts at international cooperation could prevent dark clouds of suspicion and hatred from forming on the European horizon. As the nineteenth century drew to a close, several developments made war an increasing possibility, despite continued talk of cooperation and peace. From the earliest chapters in this book, we have seen that despite man's efforts to maintain peace, "wars and rumours of war" (Matt. 24:6) persist. In his epistle, James asks, "From whence come wars and fightings among you?" They come, he says, from "your lusts that war in your members" (James 4:1). This principle helps us understand the real source of tension that produces war. The issues described below are the outward, historical expressions of the pride, fear, and greed of men and nations that led to the Great War.

Extreme Nationalism

Although love for one's country is not wrong, many Europeans during the late 1800s developed an excessive patriotism. They began to consider other cultures inferior. Unbridled nationalism, or **chauvinism**, caused many people to desire war so that they could prove their superiority over other nations. As one German put it, war "is not only a necessary element in the life of a people, but also an indispensable factor in culture, indeed the highest expression of the strength and life of a truly cultured people."

Militarism

Many European nations during this time increased their military might far beyond what was necessary for a strong national defense. National glory became the primary purpose for such military buildup; a large standing army symbolized power. In several countries—Germany, for example—the military dominated the civil government. When disputes broke out among nations, it became very easy for a government to immediately resort to the use of force. Compounding the problem was the fact that many citizens glorified war, believing that war was the noblest task in which any nation could engage. Such militaristic attitudes in Europe helped foster the full-scale war that lay ahead.

Imperialism

Another cause of antagonism among countries was competition for colonies. Many European nations, jealous of Britain's colonial empire and industrial strength, desired colonies of their own. Germany and Italy, recently unified nations, were especially eager to prove their new national strength by acquiring territory in Africa and Asia. Since colonies provided economic benefits for the mother country's growing industrial might, European nations sought territories that were rich in natural resources. Conflicting claims nearly led to war on several occasions. Usually the nations involved worked out peaceful solutions, but they were not always satisfied with the results. As competition increased, so did jealousy, hatred, and suspicion.

Rival Alliances

Deep-seated fear and distrust among European nations led to the formation of protective alliances. Two (sometimes several) nations made agreements (often in secret) promising to come to one another's aid in the event of a foreign attack. By the late nineteenth and early twentieth centuries, Europe was divided into rival alliances. This alliance system helped to drag most of Europe into war.

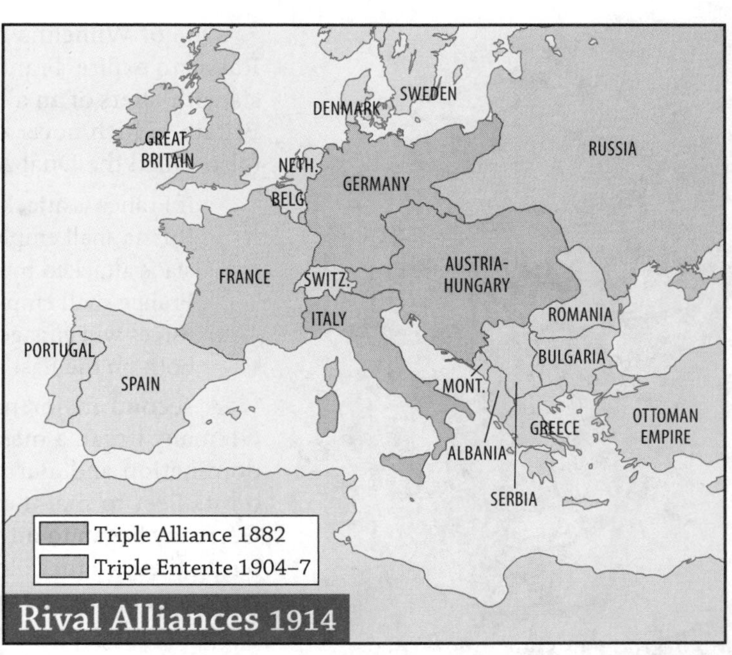

Rival Alliances 1914

Steps Toward War

The Building of Bismarck's System

Germany became a unified nation after its victory over France in the Franco-Prussian War (1870). Bismarck, who continued as chancellor of the new German state, feared that France would seek revenge for its humiliating loss. Therefore, he set out to create a system of alliances among the major nations of Europe to prevent France from finding a strong ally. By keeping France isolated diplomatically, Bismarck believed that Germany would be safe from French attack and that the political balance of power could be maintained. The system of alliances that Bismarck created is often called **Bismarck's System**.

The first alliance that Bismarck established was the **Three Emperors' League** (1873), by which Germany, Austria-Hungary, and Russia made vague promises of mutual aid in the event that war broke out with France or the Ottoman Empire. But despite its promising beginning, the league fell apart. Conflict arose between Russia and Austria-Hungary over the Balkans. Since Austria-Hungary and Russia would not cooperate, Bismarck realized that he would have to cultivate closer ties with one or the other. Fearing the growing power of Russia, he chose Austria-Hungary. In 1879, Germany and Austria-Hungary pledged mutual aid if Russia attacked one of them. This alliance, sometimes called the **Dual Alliance**, soon became the foundation of German foreign policy.

Bismarck continued his efforts to prevent France from finding a strong ally. In 1882, the **Triple Alliance** brought Germany, Austria-Hungary, and Italy together in an anti-French coalition. But Bismarck still was not satisfied; he wanted to bring Russia back into the circle of German allies. Through skillful diplomacy, he negotiated a secret alliance with Russia known as the **Reinsurance Treaty** (1887). In addition, he worked to bring England into the Triple Alliance. But England continued its long-standing policy of isolation, not wishing to get involved in European rivalries. Bismarck did not despair over the failure to create an Anglo-German alliance. As a determined foe of France and Russia, Britain was unlikely to unite with either nation. In effect, France was now isolated diplomatically.

Kaiser Wilhelm II in one of his many uniforms

The Breakdown of Bismarck's System

In July 1888, a young, impulsive **Wilhelm II** (1888–1918) became kaiser (emperor) of Germany. Not yet thirty years old, he was a proud, arrogant man who resented the domination of Bismarck in German affairs. He determined that as kaiser he would be the real leader of Germany and that no one would overshadow him. Therefore, in 1890, he forced Bismarck to resign as chancellor. Wilhelm assumed control of Germany's foreign policies, but he was not Bismarck's equal. His words and ill-advised actions only heightened European tensions.

DROPPING THE PILOT.

One of Wilhelm's first mistakes was to allow the Reinsurance Treaty with Russia to expire. France quickly capitalized on this error and approached Russia with offers of an alliance. Fearing a possible alliance between Germany and Britain (which never took place), Russia joined France in a defensive alliance (also called the Dual Alliance) in 1894. According to this treaty,

> if France is attacked by Germany, or by Italy supported by Germany, Russia shall employ all its available forces to attack Germany. If Russia is attacked by Germany or by Austria supported by Germany, France shall employ all its available forces to fight Germany. . . . These forces will engage with all their might, so that Germany has to fight both on the East and West.

A second major mistake that Wilhelm made was to antagonize Britain. Germany began a massive shipbuilding program that threatened British naval domination and alarmed the British people. Britain traditionally had to rely on its fleet to maintain its empire and to protect its homeland. In addition, Germany began to interfere with British affairs in Africa. Germany was late entering the race for colonies, but Wilhelm was determined to build an overseas empire in one generation, although it had taken other nations many generations. As a result of these developments, Britain's fear of Germany soon became stronger than its fear of France. In 1904, contrary to every German hope or expectation, Britain and France put aside their differences and came to a "friendly understanding" in what is called the ***Entente Cordiale***.

That same fear of Germany impelled Britain to patch up its differences with Russia. For some time, Russia had been trying to expand into eastern Europe to acquire an outlet to the Mediterranean Sea. It had also attempted to expand into the Persian Gulf region. The British feared that such expansion would imperil both their prize possession of India and the commercial trade going through the Suez Canal. In spite of their deep-seated rivalry, Britain and Russia signed the Anglo-Russian Entente in 1907. This agreement, like the Entente Cordiale, tended only to lessen tension and promote cooperation between the two nations. Since Britain had previously formed a friendly understanding with France, its agreement with Russia paved the way for the **Triple Entente** between Britain, France, and Russia.

Balkans 1914

The Testing of the Alliance System

By 1907, secret agreements, friendly understandings, and formal alliances had divided Europe into two rival sides. Yet many questions remained unanswered: How strong were these alliances? How long would they last? Would a nation who promised to come to another's aid in the event of war actually fulfill its promise? During the early years of the twentieth century, Europe went through a series of crises that answered many of these questions and solidified the new alliances but at the same time increased international tension and fear.

Twice, in 1905 and 1911, Germany interfered with French plans to control Morocco (a country in northwest Africa). Germany hoped not only to block France's attempt to take Morocco as a colony but also to break up the entente between Britain and France. But Germany's actions had just the opposite effect; Britain gave

Settling "The Armenian Question"

The Armenians, who came under Ottoman control in the 1400s, were a minority in both ethnicity and religion. Most Armenians were at least nominal Christians, whereas the Turks were Muslims. As a result, the Turks viewed the Armenians as infidels with no rights. In addition, some Armenians became more affluent than the Turks living around them, so the Turks tended to be jealous of their Armenian neighbors. Over time, Turkish leaders began to formulate an answer of how to settle the question "What will we do with the Armenians?"

In the two decades leading up to World War I, the Ottomans became more and more concerned that the Armenians posed a threat to Turkish rule. Their fears seemed to be confirmed when Armenians formed political organizations and voiced their desire for independence. The Turks responded with terrible and indiscriminate brutality.

The first wave of massacres occurred between 1894 and 1896, resulting in the deaths of over one hundred thousand Armenians. Renewed assaults on Armenian communities in 1909 led to the murder of another thirty thousand men, women, and children.

When World War I erupted, the Armenians may have been reluctant to support the oppressive Turkish government but answered the call when drafted. However, instead of equipping the Armenians for battle, the Ottomans marched them off to build roads and facilities to aid in the war effort. When the Armenian work crews had finished their tasks, the Turks summarily executed them or marched them to distant prison camps with immense loss of life along the way.

To prevent any threat by the surviving Armenians, Taalat Pasha, the Turkish interior minister, ordered "the elimination of the Armenian element." He ordered local leaders to "destroy completely all Armenians living in Turkey." By the end of World War I, the Turkish government had carried out the murder of an estimated one and one half to two million Armenians.

Sadly, most people have long forgotten the Armenians. When Hitler ordered the elimination of the Jews, he knew that his policy would cause revulsion and anger, but he believed that, as people had forgotten the Armenians, so they would forget the Jews. "Who does now remember the Armenians?" he asked.

© Armenian National Institute, Inc., courtesy of Sybil Stevens (daughter of Armin T. Wegner). Wegner Collection, Deutches Literaturarchiv, Marbach & United States Holocaust Memorial Museum.

France its firm support, and France succeeded in gaining Morocco. As a result, bad feelings between Germany and France mounted; they were becoming too intense to be settled peacefully.

Another series of crises occurred in the Balkans, where small national groups were struggling for their independence from Turkish control. By 1900 several Balkan nations had won their independence from the Ottoman Empire. In 1912 they joined to drive the Turks out of the Balkans. In short order, the Balkan nations smashed Turkish resistance and gained the victory. But less than a month later, a new war broke out as the Balkan nations fought among themselves to decide who would control the remaining Balkan territory.

The weakness of the Ottoman Empire and the instability of the Balkans encouraged the intervention of major European nations, especially Austria-Hungary and Russia. Austria-Hungary disliked having such unrest on its southeastern border; it also hoped to extend its borders farther into the Balkans. The Russians were of the same ethnic background (Slavic) as most of the peoples of the Balkans. By posing as the defender of its "brother Slavs," Russia, too, hoped to extend its influence in this region. While the major powers sought to keep the crisis in the Balkans a local war, their selfish interests and deep-seated hatred for one another only hastened the coming of widespread war. The Balkans were rightly called the "powder keg of Europe."

Section Quiz

1. Who established the Nobel Peace Prize to recognize those who furthered the cause of world peace?
2. Who donated funds to build the Peace Palace at the Hague, where international disputes could be settled peacefully?
3. What two countries were eager to prove their new national strength by acquiring territory in Africa and Asia?
4. What country claimed to be the defender of "brother Slavs"?
5. What area of Europe was called "powder keg of Europe"?

★ Why did European states form alliances?

II. The Pressing Conflict

The Commencement of the War

The spark that set off World War I ignited in the Balkans. On June 28, 1914, Archduke **Francis Ferdinand**, the heir to the throne of Austria-Hungary was assassinated while visiting Sarajevo, the capital of Bosnia. (Austria had annexed that Balkan province in 1908 over the opposition of the Slavic nations.) A Bosnian revolutionary, acting on behalf of the Black Hand, an anti-Austrian terrorist organization based in Serbia, shot and killed the archduke and his wife. Austria accused the Serbian government of knowing about the plot and failing to inform Austria. Meanwhile, Kaiser Wilhelm of Germany promised Austria full support in any action it might take. Austria decided to crush Serbia once and for all and on July 23 sent an **ultimatum** (a list of demands with threats) to the Serbian government. The ultimatum demanded not only an explanation and an apology for the assassination but also that Serbia undertake a thorough investigation of the crime. Austria further demanded that Serbia suppress all anti-Austrian publications and organizations.

Archduke Francis Ferdinand

Austria did not want, or expect, Serbia to meet its demands. Serbia, however, rejected outright only one of the demands; nonetheless, Austria used the assassination as an excuse to attack, and on July 28, 1914, declared war on Serbia. Two days later, Russia began to **mobilize** (make ready) its troops to come to Serbia's defense. Germany, realizing that full-scale war was imminent, warned Russia to cease mobilization within twelve hours. When Russia did not heed its warning, Germany declared war on Russia on August 1. Likewise, when France refused to give the Germans solid assurances of French neutrality, Germany declared war on France as well. Thus, the alliance system had effectively drawn the great powers into open conflict with one another. On one side were the **Central Powers** (Germany and Austria-Hungary), and on the other side were the Allies (Russia, Serbia, and France).

Much of Europe greeted the declaration of war joyfully. As the troops marched to the front, people cheered and threw flowers. In subsequent weeks, thousands of young men rushed to enlist in the army, eager to win glory on the field of battle. Since both sides expected that a few short campaigns would end the war (as had been the case in the wars of the 1860s and 1870s), neither side prepared for or expected the four terrible years of war that were to come.

Not everyone, however, cheered the outbreak of war. Sir Edward Grey, the British foreign secretary, uttered prophetic words: "The lamps are going out all over Europe; we shall not see them lit again in our lifetime." For him and many others, the apparent progress of the nineteenth century, with all of its aspirations and dreams, was soon to end on the fields of France and the plains of western Russia.

Left: British infantrymen assembled in trenches
Right: German infantrymen

War in the West

With the outbreak of war, Germany found itself in a precarious position. It had an enemy on two fronts: Russia on its eastern front (or border) and France on its western front. But the Germans had prepared for such a situation. Several years before the war, a German general named Schlieffen devised a plan to be used in such an emergency. Acting upon this **Schlieffen Plan**, the German generals decided to put most of their forces in the west and attack France first. It would take Russia longer, they believed, to organize for war because its territory was more extensive than France's. The Germans planned to surprise the French by marching through the flat plains of neutral Belgium and attacking France from the north. The German generals believed that they could encircle Paris and defeat France within six weeks. The victorious German armies could then be quickly sent to meet the advancing Russians on the eastern front.

The Germans demanded that the Belgians allow the German army to pass through their country on the way to France, but the Belgians refused. On August 4, the German army crossed into Belgium, breaking a seventy-five-year-old treaty that guaranteed Belgian neutrality. "Necessity knows no law," the German chancellor said; "we shall try to make good the wrong we have thus committed as soon as we have reached our military goal." The British, angered over Germany's disregard of the neutrality treaty, joined the Allies and declared war on Germany. The Germans soon pushed on into France and within a month were outside of Paris. But at the Marne River, the French (with reinforcements brought to the front in Paris taxicabs) stopped the German advance. By the end of the year, both sides had solidified their positions by constructing a long series of trenches that stretched from Switzerland to the English Channel.

War in the East

In the east, the Russians mobilized their forces more quickly than the Germans expected. As a result, the Russian armies achieved several initial victories against the Austrians and the Germans. In the battles of Tannenberg and the Masurian Lakes, however, the German armies, under the leadership of General **Paul von Hindenburg** (1847–1934), defeated the Russians. They captured more than 200,000 prisoners and began to push the demoralized Russian troops back toward Russia. Although they continued to fight for several more years, the Russians did not threaten German borders again during the war.

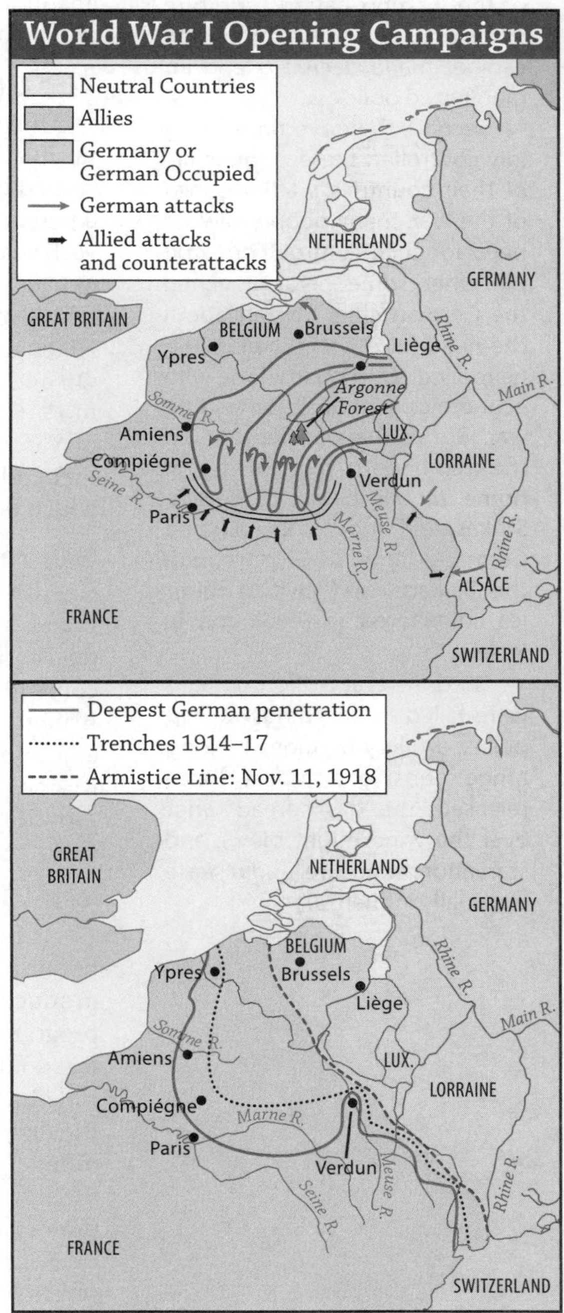

War on the Home Front

In most pre-twentieth-century warfare, civilians in the battle zones suffered, but those behind the lines often went about their business relatively unaffected. In World War I, however, the civilian population was deeply affected by what became known as total war. First, political control became more centralized. In most of the warring nations, a group of generals or a small, tightly knit cabinet made decisions and implemented policies.

Second, the governments rigidly controlled the economic life of their countries. At the outset of the war, many people saw no need for such control. For example, when someone approached the German chief of staff about the need for economic planning, he replied, "Don't bother me with economics. I am busy conducting war." But as the war dragged on, the tremendous cost was felt at home. Morale began to decline. Strikes and food riots plagued Germany, famine swept through the Balkans, and civilian miseries culminated in revolution in Russia.

Third, several million civilians were killed in bombings by zeppelins; artillery barrages by long-range guns; gas attacks (once released, the gas spread wherever the wind might blow); and starvation, exposure, and disease, especially influenza.

The inadequacy of Russian factories to produce the needed supplies fatally weakened the Russian war effort. Few supplies were available from even its allies because German warships had closed the Baltic Sea. In addition, Russia's northern ports were frozen for many months of the year. To remedy this desperate situation, the British decided to force open a sea route to Russia via the Black Sea by taking control of the Dardanelles.

The Ottoman Empire, which had entered the war in 1914 on the side of the Central Powers, controlled the straits between the Black Sea and the Aegean Sea. In 1915 Britain attempted to gain control of the strategic waterway by launching a naval attack and then landing Allied troops on the Gallipoli Peninsula. Poor planning coupled with strong Turkish resistance, however, doomed the invasion. After months of inconclusive fighting and more than 100,000 casualties, public opinion at home forced the British to withdraw their troops and abandon the project. Meanwhile, the Bulgarians had joined the Central Powers and helped to conquer Serbia by the end of 1915.

The Course of the War

During most of the war, the situation on the western front was a **stalemate** (a situation in which both sides were at a standstill). While in the east armies shifted back and forth across miles of open territory, in the west neither side could break through the intricate system of trenches that had been dug. During each year of the war, both sides conducted major offensives that cost thousands of lives but produced few gains. In 1916, for example, the British conducted an offensive along the Somme River in France. After four months of fighting, the Allies gained only 125 miles of mud while losing six hundred thousand men. On one day of that campaign, the British alone lost sixty thousand men. Earlier in 1916 the Germans had tried to break through the French lines at the fortress of Verdun. After six months of heavy bombardment and fierce fighting, the French held firm. The conflict in France became a deadly war of **attrition** in which both sides tried to wear each other down gradually.

Italy Joins the Allies

Although Italy was a member of the Triple Alliance, it remained neutral at the beginning of the war. Italy claimed that Austria and Germany were conducting an offensive, not a defensive, war; therefore, it did not feel obligated to come to their aid. Instead, Italy entered into secret negotiations with France, Britain, and Russia. The Allies promised Italy a loan and additional territory adjoining its borders if it would join them. In 1915 Italy ended its neutrality and declared war on the Central Powers. Fighting along the Italian border proved to be inconclusive, but it became yet another line for the hard-pressed Germans and Austrians to defend.

New Weapons of War

As the war continued to rage on many fronts, casualties multiplied, partly because of the introduction of new weapons. Entire industries developed to produce these weapons; nations launched major research and development programs to create more devastating weapons—and, in turn, inventions to protect soldiers against them. Infantrymen used machine guns, which dramatically increased both their firepower and the number of casualties inflicted on the enemy. For example, one Lewis machine gun could fire 450 rounds per minute. Flame throwers and poisonous gas-filled artillery shells also increased the horrors of war. Gas masks and gas-detection devices were developed to protect against the poison attacks.

Near the end of the war, the Germans began using huge guns with a range of seventy-five to eighty miles. These "Big Bertha" guns launched shells 420 mm in diameter. In 1916 the British introduced the tank to pierce the entrenched lines of the Central Powers. Although the early tanks were slow and hard to maneuver, they had such power potential that all sides eventually used them. By the end of the war, the combatants had produced more than eight thousand tanks.

In the air, both sides used airplanes to observe the enemy's position and troop movements, and, in some cases, to drop bombs. Adding a machine gun to a plane made it even more formidable. As more planes on both sides incorporated machine guns, aerial "dogfights" between opposing air forces resulted. Germany also used **zeppelins** (long, slender airships similar to modern blimps) to bomb eastern England and London. The submarine, discussed on the next page, was another important weapon.

As each new weapon was introduced or further developed, the opposing side scrambled to develop ways to defend against it and new weapons to overcome it. The new weapons forced commanders to devise new tactics and strategies for conducting war. The innovative weapons and the resulting new tactics quickly made World War I the deadliest war in history.

Above right: Soldiers firing a machine gun and wearing gas masks
Right: German zeppelin

The Red Baron

World War I was the first war in which airplanes were used as weapons. They were used not only for reconnaissance (inspection to gain military information) and bombing but also for fighting the enemy's planes in "dogfights" (air battles). Pilots who shot down at least five enemy airplanes were called aces.

The most successful ace was a German nobleman, Baron Manfred von Richthofen (1892-1918), better known as the "Red Baron" (because of the scarlet-red Fokker Dr. 1 triplane he flew). Early in the war, Richthofen transferred from the cavalry to the air service. His first efforts proved less than impressive. He crash-landed on his first solo flight and failed his first pilot's exam. Once he had learned his skill, however, Richthofen proved a deadly foe to Allied fliers. He shot down eighty Allied planes during the war, more than any other pilot on either side.

Richthofen became a national hero in wartime Germany. He formed a special fighter squadron of aces, nicknamed the "Flying Circus" because all of the pilots flew colorfully painted planes and used tents as hangars (so they could move their base of operations quickly).

On April 21, 1918, the Flying Circus encountered a squadron of Allied fighters. A Canadian pilot, Captain A. Roy Brown, fired at a German plane that was chasing a friend of his. Although Brown did not know it at the time, he might have shot down the Red Baron. (Some researchers, however, suggest that the fatal shot might have been fired by a soldier on the ground.) Wounded, Richthofen managed to land his plane behind enemy lines but died in the cockpit. Although Richthofen was an enemy pilot, the British buried him with full military honors in recognition of his bravery and gallantry.

The Red Baron was famous for his bright red Fokker Dr. 1 triplane.

Cutaway diagram of a German U-boat

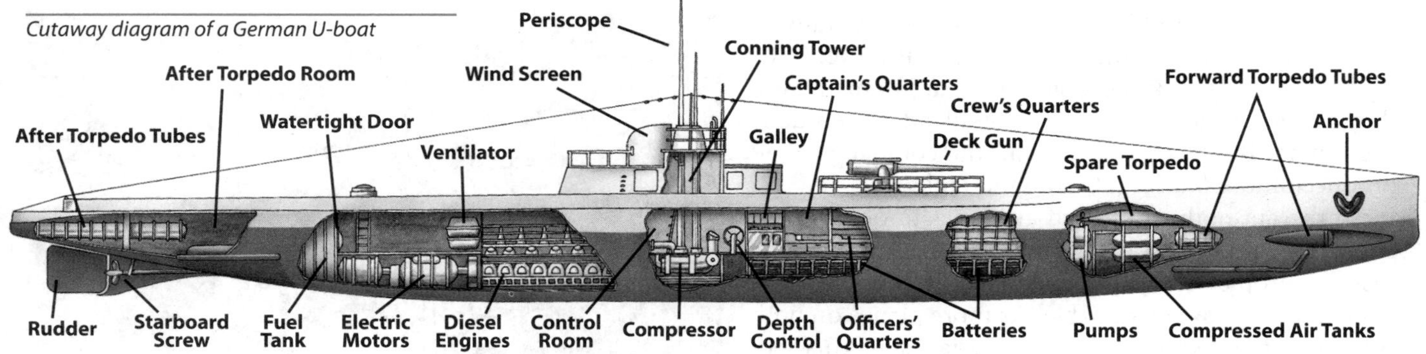

The War at Sea

Both sides realized the importance of winning the war at sea. When the fighting began, British warships implemented a blockade of Germany to keep war goods from reaching that country. Germany, on the other hand, counted on its submarines (called **U-boats**, from *Unterseeboot*) to destroy ships of both Allied and neutral nations. Soon each side was attempting to stop all imports, including food, in an effort to starve its opponent into submission.

In 1915 Germany declared a submarine blockade against Britain, threatening to sink any enemy ship that entered the "war zone" around the British Isles. On May 1 the German Embassy issued a warning to passengers planning to leave New York for Liverpool, England, aboard the British liner ***Lusitania***.

On May 7 a German submarine sank the *Lusitania* off the coast of Ireland, killing 1,198 people, including 128 Americans. The incident, as well as the sinking of various merchant ships, touched off a storm of protest in America and forced the Germans to temporarily curtail the sinking of unarmed merchant and passenger ships.

By 1916 the British had not only chased down and destroyed isolated German warships at sea but also effectively maintained their blockade of the German coastline. Facing shortages of supplies at home, the Germans decided to send their navy out to break the blockade. The fleets met in the Battle of Jutland, off the coast of Denmark. Although the British suffered more damage than the Germans, the blockade remained intact, and the German fleet returned to port, where it stayed for the rest of the war.

The Lusitania *leaving New York for England*

NOTICE!

TRAVELLERS intending to embark on the Atlantic voyage are reminded that a state of war exists between Germany and her allies and Great Britain and her allies; that the zone of war includes the waters adjacent to the British Isles; that, in accordance with formal notice given by the Imperial German Government, vessels flying the flag of Great Britain, or any of her allies, are liable to destruction in those waters and that travelers sailing in the war zone on ships of Great Britain and her allies do so at their own risk.

IMPERIAL GERMAN EMBASSY
WASHINGTON, D. C., APRIL 22, 1915

German U-Boats

In 1870 Jules Verne's novel *Twenty Thousand Leagues Under the Sea* was published. In it Verne described the fictitious adventures of the mad Captain Nemo, who sails beneath the ocean surface in his submarine, the *Nautilus*. When the novel was published, it was considered a fantasy and was received with great skepticism (even though a few primitive submarines had been invented before Verne's time). Just forty-four years later, however, the *Nautilus* became a devastating reality in the form of the German U-boat.

The Germans launched an all-out attack on British shipping to stop the flow of war supplies into Britain. The Germans found that their surface ships were no match for the large British fleet. So they relied on their U-boats to enforce the blockade around the British Isles.

The U-boat crews realized that their task was of the utmost importance to the German war effort and were willing to endure appalling conditions onboard the submarines. One historian wrote, "On long patrols . . . crews lived in an atmosphere of increasing squalor. The heat was oppressive, the air stale and foul and reeking of bilge water [water that collects in a ship's hull], wet oilskins, rubber boots, sweat, and diesel fumes so thick that a man's hair became pitchy mire."

A beached German U-boat

In the early years of the war, the German U-boats badly mauled British shipping. The British were hard-pressed to stop this deadly menace. They used merchant ships equipped with guns to combat them. These ships, called Q-ships, could quickly alter their appearance from a British freighter to one of another country. (Early in the war, the German U-boats sank only British ships.) By posing as a merchant ship of a neutral nation, the Q-ships hoped to lure unsuspecting U-boats in close and then open fire. Sometimes, however, the British ships were unsuccessful in fooling the captains of the U-boats and were sunk. As one courageous Q-ship captain said, "It was no use pretending to be something you were not unless you attended to every detail."

Later in the war, the Allies enjoyed much better success in defending against U-boat attacks. Allied ships traveled in large convoys and used blimps to spot U-boats. With the invention of depth charges, Allied surface ships had an effective means of destroying U-boats lurking beneath the ocean surface. Even so, German U-boats sank more than six thousand Allied ships during the course of the war.

The German generals persuaded Kaiser Wilhelm that an all-out submarine campaign would win the war quickly for Germany. When Wilhelm and others voiced fear that such a campaign might bring the Americans into the war, the chief of German naval operations told the kaiser, "I give Your Majesty my word as an officer that not one American will land on the continent." In February 1917 the Germans resumed unrestricted submarine warfare—the sinking of all ships, even if they were unarmed, that carried supplies to the Allies. By the end of the year, the Germans had sunk nearly three thousand ships. But the Allies overcame these losses by improving their methods of antisubmarine warfare.

Collapse of Russia

Russia was unprepared to fight a lengthy war. Its economy and government were inefficient and corrupt, and as casualties and shortages increased, the people's anger and frustration led to strikes and violence. An unplanned popular uprising that began in the Russian capital of St. Petersburg soon spread to other cities. Czar **Nicholas II** abdicated on March 15, 1917. For several months, a provisional government under Alexander Kerensky attempted to restore order and continue the war against Germany. But in November 1917 a second revolution occurred, bringing the Communists to power. In 1918 Vladimir Lenin, the new Russian leader, signed a peace treaty with the Germans. The **Treaty of Brest-Litovsk** effectively took Russia out of the war and gave Lenin time to consolidate his power. Russia gave up 1.3 million square miles of land that was inhabited by more than sixty million people (approximately one-third of its

The War and The Colonies

Although most attention in discussions of World War I focus on the major European combatants, the colonies of those nations also played critical roles in the conduct of the war. For example, France mobilized 46,000 troops from its colonies. Great Britain mobilized troops from its colonies in Australia, New Zealand, Canada, South Africa, and India. The British enlisted the services of 100,000 soldiers in the Royal Gurkha Rifles alone. Most of the British troops at the Battle of Gallipoli were Australians and New Zealanders. Belgium used its colonial troops in the Congo to attack the German colony of East Africa. The colonies of Portugal and Italy were also involved. The Allies seized most of Germany's colonies early in the war.

But the colonies were also affected economically. The same war economies that were imposed on the people in the mother countries also were imposed on their colonies. Consequently, the colonists experienced some of the same conditions and restrictions that those in the mother country felt, including higher prices and scarcity of goods. They also faced increased taxes to pay for the war.

population). In addition, it lost nearly 90 percent of its coal mines and more than 50 percent of its industry. As a result, Germany gained access to badly needed raw materials; more importantly, Germany could now concentrate its troops in the west against France and Britain and possibly win the war.

The United States Enters the War

When war broke out in 1914, the United States remained neutral. At that time, most American citizens probably agreed with President Woodrow Wilson: "The United States must be neutral in fact as well as in name. . . . We must be impartial in thought as well as in action, [we] must put a curb upon our sentiments." Yet, only a few years later, President Wilson addressed Congress and called for a declaration of war against Germany. In his speech, he stated that Americans would "fight for the ultimate peace of the world, and for the liberation of its people. . . . The world must be made safe for democracy."

What caused this shift in American sentiment? Why did Wilson, who in 1916 won reelection to the presidency with the slogan "He kept us out of war," ask for a declaration of war five months later? The following reasons help to answer these questions.

1. **German Submarine Campaign**—Many Americans were angered by the loss of life and property resulting from Germany's unrestricted submarine attacks, which reached its height in 1917. They regarded the sinking of unarmed merchant ships without warning as immoral conduct and a violation of international law.

2. **Ties with Britain and France**—The United States enjoyed bonds of language and cultural heritage with England. It believed it had a debt to repay to the French, who had helped the American colonies in their War for Independence. Furthermore, the United States had been on friendly terms with France and Britain throughout much of the preceding century.
3. **German Plot**—Great Britain uncovered a plot to bring Mexico into the war against the United States. The Germans planned to offer the Mexicans financial aid and the promise of territory in southwestern New Mexico and Arizona (territories that the United States had gained from Mexico in 1848) if Mexico would declare war on the United States.
4. **Allied Propaganda**—The turning of American opinion against the Germans was due, in part, to Allied reports of German atrocities. American newspapers received nearly all of their war news from the British, and the British often exaggerated stories and incidents to stir up anti-German sentiments.
5. **Monetary Ties**—The United States had close financial ties with the Allies. American businessmen and farmers profited from British and French purchases of American goods. In addition, American bankers had lent large sums of money to the French and British governments. These Americans did not want to lose either their markets or their investments.
6. **Balance of Power**—The United States also wanted to maintain the balance of power in Europe. Many Americans feared what would happen if a victorious Germany, with its strong militaristic ways, were to dominate Europe.

Gen. John J. Pershing, commander, American Expeditionary Force

For these reasons, and at the request of the president, the U.S. Congress declared war on Germany on April 6, 1917. Initially, American soldiers provided little help to the struggling Allies because the United States did not already have a large, well-trained army. In the last months of the war, however, more than 250,000 American troops landed in France every month. Under the leadership of General **John J. "Black Jack" Pershing**, the American Expeditionary Force (AEF) provided the necessary edge to defeat the Germans at last.

The Conclusion of the War

Germany made a last attempt to win the war before American forces could turn the tide against them. With Russia out of the war, Germany was able to send its veterans from the eastern front into France for a final series of offensives that began in March 1918. At first, the German attacks were successful; the weary French and British soldiers were on the verge of collapse. However, under General **Ferdinand Foch** (FAWSH) who had just been named commander in chief of the Allied armies in France, the Allies stopped the German advance. Then, with reinforcements from the United States, they mounted a counterattack.

While the Allies were pushing the Germans slowly out of France, Germany's allies collapsed. Revolts of subject nationalities under Turkish and Austrian control had weakened an already faltering war effort and hastened their defeat. In September, Bulgaria surrendered, and by the beginning of November, the Ottoman Empire and Austria-Hungary had surrendered. Germany saw the end coming and appealed to President Wilson for an **armistice** (a temporary cessation of fighting) based on his proposals. Wilson, however, refused to negotiate with a government that he believed did not truly represent the German people. Meanwhile, mutinies and revolts erupted across Germany. The kaiser fled to Holland, and a German republic replaced the Second German Reich. Leaders of the new government agreed to an armistice. On November 11, 1918,

Profiles in Courage

One American who emerged from the war an international hero was Sgt. Alvin C. York. A quiet, unpretentious Christian, York initially was a conscientious objector (one who believes it is wrong to fight in war). After intense soul searching, however, York went to war with his unit, determined to do his duty. During the war York displayed such courage that the U.S. military awarded him the Congressional Medal of Honor. He also received numerous foreign decorations for heroism.

Another American soldier also demonstrated unparalleled courage but did not return home to parades. Furthermore, the awarding of his Medal of Honor was delayed for nearly eighty years. Born in Sandy Springs, South Carolina, Freddie Stowers was the grandson of a slave. Like York, he was a poor southern farmer who was drafted into the army in 1917. Because of the American military's low opinion of black soldiers, Stowers and other African American soldiers were prevented from fighting with American units. Instead, they were assigned to French units who badly needed reinforcements. On the morning of September 28, 1918, Corporal Stowers and his company took part in the assault on a tall, well-defended hill known as *Côte* 188. Facing heavy German machine gun and rifle fire, Stowers's company made a steady advance against the Germans. A few minutes into the battle the Germans signaled their desire to surrender. However, when the Allied forces advanced to within one hundred meters of the Germans, the Germans suddenly dropped into their trenches and renewed their attack, killing about half of the Allied force, including the officers. Stowers then took charge and led his men, crawling toward the closest German machine gun nest. Even though Stowers was wounded during this assault, he led his men to advance toward the second line of German trenches. Stowers continued to lead his men until he was wounded a second time and then encouraged his men to continue on to victory. Stowers died during the battle and was later buried at the Meuse-Argonne American Cemetery and Memorial.

Above: First Sgt. Alvin C. York and his Congressional Medal of Honor
Below: Corporal Stowers's sisters, Georgina Palmer and Mary Bowens, with Barbara Bush and President George H.W. Bush at the Medal of Honor presentation ceremony in 1991.

Although Stowers's name was submitted for the Medal of Honor shortly after his death, no action was taken until 1990 when the Department of the Army discovered the unprocessed request. Seventy-three years after his death, his surviving sisters, Georgina and Mary, received Stowers's Medal of Honor at the White House from President George H.W. Bush.

at 11:00 a.m., German and Allied officials met in a railroad car in the Compiègne Forest in France and signed the armistice ending World War I.

Although the armistice brought an end to the fighting, it could in no way repair the damage that the war had done. The cost of the war in terms of human lives was staggering. Ten million of the approximately sixty-four million men who were mobilized died; approximately twenty million were wounded, and about six million were missing or unaccounted for. Civilian deaths through starvation, disease, massacres, submarine attacks, and so on probably equaled battlefield deaths. The average daily loss of life during the war was approximately fifteen thousand. In financial terms, the total direct cost of the war neared $200 billion; indirect costs totaled more than $151 billion. Combined, the war cost approximately $9 million an hour.

While these figures give a somewhat cold and approximate account of the cost of the war in lives and dollars, one cannot measure the total effect that the war had on the world, especially Europe. How does one measure personal suffering or the loss of a generation of young men? How does one measure the devastation to industry, countryside, and economy?

The only difference between this war and previous wars was that new technology increased man's destructive power. In fact, some people foolishly believed that the war had been so destructive that men would never again resort to warfare to settle their disputes. Their error would soon be exposed by yet another world war.

Section Quiz

1. Who was assassinated on June 28, 1914?
2. What country's neutrality did the Germans violate as they invaded France? What European country declared war on Germany as a result of that attack on a neutral country?
3. What was the German policy that called for the sinking of all ships, armed or not, that carried supplies to the Allies?
4. What country left the struggle against Germany in 1918?
5. What country joined the struggle against Germany in 1917?

★ Why did World War I utterly shatter European optimism about the goodness of humanity and the progress of civilization?

III. The Pursuit of Peace

The Paris Peace Conference

In January 1919 the **Paris Peace Conference** opened. Seventy delegates representing thirty-two nations met to negotiate the peace settlement for World War I. Unlike the victorious nations at the Congress of Vienna, which had allowed France (the defeated nation) to participate in the negotiations (see p. 373), the Allies excluded the defeated Central Powers from the conference. Nor was Russia invited because it had withdrawn from the war in 1918 after the Communist revolution.

The "Big Four" at the League of Nations negotiations: (from left) David Lloyd George, Great Britain; Vittorio Orlando, Italy; Georges Clemenceau, France; Woodrow Wilson, United States.

The dominant leaders at the conference were U.S. president **Woodrow Wilson**, French premier **Georges Clemenceau**, British prime minister **David Lloyd George**, and Italian prime minister **Vittorio Orlando**. These men largely determined the character and content of the peace treaties.

When the Germans signed the armistice ending World War I, they did so with the understanding that Wilson's peace program would be the basis of the peace treaty. Wilson had advocated a moderate settlement, known as the **Fourteen Points**, which would not seek revenge upon the defeated powers. When Wilson arrived in Europe, enthusiastic crowds welcomed him wherever he went. He did not receive such a hearty welcome by the diplomats at the conference, however; many of them considered him an idealist and found him stubborn and preachy.

Clemenceau, the leader of the French delegation, was known as the "Old Tiger." He was a cynical and crafty politician who had no use for Wilson's idealism. He once commented that "even God was satisfied with Ten Commandments, but Wilson insists on fourteen." Clemenceau's main concern was the security of France. He desired to keep Germany militarily weak and to make it pay for the war damages inflicted on France.

Lloyd George of Great Britain also wanted to see Germany punished, but his treaty proposals were not as severe as Clemenceau's. He hoped that German industry could soon be revived, since the staggering British economy desperately needed as many markets as possible. At the same time, he wanted to protect British colonial and naval interests.

The Treaty of Versailles

The Allies drew up five major treaties ending the war, the most important of which was the Treaty of Versailles—the treaty between the Allies and Germany. The Germans had expected the treaty to be in accord with Wilson's moderate proposals; instead, its provisions were very harsh.

Territorial Provisions—According to the Treaty of Versailles, Germany had to return Alsace and Lorraine to France and grant smaller amounts of land to Belgium and Denmark. Clemenceau had originally demanded that all German territory west of the Rhine River come under French control, but the United States and Britain would not agree to such a demand. So the Allies worked out a compromise whereby they would jointly occupy the Rhineland for fifteen years. During that time the French would be allowed to control the rich Saar coal field located in the Rhineland.

In the east, the treaty reestablished an independent Polish nation. East Prussia was detached from the rest of Germany to give Poland an outlet to the Baltic Sea. This territory became known as the Polish Corridor and included the port city of Danzig (Gdańsk), which came under the control of the League of Nations. A portion of the coal-rich province of Silesia went to Poland, and Lithuania received the German port of Memel. In addition, Germany lost all of its Asian and African colonies. Altogether, the Germans lost twenty-five thousand square miles of territory inhabited by six million people. (See map on p. 463.)

Economic Provisions—The Treaty of Versailles also specified that large amounts of coal from German mines had to be sent to several of the Allied nations for ten years. It required the Germans to turn over many of their merchant ships and fishing vessels to the Allies, in addition to building new ships for them. But the most damaging economic provision of the treaty was the Allied demand that Germany pay **reparations** (payment for war damages). In spite of the fact that the Allies could not agree on the amount of the war damages, the treaty demanded an immediate payment of $5 billion. The delegates established a special commission to decide on the final amount later.

The signing of the peace treaty at the Palace of Versailles

Military Provisions—The German army was limited to one hundred thousand men. A thirty-mile-wide zone east of the Rhine River was to remain **demilitarized** (no armies could be in that area at any time). The army could have no tanks or large guns; the navy could have no submarines and only six warships. All military aircraft had to be destroyed; no new ones could be built.

The "War Guilt" Clause—The basis for all of these repressive provisions was Article 231 of the treaty, which stated, "The Allied and Associated Governments affirm and Germany accepts the responsibility of Germany and its allies for causing all the loss and damage to which the Allied and Associated Governments and their nationals have been subjected as a consequence of the war

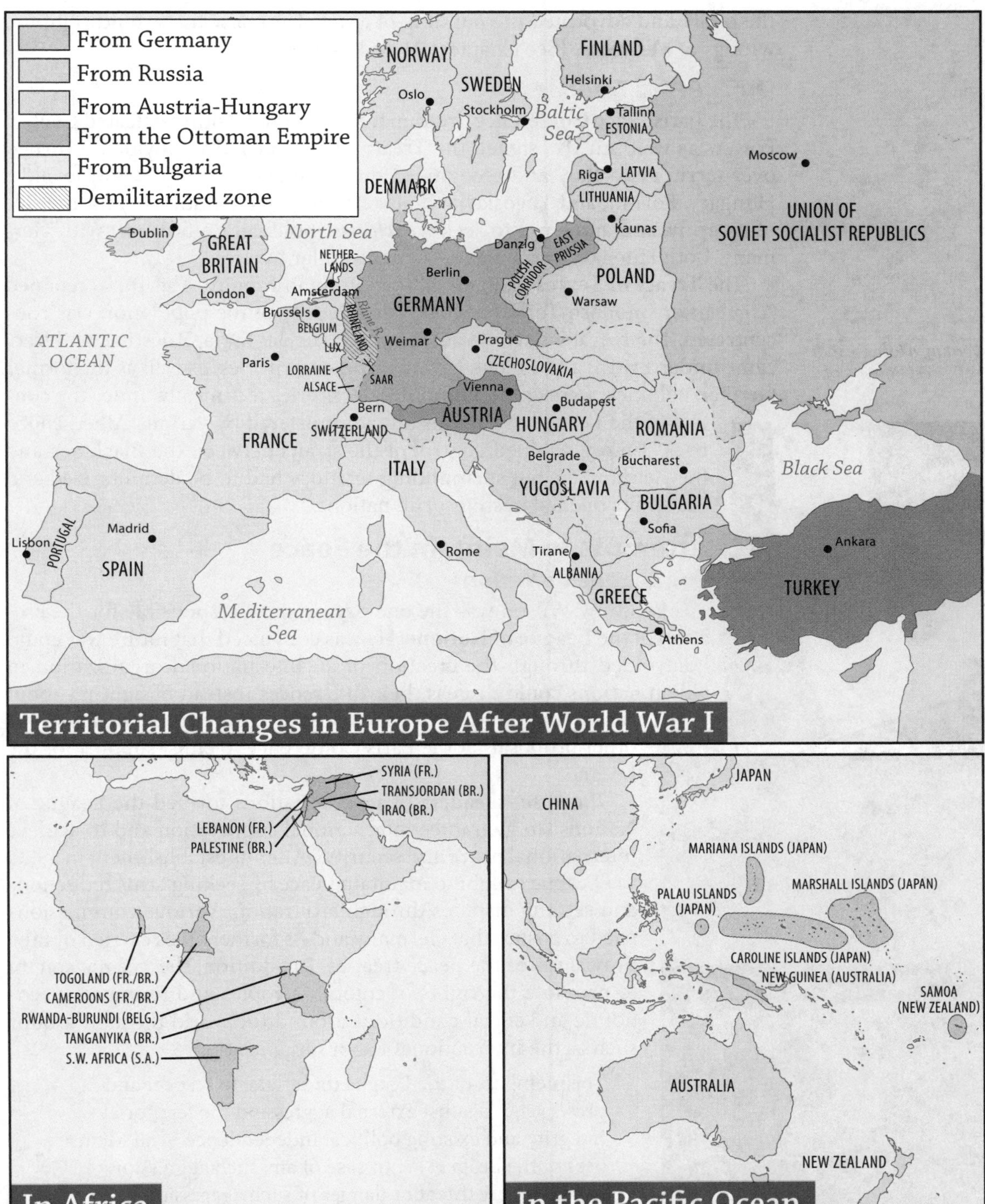

imposed upon them by the aggression of Germany and its allies." This so-called **war guilt clause** placed the entire blame for the war on Germany and its allies.

Germany at first refused to sign the treaty. Although it was willing to accept some blame for the war, it believed it unjust to shoulder all the blame. But when the Allies threatened to continue the war if the Germans would not cooperate, a German delegation at Versailles signed under protest. In the years following Versailles, German resentment and anger at this unjust provision soon changed to hatred, and thoughts of revenge began to mount. Before long, many Germans began to listen seriously to Adolf Hitler as he fiercely condemned the treaty and advocated the building of a new Germany that would right the wrongs of Versailles. (See Chapters 21 and 22.)

Other Peace Treaties

The Paris Peace Conference drew up treaties with the other defeated Central Powers as well. Austria signed the **Treaty of St. Germain**, in which it turned over territory to Italy and recognized the independence of Czechoslovakia, Hungary, Poland, and Yugoslavia. It also had to pay reparations, limit the size of its army, and agree not to seek ***Anschluss*** (political unification) with Germany. Both Hungary and Bulgaria signed similar treaties.

The **Treaty of Sèvres** dismantled the Ottoman Empire. The Turks retained Asia Minor (modern Turkey), where the majority of the population was concentrated. Their Arabian territories, however, such as Syria, Palestine, and Iraq, came under British and French control. These territories, as well as the former German colonies, were called **mandates**, territories technically under the control of the League of Nations but administered by various Allied countries. Turkey retained control of the straits between the Black Sea and the Aegean Sea, but surrounding territory had to be demilitarized and the straits opened to ships of all nations.

World War I cemetery at Verdun, a fortress that was the site of some of the fiercest fighting of the war

Attempts to Maintain the Peace

The League of Nations

Woodrow Wilson was the one person most responsible for the creation of the **League of Nations**. He was convinced that future war could be avoided through the creation of an international organization in which nations could discuss their differences instead of fighting about them. Therefore, he was willing to compromise many of his other proposals at the Paris Conference to enlist support for the League.

Purpose—Leaders of several nations formed the League of Nations "to guarantee international cooperation and to achieve international peace and security." After its establishment in 1920, the League sought to maintain peace by seeking arms reductions and settling disputes through arbitration. Various commissions tried to ensure that Germany and its former allies carried out the provisions of the peace treaties. In addition, the League sought to promote the rights of colonial peoples and to improve economic and social conditions around the world through groups such as the International Labor Organization.

> The members of the League undertake to respect and preserve . . . against external aggression the territorial integrity and existing political independence of all Members of the League. . . . In case of any such aggression or in case of any threat or danger of such aggression the Council shall advise upon the means by which this obligation shall be fulfilled.
>
> —League Covenant, Article X

Ultimate Failure—Despite the League's success in settling minor disputes among weaker nations, it lacked the authority to settle major crises among powerful nations. Strong nations simply ignored or defied the League, and later some of them even withdrew their membership in the organization.

Compounding the problem was the ineffectiveness of the organization. The League had the power only to recommend action on the part of its members; it could not require them to take action. In addition, important decisions required unanimous approval on the part of every member nation. In the unlikely event that the League could get every member to approve an action, it had no armed forces of its own to police troubled areas. Even when member nations had the military capacity to enforce a decision, they were hesitant about using force, fearing it might lead to another war.

The League suffered a serious blow when the United States refused to join. Even though President Wilson was the chief proponent of the League, the U.S. Senate would not ratify the treaty. The mood in the United States after the war was one of isolation from foreign involvement. Thus, the nation that emerged from the war as the strongest power did not become a member of the League.

Reparation Revisions

The Paris Peace Conference set up a special commission to determine how much Germany owed in reparations. In addition to the $5 billion that the Allies originally demanded, the reparations commission finally settled on an additional sum of $32 billion. Germany made several payments but soon stopped because its economy was not strong enough to bear the burden. When payments did not resume, France retaliated by invading the Ruhr Valley (an industrial district in Germany). British and American opposition forced France to withdraw.

Realizing Germany's financial problems, American banker **Charles Dawes** formed a committee in 1924 to find a solution. Taking as its slogan "Business, not politics," the committee decided to lend Germany money and allow it to spread the reparation payments out over a longer period. In 1929, **Owen Young**, an American lawyer, devised another plan that reduced the amount of reparations and gave Germany until 1988 to complete its payments. When economic problems continued, President Herbert Hoover in 1931 advocated a one-year **moratorium** (suspension) on all reparations payments. After this moratorium, however, Germany never resumed payments.

Closely associated with the German failure to pay reparations was the failure of Britain and France to pay their own **war debts** to the United States. During the war, Britain, France, and other countries had borrowed huge amounts of money from the United States. The Allies had planned to use some of the money Germany paid them in reparations to repay their war debt. But when Germany could not meet its reparation payments, the Allies in turn could not repay their creditors. Intending to reduce the problem, American and British bankers made loans to Germany, hoping that it would invest that money in its economy. As its economy became stronger, it would better be able to meet the reparation payments. But instead of investing the money, Germany immediately used most of it for reparation payments to Britain and France. Britain and France, in turn, used the money to pay off their war debts to the United States, and again Germany needed another loan. The Allies found this reparations/war-debt cycle impossible to

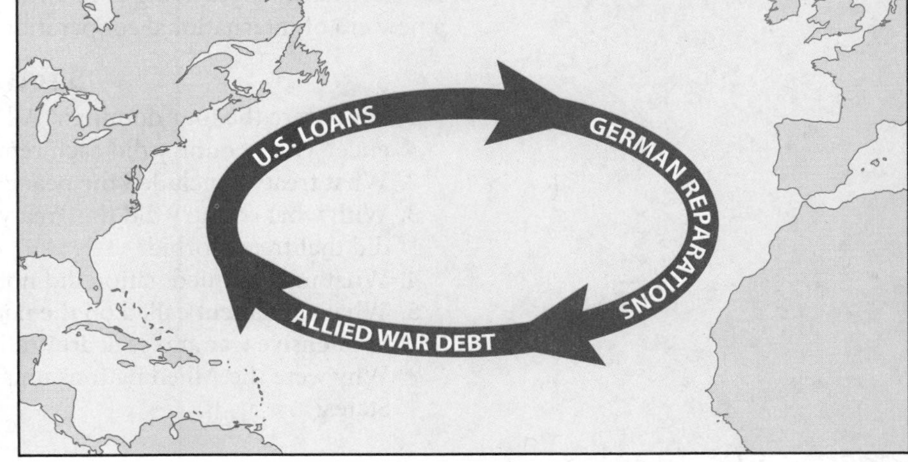

break, and before long all war-debt and reparation payments ceased. This cycle contributed to the worldwide depression of the 1930s.

Disarmament and Nonaggression Pacts

The Locarno Pact—To a Europe apprehensive about the possibility of another war, the Locarno Conference seemed to offer hope. In the fall of 1925, several European nations met in Locarno, Switzerland. At this conference, Germany signed a treaty with France and Belgium in which it agreed to recognize its present borders with those two nations as permanent. In addition, all three nations promised not to go to war with one another except in self-defense. Although Germany did not recognize its eastern border as permanent, it did agree not to seek any change in that border through war. This **Locarno Pact**, which involved other agreements as well, seemed to hold the promise of peace in Europe. Nations that hated each other now seemed, at least on the surface, to be friends. European tensions relaxed somewhat, and for several years this "spirit of Locarno" gave Europeans a false sense of security.

Washington Naval Conference—Those who refuse to believe that wars result from the natural sinfulness of man will sometimes conclude that wars are caused by weapons. They believe that if they eliminate weapons, they can eliminate war. This elimination of weapons or arms is called **disarmament**. The best example of an attempt at disarmament in the 1920s was the **Washington Naval Conference** (1921–22). The great naval powers—Britain, the United States, Japan, and others—agreed to limit the number of warships each could build. They also established a ratio by which to limit the buildup of large warships. They decided, for example, that for every five tons of American shipping, Britain could have five tons, and Japan three tons. The conference failed, however, to reach any agreement on limiting the number of smaller warships and submarines. Ultimately, the conference was a failure; its participants—notably Japan—kept the agreement only when it suited their purposes.

Kellogg-Briand Pact—The crowning effort to preserve the peace in the post–World War I period came in 1928. Frank Kellogg, the American secretary of state, working with Aristide Briand, the French minister of foreign affairs, proposed an agreement calling upon the nations of the world to renounce the use of offensive war. Nations that signed the document pledged to use arbitration rather than force to settle their disputes. In short, this document, known as the **Kellogg-Briand Pact**, sought to unite "the civilized nations of the world in a common renunciation of war as an instrument of their national policy." Sixty-two nations eventually signed this idealistic agreement, which simply made war illegal. Three years later, one signatory—Japan—invaded Manchuria. Yet many people living at that time looked to this agreement as the start of a new era of international cooperation.

Section Quiz

1. Who were the four dominant Allied leaders at the Paris Peace Conference? What country did each represent?
2. What treaty concluded the peace between the Allies and Germany?
3. With what country did the Treaty of St. Germain settle the peace? What did that treaty forbid?
4. What major Allied nation did not join the League of Nations?
5. What agreement called on the nations of the world to renounce the use of offensive war and seek arbitration to settle international disputes?

☆ Why were the Allied nations unable to repay their debts to the United States?

Chapter 20 Review

Making Connections

1–3. Why did the U.S. enter the war on the side of the Allies? (List three reasons.)

4–5. Why was the League of Nations doomed to fail? (List two reasons.)

Developing History Skills

1. Defend or refute the following statement, "The peace settlements of World War I increased the likelihood of another major war."
2. Summarize the reasons Germany did not resume reparation payments following the one-year moratorium in 1931. You might need to look at the next chapter to answer this question.

Thinking Critically

1. Why did the United States refuse to join the League of Nations? Were these reasons valid?
2. Evaluate the disarmament and non-aggression pacts and their ability to prevent war based on the information in this chapter.

Living in God's World

1. Given James 4:1–3 and Matthew 5:9, write a brief Christian perspective on war and peace.
2. Given Matthew 5:7, write a proposal for how nations ought to treat each other after war.

People, Places, and Things to Know

Alfred Nobel
Andrew Carnegie
chauvinism
Bismarck's System
Three Emperors' League
Dual Alliance
Triple Alliance
Reinsurance Treaty
Wilhelm II
Entente Cordiale
Triple Entente
Francis Ferdinand
ultimatum
mobilize
Central Powers
Schlieffen Plan
Paul von Hindenburg
stalemate
attrition
zeppelins
U-boats
Lusitania
Nicholas II
Treaty of Brest-Litovsk
John J. "Black Jack" Pershing
Ferdinand Foch
armistice
Paris Peace Conference
Woodrow Wilson
Georges Clemenceau
David Lloyd George
Vittorio Orlando
Fourteen Points
reparations
demilitarized
war guilt clause
Treaty of St. Germain
Anschluss
Treaty of Sèvres
mandates
League of Nations
Charles Dawes
Owen Young
moratorium
war debts
Locarno Pact
disarmament
Washington Naval Conference
Kellogg-Briand Pact

21

DISCONTENT AND EXPERIMENTATION

I. Weakness Within the Democracies

II. Rise of Totalitarian Dictatorships

III. Era of Disillusionment

Adolf Hitler, the Nazi party, and the swastika came to symbolize the rise of totalitarian regimes in Europe after World War I.

Shifting from war to peace proved to be extremely difficult for a world that was tired and disillusioned from four years of bloodshed. Economic weakness, political instability, and changing moral values multiplied in the years following World War I. During the 1920s, world leaders attempted to solve these problems through peace treaties and economic agreements. By the 1930s, however, everyone could see that those efforts had failed. The Great Depression brought worldwide economic chaos. The rise of new dictators shattered President Wilson's idealistic promise of a world "safe for democracy." Standards of morality declined, and moral decay increased as a growing number of people abandoned belief in the authority of God's Word.

Edmund Burke, an eighteenth-century British statesman, said, "All that is necessary for the triumph of evil is that good men do nothing." The two decades following World War I were marked by widespread apathy, especially among the victorious Allied nations. Individual citizens and national governments allowed evil to multiply. Socialist ideas crept into the economies of many countries. Self-serving dictators captured control of the governments of both small and large countries. Religious liberals infiltrated the churches, turning many away from the truth of God's Word. The attitude of indifference that allowed these forces of evil to triumph eventually led to the outbreak of World War II.

Economic and social disorder as well as national pride helped bring to power charismatic dictators such as Adolf Hitler and Benito Mussolini.

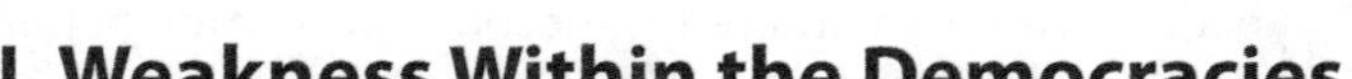

I. Weakness Within the Democracies

One of the most serious problems facing Europe and America after World War I was the change from wartime to peacetime economies. Once the fighting stopped, governments relaxed their economic controls. But as inflation and then depression struck, many governments reestablished those controls.

Great Britain

As veterans returned home from the war, British prime minister Lloyd George promised that Britain would be a land "fit for heroes." The two decades between the world wars, however, did not match his optimistic promise. Britons witnessed the steady decline of their empire. In addition, the British economy suffered greatly; the war had seriously hurt the nation's trade, and debt was ten times greater than it had been in 1914. Hardest hit was the coal-mining industry. Strong foreign competition and increased use of other energy sources resulted in diminished demands for coal. Layoffs and miners' strikes resulted. Unemployment in all industries increased so dramatically that by 1932 almost one Briton in four was out of work. Many were on the dole (government relief for the unemployed). In the same year, Britain abandoned its policy of free trade and initiated protective tariffs (taxes on imported goods).

Ramsay MacDonald

As economic problems deepened, Britain gradually developed into a welfare state. Parliamentary appropriations for social welfare programs dramatically increased during the 1920s and 1930s. Another indication of the trend toward socialism was the rise of the Labour Party led by **Ramsay MacDonald** (1866–1937). In 1924, MacDonald became the first Labour Party prime minister of Britain. Although he held the office for less than a year, the Labour Party established itself as a major force in British politics.

The war had not only increased Britain's economic woes but also stimulated demands for home rule, or complete independence, by several British possessions. After several years of fierce fighting, Britain finally gave in to Irish demands for independence and created the Irish Free State in 1921. (Northern Ireland—called Ulster—remained under British control.) In Egypt, strong nationalism forced the British to recognize that country's independence, although

Britain still maintained a naval base there to protect the Suez Canal. Nationalists in India continued clamoring for independence. In 1935, the British Parliament passed the Government of India Act, which granted the Indians greater self-government. In the **Statute of Westminster** (1931), Britain approved a 1926 report that had declared Canada, Australia, New Zealand, and South Africa to be "autonomous communities within the British Empire, equal in status, in no way subordinate one to another in any aspect of their domestic or external affairs, though united by common allegiance to the crown and freely associated as members of the British Commonwealth of Nations."

In 1940 the French show their British allies a gun emplacement along the supposedly impregnable Maginot Line.

France

During World War I, France suffered heavier losses in life and property than Great Britain did, yet France achieved greater economic recovery. New factories replaced those destroyed during the war. The recently returned territories of Alsace and Lorraine provided rich mineral deposits and important industrial plants. Even in the face of worldwide economic problems, unemployment never became as severe in France as it was in Britain. Most of the French people were small businessmen or farmers, and although violent strikes did occur, France weathered the economic storms better than much of the rest of Europe.

Nevertheless, France remained politically unstable. The Third French Republic (established after the French defeat in the Franco-Prussian War) was plagued by so many political parties that none was able to gain a majority. As a result, the government was established on shaky coalitions of several political parties. Between 1920 and 1940, France changed prime ministers some forty times. As successive governments failed to solve France's domestic problems, discontented radical groups, which threatened the republic, became increasingly popular. During this period various Socialist and Communist political parties became stronger. These parties, calling themselves the Popular Front, managed to gain control of the government in 1936, naming **Léon Blum** (1872–1950) as prime minister. This coalition soon fell apart, however, and France returned to more conservative control.

The Maginot Line was a line of fortifications that included an elaborate system of underground chambers containing whatever the soldiers might need or want.

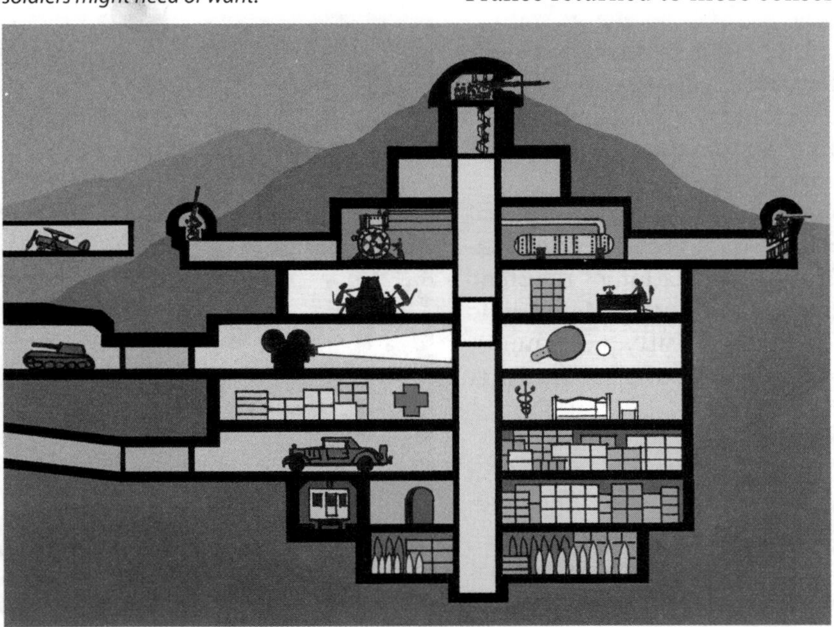

In foreign affairs, the French remained wary of Germany. They were determined to protect their border with Germany and questioned the League's ability to provide protection in case of another war. Furthermore, Britain and the United States refused to guarantee aid to France in the event of renewed German aggression, so France formed defensive alliances with some of the smaller European nations. Between 1924 and 1927, for example, France signed agreements with Czechoslovakia, Romania, and Yugoslavia.

In 1929, under the leadership of André Maginot, the French began building a line of fortifications stretching 560 miles, from Switzerland to the Belgian border, along its border with Germany. Below the fortifications was a network of underground chambers containing power stations, ammunition supplies, hospitals, recreation halls, theaters, and living quarters. Each fortification was joined to the others by an underground subway, which made possible quick and safe transportation of troops anywhere along the line. Those fortifications became France's main line of defense on the east. Many Frenchmen confidently believed that the **Maginot Line**, as it was called, would stop any German attack. During World War II, however, the Germans simply bypassed those fortifications, rendering them useless.

Top: Warren G. Harding
Bottom: Calvin Coolidge

The United States

World War I had thrust the United States into a strong leadership role in world affairs. After the war, however, many Americans wanted to return to a policy of isolationism. Although Wilson advocated U.S. participation in world affairs through the League of Nations, the Senate twice refused to ratify the Versailles Treaty, which contained the League provisions. In 1920 Americans turned away from the idealism and internationalism of Wilson. They elected as president Warren G. Harding, who promised a "return to normalcy." Harding's successor, Calvin Coolidge, continued to emphasize domestic well-being over foreign involvement. (That is what Harding meant by "normalcy.") Coolidge declared, "The business of the United States is business." By the end of the 1920s, conditions seemed so favorable that President Herbert Hoover stated in his 1929 inaugural address, "I have no fears for the future of our country. It is bright with hope."

The Great Depression

On the surface, all seemed to be going well in the United States. New technology enabled factories to mass-produce a variety of consumer goods. People were enjoying more leisure time. But under the surface of this period known as the "Roaring Twenties" was great decay in the moral life of the nation. This decay became evident by the end of the decade. One of the characters in John Steinbeck's novel *The Grapes of Wrath* summarized the popular moral attitude of the day:

> There ain't no sin and there ain't no virtue, there's just stuff people do. . . . Some of the things folks do is nice and some ain't nice, but that's as far as any man got a right to say.

Heavy advertising and credit purchases helped to weaken old ideas about thrift. America was fast becoming a nation in which the rush for wealth and pleasure was the most important pursuit in life. But in 1929 the seeming prosperity of the 1920s came to a sudden end. The collapse of the stock market in October triggered a drop in prices, a decline in foreign trade, the closing of factories, the failure of banks, and a dramatic rise in unemployment. Unemployed workers receiving food in bread lines and soup lines became a common sight in many American cities. By the winter of 1932–33, an estimated thirteen to seventeen million people (approximately one-third of the work force) were unemployed. Though the crash occurred only a few months into his presidency, Herbert Hoover received most of the blame for America's economic woes. Looking for a solution to their problems, the American people elected **Franklin Roosevelt** (1882–1945) to the presidency in 1932.

The New Deal

After his inauguration, Roosevelt immediately began to promote his program of relief, recovery, and reform as a "**New Deal**." Job programs such as those connected with the Works Progress Administration sought to provide immediate relief for the millions of unemployed. Other organizations, such

Hoover and FDR on Inauguration Day, 1933

as the Agricultural Adjustment Administration, were designed to meet long-term goals. Roosevelt promoted many economic changes that he hoped would end the threat of another depression and at the same time provide financial security for Americans. The Securities and Exchange Commission was established to regulate stock exchanges, and Congress passed the Social Security Act (1935).

Historians, economists, and politicians have debated the value of the New Deal. No one doubts that Roosevelt's policies dramatically affected the United States. The key question is whether that effect has been positive or negative. In retrospect, many people have concluded that the New Deal did more harm than good. It provided temporary relief for many Americans but failed to end the Depression or provide any real economic recovery. In addition, Roosevelt's policies were often experimental and increased government spending and the power of federal bureaucrats (the nonelected officials who handle government affairs). This led to increased government involvement in economic and social matters without resolving the core economic problems.

Section Quiz

1. List three possessions of Great Britain that were given self-rule, or complete independence, after World War I.
2. What factor contributed to political instability within the Third French Republic following World War I?
3. What was the name of the French line of defense that protected the length of France's border from Switzerland to Belgium?
4. Which U.S. president sought to promote relief, recovery, and reform to get the country out of the Great Depression? What name was given to his programs?
5. What are the nonelected officials who handle government affairs called?

II. Rise of Totalitarian Dictatorships

People often rely on strong leaders without being appropriately discerning of their integrity. The Bible teaches that no matter what challenges a nation may face, the most important qualification for leadership is righteousness: "When the righteous are in authority, the people rejoice: but when the wicked beareth rule, the people mourn" (Prov. 29:2). As Europe struggled to overcome postwar problems, dictatorial governments became more common. Many Europeans supported ambitious, power-seeking men in hopes that they would bring economic and political stability to their countries. Despite the early successes of such rulers, their nations were brought to bitter mourning.

Once in power, these dictators established **totalitarian states**. Although no two such states were exactly alike, they did share the following characteristics:

1. The use of propaganda (materials and methods of indoctrination) to promote the ideas and programs of the state.
2. The use of an efficient secret police to arrest or assassinate those who opposed the state and its policies.
3. Emphasis on the goals of the state rather than on individual rights or concerns.
4. State control of every aspect of life—political, economic, cultural, educational, and religious.

5. A government maintained by force and not accountable to the people for its actions.
6. A one-party political system led by a powerful dictator.

All across Europe, in both established countries and newly created countries, dictators came to power. For example, Antonio de Oliveira Salazar became dictator in Portugal. In Spain, following a bloody civil war, Francisco Franco gained control of the government. In Turkey, Mustafa Kemal (keh MAHL), a champion of Turkish nationalism, established himself as dictator. But it was under dictators in Russia, Italy, and Germany that totalitarianism assumed its most terrible forms between the world wars.

Communism in Russia

Collapse of Czarist Russia

The reforms of Czar Alexander II came to an end with his assassination in 1881 (see p. 388). His successor, **Alexander III** (1881–94), attempted to suppress revolutionary ideas and activities. He ordered the state police and courts to intensify their efforts and demanded a strict censorship of the press. Alexander also persecuted various minority national groups, such as the Poles and the Finns. He wanted to force them to become "Russian" in language, religion, and attitude. Alexander also supported organized government massacres called **pogroms**, which killed thousands of Jews living in Russia, in an effort to redirect Russian anger away from his abusive rule.

Czar Nicholas II

The harsh policies of Alexander III were continued under his son **Nicholas II** (1894–1917). During his reign, popular discontent burst into revolutionary activity. Radicals and liberals of all kinds organized themselves into political parties, one of the most radical of which was the Social Democratic Party (1898). To escape arrest and imprisonment, some of its members fled to Switzerland, where they carried on their work and awaited an opportunity to return to Russia. But philosophical differences within the party caused a small group called the **Bolsheviks** to break away from the larger, more moderate group known as the **Mensheviks**. The Bolsheviks advocated change through violence; the Mensheviks desired change through more peaceful measures.

Prelude to Revolution—For a while, Nicholas II was able to maintain the authority and stability of the government. But disasters in the **Russo-Japanese War** (1904–5) brought popular discontent to the surface. Russian expansion in the Far East during the late nineteenth century had clashed with Japanese expansionist interest, leading to open hostility. Fighting broke out, but the war was brief; poor organization, incompetence, and low morale among the Russian troops helped Japan gain several important victories. At the urging of U.S. president Theodore Roosevelt, a humiliated and shaken Russian government met with Japanese leaders and signed the Treaty of Portsmouth. Russia surrendered both territory and economic advantages in the Far East to Japan.

The most dramatic illustration of popular discontent during the war was a workers' march to the czar's winter palace in St. Petersburg. On January 22, 1905, a procession of two hundred thousand men, women, and children moved toward the palace. They carried a petition calling on Nicholas II to improve the lot of the workers, convene a national assembly, and order elections in which all the people could vote. But the marchers never saw the czar; instead, government soldiers met the marchers and opened fire, killing scores of people and wounding many more. The violent events of that day, known as **Bloody Sunday**, turned the loyalty of many Russians from the czar. They began to look elsewhere for an answer to their suffering.

In the following months, unrest and disorder increased as peasant uprisings, strikes in the factories, and mutinies within the armed forces spread throughout the country. In October a strike among railway workers triggered strikes in all areas of the economy. To direct and maintain the general strike more efficiently, the workers in St. Petersburg organized themselves into a **soviet** (council). Groups of workers in other cities soon followed their example. After a few days, the czar's government yielded to the strikers. Nicholas issued the October Manifesto, promising a constitutional government with free speech and a national assembly, called the **Duma**, to be elected by the people.

Outbreak of Revolution—Over the next several years, however, the czar worked against the Duma while promoting his own social reforms. Economic expansion and industrialism resumed, but local strikes and other symptoms of unrest continued. Dissatisfaction with the czar's government remained strong, and the hardships and sufferings of World War I stirred that discontent into revolutionary action.

Top: Rasputin
Bottom: Aleksandr Kerensky

The Russian people at first seemed to support the war. But early disastrous defeats (see p. 453) caused serious morale problems. Poor planning created food shortages in the cities, and heavy casualties among the soldiers weakened Russia's ability to continue fighting. To try to save the military situation, Nicholas II personally took command of the troops, leaving the empress at home under the evil influence of the monk **Rasputin**. Rasputin was a religious fraud who won the favor of the empress when it appeared that he had healed her son of a blood disorder. He became an advisor to the royal family, but his greedy desires and corrupt influence only further weakened the czar's government. With Nicholas gone from the capital, the political situation rapidly deteriorated. Several Russian nobles murdered Rasputin, hoping that their action would restore public confidence in the government, but even this did not accomplish their purpose.

On March 8, 1917, the people's anger and frustration erupted. Strikes and riots broke out in the capital of St. Petersburg. As chaos gripped the city, the troops which had been ordered to quell the disturbances joined with the strikers. News of the uprisings spread quickly throughout the country, and in city after city, workers overthrew local authorities and organized revolutionary soviets. In St. Petersburg, Nicholas disbanded the Duma, but its members ignored his order and established a provisional government. Four days later, on March 15, Nicholas II abdicated, bringing to an end over three hundred years of Romanov rule.

In the months following the fall of the czar, a provisional government headed by Menshevik **Aleksandr Kerensky** tried its best to restore order. But the radical Bolsheviks organized workers in opposition to his government. They sought an immediate end to the war and the implementation of radical social reforms. Worker opposition at home and the war abroad made the situation very difficult.

To make matters worse, the Germans, eager to remove the Russians from the war, helped exiled Bolshevik leaders return to their homeland. The Germans hoped that these extremist leaders would further disrupt Russia's internal affairs and thereby disrupt Russia's war effort. Their plan succeeded.

Founding of the USSR

Bolsheviks Seize the Revolution—The leader of the Bolsheviks was **Vladimir Lenin** (1870–1924), a brilliant young man who became involved in revolutionary activities while attending a Russian university. Through his study of Karl Marx, he became a dedicated member of the Social Democratic Party and

Above left: Demonstrators in St. Petersburg flee after Russian soldiers fire into the crowd, July 1917.
Above: Lenin

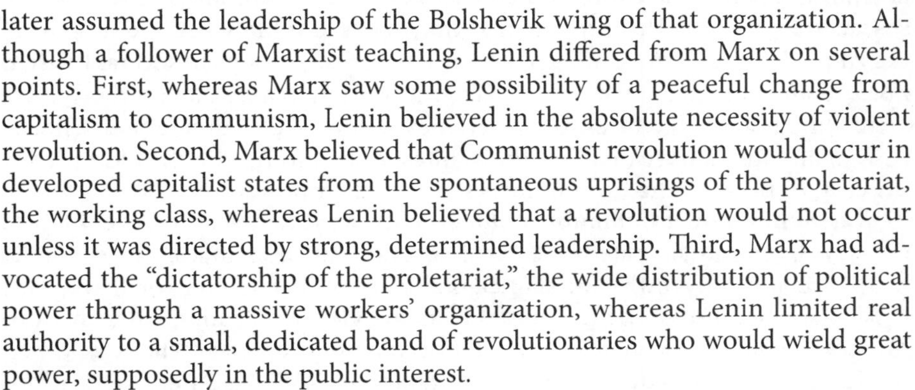

later assumed the leadership of the Bolshevik wing of that organization. Although a follower of Marxist teaching, Lenin differed from Marx on several points. First, whereas Marx saw some possibility of a peaceful change from capitalism to communism, Lenin believed in the absolute necessity of violent revolution. Second, Marx believed that Communist revolution would occur in developed capitalist states from the spontaneous uprisings of the proletariat, the working class, whereas Lenin believed that a revolution would not occur unless it was directed by strong, determined leadership. Third, Marx had advocated the "dictatorship of the proletariat," the wide distribution of political power through a massive workers' organization, whereas Lenin limited real authority to a small, dedicated band of revolutionaries who would wield great power, supposedly in the public interest.

Returning to Russia from exile in Switzerland with the help of the Germans in April 1917, Lenin rallied his followers in opposition to the provisional government. They championed such slogans as "All power to the soviets" and "Peace, land, and bread." For the downtrodden Russian people, the Bolsheviks seemed to offer hope for a brighter future. Urban labor organizations, which were more radical and better organized than any other group in Russian society, proved to be most susceptible to Bolshevik propaganda.

On the morning of November 7, 1917, Lenin's followers seized the government offices in St. Petersburg and arrested many of the leaders of the provisional government. With very little bloodshed, the Bolsheviks came to power, with Lenin as a virtual dictator.

Lenin was successful for several reasons. The Russian people had not wholeheartedly supported the provisional government, which wanted to continue the war against Germany. Most of the Russian people, including the soldiers, desired an immediate end to the fighting. Discipline was so low among the armed forces that officers who might have opposed the Bolshevik takeover did not have the support of their troops. (In 1917 more than two million soldiers deserted.) Besides wanting to end the war, the peasants and industrial workers expected the provisional government to provide immediate solutions to Russia's economic problems. When the government failed to do so, many Russians turned to Lenin and the Bolsheviks.

Japanese troops in Vladivostok, Russia, 1921. The Allied nations of World War I intervened in the Russian civil war to help the anti-Communist forces.

Civil War Erupts—Once the Bolsheviks seized power, they faced serious problems of their own, the most serious of which was the war with Germany. Lenin realized that the Communists (the name that the Bolsheviks had adopted in 1918) could not consolidate their power and fight a war at the same time. Therefore, in 1918 they signed the Treaty of Brest-Litovsk, exchanging large amounts of Russian territory for peace. The Allies were angered that Russia had deserted the war effort and were disheartened by the radical change that had swept over Russia.

For the next four years, Russia suffered through a bloody civil war which raged throughout the country. Initially, the Communists seemed to be at a disadvantage; they lacked a strong, well-trained army. But through the efforts of **Leon Trotsky**, the Communists organized the so-called Red Army. Their opponents, known as the Whites, had the support of the Allies, including the United States. The Allies sent troops to several Russian ports in an effort to aid anti-Bolshevik groups in Russia. Although the Whites won some notable victories, they were never able to coordinate their efforts. Also, many Russians feared that the Whites wished to restore the old order of the czar. In the end, the Communists retained their power.

Russia Becomes a Communist State—Within the first years of its existence, the new Communist state underwent several official changes. For example, in 1918 Lenin moved the Russian capital from St. Petersburg (or Petrograd) to Moscow because of the threat of advancing German armies. After the war, Moscow remained the new capital and became the center of what was called the Russian Soviet Federated Socialist Republic (RSFSR). After the death of Lenin in 1924, the official name of the country became the Union of Soviet Socialist Republics (**USSR**). This new country was composed of fifteen republics. But the central government controlled virtually every aspect of the country, dominating the individual republics and leaving the people with no real voice in their government.

During the violent days of civil war, Lenin instituted a tightly regulated system of economic controls that he called "war communism." In Lenin's words, it was "a frontal attack" on "the citadel of capitalism" designed to implement pure Marxist economic principles. Among other things, the government nationalized (placed under state ownership) Russian industry and demanded that the peasants turn over all of their surplus crops to the state for a set price. Forced labor and lack of incentives brought an already ailing economy to the point of collapse. For example, by 1920 the production of iron ore had dropped 98.4 percent from its 1913 level; the manufacture of cotton goods had fallen 95 percent. Overall, industrial production was only 13 percent of what it had been in 1913. As signs of deep resentment against the Communist system began mounting, the government abandoned its policy of war communism and in 1921 instituted the **New Economic Policy** (NEP).

The NEP, which lasted from 1921 to 1928, was nothing new at all; it was simply a temporary retreat from communism to rescue the Russian economy and to quiet growing anti-Communist sentiment within the country. Various aspects of capitalism, such as private trade and profit-making, became legal

once again. By the time the program ended, the Russian economy had significantly improved. Ironically, Lenin used the capitalistic principles that he had vowed to destroy to save the Communist government and economy.

Strengthening of the USSR

When Lenin died in 1924, a power struggle developed between Leon Trotsky and **Joseph Stalin** (1879–1953). Trotsky was a brilliant and egotistical man known for his fiery speeches. Stalin, on the other hand, was a quiet, dependable, yet ruthless party man, little known outside the Soviet Union. By 1927 Stalin had established himself as the new dictator of the USSR. In the years before Lenin's death, Stalin had appointed many of his supporters to high government positions. After Lenin's death, he used his influence to force Trotsky and his supporters from the government.

Five-Year Plans—In 1928 Stalin ended the NEP and embarked on a series of programs called the **Five-Year Plans**. These programs, designed to build up industrial production and **collectivize** (bring under central government control) agriculture, turned the country back toward socialism. The government established production goals for each industry. Although some of the heavy industries met the government's demands, many other industries did not. Manufactured products were always in short supply. Inefficient bureaucratic mismanagement further illustrated the serious weaknesses in Communist economic theory.

Stalin's program to collectivize agriculture met with hostile resistance on the part of many peasants. The secret police and the army used whatever means they deemed necessary—execution, deportation, or the burning of peasants' homes—to force compliance with government demands. In desperation, the peasants fought back, burning their crops and killing their livestock. Yet, in the end, their resistance was crushed. The struggle had been so severe that between 1928 and 1933 more than half of the homes in the Soviet Union were destroyed. In addition, a severe famine struck the country during 1932 and

Lenin and Stalin

The Soviet Union's first two Communist dictators—Vladimir Lenin and Joseph Stalin—were not actually named Lenin and Stalin. In 1901, Vladimir Ilyich Ulyanov assumed the alias Lenin in an effort to confuse the Russian police. Joseph Stalin was really named Iosif Vissarionovich Dzhugashvili. In his early writings, he used several pseudonymns, but his favorite was Stalin ("man of steel").

Lenin and Stalin

1933. This, along with the struggle over collectivization, led to the deaths of more than five million people.

Stalin's Five-Year Plans had several other significant results. First, as economic depression hit the Western democratic countries in the 1930s, many of them followed the example of Stalin and turned to a planned economy. Many naive Western leaders, blind to the failures of Stalin's program and the terrible cost in human life, marveled that a backward nation like Russia could make such apparent industrial progress. Second, the most significant result of what has been called Russia's Second Revolution was the ever-tightening grip of the state over the people. What little liberty the people may have had under Lenin disappeared rapidly under Stalin.

Reign of Terror—As we have seen, Stalin often resorted to violence and terror to force his will on the Russian people. During 1936–38, he turned on his own Communist Party, determined to wipe out anyone who might prove disloyal to his regime. To accomplish his goal, Stalin instituted a system of **purges** in which eight hundred thousand Communist Party members were murdered, including many of the ruling elite. Even the military suffered, as Stalin ordered the execution of most of the army's top leaders and many of the lesser officers. These events created such fear in the Soviet Union that Stalin's power became more secure than ever.

Because communism seeks to control every aspect of life, the Soviet state under both Lenin and Stalin made a strong effort to wipe out any form of Christianity within its territory. Within twenty years, the government had forced the closure of thousands of churches and schools and had killed many pastors and priests. The Soviet government's cruelty stemmed from the realization that Christian virtues (including love for one's neighbor and individual responsibility) posed a threat to Communist ideas and goals. The Communists' hatred for Christianity is well illustrated by Lenin who described the idea of God as "unutterable vileness."

Foreign Policy—After the Bolshevik revolution, Lenin believed that Communist revolutions would soon sweep across Europe. To further his goal, he established the "Communist International," commonly called the **Comintern**, to found Communist parties in other countries and to take an active role in stirring up discontent in hopes of producing revolution.

Under Stalin, Soviet foreign policy shifted away from the open radicalism of its early years. Stalin, like Lenin, hoped to see communism spread throughout the world; unlike Lenin, however, he believed that the priority for the Soviet Union was to build up communism at home. Once that was accomplished, the USSR could take a more active role in promoting world revolution. Despite the Soviet Union's stated intention to destroy Western democratic governments, many Western nations granted diplomatic recognition to the Soviet government. By the end of 1924, Britain, France, and Italy, among others, had granted such recognition. In 1933 the United States followed their example, officially recognizing the Soviet Union and establishing trade relations.

Section Quiz

1. Who was the last czar of Russia? In what year was his government overthrown?
2. What Communist leader instituted "war communism"?

3. When "war communism" failed and the Russian economy faced collapse, what did Lenin institute? What economic system was he restoring?
4. What Communist leader instituted a system of purges, eliminating all whom he considered a threat to his regime?

★ Why did some Western democratic countries imitate Stalin's Five-Year Plans?

Fascism in Italy and Germany

After the rise of communism in Russia, a new type of totalitarian government called **fascism** (FASH iz um) came to power in Italy and Germany. (German fascism is usually called **Nazism**.) Many of the citizens in those countries had grown discouraged with representative government, yet they feared communism. Fascism seemed to provide an attractive alternative because it promised stability and security.

Peter Vins: "Choosing Rather to Suffer Affliction"

The suffering of Soviet Christians at the hands of their Communist government is well illustrated by the life of Russian Baptist pastor Peter Vins. He was born in 1898 into the family of Jacob Vins (or Wiens), a pastor among the Mennonites and Baptists in Russia. Persecuted by the czarist government, Jacob went into voluntary exile in North America in 1911, and his family joined him the following year. In 1919, after the Bolshevik Revolution, Jacob Vins returned to his homeland. Peter remained in the United States to attend seminary and prepare for the ministry. In 1926 he joined his father as an "American missionary" holding American citizenship.

In the years immediately following the Bolshevik Revolution, a surprising degree of religious freedom existed in the Soviet Union. The Communists allowed some liberty to win supporters to their side during the civil war. Jacob Vins began his ministry in 1919, for example, in a section of eastern Russia that was temporarily occupied by the Japanese.

Lenin had written, "We require that religion should be a private matter as far as the state is concerned. The state must have nothing to do with religion. . . . Religious and church societies must be completely free unions of like-minded citizens independent of the authorities." Although the atheistic Lenin found it convenient to accommodate religion for a while, his successor Joseph Stalin moved ruthlessly to transform the Soviet Union into a religion-free state. When persecution began, Christians with foreign citizenship had the choice of leaving or becoming Soviet citizens. Peter, now with a wife and son, chose to give up his American citizenship and remain.

Peter Vins was able to minister to the Russian people for only two years before he was arrested and sentenced to three years in a labor camp. After his release, he moved to the city of Omsk. With meetings for worship forbidden, he sought to encourage believers privately in their homes, but he knew that it was only a matter of time before he was arrested again. He and his wife sewed parts of the Bible into his clothing so that he would have the Scriptures with him when he returned to prison.

In 1936 Peter Vins was arrested, served ten months, was released, and then was arrested again in 1937. This time he received a ten-year sentence for "anti-Soviet" views. He was denied visitors. Instead, his wife and young son would come to the street outside the prison, where they could look at him through the barred windows. The prison authorities, disliking even this distant contact between prisoners and their families, began building boxes around the windows. These boxes allowed light in from the top but did not permit anyone to see in or out. Each time Peter's family visited, they saw the boxes getting closer to his window. Finally, his window was covered. Only many years later did his son learn that shortly after this, Soviet authorities had shot Peter Vins.

Appropriately, Peter Vins's favorite Scripture passage was Hebrews 11:24–26: "By faith Moses, when he was come to years, refused to be called the son of Pharaoh's daughter; choosing rather to suffer affliction with the people of God, than to enjoy the pleasures of sin for a season; esteeming the reproach of Christ greater riches than the treasures in Egypt."

In theory, communism and fascism differ in the following ways.

1. Under fascism, businesses are privately owned but rigorously controlled by the government. (A fascist economy is often referred to as a corporate economy.) Under communism, however, the government both owns and controls business.
2. Fascism is highly nationalistic; communism ideally seeks a classless, international society.
3. A military dictatorship usually openly governs a fascist state; communism deceptively emphasizes the "dictatorship of the proletariat."
4. Fascism glorifies the state; communism teaches that the state will gradually wither away.

Despite the theoretical differences between communism and fascism, however, there is little difference in the everyday life of people living under these forms of governments. Both firmly control the people and greatly restrict their liberties.

Benito Mussolini, Il Duce

Mussolini in Italy

Italy entered the postwar era a disappointed and dispirited nation. Despite significant sacrifices in the Great War—including the loss of five hundred thousand men—the country gained very little in return, except additional problems. While Britain and France received former German and Turkish territory as mandates, Italy received none. Furthermore, Italy's borders were not expanded as many Italians believed they should be (because of Italy's support for the Allies). Strikes, inflation, and debt plagued the Italian economy. Politically, small factions created disunity and hindered government action.

In the midst of the turmoil and confusion, the Italian people became increasingly disenchanted with the country's direction. Wealthy landowners and industrialists, fearful of a Communist revolution, wanted protection for their businesses and property. Returning war veterans found that jobs were in short supply and that few Italians appreciated their wartime services. Strong nationalists wanted Italy to become a great military power, to expand its borders, and to acquire additional colonies. The man who seemed to draw these groups together was **Benito Mussolini** (1883–1945).

Mussolini and the Fascist Party—Mussolini, the son of a blacksmith, became a well-known Socialist while still in his twenties. He wrote for several Socialist newspapers. But his violent articles incurred the wrath of the authorities, and they imprisoned him on several occasions. He soon fell out of favor with the Socialists because he supported Italy's entrance into World War I. His political career, however, did not end. In 1921 Mussolini helped to organize the Fascist Party, which took as its emblem the symbol of authority in ancient Rome, the *fasces* (see p. 67); hence, the name *Fascists*.

Most Italians were not Fascists, but they were tired of the unrest and trouble caused by labor unions and Socialist political groups. Mussolini seemed to offer some promise of stability and order. He decided that the time was ripe to seize power. In October 1922 thousands of his followers marched on Rome and demanded that King Victor Emmanuel III appoint Mussolini premier of Italy. The king, believing he had no other choice, agreed to the Fascists' demands, and Mussolini became the new leader of Italy.

Mussolini and the Fascist State—Once in power, Mussolini slowly turned Italy into a totalitarian state. He established his authority by appointing Fascists to numerous government posts. By the end of 1925, he had manipulated the political process so completely that he had a firm grasp on the affairs of the state. Mussolini was now a dictator, but he maintained the appearance of a representative government.

In Fascist Italy, as in Communist Russia, the party was the real source of political power. Fascist political organizations began on the local level and provided the basis for a highly structured hierarchy that culminated in the Fascist Grand Council. In theory, that group of approximately twenty individuals ran the Italian government. The final authority, however, lay in the hands of ***Il Duce*** ("leader" or "commander"), a title that Mussolini used for himself.

One of Mussolini's major goals was to make Italy economically self-sufficient. He wanted Italy to be able to produce everything it needed, including manufactured goods and food. To achieve this program of **autarky**, as it was called, he organized Italy's entire work force into thirteen groups, or **syndicates**, each of which represented a different division of the work force. Under the watchful eye of the government, the syndicates established wages, prices, business policies, and working conditions.

Unlike Stalin or Hitler, however, Mussolini had no clearly defined political program. Like most dictators, he suppressed freedom of speech, freedom of the press, and opposing political parties. But Mussolini's own political philosophy was rather vague and, according to one of his government officials, was based on "mystic sentiment" rather than "distinct ideas."

As dictator, Mussolini enacted a series of popular agreements known as the **Lateran Treaties** with the Roman Catholic Church. Since 1870, relations between the Roman Church and the Italian state had been strained. The state had taken territory that for centuries had been controlled by the papacy. With the unification of Italy, that territory became part of the Italian state. In retaliation, the Roman Church refused to recognize or cooperate with the new state. For nearly sixty years, successive popes remained isolated in the Vatican. In 1929, after lengthy negotiations, Mussolini and the Roman Church finally reached an agreement. The pope agreed to recognize the Italian government and to renounce all territorial claims. In return, the government granted the pope a large sum of money and established a small independent state known as the Vatican City and placed it under the pope's control. The Lateran Treaties remain in effect.

Adolf Hitler, der Führer

Hitler in Germany

As World War I was coming to an end, German Kaiser Wilhelm II abdicated. Spontaneous revolutions had erupted throughout the country, forcing him to flee to Holland. The German people organized a republic to replace the monarchy. In 1919 delegates from around Germany assembled in the town of Weimar and drew up a constitution for the young republic. Among other things, the new constitution granted the German people the right to freely elect representatives to the Reichstag and to elect a president to a seven-year term. The president appointed a chancellor from the strongest political party in the Reichstag. In turn, the chancellor selected people to fill the various cabinet posts of the government. In addition, the constitution guaranteed the German people a number of basic freedoms, including the freedoms of speech, press, and religion.

The Collapse of the German Mark

After World War I, Germany had severe economic problems that fueled discontent and created support for Nazism. Not only were government expenditures high, but Germany had a huge debt resulting from the war. One indication of the country's plight was the high rate of inflation. During World War I, prices had risen about 100 percent, but in the early 1920s, inflation increased at an even more alarming rate.

When French troops invaded the Ruhr Valley in 1923, many Germans in that region went on strike. To support the strikers while they were unemployed, the government began printing large amounts of paper money. Consequently, prices skyrocketed, bringing about the collapse of the German mark (the German monetary unit, similar to the American dollar).

As inflation climbed in 1923, more than three hundred paper mills and two thousand printing establishments worked twenty-four hours a day to supply the necessary paper money. By August 1923, the government was printing 46 billion marks per day. In light of the worsening conditions, employers began paying their employees twice a day and allowing them time off from work to rush to the stores and buy what they needed before prices rose again. Restaurants did not even price items on their menus. They figured a customer's bill only when he was ready to leave because the value of the mark might have declined from the time he sat down at a table.

The following example may help illustrate the devastating nature of German inflation. In 1914, if someone possessed 100,000 marks, he could have exchanged them for nearly 24,000 American dollars. In November 1923, that same 100,000 marks would have been worth only a minute fraction of a cent—$0.00000024.

Finally, the German government abolished the old currency and instituted a new mark—the Rentenmark. People with the old currency could trade in one trillion of their old marks for the new Rentenmark. As a result of such terrible inflation, many Germans lost both their savings and their confidence in the Weimar Republic. As they searched for answers to their country's problems, many people began to listen to a man named Adolf Hitler, who promised a new and better Germany.

Date	Number of marks equal to a dollar (monthly average)
July 1914	4.2
Jan. 1919	8.9
Jan. 1921	64.9
Jan. 1922	191.8
July 1922	493.2
Jan. 1923	17,972
July 1923	353,412
Aug. 1923	4,620,455
Sept. 1923	98,860,000
Oct. 1923	25,260,208,000
Nov. 15, 1923	4,200,000,000,000

Despite its promising start, the **Weimar Republic** had serious weaknesses. Many Germans did not support the republic; they were generally apathetic toward government. The German people also had no experience running a republic, nor did they have a strong traditional attachment to its ideals. Furthermore, having numerous political parties made it difficult for the government to function effectively because no party ever won a majority in the national elections. These weaknesses helped prepare the way for one of the worst dictators of modern history, **Adolf Hitler** (1889–1945).

Hitler and the Nazi Party—As a young man, Adolf Hitler had shown little promise. When his hopes of becoming an artist or architect ended in failure, he wandered about the city of Vienna, barely making a living. At the outbreak of World War I, he tried to enlist in the Austrian forces but was found unfit. He then volunteered for service in the Bavarian Reserve Infantry and was assigned to the messenger service. During the war, he was wounded in the leg, promoted to lance corporal, and awarded two Iron Crosses.

Hitler reacted bitterly to news of the armistice. After the war, he came in contact with a small political organization that soon became known as the National Socialist German Workers' Party, or Nazi Party. Finding many of its ideas to his liking, he promptly joined the group in 1920; a year later, he became its leader.

The name National Socialist German Workers' Party (*Nationalsozialistische deutsche Arbeiter Partei*) was chosen to appeal to a wide range of Germans. In 1920 the Nazis formed the *Sturmabteilungen* (SA), also known as stormtroopers and Brownshirts, to help preserve order at party rallies. They were essentially street thugs.

As the Nazis increased in power, Hitler found it expedient to reduce the SA's power and purged it, killing many of its leaders. He later created an elite guard called the *Schutzstaffel* (SS). They were identified by their black shirts and special daggers. Their initial purpose was to protect Hitler. Later, under the leadership of Heinrich Himmler, the SS also operated both a secret police organization known as the **Gestapo** and a system of concentration camps. The SS military units were among the most fanatical and formidable fighters during World War II and were responsible for horrendous war crimes in the concentration camps.

Poster for a national competition of the storm troopers (SA)

In 1923 Hitler led an uprising (called the "beer hall putsch" after where it was planned) in the city of Munich, attempting to overthrow the government. Popular support was not behind the idea, however, and the revolt was short-lived. The government arrested the leaders of the revolt, and the courts sentenced Hitler and several other Nazis to prison. Hitler, who served less than a year of his five-year sentence, did not remain idle while in prison; he dictated a book to his cell mate titled ***Mein Kampf*** ("My Struggle"), in which he attacked the Weimar Republic, blamed the Jews for Germany's problems, and demanded the renunciation of the Versailles Treaty. He also proclaimed that the Germanic peoples were a "master race" called the Aryans. Once out of prison, Hitler continued to spread these ideas in public speeches, and before long, large numbers of Germans began to believe him. He began reorganizing the party and planning a propaganda campaign designed to gain power without reliance on force alone. The Nazi movement was filled with symbolism, with no symbol more infamous than the **swastika**, or "broken cross."

Hitler's Rise to Power—The reasons for Hitler's amazing rise to power are varied. (1) As we have seen, the Weimar Republic was weak and inefficient. The Nazis realized this fact and exploited those political weaknesses. (2) The Nazis exploited the anger of many Germans against the "war guilt" clause of the Versailles Treaty, using every opportunity to condemn it. (3) Economic problems, especially inflation and unemployment, caused many people to listen to the Nazi promises of economic recovery. (4) Hitler and the Nazis were violently anti-Communist, a position that reassured Germans who worried about their wealth. (5) Hitler's charisma, personal leadership, and brilliant use of propaganda techniques drew to the Nazi Party people who otherwise would have had little use for the organization.

Hitler was a powerful orator. To increase his effectiveness, he studied films of himself experimenting with various gestures and facial expressions. He selected the most dramatic gestures and expressions for use in his speeches.

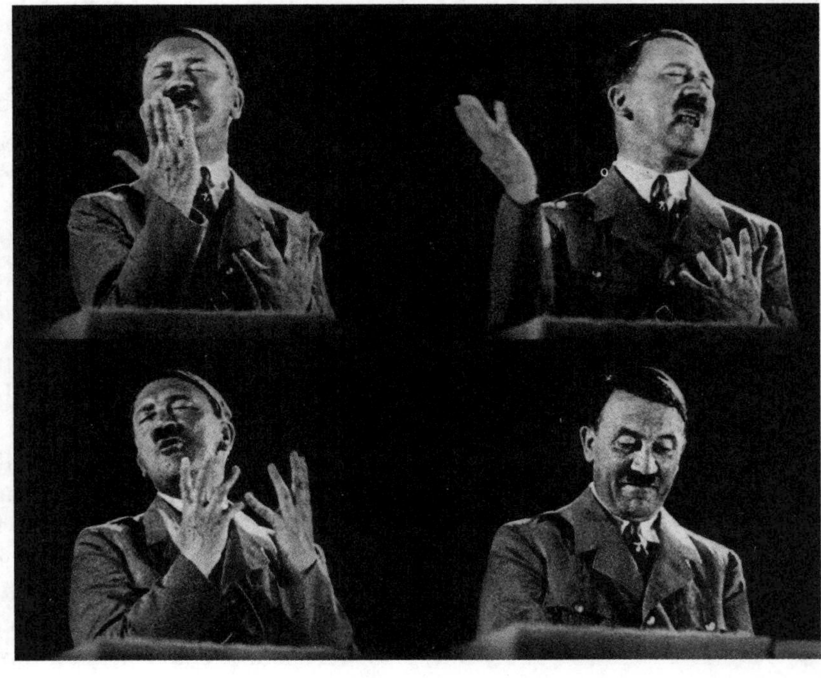

As economic problems became more severe after 1930 because of worldwide depression, the Nazis steadily increased in strength and numbers. After each election, the number of Nazis in the Reichstag grew, until by July 1932 they were the largest party in the German republic, although still not a majority. Because the Nazis had won such a large number

Above: Paul von Hindenburg
Above right: Members of the Reichstag saluting Hitler

of seats, however, the president of the republic, **Paul von Hindenburg**, asked Hitler to join a coalition government as vice-chancellor, but Hitler refused. Because no party held a majority of seats, his refusal made it difficult to form a government. New elections had to be held in November. When the results were in, the Nazis had received two million *fewer* votes than they had received in the July elections. In addition, they had lost thirty-four seats in the Reichstag. Despite the decline in Nazi strength, Hitler demanded the position of chancellor. Hindenburg, who saw no other way out of the political impasse, appointed Hitler chancellor of Germany on January 30, 1933.

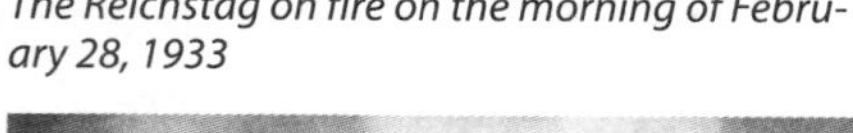

The Reichstag on fire on the morning of February 28, 1933

Hitler then realized that the power he craved was within reach. New elections would be held in March. In an effort to win a majority of the votes, the Nazis used propaganda, violence, and threats. The culmination of the election campaign occurred six days before the voting took place. A fire broke out in the Reichstag building, partially destroying it. The Nazis blamed the Communists and tried to whip up mass hysteria. (There was strong suspicion that the Nazis may have set the fire themselves.) When the election results came in, the Nazis found that they had won only 44 percent of the vote. Although they still lacked a majority, the Nazis persuaded enough Reichstag members to pass the Enabling Act, which suspended the republic and made Hitler dictator of Germany. He established the so-called Third Reich, an empire that he said would last for a thousand years.

Germany Under Nazi Rule—Once in power, Hitler clearly manifested the racist beliefs of Nazi ideology. Hitler blamed the Jews for causing Germany's defeat in the First World War. He accused them of corrupting the pure Aryan race and plotting to rule the world. "The wretched Jew," said Hitler, is the "enemy of the human race" and the "cause of all our miseries." Within months after coming to power, the Nazis turned this hatred of Jews into action. Initially, they deprived Jews of citizenship and forbade their marriage to other Germans. Then, on the night of November 9–10, which was later called *Kristallnacht,* the Nazis severely damaged or destroyed 7,500 Jewish businesses, 155 synagogues, and numerous homes of Jews and killed 35 Jews. Afterward, they rounded up thirty thousand Jews (for their own "protection") and put them into concentration camps. Before long, many more Jews were sent to concentration camps and ruthlessly exterminated.

Christians also came under Nazi persecution. Hitler attempted to close all church-run schools. The Gestapo arrested pastors who opposed the state. To the Nazis, Christian virtues such as humility and gentleness encouraged a slave mentality and had to be eliminated.

To their shame, some German Protestants supported Hitler, and, under Nazi sponsorship, organized what they called the German Christians. Their motto was "The Swastika on our breasts, the Cross in our hearts." These religious leaders discarded most of the Bible because it was written by Jews. They allowed only Aryans to be members of their churches. These pastors claimed that Christ was not really a Jew and that through His death He had preserved the world from Jewish domination. To them, Hitler was a second messiah destined to perfect the work that Jesus had begun. One German pastor said, "Christ has come to us through Adolf Hitler. . . . We know today the Savior has come. . . . We have only one task: be German, not be Christian." As if the blasphemy of these so-called German Christians were not enough, some Nazis even abandoned all pretense of Christianity and openly promoted a return to the pagan idols of the ancient Germanic tribes.

Germans look at the results of Kristallnacht the next morning.

United States Holocaust Memorial Museum

On the economic front, Hitler advanced a series of Four-Year Plans. The first, begun in 1933, sought to end unemployment through a massive rearmament program and the building of public works such as the famous *Autobahnen* (superhighways). The *Autobahnen* provided a military highway system throughout Germany in anticipation of another two-front war. The second Four-Year Plan attempted to make Germany economically self-sufficient so that, in the event of war, Germany could not be hurt by a blockade. To accomplish these goals, the government outlawed strikes. In addition, all workers and employers came under the direction of the German Labor Front, which had the power to determine wages and settle labor disputes. To gain the cooperation of labor, the Nazis established the "Strength Through Joy" movement, which provided vacations and entertainment at low cost. The Nazis also intensely labored to indoctrinate young people with Nazi propaganda, organizing them into Hitler

Left: Nazi anti-Jewish propaganda poster (The Jew—war instigator, war prolonger)
Middle: Nazi poster presenting Hitler as a messianic character (Long live Germany!)
Right: Nazi propaganda poster of Hitler as der Führer *(One people, one realm, one leader!)*

Hitler Youth forming a Nazi swastika, 1933

Youth clubs. Thus, Hitler successfully brought Germany under Nazi control, establishing a strong totalitarian state. Before long, he would attempt to expand the territory of his Third Reich (see Chapter 22).

Section Quiz

1. Who was the leader of the Fascist Party in Italy? In what year did he come to power?
2. In what series of treaties did Mussolini make peace with the Roman Catholic Church?
3. What was the name of the fascist movement in Germany? Who became its leader?
4. Whom did Hitler call the "master race"? What people did Hitler blame for Germany's problems?

★ Why did the German people allow Hitler to control their lives?

III. Era of Disillusionment

During the latter half of the nineteenth century, many artists and writers reacted against the impact of industrialism on society. They rejected conventional art forms and embraced new, experimental techniques. This reaction continued in the early twentieth century as the arts reflected the death and destruction of the war period. The devastation of war, economic depression, and moral decay led to feelings of despair. As this mood affected modern art and literature, artists and writers portrayed a pessimistic and disjointed view of man, his world, and the future.

A Small House in the Garden, *Pablo Picasso, 1909*

Painting

Expressionism

In art, two of the best-known twentieth-century movements (or schools) were expressionism and cubism. In **expressionism**, the artist tried to paint how he felt about his subject rather than trying to realistically reproduce what he saw. **Henri Matisse** (1869–1954) was the best representative of this school. Figures in expressionistic paintings were of secondary importance. Color was the real subject; through this medium the artist could most graphically express his emotions. Bright colors, simplified designs, and clearly outlined figures characterized Matisse's work.

Cubism

The second major artistic movement of the twentieth century was **cubism**. Its best representative was the Spanish-born **Pablo Picasso** (1881–1973). To a much greater degree than Matisse, Picasso abandoned the Renaissance ideal that a painter should portray on canvas what he saw in nature. Picasso believed that what we see might not be final reality; therefore, he contended that art that simply copied the visible world was useless. Instead, he often reduced his figures to various geometric shapes (hence, the name cubism), which he portrayed from several different perspectives at once. His technique distorted the figures in his paintings. His approach, however, was not as radical as that of a fellow cubist who said, "My aim is to create new objects which cannot be compared to any object in actuality." Picasso, as well as many other twentieth-century artists, tried deliberately to shock viewers and challenge their perception of the world.

Architecture

During the twentieth century, architecture underwent a drastic change. New building materials—concrete, glass, and steel—revolutionized architectural design. In large cities, soaring steel and glass skyscrapers dominated the skyline. Since steel eliminated the need for heavy stone or brick walls to support a building, most architects tried to convey a sense of openness through the extensive use of glass. In many ways, modern architecture reflected the mechanized and urban society of the twentieth century.

Of the men who helped establish these modern architectural trends, three are especially noteworthy. **Louis Sullivan** (1856–1924), an American architect, is credited with developing the skyscraper. His motto was "form ever follows function"; that is, the design of a building should match the purpose for which it is built. Excessive decoration is eliminated to achieve a clean, simple appearance. **Walter Gropius** (1883–1969), also a functionalist, helped to popularize that style in Europe. American architect **Frank Lloyd Wright** (1869–1959) followed a variation on the functionalist approach. He believed that for form to follow function, the design of a building should blend with its surroundings.

The Kaufmann House, Mill Run, Pa.; an example of Frank Lloyd Wright's architectural philosophy of blending structures with the surrounding environment

Courtesy of Western Pennsylvania Conservancy

Music

Music in the twentieth century was extremely varied, encompassing everything from jazz (which reached its peak of popularity in the 1920s) to electronic music. As in other art forms, radical experimentation increased after World War I as many composers abandoned traditional musical concepts. Russian composer **Igor Stravinsky** (struh VIN skee; 1882–1971) and Austrian **Arnold Schönberg** (SHURN behrg; 1874–1951) influenced modern musical trends. Stravinsky is sometimes considered the father of modern music. He developed a new musical theory known as **polytonality**, which involves the use of several keys simultaneously. In the past, composers had used only one musical key at a time. Stravinsky used polytonality in his famous orchestral work *The Rite of Spring*. Arnold Schönberg, on the other hand, abandoned all fixed tone patterns or keys and created what is called atonal music. Instead of using one of the common eight-tone scales, Schönberg based his compositions on a twelve-tone scale, giving no special emphasis to any one tone.

Igor Stravinsky

In spite of several technical differences among modern composers, their music exhibited certain common characteristics—and contrasted markedly with the music of earlier eras. For example, the melody line often contained unusual intervals (jumps in pitch), and musical phrases were often nonsymmetrical (lacking balanced proportions). Odd and complex meters (the number of beats to a musical measure) became increasingly common and often changed constantly throughout a musical composition. Likewise, modern rhythms were often jarring and violent. In contrast to the harmony of earlier periods, modern music made greater use of dissonance (clashing tones). Composers during the twentieth century also experimented with widely divergent musical styles, such as jazz and rock.

T. S. Eliot

Literature

Like music, the literature of the 1920s and 1930s reflects the attitudes prevalent between the wars. For example, poet **T. S. Eliot** (1888–1965), in his complex major work "The Waste Land," tries to portray the desolation and meaninglessness of modern life. In his poem "The Hollow Men," Eliot replaces the cataclysmic view of the end of the world taught in Scripture (2 Peter 3:10, 12–13) with a bleak, feeble one: "*This is the way the world ends / Not with a bang but a whimper.*" Another author, German novelist **Thomas Mann** (1875–1955), presents his central characters as passive figures, victimized by the uncontrollable forces that surround them.

Much of the literature of the first half of the twentieth century was filled with hopelessness, pessimism, and pacifism. Many writers rejected the concept that literature should teach moral lessons. The techniques they used also demonstrated a break with the past. Modern poetry, for example, often lacked a rhyme scheme and a regular rhythm pattern. In addition, some prose writers and poets tended to be deliberately obscure. This tendency was illustrated by the work of novelist **James Joyce** (1882–1941), who developed the stream-of-consciousness technique in which the reader is forced to decipher the fragmented and often rambling thoughts of the major character. Despite their diverse forms and styles, painters, composers, and writers united in portraying a world that was hopeless, barren, and dehumanizing.

Section Quiz

1. What were two well-known movements, or schools, of painting in the twentieth century?
2. Identify the three noteworthy architects who helped establish modern architectural trends.
3. What is the name for the musical theory that uses several keys simultaneously? Who developed this modern musical style?
4. What poet sought to describe the desolation and meaninglessness of life prevalent between the world wars? What was the name of his major work?

★ How did the music of this period reflect the attitude of many people after World War I?

Chapter 21 Review

Making Connections

1. Why are the apparent differences between communism and fascism irrelevant to the average citizen?

2–5. Why did Hitler rapidly rise to power in Germany? (List four reasons.)

Developing History Skills

1. Evaluate the effects of Lenin's policy of war communism on the Russian economy.
2. Consider the following statement, "During difficult times, people often seek immediate solutions to their problems. Some 'solutions', however, often bring harm rather than good." Support or refute this statement by providing examples from the leading democratic nations following the First World War.

Thinking Critically

1. Assess the benefits or dangers of a welfare state.
2. Compare the art produced during the Era of Disillusionment with the art produced during the Romantic Era (Chapter 17).

Living in God's World

1. Both Communists and Fascists realized that Christian virtues stood in contrast to their forms of government. Make a list of key Christian virtues that relate to government and write a proposal for a form of government that matches those virtues.
2. Choose one piece of art mentioned in this chapter and research it. Describe how it reflects the worldview of the creator. Be prepared to give a brief presentation to the class.

People, Places, and Things to Know

Ramsay MacDonald
Statute of Wesminster
Léon Blum
Maginot Line
Franklin Roosevelt
New Deal
totalitarian states
Alexander III
pogroms
Nicholas II
Bolsheviks
Mensheviks
Russo-Japanese War
Bloody Sunday
soviet
Duma
Rasputin
Aleksandr Kerensky
Vladimir Lenin
Leon Trotsky
USSR
New Economic Policy
Joseph Stalin
Five-Year Plans
collectivize
purges
Comintern
fascism
Nazism
Benito Mussolini
Il Duce
autarky
syndicates
Lateran Treaties
Weimar Republic
Adolf Hitler
Gestapo
Mein Kampf
swastika
Paul von Hindenburg
expressionism
Henri Matisse
cubism
Pablo Picasso
Louis Sullivan
Walter Gropius
Frank Lloyd Wright
Igor Stravinsky
Arnold Schönberg
polytonality
T. S. Eliot
Thomas Mann
James Joyce

22

The Second World War

- I. Global Tension
- II. Global Conflict
- III. Efforts for Global Peace

American SBD Dauntless dive-bomber over Wake Island

Despite World War I being called "the war to end all wars," it was not long before the nations of the world faced an even more devastating conflict—World War II. For two decades, people had relied on vague promises of peace made by world leaders. They had trusted in well-meaning but ineffective treaties and organizations. But, as in the days of the prophet Jeremiah, people were crying, "Peace, peace; when there [was] no peace" (Jer. 6:14). Had they been alert, the leaders could have seen the signs of approaching war. Power-thirsty dictators were on the march, building large armies and stockpiling weapons. By the time the rest of the world realized the danger, it was too late to avert the outbreak of a war that was truly a "world war."

President Roosevelt signed the declaration of war against Japan on December 8, 1941.

I. Global Tension

Dictators Defy the League of Nations

After World War I, world leaders met to organize the League of Nations. They hoped this organization would thwart any new military aggression and thus maintain world peace and security. But during the 1930s, the militaristic governments of Italy, Germany, and Japan began to threaten world peace. For Mussolini in Italy, Hitler in Germany, and the leaders in Japan, war became an accepted and legitimate means of achieving their personal and national goals. Although the League of Nations made several feeble attempts to stop such aggression, its system of collective security failed.

Japanese Expansion in Asia

Japan entered the twentieth century as a greatly transformed country. During the Meiji Period (see p. 434), Japan had thrown off centuries-old feudalistic customs and had adopted many modern ways. Its new industrial and military might enabled Japan to win decisive victories over the much larger countries of China and Russia. In the years before World War I, Japan continued to develop its industry and modernize its military forces. When World War I broke out, Japan joined the side of the Allies. In spite of its limited role, Japan emerged from the war a major power.

After World War I, the office of emperor became largely ceremonial, and civilian officials led the Japanese government. They followed a more restrained and conciliatory policy than that which Japan was accustomed to. In 1922, Japanese leaders signed the Nine Power Treaty, agreeing with other major powers to respect the sovereignty and territory of China. Japan also joined and participated in the activities of the League of Nations. But by the end of the decade, the young emperor allied with the military with the goal of gaining control of the country. Emperor **Hirohito** and the military leaders believed that Japan should take advantage of its position of strength and extend Japanese influence in the Pacific. They sought to use Japan's military might to create a "new order" in Asia. When Japan's civilian government collapsed in the 1930s, Hirohito used the military to seize control of the government. Under his leadership, Japan actively embarked on a program of territorial expansion.

Emperor Hirohito

Chinese Weakness—Japan conducted its expansionist policy at the expense of China. China lacked a strong central government and was seething with internal political turmoil. In 1911, there had been a revolt against the ruling Manchu dynasty. Within four months, the Manchu had fallen from power and a Chinese republic was proclaimed. **Sun Yat-sen**, the organizer of the Kuomintang (KWO min TAHNG), or Nationalist Party, led the revolt. To give direction to this new party, Sun enunciated what he called the Three Principles of the People: nationalism, democracy, and

Top: Chiang Kai-shek
Bottom: Mao Zedong (1949)

social progress. But Sun never gained the support he needed to establish a stable government. Years of anarchy ensued as local leaders known as warlords fought one another for political power.

After the death of Sun Yat-sen, **Chiang Kai-shek** (CHANG KYE-SHEK; 1887–1975) took control of the Kuomintang. He began a military campaign to reunite China under a national government. But in 1927 rival factions within the Kuomintang caused a split in the party. Civil war broke out between Chiang's conservative forces and the Communist forces led by **Mao Zedong** (MOU DZUH-DONG; 1893–1976). By stirring up peasant uprisings, Mao hoped to bring about a Communist revolution. Chiang countered by launching an all-out effort to drive the Communists from their strongholds in southern China. But the Communist forces slipped past Chiang's lines and in their famous Long March traveled some six thousand miles to northwestern China. Further attempts by Chiang to drive the Communists out of the country failed because he had to focus his military forces on defending China from Japanese aggression during the 1930s.

Japanese Invasion—Japan's easy defeat of China in the Sino-Japanese War (1894–95) had revealed just how weak and vulnerable China was. Working through the military, the Japanese emperor launched a daring program of territorial expansion. In 1931, Japanese troops seized the entire province of Manchuria, which had been under nominal Chinese control. The Chinese government protested the Japanese action to the League of Nations. But the League did little except pass several resolutions urging Japan and China to settle their differences through negotiations. In the end, Japan refused to withdraw from Manchuria but withdrew from the League of Nations instead.

Realizing that Japan was a continuing threat to China, the Communists under Mao and the Nationalists under Chiang called a truce in their civil war and united to defeat the Japanese. But even a united Chinese front could not withstand Japan's full-scale invasion of China, which began in 1937. The Japanese captured several major Chinese cities and most of China's valuable economic resources. Although the League of Nations condemned the invasion, no country was willing to go to war to halt Japanese aggression.

Italian Revenge in Africa

Italy was the second major nation to successfully defy the League of Nations. Mussolini sought to re-create the grandeur of the Roman Empire by building a new Italian empire. In doing so, he hoped also to illustrate the vitality of fascism. His first target was Ethiopia—an independent African nation that had defeated an invading Italian army in the late nineteenth century. In 1935, a large, well-equipped Italian army invaded Ethiopia. The Ethiopians, who fought with primitive weapons such as bows and arrows, were no match for the Italians. Using a combination of air power, tanks, and poison gas, the Italians easily conquered the country.

The League of Nations was unwilling to use military force against Mussolini because its most important members, Britain and France, wanted to stay on good terms with Italy to isolate Hitler's Germany. Instead, the League decided to impose economic sanctions—forbidding the sale of certain materials to Italy. These sanctions, however, did little to hinder Italy's war effort because they did not include oil, which fueled Mussolini's tanks, planes, and other motorized vehicles. Mussolini defied every effort of the League to halt his invasion and made Ethiopia a part of his growing empire. In addition, he seized the small Balkan nation of Albania in April 1939.

German Rearmament in Europe

Like Mussolini, Hitler also sought to build a new empire. Once he had firmly established himself in power, he began laying the foundation for a new German empire—the **Third Reich**. Hitler wished to provide the German people with additional ***lebensraum*** ("living space"). To accomplish this goal, he knew that he had to rearm Germany. In 1933, Hitler ended German participation in the Geneva Disarmament Conference (1932–33). He also pulled Germany out of the League of Nations. Two years later, in violation of the Versailles Treaty, he reestablished the German General Staff and reintroduced a military draft.

Only one task then remained before Hitler could begin actively building his empire—he had to fortify the Rhineland. According to the Treaty of Versailles and the Locarno Pact, German territory west of the Rhine River had to be demilitarized (kept free of troops and military equipment). But Hitler had no intention of abiding by these treaty provisions. On March 7, 1936, he ordered German troops to march into the Rhineland. France reacted angrily to Hitler's conduct but took no action against Germany. Furthermore, the League once again proved itself unable to prevent or solve an international crisis. No significant check was placed on Hitler's action.

Adolf Hitler

Hitler Challenges European Security

Germany Forms Alliances

Until 1935, Germany remained diplomatically isolated in Europe; even Italy sided with Britain and France in verbal opposition to Hitler. European displeasure with Italy's conquest of Ethiopia, however, drove Mussolini closer to Hitler. In 1936, Germany and Italy formed an alliance known as the **Rome-Berlin Axis**, taking its name from a speech by Mussolini. Mussolini had described a "line" running between Berlin and Rome, a line that was "not a partition but rather an axis round which all European states animated by the will to collaboration and peace can also collaborate." That same year, Germany and Japan signed the **Anti-Comintern Pact**, which on the surface was an agreement generally directed against communism but in reality was aimed specifically at Russia. The following year, Italy and Japan signed a similar agreement, bringing together the three major nations that would constitute the Axis powers in World War II. The opponents of this Rome-Berlin-Tokyo Axis would come to be known as the Allies.

The Third Reich

German history has included three *reichs* (empires or kingdoms). Otto the Great established the first one in 962, when he became the first Holy Roman emperor. This reich lasted until 1806, when Napoleon abolished it. Later, Otto von Bismarck helped unify Germany, creating a second German empire that lasted from 1871 to 1918. Adolf Hitler created what he called the Third Reich. Although he declared that it would last for a thousand years, it lasted for only twelve (1933–45).

The Spanish Civil War

The outbreak of civil war in Spain in 1936 provided the opportunity to bring Germany and Italy together. The Fascist followers of General **Francisco Franco** (1892–1975) revolted against Spain's republican government. Recognizing that Franco had a political philosophy similar to theirs, Mussolini and Hitler supported his war effort. The Germans provided primarily planes and tanks; Italy supplied fifty to seventy thousand troops and one thousand planes. Russia offered some material assistance to the Loyalists (supporters of the Spanish government), but France and

Benito Mussolini and Adolf Hitler in Munich, Germany, 1938

Britain followed a policy of nonintervention in Spain's affairs. Despite a lack of supplies and foreign support, the Loyalists resisted stubbornly; but when Madrid fell to the rebel forces in early 1939, the war ended. The victorious Franco became dictator of Spain.

In addition to the tremendous significance that this civil war had for the history of Spain, it also proved to be a "dress rehearsal" for World War II. By assisting Franco, Germany and Italy were able to try out new weapons under actual battle conditions and to learn how to use them effectively. One such weapon was the dreaded *Stuka* dive-bomber, which Germany would soon use to terrorize its enemies. Consequently, when World War II broke out in Europe, these nations—Germany in particular—had an initial advantage over their opponents.

Hitler Takes Austria

According to a post–World War I treaty, Austria was forbidden to join Germany in a political union. Yet Austria was the first area of Europe that Hitler sought to add to his Reich. During the interwar years, economic and political weakness hindered the growth of a stable economy and threatened to undermine the new Austrian republic.

In 1934, Hitler had attempted to seize Austria, but his effort had failed, partly because of Mussolini's opposition. To soothe Austria's fear, Hitler promised to respect Austrian independence. This promise, however, was only one of many that he did not intend to keep. In 1938, Hitler was ready to try again. Taking advantage of political turmoil in Austria, Hitler demanded that a Nazi be installed as chancellor of the country. Mussolini, by then on friendlier terms with Hitler, was heavily involved in the Spanish Civil War and did not give the Austrian government his support as he had in 1934. Austria was too weak to resist Hitler's demands. When the new Nazi chancellor of Austria was installed, he "requested" that Hitler send troops into Austria and reestablish order. As Europe stood by, Hitler seized the entire country, effecting the *Anschluss* ("union").

Sudetenland Sacrificed at Munich—Encouraged by his success in Austria, Hitler next turned his attention to Czechoslovakia, where 3.5 million of the inhabitants were German. Most of them lived near the border of Germany and Austria in an area known as the Sudetenland (named after the Sudeten Mountains). Unlike Austria, Czechoslovakia had a strong economy and a stable, republican government. Nevertheless, Hitler's agents stirred up discontent among the German inhabitants of the country. Hitler openly demanded that the Sudetenland become a part of the German Reich.

As tension between Czechoslovakia and Germany increased, **Neville Chamberlain** (1869–1940), prime minister of Great Britain, met with Hitler several times to seek a solution to the Czech crisis. Convinced that Hitler was willing to go to war over the Sudetenland, Chamberlain—with the support of the French government—pressured Czechoslovakia to capitulate to Hitler's demands. In his efforts to avoid war, Chamberlain foolishly believed Hitler's promise that "after the Sudeten German question is regulated, we have no further territorial claims to make in Europe."

Although bordered by German territory on three sides, Czechoslovakia refused to surrender to Hitler's wishes. War seemed imminent. At the last minute, Hitler, at Mussolini's urging, invited Chamberlain and **Édouard Daladier** (the prime minister of France) to meet in Munich and settle the crisis. On September 29, 1938, after hours of negotiations, the other leaders gave Hitler the Sudetenland. Incredibly, representatives from Czechoslovakia had not even been allowed to participate in the **Munich Conference**.

When Chamberlain returned to Britain, he told an enthusiastic crowd, "I return from Germany bringing peace with honor." However, Chamberlain sought to halt Hitler's expansionistic plans through a policy of **appeasement** (buying off an aggressor by making concessions). Chamberlain believed that he had helped to establish "peace for our time"; but within a year, Europe had plunged into World War II.

Czechoslovakia Falls to the Germans—On October 3, 1938, Chamberlain stood in the House of Commons and spoke in defense of his appeasement policy. He claimed that the "great and imminent menace" of war had been removed and that "the new Czechoslovakia [would] find a greater security than she [had] ever enjoyed in the past."

Although the road to peace might be difficult, he said, "I believe that there is sincerity and good will on both sides." Two days later, **Winston Churchill**, (1874–1965), a member of the House of Commons, stood in the same place and denounced appeasement. "We have sustained a total and unmitigated defeat," he declared. He predicted that all of eastern Europe would be subjected to Nazi tyranny. Furthermore, he concluded with a somber warning and challenge:

> And do not suppose that this is the end. This is only the beginning of the reckoning. This is only the first sip, the first foretaste of a bitter cup which will be proffered to us

British prime minister Neville Chamberlain trusted Hitler's signature and declared "peace for our time."

British prime minister Winston Churchill

year by year unless by a supreme recovery of moral health and martial vigor, we arise again and take our stand for freedom as in the olden time.

Time was to prove Churchill right. On March 15, 1939, German troops marched into Prague (the capital of Czechoslovakia) and brought most of the country under Nazi rule. Poland and Hungary occupied the rest of Czechoslovakia.

In the past, Hitler had claimed that all he wanted to do was to bring all Germans in Europe under one rule. Several European nations, particularly Britain, thought that Germany had been treated unfairly in the Versailles Treaty. Many leaders regarded Hitler's seizure of "German" territory as a means of correcting that injustice. In addition, the people of Europe remembered the last great war. They wanted to avoid renewed bloodshed at all costs.

As it turned out, however, the policy of appeasement only made war certain. Following Hitler's seizure of Czechoslovakia, even the most naive of political leaders (including Chamberlain) finally realized that appeasement had failed. Hitler did not intend to confine his territorial demands; instead he sought to incorporate as much territory into his empire as possible with little regard for boundaries. Afraid for their own safety, Britain and France now determined to use force if necessary to oppose any further Nazi aggression.

Stage Set For War

Hitler's next target was Poland. Within a week after taking Czechoslovakia, he demanded that Poland cede to Germany a strip of territory known as the "Polish Corridor," which would connect East Prussia with the rest of Germany. This time, however, France and Britain decided to resist German demands regardless of the cost. Chamberlain, in a complete reversal of his earlier appeasement policy, stated that in the event "of any action which clearly threatened Polish independence, and which the Polish government accordingly considered it vital to resist with their national forces, His Majesty's Government would feel themselves bound at once to lend the Polish government all the support in their power."

Hitler addressing the Reichstag

To increase their effectiveness against Hitler, Britain and France tried to reach a military agreement with the Soviet Union. They ran into difficulty, however. Not only had they ignored the Soviets in the crisis over Czechoslovakia, but Stalin also thought that the Soviets had been snubbed by Chamberlain all along. He was not about to meekly cooperate with Britain now.

Meanwhile, Hitler was not idle. In May, he and Mussolini finalized a military alliance known as the **Pact of Steel**. Then, on August 23, Hitler shocked the world by announcing that Germany and the Soviet Union had signed a nonaggression pact. Both sides agreed that for ten years they would "refrain from any violence, from any aggressive action, and any attack against each other, individually or jointly with other powers." Two nations that had been sworn enemies now seemed to be on friendly terms. As William Shakespeare once wrote, "'Tis time to fear when tyrants seem to kiss."

With this agreement, Hitler confidently believed that Britain and France would not try to stop him if he invaded Poland. He had seen them weakly give in to his demands in the past. He had no doubt that in spite of their promise to defend Poland they would back down once again. Hitler miscalculated, however, and Europe was plunged into another war.

Section Quiz

1. What areas did Japan invade in 1931 and 1937?
2. What country did the Italians invade in 1935? How did the League of Nations respond?
3. What country experienced a civil war in which other nations—especially Germany and Italy—helped shape the outcome?
4. Where did European leaders meet in 1938 to settle the question of the Sudetenland? To what country did this territory belong?
5. With what country did Hitler sign a nonaggression pact before his invasion of Poland?

★ Why did Britain and France continue to give in to German demands?

II. Global Conflict

Axis Successes

Sweep into Poland

On September 1, 1939, German forces numbering 1.7 million suddenly attacked Poland and rapidly advanced across the country. Contrary to Hitler's expectation, Britain and France immediately demanded that Germany cease hostilities. When the German government did not respond, Britain and France declared war on Germany. It was now too late for Hitler to turn back—World War II had officially begun. In less than four weeks, Germany, using its powerful armored, or **panzer**, divisions and superior air force—the **Luftwaffe**—defeated Poland. This fast-moving attack became known as **blitzkrieg** ("lightning war").

German Stuka *Ju-87 dive-bomber attacking Poland, September 1, 1939*

As the Germans were invading Poland from the west, the Soviets were invading Poland from the east. According to the Nazi-Soviet Pact, the two countries divided Polish territory between themselves. In addition, Hitler agreed to recognize the Soviet claim to the small Baltic nations of Estonia, Latvia, and Lithuania. The Soviets forced those nations to allow the establishment of Soviet military bases within their countries. The Soviets then demanded that Finland grant them the same military concessions. When Finland refused, fighting broke out in late 1939. Although outnumbered five to one, the Finns held off the Russians for a while and won several victories. In the end, the Soviets broke the Finnish resistance and forced the Finns to give up territory. The conflict, however, cast grave doubts on Russia's ability to wage war.

Invasion of Scandinavia

Meanwhile, little was happening in western Europe. The Allies, unprepared for a full-scale war, decided that a blockade of Germany would be the most effective strategy while they waited for the next German move. On the German side, Hitler wanted to attack in the west, but severe winter weather hampered his plans. For seven months a "phony war," or ***sitzkrieg*** (literally, "sitting war"), continued without either side launching a major offensive.

In April 1940, Germany ended the military inactivity on the western front by attacking Denmark and Norway. Hitler feared the Allies would establish military bases in Norway, so he attacked and seized the country for the Axis powers. Both Norway and Denmark were caught by surprise and were easily conquered. Denmark, in fact, surrendered after only a few hours of fighting.

One factor that particularly aided the German conquest of Norway was the presence within the country of traitors known as **fifth columnists** (a term coined during the Spanish Civil War to refer to individuals within a country who secretly aid the enemy by spying, spreading enemy propaganda, and committing sabotage). In Norway, **Vidkun Quisling** became the most notorious of the fifth columnists. His subversive activities helped the Germans conquer his country. Today his name is a synonym for *traitor*.

The Fall of France

After the conquest of Norway and Denmark, Hitler began his long-awaited offensive in the west. Although the Low Countries (Belgium, the Netherlands, and Luxembourg) could provide little resistance, most observers thought that France would prove much more formidable than Germany's other foes. The French and the British had several thousand troops on the French-Belgian border to protect against a German attack across the flatlands of central Belgium. Also, along the French-German border, the French had established the **Maginot Line** (see pp. 470–71). No one expected a stunning blitzkrieg like the one in Poland.

On May 10, 1940, German forces attacked, easily crushing the Low Countries; Holland and Luxembourg fell in less than a week, and the Belgians held out for only two weeks. Meanwhile, the Allies swept into Belgium to meet the Germans. Britain and France had made a serious error, however. While they strongly defended most of the French border, the Allies stationed very few troops in the Ardennes region by southern Belgium. The Allies thought that the heavy forests there would be enough to stop any German attack through the Ardennes. Hitler thought otherwise and sent a large armored force through the forests, bypassing both the heavy fortifications of the Maginot Line along the French-German border and the massive buildup of Allied troops along the French-Belgian border. The heavy tanks pushed through the Ardennes with only minor difficulty and attacked a small and very surprised Allied force near the city of Sedan.

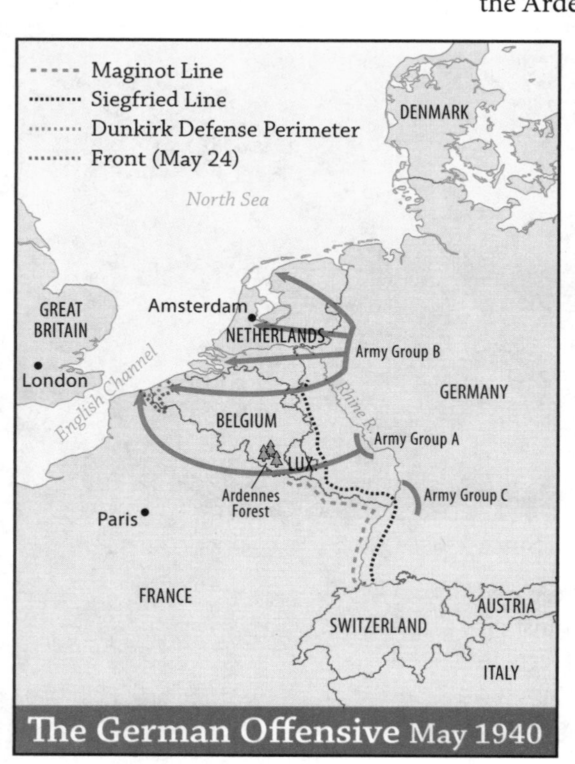

The German Offensive May 1940

The German forces broke through the Allied lines and soon had a large Allied army encircled in northwestern France. The Allies had their backs to the English Channel and seemed doomed as the Germans pushed them relentlessly toward the coast. Before long, the French and the British found themselves on the beaches at the port city of Dunkirk. Surprisingly, the Germans halted their advance, thereby giving the British time to send out a call for help. From all along the British coast, sailors and civilians came in barges, tugboats, and private yachts—more than eight hundred boats of all types and sizes—and ferried the Allied soldiers across the channel to Britain. Thus, an entire army of more than 350,000 men was saved from almost certain destruction. Churchill, however, told the House of Commons, "We must be very careful not to assign to this deliverance the attributes of a victory. Wars are not won by evacuation."

Meanwhile, another German force pushed southward into France. As a French defeat became more certain, Italy, hoping to gain more territory, declared war on France and Great Britain. "I need a few thousand dead," said Mussolini, "so that I can attend the peace

Deliverance at Dunkirk

In May of 1940, news reached Britain that Hitler's panzer divisions had pushed through the Ardennes Forest into France. The surprised British Expeditionary Force and thousands of other Allied troops were forced to retreat to the port city of Dunkirk, and Christians throughout the British Empire began praying for God to deliver them. A close examination of the events of the rescue at Dunkirk shows how God granted deliverance in the midst of seemingly hopeless circumstances.

When the commander of the British forces realized that his army could not withstand the waves of German troops and tanks, he ordered the retreat to Dunkirk. Although this action was contrary to orders from Britain, he reasoned that at Dunkirk there would be a chance of escaping by sea. Had he remained in his present position, he would have been surrounded, with no means of escape.

To the surprise of the Allies, the advancing German panzer divisions stopped twelve miles short of Dunkirk. Hitler, thinking that the Allies had little hope of escaping, ordered the halt. He agreed with many of his top aides that the annihilation of the trapped Allied army should be left to the Luftwaffe, which could annihilate the British army in only three days.

But the Luftwaffe was thwarted by bad weather. Pouring rain, thick fog, and low cloud cover hindered their efforts. The British seized the opportunity to send for help. A flotilla of more than eight hundred ships, manned by British soldiers and private citizens, crossed the channel to ferry the men back to England.

The notoriously treacherous channel weather was unusually cooperative. Prevailing winds were light and westerly—had they been strong and northerly, which is often the case, the rescue would have been much more difficult. In addition, wave heights were lower than normal. Above the rescue operation, haze and dense fog obscured the beaches from the Luftwaffe pilots. Luftwaffe records state that wave after wave of bombers reported "lack of good bombing conditions" and returned to base with their bombs.

For nine days—from May 26 to June 4, 1940—the rescue operation went on. In the end, more than 350,000 soldiers, two-thirds of whom were British, were rescued. This amazing evacuation was known as the "miracle at Dunkirk." God used both human instruments and the forces of nature to answer the prayers of concerned, but trusting, British Christians. Truly, "the effectual fervent prayer of a righteous man availeth much" (James 5:16).

conference as a belligerent [a nation that is responsible for beginning a war]." The French government, which had already fled Paris, rejected Britain's plea that the French army withdraw to North Africa and continue fighting. Instead, the political parties appointed Marshal **Henri Pétain** (1856–1951), a hero of World War I, to head a new French government. Pétain immediately asked the Germans for an armistice. On June 22, 1940, the French signed the surrender documents in the same railroad car in which the Germans had surrendered to the Allies in World War I. France had fallen in just forty-two days.

Hitler and some of his senior officers standing in front of the railroad car where France signed the terms of surrender

According to the agreement with France, the Germans would occupy more than half of France, including Paris, the entire Atlantic coastline, and the northern section of the country. The rest of France would remain unoccupied, and a government under Marshal Pétain would rule for the Germans. Since the city of Vichy became the new seat of government, the entire region under Pétain's rule became known as **Vichy France**. Many of the Frenchmen who had escaped to Britain refused to recognize the leadership of the Vichy government. Instead, they joined the Free French movement led by **Charles de Gaulle** (1890–1970). These Frenchmen continued to wage war against the Axis powers.

Left: Gen. Charles de Gaulle
Right: Gen. Erwin Rommel

Invasion of North Africa

Inspired by Hitler's impressive victories in Europe, Mussolini attempted to duplicate them in North Africa. He knew that Britain was facing terrific pressure from Hitler in Europe and therefore would not be able to send many additional troops to Africa. Consequently, Mussolini launched an invasion of Egypt. Such an invasion, he hoped, would not only seriously weaken Britain's position in the Mediterranean but also provide access to the oil fields of the Middle East. But Mussolini had underestimated the British, and his invasion proved a disaster. The British pushed the Italian invaders out of Egypt and back into Libya and captured more than 100,000 prisoners and much valuable war materiel.

To prevent a total Italian collapse, Hitler intervened. In the spring of 1941, a brilliant German commander, General **Erwin Rommel**, arrived in North Africa with specially trained German forces. Rommel, known as the "Desert Fox," often displayed tactical ability but was unable to win a crushing victory; he lacked sufficient supplies and reinforcements. Nonetheless, by 1942, his forces had advanced into Egypt, coming within seventy miles of the British naval base at Alexandria. Both sides were exhausted, however, and for four months there was a lull in the fighting.

Axis Blunders

At the beginning of Hitler's rule, many of his generals did not trust his military judgment or strategy. After the fall of France, however, his military prestige increased to the point that his ideas were rarely challenged. But Hitler's military success did not continue. We can now look back and see that many of his decisions proved to be military blunders.

The Battle of Britain

Although France was defeated, Hitler could not immediately direct his attention toward Britain. German troops had to first consolidate their position in the newly conquered territories. The British knew that the lull in the fighting was only temporary and that soon they too would experience the fierceness of Hitler's attack. Like France, they were in a precarious position, having already suffered several military setbacks and having little with which to defend themselves.

Although the future seemed dark, the British found hope in the courageous and energetic leadership of Winston Churchill, who had replaced Neville Chamberlain as prime minister. Churchill encouraged the British people with these words:

> We shall not flag or fail. We shall go on to the end. We shall fight in France, we shall fight on the seas and oceans, we shall fight with growing confidence and growing strength in the air. We shall defend our island, whatever the cost may be. We shall fight on the beaches, we shall fight in the fields and in the streets, we shall fight in the hills. We shall never surrender.

The will of the British people to withstand the Nazis was soon tested. Hitler ordered not only a complete air and submarine blockade around Great Britain but also a Luftwaffe bombing campaign in preparation for an invasion. While

Britain Prepares for Invasion

Soon after the fall of France, the British were keenly aware of the threat of a German invasion and began making careful preparations. In a radio address, Anthony Eden, the secretary of war, said, "Those of you who are not in the Forces: Stay where you are! Refugees on roads and railways hamstring those upon whom your defense depends. . . . The mass of refugees helped to lose the battle of France; they will not lose the battle of Britain."

All across Britain, obstacles were placed on roads and in fields to prevent the enemy from landing planes. People were instructed to immobilize their cars and trucks by removing and hiding vital engine parts, thus denying the invading enemy an additional means of transportation. Public information leaflets further instructed the British people: "Do not give any German anything. Do not tell him anything. Hide your food and your bicycles. Hide your maps. . . . Think always of your country before you think of yourself." School children were taught that if Germans soldiers asked them for directions they should answer only "I can't say."

To confuse the Germans further in the event of an invasion, the government ordered that "no person should display or cause or permit to be displayed any sign which furnishes any indication of the name of, or the situation or the direction of, or the distance to any place." Consequently, all signposts were removed from the roads; wherever the name of a town was written, it was painted over. As it turned out, however, the invasion did not come, and the British people did not have to test their precautionary measures.

American poster expressing Allied concerns for the security of their armed forces

the Luftwaffe bombed British airfields and radar installations, Hitler's generals began gathering a fleet of barges and training their troops for an **amphibious** (invasion by sea) assault. He believed that once the Nazis had control of the skies over Britain, Operation Sea Lion (the code name for the invasion) could proceed.

Even though the German attacks against British airfields seemed to be succeeding, the Luftwaffe changed targets in early September. German bombers began dropping their loads on British cities. At the height of the bombing, three hundred to six hundred Londoners were killed daily. Hitler hoped that bombing civilian targets would destroy the British people's morale and thus break their will. But British morale did not weaken.

Hitler had underestimated the spirit of the British people. Their determined effort to resist the Nazis was demonstrated by the heroism of the British Royal Air Force (**RAF**). The Luftwaffe outnumbered the British fighters, but the British had better planes and the advantage of the newly invented radar. Before the war, Britain had begun to build an air defense system that allowed the RAF to track enemy planes and then direct the British planes to meet the attackers. Also, whenever a British plane was shot down, the pilot could parachute to safety and fly again another day. Downed German pilots, however, were captured and lost to the Nazi cause. Time after time, the RAF met the oncoming waves of bombers and inflicted heavy losses. Between August 8 and October 31, 1940, official government estimates placed the number of German planes shot down at nearly 1,400 in contrast to 800 British planes. The German air force never recovered from these terrific losses. With each passing week, Hitler's invasion plans became less and less likely to succeed. Summarizing the work of the British pilots, Winston Churchill said, "Never in the field of human conflict was so much owed by so many to so few."

This British poster combines two symbols of British patriotism and determination—the British flag and Churchill, whose tenacity was like that of a bulldog.

Although the United States was not yet at war with the Axis powers, America clearly indicated its support for the Allied cause. First, the United States gave Britain fifty World War I destroyers in return for a ninety-nine-year lease on eight British military bases in the Western Hemisphere. Second, the U.S. Congress passed the so-called **Lend-Lease Act** in 1941, authorizing the president to "sell, transfer title to, exchange, lease, lend, or otherwise dispose of" military supplies to any country whose security was important to the United States. Third, Winston Churchill and Franklin Roosevelt drew up and signed the **Atlantic Charter**, an eight-point document that set forth the "common principles" on which both countries "base[d] their hopes for a better future for the world." The charter provided that after the "final destruction of the Nazi tyranny," the signatories would seek such things as the disarmament of aggressor nations, freedom of the seas, and equal economic opportunities.

The Atlantic Charter

The President of the United States of America and the Prime Minister, Mr. Churchill, representing His Majesty's Government in the United Kingdom, being met together, deem it right to make known certain common principles in the national policies of their respective countries on which they base their hopes for a better future for the world.

First, their countries seek no aggrandizement, territorial or other;

Second, they desire to see no territorial changes that do not accord with the freely expressed wishes of the peoples concerned;

Third, they respect the right of all peoples to choose the form of government under which they will live; and they wish to see sovereign rights and self government restored to those who have been forcibly deprived of them;

Fourth, they will endeavor, with due respect for their existing obligations, to further the enjoyment by all States, great or small, victor or vanquished, of access, on equal terms, to the trade and to the raw materials of the world which are needed for their economic prosperity;

Fifth, they desire to bring about the fullest collaboration between all nations in the economic field with the object of securing, for all, improved labor standards, economic advancement and social security;

Top: Franklin D. Roosevelt
Bottom: Winston S. Churchill

Sixth, after the final destruction of the Nazi tyranny, they hope to see established a peace which will afford to all nations the means of dwelling in safety within their own boundaries, and which will afford assurance that all the men in all lands may live out their lives in freedom from fear and want;

Seventh, such a peace should enable all men to traverse the high seas and oceans without hindrance;

Eighth, they believe that all of the nations of the world, for realistic as well as spiritual reasons must come to the abandonment of the use of force. Since no future peace can be maintained if land, sea or air armaments continue to be employed by nations which threaten, or may threaten, aggression outside of their frontiers, they believe, pending the establishment of a wider and permanent system of general security, that the disarmament of such nations is essential. They will likewise aid and encourage all other practicable measure which will lighten for peace-loving peoples the crushing burden of armaments.

The Invasion of Russia

Late in 1940, Hitler issued an order directing his generals to begin "preparation to crush Soviet Russia in a lightning campaign even before the termination of hostilities with Great Britain." Under the code name Operation Barbarossa, plans went forward in the spring of 1941 for an invasion of Russia. Although Stalin and Hitler had signed a nonaggression pact in 1939, Hitler decided to attack Russia to secure both *lebensraum* and needed natural resources such as oil. (The British naval blockade was preventing the German importation of needed raw materials.) In addition, Hitler hoped that a Russian surrender would put increased pressure on Britain by removing its last hope of finding a European ally.

But the attack on Russia proved to be another serious blunder. The Nazis underestimated not only the Soviet industrial capacity but also the length of time necessary to win a victory. Although some Russians initially welcomed the Germans as liberators from the cruel Stalin regime, the harshness of the German conquerors soon united the Russian people to fight for "Mother Russia." Like Napoleon in 1812, the Nazis made no provision for the severe Russian winters, and, like Napoleon, they found that in the end the weather helped defeat them.

German panzer unit and soldiers invading Russia in Operation Barbarossa

The invasion was delayed one month while the Germans established Nazi control over Greece and Yugoslavia, but Hitler finally launched his attack on June 22, 1941. With thousands of planes and tanks and more than 600,000 other motor vehicles, three million Nazi soldiers advanced into Russia along an eighteen-hundred-mile front. For the first several months, the Nazi forces advanced rapidly, capturing thousands of prisoners and more than 500,000 square miles of territory. As the Russians retreated, however, they carried out a scorched-earth policy, just as they had done when Napoleon invaded in 1812. They destroyed or removed anything that the invading Germans might have used as supplies.

By December 1, the Russian armed forces had suffered four to five million casualties, including more than one million prisoners of war. German forces had besieged Leningrad and had nearly reached Moscow, but the coming of winter ended their advance. Temperatures in early December fell to $^{-}40°$ F, bringing in the earliest and coldest winter of the century. Machinery would not function, and soldiers suffered from lack of winter clothing. Hitler's campaign failed to knock Russia out of the war quickly. Now he had to wait until spring to try again.

In the spring, Nazi troops pushed farther into southern Russia, toward the oil fields. At the same time, they attacked Stalingrad, which not only was a strategic transportation center but also carried Stalin's name. Therefore, Hitler was determined to capture the city at all costs. For months, German troops shelled Stalingrad, but the Soviets refused to surrender. As the Nazis advanced slowly into the city, they found that the Russians were using the rubble of the destroyed buildings as fortresses. For several more months, desperate hand-to-hand fighting raged in the city. Neither side was able to defeat the other. Finally, the Russians managed to surround the Germans, and what was left of the German army surrendered in February 1943. Several days earlier, the Russians had also broken the German siege of Leningrad.

Concentration camp at Dachau, Bavaria

To this point, Russia had received only a limited amount of aid from the West. In a speech broadcast at the start of the German invasion of Russia, Churchill had promised that

> any man or state who fights against Nazism will have our aid. . . . We shall give whatever help we can to Russia and to the Russian people. . . . We have offered to the government of Soviet Russia any technical or economic assistance which is in our power.

The Holocaust

In both *Mein Kampf* and his many speeches, Hitler said that the Jews were "culture destroyers" and had to be annihilated to save the "master race" (the Germans) from contamination. However, although the Jews were horribly mistreated and frequently placed in concentration camps, few people outside of Germany (and only a few in Germany) believed that Hitler really meant what he said.

Early in the war, Hitler ordered that all Jews be rounded up and forced to live in restricted areas called *ghettos*. These areas were sealed off from the rest of the city, and the Jews were forced to live in deplorable conditions and given rationed food allotments. They were also forced to work in nearly unbearable conditions. The Nazis called the ghettos "death boxes."

When the German invasion of Russia began, Hitler instructed the SS to eliminate all Soviet Jews. In town after town and village after village, the Nazis systematically rounded up the Jews and shot them. In Kiev, for example, they herded the Jews to the cemetery, forced them to dig a large communal grave, undress, and then in groups climb into the grave. Each group was machine-gunned and covered with a layer of dirt.

In January 1942, Hitler called for a meeting of his top advisers to devise a way to annihilate the entire European Jewish community as quickly as possible. They rejected starvation and shooting; the first method was too slow and the second too costly. The Nazis decided that the most economical and efficient method was to build large gas chambers at the existing concentration camps. In those chambers, hundreds of Jews could be gassed at once. The disposal of the bodies, however, was a problem. In one camp, they were just stacked and allowed to decay, and in another they were placed in huge graves. But in most of the other camps, the Nazis built large crematoriums (furnaces for cremating bodies).

The Germans built the largest "disposal" center in the Polish village of Oswiecim (in German, *Auschwitz*). Three camps were built there to receive thousands of Jews from all over eastern Europe. They were brought to the camps in closed railroad cars made to accommodate forty people, but as many as one hundred fifty people were crammed into each car. With little food or water and no toilet facilities, the Jews traveled for days before reaching the camp. Usually by the time the train reached its destination, scores of people in each car were dead. Upon arrival at the camp, the Nazis divided the victims into two groups: those who were fit to work and those who were not (the old, sick, or very young). The Nazis took the second group to the "showers," as the gas chambers were called, and disposed of them. They put the rest to work until they were no longer useful, and then they sent them to the "showers" as well.

Toward the end of the war, as the Germans grew desperate, most incoming victims were sent directly to the gas chambers. The slaughter was so immense that the crematoriums could not keep up with the demand.

Millions of Europeans (including communists, Gypsies, mentally and physically handicapped, Jehovah's Witnesses, and members of many other groups) died in the Nazi concentration camps from the awful brutality of the SS. But the Jewish people remained Hitler's primary target. An estimated six million Jews (two and a half million at Auschwitz alone) were methodically murdered, supposedly to save the "master race" from destruction.

This horrible event has become known as the Holocaust by many. However, many Jews prefer the term *shoah* which means "calamity." They reject the term *holocaust* because it refers to a burnt sacrifice, and some Jews find this image objectionable.

Two German soldiers supervise a group of Jews as they are forced to pump water in an unidentified ghetto.

United States Holocaust Museum, courtesy of Ralf Rossmeissl
THE VIEWS OR OPINIONS EXPRESSED IN THIS BOOK, AND THE CONTEXT IN WHICH THE IMAGES ARE USED, DO NOT NECESSARILY REFLECT THE VIEWS OR POLICY OF, NOR IMPLY APPROVAL OR ENDORSEMENT BY, THE UNITED STATES HOLOCAUST MEMORIAL MUSEUM.

Yet supply routes were few. British and American supply ships sailed regularly around Norway to the northern Russian ports of Murmansk and Archangel, but the ships were in danger from Nazi submarine and air attacks. Consequently, the Allies opened up an alternative supply route into southern Russia through Iran. By 1943, supplies began to pour into Russia. By the end of the war, the United States alone had supplied the Soviets with $11 billion in Lend-Lease aid.

Attack on Pearl Harbor

Japan was already at war in Asia before World War II officially began. In September 1939, when war broke out in Europe, Japan took advantage of the situation and moved into Southeast Asia. The free nations of Europe were struggling against Hitler for their very survival and could do little to halt Japanese aggression. Japan needed only to neutralize the military power of the USSR and the United States to proceed with its plans of conquest in the Pacific. In April 1941, Japan and Russia signed a nonaggression pact. Only the United States remained an obstacle.

Although U.S.-Japan relations had become increasingly strained because of Japanese aggression, the United States remained officially neutral. However, in the fall of 1941, Japanese emperor Hirohito appointed **Hideki Tojo** (1885–1948) to serve as the virtual dictator of Japan. With the emperor's approval, he and his fellow generals decided that if the American fleet stationed at Pearl Harbor, Hawaii, were destroyed, there would be no power strong enough to stop Japanese expansion into Southeast Asia. Such expansion was necessary, they believed, if Japan was to become economically self-sufficient.

Just before 8:00 a.m. on Sunday morning, December 7, 1941, nearly four hundred Japanese planes descended on Pearl Harbor. In a well-coordinated surprise attack, the Japanese knocked out American airfields and seriously crippled the U.S. Pacific Fleet, which was anchored in the harbor. Through a combination of carelessness and miscalculation, the Americans at Pearl Harbor were caught by surprise. The Japanese attack killed more than two thousand Americans, destroyed two-thirds of the American aircraft, and sank or seriously damaged five battleships and three cruisers.

In a day when a nation's naval strength rested on its battleships, the American losses seemed insurmountable. But the American aircraft carriers were not at Pearl Harbor and thereby escaped the devastation of the Japanese attack. These carriers would play a critical role in defeating the Japanese in the Pacific.

Although the Japanese considered their attack on Pearl Harbor a resounding success, it stirred the American people to action. On December 8, President Roosevelt declared the unprovoked attack a "date which will live in infamy" and asked Congress to declare war on Japan, which it did. Three days later, Germany and Italy declared war on the United States. The entrance of the United States into the war brought renewed vigor to the Allies in Europe. Soon, the U.S. Navy—led by its aircraft carriers—began to turn back Japanese expansion in the Pacific. The fears of the Japanese admiral Yamamoto had come true: the attack on Pearl Harbor had awakened a "sleeping giant."

Top left: This Japanese propaganda poster uses a samurai warrior to symbolize the power of the Axis alliance.
Top right: A World War II poster uses the Pearl Harbor attack as a rallying point.
Above: Smoke billows from the USS West Virginia *after the Japanese attack on Pearl Harbor.*

Section Quiz

1. The German invasion of what country led to the official beginning of World War II? When did that invasion—and thus the war—begin?
2. At what port city were more than 350,000 Allied soldiers rescued from almost certain destruction?
3. What prime minister of Great Britain encouraged the British people never to surrender despite the gloomy prospects?
4. What people, whose systematic extermination he ordered, did Hitler label as "culture destroyers"?
5. When (month, day, and year) did the Japanese attack Pearl Harbor?

★ Why did Japan attack American forces at Pearl Harbor?

The United States Strikes Back

Unprepared for war and reeling from the attack on Pearl Harbor, the United States was fighting a purely defensive war against both Germany and Japan. The first two U.S. offensive actions occurred in the Pacific. In China, the American Volunteer Group, a small band of fighter pilots led by Col. Claire Chennault, helped China oppose the Japanese invasion there. Flying P-40 Warhawks, the noses of which they painted with a distinctive shark's mouth, the American pilots became known as the Flying Tigers. In China they developed the techniques that American pilots would use throughout the war.

But America needed the boost in morale that could come only from striking the enemy on his own soil. That opportunity came with a top-secret bombing raid led by Gen. Jimmy Doolittle, who trained Army pilots to fly B-25 bombers from the deck of an aircraft carrier. Doolittle and his "raiders" steamed secretly across the Pacific and bombed Tokyo on April 18, 1942. Although the raid did little actual damage, it shook the confidence of Japan's military leaders and forced them to keep at home some of the military resources they might otherwise have used elsewhere in the Pacific.

The American Volunteer Group, or "Flying Tigers," used Curtis P-40 Warhawk fighters, bearing their famous shark-face design and the emblem of Nationalist China under the wings, against the Japanese in China early in the war.

Allied Advances

From North Africa to Italy

The year 1942 witnessed the halt of the Axis advance and proved to be the turning point for the Allies. In spite of Rommel's brilliant leadership in North Africa, the Germans were defeated by the British commander General **Bernard L. Montgomery** at the battle of El Alamein. At the same time, an American invasion force under General **Dwight D. Eisenhower** landed on the Algerian coast. By May 1943, the outnumbered Axis troops in Africa had surrendered.

Two months later, a force of 160,000 men under Eisenhower landed in Sicily, bringing the war directly to the Italian people. This invasion not only cost Mussolini what little popular support he still had but also turned some of the top-ranking members of his own Fascist Party against him. Having no alternative, Mussolini resigned his position and was quickly imprisoned. A new Italian government headed by one of his former associates immediately began secret negotiations with the Allies about terms of surrender. As Allied troops landed on the Italian peninsula itself, Italy surrendered unconditionally in September 1943. Nevertheless, hundreds of thousands of German troops continued fighting in Italy until the surrender of Germany.

Mussolini himself met a violent end. German troops rescued him from prison and established him as a puppet ruler in the German-controlled areas of Italy. As the Axis collapsed, Mussolini, his mistress, and some friends attempted to escape to Switzerland. But Italian **partisans** (fighters who harass an enemy occupying their territory) captured them. They shot both Mussolini and his mistress, took their bodies to Milan, and hung them upside down in front of a gas station.

From Britain to Normandy

Allied Summit Conferences—In 1943, the Allies held two conferences that greatly influenced the outcome of the war. In January, Churchill and Roosevelt met for ten days at Casablanca, Morocco, where they declared that nothing less than the "unconditional surrender" of the Axis would be acceptable to them. The reason for such a declaration was that after World War I many Germans began to believe the myth that they had not really been defeated; Churchill and Roosevelt wanted to ensure that this time Germany would *know* without question that it had been beaten. But by establishing the principle of unconditional surrender, the Allies unintentionally lengthened the war, uniting the Germans more firmly behind their government.

In late 1943, the so-called **"Big Three"** (Churchill, Roosevelt, and Stalin) held a major summit (a conference of high-level officials) at Teheran, Iran, to discuss military strategy. Churchill wanted the Western Allies to concentrate their military efforts in the Mediterranean to check Soviet expansion there and in Eastern Europe. Stalin, on the other hand, wanted to control Eastern Europe, so he opposed any plans that would call for American and British troops in Eastern Europe. Roosevelt sided with Stalin, so Churchill had to abandon his ideas and agree to an invasion of France instead.

Montgomery's British tanks cross the North African desert to engage Rommel's Afrika Korps.

The Normandy Invasion—After the Teheran Conference, the United States and Britain began planning an invasion of France under the code name **Operation Overlord**. It would be impossible to conceal from the Germans the countless tons of supplies and thousands of aircraft and motor vehicles being stockpiled in Britain, so the Allies attempted to mislead the Germans as to the time and place of the invasion. To accomplish that deception, work crews built fake military installations in southeastern England across from Calais in France. They even constructed rows of dummy tanks that looked real to German airmen flying over the island. The military then created a nonexistent invasion force complete with its own commander, sent false messages, which they allowed the Germans to intercept, and even conducted naval movements off that section of the French coast. All of this activity was designed to make the Germans believe that an attack was coming near the French-Belgian border. The plan succeeded, for when the real Allied attack came, the Germans had amassed their best troops in the area of France where they expected the invasion to come.

The Allies actually planned to invade Europe by way of Normandy. Dwight Eisenhower, the supreme Allied commander, decided to plan **D-day** (the day when an attack is to be launched) for June. Everything had to be just right for the attack, including the weather, the tides, and the amount of moonlight. Finally, on June 6, 1944, in spite of threatening weather, Eisenhower ordered the attack to proceed on five different Normandy beaches. The assault, the greatest amphibious operation in history, had been thoroughly rehearsed to ensure its success. More than ten thousand planes bombed coastal targets and provided aerial cover for the invasion forces. Battleships shelled the enemy's beach defenses. Paratroopers landed behind the German lines before the amphibious assault and secured important objectives. Five thousand large ships and four thousand smaller

American soldiers wade ashore at Omaha Beach in Normandy on D-day, June 6, 1944.

Top: Artist's rendition of a German V-1 buzz bomb being launched toward Allied forces
Middle: Artist's rendition of the aircraft carrier USS Yorktown *under attack by Japanese planes during the Battle of Midway*
Bottom: Midway Atoll

landing craft followed minesweepers across the English Channel to the designated landing spots.

In the end, D-day succeeded in spite of underwater barriers, explosive mines, and stiff German resistance at several of the beaches. Within three weeks after the invasion, the Allies had landed nearly 1 million men, 500,000 tons of supplies, and 177,000 vehicles in France. Germany's defeat was assured; it was only a matter of time before the Germans surrendered.

If defeat seemed so certain, why did the Germans continue fighting for another year? First, Hitler and his staff believed that new "miracle weapons" would turn the tide and save Germany from defeat. For example, in 1944, the Nazis began launching rocket bombs (the British called them "buzz bombs") against the Allies. But the V-1 rockets (short for *Vergeltungswaffe*, "retaliatory weapon"), the more sophisticated V-2 rockets, and the newly developed jet aircraft all came too late to save the Nazis from defeat. Had German scientists succeeded in their efforts to develop the atomic bomb before the end of the war, the outcome might have been different.

A second reason that the Nazis prolonged the war is that Hitler expected the United States and Britain to fall into serious disagreement with Russia and split their alliance. He and his staff did not believe that the Western democracies would allow the Soviet Union to conquer Germany.

Third, the Nazis stirred up a fear of Russian communism among the German people. Nazi propaganda began to emphasize the importance of Fortress Europe (*Festung Europa*) rather than the concept of *lebensraum*, which had been so prominent in their ideology a few years earlier. With the cry of "Victory or Bolshevism" ringing in their ears, many Germans tried wearily to do their part in salvaging the collapsing Third Reich.

From Island to Island

The Fall of the Philippines—After the attack on Pearl Harbor, the Japanese military command ordered attacks throughout the Pacific. One of those attacks struck the Philippines. American defenders on the islands had too few aircraft and too few men to defend the entire territory, so they decided to concentrate on defending the largest and most important of the islands, Luzon. American and Filipino forces on the Bataan peninsula held out for several months, making their final stand on the fortress island of Corregidor. With surrender in May 1942, however, all organized resistance in the Philippines ceased. The American commander, General **Douglas MacArthur**, escaped but vowed, "I shall return." The Japanese forced the prisoners they captured on Bataan and Corregidor to march nearly a hundred miles through the jungle and under the most inhumane conditions to a prison camp. Brutality on the "Bataan

Breaking the Japanese Codes

Because radio transmissions can be intercepted easily by an enemy, both the Allies and the Axis forces took pains to maintain the secrecy of their communications. Most often they used ciphers and codes in transmitting their radio messages. (In a cipher, the letters and numbers in a message are exchanged for different letters and numbers. In a code, a word, phrase, or sentence is replaced by one letter or several letters or numbers.) Most messages are sent in both cipher and code.

By World War II, Americans had broken many of the Japanese military ciphers and codes. This knowledge became a vital help to the Allied war effort, especially after the devastating American losses at Pearl Harbor. The significance of such code breaking is illustrated by the Battle of Midway.

Having cracked a new Japanese code, the Americans learned of a planned Japanese attack on an undisclosed target coded "AF." Though Navy intelligence had a hunch that "AF" referred to Midway Island, they were not certain. They had to be sure if they were to stop the Japanese invasion. To confirm their suspicions, Navy intelligence had personnel at Midway send an uncoded message to headquarters at Pearl Harbor stating that the fresh-water distilling plant on Midway was broken. Pearl Harbor radioed back that they would send a barge with fresh water. Knowing that the Japanese monitored such messages and reported such routine matters to Tokyo, the Americans waited for the Japanese transmission. Soon, the Americans intercepted a Japanese message that said that "AF" was short of fresh water. Now the Americans knew for sure that the target was Midway.

Because of this advance warning, the American fleet—led by three aircraft carriers—was able to surprise the Japanese invasion fleet and severely cripple it. Midway was saved, and the tide of Japanese expansion was stopped.

Death March" was commonplace, and thousands died. A few managed to escape and became guerrilla fighters.

Elsewhere in the Pacific, Japanese troops overran the British colonies of Hong Kong, Malaya, Singapore, Burma, and the Dutch East Indies (Indonesia). Other nations were also unprepared for war, and Japan won a series of relatively easy victories.

But Japan had overextended itself. Its resources were no match for America's industrial potential. Before long, American war production surpassed that of the Japanese. By the end of 1942, only one year after the attack, most of the ships that had been damaged at Pearl Harbor had been repaired or replaced. The Allies had suffered serious reverses, but under the leadership of General MacArthur, who became the supreme Allied commander in the Pacific, the tide turned against Japan.

The Navajo "Code Talkers"

Just as American code experts worked to break Japan's codes, the Japanese tried to break U.S. military codes—and Americans tried to prevent it. Philip Johnson, the son of a missionary to the Navajo Indians in the American Southwest, suggested a method by which the American code was never broken: using Navajos speaking their own language.

Navajo has no alphabet or symbols, so it is not written. It is also very complicated, and few people knew it. In early tests of the method, Navajos could decode a three-line message in only twenty seconds, whereas a decoding machine required thirty minutes to decode the same message.

The U.S. Marine Corps recruited and trained more than 375 Navajos as "code talkers," and they served in every major engagement in the Pacific. For example, during the first two days of the battle for Iwo Jima, six code talkers worked around the clock, sending and decoding more than eight hundred messages without making any mistakes.

The Navajo code talkers were critical to the Allied victory over Japan. For years, few people knew about their invaluable contribution because the program was so secret. They were finally honored for their service in 1992.

Marine Pfc. Preston Toledo and Pfc. Frank Toledo relaying orders in their native language

General Douglas MacArthur wades ashore at Lingayen Gulf in the Philippines, fulfilling his vow to return to the islands.

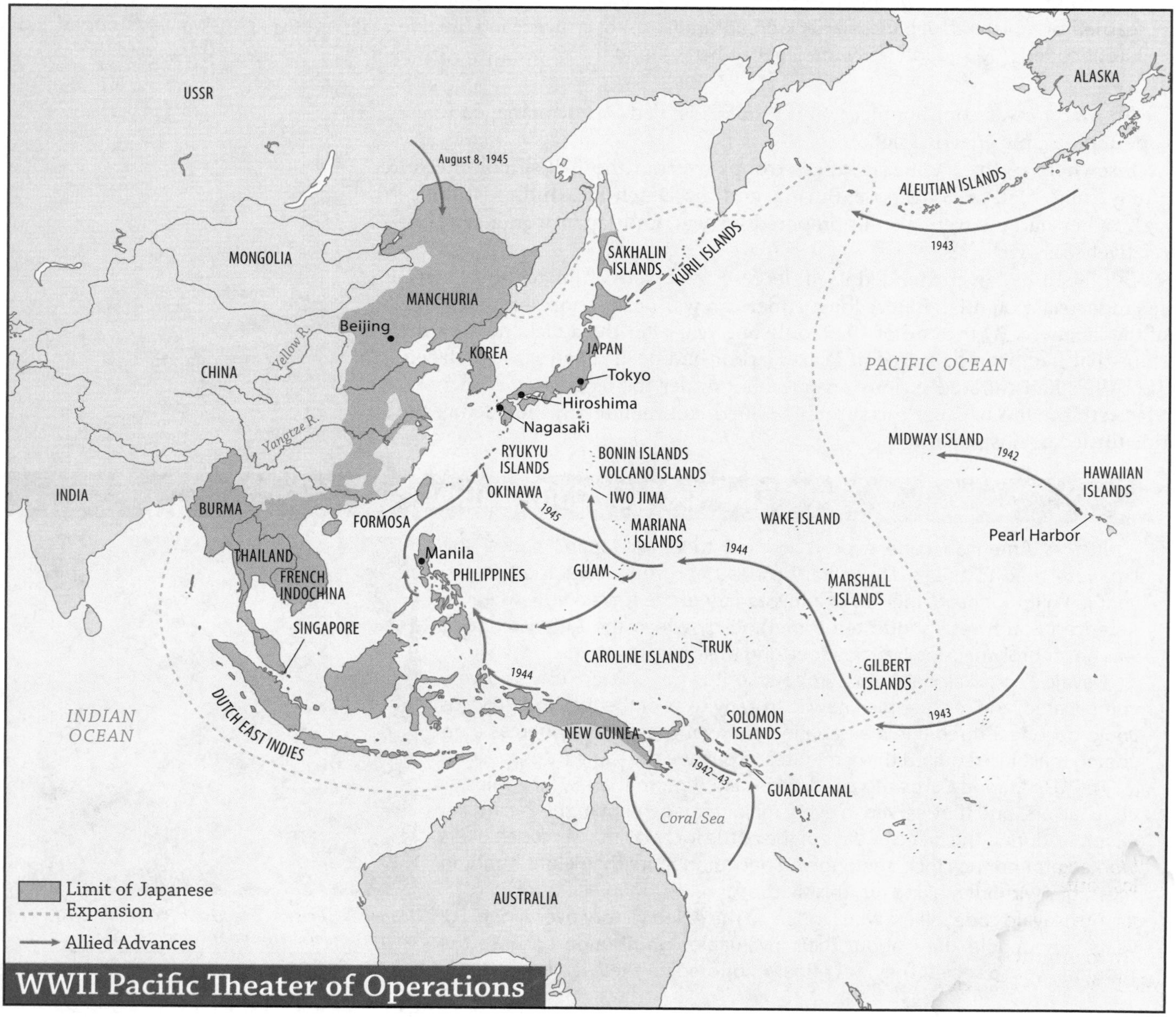

USSR
ALASKA
August 8, 1945
ALEUTIAN ISLANDS
1943
MONGOLIA
SAKHALIN ISLANDS
KURIL ISLANDS
MANCHURIA
Beijing
Yellow R.
CHINA
KOREA
JAPAN
Tokyo
Hiroshima
Nagasaki
PACIFIC OCEAN
Yangtze R.
RYUKYU ISLANDS
BONIN ISLANDS
VOLCANO ISLANDS
MIDWAY ISLAND
1942
HAWAIIAN ISLANDS
INDIA
OKINAWA
IWO JIMA
1945
BURMA
FORMOSA
MARIANA ISLANDS
WAKE ISLAND
Pearl Harbor
THAILAND
Manila
1944
FRENCH INDOCHINA
PHILIPPINES
GUAM
MARSHALL ISLANDS
SINGAPORE
TRUK
CAROLINE ISLANDS
GILBERT ISLANDS
1944
INDIAN OCEAN
DUTCH EAST INDIES
NEW GUINEA
SOLOMON ISLANDS
1943
1942–43
GUADALCANAL
Coral Sea
AUSTRALIA

Limit of Japanese Expansion
Allied Advances

WWII Pacific Theater of Operations

Island-Hopping Campaign—In 1942, the United States defeated Japan in two major naval battles, halting further Japanese expansion. In the first battle, the Battle of the Coral Sea, American planes launched from aircraft carriers sank 100,000 tons of Japanese shipping. These losses prevented the Japanese from launching a full-scale invasion of Australia. A month later, a Japanese force of eighty ships converged on Midway Island, an American naval base 1,300 miles northwest of Honolulu, Hawaii. Although seriously outnumbered, the Americans struck first, sinking several Japanese aircraft carriers and turning back the Japanese attack. After that defeat, Japan was on the defensive for the rest of the war.

American forces soon began an island-hopping campaign, recapturing strategic Japanese-held islands in the Pacific. Instead of conquering every island in their path, however, the Americans seized only those that offered good sites for air bases. They simply bypassed Japanese troops on other islands. Fighting was intense, with great loss of life on both sides. Few Japanese troops surrendered, and most chose to die in battle or to commit suicide rather than face the dishonor of surrender.

As American forces moved ever closer to the home islands of Japan, some Japanese soldiers engaged in suicide attacks against U.S. forces. For example, American forces sometimes faced **banzai** charges (so named because of the war cry shouted by the Japanese troops). Waves of Japanese soldiers, some with improvised weapons, charged American infantry positions only to be slaughtered. In the air, Japanese suicide pilots, known as **kamikaze** pilots, crashed their bomb-laden planes into American ships in desperate attempts to sink them. Although such attacks caused great damage, they failed to halt America's advance toward Japan. They did, however, illustrate just how determined the Japanese forces were.

In the fall of 1944, General MacArthur returned to the Philippines as promised, bringing a large American force. As his troops advanced on the ground, American naval forces engaged the Japanese off the coast in the Battle of Leyte Gulf. In three days of fighting, the Japanese navy lost forty ships and any opportunity to launch another naval attack. On the ground, American forces had some success, but Japanese resistance continued in the Philippines until the end of the war.

Marines raising the flag atop Mount Suribachi on Iwo Jima

In 1945, U.S. troops targeted two strategic islands—Iwo Jima and Okinawa—that would provide good air bases on which pilots could land safely and from which they could launch bombing raids and even an invasion of the main islands of Japan. Iwo Jima was less than 700 miles from Tokyo. For seventy-two days American planes bombed Iwo Jima, hoping to "soften up" the defenses before ground troops landed on the beaches. Nevertheless, American casualties during the invasion were high. After five weeks of intense fighting, Iwo Jima was in American hands. Of the estimated 21,000 to 23,000 Japanese troops on the island, only 216 surrendered. In June 1945, American forces also captured Okinawa, a large island only 350 miles south of Japan.

Allied Victory

Throughout 1943 and 1944, Soviet troops, well-supplied by the West, relentlessly pushed the German troops

Yalta Conference

The Yalta Conference recognized Soviet control of eastern Europe. In fact, at the time of the conference, Russian troops already controlled large portions of that region. Unless the United States and Great Britain wanted war with Russia, Stalin intended to maintain Russian control over the area. Roosevelt and Churchill were eager to gain Soviet aid in the war against Japan; therefore, they tried consciously not to antagonize Stalin. Stalin promised Churchill and Roosevelt that he would allow free elections in eastern Europe following the war, but within a few years even the most naive Western observers realized that Stalin did not intend to keep his word.

Churchill, Roosevelt, and Stalin

back toward Germany. They drove the Nazis out of eastern Europe and established their own form of totalitarianism over that region. In western Europe, Allied troops liberated Paris. They intensified their bombing of German cities and by December 1944 had reached the border of Germany. Hitler decided to order one final effort to shatter the Allied advance. In December, German armored troops suddenly attacked a weakly held section of the Allied line and pushed back the American forces there. Despite some initial success, the German drive halted as the Allies forced the Germans back to their original position. The **Battle of the Bulge** (as it came to be known) wasted much of Germany's remaining strength and probably hastened the end of the war in Europe.

In February 1945, as Allied victory seemed certain, Churchill, Roosevelt, and Stalin met at the **Yalta Conference** in the Crimea to determine the policies they would follow in the months ahead. "We have considered and determined the military plans for the final defeat of the common enemy," they proclaimed. Although they had agreed on surrender terms, they said, "these terms [would] not be made known until the defeat of Germany has been accomplished." Although they avoided specific public statements, the Allies did make certain general principles clear to the public: Germany would have to pay reparations, German war criminals would be brought to trial, all German forces would be disarmed and disbanded, and Germany would be divided into zones of occupation. Stalin also secretly promised America and Britain that he would go to war against Japan within three months after the war ended in Europe.

Advance to Berlin—Although American forces could easily have taken Berlin, Eisenhower ordered American troops to halt on the Elbe River, in fulfillment of a promise made at Yalta, to allow the Russians to close in on the city. On April 30, 1945, before Russian troops arrived, Adolf Hitler committed suicide in his underground bunker in Berlin. His aides then burned his body with gasoline. The next day, however, German radio announced that Hitler had died at the head of his troops, fighting to his last breath against bolshevism. On May 7, the Germans surrendered unconditionally, and the Allies declared **May 8, 1945**, "V-E" Day ("Victory in Europe"). The war in Europe was over.

Amid the jubilation, however, was the discovery of unbelievable horrors and atrocities committed by the Third Reich in the numerous concentration camps the Nazis had run. The Allies forced captured German guards from the

WWII European Theater of Operations

camps and civilians who had lived near the camps to look on their ghastly work and then bury the dead. These and other atrocities became known as the **Holocaust**. Jews and Gentiles the world over vowed, "Never again."

Two months later, the leaders of the three victorious powers met at Potsdam, Germany, where they drew up a declaration charting the future course of Germany according to the decisions reached at Yalta. Roosevelt had died in April 1945, so President **Harry Truman** represented the United States. Near the end of the conference, **Clement Attlee**, who had been elected the new British prime minister, replaced Churchill at Potsdam. In addition to discussing Germany, the United States and Britain issued an ultimatum to Japan, warning that unless the country surrendered, it would face serious consequences: the United States had developed the atomic bomb.

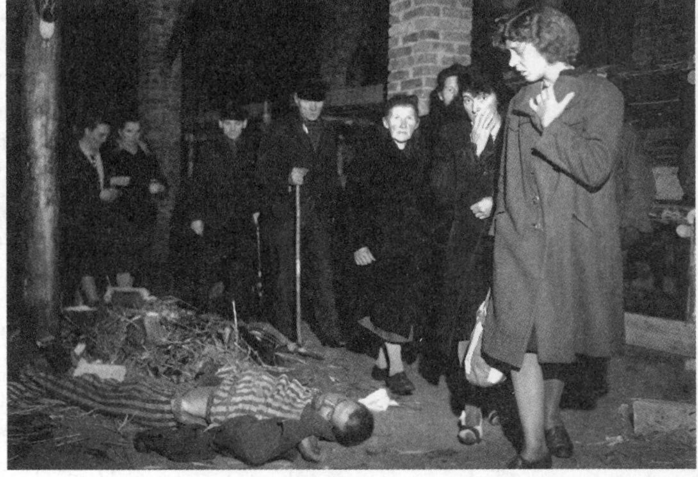

The Allies forced German civilians to view the victims of war crimes at Buchenwald concentration camp.

Left: Harry Truman
Right: The mushroom cloud from the atomic explosion over Nagasaki

Victory in the Pacific

After the surrender of Germany, war continued in the Pacific. American bombers leveled whole sections of Japanese cities using incendiary bombs (bombs designed to start fires). In a one-night raid against Tokyo, for example, fire destroyed nearly sixteen square miles of the city, and more than eighty thousand people died. Although many Japanese people wanted to see the war end, Japan's emperor and military leaders refused to surrender. Instead, they gathered as much war materiel as they could, including eight thousand planes, which they intended to use against the Americans should they attempt to invade Japan.

The two atomic bombs dropped on Japan: "Little Boy" (top) and "Fat Man" (bottom)

American and British troops advanced steadily toward Japan. Allied leaders, however, dreaded the long and bloody struggle that lay ahead of them. President Truman and his military staff believed that Japanese and American casualties would reach into the hundreds of thousands if American troops actually invaded the home islands of Japan. In an effort to shorten the war and save lives, Truman ordered that an atomic bomb be dropped on the Japanese city of Hiroshima. On August 6, 1945, the bomb was dropped. Its blast wiped out 4.7 square miles of the city and killed an estimated seventy thousand people; another seventy thousand were injured. When Truman announced the dropping of the bomb to the American people, he issued another stern warning to Japan: "We are now prepared to obliterate more rapidly and completely every productive enterprise the Japanese have above ground in any city." If the Japanese leaders did not accept Allied terms of surrender, they could "expect a rain of ruin from the air, the like of which has never been seen on this earth."

Realizing that the war against Japan would end quickly and wanting to gain territory in the peace negotiations, the Soviets finally declared war on Japan on August 8. Since the Japanese leaders still refused to surrender, the United States dropped a second atomic bomb on the city of Nagasaki on August 9. Five days later on August 14, the Japanese government surrendered with the sole condition that their emperor be allowed to retain his throne. On September 2, 1945 ("V-J" Day), hostilities formally ended as Japanese and Allied representatives signed the surrender document aboard the USS *Missouri* anchored in Tokyo Bay. World War II was finally over.

Section Quiz

1. Which "Big Three" Allied leaders met at Teheran in 1943?
2. Where did the Big Three decide to invade Europe to get a foothold on the Continent?
3. Who was the Allied leader of the Normandy invasion?
4. What strategy did American forces employ as they began to recapture strategic Japanese-held islands in the Pacific?
5. What new weapon did the United States use against two Japanese cities in August 1945?

★ Why do you think the Japanese emperor and military leaders refused to surrender until the United States dropped two atomic bombs?

III. Efforts for Global Peace

Even before the end of World War II, the Allies had called for the formation of an international peace-keeping organization. The "Big Three" Allied powers discussed that hope in conferences in Teheran (1943), Dumbarton Oaks (1944), Yalta (1945), and San Francisco (1945).

At the San Francisco conference, representatives of fifty governments formally organized the **United Nations** (UN). The UN Charter defined its purpose as the maintenance of international peace and security. In addition, the UN sought to foster cooperation among nations in solving worldwide social, economic, and humanitarian problems. These goals expressed the same kind of optimism that had characterized the ill-fated League of Nations after World War I—the desire for lasting world peace and cooperation among all nations. The verse inscribed on the UN headquarters building in New York City summarizes the organization's dream:

> They shall beat their swords into plowshares, and their spears into pruninghooks: nation shall not lift up sword against nation, neither shall they learn war any more. (Isa. 2:4)

To accomplish their goals, member nations created three major bodies within the UN: the **Secretariat**, the **General Assembly**, and the **Security Council**. The Secretariat, headed by the Secretary General, is the administrative arm of the UN. All member nations are represented in the General Assembly, where they debate world issues in annual sessions. The Security Council embodies the executive, or enforcement, power of the UN. Five permanent members—the United States, Russia (formerly the Soviet Union), China, Great Britain, and France—and ten nonpermanent members, elected by the General Assembly to two-year rotating terms, make up the Security Council.

In addition to these bodies, the UN bureaucracy includes various special agencies. For example, the Economic and Social Council promotes better living standards and human rights throughout the world, the Trusteeship Council

Top: The Japanese signing the terms of surrender aboard the battleship USS Missouri
Bottom: The Secretariat building of the United Nations

assists colonial peoples, and the International Court of Justice resolves disputes among nations as the judicial arm of the UN. Other specialized agencies include the International Labor Organization; the World Health Organization; and the UN Educational, Scientific, and Cultural Organization (UNESCO). The United States, which earlier had shunned the League of Nations, not only joined the UN but became its host as well.

The UN displays the shortcomings that often characterize international organizations. As with the League of Nations, the primary weakness of the UN has been its lack of authority. As a voluntary international organization, it has lacked the power to enforce its actions, even upon member nations. Furthermore, each of the five permanent members of the Security Council has veto power over any council decision. In the first ten years of the UN, the council experienced seventy-eight vetoes, seventy-five of them by the Soviet Union. During the Cold War era that followed World War II, the superpowers clearly dominated the world organization, but their competing differences rendered the Security Council ineffective. The threat of nuclear war, not the UN, prevented the outbreak of another world war.

Section Quiz

1. How many nations were represented in the formal organization of the United Nations?
2. What five nations are permanent members of the Security Council?
3. What is a primary weakness of the United Nations?
4. What country exercised the veto more than any other nation during the first ten years of the UN?
5. What effectively prevented the outbreak of another world war?

★ Why do nations not turn their weapons into farm implements?

Chapter 22 Review

Making Connections

1–3. What steps did Japan take to control the Pacific region? (List three.)

4–5. What new techniques did Germany use effectively leading up to and during World War II? (List two.)

Developing History Skills

1. Why did the Allied declaration of war surprise Hitler?
2. Evaluate the overall effectiveness of the United Nations in keeping peace in the world. Defend your answer.

Thinking Critically

1. Defend or refute the following statement: "The dropping of the atomic bombs saved many lives and was justified."
2. Why did the Axis powers have an advantage at the beginning of the war? Why do you think they were unable to maintain that advantage?

Living in God's World

1. Imagine you are a Christian living in Germany during World War II. What would your responsibility toward the government be?

People, Places, and Things to Know

Hirohito
Sun Yat-sen
Chiang Kai-shek
Mao Zedong
Third Reich
lebensraum
Rome-Berlin Axis
Anti-Comintern Pact
Francisco Franco
Neville Chamberlain
Édouard Daladier
Munich Conference
appeasement
Winston Churchill
Pact of Steel
panzer
Luftwaffe
blitzkrieg
sitzkrieg
fifth columnists
Vidkun Quisling
Maginot Line
Henri Pétain
Vichy France
Charles de Gaulle
Erwin Rommel
amphibious
RAF
Lend-Lease Act
Atlantic Charter
Hideki Tojo
Bernard L. Montgomery
Dwight D. Eisenhower
partisans
"Big Three"
Operation Overlord
D-day
Douglas MacArthur
banzai
kamikaze
Battle of the Bulge
Yalta Conference
May 8, 1945
Holocaust
Harry Truman
Clement Attlee
United Nations
Secretariat
General Assembly
Security Council

23

THE COLD WAR ERA

I. Postwar Confrontation
II. Spread of Communism
III. Showdown Between the Superpowers
IV. Aftermath of the Cold War
V. Other Post–World War II Developments

Berlin Wall in November 1989

During the months following World War II, Soviet expansion threatened to enslave the Europe that the Allies had so recently freed from the grips of Hitler and Mussolini. "Nobody knows what Soviet Russia and its Communist international organization intends to do in the immediate future, or what are the limits, if any, to their expansive and proselytizing tendencies," Churchill warned. But what was already apparent to Churchill was that much of Europe had fallen under Soviet domination. "From Stettin in the Baltic to Trieste in the Adriatic," Churchill observed, "an iron curtain has descended across the Continent."

Before long, that so-called **iron curtain** came to symbolize an even greater division. The world that emerged from World War II split into two competing camps—the Communist world, dominated by the Soviet Union, and the free world, led by the United States. Decades of apprehension, hostility, and competition between the Soviet Union and the United States followed. Because those superpowers never actually fought each other in open combat, people referred to the decades following World War II as the **Cold War**. After forty-five years of costly struggle, communism proved to be a failure, and the Soviet Union dissolved.

I. Postwar Confrontation

Background of the Cold War

The end of World War II brought a new set of challenges. The United States and the Soviet Union emerged as the world's greatest military powers, or superpowers. The world was divided politically and economically into three groups: the "industrialized nations," comprising North America, Western Europe, and Japan, which combined democratic government with capitalistic economies; the Communist world of the Soviet Union, Eastern Europe, and China, all of which were controlled economies; and the developing countries of Africa, Asia, and the Middle East, which were known collectively as the third world and were a mixture of military dictatorships and fledgling democracies.

A Heritage of Mistrust

Since the Bolshevik Revolution of 1917, relations between the Soviet Union and the West had been characterized by suspicion and mistrust. Lenin created ill will among the Allies when he pulled Russia from World War I and made a separate peace with Germany.

Relations between the Soviets and the West worsened when the Soviets signed a nonaggression pact with Nazi Germany in 1939. In June 1941, when Hitler violated that pact and invaded the Soviet Union, Britain and the United States joined the Communists to fight the common threat of Nazism and remained allies throughout the war.

Communist Motives

Three motivations fueled Soviet expansion. First, the Soviet Union remained suspicious of the West, in part because of centuries of Russian isolation but even more because of the nature of the totalitarian Communist system. Since their own rule was built on fear and repression, the Soviets assumed the worst motives in their opponents.

A second factor was Communist ideology. Communist philosophy required its expansion around the world. In fact, one of Lenin's greatest "contributions" to Communist thought was his conviction that violence was the primary means of spreading the Communist revolution. If the workers of the

The Iron Curtain

Beware, I say, time may be short. . . . A shadow has fallen upon the scenes so lately lighted by the Allied victory. Nobody knows what Soviet Russia and its Communist international organization intends to do in the immediate future, or what are the limits, if any, to their expansive and proselytizing tendencies. . . . From Stettin in the Baltic to Trieste in the Adriatic, an iron curtain has descended across the Continent. Behind that line lie all the capitals of the ancient states of central and eastern Europe. Warsaw, Berlin, Prague, Vienna, Budapest, Belgrade, Bucharest, and Sofia, all these famous cities and the populations around them lie in what I must call the Soviet sphere, and all are subject, in one form or another, not only to Soviet influence but to a very high and, in many cases, increasing measure of control from Moscow. . . . In a great number of countries, far from the Russian frontiers and throughout the world, Communist fifth columns are established and work in complete unity and absolute obedience to the directions they receive from the Communist center. Except in the British Commonwealth and in the United States, where communism is in its infancy, the Communist parties, or fifth columns, constitute a growing challenge and peril to Christian civilization. These are sober facts. . . . But we should be most unwise not to face them squarely while time remains. . . . What the Russians desire is . . . the indefinite expansion of their power and doctrines.

—Winston Churchill, March 5, 1946

Churchill delivering his "iron curtain" speech at Westminster College

free world would not overthrow their governments, then the Communist powers would do so by force.

Finally, a simple desire for power motivated the Communists. Like the Nazis, they wanted to increase their empire's wealth, power, and prestige by adding territories. Although they constantly criticized Western imperialism, the Communists built an empire that dwarfed the ancient empires of Persia and Rome.

Soviet Expansionist Policies

The Soviet Union was especially interested in Eastern Europe. Twice in the twentieth century, Germany had invaded Russia; Soviet leaders wanted to ensure that it never happened again. The Soviet Union sought to extend its sphere of influence over the bordering territories in Eastern Europe, creating a buffer zone between the Soviet Union and the West. Soviet control over this territory also would supply raw materials for rebuilding the Soviet economy, which had been devastated by the war.

Marshal Tito

In the wartime conferences at Teheran, Yalta, and Potsdam, the Allied leaders had wrestled with the question of what to do with Germany and Eastern Europe. They agreed that Germany should be divided and occupied by Western and Soviet forces. They could not agree, however, on the issue of Eastern Europe. Great Britain and the United States wanted to set up democratic republics, but the Soviet Union, with its Red Army already in that region, insisted on regimes friendly to Soviet interests.

The Soviets managed to place Communists in power in several countries in Eastern Europe. In 1945 both Poland and Romania fell under Communist control. Soviet puppet governments were established the following year in Bulgaria and Albania. In 1947 Hungary succumbed to Soviet domination, as did Czechoslovakia in 1948. In Yugoslavia, Josip Broz (1892–1980), better known as Marshal Tito, came to power. Tito established a Communist government but dismayed Stalin by insisting on a greater degree of independence from Moscow

Cold War Europe

than did other Eastern European countries. Since Stalin had no common border with Yugoslavia, he could not use his army to enforce his will. The Soviet dictator could only fume and denounce Tito.

Elsewhere in Eastern Europe, though, the Soviet Union exercised virtual colonial control over the Communist-bloc countries for nearly fifty years. Soviet leaders dictated the political, economic, and social affairs of their satellite states. When any Soviet-dominated country in Eastern Europe attempted to overthrow the imperialistic yoke, Soviet tanks and troops crushed the revolt swiftly and brutally. Such was the case in both Hungary in 1956 and Czechoslovakia in 1968. And the free countries of the world did nothing to help those people gain their freedom. Although leaders in the United States hinted that they would support the Hungarians, they did not deliver on those perceived promises.

American Containment Policies

American Ideals

When World War II ended, the United States was undoubtedly the most powerful nation in the world; its economic and military might were without equal. The only nation with the atomic bomb, the United States could not retreat to its traditional prewar isolationism. In another break with tradition, America began a peacetime defense buildup.

Scenes from the Hungarian and Czech uprisings: toppled statue of Stalin in Hungary (left) and Soviet tanks in Prague (right)

The United States enjoyed an enormous amount of prestige and goodwill among the nations that benefited from its assistance during the war. America entered the postwar period with a clear sense of superiority and mission. Its goal was to spread democracy and promote free trade throughout the world. In actions unprecedented in history, the United States began to rebuild its defeated foes, helping them recover from the ravages of war and get back on their feet economically and politically.

Containment

Americans became alarmed, however, at the spread of communism. They denounced Soviet aggression. When President Harry S. Truman (1884–1972) sternly lectured the Soviet foreign minister about the issue, the Soviet official indignantly replied that he had never been talked to like that in his life. Truman shot back, "Carry out your agreements and you won't get talked to like that." But little changed. With a dwindling Allied presence in Eastern Europe and the continued influence of the Soviet Union, one country after another fell to communism. In response, Truman implemented a foreign policy designed to contain the spread of communism.

The **Truman Doctrine** underscored the major objective of American foreign policy during the Cold War—**containment**. This policy, developed by George Kennan, stated that the best strategy against Soviet power would be "long term, patient but firm . . . containment of Russian expansive tendencies." Kennan also noted prophetically that Soviet power bore within itself the seeds of its own destruction.

The Marshall Plan

The United States also worried about Western Europe, where the economic chaos following the war encouraged the growth of Communist parties in Italy and France. In June 1947, one month after Truman signed the bill of aid to Greece and Turkey, U.S. secretary of state George Marshall announced plans to provide massive economic assistance to war-ravaged Europe. In April 1948 Truman signed the European Recovery Act, or **Marshall Plan**, as it was popularly called, which provided $5.3 billion for the program. Western European countries eagerly accepted the funds. Over the next four years, their economies dramatically improved.

The long-term purpose of the Marshall Plan was to thwart any advance of communism in Western Europe by rebuilding those countries economically. This plan not only reduced the appeal of communism in Western Europe but also helped create strong trade partners. Not surprisingly, the act further intensified the Cold War. The Soviet Union and the puppet governments of its

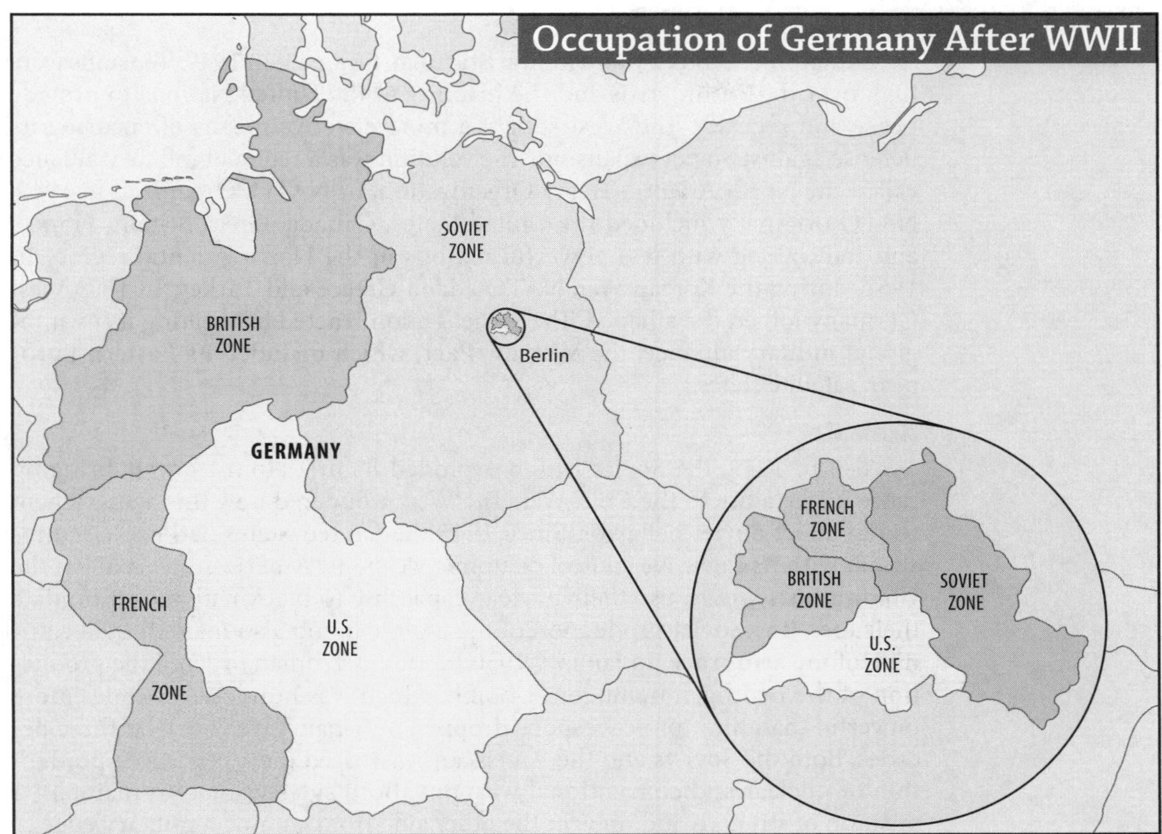

satellites rejected the American offer of economic assistance, fearing a scheme that meant greater American influence. Acceptance or rejection of the aid divided Europe into pro-American and pro-Soviet sides.

U.S./Soviet Confrontation

Germany

After World War II, the Allies divided Germany into zones, each occupied by France, Great Britain, the United States, or the Soviet Union. Berlin, the German capital, was also divided: the Western Allies occupied West Berlin, and the Soviets occupied East Berlin. The Western Allies organized the Federal Republic of Germany, which included West Germany and West Berlin, with Bonn as its capital. The Soviet Union responded by establishing the German Democratic Republic, composed of East Germany and East Berlin. Unfortunately, West Berlin lay deep inside hostile East Germany.

In 1948 Berlin became a test for the policy of containment. The Soviets, upset with the Marshall Plan and the unification of West Germany, cut off all highway and rail access between West Berlin and Western Europe, bringing the Communist-bloc nations and the free world to the brink of war. With Truman's leadership, American and British authorities ordered an airlift to provide the people of West Berlin with vital supplies. For nearly a year, the West flew fuel and food to the besieged city. At the height of the airlift, planes were landing every ninety seconds, twenty-four hours a day. So successful was the airlift that the Soviet Union lifted the blockade. The West had scored a major victory in the Cold War without resorting to armed conflict.

Artist's rendering of American flight into Berlin during the airlift

NATO

Containment took a more militaristic turn, however, in 1949. Tensions were high over the Berlin crisis and the inability of the United Nations to provide peace and security. The West sought a more effective means of ensuring its defense against Soviet expansion. The solution was a regional military alliance called the North Atlantic Treaty Organization, or **NATO**. Organized in 1949, NATO originally included the United States, Canada, Great Britain, France, and Italy, along with less powerful nations in the North Atlantic region. In 1952, during the Korean War, NATO added Greece and Turkey. In 1955 West Germany joined the alliance. The Soviet Union reacted by creating its own regional military alliance, the **Warsaw Pact**, which included its Eastern European satellite states.

Arms Race

Also in 1949, the Soviet Union exploded its first atomic bomb, bringing more uncertainty to the Cold War. The West wondered how this achievement would affect Soviet behavior. Since 1945 the United States had exercised restraint with its exclusive control of atomic weapons. Americans feared that the Communists would use their nuclear capability to blackmail and intimidate their foes. The Soviet production of the atomic bomb also marked the beginning of the **arms race**. In January 1950 President Truman ordered the production of the hydrogen bomb, or H-bomb, which was hundreds of times more powerful than the atomic weapons dropped on Japan. Over the next three decades, both the Soviets and the Americans increased their peacetime production of nuclear and conventional weapons. Both sides wanted to maintain a position of strength and prevent the other side from gaining a military edge.

Section Quiz

1. Define the term *Cold War*.
2. List the three reasons the Soviet Union sought to extend its sphere of influence over Eastern Europe.
3. What was the purpose of the Truman Doctrine?
4. What divided city was the focus of a blockade and an airlift?
5. What Western regional military alliance was organized in 1949? What was its Soviet counterpart?

★ Why do you think American authorities failed to provide military support to Hungary in 1956?

II. Spread of Communism

Eastern Europe was not the only critical region in the Cold War era. Bolstered by the Soviet Union, the unrelenting march of communism continued around the world. From the Orient, through the Middle East, in Africa, to Latin America, country after country fell under the yoke of communism. The Soviet empire alone encompassed one-fourth of the world's land area and one-third of its population. During the postwar period, tension between the free world and the Communist bloc flared several times into wars limited to specific geographic areas, often called contained or **limited wars**. Instead of confronting each other directly in these military actions, the United States and the Soviet Union supported other nations to protect and maintain their respective spheres of influence around the world. For example, the Soviets supported North Vietnam against the United States in the 1960s and early 1970s, and the United States aided Afghan forces against the Soviets in the 1980s.

The Fall of China

One of the first areas outside Europe to face the threat of communism was China. After the defeat of Japan, civil war between the Nationalist forces of Chiang Kai-shek and the Communist forces of Mao Zedong resumed in China. (See page 492.) The conflict continued until 1949. Despite receiving more than $2 billion in American aid, the Nationalist forces could not defeat the Communists. As that aid was reduced, the leaders of China, who had relied on American help to defeat the Communists, found themselves militarily and economically vulnerable. By 1949 Mao's forces had captured the major cities of China, sealing the fate of Chiang. The Communist forces drove the Nationalist armies off the mainland and to the nearby island of Formosa (Taiwan).

Mao Zedong with his fourth wife Jiang Qing in 1946

Chiang's collapse was a major blow to American interests in Asia. America had fought World War II, in part, to secure the freedom of China from Japanese militarism, but the country fell to the Communists. For the next thirty years, the United States recognized Taiwan as the "real" China and refused diplomatic ties with the Communist government in Beijing. A huge landmass encompassing the Soviet Union and China was under Communist rule, posing a serious problem for the West during the Cold War era.

The Korean War

Invasion and Reaction

Asia remained a hot spot in the East-West confrontation when Communist North Korea invaded South Korea and sparked the **Korean War** (1950–53). At the close of World War II, Korea had been divided, like Germany, into Communist and non-Communist occupation zones. North Korean forces, trained and financed by the Soviet Union, now sought to unite all of Korea under Communist rule. In June 1950 North Korean forces invaded South Korea, confirming the worst fears of the West—the Communists intended to continue expanding their influence.

President Truman viewed this invasion as another example of Soviet expansion; such aggression, he believed, had to be stopped. Therefore, he called on the free world, led by the United States, to halt the Communist conquest of South Korea. Rather than appealing to Congress for a declaration of war, however, President Truman appealed to the United Nations. Although other nations joined the fight against the North Koreans, the war was primarily an American effort.

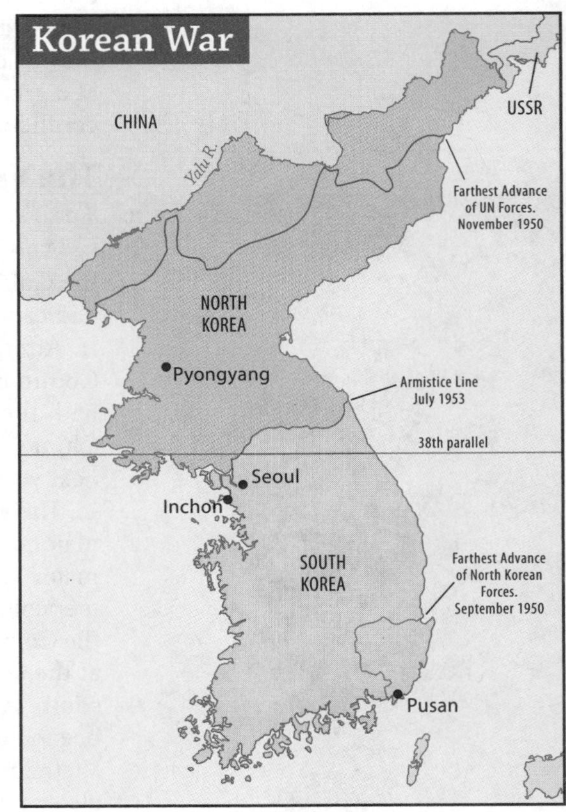

Success and Stalemate

The initial North Korean advance had overrun most of the Korean peninsula. However, under the command of General **Douglas MacArthur**, UN forces composed primarily of American and South Korean troops mounted a daring counteroffensive. Following an amphibious assault at Inchon, UN forces secured South Korea, driving the enemy across the **38th parallel** (the border between North and South Korea). They pursued the enemy deep into North Korea, pushing all the way to the Yalu River (the border between North Korea and Communist China). Just as the UN forces seemed on the verge of victory, waves of Communist Chinese troops swept across the Chinese border, overwhelming MacArthur's army and forcing a retreat to the 38th parallel.

General MacArthur, wanting to gain a military victory, proposed a major assault on North Korea that would have included bombing Chinese bases in Manchuria. Such action would escalate the conflict but would be necessary for ultimate victory. However, the risk

U.S. troops in Korea

of widening the war in Asia and possibly involving both China and the Soviet Union led Truman to fight a limited war with a negotiated settlement. Truman's chairman of the Joint Chiefs of Staff, General Omar Bradley, expressed the administration's sentiment that MacArthur's plan would provoke "the wrong war, at the wrong place, at the wrong time, and with the wrong enemy." Frustrated, MacArthur bypassed regular channels for expressing his views to the government and made his views public. On April 11, 1951, an angry Truman responded by relieving MacArthur of his command. That same year, negotiations to end the war began.

For two years, both hostilities and peace negotiations continued. Finally, in July 1953, an armistice was signed, ending the war. It provided for a demilitarized zone between North and South Korea and called for a conference to settle questions about Korea's future, but the conference was never held. The years of bloodshed ended in a stalemate with the Korean peninsula returning to its prewar divided state. Communism had been "contained"—not defeated—but at a great price. More than a million Koreans and Chinese lay dead from the conflict; about 54,000 Americans would not return home.

Ho Chi Minh

The Vietnam War

The French Phase

Another significant challenge to the containment of communism during the Cold War came in the Southeast Asian country of Vietnam. The Japanese had captured French Indochina, which included Vietnam, during World War II. After the war, the French wanted to recover their colony, but Vietnamese Communist **Ho Chi Minh** declared his country's independence, and a struggle with the French ensued. The Indochinese war increased in significance with China's fall to communism in 1949 and the beginning of the Korean War the next year.

The year after the Korean armistice, the Vietnamese Communists scored a major victory over the French in the **Battle of Dien Bien Phu**, annihilating a major French army. The French, no longer able or willing to reclaim their former colony, sought a negotiated settlement. At the Geneva Conference of 1954, the Communists won a diplomatic victory: Vietnam was divided into two parts at the seventeenth parallel—the Communist north and the non-Communist south. Almost immediately, Communist guerrillas, known as the **Viet Cong**, began subversive activity in the south. Their goal was to weaken the South Vietnamese government so that they could unite Vietnam under a Communist government led by Ho Chi Minh.

To keep South Vietnam and other Asian nations free from communism, the United States, Great Britain, France, and several non-Communist Asian nations formed the Southeast Asia Treaty Organization (**SEATO**) in 1954. In theory, the member nations agreed to "consult" with each other concerning any Communist aggression in that part of the world. In practice, they were pledging military assistance against the Communist menace.

As the chief member of SEATO, the United States began supporting the non-Communist government in South Vietnam economically and militarily. Behind America's foreign policy lay what U.S. president Dwight Eisenhower called the **domino theory**: if Vietnam fell to communism, then other countries of Asia would fall like dominos. The United States was determined that Vietnam would not be that first "domino." Although presidents Eisenhower and Kennedy sent only a limited number of American military advisers to help South Vietnam, their aid marked the beginning of a major military commitment. American leaders had decided to settle the conflict through direct military involvement.

The American Phase

In 1964 three North Vietnamese torpedo boats attacked American destroyers that were in international waters in the Gulf of Tonkin. Through the **Gulf of Tonkin Resolution**, the American Congress authorized President Lyndon Johnson to "take all necessary measures to repel any armed attack against forces of the United States and to prevent further aggression." Congress also authorized the president to take "all necessary steps, including the use of armed force, to assist any member . . . of the Southeast Asia Collective Defense Treaty requesting assistance in defense of its freedom." The number of American military personnel in Vietnam jumped from 23,000 in 1964 to a high of 542,000 in 1969. In 1965 the United States also began bombing Communist supply routes and bases in North Vietnam.

A pivotal year in American involvement in the Vietnam War was 1968. Military officials believed that they were making progress against the Communist enemy. But the Viet Cong demonstrated surprising strength in their **Tet** (New Year) **offensive** on South Vietnamese cities. In that coordinated attack, the Communists temporarily occupied many major cities of South Vietnam and even briefly captured part of the American embassy. In purely military terms, the offensive was a failure; American and South Vietnamese forces drove the Communists back and inflicted heavy casualties. Its propaganda value, however, was enormous. Tet showed that the war was not almost won, as the American government was claiming. For many Americans, frustration increased, and victory seemed even further away.

U.S. troops in Vietnam run across a landing zone to board a waiting helicopter.

President Johnson, faced with growing public dissatisfaction with American involvement in the war, saw no likely prospect of military success through limited war. He decided not to seek reelection, halted the bombing of North Vietnam, and initiated peace talks with the Communists.

Richard Nixon, who won the 1968 presidential election, began a gradual American withdrawal from Vietnam and turned the burden of the fighting over to the South Vietnamese in a program that he called **Vietnamization**. However, to keep pressure on the North, he continued heavy bombing in that region and in the spring of 1970 ordered an invasion of Cambodia to cut Communist supply routes. Nixon finally achieved what he called "peace with honor" by negotiating a peace settlement with the North Vietnamese in January 1973. According to that agreement, U.S. troops evacuated South Vietnam. However, without American troops, the South Vietnamese could neither defeat the Communists nor hold on to their own country. In 1975 the war ended with the achievement of Ho Chi Minh's goal: a unified Vietnam under Communist control. The Communists also took over the neighboring countries of Laos and Cambodia. The domino theory had proved true.

Communism in Africa and Latin America

Africa

As in Asia, Moscow had an opportunity to extend its influence in Africa in the wake of the disintegration of European colonial empires. (See pp. 551–54.) Following World War II, one African country after another gained its independence from European colonial rule. Many of these countries turned to the Soviets for assistance in their struggle against the imperialistic forces of the West. In other countries, Communist forces used the turmoil and discontent to encourage revolution. Communist regimes enjoyed some success in Ethiopia, Mozambique, and Angola. Newly independent countries also sought financial and military assistance from the Soviet Union and its Communist allies. Many African countries soon began to realize that their pro-Soviet alliances came with strings attached. These countries fell prey to a new form of colonial control: Soviet, Cuban, and Chinese Communists. However, the West responded to Communist expansion in Africa with little more than words.

Latin America

The cause of containing the spread of communism moved closer to home for the United States as communism gained a foothold in Latin America. In the decades following World War II, Latin American countries were still faced with social and political inequality, poverty, poor education, and dictatorial governments. As the Communists began to exploit the unsettled conditions in the region, Americans became more alarmed. Some Latin American countries looked to the Soviets instead of the United States for economic assistance in reaction to what they called "Yankee imperialism."

Fidel Castro (seated) during his revolution against the Batista regime in Cuba

In 1959 Communist dictator **Fidel Castro** seized power in Cuba and allied his country with the Soviet Union. Cuban exiles, supported by the U.S. Central Intelligence Agency (CIA), attempted an invasion to oust Castro in 1961, but President Kennedy aborted the American support of the mission, resulting in a fiasco known as the **Bay of Pigs**.

Castro-backed guerrilla groups began stirring up revolutionary activity throughout the region. Communism threatened the Central American countries of Nicaragua, El Salvador, and Panama. In Nicaragua, the Sandinistas, a left-wing group, came to power in 1979 and ruled the country for ten years. No longer was the Communist threat halfway around the world; it was being nurtured in the United States' backyard.

The United States showed stronger resolve in dealing with communism in Latin America than it had in Africa. In 1965 President Johnson sent American Marines into the Dominican Republic to halt a Communist takeover. The CIA supported the overthrow of a Marxist government in Chile in 1973. In the

1980s President Ronald Reagan responded to the Communist threat in Latin America by encouraging free and democratic elections, providing economic assistance to faltering economies, and offering military assistance to countries threatened by Communist aggression. His firm stand ultimately began to pay dividends in the collapse of Marxist regimes south of the U.S. border.

Section Quiz

1. To where did the Nationalist forces of Chiang Kai-shek flee at the end of the Chinese civil war?
2. What country provided a large number of troops to aid the North Koreans during the Korean War?
3. What theory maintains that if one country is allowed to fall to communism, then others near it will also topple?
4. What resolution authorized the American president to take whatever steps necessary to stop further acts of aggression by the Viet Cong?
5. What Latin American country allied itself to the Soviet Union in the 1950s and stirred up revolutionary activity throughout the region? Who was its leader?

★ Why did the United States respond more aggressively to the Communist threat in Latin America than it had in Africa?

III. Showdown Between the Superpowers

"Coexistence" and Tension

Despite the ongoing struggle between the free and Communist worlds over the spread of communism, relations between the United States and the Soviet Union improved during the 1950s. In 1953 Stalin died and **Nikita Khrushchev** (KROOSH chef) emerged as the new leader of the Soviet Union. He and the new American president, Dwight Eisenhower, pursued a course of "**peaceful coexistence**." According to Khrushchev, "The main thing is to keep to the positions of ideological struggle without resorting to arms to prove that one is right."

Top: Nikita Khrushchev
Bottom: Sputnik

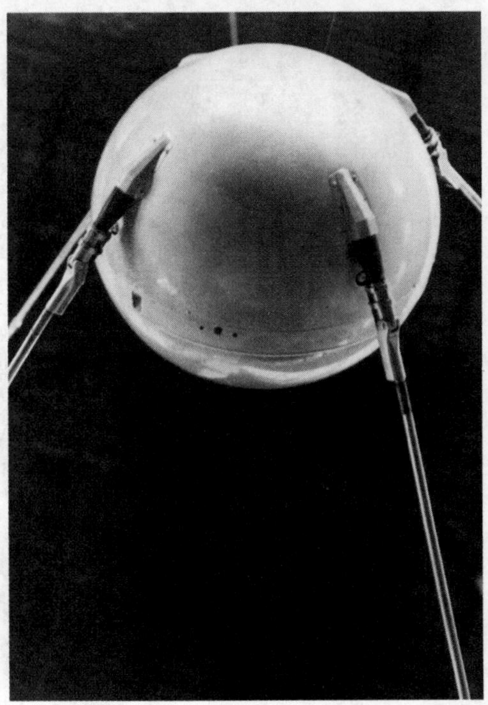

The prospect of peaceful coexistence was short-lived, however. By the late 1950s, East-West relations were once again stormy. In 1957 the Russians launched ***Sputnik***, the first man-made earth satellite, causing great alarm for the people of the United States. Americans looked upon their country as the world leader in science and technology; they now found themselves in second place in the race for space. They particularly feared that the Soviets would use this new capability for a possible nuclear missile strike.

America responded with a renewed resolve to strengthen education (especially in science) and an intense acceleration of its own space program. President Kennedy pledged to put a man on the moon by the end of the 1960s—a promise that the government fulfilled during the Nixon presidency.

While attempting to keep track of Soviet activities, the United States suffered an embarrassing setback in May 1960. Two weeks before a major summit conference between the Western allies and the Soviet Union, an American U-2 reconnaissance (spy) plane piloted by Gary Powers was shot down while flying over Russian territory. Khrushchev used the "**U-2 incident**" as an excuse for breaking off talks at the Paris summit conference. The Soviet defense minister announced that if further flights over the USSR occurred, the Soviets would fire rockets on the base from which the plane took off. Powers was tried by the Russians and found guilty of espionage and imprisoned. He was released in 1962 in a prisoner exchange.

A U-2 spy plane

The U-2 incident was only a mild prelude to clashes between the free world and Soviet totalitarianism in the early 1960s. The first center of tension was Berlin. The constant flow of refugees from Communist East Germany into Western Europe was a living testimony to the failures of communism. Irked and embarrassed, the Soviets in August 1961 built a concrete-and-barbed-wire wall separating East and West Berlin. The **Berlin Wall** became the most recognizable symbol of the Cold War struggle between the free world and communism. In a sense, it was an admission of failure by the Communists, but it kept their most productive citizens within the Communist bloc.

Top: An East German guard leaps over barbed wire to freedom during the early stages of construction of the Berlin Wall in 1961. Bottom: Memorial markers for people shot while trying to escape over the Berlin Wall

In addition to the wall itself, would-be escapees had to contend with more barbed wire, attack dogs, land mines, and armed guards with shoot-to-kill orders. But that did not keep people from trying to escape. Some people tried to climb over, jump over from nearby multistoried buildings, tunnel under, or even sail over in a homemade hot-air balloon, but many died in their attempts.

The Cold War heated up briefly in 1962 when the United States discovered that the Soviets were installing nuclear missiles in Castro's Cuba. In what has been called the **Cuban missile crisis**, President Kennedy insisted that the Soviets remove the missiles. To enforce his demand, he ordered a blockade of the island. Khrushchev backed down and had the missiles removed. The United States and the Soviet Union narrowly avoided a full-scale war.

"Thaws" in the Cold War

In the early 1970s, President Nixon took dramatic steps to end the Cold War. In 1972 he became the first American president to visit mainland China, even though the United States at that time did not recognize the Communist Chinese government. His secretary of state, Henry Kissinger, worked toward a policy of **détente** (relaxation of tensions) with the Soviet Union. Cooperation and summit meetings replaced the harsh language and hostile positions of the superpowers. In

Left: Richard Nixon visits the Great Wall during his historic trip to China in 1972.
Right: President Ronald Reagan

1972 Nixon visited the Soviet Union and signed the Strategic Arms Limitations Talks (**SALT**) treaty with the Soviets, which limited the number of nuclear weapons that each superpower could possess.

The United States entered the 1980s in a weakened position. Economically, recession gripped the country. Militarily, years of disarmament talks and broken Soviet promises left the United States in a precarious position of having to catch up with the military production of its Soviet counterpart. But the American resolve to stand against the threat of communism found a champion in President **Ronald Reagan**, elected in 1980. He was determined to restore America's prestige in the world; at the same time, he denounced the evils of communism. Wanting to deal with the Soviets from a position of strength, Reagan gained support for a buildup of America's military. He initiated a new weapons system, the Strategic Defense Initiative (**SDI**), called "Star Wars" by its detractors, which was designed to use American space, laser, and satellite technology to provide a shield against incoming Soviet missiles.

Although some people in the United States were skeptical of SDI, the Soviets were alarmed. The arms race, which had for so long been balanced in their favor, was now tipping toward the United States. They withdrew from arms-control negotiations, insisting that they would not return until the United States was willing to stop work on SDI. Relations between the two superpowers further deteriorated when in 1983 the Soviets shot down a Korean passenger plane, claiming that they thought it was a spy plane.

True Soviet Intentions

By the end of the 1970s, it was apparent that the Soviets were violating the arms treaties and were still intent on military aggression. This was clearly demonstrated in December 1979 when Soviet troops invaded neighboring Afghanistan. The free world was alarmed over not only the Soviet invasion of Afghanistan but also the possible Soviet threat to the world's oil supplies in the Persian Gulf region.

Collapse of the Soviet Empire

Reasons for Decline

In spite of this renewed confrontation between the superpowers, the relationship between the Soviet Union and the free world began to change. Several factors made this dramatic development possible. One was the growing unrest of Eastern Europeans who suffered under the yoke of Soviet rule. They expressed their opposition to Soviet control through demonstrations and uprisings.

Another factor contributing to change was unsettled leadership in the Soviet Union. In the first five and a half decades following the creation of Communist Russia, the leadership of the Soviet government had been vested mainly in the hands of three brutal and deceptive men: Lenin, Stalin, and Khrushchev. When Khrushchev left office in 1964, a brief power struggle occurred between

Alexi Kosygin and Leonid Brezhnev (1906–82). Kosygin thought that the Soviet Union should relax tensions with the West while strengthening the Soviet economy. Brezhnev, however, favored a hard line toward the West, an extensive development of the Soviet military, and continued export of communism to other countries. Brezhnev's views won out, Kosygin passed into oblivion, and Brezhnev ruled with an iron hand for almost twenty years. But the continuity and longevity of leadership was broken in 1982 with the death of Brezhnev. Over the next three years, two men headed the Soviet state: Yuri Andropov and Konstantin Chernenko, neither of whom was in office for much more than a year. When Ronald Reagan was criticized for his lack of success in negotiating with the Soviets, he replied with exasperation, "Well, they keep dying on me!" This rapid change in Soviet leadership was partially the result of the advancing age of the elite within the Communist Party. A battle began to emerge between the younger, more pragmatic leaders and the aging "hard-liners."

The economic woes so prevalent under the Communist system caused many younger Soviets to recognize the need for reform. Communism had built basic industries in Russia early in the century but could not match the material abundance of the West's consumer society. Soviet farms consistently performed poorly. Central planning rather than market forces guided the economy, and the lack of incentives for Soviet workers resulted in low productivity. In the high-technology, scientific world of the 1980s, the Soviets were lagging far behind the West.

Contributing to the Soviet economic decline was the enormous drain of national wealth spent on defense. The arms race during the Cold War ultimately bankrupted the Soviet Union, especially in the 1980s after Reagan increased the pressure with America's defensive buildup.

Perestroika *and* Glasnost

By the mid-1980s, the defects in the Soviet political and economic system could no longer be hidden. The new Soviet premier, **Mikhail Gorbachev**, called for a wide range of social, political, and economic reforms called ***perestroika***, or "restructuring." Through *perestroika*, he sought to increase industrial productivity; stimulate technological development; restructure the stagnant, inefficient bureaucracy; decentralize management of the economy; and experiment with a free market system.

Disappointment is evident on the faces of Ronald Reagan and Mikhail Gorbachev after their failure to agree on arms reductions. Many credit Reagan's unwillingness to compromise with bringing about the end of the Cold War.

Gorbachev knew that his quest for reform would be in vain unless he could gain public support to put pressure on the "Old Guard" in the Communist Party. In addition, he desperately needed financial assistance from the West to implement his programs. Therefore, he linked to *perestroika* the concept of ***glasnost***, or "openness." Gorbachev hoped to create a more democratic atmosphere in which the Soviet government would be more forthright and accountable to the people. He encouraged open discussions of the problems facing the country and a self-examination of the Soviet state. Under *glasnost*, the Soviet people were encouraged to evaluate and even criticize their leaders to promote better government. But given an opportunity they had not experienced for more than seventy years, the Soviet people voiced opposition to the very foundation of the Soviet state—communism. They did not want to reform that corrupt system; they wanted to abolish it.

Gorbachev, whether purposely or inadvertently, set in motion forces that led to the undoing of the Soviet state and the rejection of communism. As a former White House official said, "Gorbachev has let the genie out of the bottle, and his successors will not be able to stuff it back in."

The Fall of the Berlin Wall

On June 12, 1987, President Reagan stood on the West German side of the Berlin Wall and challenged the Soviet leader: "General Secretary Gorbachev, if you seek peace, if you seek prosperity for the Soviet Union and Eastern Europe, if you seek liberalization: Come here to this gate! Mr. Gorbachev, open this gate! Mr. Gorbachev, tear down this wall!" In November 1989 East German protestors attacked that symbol of Communist isolationism and totalitarianism. They began hammering away at the concrete structure. Soon even the guards, who had once shot people for getting too close to the wall, joined the protestors in tearing it down. Through its breaches, East Germans poured into West Berlin, reuniting with family members and experiencing freedom for the first time. The government of East Germany collapsed, and in 1990 the two Germanys became one nation.

Reagan at the Brandenburg Gate following his challenge to Gorbachev: "Tear down this wall!"

Unrest in Eastern Europe

As the 1980s drew to a close, the Soviet empire began unraveling with amazing speed. Gorbachev's internal reforms encouraged new waves of protest against the Soviet Union in Soviet-dominated Eastern Europe. In Poland, resistance to the Communist government had been maintained by **Solidarity**, a powerful labor union. In 1989 Solidarity-led forces secured the election of the first non-Communist prime minister in Poland since World War II. In 1990 **Lech Walesa**, the head of Solidarity and leader of the movement for reform and resistance, was elected president. Hungary and Czechoslovakia, nations in which the Soviets had crushed democratic movements in 1956 and 1968 respectively, began distancing themselves from the Soviets and repudiated communism.

Hungary and Czechoslovakia opened their borders to the West. This action had an unexpected effect on East Germany, supposedly one of the most prosperous Soviet-bloc countries. The East Germans expressed discontent with the Communist regime by a mass exodus. By hundreds and then thousands, they went around the Berlin Wall, escaping to the West through Hungary and Czechoslovakia. By the time the Communist government tried to act, it was too late. The momentum of protest was out of hand and would not be satisfied until communism and Soviet control were overthrown. The Berlin Wall fell in 1989, and freedom became contagious.

Below left: East German border guards stand idle while hundreds of West Berliners sit and stand on the formerly forbidden area atop the Berlin Wall.
Below: Lech Walesa

Boris Yeltsin, Russia's first freely elected president

Unrest in the USSR

While Soviet leaders witnessed the disintegration of their domination over Eastern Europe, they struggled to maintain control at home. Many internal challenges threatened to tear the country apart. Ethnic unrest in the Soviet republics of Armenia and Azerbaijan led to widespread violence. The Baltic republics of Latvia, Lithuania, and Estonia moved toward separation from the Soviet Union. Reformers, upset at the slow pace of Gorbachev's reforms, called for his resignation. They supported decentralization of government, the independence movements of the republics, a speedier transition toward a free-market economy, and more freedom of expression. Leading the opposition to Gorbachev was **Boris Yeltsin**, an ex-Communist whose support of reform helped him to be elected president of Russia, the largest of the Soviet republics.

In August 1991 the hard-line Communists made a last stand. Soviet Communist leaders detained Gorbachev and announced that he was ill. Furthermore, the Communist Party ordered a six-month "state of emergency." Soviet citizens, led by Yeltsin, resisted, launching a general strike as Yeltsin denounced the action of the hard-liners. The army refused to obey orders to fire on the crowds, and the Communist coup collapsed.

In December 1991 eleven of the Soviet republics declared their independence from the Soviet Union. Following the leadership of Russia, they formed the **Commonwealth of Independent States (CIS)**. Gorbachev was a ruler without a country. On December 25, with little fanfare, he resigned. The Soviet Union dissolved into independent republics, and, with its demise, communism was repudiated.

Section Quiz

1. What term did Khrushchev use to indicate that the United States and the Soviet Union could agree to disagree without resorting to arms?
2. What crisis close to the U.S. border almost led to war between the United States and the Soviet Union in 1962?
3. What word means the "restructuring" of the Soviet government and economy to bring about badly needed reforms?
4. What term means a new spirit of "openness" within the Soviet Union in which the government would be more forthright and accountable to the people?
5. Who was the last leader of the Soviet Union?

★ Why did the Soviet invasion of Afghanistan potentially threaten much of the world's oil supplies?

IV. Aftermath of the Cold War

The collapse of the Soviet Union signaled "a new birth of freedom" for many oppressed peoples. With that freedom, however, came many problems. The people in some countries noticed little difference in their lives; the change in governments was more like the changing of jailers in a prison than the opening of the prison doors. In some cases, not even the jailers changed.

The Former Soviet Union

The events within the former Soviet Union illustrated the blessings and difficulties of the collapse of communism. Some former republics of the USSR—notably the Baltic states of Estonia, Latvia, and Lithuania—wanted little to do with their former overlords. Some of the newly independent republics merely maintained repressive rule under another name. Three republics in particular dominated the new Commonwealth of Independent States. Ukraine and Belarus, located the farthest west, were among the most populous, most

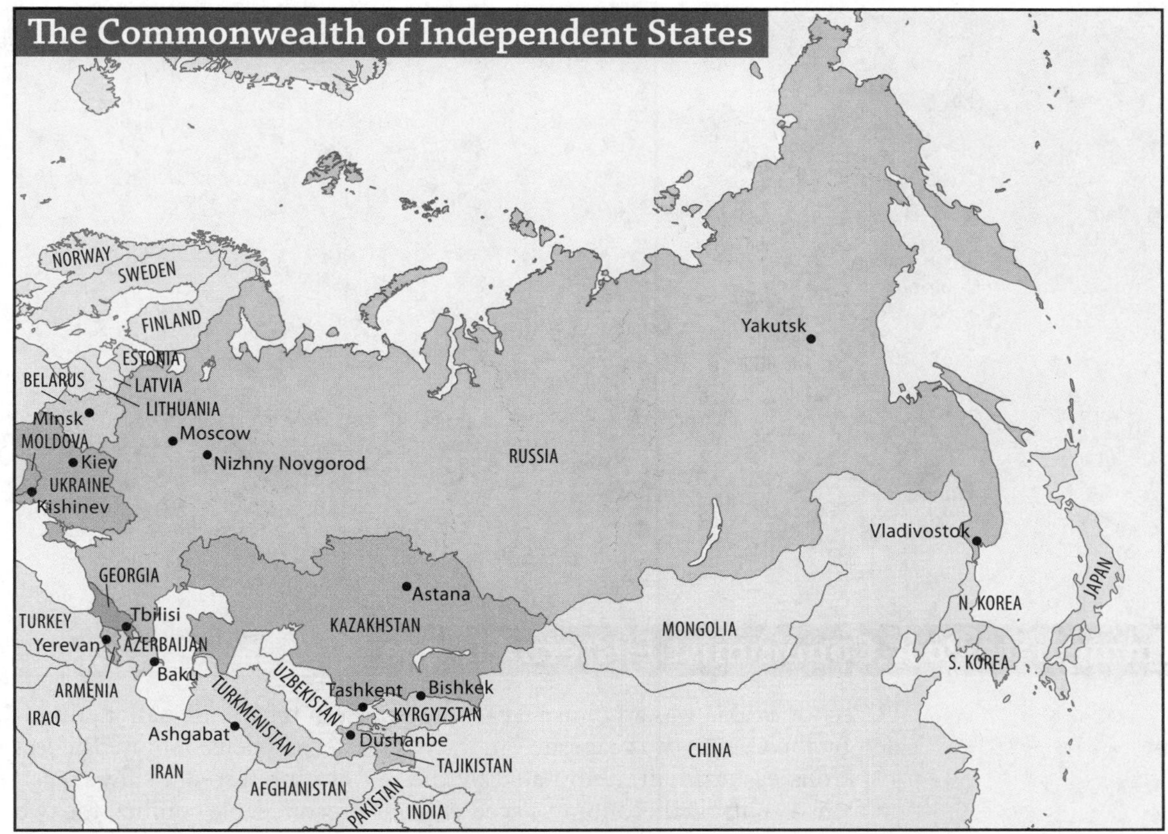

prosperous, and most industrialized of the new republics. Their transition to independence, therefore, was a little easier. The most important of the new republics, however, was Russia. With more than half of the population and more than three-fourths of the landmass of the former Soviet Union, Russia is a notable world power on its own. The United Nations recognized this fact by granting Russia the Soviet Union's seat on the UN Security Council.

The Russians now enjoyed greater freedom than they had at any other time in their history, but the drastic change from communism to a free-market economy created inflation and unemployment. The troubles of the Soviet economy, which had sparked the drastic political changes, did not disappear with the overthrow of communism. With its antiquated technology, inefficient management policies, poor system of transportation, and nearly worthless currency, Russia had to begin almost from scratch to rebuild its economy. President Boris Yeltsin, who had been praised for standing up to the Communist coup in August 1991, found himself roundly criticized for problems that he could do little to solve. Shortages and unrest marked the difficult transition from tyranny to freedom.

Eastern Europe

The former Soviet empire in Eastern Europe likewise endured a difficult transition. Some nations, such as Poland and Hungary, made the transition to democratic government and a free economy without violence, though not always without pain. In other nations, economic suffering was overshadowed by physical suffering. Romania overthrew its Communist leader in violent revolution, executing dictator Nicolae Ceausescu and his wife on Christmas Day 1989. The violence did not stop with that act, however. Riots continued to rend the nation after the Communist overthrow, and Romania found itself exchanging one form of dictatorship for another.

Immediate Post-Communist Eastern Europe

Czechoslovakia was an unusual case. The western half of the nation, dominated by the Czechs, was eager to embrace a Western-style economy. The less prosperous eastern half, dominated by the Slovaks, preferred a slow transition from a controlled economy. Faced with an irreconcilable conflict, the two halves decided peacefully to pursue separate paths. In 1993 Czechoslovakia became two nations: the Czech Republic and Slovakia.

The division of Yugoslavia, however, was not peaceful. Ever since its creation after World War I, Yugoslavia had been an uneasy mixture of different ethnic groups (including Serbs, Croats, and Slovenes) and religious groups (Eastern Orthodox, Roman Catholic, and Muslim). Without the unifying force of the Communist regime, the different regions of that nation began to pursue independence. Slovenia, Croatia, Macedonia, and Bosnia and Herzegovina claimed independence in 1991. Only Serbia and Montenegro remained together under the name "Federal Republic of Yugoslavia." Violence marred the breakup of Yugoslavia. The Serbs particularly resented the reduction of their power and feared for the fate of Serbs, who were now minorities in the other former Yugoslav republics.

The result was bloody civil war. Thousands of civilians died, particularly in Bosnia, where the Serbs sent arms and troops to "protect" Serb minorities—and carve out more territory for the Serb-dominated government of Yugoslavia. To help knit the acquired regions to Yugoslavia, the Serbs began "cleansing" those areas of non-Serbs, particularly Muslims. By "cleansing," they meant the forced removal or even killing of non-Serbs in the conquered regions. Anarchy reigned even as the UN sought a peaceful solution. Described as the "powder keg of Europe" before World War I, the Balkans had again become a center of terror and violence by the end of the twentieth century. Years of Communist rule had done little to bring a sense of unity to that troubled region.

Section Quiz

1. Which of the former Soviet republics became the most important player in world politics? Who was its first president?
2. Over what European country did dictator Nicolae Ceausescu rule? How did his rule end?

3. After the collapse of communism in Eastern Europe, what former Communist nation broke into several smaller republics and engaged in ethnic civil war?

★ Why has the Balkans been described as the "powder keg of Europe"?

V. Other Post–World War II Developments

China

After taking over the mainland from the Nationalist government in 1949, Mao Zedong and his Communist forces established a cruel dictatorship in China. Thousands of people who were considered "dangers" to the Communist state—former Nationalists, intellectuals, businessmen, Christians—were sent to prison camps or executed. Like the Soviet Communists in the 1920s, the Chinese sought to establish an atheistic state through force and repression.

Seeing the need to compete with the free world and the Soviet Union, Mao launched great crusades to modernize and thoroughly revolutionize China. With the "**Great Leap Forward**" in the late 1950s, Mao sought to improve Chinese agriculture and bring the steel industry up to Western standards. Instead, his ill-planned reforms wrecked the Chinese steel industry and caused a famine that resulted in the deaths of twenty to thirty million Chinese. In the late 1960s, Mao launched the "**Cultural Revolution**," an attempt to stir up zeal for radical communism. Young Communists, called the Red Guard, held rallies and indulged in acts of violence designed to promote revolutionary fervor. They disrupted the Chinese educational system until it could be "purified" in an acceptably radical manner. The result of the Cultural Revolution was civil chaos and economic decline. Mao abandoned it after only a few years, and he allowed his former radical supporters to be suppressed.

Propaganda poster promoting Mao Zedong and the Cultural Revolution

Western leaders were somewhat relieved when Mao died in 1976. The Communist leaders who succeeded him—Deng Xiaoping, Hu Yaobang, and Zhao Ziyang—seemed to be more "realistic" in their rule. China's Communist overlords allowed limited free-market reforms and scaled back some of Mao's more repressive measures.

The true nature of the Communist state had not changed, however, as was shown tragically in 1989. In a year when communism seemed to be collapsing around the world, a reform movement sprang up among Chinese students. They called for the reform of the Chinese state, particularly the granting of greater political freedom. In April 1989 a group of students began a demonstration in **Tiananmen Square** in the Chinese capital of Beijing. More and more people joined the demonstration, and people around the world watched on television as the students protested repressive rule. News of the event quickly spread around the world, making it difficult for the Communists to misinform the world or "spin" the events in their favor. Then the Communist authorities cracked down. In early June tanks rolled into Tiananmen Square. More than two thousand people were killed as the government quashed the student movement. There was no rebirth of freedom in China as there had been elsewhere in the former Communist bloc. The students, though, had demonstrated that strong dissent still existed within Communist China despite forty years of oppression.

Often overlooked in many histories of China is the violent persecution that Chinese Christians have endured under Communism. Many stories have emerged of arrests, imprisonment, and brutal treatment of Christians by the

A lone Chinese student challenges tanks in Tiananmen Square. Shortly after this photo was taken, Communist troops quashed the demonstration, killing more than two thousand demonstrators.

Communist Chinese. However, many of those Christians have stood firm and spread the gospel even under the most trying circumstances. Despite harsh treatment by authorities, the church in China has emerged triumphant and is thriving. Chinese Christians are now estimated to number over one hundred million and continue to multiply even as the Communist authorities harass and imprison the leaders of the church.

Japan

Like West Germany, Japan made great strides politically and economically after World War II. General MacArthur headed the occupation government that oversaw the rebuilding of the devastated nation. When Emperor Hirohito publicly repudiated claims to deity, MacArthur became the real leader of the Japanese nation. Launching a massive reform movement, he called for women's suffrage, promoted the formation of labor unions, requested Christian missionaries to come to Japan, and, ultimately, imposed a new constitution on Japan. The result was a stable democracy, a remarkable contrast to Japan's recent militaristic tradition.

With the removal of the occupation government, Japan proved competent to rule itself. The Liberal-Democratic Party took control in 1955 and held power continuously until 1993. Political stability contributed to striking economic growth. In addition to providing billions of dollars in financial aid to Japan, America supplied technology, markets, and raw materials for a strong industrial base. Military protection by the West allowed Japan to pour its wealth into industrial development. (The new constitution strictly forbade Japan to have an army.)

Japanese high-tech bullet train

In addition, Japan's own hard work and a superior educational system pushed the Japanese to the economic forefront. The Japanese excelled in heavy industry. In automobile manufacturing, their well-built, fuel-efficient cars allowed the nation to displace the United States as the leader in auto production. The Japanese pioneered the development of electronics by stressing the use of transistors and other technological innovations. In the 1950s critics joked that "Made in Japan" was a synonym for cheap, shoddy products; by the 1980s Japan was cornering the world market in high-quality televisions, stereos, radios, and other electronic equipment.

Japanese companies such as Mitsubishi, Toyota, Sony, and Nintendo became household words around the world. The Japanese passenger rail system became the envy of the industrialized world.

Japan still faced problems, however. Foreign nations resented the Japanese government's high tariffs and trade restrictions that protected Japanese industries from competition. Although such actions did protect Japan, they prompted Japanese trading partners to retaliate with their own trade barriers. Still, the rise of a prosperous, democratic Japan from the rubble of totalitarianism and military defeat was one of the great success stories of the postwar era.

Section Quiz

1. Who was the first major leader of Communist China? With what program did he attempt to improve Chinese agriculture and industry in the 1950s?
2. Where in Beijing was a student rally for reform held?
3. Who headed the occupation government of postwar Japan?

★ Why did the Chinese Communist rulers respond violently to the student protests?

The United States

Some experts predicted economic decline in the United States after World War II. Instead, what followed was an economic boom. Consumers demanded items that they could not purchase during the war. They had sacrificed consumer goods for the greater good of the war effort; now they wanted to make up for it. One writer nicknamed American culture "the affluent society" because of its enormous wealth and productivity.

Along with this economic prosperity was a continuation of Franklin Roosevelt's big-government policies. This trend continued with Lyndon Johnson's **Great Society** in the 1960s. Like some earlier leaders, Johnson assumed that American wealth and government action could solve the nation's problems. He spent billions of dollars on federal health, housing, and education programs to fight what he called the "war on poverty" in hopes of creating the ideal welfare state. American technology outstripped that of all other nations and was symbolized by America's successful landing on the moon in 1969. The United States was the undisputed leader among nations during the first twenty years following the war.

Martin Luther King Jr.

Nonetheless, internal difficulties troubled the nation. Many black Americans still did not receive equal treatment. Launching what became known as the **civil rights movement**, African Americans began to make significant gains in politics and society. The U.S. Supreme Court declared segregation of public schools by race to be unconstitutional. Martin Luther King Jr., the movement's most visible spokesman, emerged in the 1950s and 1960s to lead a crusade for voting rights and equal access to public facilities for blacks. Congress passed the 1964 Civil Rights Act and the 1965 Voting Rights Act. But violence also erupted as different ethnic groups clashed during civil rights protests. Riots tore apart poor sections of large American cities.

Added to the ethnic conflict was a generational conflict. In the 1960s many young people revolted against authority—parental, educational, and governmental. Long hair, rock music, drugs, and sexual immorality symbolized their revolt. The Vietnam War particularly divided the older and younger

Reagan's Legacy

Whereas America was in an economic malaise when Reagan took office, by the end of his administration, his policies had reduced inflation to single digits, lowered interest rates, and decreased unemployment. The economy was booming. He strengthened the military and pursued a vigorous and consistent foreign policy, restoring America's image abroad. Reagan defeated attempts to establish Communist footholds in Latin America and encouraged the Soviet Union to be more open with both its own people and the international community. He also rejuvenated the freedom philosophy both in the United State and around the world, offering hope to both struggling capitalist countries and the developing nations of the third world.

generations. Demonstrations against the war sometimes ended in bloodshed, and many young men refused to serve in the armed forces, "dodging" the draft by fleeing to Canada.

Vietnam did more than divide Americans; it diminished their prosperity. Johnson attempted to pay for the war without cutting the massive spending needed to build his Great Society. Before long, economic stagnation set in, and the United States suffered high unemployment and high inflation in the 1970s.

A national drift occurred in leadership as well. Johnson's successor, Richard Nixon, was forced to resign in 1974 amid charges of political corruption. His successors, Gerald Ford and Jimmy Carter, were uninspiring, and voters rejected them. The apparently growing military strength of the Soviet Union seemed only to heighten the perception that the United States was on the decline.

A change occurred, however, with the election of Ronald Reagan in 1980. He was the first president since the 1930s to question the premise of the welfare state. He sought to reduce government regulation and lower taxes, and Congress obliged with huge tax cuts. Reagan enjoyed the support of religious and social conservatives who were offended by the radicalism of the 1960s. He supported issues important to such conservatives, notably an end to legalized abortion.

Reagan's successor, George H. W. Bush, continued Reagan's policies. During his term, the Soviet Union collapsed, and he led a successful war against Iraqi dictator Saddam Hussein. Yet, in 1992, a sluggish economy and an uninspiring campaign resulted in the rejection of Bush in favor of the Democrat **Bill Clinton**.

Above: President Bill Clinton
Below: West German chancellor Konrad Adenauer

Western Europe

The postwar era saw the decline of the remaining dictatorships in Western Europe. When Spanish dictator Francisco Franco, who had seized power in the Spanish Civil War in the 1930s (see Chapter 22), died in 1975, Spain restored the monarchy under King Juan Carlos. The new king restored democratic government to the nation, paving the way for Spain to join the European Community in 1985.

The end of the dictators did not mean the end of strong rulers in Europe. Within the democracies, leaders with strong views and even stronger character dominated the politics of their countries as well as the Continent.

Germany

Germany traveled a remarkable road after the war—from a ruined shell of a nation to a world economic giant. The Cold War, however, divided Germany. West Germany had the fastest-growing economy in Europe by the 1950s, in large part because of the policies of Chancellor **Konrad Adenauer**. The mayor of Cologne from 1917, Adenauer had been dismissed from his office by the Nazis in 1933. In 1944 the Gestapo put him in prison, where the warden told him, "Now, please do not commit suicide. You would cause me no end of trouble. You're sixty-eight years old, and your life is over anyway."

Adenauer's life was far from over, however. In 1949 he became the first chancellor of West Germany, an office he held for fourteen years. The chancellor fashioned what was called the *Wirtschaftswunder* ("economic miracle"). Rejecting socialism and following free-market principles, he rebuilt Germany. Income tripled while he was chancellor, and by 1955 the nation was producing more goods than it had before the war, despite West Germany's being only about half the size of prewar Germany. Although not a military power, West Germany became an economic superpower.

France

France experienced two new governments in the decades after World War II. After the liberation of the French from the Nazis in 1944, **Charles de Gaulle**, leader of the Free French during the war, led a provisional government until 1946. He angrily rejected the new constitution for the Fourth Republic, however, because it did not give sufficient power to the president. De Gaulle retired, and his predictions about the weaknesses of the Fourth Republic proved true. Multiple parties dominated the legislative branch, and a succession of cabinets made it difficult to solve major problems. The French army, humiliated by the Germans in 1940, sought to restore its honor by holding on to the empire. Instead, the army endured bitter defeat at the hands of Vietnamese Communists and had to pull out of Indochina in 1954. In 1956 the French joined the British and the Israelis in an attempt to recapture the Suez Canal from Egypt, but international opposition forced France and Britain to relinquish their gains, further humiliating the French.

French president Charles de Gaulle

Following a crisis in Algeria in 1958, the French army forced the government to recall de Gaulle. He led the French to replace the Fourth Republic with the **Fifth Republic**, a government with a constitution that provided for a strong president. De Gaulle and the new government brought stability and order to France. It became the leading military power of the Continent and was surpassed by only West Germany in economic might. After de Gaulle's retirement in 1969, his system endured. Even the 1981 election of François Mitterand, the first socialist president of the Fifth Republic, did not shake the nation. Since the French Revolution in 1789, the Third Republic (1870–1940) is the only French government to have lasted longer than the Fifth Republic.

Great Britain

The postwar era was a period of transition and decline for Great Britain. The sun finally set on the British Empire as her once-glorious holdings began to slip away. India, Pakistan, and Burma gained independence in the late 1940s, and by the 1960s few territories remained under British rule.

British prime minister Margaret Thatcher

The weak British economy was not helped when the Labour Party took power after World War II and began to pursue socialist policies to build a welfare state. While the British people welcomed greater personal security through reforms such as a national health insurance plan, they learned too late that the cost included higher taxes and stifling government regulation. Labour "nationalized" many major industries, such as coal and the railways. Government control resulted in inefficient industries, which reduced Britain's competitiveness.

In 1975 **Margaret Thatcher** became leader of the Conservative Party and campaigned against Great Britain's "slither and slide toward socialism." Voters swept her and her party into power in 1979, marking a sense of renewal in the nation. Thatcher sold many of the nationalized industries to private investors and slashed the nation's tax rates, spurring economic growth. She confronted the powerful labor unions, which were stifling economic growth, and broke their power. Thatcher appropriately became known as the "Iron Lady."

In foreign affairs Thatcher supported the anti-Communist policies of the Reagan administration. She also led Britain to victory in a war against Argentina over the Falkland Islands in 1982. To her opponents and those who warned of possible defeat in the war, Thatcher responded, "Defeat—I do not recognize the meaning of the word." Likewise, when Iraq invaded Kuwait in 1991, she provided invaluable support to the international coalition created by George Bush.

Winning three elections and holding office from 1979 to 1990, Thatcher served longer than any other British prime minister since the early nineteenth century. Next to Winston Churchill, she is considered by many people to have been the most important British political leader in the twentieth century.

Section Quiz

1. Who was the most important leader of the American civil rights movement?
2. What new French government arose in 1958? Who was its first president?
3. What word refers to a government's taking over a private business and making it part of the government?
4. What two nations fought over control of the Falkland Islands in 1982? Which nation won?

★ Why was Margaret Thatcher able to govern Britain for eleven years and make radical changes in the country?

Chapter 23 Review

Making Connections

1–5. Why was this period in history referred to as the Cold War? List five events that could have led to another major war.

Developing History Skills

1. Briefly summarize the consequences of Mao Zedong's victory over Chiang Kai-shek in China. (You may want to refer to Chapter 22 to help answer this question.)
2. Review the reasons for the collapse of the Soviet Union.

Thinking Critically

1. Assess the decision of President Truman to relieve General MacArthur of his command during the Korean War.
2. Why was the United States in such a weak military position when Ronald Reagan became president?

Living in God's World

1. The Soviet Union was a military threat to the United States during much of the last half of the twentieth century, yet it fell swiftly. What are some biblical reasons the Soviet Union may have fallen so quickly?
2. During the Cold War, Americans championed the ideals of liberty rather than oppressive communism. What are some of the dangers that America faces in its emphasis on freedom?

People, Places, and Things to Know

iron curtain
Cold War
Truman Doctrine
containment
Marshall Plan
NATO
Warsaw Pact
arms race
limited wars
Korean War
Douglas MacArthur
38th parallel
Ho Chi Minh
Battle of Dien Bien Phu
Viet Cong
SEATO
domino theory
Gulf of Tonkin Resolution
Tet offensive
Vietnamization
Fidel Castro
Bay of Pigs
Nikita Khrushchev
peaceful coexistence
Sputnik
U-2 incident
Berlin Wall
Cuban missile crisis
détente
SALT
Ronald Reagan
SDI
Mikhail Gorbachev
perestroika
glasnost
Solidarity
Lech Walesa
Boris Yeltsin
Commonwealth of Independent States (CIS)
Great Leap Forward
Cultural Revolution
Tiananmen Square
Great Society
civil rights movement
Bill Clinton
Konrad Adenauer
Charles de Gaulle
Fifth Republic
Margaret Thatcher

24

To the Present

I. Struggling Democracies

II. Communist and Post-Communist Countries

III. Developing Nations

IV. The Middle East

Cape Town, South Africa

Since the end of the Cold War, several trends have emerged. One is **globalization**: nations now tend to have an international focus rather than a purely national focus. The United States remains a leader in the West, while European states have struggled to play a significant role. In the East, China and India have become leading economic and political powers.

A second trend is the spread of democracy. Having survived in many of the former Communist countries, democracy has now spread to countries in Africa and Asia. An exception to this trend is Communist China, which has staunchly resisted democratic movements. Nevertheless, Communist China has emerged from self-imposed isolation to develop trade ties with the West.

The advancement of Christianity around the world is a third trend. The most significant growth has occurred in developing countries, though persecution often accompanies this growth.

Finally, even though the Cold War ended more than twenty years ago, conflict remains. Conflicts in this new era have tended to be regional, as evidenced by flare-ups in parts of Africa, Eastern Europe, and the Middle East. In addition, acts of terrorism—the use of indiscriminate violence, or the threat of its use, for political ends—have been on the rise. Terrorism, often in the form of militant Islam, has replaced communism as the primary international threat.

I. Struggling Democracies

In the years following the Cold War, the industrialized nations enjoyed relative peace and prosperity. Although minor local conflicts occurred in the world, no general confrontation raged on the scale of the East-West rivalry of the Cold War era. Both democracy and capitalism rode a wave of popularity and success across much of the globe. For example, many countries in Eastern Europe embraced political freedom for the first time in generations. With trade barriers lowered, the economies of the major nations generally enjoyed significant growth. Even leaders of nations that had nominally liberal or left-wing governments initially adopted some conservative programs. However, many European states, along with the United States, continued to appease a growing percentage of their citizens with expensive social programs. In addition, the threat of terrorism at the beginning of the twenty-first century has begun to shift the focus from political issues to questions of security and survival. The global economy is dependent on free trade and sound currency. Anything that threatens either will have disastrous results for all.

United States

Economic problems of the early 1990s made it challenging for President George H. W. Bush to continue Reagan's bold legacy, which had emphasized tax and spending cuts. Facing a recession and budget deficit, President Bush signed off on congressional tax increases despite his pledge not to do so. In 1992, following an uninspiring campaign, Bush lost to the Democratic nominee, Bill Clinton, who made the economy the central issue of the election.

During the Clinton years, the government made or attempted to make changes that would have long-term consequences. Under the leadership of Hillary Clinton, a government task force attempted to impose socialized medicine under the title of "universal health care." Dubbed "Hillary Care" by its opponents, the plan drew increasing opposition, and the Clintons were forced to abandon it. Clinton also sought to open the military to homosexuals. Again, many groups opposed the effort. The compromise "Don't Ask, Don't Tell"

Top: President George W. Bush
Middle: President Barack Obama
Bottom: British prime minister Tony Blair

became the standard until it was ended by President Barack Obama in 2011. Various scandals surfaced during Clinton's two terms in office, and many people viewed Clinton's presidency as a reflection of the declining morals of the nation.

The economy continued to grow, and foreign affairs appeared to have little impact on people's daily lives. As a result, Americans faced the new millennium with great hopes. The 2000 presidential election, however, proved controversial. **George W. Bush**, son of the previous President Bush, battled former vice president Albert Gore in one of the closest presidential elections in American history. Gore won the popular vote, but the electoral vote hung on disputed results in Florida. After a month of heated debate, the Supreme Court ended the uncertainty with a legal decision favoring Bush, who, with Florida's electoral votes, won the election.

Eight months after Bush was sworn into office, the 9/11 attack occurred. This assault on America by Muslim terrorists, in large part, set the course of Bush's time in office. In addition, Bush urged tax reform, and Congress passed what became known as the "Bush tax cuts." In this pro-business climate, the nation enjoyed reduced unemployment (below 5%) and steady economic growth, although deficits continued to grow due to increased congressional spending. Bush won reelection in 2004 primarily because of popular support for his anti-terror policies, a thriving economy, and his advocacy of traditional moral values.

By the end of Bush's second term in office, many people in America looked for new leadership. Reasons for the discontent included rejection of moderate Republican policies and economic concerns. In 2008 the nation elected **Barack Obama** by a wide margin over Republican candidate John McCain. Obama promised to bring about fundamental changes and consistently worked to bring about these alterations. However, a majority of Americans were unhappy with the modifications proposed or enacted by Obama. Many expressed concern that he was leading the country in the wrong direction, while others complained that Obama had not accomplished the transformation that he promised. The 2012 election would be pivotal in determining the long-term direction of the United States.

Great Britain

Though conservatism continued to dominate western Europe after the Cold War, Great Britain lost much of the dynamism it had shown under Thatcher. In 1990 the Conservatives chose John Major to be their leader and prime minister. Major shared Thatcher's commitment to the American alliance but wanted greater integration with the European Union. Major never developed a strong popular following like that of his predecessor.

In May 1997 **Tony Blair** and the Labour Party crushed the Conservatives, and a new era began for Great Britain. Blair, like Clinton, his contemporary in the United States, sought a pragmatic, centrist approach to politics because the British public favored it, and it made Blair and the Labour Party more acceptable to the business community. Blair's **"New Labour" Party** distanced itself from unions and stopped calling for nationalization of British business and industry. His government maintained the spending limits of the Conservative era and limited the rate of expansion of the welfare state. The British economy remained strong, and Blair's Labour Party won its second major victory in 2001. Blair stepped down as prime minister in 2007.

Gordon Brown served briefly as prime minister, representing the Labour Party. His austere reforms to strengthen Britain's financial standing resulted in a dramatic loss of popularity. In 2010 the Conservative Party returned to power when its candidate, David Cameron, won the national election, in part by agreeing to a coalition with the Liberal Democrat Party.

Britain continues its attempt to balance a welfare state with the need to maintain a viable economy. As a result, increasing welfare benefits, generous retirement for government workers, and universal health care continue to drain the national coffers. In addition, the quality of health care has declined as socialized medicine in Britain has resulted in reduced services and longer waits for medical care.

Some are concerned that the presence of a large Muslim minority also threatens the stability of the nation. Some Muslim leaders in Britain demand the right to practice sharia law, and many Muslim citizens have chosen not to assimilate. Some Muslim communities have also become a breeding ground for terrorism.

Germany

Conservative leaders in West Germany built on Konrad Adenauer's foundation and made the nation the dominant force in Western Europe. German leadership continues to shift between a conservative socialist approach and a more aggressive socialist style.

In 1982 conservatives returned to power with Helmut Kohl as chancellor and dominated German politics for the next sixteen years. A strong ally of the United States, he allowed Ronald Reagan to place missiles in West Germany, an act that the Soviet Union perceived as a major threat. Kohl also played a key role in Europe as he developed, with the emergence of the European Union, strong ties with France.

In 1998 Gerhard Schroeder, a socialist, became the next chancellor. Like Clinton and Major, Schroeder did not make any major changes. However, he failed to resolve continuing economic problems as Germany struggled through a recession with a lingering high unemployment rate. As a result, Schroeder and his party failed to receive a majority vote in 2005.

Angela Merkel assembled a majority by combining her Christian Democratic Union (CDU) party with two other parties and became the chancellor in 2005. Her stated goal was to reduce unemployment. Merkel was consistently pro-market and supported changes in German law to allow companies to lay off workers and increase working hours in order to become more competitive. While her decisions were not without controversy, Merkel led Germany to renewed economic prosperity and easily won reelection in 2009.

France

In 1981 François Mitterrand became the first socialist president of the Fifth Republic. He nationalized some industries and instituted social reforms. When inflation and unemployment returned, however, he abandoned some of his programs and returned to more conservative methods. Mitterrand served until 1995 when he stepped down because of cancer from which he died the following year.

In 1995 Jacques Chirac became president and returned France to a centrist government. Like Mitterrand, he governed with both conservative and socialist prime ministers. The French shortened the presidential term from seven to five years, and Chirac won reelection in 2002. Chirac chose not to run for a third term, and the French elected **Nicolas Sarkozy** as the president of France in 2007. Sarkozy became a one-term predident when he lost to an openly socialist opponent in 2012.

In recent decades, France has had difficulty finding its role in the world. During the Cold War, it tried to be neutral and speak for nations not aligned

Top: David Cameron became Britain's prime minister in 2010.
Middle: Angela Merkel became chancellor of Germany in 2005.
Bottom: Nicolas Sarkozy became president of France in 2007.

Following an earthquake near Japan in 2011, a tsunami caused extensive loss of life and destruction of property.

with either of the superpowers. Since then, however, France and Germany have dominated the European Union and have tried to counter the international power of the United States. The French worry about the decline of French language and culture. Fiercely independent, and with a growing Muslim population, the French have resisted helping the United States fight terrorism.

Japan

After World War II, Japan experienced a remarkable economic recovery. Although it is still one of the leading economies in the world, it has had significant problems in recent years. From 1990 to the early twenty-first century, Japan suffered its longest economic downturn since 1945. Critics blamed bureaucratic regulation and recommended greater economic freedom. Bad loans during the good economic times of the 1970s and 1980s weakened banking in Japan. Competition from South Korea, Taiwan, Hong Kong, and Singapore also hurt Japan's economy. Ironically, the success of those Asian neighbors came from their imitating Japanese industry.

In addition, Japan faced traditional challenges. Its 127.4 million people (2010) live on a relatively small area of land, and its natural resources are limited. The Japanese must import most of their food and raw materials for their factories. In addition, trade with the world remains vital for both importing and exporting. If the Asian, European, or American economies suffer, so does the Japanese economy.

However, Japan stands apart from most of Asia, not only as a democracy and a major economic power but also because its culture and society have certain special characteristics. Most Asian countries are very traditional, but urbanization is changing Japan rapidly. Young people, moving to the cities for work, often leave their rural customs behind. When they marry, they establish their own homes rather than living with their extended families, and Western influences, especially American popular culture, are strong.

Section Quiz

1. What judicial body settled the controversy over the presidential election in the United States in 2000?
2. Who received the most popular votes during the U.S. presidential race in 2000?
3. Who led the Labour Party in Britain to victory in 1997?
4. Who gained a majority and was elected to serve as chancellor of Germany in 2005?

★ Why has France had trouble finding its role in the world?

II. Communist and Post-Communist Countries

The end of the Cold War resulted in a great decline in the influence of communism and an expanded influence of various forms of democracy. However, communism remains a repressive and brutal reality for more than a billion people.

China

China remains the only major Communist nation, with North Korea, Vietnam, and Cuba continuing their totalitarian ways in its shadow. Since the 1990s, despite the challenge of having a population of more than one billion, China has developed one of the largest and fastest-growing economies in the world. This growth is due primarily to increased world trade and foreign investment.

Beginning in the 1990s, China's leaders embraced modernization and some capitalism so their nation could improve its standard of living. In 1997 Great Britain's control of Hong Kong ended, and it passed into China's hands. The Chinese shrewdly let Hong Kong keep its capitalist economy, one of the best in Asia, while exercising firm political control. In 2001 China joined the World Trade Organization, another measure of its economic progress. Wal-Mart opened its first store in China in 1996, and the company became a major employer through its 354 retail units by the end of 2011. So-called "big box" stores, including Home Depot and Best Buy, opened several stores in China with mixed results.

The Chinese military benefited from the growing wealth of the nation. The military made significant advances in missile technology, purchased and refitted Soviet aircraft carriers, and built stealth fighters and bombers. While much of this technology was appropriated from the West, the Chinese have aggressively used this technology to increase their political and military clout in Asia.

An Unlikely Alliance

China's neighbor, Taiwan, to which the non-Communists fled in 1949, remains democratic and capitalist and is, along with Hong Kong, an Asian success story. While living under an ongoing threat of invasion from mainland China, the Taiwanese have transformed their economy into what has become known as the "Taiwan Miracle." This tiny island nation has developed a dynamic economy that has averaged eight percent growth for the past thirty years. Thus, despite the official animosity of Communist China, a large number of Taiwanese business people and their families live on the mainland and play a role in the commercial growth of China.

One of the ongoing tragedies is China's attempt to stabilize its population growth. In the 1970s the Communist government instituted a single-child policy. This innocent-sounding policy has resulted in the murder through abortion of up to thirteen million Chinese babies each year for the last forty years. One unintended consequence of this slaughter has been the imbalance of male and female babies born. Since many Chinese families prefer a male child so that the parents will be provided for in their final years, gender-selective abortion resulted in the murder of many Chinese baby girls. There are now millions more Chinese men looking for wives than there are Chinese women to meet this need. It is projected that by 2025 China will have 96.5 million men in their twenties but only 80.3 million young women. One of the long-term consequences of this imbalance is that by 2050 there will not be enough workers to support an aging Chinese society. Yet the use of abortion continues as official policy in China.

Chinese aircraft carrier purchased from the former Soviet Union

In addition, Communist China continues to persecute religious groups, from Christians and Tibetan Buddhists to sects such as the Falun Gong. However, despite growing persecution of Christians and brutal prison conditions imposed upon believers, the number of Christians in China has exceeded one hundred million and shows no sign of decline. One of the reasons for official concern about the growing church is that there are now more Christians than Communists (estimated to be around eighty million) in Communist China.

Top: Russian president Vladimir Putin
Above: Russian prime minister Dmitry Medvedev

Russia

During the 1990s Russia struggled economically and politically. After the collapse of the Soviet Union in 1991, Russia's president, Boris Yeltsin, led the nation in the transition from communism to capitalism and democracy. He encountered the enormous task of privatizing state-owned businesses and industries and preparing Russia for international trade. During this difficult transition Yeltsin remained personally popular, and in 1996 Russians reelected him. In 1999, however, Yeltsin resigned because of bad health and suspicions about corruption. He named his prime minister, **Vladimir Putin**, a former KGB (Soviet secret police) official, acting president.

In 2000 Russians elected Putin president, and he continued reforms, making steady progress in a few areas. Under Putin's leadership the Russian economy grew. Development of gas and oil reserves created great wealth and raised the living standards of many in Russia. However, Putin also used undemocratic tactics, such as putting opponents in prison and controlling the media. Putin strengthened the government in Moscow and steadily moved toward greater centralized control.

Putin temporarily improved Russia's relations with the West and cooperated somewhat with the United States in the war on terror although he opposed the war in Iraq. During Putin's first tenure, Russia tolerated the expansion of NATO into Eastern Europe. He remained popular and easily won reelection in 2004. Forced by constitutional limits to step down as president in 2008, Putin was appointed Prime Minister of Russia by his successor, Dmitry Medvedev. In 2012 Putin again ran for president and easily won. Then Putin appointed Medvedev to his former position as prime minister. Despite Putin's victory, he faces growing opposition and the challenges of a sluggish economy.

Eastern Europe

At the beginning of the twenty-first century, Eastern Europe continued to be a source of both hope and despair. Freedom from communism meant a better life for some people but strife and trouble for others. One measure of economic progress was the entry of several countries into the European Union in 2004.

Poland, after suffering at the hands of first Nazi Germany and then the Soviet Union, achieved independence in the 1990s after it embraced capitalism and democracy. In 1993 the Social Democrats (former Communists) won elections and maintained Poland's commitment to a market economy. The Polish economy grew and attracted foreign investment at a rate remarkable by Eastern European standards but still behind the industrialized nations of the West. The Czech Republic also enjoyed some economic success, but many of its neighbors—including Slovakia, Bulgaria, and Romania—suffered terribly. Albania continues to be the poorest country on the continent but is beginning to attract foreign investment.

Another measure of progress is the expansion of NATO in Eastern Europe. Created to prevent the advance of communism, NATO now provides a means for the West to coordinate military action where necessary. Poland, the Czech Republic, Slovakia, Hungary, Estonia, Latvia, Lithuania, Bulgaria, Romania, and Slovenia are now members.

In the 1990s NATO intervened in the former Yugoslavia to stop ethnic and religious war between the dominant Serbs and other groups. Serbia, populated by Orthodox Christians and Slavs, had dominated the area for centuries and tried to maintain its dominance over Muslims and Catholics there, even if it meant wholesale slaughter. One simmering battleground was Bosnia, where Serbs fought Muslims. The United States and Europe, including Russia, intervened, and in 1995 a peace agreement was signed in Dayton, Ohio. Peacekeepers stayed in Bosnia to control the violence.

In 1998 Serbian president **Slobodan Milosević** began a campaign of mass murder and ethnic cleansing in nearby Kosovo, where mostly Kosovar Albanians lived. During 1998 and 1999, the West, again with Russia's help, tried to end the violence with diplomacy, but when that failed, NATO intervened militarily against Serbia. UN peacekeepers continue to monitor the area.

In 2000 a revolution ended Milosević's tyranny in Serbia, and his party was defeated in elections later that year. Milosević was captured in 2001 and taken to The Hague in Holland, where he was tried for war crimes. In 2006 Milosević died of a heart attack while in prison.

Slobodan Milosević

Section Quiz

1. How has China's economy performed in recent years?
2. Which leader stabilized Russia in the early twenty-first century?
3. What military organization expanded into Eastern Europe?
4. Who was the Serbian dictator who instituted a campaign of mass murder and ethnic cleansing in Kosovo?

★ How has Taiwan played a role in China's economic prosperity?

III. Developing Nations

During the Cold War, nations that were part of neither the "first world," the industrialized bloc, or the "second world," the Communist Soviet bloc, were labeled the "third world." The emergence of these **developing nations** was a major theme of the late twentieth century. The first step in their formation was **decolonization**, when imperialist nations granted independence to their colonies.

In a remarkably peaceful process, 120 nations eventually emerged from the old European empires after 1945, but they faced many obstacles, including the challenge of meeting the housing, sanitary, and transportation needs of a growing population. The threat of communism and a general political instability caused by lack of experience with self-rule posed other problems.

Nations labeled *less-developed* are varied. Some countries have modern economies, whereas others still live in what many consider to be a primitive state. Politically, some of those nations are democratic, while others have brutal dictators.

Mohandas Gandhi

Asia

Indian Subcontinent

The first major developing nation to gain independence was India, the "Jewel in the Crown" of the British Empire. **Mohandas Gandhi**, the leader of the Indian nationalists, mounted a campaign of **passive resistance**, a nonviolent program designed to defy British rule through strikes (including hunger strikes and sit-down strikes), mass demonstrations, and refusal to pay taxes. Between the world wars, the British government granted the Indian people more political power, but not until 1947 did India achieve full independence.

Because of the sharp division between India's Hindu and Muslim factions, the British divided India into two sovereign nations: India and Pakistan. War followed, leaving more than half a million dead. Predominantly Hindu India became a federal republic in 1949 under the leadership of Jawaharlal Nehru, a close associate of Gandhi. Pakistan, with its Muslim majority and military government, was separated geographically into East and West Pakistan on opposite sides of India. In 1971 East Pakistan, believing itself to be mistreated by the government in West Pakistan, rebelled. With Indian aid the region fought for and won independence and became Bangladesh, only to emerge as one of the poorest nations in the world.

Muslim Pakistan and Hindu India have frequently clashed over dominance in the Indian subcontinent. With a few exceptions, the military has ruled Pakistan since it gained its independence. In addition, a growing Islamic influence continues to threaten the stability of that young country.

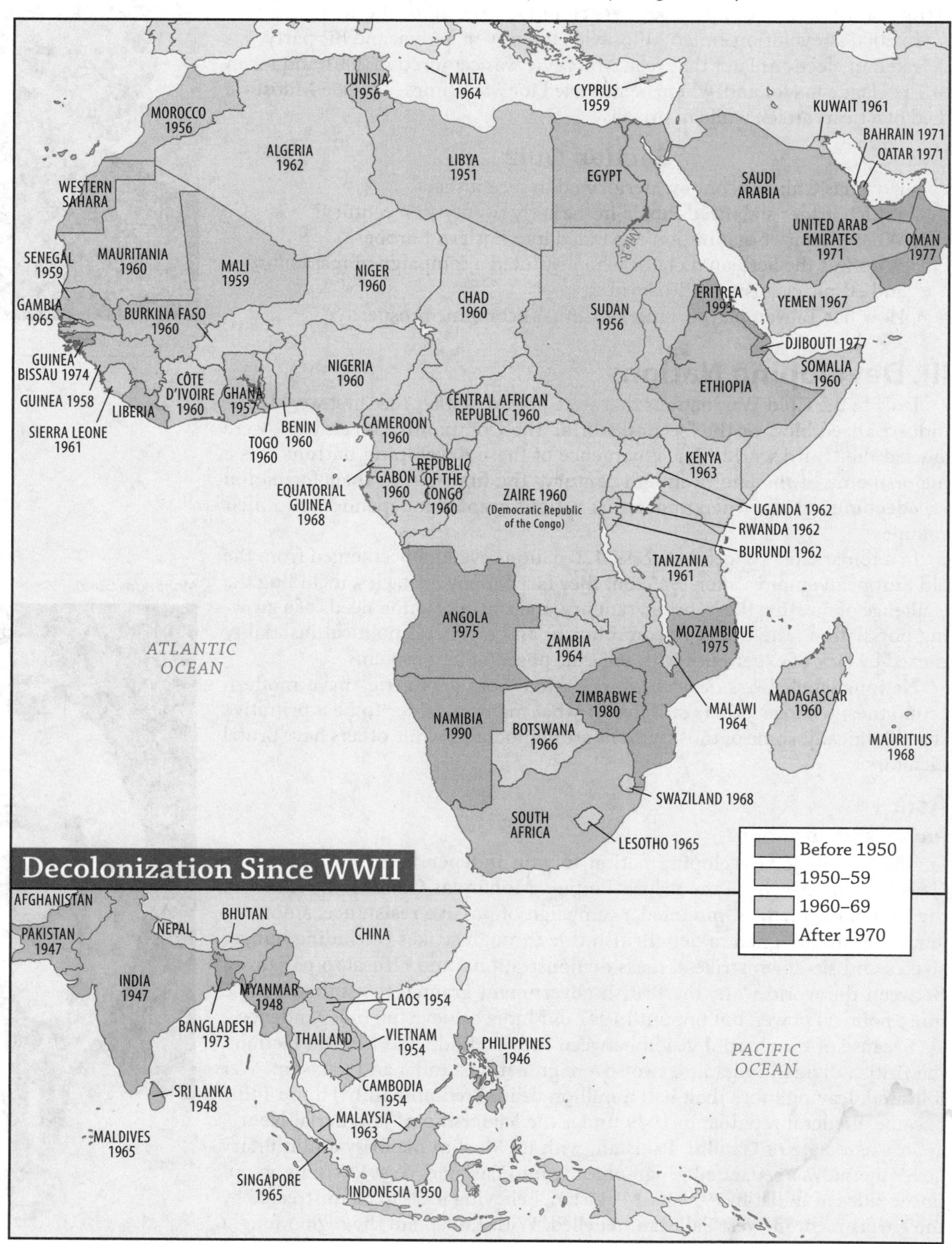

Decolonization Since WWII

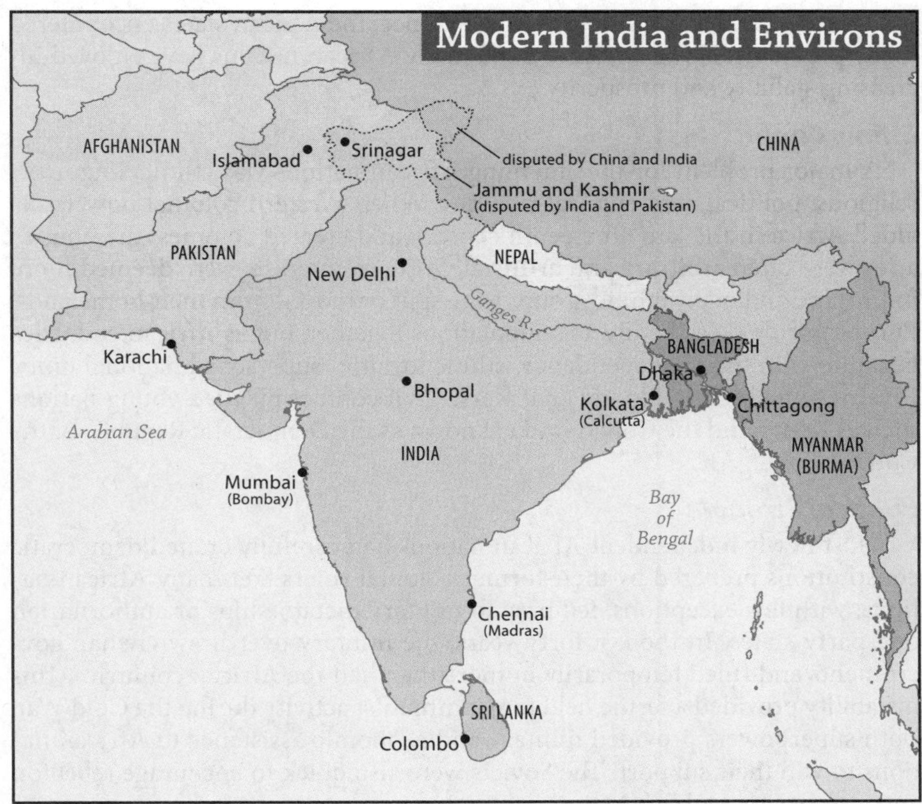

India, the "world's largest democracy," has struggled to remain a representative government, while leaders in India have increasingly embraced capitalism over socialism. One result is the emergence of areas with strong economic growth, including Mumbai, Gujarat, Haryana, and Delhi. Leadership has shifted from the Nehru family to Hindu nationalists, who won elections in 1998.

India has also tried to remain a secular state, but religion continues to play a dominant role in every aspect of Indian society. Tension between the sizable Muslim minority, the Hindu majority, and a growing Christian population is ongoing, and violence against Christians has continued to escalate. Since the creation of India and Pakistan, both countries have struggled for control of the state of Kashmir, technically given to India but also claimed by Pakistan. With both India and Pakistan possessing nuclear power, these conflicts cause great concern for Asia and the world.

Southeast Asia

Nationalist movements also grew stronger in Southeast Asia, which had been under Japanese domination since the 1930s. Its people did not want to return to colonial rule under Western nations after World War II. Southeast Asia continues to face serious problems as ethnic and religious tensions plague the region. Terrorism and separatist movements also threaten the stability of governments. While the economies of some of those nations improved dramatically in the late twentieth century, by the late 1990s severe economic decline gripped the area, worsening social and political conditions. Their economies remain fragile and subject to the instability of world markets.

Africa

Africa also witnessed a rapid series of independence movements in the postwar period. In 1950 only four states on the continent were free; by the 1990s more than fifty were free. In 1960 alone eighteen former colonies gained independence. In their rush for independence, the African states encountered many problems. However, since 2000 many African nations have enjoyed increasing stability and prosperity.

Ethnic Conflict

A major problem for the emerging African nations was ethnic, linguistic, religious, political, and cultural rivalries. When Western colonial powers divided Africa in the late nineteenth century and created colonies, the boundaries were often arbitrary and artificial. Western interests were deemed more important, and many ethnic groups were split or moved from their homelands. European rule held the diverse populations together, but as African countries began to gain their independence, ethnic loyalties superseded national unity. Rivalries often led to bloody civil wars. Civil conflict plagued young nations such as Kenya and the Congo (today known as the Democratic Republic of the Congo).

Political Struggle

Most newly independent African nations had carefully crafted democratic constitutions prepared by their former colonial rulers. Yet many African nations, with few exceptions, fell prey to military dictatorships or authoritarian one-party states. In the last forty years, the military overthrew civilian governments and ruled temporarily in more than half the African countries. This instability provided a fertile field for Communist activity during the Cold War. Both superpowers provided military and economic assistance to African nations to win their support. The Soviets were also quick to encourage rebellion and violence to establish Marxist states.

The road to democracy—black majority rule—has been rocky for some African nations, but few have exceeded the struggle witnessed in South Africa. After generations of suppression by the white minority, black resentment led to

Nelson Mandela

South African president Nelson Mandela

Winner of the 1993 Nobel Peace Prize and the first black president of South Africa, Nelson Mandela is one of the most admired world figures. The son of a chief, he attended a university and studied law, and he and a friend became the first blacks to open a law office in South Africa.

Mandela, however, is most known for his decades-long leadership of the African National Congress (ANC), a multiracial political party that pushed for democracy for everyone in the country and an end to apartheid. Mandela and the ANC eventually embraced violence as the only way for blacks to achieve their goals. His actions led to his imprisonment for almost three decades. During that time he became a symbol of resistance to apartheid not only in South Africa but throughout the world.

Suffering from economic sanctions imposed by other nations, the white-minority government released Mandela from prison in 1990 and started work on a constitution for a true democracy in South Africa. In 1994, in their first multiracial elections, South Africans chose Mandela as president. Instead of revenge he focused on forgiving his opponents and reassured whites in the country as well as possible foreign investors. Mandela served only one term, which ended in 1999. By then he had begun the process of transforming the image of South Africa from one of oppression to hope.

protests and riots. **Nelson Mandela** emerged as the leader for black majority rule, and the white government imprisoned him for nearly three decades.

Meanwhile, international pressure mounted against the white South African government. In 1990 the government, led by Frederick Willem de Klerk, announced the release of Nelson Mandela and both a commitment to majority rule and an end to apartheid. Work on a new constitution followed. In 1994 in their first truly democratic elections, South Africans elected Mandela president and Thabo Mbeki vice president. In 1999 Mbeki was elected president.

Fortunately, South Africa's ultimate success is the rule and not the exception, and many African states have made political progress. The 1990s brought a new era of democracy. By 2000 forty-two nations held multiparty elections, although majority parties and military leaders in some nations continued to intimidate opposition groups.

In most of Africa, religious groups live peacefully together, but in some parts religious conflict threatens political stability. In Nigeria and the Sudan, for example, Christians have struggled against Muslims who want to impose Islamic law on Christian areas. In the Sudan, Muslim forces have been particularly brutal in their attacks on Christians and followers of traditional African religions in the south. A peace agreement in 2004 promised an end to the fighting, but the fighting did not end. The latest attempt to end the violence resulted in secession of southern Sudan in order to form a separate nation. On July 9, 2011, South Sudan became a nation. However, the violence against Christians and traditional African religions continued.

Continuing Tragedy in Zimbabwe

Zimbabwe was once the center of a thriving civilization in Africa. However, its emergence from British colonial control after World War II did not result in prosperity or stability. One of the reasons for Zimbabwe's problems was three decades of rule by Robert Mugabe. Mugabe came to power in 1980 and pursued policies that divided the European and black populations. For example, in 2000 Mugabe began to seize land from white farmers and redistribute it to native Africans. His policies, while popular in the short run, led to hyperinflation and chronic shortages. Yet Mugabe remained in power, despite the social and political upheaval that plagued Zimbabwe. In 2008 Mugabe won reelection after a questionable recount provided him with a majority.

Recent Growth

Between 2000 and 2010, six of the fastest growing countries in the world were found in Africa. Africa's population of one billion is expected to double in the next forty years. This growth is due, in part, to the decline of deaths from HIV/AIDS, resulting from effective medicines, and to the greater use of mosquito nets to prevent the spread of malaria.

South Africa is one of the fastest growing countries in Africa.

The wealth of Africa is also steadily increasing. While some Africans continue to live on less than two dollars a day, more and more are moving into the middle class and earning around three thousand dollars a year. Part of the reason for the economic growth is a dramatic increase in foreign investment since 2000. In addition, Africans are increasingly turning natural resources, including copper, gold, and oil, into wealth. More Africans are using technology to boost potential earnings, productivity is steadily rising, and trade with other countries increasing. While Africans have many hurdles yet to overcome, the economic potential for many countries on this continent is great.

Hugo Chavez, socialist ruler of Venezuela who is a vocal anti-American leader in Latin America

Latin America

Since World War II, Latin America has experienced political revolutions, economic crises, and social upheaval. Possessing one of the world's fastest-growing populations, the region consists of poor masses and a small but rich land-owning class. Many Latin American countries have based their economies on a single export, such as coffee, bananas, or sugar. They have generally suffered from high inflation, stagnant socialist economies, and large foreign debts. Some countries, however, are developing industries, are becoming more productive in agriculture, and are fostering a larger middle class. Brazil, for example, has enjoyed one of the highest economic growth rates in the developing world. The production of oil also has helped enrich countries such as Mexico and Ecuador.

Military dictatorships have been a major political problem for Latin America. Argentina, for instance, endured the rule of several military rulers, notably Juan Perón (1946–55, 1973–74). Although that country developed a democratic government in 1983, it continued to suffer from high inflation and an unstable economy. Recent global economic problems have had a major negative impact on Argentina and other Latin American nations.

Two nations built strong democratic traditions. Costa Rica, with a stable democracy and relatively high standard of living, is a shining example of democracy in Central America. Mexico endured a series of revolutions and dictatorships in the first hundred years of its independence. Then, during World War I, the nation adopted a new constitution that has provided a relatively stable government to the present.

Section Quiz

1. What was the first step in the emergence of developing nations after World War II?
2. What is the world's largest democracy?
3. Who was the first democratically elected president of South Africa?
4. What two factors contribute to a potential doubling of the population in Africa?

★ Why do you think many states in Latin America have historically had problems with military dictators?

IV. The Middle East

The Middle East is also part of the developing world. The region is important as a strategic source of wealth and a troubled center of conflict, and it has great significance for the Western industrial nations because it holds some of the world's largest oil reserves. In addition, several countries in the Middle East are or have been controlled until recently by brutal dictators or radical groups.

Two of the most disruptive elements in the Middle East are ethnic and religious. Except for Iran and Turkey, most countries in the area are Arab. Israel, though controlled by Jews, also has a large Arab population. Islam is the dominant religion in the region, although pockets of orthodox Jews and nominal Christians also exist there.

All of these features combine to make the Middle East a volatile region. This should come as no surprise for the Christian since history after the Flood began in the Middle East and will end in the Middle East with the return of Christ (Rev. 19).

The Arab-Israeli Conflict

Much of the postwar tension in the Middle East has resulted from the return of the Jews to Palestine and the creation of the national state of Israel. The history of Israel and its neighbors has been one of armed truces punctuated by open warfare. In each conflict Israel has shown amazing strength and military cunning to overcome its more numerous foes, but military victory has not brought peace.

Arab-Israeli Wars

The modern state of Israel was literally born of war in 1948. The United Nations attempted to divide Palestine peacefully between the Jews and the Arabs. Instead, war followed as Arab forces from Egypt, Jordan, Syria, Lebanon, and Iraq tried to drive the Jews from Palestine. Against great odds, the Israelis defeated their opponents and won their war for independence. However, the uneasy peace provided no final settlement. The Arab states refused to recognize the existence of Israel and dedicated themselves to Israel's destruction.

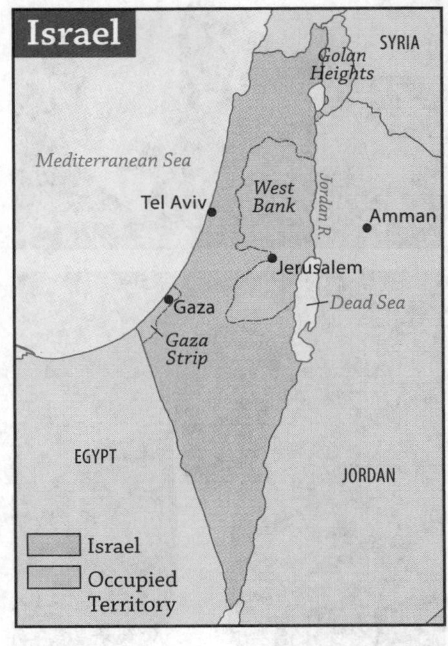

The Suez Crisis—The tension between Israel and the Arab community led to war again in 1956, when Egypt seized control of the Suez Canal. Fearing Egyptian moves against their nation, the Israelis agreed to aid Britain and France by moving into the Sinai Peninsula, thereby giving those nations an excuse to take control of the Suez Canal. The Israeli army conquered Sinai with surprising ease, but it had to withdraw when international pressure forced Britain and France to back down.

The Six-Day War—A UN peacekeeping force remained in Sinai until 1967, when the Egyptian government asked them to leave before it launched a new attack on Israel. Realizing that Egypt, Syria, and Jordan were preparing to attack, Israel launched a preemptive strike. The Israeli air force caught the Egyptian planes on the ground, destroyed them, and then turned on Syria and Jordan. The Israelis again routed a larger foe. They captured the Sinai Peninsula, the West Bank (Arab territory on the west bank of the Jordan River, including Jerusalem), the Gaza Strip (along the Mediterranean coast), and the Golan Heights (along the Israeli-Syrian border).

The Yom Kippur War—Victory still did not bring peace. In 1973 Egypt and Syria attacked without warning on October 6, Yom Kippur, the Jewish Day of Atonement. In that war the Arab allies enjoyed initial success, but the Israelis, led by defense minister Moshe Dayan and resupplied by the United States, ultimately repulsed the Arab forces.

Mahmoud Abbas, leader of the PLO since 2009

The Palestinian Question

While there are various opinions about what *Palestinian* means, the term usually refers to a group of Arab-speaking people who trace their lineage to people who, over the past several centuries, lived in Palestine. Since the creation of the modern state of Israel, many from this group have demanded their own country. Organized as the Palestine Liberation Organization (**PLO**) in 1964 under the leadership of **Yasir Arafat**, the Palestinians have consistently demanded that Israel give them land in order to form a separate Palestinian state. During two periods, 1987–93 and 2000–05, the war of words escalated to a violent outburst known as ***intifada*** ("uprising"), resulting in several thousand deaths. Despite seemingly endless peace negotiations and U.S. diplomatic involvement at the highest levels, peace has eluded this region.

Top: Mahmoud Ahmadinejad, President of Iran, took office in 2005.
Middle: Osama bin Laden, leader of al-Qaeda
Bottom: Muammar Gaddafi, former dictator of Libya who actively supported terrorist activity, including the bombing of a Boeing 747 over Lockerbie, Scotland, in 1988

Other Sources of Tension

Iran

Beginning in the 1970s, Islamic elements stirred hostilities in the Middle East. Iran, for example, had been a long-time ally of the United States. However, in 1979 Islamic forces overthrew the shah and installed the **Ayatollah Khomeini** as ruler. (*Ayatollah*, Persian for "reflection, or sign, of Allah," is the highest title of honor that a Shiite Muslim can hold.) Iranian radicals instituted an Islamic republic in which Muslim religious law guides the state. The Iranians viewed their revolution as a first step toward worldwide change.

Iran returned to the spotlight in 2005 with the election of **Mahmoud Ahmadinejad** as president. He frequently attacked the West in defiant speeches. Ahmadinejad also led his country to develop nuclear technology, with the suspected goals being to strengthen Iran's military capabilities and to support terrorist groups abroad. He won reelection in 2009, despite large protests in Iran. Many protestors were detained or murdered by Iranian security forces.

In addition to having Iraq on its western border, Iran has Afghanistan and Pakistan on its eastern border. Across its long borders, Iran has extended its influence into these other troubled countries. Leaders in Iran have worked tirelessly to destabilize this region and have opposed Western attempts to develop democracies.

Spread of Islam

The growth of Islam is widespread and appears to be well-organized, particularly in Europe. Although the countries with the highest concentrations of Muslims are in Africa, the Middle East, and Southeast Asia, Islam is growing rapidly in the West. Some experts predict that Islam will be the majority religion in Europe by the end of the twenty-first century. The Islamization of Europe holds serious consequences for the rest of the Western world.

Beginning in the late 1990s, the **Taliban** ("students" trained in not only radical Islamic doctrine but also terrorist tactics) gained control in Afghanistan, enforcing radical Muslim rule and providing safe haven and training camps for Muslim terrorists. These and other groups committed acts of terrorism to undermine secular Muslim regimes. Saudi Arabia has a large number of such radicals. With the decline of communism, many people view Islamic expansion as the new ideological threat to international peace and stability.

Islamic Terrorism

The inability to destroy Israel and the presence of Western military forces in the Persian Gulf region led to the rise of extremist Muslim groups. To advance their causes, terrorist groups have often staged attacks on innocent civilians. Since these groups cannot match the military might and technology of wealthier nations, they resort to unconventional means. Terror, they believe, is an equalizer.

With the rise of **Osama bin Laden**'s **al-Qaeda** network, terrorism took on an even more sinister and international character in the 1990s. A wealthy Saudi, bin Laden was forced to flee his homeland due to his attempts to overthrow the Saudi monarchy. Bin Laden found haven in Taliban-run Afghanistan, where he trained terrorists and masterminded terrorist plots. He shared the Muslim anger against secular and Western-oriented Arab governments that had failed to keep their promises of economic progress. However, he also harbored a particular hatred of the United States. Bin Laden despised America's military and commercial presence in Saudi Arabia, home to Islam's holiest sites. He also hated America for its support of the nation of Israel.

Top left: The Pentagon burns following the crash of a plane hijacked by al-Qaeda terrorists.
Top: As one of the World Trade Center towers burns from the first terrorist attack, a second hijacked plane is about to crash into the other tower.
Above: Popularly known as the Freedom Tower, One World Trade Center is part of a new complex of high-rise buildings being constructed on the site where the twin towers stood.

Bin Laden declared that the Palestinians and the Iraqis were oppressed by American power. He wanted an Islam that was free from foreign influence. Bin Laden viewed Western popular culture as a threat to the Muslim way of life. He supported a literal interpretation of Islam, which would force women to return to traditional dress, renounce any desire to be educated or have careers, and give up the right to vote. Bin Laden adopted the model established by the Iranian Islamic republic in the 1970s (see p. 560).

Under bin Laden's leadership, al-Qaeda executed its most ambitious terrorist act on September 11, 2001, launching multiple attacks on the United States. Al-Qaeda had managed to stage smaller attacks against U.S. interests before, including an attempt in 1993 to destroy the World Trade Center and the bombing of the warship U.S.S. *Cole* in 2000. But the September 11 attacks changed America and the world. On that date Islamic terrorists affiliated with the al-Qaeda network flew two hijacked passenger jets into the World Trade Center towers in New York, killing almost 3,000 people in the most devastating attack to date on American soil by a foreign group. A third jet crashed into the Pentagon, killing 125 people. A fourth plane, apparently headed for the White House or the Capitol, crashed in Pennsylvania after passengers wrested control of the plane from the hijackers. These harrowing events temporarily united Americans, and the country fought back. American and Allied forces hunted down and captured or killed many of those responsible for the attacks. Even the elusive bin Laden failed to evade American forces; in 2011 a Navy Seal team entered his compound in Pakistan and killed him during a raid.

The Gulf Wars

Seeking power and fame, dictator Saddam Hussein of Iraq invaded Kuwait in August 1990, seizing Kuwait's huge oil reserves and threatening the security of Saudi Arabia. Led by the United States, under President George H.W. Bush, and Great Britain and authorized by the United Nations, a coalition launched massive air strikes against Iraqi forces in Kuwait in January 1991. For five weeks coalition forces pounded Iraqi forces in Kuwait and even struck targets in Iraq with bombs and missiles. In February coalition ground forces attacked, drove Iraqi forces from Kuwait, and defeated Hussein's army, all within one hundred hours. Iraq lost tens of thousands of soldiers; coalition forces lost fewer than two hundred. High-tech weaponry and superior

Top: Hamid Karzai, president of Afghanistan, took office in 2004.
Above: Nouri al-Maliki, prime minister of Iraq, took office in 2006.

firepower made it possible for the war to be concluded so quickly. Although Kuwait was liberated, the terrorist threat remained.

Following the terrorist attack on September 11, 2001, President George W. Bush launched the United States and much of the world into a second war in the Persian Gulf region. A U.S.-led multinational coalition invaded Afghanistan, destroyed terrorist training camps, and toppled the Taliban government, which had hosted bin Laden and al-Qaeda. Coalition forces secured areas of the country and began the process of establishing a representative government. Afghanistan had its first free presidential election in 2004. In December of that year, **Hamid Karzai** was inaugurated as Afghanistan's president.

Bush warned the world, as had President Clinton, that Saddam Hussein was developing weapons of mass destruction (WMD). The UN passed a resolution threatening dire consequences if Iraq did not allow UN inspectors to have access to suspected WMD sites, but the UN did nothing to enforce the resolution because France, Germany, and Russia objected to such action. In 2003 Bush took the initiative and led a "coalition of the willing" against Iraq to remove Hussein from power and prevent any possible WMDs from falling into the hands of terrorists (but no WMDs were ever found). The coalition quickly crushed Iraqi military opposition, removed Hussein's Ba'athist party from power, and captured Hussein and his major lieutenants. A newly established Iraqi government held war crimes trials in 2005, after which several leaders, including Hussein, were executed by the Iraqi government, while others were given long prison sentences.

Following the initial conquest of Iraq, U.S. forces quickly found themselves in the middle of violent clashes between Shia and Sunni Muslims who have been at war for centuries. In addition, elements of al-Qaeda and groups supported by Iran took every opportunity to wound or kill American forces and destabilize Iraq. President Bush responded by sending in additional troops to stabilize the country. President Obama initially called for the withdrawal of U.S. forces; then he briefly supported the build-up of forces before abruptly calling for the pull-out of American troops when an agreement with Iraq on a continued American presence was not reached. The last U.S. forces left Iraq in December 2011. Violence between Shia and Sunni Muslims resumed shortly after the departure of U.S. forces.

Section Quiz

1–2. What are two reasons for Western interest in the Middle East?
3. When was Israel founded as a modern state?
4. Who led al-Qaeda to attack the United States in 2001?
★ Why does Iran pose a significant threat to peace in the Middle East?

Chapter 24 Review

Making Connections

1–2. Why were Tony Blair and the New Labour Party able to remain in power for a decade? (Give two reasons.)

3. How did Vladimir Putin become a popular Russian leader?
4. Why have many African countries endured ethnic conflict since World War II?
5. What role did the Taliban play in the growing influence of Osama bin Laden?

Developing History Skills

1. Develop a timeline from 1975 to 2001 that includes ten significant terrorist attacks on the U.S., and identify the presidents during whose administration the attacks occurred.

Thinking Critically

1. Evaluate the "war on terror" declared by President George W. Bush following the attacks on September 11, 2001.

Living in God's World

1. Globalization has affected not only trade but also religion. You are more likely to work or associate with people from other religions than previous generations of Americans. Research a religion such as Islam or Buddhism, and write a gospel tract that addresses the gospel specifically to adherents of that religion.
2. Most people recognize the horrors that totalitarian governments have brought about in the last 100 years. Is democracy the solution to these horrors? Why or why not?

People, Places, and Things to Know

globalization
George W. Bush
Barack Obama
Tony Blair
"New Labour" Party
Angela Merkel
Nicolas Sarkozy
Vladimir Putin
Slobodan Milosević
developing nations
decolonization
Mohandas Gandhi
passive resistance
Nelson Mandela
PLO
Yasir Arafat
intifada
Ayatollah Khomeini
Mahmoud Ahmadinejad
Taliban
Osama bin Laden
al-Qaeda
Hamid Karzai

GLOSSARY

A

Abbasid caliphate that marked the peak of the **Muslim** empire; during this caliphate the political unity of the Muslim world collapsed (Ch. 6)

Abrahamic Covenant God's covenant to Abraham in which He promised Abraham descendants, a land for his descendants, and a Messiah that would come through his seed (Ch. 2)

absolute power unlimited and unrestrained power (Ch. 14)

Act of Settlement Act of Parliament that established its right to grant the throne to whomever it wished (Ch. 14)

Afrikaners South African whites of Dutch descent who instituted **apartheid** and controlled the country's government and economy from World War II to the end of apartheid in 1990 (Ch. 24)

Age of Reason a term for the seventeenth and eighteenth centuries (Ch. 15)

AIDS acquired immune deficiency syndrome (Ch. 24)

Allah the god of **Islam** (Ch. 6)

al-Qaeda terrorist network headed by Osama bin Laden; attacked the United States on September 11, 2001 (Ch. 24)

amphibious land and sea (Ch. 22)

Anabaptists group that rejected infant baptism and rebaptized each other (Ch. 12)

anarchy the breakdown of government and order (Ch. 3)

ancestor worship worship of a family's ancestors (Ch. 7)

Anglican Church Church of England; the established state church of England which has as its creed the Thirty-nine Articles (Ch. 12)

Anglo-Russian Entente 1907 agreement between England and Russia; divided Persia into three zones of control (Ch. 19)

Anglo-Saxon Chronicle document that traces the history of England from Roman times to Alfred's day (Ch. 9)

Anglo-Saxons Germanic tribes from northern Europe who invaded Britain after the Romans left (Ch. 9)

Anschluss political unification between Austria and Germany that the **Treaty of Versailles** forbade but was later accomplished by Hitler (Ch. 20)

anthropomorphic having human forms or attributes (Ch. 3)

Anti-Comintern Pact 1936 treaty between Germany and Japan directed against communism, specifically Russia (Ch. 22)

apartheid a rigid system of racial separation in South Africa initiated by the **Afrikaners** (Ch. 24)

appeasement buying off an aggressor by territorial concession (Ch. 22)

apprentice first class in a craft **guild**; lived in the home of a **master** and learned trade skills and proper conduct (Ch. 10)

aqueducts engineering works to supply water to cities (Ch. 5)

archon chief magistrate of the Athenian council of nobles (Ch. 3)

armistice a temporary cessation of fighting (Ch. 20)

arms race a build-up of weapons between two or more nations in order to maintain a position of strength and to prevent the other side from gaining a military edge (Ch. 23)

artifacts objects made by people (Ch. 1)

Aryans a fair-skinned people who came from central Asia sometime after 1500 BC and subdued the non-Aryan people of northwest India; established Sanskrit (Ch. 7)

assembly line workers stationed along a conveyer belt assembling specific parts of a product as the item moves down the line (Ch. 18)

assignats French Revolutionary paper money backed by Roman Catholic land that was confiscated (Ch. 16)

astrology the practice of trying to interpret human events and destiny by the position of the planets and stars (Ch. 2)

astronomy the study of celestial bodies (Ch. 2)

Athena patron of the city of Athens; goddess of wisdom (Ch. 3)

Atlantic Charter eight-point document between Winston Churchill and Franklin Roosevelt that set forth the "common principles" on which both countries "based their hopes for a better future for the world" (Ch. 22)

atonal music abandoned fixed tone patterns or keys; no special emphasis to any one note (Ch. 21)

attrition war in which each side tried to gradually wear the other down (Ch. 20)

Augsburg Confession a confession written by Philipp Melanchthon that set forth the chief doctrines that Luther and his followers contended (Ch. 12)

augustus co-emperor of half the Roman Empire under Diocletian's plan (Ch. 5)

Austro-Prussian War also called Seven Weeks' War; 1866 war in which Prussia defeated Austria (Ch. 17)

autarky self-sufficiency of a nation (Ch. 21)

Autobahnen superhighway in Germany (Ch. 21)

autocratic ruling with unlimited authority (Ch. 7)

automation machines running the machines that make the products (Ch. 18)

Avesta the sacred writings of Zoroastrianism (Ch. 2)

Aztec Central American civilization that flourished after the Mayan civilization; conquered by the Spanish (Ch. 13)

B

Baal pagan god of the Canaanites (Ch. 2)

Babel city in Shinar (southeastern Mesopotamia) that had a great tower; place where languages were formed (Ch. 1)

Babylonian Captivity (1) seventy-year exile of Israel in Babylon (Ch. 2) (2) the period from 1309 to 1377 when the papal court dwelt in Avignon, France (Ch. 10)

baillis French royal officials whom the king appointed and paid (Ch. 9)

balance of power the goal of European nations to ensure that no nation would dominate Europe; involved the formation of alliances (Ch. 14)

Balfour Declaration British declaration to provide a home for the Jews in Palestine (Ch. 24)

banca "bench"; the table of the moneychangers (Ch. 10)

banzai war cry shouted by Japanese troops (Ch. 22)

barbarians a Roman term for all those outside the empire who did not share in the Greek or Roman cultures (Ch. 5)

baroque period in art history from 1600 to about 1750; having a grand, dynamic, heroic, active, swirling, sensual, and emotional style (Ch. 15)

barter exchanging goods for goods (Ch. 10)

Battle of Dien Bien Phu battle where the Communist Vietnamese annihilated the French army (Ch. 23)

Battle of Hastings battle in England between the Normans and the Anglo-Saxons; William "the Conqueror" established the Norman dynasty (Ch. 9)

Battle of Manzikert battle in Asia Minor between the **Seljuk Turks** and the Byzantines; established Turkish control of Asia Minor (Ch. 6)

Battle of Plassey battle where the British defeated an Indian ruler during the **Seven Years' War** (Ch. 19)

Battle of the Bulge Germany's final attempt to push back the Allied advance into Germany after **D-day** (Ch. 22)

Battle of Tours defeat of the **Muslims** by the Franks; stopped the Muslim advance into Europe (Ch. 6)

Bay of Pigs failed American attempt to invade Cuba (Ch. 23)

Bedouins Arab nomads who traveled through the harsh desert wilderness in independent bands searching for pastureland and water for their livestock (Ch. 6)

Benedictine Rule a standard of discipline and order that strictly regulated the life of monks; the most popular system of rules in medieval Europe; designed by Benedict of Nursia (Ch. 8)

Berlin Wall a concrete and barbed wire wall physically separating East and West Berlin; most recognizable symbol of the **Cold War** (Ch. 23)

"Big Three" Winston Churchill, Franklin D. Roosevelt, and Joseph Stalin (Ch. 22)

Bill of Rights (1) 1689 English document that limited royal power, established certain civil liberties, and forbade future kings or queens from being Roman Catholics (Ch. 14) (2) the first ten amendments of the United States Constitution that defined liberties and placed restraints on governmental interference (Ch. 16)

Bismarck's System German system of alliances created by Bismarck to prevent French attack and to maintain the **balance of power** (Ch. 20)

blitzkrieg "lightning war"; fast-moving attack that sought to penetrate enemy lines (Ch. 22)

Bloody Sunday January 22, 1905; when the troops of the Russian **czar** massacred peaceful protesters (Ch. 21)

Boers Dutch colonists in South Africa (Ch. 19)

Boer War conflict between the **Boers** and the British; the British won and gained control over the Orange Free State and the Transvaal (Ch. 19)

Bolsheviks wing of the Social Democratic Party in Russia who advocated change through violence (Ch. 21)

Bourbon French royal family; descended from Louis IX (Ch. 12)

bourgeoisie French middle class property owners, capitalists, and industrialists or factory owners (Ch. 18)

Boxer Rebellion Chinese uprising against Western influences; put down by European and American troops (Ch. 19)

Brahman the great Hindu god who permeates everything in the universe (Ch. 7)

British North America Act Act of Parliament creating the Dominion of Canada (Ch. 19)

Brunswick Manifesto declaration of the Duke of Brunswick calling upon the French people to rally behind their king and to protect him from the leaders of the Revolution (Ch. 16)

Buddhism Eastern religion founded by Siddhartha Gautama (Buddha); a religion built upon works and moral behavior (Ch. 7)

bull an official papal document (Ch. 10)

bureaucracy the nonelected officials who handle government affairs (Ch. 21)

Bushido an unwritten military code that governed the conduct of the **samurai** (Ch. 7)

Byzantine Empire the Eastern Roman Empire after the Western Roman Empire fell (Ch. 6)

C

cabinet government a group of advisors to the English king who met to discuss matters of state (Ch. 14)

caesar the assistant of an **augustus** (Ch. 5)

cahiers lists of grievances (Ch. 16)

caliphs successors of Muhammad who directed the affairs of **Islam** and exercised spiritual, political, and military authority (Ch. 6)

calligraphy the art of beautiful writing (Ch. 6)

capital supply of money (Ch. 13)

capitalism economic system designed to advance wealth (Ch. 13)

caravel a ship with large square sails to provide power and smaller triangular sails to provide maneuverability (Ch. 13)

Carolingian House the Frankish royal house named after Charlemagne (Ch. 8)

Carolingian Miniscule clean and simple writing style developed during Charlemagne's reign; became the model for much of our "lowercase" writing today (Ch. 8)

caste system a system of rigid social groups in India (Ch. 7)

castle the center of life for the nobility; the **lord**'s home, the local jail, the treasury, the armory, the court, and the seat of government (Ch. 8)

catholic "universal"; "encompassing all"; the term of early Christians for the universal church (Ch. 8)

caudillos ambitious military leaders who ruled as dictators (Ch. 19)

Cavaliers supporters of the king in the English Civil War (Ch. 14)

Central Powers Germany, Austria-Hungary, and the Ottoman Empire during World War I (Ch. 20)

chansons lighthearted songs that set secular lyric poems to music (Ch. 11)

charter a legal document that outlined the privileges granted to a town by a feudal **lord** (Ch. 10)

Chartism nineteenth-century British reform movement (Ch. 18)

chauvinism unbridled nationalism (Ch. 20)

Chinese characters sixty-five thousand characters that represent complete ideas, objects, and sounds (Ch. 7)

chivalry a **knight's** strict code of behavior (Ch. 8)

Christian socialism philosophy held by theological liberals who viewed socialism as "the embodiment of Christianity in our culture" (Ch. 18)

Christian worldview composed of three central truths: (1) God made the world and everything in it; (2) this world has fallen into a sad and broken condition because of human sin; and (3) God is working to redeem this world to Himself; see **worldview** (Ch. 1)

circumnavigation sailing around the world (Ch. 13)

Cistercians monastic order that adopted lives of seclusion and strict discipline; made popular by Bernard of Clairvaux (Ch. 9)

Civil Constitution of the Clergy placed the French church under state control, provided for the election of all the clergy by the people, and required the clergy to take an oath of loyalty to the state (Ch. 16)

civilization human existence lived in cities or under their influence (Ch. 1)

civil rights movement African American movement to gain fair and equal treatment in matters such as voting and access to public facilities (Ch. 23)

clan (1) a number of families from a common ancestor (Ch. 4) (2) a group of families claiming descent from a common ancestor; the basic social, political, and religious unit in Japan (Ch. 7)

clergy those who took "Holy Orders" in special service to the church (Ch. 8)

clique an exclusive, elite group (Ch. 22)

coalition a temporary alliance of nations (Ch. 16)

Code Napoleon Napoleon's codification of French laws (Ch. 16)

Cold War post-World War II state of apprehension, hostility, and competition between the Soviet Union and the United States (Ch. 23)

collectivize bring under central government control (Ch. 21)

College of Cardinals a Roman Catholic assembly of cardinals that chooses a new **pope** (Ch. 9)

Comintern "Communist International"; a group established to found Communist parties in other countries and to take an active role in stirring up discontent in hopes of producing revolution (Ch. 21)

Commercial Revolution the economic changes in European business practice and thinking during the fifteenth and sixteenth centuries (Ch. 13)

Committee of Public Safety twelve-man committee headed by Robespierre who managed the everyday affairs of the French Revolutionary government; see **Reign of Terror** (Ch. 16)

common law uniform laws in England determined by justices (Ch. 9)

Commonwealth of Independent States CIS; organization of former countries of the **USSR** (Ch. 23)

company an organization of men who pooled their resources, sharing gains as well as losses (Ch. 13)

compass a magnetized navigation device that greatly aided sailors during the age of exploration (Ch. 13)

Concert of Europe international cooperation set up through the **congress system** to avoid major wars and to suppress nationalism and liberalism (Ch. 17)

Concordat of Worms recognized the right of the church to elect its own bishops and abbots and to invest them with spiritual authority; the elections had to be held in the presence of the emperor or his representatives (Ch. 9)

condottière leaders of mercenaries that fought in Italy during the late fifteenth and sixteenth centuries (Ch. 11)

Confucianism Eastern religion founded by Confucius that was based on relationships (Ch. 7)

Congress of Vienna a meeting of European statesmen at the end of the Napoleonic Wars (Ch. 17)

congress system an international agreement to convene new congresses when necessary to resolve problems affecting the peace and stability of Europe; see **Concert of Europe** (Ch. 17)

conquistadors "conquerors" sent from Spain to the New World to search for riches, to evangelize the Indians, and to establish Spanish authority (Ch. 13)

conservatism political theory that supports maintaining the status quo, which in early nineteenth-century Europe was usually a strong monarchical or despotic central government (Ch. 17)

consul annually elected leaders of the Roman Republic who held the **imperium** (Ch. 4)

containment the use of military, economic, diplomatic, and psychological means to curtail the further advance of communism (Ch. 23)

Continental System attempt by Napoleon to blockade British trade by closing Europe's ports to British ships (Ch. 16)

Corn Laws laws that placed a high tariff on imported grain (Ch. 18)

Cortés Spanish council composed of nobles, **clergy**, and representatives of the cities (Ch. 10)

corvée French system of forced labor (Ch. 16)

Council of Constance fifteenth-century Roman Catholic Church council that ended the **Great Schism** and burned John Huss (Ch. 10, 12)

Council of Nicaea church council in 325 that affirmed the doctrines of Christ's deity and the Trinity (Ch. 5)

Council of Trent the **Counter-Reformation** council that condemned justification by faith alone and the sole authority of Scripture, set forth a complete doctrinal position of the Roman Church, and sealed the break between Protestant and Roman Catholic churches (Ch. 12)

Counter-Reformation another term for the Catholic Reformation that opposed the Protestant Reformation (Ch. 12)

coup d'état a sudden and illegal seizure of power by force (Ch. 16)

Creation Mandate first command from God revealing that man's reason for being is to subdue the earth and exercise dominion over it; found in Genesis 1:28 (Ch. 1)

Crimean War war in which Britain, France, and the Kingdom of Sardinia defeated Russia (Ch. 17)

criollos Spaniards born in the New World (Ch. 19)

crucifixion death on a cross (Ch. 5)

Crusades military expeditions from the West to free the East from the **Muslims** (Ch. 6, 9)

Cuban Missile Crisis confrontation between the United States and the **USSR** after the USSR placed offensive missiles on Cuba (Ch. 23)

cubism second major artistic movement of the twentieth century; often portrayed reality by various geometric shapes seen from various perspectives at once (Ch. 21)

Cultural Revolution Communist China's attempt to stir up zeal for radical communism; resulted in civil chaos and economic decline (Ch. 23)

culture the physical and mental environment developed through human thought and labor (Ch. 1)

culture system Dutch colonial system which required natives to use one-fifth of their land and one-fifth of their time in growing crops for the Dutch (Ch. 19)

cuneiform the earliest known form of writing (Ch. 2)

curia regis the Great Council; an English feudal body composed of chief **vassals**; "king's council"(Ch. 9)

czar emperor of Russia; comes from the word *casear* (Ch. 14)

D

D-day the day when an attack is to be launched; June 6, 1944, the day that the Allied forces invaded France (Ch. 22)

Declaration of Independence document whereby the American colonies declared their independence from Britain (Ch. 16)

Declaration of the Rights of Man French Revolution document that outlined what the National Assembly considered to be the natural rights of all people and the rights that they possessed as citizens (Ch. 16)

decolonization the winning of independence by colonies in Asia and Africa from Western imperial nations (Ch. 24)

deductive method reasoning from the general to the specific (Ch. 15)

deism belief in God as the First Cause; denied supernatural prophecy and miracles; taught that man is born good; regarded reason as the standard for truth (Ch. 15)

Delian League defensive alliance of Greek city-states led by Athens against the Persians (Ch. 3)

demesne the land reserved for the **lord** (Ch. 8)

democracy rule by the people (Ch. 3)

détente relaxation of tensions (Ch. 23)

developing nations third world; generally characterized by poverty, lack of production, and political instability (Ch. 24)

Diaspora the scattering of the Jewish people (Ch. 2)

Diet the German equivalent of the English Parliament and the French **Estates-General** (Ch. 10)

Diet of Worms the **Diet** in 1521 at which Martin Luther held to the contents of the books that he had written (Ch. 12)

Diplomatic Revolution radical changes in traditional European alliances prior to the **Seven Years' War** (Ch. 14)

Directory French revolutionary government after the National Convention; two chamber legislature; five Directors; overthrown by Napoleon (Ch. 16)

disarmament elimination of weapons or arms (Ch. 20)

dividends profit given to the stockholders of a **joint-stock company** (Ch. 13)

divine providence biblical teaching that God has planned all of human history (Ch. 1)

divine right belief that the king was established by God and therefore had **absolute power** and was not bound by human law (Ch. 14)

divine sovereignty God's complete and permanent authority over this world (Ch. 1)

division of labor dividing the manufacturing process into several simple procedures among a number of workers (Ch. 18)

dole government relief for the unemployed (Ch. 21)

"do-nothing kings" seventh-century **Merovingian** kings who reigned but did not rule; the power went to the **mayor of the palace** (Ch. 8)

Domesday Book a survey of property taken in England when William "the Conqueror" conquered England (Ch. 9)

domestic system workers living at home and working there with their own hand tools (Ch. 18)

domino theory the **Cold War** theory that once Vietnam fell to communism, then other countries of Asia would fall like dominos toppling against one another (Ch. 23)

Donation of Pepin the lands of the **Lombards** that were given to the **pope** by Pepin the Short; became the Papal States (Ch. 8)

Dorians invaders that conquered the **Mycenaean civilization** around 1200 BC (Ch. 3)

Dual Alliance alliance between Germany and Austria-Hungary; the foundation of pre-World War I German foreign policy (Ch. 20)

Dual Monarchy the Austro-Hungarian Empire under one crown (Ch. 17)

dualism philosophical system in which there are two types of reality (e.g., spiritual and physical) (Ch. 15)

duchy a **duke**'s territory (Ch. 9)

duke local Germanic tribal leader (Ch. 9)

Duma Russian national assembly (Ch. 21)

dynastic rule the rule of one family (Ch. 7)

E

Eastern Orthodox Church made up of various national churches that refused to recognize the Church of Rome's claim of control (Ch. 6)

ecumenical movement attempt to gain the union of all professing Christians in the world (Ch. 24)

Edict of Milan edict of Constantine in 313 that made Christianity legal (Ch. 5)

Edict of Nantes edict of Henry IV that gave the **Huguenots** a certain amount of religious toleration (Ch. 12)

Elizabethan Settlement the attempt by Elizabeth to settle England's religious problems through compromise (Ch. 12)

empire the rule of one people over another (Ch. 2)

empiricism the idea that all knowledge comes through experience (Ch. 15)

Ems dispatch report of a meeting between William I of Prussia and a French ambassador that was altered and published by Bismarck; immediate cause of the **Franco-Prussian War** (Ch. 17)

enclosure movement the incorporation of common grazing lands into the estates of wealthy landowners to form large farms (Ch. 18)

Enlightenment eighteenth-century intellectual movement that looked to reason as the solution for all of life's problems (Ch. 15)

Entente Cordiale agreement between Britain, France, and Russia (Ch. 20)

Epic of Gilgamesh epic Babylonian poem that describes the adventures of Gilgamesh and includes an account of a universal flood (Ch. 2)

Epicureanism philosophy that teaches that true happiness comes only as man frees his mind from fear and his body from pain (Ch. 5)

Estates-General French representative body composed of **clergy**, nobility, and townspeople (Ch. 9)

Etruscans one of Italy's earliest civilizations, they lived in northern Italy and contributed to the development of Roman culture (Ch. 4)

euro single currency of the member nations of the **European Union** (Ch. 24)

European Union EU; union of European countries (Ch. 24)

evaluation of historical sources examination of a given record for its internal consistency and believability (Ch. 1)

excommunicate to punish an individual by depriving him of the sacraments and excluding him from the fellowship of the church (Ch. 9)

expressionism artistic movement in which the artist tries to paint how he feels about his subject rather than trying to reproduce realistically what he sees (Ch. 21)

extraterritoriality an individual's right to be tried in his own national court for breaking the law of another country (Ch. 19)

F

Fabian socialism British socialists who sought to achieve a socialist society without revolution (Ch. 18)

factory system production system that brought the workers, raw materials, and machinery under one roof (Ch. 18)

fasces a small bundle of rods which enclosed an axe; symbol of the **imperium** (Ch. 4)

fascism totalitarian government characterized by corporate economy, strong nationalism, military dictatorship, and a glorification of the state (Ch. 21)

federalism delegating specified powers to the national government and reserving all other powers for the state governments (Ch. 16)

Fertile Crescent crescent-shaped fertile region encompassing Mesopotamia and the land of Canaan (Ch. 2)

feudalism a political system in which local rulers offered the people protection in return for their services (Ch. 8)

fief land grants given in return for services (Ch. 8)

fifth columnists individuals within a country who secretly aid the enemy by spying, spreading enemy propaganda, carrying out acts of sabotage, or other similar activities (Ch. 22)

Fifth Republic French government established by Charles de Gaulle that provided for a strong president; occasioned by the French presence in Algeria (Ch. 23)

First Estate clergy of the Roman Catholic Church; aspect of French society (Ch. 16)

Five Pillars of Islam certain religious duties that **Islam** requires every **Muslim** to perform in order to reach heaven; (1) reciting the simple confession "There is no God but **Allah**, and Muhammad is his prophet"; (2) reciting prayers five times daily while facing toward Mecca; (3) giving alms (money) to the poor; (4) fasting from sunrise to sunset during the sacred month of Ramadan; (5) making a pilgrimage to Mecca (Ch. 6)

Five-Year Plans economic program of Joseph Stalin that increased the socialization of the Russian economy (Ch. 21)

florin a gold coin minted by the city of Florence (Ch. 10)

Foreign Legion elite French army that was used throughout France's colonial empire (Ch. 19)

Four Noble Truths the center of Buddha's teachings; (1) Suffering is part of all existence; (2) Suffering has a cause—selfish desires; (3) Suffering can be overcome by destroying selfish desires; (4) If man follows the Eightfold Path, he will destroy selfish desires and end all suffering (Ch. 7)

Fourteen Points Woodrow Wilson's peace plan after World War I (Ch. 20)

Franco-Prussian War war between France and Prussia immediately caused by the **Ems dispatch**; Prussia won and the Second French Empire ended (Ch. 17)

Franks the most powerful Germanic people in the early Middle Ages; kingdom ruled by the **Merovingian House** and the **Carolingian House** (Ch. 8)

freemen more privileged peasants who served as manorial officials or provided skilled labor, such as blacksmiths, millers, and carpenters (Ch. 8)

frescoes paintings on wet plaster (Ch. 11)

friars members of the **mendicant orders** (Ch. 9)

Frondes French political upheavals between 1648 and 1653 aimed at challenging the power of the king; last serious attempt to limit the power of the king until the French Revolution (Ch. 14)

Fujiwara a **clan** that took over Japan by marrying their daughters to the sons of the imperial family (Ch. 7)

G

General Assembly body of the United Nations where all member nations have representation (Ch. 22)

genocide the systematic extermination of a race or ethnic or religious group (Ch. 24)

genre painting a type of painting that depicts scenes of everyday life (Ch. 11)

geocentric theory earth-centered theory of the universe (Ch. 5)

Gestapo Nazi secret police (Ch. 21)

ghettos Jewish area of a city sealed off from the rest of the city (Ch. 22)

gladiator warrior who fought in the Roman Colosseum (Ch. 5)

glasnost "openness"; Soviet policy of encouraging open discussions of the problems facing the USSR (Ch. 23)

globalization characterized by an international rather than a purely national focus (Ch. 24)

Glorious Revolution peaceful revolution in which Parliament dethroned James II and installed William and Mary as corulers (Ch. 14)

Golden Bull established the **Diet** of the Holy Roman Empire (Ch. 10)

Golden Horde Mongol state based in Russia; founded by Batu Khan; the strongest Mongol state in western Asia (Ch. 7)

gospel the teaching that Jesus Christ died in the place of sinful humans so that they might be forgiven of their sins and be able to claim as their own the righteousness of Jesus Christ (Ch. 5)

Gothic light and delicate fourteenth-century architecture with flying buttresses, higher ceilings, thinner walls, larger windows and doors, and stained glass windows (Ch. 10)

Grand Alliance an alliance of European nations—especially England and the Netherlands—against Louis XIV of France (Ch. 14)

Great Awakening eighteenth-century revival in Britain's American colonies (Ch. 15)

Great Leap Forward Mao's attempt to modernize Chinese agrarian economy; wrecked the Chinese steel industry and caused a famine (Ch. 23)

Great Northern War war in which the Russians, led by Peter the Great, defeated Sweden and won additional territory along the Baltic Sea (Ch. 14)

Great Schism the period from the late fourteenth to early fifteenth century during which the Roman Catholic Church had two to three men claiming to be the pope (Ch. 10)

Great Society American social program led by Lyndon Johnson that sought to eliminate poverty (Ch. 23)

Great Trek migration of the **Boers** northward from Cape Colony in South Africa (Ch. 19)

"Greek fire" an explosive mixture of naphtha oil, sulfur, and saltpeter (Ch. 6)

guerrillas "little wars"; small bands of troops that attack a superior force (Ch. 16)

guilds organizations whose primary function was to regulate the business activity of a given town (Ch. 10)

Gulf of Tonkin Resolution congressional authorization for American president Lyndon Johnson to "take all necessary measures to repel any armed attack against forces of the United States and to prevent further aggression" (Ch. 23)

Gupta Empire fourth-century Indian empire under which India had perhaps its greatest era of prosperity and achievement (Ch. 7)

H

Habeas Corpus Act made it illegal for the British government to arbitrarily hold someone in jail (Ch. 14)

Hagia Sophia finest example of Byzantine architecture; built by Justinian (Ch. 6)

Hanseatic League an association composed of more than seventy German cities in northwestern Europe; sought to organize and control trade in Sweden, Russia, Flanders, and England (Ch. 10)

Habsburgs German noble family who built a strong base of power (Austria) among the southern German states; ruled the **Holy Roman Empire** after 1438 (Ch. 10); rulers of Austria; rivals of the **Hoehnzollern**; held the title of Holy Roman Emperor (Ch. 14)

Hegira the flight of Muhammad from Mecca to Medina; year 1 of the **Muslim** calendar (Ch. 6)

heliocentric theory theory that the earth orbits the sun; promoted by Copernicus (Ch. 15)

Hellenic Greek culture (Ch. 3)

Hellenistic similar to Greek culture (Ch. 3)

Helots original Spartans who were enslaved by the Dorians (Ch. 3)

hierarchical structure with levels of authority (Ch. 5)

hieroglyphics a form of picture writing (Ch. 2)

Hinduism Indian religion that has no formal statement of doctrine but is based on the ***Vedas*** and ***Upanishads***; serves as the unifying influence in India's diverse society (Ch. 7)

historical interpretation interpreting events by integrating the perceived meaning and significance of the events (Ch. 1)

historical synthesis gathering the useful information and weaving the facts together into a narrative of the past (Ch. 1)

history the study of the record of the past acts of God and man on earth from its creation to the present, based on the best surviving evidence (Ch. 1)

Hohenstaufens German royal family that rose to prominence in the twelfth century (Ch. 9)

Hohenzollern rulers of Prussia; rivals of the **Hapsburgs**; united the German states into one country in the nineteenth century (Ch. 14)

Holocaust Nazi Germany's attempt to exterminate the Jews (Ch. 22)

Holy Roman Empire the name of the German empire because of its alliance with the Roman Catholic Church and its symbolic association with the empire of ancient Rome (Ch. 9)

homage the ceremony by which a man became a **vassal** and thus eligible for a **fief** (Ch. 8)

homophony music with one basic melody line and several supporting harmony parts (Ch. 15)

Huguenots French Protestants (Ch. 12)

human depravity the doctrine that every aspect of every human's being (body, mind, will, and emotions) has been marred by the Fall and is opposed to God's will (Ch. 1)

humanism a renewed focus on man's capacities (Ch. 11)

humanists those who studied the liberal arts (Ch. 11)

humanities (1) formal study of human thought and culture (Ch. 3) (2) the liberal arts; the study of history, science, and grammar, as well as classical literature and philosophy (Ch. 11)

Hundred Years' War war between England and France during the fourteenth and fifteenth centuries; won by the French (Ch. 10)

Huns nomadic tribe led by Attila whose advance west forced Germanic tribes to seek refuge in Roman territory (Ch. 5)

I

icon painted images of Christ and the saints (Ch. 6)

Il Duce title of Mussolini; head of the Italian Fascist government (Ch. 21)

Ile-de-France the small area around Paris owned by the Capetians (Ch. 9)

Iliad an epic poem of the Greek Dark Ages written by Homer (Ch. 3)

image of God a complex of qualities possessed by all humans that reflects part of God's own personality (Ch. 1)

imperator an ancient title given to the commander of a victorious army; head of the Roman Empire (Ch. 4)

imperialism the extension of power by one people or country over another country (Ch. 19)

imperium the king's authority in Rome (Ch. 4)

impressionism nineteenth-century French art style; focused on light and color using short, choppy brush strokes (Ch. 18)

Inca South American **empire** from the fourteenth to sixteenth centuries (Ch. 13)

indemnities compensation to other nations for war damages (Ch. 17)

Index of Prohibited Books a list of books that the Roman Catholic Church has condemned (Ch. 12)

indictment accusation (Ch. 9)

inductive method reasoning from specific cases to a general conclusion (Ch. 15)

indulgences certificates that supposedly granted pardon from the punishment of sins (Ch. 12)

Industrial Revolution a period in the late eighteenth-century and early nineteenth-century when technological developments radically changed industry (Ch. 18)

Inquisition a special church court commissioned by the pope to stamp out heresy (Ch. 9, 12)

The Institutes of the Christian Religion theological book written by John Calvin; one of the most significant and influential books on theology ever written (Ch. 12)

intendents officials directly responsible to the French king (Ch. 14)

interchangeable parts identical parts that could be used to replace broken parts in manufactured goods (Ch. 18)

interdict the suspension of public church services and of the administration of all sacraments (except baptism and extreme unction) in a given location (Ch. 9)

intifada the "uprising" of the Palestinians against the Israelis (Ch. 24)

investiture symbolic act by which the **lord** gave to the **vassal** the right of use of a **fief** (Ch. 8)

iron curtain the dividing line between Western Europe and Communist Eastern Europe (Ch. 23)

Islam a religion based on the teaching of Muhammad (Ch. 6)

J

Jacobins French revolutionaries who advocated the most radical changes; appealed to the **sans-culottes** (Ch. 16)

Jamestown first English permanent settlement in the New World; located in Virginia (Ch. 13)

Jesuits Roman Catholic religious order founded by Ignatius Loyola that suppressed heresy and promoted Roman Catholic education (Ch. 12)

jihad Islamic "holy war" (Ch. 6)

joint family extended family that includes the children, grandchildren, wives, and close blood relatives of a common ancestor (Ch. 7)

joint-stock company a company in which people invested money and in return were issued stock certificates showing the amount of money they invested (Ch. 13)

journeyman second class of a craft **guild**; "day laborer"; could seek employment and earn wages as a skilled worker (Ch. 10)

July Revolution revolution in France that brought down Charles X and established Louis Philippe as king; sparked other revolutions throughout Europe (Ch. 17)

June Days attempted overthrow of the French government in June 1848 (Ch. 17)

Junkers Prussian nobility who worked closely with the electors in governing the country and serving as officers in the Prussian army (Ch. 14)

"just price" a price that included the cost of materials, a fair return for the labor expended, and a reasonable profit (Ch. 10)

Justinian Code a systematic arrangement of laws that clarified Roman legal principles (Ch. 6)

K

Kaaba a sacred shrine at Mecca that housed hundreds of pagan idols; Muhammad destroyed the idols of the Kaaba and turned it into the center of Islamic worship (Ch. 6)

kamikaze Japanese suicide pilots (Ch. 22)

Kellogg-Briand Pact document that outlawed war; crowning effort to preserve peace in the post-World War I period (Ch. 20)

knight medieval warriors who protected life and property and lived by the "code of **chivalry**" (Ch. 8)

Korean War war between Communist North Korea and democratic South Korea (Ch. 23)

L

laity those who did not take "Holy Orders" (Ch. 8)

Lateran Treaties treaties between Benito Mussolini and the Roman Catholic Church that established Vatican City and gave Italy's government recognition by the Roman Catholic Church (Ch. 21)

latitude distance from the equator (Ch. 13)

Law of the Twelve Tables foundation of Roman civil law; the first written law code in Rome; hung in the **Roman Forum** (Ch. 4)

lay investiture claim of kings and nobles not only to appoint church officials but also to invest them with their religious authority (Ch. 9)

LDP Liberal Democratic Party; major political party in Japan (Ch. 24)

League of Nations post-World War I international organization that sought to guarantee international cooperation and to achieve international peace and security (Ch. 20)

League of the Seven Hills league of seven villages on the banks of the Tiber River; the beginning of the city of Rome (Ch. 4)

lebensraum "living space"; Hitler's early reason for expanding German territory (Ch. 22)

Lend-Lease Act Act of Congress authorizing the president to "sell, transfer title to, exchange, lease, lend, or otherwise dispose of" military supplies to any country whose security was important to the United States (Ch. 22)

levée en masse a nation calling upon all its citizens to take an active part in the war effort; first employed during the French Revolution (Ch. 16)

liberalism political theory supporting an increase in civil and political freedoms and less government interference with the individual (Ch. 17)

lieutenants French officers responsible to the king by whom the king gained control of the army (Ch. 14)

limited wars wars limited to specific geographic areas (Ch. 23)

Line of Demarcation line of separation in the Atlantic Ocean that decided the areas that could be colonized by Spain and Portugal (Ch. 13)

Locarno Pact 1925 treaty in which Germany agreed to recognize its post-World War I boundaries as permanent (Ch. 20)

Lollards followers of John Wycliffe (Ch. 12)

Lombards Germanic people who through conquest moved into northern Italy (Ch. 8)

longbow English bow that could shoot arrows able to penetrate suits of armor (Ch. 10)

lord landholding noble in **feudalism** (Ch. 8)

Louisiana Purchase 1803 land purchase by the United States that almost doubled the size of that nation (Ch. 19)

Luftwaffe Nazi Germany's air force (Ch. 22)

Lusitania British ocean liner that was sunk by a German submarine in 1915 (Ch. 20)

M

Maastricht Treaty treaty between members of the European Common Market to form the European Union (Ch. 24)

Maginot Line a series of French fortifications along her border with Germany (Ch. 21)

Magna Carta a guarantee of feudal rights; one of the most important documents in English history because it showed that the king was under the law (Ch. 9)

Magyars a group of Asiatic nomads who later became known as the Hungarians (Ch. 8)

Manchu dynasty ruling dynasty in China from 1644 to 1911/12 (Ch. 19)

mandates territories technically under the control of the League of Nations but administered by various Allied countries (Ch. 20)

mannerism artistic style throughout much of the sixteenth century; characterized by distortions and exaggerations (Ch. 15)

manor the center of medieval society, a self-contained farming community controlled by a **lord** and farmed by peasants (Ch. 8)

Maoris New Zealand natives; eventually won representation in the New Zealand government (Ch. 19)

Mare Nostrum the Roman term for the Mediterranean Sea; "our sea" (Ch. 4)

Marshall Plan European Recovery Act; provided massive economic assistance for post-World War II Europe; the western nations accepted the funds and the eastern nations did not (Ch. 23)

Marxism theory that every social, political, or religious movement springs from a desire by one group of people to take economic advantage of another group; taught that history would naturally progress toward perfection (communism) (Ch. 18)

mass the Roman Catholic service in which the Holy Eucharist is offered (Ch. 8)

master third class of a craft guild; could open his own shop and take on apprentices and journeymen (Ch. 10)

Maya Central American civilization from the fourth through the tenth centuries; noted for its artistic and intellectual achievements (Ch. 13)

Mayflower Compact a temporary agreement establishing civil authority for the Plymouth Colony (Ch. 16)

mayor of the palace principal palace official under the Merovingian House (Ch. 8)

Medici family prominent Italians who had become extremely wealthy through commerce and banking; controlled the city of Florence (Ch. 11)

Meiji Period period during which Japan was transformed from a feudal society to a major industrial power (Ch. 19)

Mein Kampf "My Struggle"; book by Adolf Hitler (Ch. 21)

mendicant orders monastic orders who labored to bring about reform by living and preaching among the people; they begged for their daily sustenance (Ch. 9)

Mensheviks wing of the Social Democratic Party in Russia that advocated change through peaceful measures (Ch. 21)

mercantilism economic system that held that the wealth of colonies should benefit the mother country (Ch. 13)

Merovingian House first royal line of the Franks (Ch. 8)

mestizos those of mixed Spanish and Indian blood (Ch. 19)

middle class social class primarily composed of merchants, bankers, craftsmen, and skilled laborers (Ch. 10)

Middle Kingdom Chinese term reflecting the belief that China was the center of the earth (Ch. 7)

minaret a tower that is a part of or adjacent to a **mosque** (Ch. 6)

Minoan civilization an early civilization in the Aegean region based on the island of Crete; established trade with the **Fertile Crescent** and Egypt (Ch. 3)

missi dominici messengers sent in pairs by Charlemagne throughout his **empire** to ensure the enforcement of his policies on the local level (Ch. 8)

mobilize make ready troops (Ch. 20)

monarchy rule by one (Ch. 3)

monasticism the lifestyle of withdrawing from all worldly cares and possessions and practicing strict discipline and religious exercises (Ch. 5)

moneychangers men experienced in judging the approximate value of coins, discovering counterfeit currency, and determining one currency's value in relation to another (Ch. 10)

monotheism belief in only one God (Ch. 2)

Monroe Doctrine warning by James Monroe that the United States would resist any efforts to colonize the Americas (Ch. 17, 19)

Moors Spanish **Muslims** (Ch. 10)

moratorium suspension (Ch. 20)

mosaic inlaid pieces of glass or stone in wet cement or plaster (Ch. 6)

mosque place of **Muslim** worship (Ch. 6)

motets unaccompanied Latin songs that combined different melodies and words with a plainsong melody (Ch. 11)

movable type separate printing blocks for each character (Ch. 7)

muezzin one who calls faithful **Muslims** to prayer five times a day from a minaret (Ch. 6)

Mughal Turkish-Mongol dynasty in India around the sixteenth century; founded by Babur (Ch. 7)

Munich Conference conference in which Britain and France gave the Sudetenland to Hitler (Ch. 22)

Muslim follower of **Islam**; "submitter to **Allah**" (Ch. 6)

Mycenaean civilization early Greek civilization on the mainland of Greece; borrowed heavily from the **Minoan civilization** (Ch. 3)

N

nation very large group of people (usually including many cities) who have in common the same land area and the same language (Ch. 1)

nationalism a longing for independence and local autonomy (Ch. 17)

nation-state an independent group of people having common interests and ruled by a king (Ch. 10)

NATO North Atlantic Treaty Organization; a regional military alliance to defend against Soviet expansion (Ch. 23)

Nazism German fascism (Ch. 21)

neoclassical eighteenth-century artistic style that imitated the classical ideals of ancient Greece and Rome (Ch. 15)

New Deal Franklin Roosevelt's program of relief, recovery, and reform (Ch. 21)

New Economic Policy capitalistic program to revitalize the economy of the **USSR** (Ch. 21)

"New Labour" Party British political party (Ch. 24)

"New Rome" Constantine's name for Constantinople (Ch. 6)

Nika Revolt a popular uprising crushed by Justinian early in his reign; the turning point of Justinian's reign (Ch. 6)

Ninety-five Theses a list of statements concerning the sale of indulgences that Martin Luther proposed as topics for a scholarly debate (Ch. 12)

O

OAS Organization of American States; a regional organization designed to prevent Communist expansion in the Western Hemisphere (Ch. 24)

Odyssey an epic poem of the Greek Dark Ages written by Homer (Ch. 3)

Old Regime political and social order in France before the French Revolution (Ch. 16)

oligarchy rule of a few (Ch. 3)

Olympiad four-year period between Olympic games; became a Greek means of dating historical events (Ch. 3)

Operation Overlord code name for the Allied invasion of France during World War II (Ch. 22)

Opium Wars wars between China and European powers led by Great Britain; fought over the issue of importing opium into China (Ch. 19)

oratorio musical composition for solo singers, chorus, and orchestra that tells a sacred story without the dramatic action employed in operas (Ch. 15)

organization a system of rules, regulations, and accountability that governs all who take part in the functions of a city (Ch. 1)

Ottoman Turks the **Muslim** invaders who sacked Constantinople and killed the last Byzantine emperor (Ch. 6)

P

pacifism refusal to take up arms against anyone, even in time of war (Ch. 12)

Pact of Steel German-Italian military alliance prior to World War II (Ch. 22)

page a boy placed under the care of a **knight** for the purpose of becoming a knight (Ch. 8)

pantheism the belief that everything in the universe, whether it be spiritual or physical, is all part of one great substance called "God" (Ch. 15)

panzer German armored vehicle (Ch. 22)

Paris Peace Conference conference that negotiated the peace settlement for World War I (Ch. 20)

Parliament the English representative body consisting of two houses, the House of Commons and the House of Lords; had the **"power of the purse"** (Ch. 9)

Parliament Bill capstone of Britain's political development; made the House of Commons dominant; limited the House of Lords (Ch. 18)

partisans fighters who harass an enemy occupying their territory (Ch. 22)

passive resistance a nonviolent program defying the current rule through strikes (including hunger strikes and sit-down strikes), mass demonstrations, and refusal to pay taxes (Ch. 24)

pater the father in the Roman family; exercised sole authority in the family (Ch. 4)

Parthenon most spectacular temple in Athens; dedicated to **Athena** (Ch. 3)

patriarch bishop of one of the most important cities of the empire—Jerusalem, Antioch, Alexandria, Rome, and Constantinople (Ch. 5)

patrician the aristocratic class in Rome made up of wealthy landowners and noble families (Ch. 4)

patrons sponsors of artists (Ch. 11)

Pax Romana "Roman Peace"; 31 BC to 180 (Ch. 5)

Pax Sinica "Chinese Peace" established by the Han Dynasty (Ch. 7)

"peaceful coexistence" the Cold War policy that sought "to keep to the positions of ideological struggle without resorting to arms" (Ch. 23)

Peace of Augsburg allowed each German prince the right to choose whether his territory would be Lutheran or Roman Catholic (Ch. 12)

Peace of God decree by which the church forbade the pillage of its property and extended protection to all noncombatants in society (Ch. 8)

Peloponnesian League a league of Greek city-states led by Sparta with the intention of thwarting the goals of Athenian democracy (Ch. 3)

Peloponnesian War Greek civil war between Athens and her allies and Sparta and her allies (Ch. 3)

peninsulares Spaniards born and raised in Spain (Ch. 19)

perestroika Soviet policy during the 1980s of a wide range of social, political, and economic reforms (Ch. 23)

perspective artistic technique of portraying a three-dimensional appearance on a flat surface (Ch. 11)

Petition of Right document that Parliament sent to Charles I which stated that the king did not have the right to make people pay taxes without parliamentary consent and that Parliament would not tolerate arbitrary imprisonment of any subjects (Ch. 14)

Petrine theory the Roman Catholic theory that Christ made Peter the first **pope** and gave him supreme authority over the church on earth; Peter subsequently transferred this office and its authority to those who succeeded him as bishop of Rome (Ch. 8)

pharaoh ruler of Egypt (Ch. 2)

philosophers men who sought the answers to the basic questions of life through human reasoning ability (Ch. 3)

philosophes eighteenth-century French writers and social critics (Ch. 15)

Pietism seventeenth- and eighteenth-century movement dedicated to spiritual renewal (Ch. 15)

Pilgrims group of English Separatists that left for the New World in 1620 (Ch. 16)

plainsong Gregorian chant; simple, single-lined melody (Ch. 11)

plebeian the "common" class in Rome made up of farmers, traders, and craftsmen (Ch. 4)

plebiscite a resolution of the Council of Plebeians (Ch. 4)

PLO Palestinian Liberation Organization; demanded a separate Palestinian state and initiated **intifada** (Ch. 24)

pogroms organized government massacres in Russia (Ch. 21)

polis "city-state"; basic political unit of Greece (Ch. 3)

polygamy marriage of a husband to more than one wife (Ch. 7)

polyphonic consisting of many melodies (Ch. 11)

polyphony music in which several melody lines of equal importance are intertwined (Ch. 15)

polytheism belief in many gods (Ch. 2)

polytonality the use of several musical keys simultaneously (Ch. 21)

pontifex maximus "greatest pontiff"; title of the Roman emperors (Ch. 5)

pope the bishop of Rome; first used of the bishop of Rome in 452 and generally accepted as his title by the end of the sixth century (Ch. 8)

popular sovereignty government based upon the consent of the governed (Ch. 16)

post-impressionism eighteenth-century artistic style that emphasized universal themes and tried to outline more clearly than impressionism the figures in paintings (Ch. 18)

"power of the purse" a representative body's power to approve all new taxes; a means of forcing the king to hear grievances (Ch. 9)

Pragmatic Sanction agreement among European rulers to respect the territorial boundaries of Austria upon the ascension of Maria Theresa (Ch. 14)

primary sources records produced during the time period being studied; usually by those involved in the events being studied (Ch. 1)

princeps "first citizen" (Ch. 5)

proletariat the workers in Marxism (Ch. 18)

propaganda materials and methods of indoctrination (Ch. 21)

prospectus details of a proposed business venture (Ch. 13)

Protectorate English government established by Oliver Cromwell (Ch. 14)

publican tax collector for the Roman Republic in provinces (Ch. 4)

Punic Wars three wars between Carthage and Rome (Ch. 4)

purgatory a place of temporary punishment where souls bound for heaven must go after death to atone for their "minor" unconfessed sins or for sins for which they have not done sufficient penance (Ch. 8)

purges Stalin's practice of murdering those who might threaten his power (Ch. 21)

Puritans those who wanted to purify the **Anglican Church** of those practices that reminded them of Roman Catholicism (Ch. 12); Anglicans who sought to purify the Church of England (Ch. 14)

Q

quadrivium liberal arts curriculum consisting of arithmetic, geometry, astronomy, and music (Ch. 10)

Quadruple Alliance alliance between Austria, Prussia, Russia, and Great Britain to maintain the **Congress of Vienna**'s sentiments (Ch. 17)

Quebec Act act permitting French Canadians to retain their language, law, and customs, and to freely practice their Roman Catholic religion (Ch. 19)

Qur'an the sacred book of the **Muslims** (Ch. 6)

R

RAF British Royal Air Force (Ch. 22)

rationalism the belief that reason is the only sure source of knowledge and truth (Ch. 15)

realism an artistic style that sought to portray life as it really is (Ch. 18)

realpolitik "politics of reality"; using whatever political means necessary—including force—to advance national goals (Ch. 17)

recant renounce one's beliefs (Ch. 12)

Reconquista the reconquest of the Iberian Peninsula, which was held by the **Muslims** (Ch. 10)

Reform Bill 1832 bill that reorganized the electoral system for the House of Commons (Ch. 18)

regular clergy clergy who lived according to a monastic rule (Ch. 8)

Reichstag German legislative body (Ch. 21)

Reign of Terror most destructive and violent phase of the French Revolution (Ch. 16)

Reinsurance Treaty Bismarck's alliance with Russia (Ch. 20)

Renaissance the revival of learning in Europe from the fourteenth century through the sixteenth century (Ch. 11)

reparations payments for war damages (Ch. 20)

republic form of government in which voting citizens exercise power through elected officials under law (Ch. 4)

requerimento statement that the **conquistadors** read to the Indians explaining that the **pope** had given Spain authority over the New World (Ch. 13)

Restoration reestablishment of the Stuart monarchy in 1660 (Ch. 14)

Risorgimento Italian nationalist movement (Ch. 17)

rococo an artistic style that is characterized by refined elegance (Ch. 15)

Roman Forum the center of Roman government (Ch. 4)

Romanov Russian royal dynasty; deposed in the Revolution of 1917 (Ch. 14)

Roman sacramental system a system of religious acts which Roman Catholics believe automatically grant grace (spiritual benefit) by their very performance; see **seven sacraments** (Ch. 8)

Romanesque the prevalent architectural style in Europe from 1050 to 1150 (Ch. 10)

romanticism late-eighteenth-century European literary and artistic movement characterized by a reaction against rationalism and an embrace of idealism and emotions (Ch. 17)

Rome-Berlin Axis alliance between Nazi Germany and fascist Italy (Ch. 22)

Roosevelt Corollary corollary to the Monroe doctrine proclaimed by Theodore Roosevelt; in the case of wrongdoing on the part of any Latin American state, the United States claimed the right to intervene in that country and set its affairs in order (Ch. 19)

Roundheads supporters of Parliament in the English Civil War (Ch. 14)

Rus the Slavic designation of the Norsemen; "rowers" or "seafarers" (Ch. 6)

Russification Nicholas I's policy of uniting the diverse national groups within Nicholas's territory around the culture and traditions of Russia (Ch. 17)

Russo-Japanese War war between Japan and Russia; Japan won and became a major world power (Ch. 19, 21)

Rwandan genocide the systematic extermination of tribal groups in Rwanda during the 1990s (Ch. 24)

S

St. Bartholomew's Day Massacre massacre of **Huguenots** throughout France on August 27, 1572 (Ch. 12)

St. Lawrence Seaway seaway that fostered economic growth between Canada and the United States (Ch. 23)

Salian House German royal house that tried to bring the German nobles under royal control (Ch. 9)

SALT Strategic Arms Limitation Talks; limited the number of nuclear weapons that the United States and the **USSR** could possess (Ch. 23)

samurai Japanese warrior (Ch. 7)

sanctions forbidding the sale of certain materials to a country (Ch. 22)

sans-culottes "without breeches"; Paris workers (Ch. 16)

Sanskrit early Indian language established by the **Aryans** (Ch. 7)

satrapies provinces in the Persian Empire (Ch. 2)

Schlieffen Plan Germany's plan for a two-front war (Ch. 20)

Scholasticism a twelfth-century intellectual movement that was characterized by a renewed interest in theology and philosophy (Ch. 10)

scientific method a pattern of thinking that scientists use when seeking answers to their questions about the physical universe (Ch. 15)

scientific revolution a period from the Renaissance to the eighteenth century when scientific inquiry and achievement advanced rapidly (Ch. 15)

scorched-earth policy burning everything that might be of value to the enemy (Ch. 16)

SDI Strategic Defense Initiative; American defense program designed to use American space, laser, and satellite technology to provide a shield in space against incoming Soviet missiles (Ch. 23)

SEATO Southeast Asia Treaty Organization; formed to keep Asian nations free from communism (Ch. 23)

secondary sources records that explain or interpret **primary sources** (Ch. 1)

Second Estate nobility; aspect of French society (Ch. 16)

Second Vatican Council also called Vatican II; Roman Catholic council that encouraged ecumenism (Ch. 24)

Secretariat administrative arm of the **United Nations** (Ch. 22)

secular clergy conducted religious services, administered the sacraments to the laity, and supervised the business and secular clergy of the church (Ch. 8)

Security Council the executive, or enforcement, power of the **United Nations**; consists of five permanent members and ten non-permanent members (Ch. 22)

seed of the serpent humans yet to be born who would prove to have the same deceptive, God-defying nature that Satan evidenced that day in the garden (Ch. 1)

seed of the woman future humans who would prove to be loyal to their Creator (Ch. 1)

Seljuk Turks nomadic tribes from central Asia that adopted Arab culture and the Islamic religion (Ch. 6)

Senate the most important and most powerful body of the Roman Republic (Ch. 4)

Separatists those who removed themselves from the **Anglican Church** (Ch. 12)

Sepoy Mutiny the 1857 revolt by the sepoys, the native Indian troops employed by the East India Company (Ch. 19)

Septuagint Greek translation of the Hebrew Old Testament (Ch. 5)

serfs majority of those living on a **manor**; their status was midway between the ancient slave and the medieval freeman (Ch. 8)

seven sacraments baptism, confirmation, penance, the Holy Eucharist, matrimony, holy orders, and extreme unction; see **Roman sacramental system** (Ch. 8)

Seven Years' War war with Britain and Prussia on one side and France, Russia, and Austria on the other; won by Britain and Prussia (Ch. 14)

17th parallel the 1954 border between North Vietnam and South Vietnam (Ch. 23)

sheriff one who governed a **shire** (Ch. 9)

Shintoism originally a form of nature worship that attributed deity to anything in nature that was awe-inspiring or extraordinary; stressed the supremacy of the sun goddess and the divine descent of the emperor; a religion of feeling (Ch. 7)

shires districts in England set up by Alfred the Great (Ch. 9)

shogun "great general"; military ruler of Japan; held the real power over the Japanese government from 1192 to 1868 (Ch. 7)

simony the buying and selling of religious or blessed articles as well as church offices (Ch. 9)

Sino-Japanese War war between China and Japan (1894–95); won by Japan (Ch. 19)

Sistine Chapel a chapel in the Vatican; Michelangelo painted the ceiling (Ch. 11)

sitzkrieg "sitting war"; the beginning of World War II in the West when there were no major offensives (Ch. 22)

Six-Day War war in which Israel launched a preemptive strike against Egypt, Syria, and Jordan; won by Israel (Ch. 24)

Slavs a group that settled in Eastern Europe after the Germanic tribes migrated west; the largest people group in Russia (Ch. 6)

socialism government ownership of the means of production and the distribution of goods for the presumed welfare of society (Ch. 18)

sola fide justification by faith alone; Reformation doctrine that a man is not justified before God by his works or by faith and works but by faith alone (Ch. 12)

Solidarity a powerful labor union in Poland that opposed the Polish Communist government (Ch. 23)

soviet Communist organization of workers (Ch. 21)

Spanish Armada a great fleet of 130 ships that was to sail to the Netherlands, pick up a large Spanish army, and transport the invasion force to England; defeated by the English and storms in 1588 (Ch. 12)

specialization an individuals' commitment to concentrate on a given endeavor necessary for human existence (Ch. 1)

Sputnik the Russian satellite that was the first manmade satellite launched into space (Ch. 23)

squire the personal servant of a **knight** (Ch. 8)

stalemate a situation in which both sides are at a standstill (Ch. 20)

status quo ante bellum how things were before the war (Ch. 14)

Statute of Westminster act of Parliament declaring Canada, Australia, New Zealand, and South Africa to be "autonomous communities within the British Empire" and "members of the British Commonwealth of Nations" (Ch. 21)

steppes vast grassy plains from western China to eastern Europe (Ch. 7)

Stoicism philosophy that taught that the highest good is the pursuit of courage, dignity, duty, simplicity of life, and service to fellow men (Ch. 5)

sub-Saharan Africa the part of Africa south of the Sahara (Ch. 7)

subinfeudation parceling out portions of a **fief** to gain the services of lesser nobles (Ch. 8)

Suez Crisis the time in which Egypt took control of the Suez Canal in 1956 and Israel took control of the Sinai Peninsula (Ch. 24)

summit conference of high-level officials (Ch. 22)

Swahili the native African language of the east African city-states; contained elements of Arabic, Persian, and Indian (Ch. 7)

swastika Nazi symbol; "broken cross" (Ch. 21)

syllogism a three-step logical process of thinking (Ch. 3)

synagogues centers of worship of the "scattered" Jews (Ch. 5)

syndicates groups in the work force (Ch. 21)

T

Table of Nations Genesis 10; lists the descendants of Shem, Ham, and Japheth according to the nations that arose from their families (Ch. 1)

Taika Reform mid-seventh century restructuring of Japanese government to weaken the strength of the local **clan** chieftains; known as the "Great Change" (Ch. 7)

taille French royal land tax (Ch. 10)

Taliban radical Muslims that gained control in Afghanistan (Ch. 24)

Taoism founded by Lao-tzu; encouraged men to live in harmony with nature ; became the basis of mystical, magical, and superstitious elements in Chinese society (Ch. 7)

Tartars fierce Mongolian warriors from central Asia that attacked Russia in the thirteenth century (Ch. 6)

tenants-in-chief military followers who were feudal **vassals** (Ch. 9)

Tennis Court Oath oath of the **Third Estate** declaring that they would not disband until a written constitution was established (Ch. 16)

terrorism the use of indiscriminate violence, or the threat of its use, for political ends (Ch. 24)

Tet Offensive failed surprise attack of the North Vietnamese on South Vietnam; affected the American attitude toward the **Vietnam War** (Ch. 23)

theocracy government directly by God (Ch. 2)

Third Estate largest estate in France comprising all who were not clergy or nobility (Ch. 16)

Third Reich empire of Nazi Germany from 1933 to 1945 (Ch. 22)

Thirty Years' War the last great religious war fought in Europe; won by the Protestants with France's aid (Ch. 14)

38th parallel the border between North and South Korea (Ch. 23)

Three Emperors' League pre-World War I alliance between Germany, Russia, and Austria-Hungary (Ch. 20)

three-field system a pattern of rotating planting among three fields leaving one fallow each year (Ch. 8)

Tiananmen Square square in Beijing, China; site of a deadly confrontation between the Chinese army and college-aged dissidents (Ch. 23)

Tokugawa family of shoguns that ruled Japan since the beginning of the seventeenth-century (Ch. 19)

topography the physical features of a land (Ch. 7)

total war war that affects those in the battlefield and those at home (Ch. 20)

totalitarian states one-party political system led by a powerful dictator who typically maintains control by force (Ch. 21)

tournament a mock war; included two types of contests, the joust and the melee (Ch. 8)

tradition the handing down of information by word of mouth from generation to generation (Ch. 1)

transubstantiation Roman Catholic belief that during the Holy Eucharist the priest transforms the bread and wine into the actual body and blood of Christ (Ch. 8)

treasury of saints Roman Catholic doctrine of the storehouse of the "excess works" of the saints and the works of Christ; used in the dispensing of **indulgences** (Ch. 12)

Treaty of Aix-la-Chapelle treaty ending the **War of Austrian Succession**; except for Silesia being given to Prussia, it returned Europe to **status quo ante bellum** (Ch. 14)

Treaty of Brest Litovsk treaty between Russia and Germany after the Russian Revolution; pulled Russia out of World War I (Ch. 20)

Treaty of Kanagawa treaty between Japan and the United States; first treaty Japan ever signed with a Western nation (Ch. 19)

Treaty of London treaty that recognized the independence and perpetual neutrality of Belgium (Ch. 17)

Treaty of Paris (1) treaty ending the **Seven Years' War** (Ch. 14) (2) treaty ending the War for Independence between the United States and Britain (Ch. 16)

Treaty of Sèvres treaty between the Ottoman Empire and the Allied Powers of World War I; dismantled the Ottoman Empire (Ch. 20)

Treaty of St. Germain treaty between Austria and the Allied Powers of World War I (Ch. 20)

Treaty of Utrecht ended the **War of the Spanish Succession** (Ch. 14)

Treaty of Verdun treaty between Charles the Bald, Louis the German, and Lothair to divide Louis the Pious's kingdom (Ch. 8)

Treaty of Versailles treaty between Germany and the Allied Powers of World War I; included the **war guilt clause**, which demanded that Germany pay **reparations** (Ch. 20)

Tribal Assembly another name for the **plebeian** assembly in Rome (Ch. 4)

tribe a number of **clans** united by common beliefs and living in a particular region (Ch. 4)

tribunes ten men, elected by the Council of Plebeians, who protected the rights and interests of the common people (Ch. 4)

Triple Alliance anti-French coalition of Germany, Austria-Hungary, and Italy (Ch. 20)

Triple Entente pre-World War I agreement between Britain, France, and Russia (Ch. 20)

triumvirate rule of three men (Ch. 4)

trivium liberal arts curriculum consisting of grammar, rhetoric, and logic (Ch. 10)

troubadours wandering minstrels who popularized the vernacular in lyric poetry (Ch. 10)

Truce of God decree which limited fighting to specified weekdays by forbidding combat from Wednesday evening to Monday morning (Ch. 8)

Truman Doctrine the principle, enunciated by Harry S. Truman, of assisting countries in a struggle against communism (Ch. 23)

Tudor family the ruling family of England during the sixteenth century (Ch. 12)

two-field system planting crops on only half of the cultivated land, leaving the other half to lie fallow for a year to recover its fertility (Ch. 8)

tyranny government headed by a tyrant who gained complete control of it—usually by force (Ch. 3)

U

U-2 incident the shooting down of an American U-2 reconnaissance (spy) plane over the Soviet Union in 1960 (Ch. 23)

U-boat *unterseeboot*; German submarine (Ch. 20)

ultimatum a list of demands with threats (Ch. 20)

Umayyad caliphate that was a hereditary dynasty centered in Damascus (Ch. 6)

Unam Sanctam papal **bull** by Boniface VIII; stated that obedience to the pontiff was necessary for salvation (Ch. 10)

underwriter one who wrote his name below the **prospectus**, pledging to help share the cost of the enterprise (Ch. 13)

United Nations an international organization founded in 1945 that seeks the maintenance of international peace and security (Ch. 22)

universitas those united for the common purpose of education (Ch. 10)

unrestricted submarine warfare the sinking of all enemy ships, whether armed or not (Ch. 20)

Upanishads philosophical essays elaborating on the teaching of the ***Vedas*** (Ch. 7)

USSR Union of Soviet Socialist Republics (Ch. 21)

usury the practice of charging interest for the use of lent money (Ch. 10)

utopian socialism belief that if the inequities in society could be abolished, man's natural goodness could be perfected (Ch. 18)

V

Vandals a Germanic tribe that established a kingdom in North Africa; sacked Rome after the **Visigoths** (Ch. 5)

Varangians Swedish Norsemen who plundered Slavic villages during the eighth and ninth centuries (Ch. 6)

vassal recipient of a **fief** who owed allegiance to a **lord** (Ch. 8)

Vedas collection of religious literature that contains the early traditions and religious beliefs of the Indians (Ch. 7)

vernacular common spoken language (Ch. 10)

Versailles palace of Louis XIV; built twelve miles southwest of Paris (Ch. 14)

viceroy an "assistant king" that the Spanish king appointed to oversee affairs in the New World (Ch. 13)

veto a way for tribunes to could stop unjust acts of **patrician** officials (Ch. 4)

Vichy France area of France unoccupied by Nazi Germany; Vichy became the seat of the new government (Ch. 22)

Viet Cong Communist **guerillas** who launched subversive activity in South Vietnam (Ch. 23)

Vietnam War war between the Communist North Vietnam and the democratic South Vietnam (Ch. 23)

Vietnamization the policy of gradually turning the burden of the fighting of the Vietnam War over to the South Vietnamese (Ch. 23)

Vikings Germanic tribes from Scandinavia that were explorers and warriors; the most feared invaders of their day (Ch. 8)

Visigoths a Germanic tribe that settled in the Eastern Roman Empire; defeated Rome at the battle of Adrianople and later sacked Rome (Ch. 5)

W

war communism tightly regulated system of economic controls imposed on Russia by Lenin (Ch. 21)

war debts debts incurred during the course of a war (Ch. 20)

war guilt clause clause in the **Treaty of Versailles** that placed the blame for World War I on the Germans (Ch. 20)

War of the Austrian Succession war with Great Britain and Austria on the one side and Prussia, Spain, and France on the other; fought when Maria Theresa ascended the Austrian throne (Ch. 14)

War of the Spanish Succession war between the **Grand Alliance** and Louis XIV over the succession to the throne of Spain (Ch. 14)

Warsaw Pact Soviet regional military alliance that included Soviet satellite states in Eastern Europe; organized to counter **NATO** (Ch. 23)

Wars of the Roses series of conflicts between the houses of York and Lancaster over the English throne (Ch. 10)

Washington Naval Conference the 1922 conference that limited the number of warships that each maritime nation could build; made a ratio to limit the number of large warships (Ch. 20)

week work obligation of **serfs**; devoting two or three days a week to work for the **lord** (Ch. 8)

Weimar Republic German government after World War I (Ch. 21)

welfare state a state in which the government assumes the responsibility for the material and social well-being of every individual "from the cradle to the grave" (Ch. 18)

wheel of life cycle of rebirths in reincarnation (Ch. 7)

witan Anglo-Saxon assembly of the great men of the kingdom (Ch. 9)

world soul another name for the **Brahman** (Ch. 7)

worldview a perspective from which we may examine and interpret the universe and everything in it (Ch. 1)

written records more accurate records of the past such as private letters, inventory lists, inscriptions, diaries, and journals (Ch. 1)

Y

Yalta Conference meeting between Churchill, Roosevelt, and Stalin that recognized Soviet control of eastern Europe (Ch. 22)

Yamato clan Japanese **clan** that forged a unified state; claimed divine lineage for the emperor (Ch. 7)

YMCA Young Men's Christian Association (Ch. 18)

Yom Kippur War 1973 war between Israel and the combined forces of Egypt and Syria that began on the Jewish Day of Atonement; won by Israel (Ch. 24)

Z

zeppelins long, slender airships similar to modern blimps (Ch. 20)

Zeus "king of gods and man"; ruler of Mount Olympus (Ch. 3)

ziggurats pyramid-like structures that had terraces at different levels along their exterior (Ch. 2)

Zollverein nineteenth-century German trade union under the leadership of Prussia (Ch. 17)

INDEX

C

N

O

P

Q

R

PHOTOGRAPH CREDITS

The following agencies and individuals have furnished materials to meet the photographic needs of this textbook. We wish to express our gratitude to them for their important contribution.

Alamy
Andrés Morya – Hinojosa
APVA Preservation Virginia
Architect of the Capitol
Art Renewal Center
Art Resource
Ashmolean Museum, University of Oxford
ASSOCIATED PRESS
John Bean
Nathan Benn
BiblePlaces.com
BJU Photo Services
BJU Press Files
Bob Jones University Museum and Gallery
Dennis Bollinger
Calvin College
Clipart.com
George R. Collins
Corel Corporation
Dr. Stewart Custer
Department of Defense
DigitalSTOCK
Dundee Central Library
Egyptian Tourist Authority
Fotolia
German Information Center
Getty Images
Harry S. Truman Library
Hemera Technologies, Inc.
Herbert Hoover Library
Webb Hudspeth
Institute of Human Origins
iStockphoto
Jupiter Images
Library and Archives Canada
Library of Congress
Mexican Government Tourism Office
Musée cantonal des Beaux-Arts de Lausanne
NASA
National Archives
The National Churchill Museum Photographic Collection
National Gallery of Art
National Maritime Museum, Greenwich, UK
National Park Service
New Netherland Museum/ www.newnetherland.org
The New York Public Library
North Wind Picture Archives
Gerald Oskoboiny
Overseas Missionary Fellowship
The Oxyrhynchus Papyri Project, Oxford/Egypt Exploration Society
Palace of Westminster Collection
PhotoDisc, Inc.
Photo Office de Tourisme de Nimes, France
Punch Cartoon Library
Wade Ramsay
Reading Museum (Reading Borough Council)
REUTERS
Ed Richards
Ronald Reagan Presidential Library
Russian Gospel Ministries
Saudia Aramco World
Shutterstock
Mark Sidwell
SuperStock
Swabian Tourism Bureau
Sword of the Lord
Thinkstock
TrekEarth.com
United States Air Force
United States Army
United States Holocaust Memorial Museum
University of Bologna
University of Michigan Health System
Unusual Films
Western Pennsylvania Conservancy
The White House
Wikimedia Commons
Wikipedia
William J. Clinton Presidential Library
Wittenberg Culture, www.wittenberg.de
www.HolyLandPhotos.org
Yale Divinity School Library

Cover
iStockphoto.com/Konstantin Yolshin; IStockphoto.com/ naphtalina; iStockphoto.com/ emrah_oztas

Front Matter
Getty Images/Hemera/ Thinkstock vi (top); "Ajanta caves, Maharashtra"/Soman/ Wikimedia Commons/ GNUFDL 1.2/CC-BY-SA 3.0 vi (bottom); "Kovář při práci (Velikonoční trhy na Václavském náměstí)" by Matěj Baťha/Wikimedia Commons/ CC BY-SA 3.0 vii (blacksmith); "Braine-le-Château" by Jean-Pol GRANDMONT/Wikimedia Commons/CC BY 2.0 vii (watermill); "Flour mill" by Jonas Bergsten/Wikimedia Commons/ Public Domain vii (grist mill); "Confuciustempleapricot-platform" by Rolf Müller/ Wikimedia Commons/ GNUFDL 1.2/ CC-BY-SA 3.0 viii (Pavilion); PhotoDisc/Getty Images viii (African Sunrise)

Unit One Opener
Getty Images/iStockphoto/ Thinkstock xii–1

Chapter 1
NASA Glenn Research Center (SASA-GRC) 2; Mexican Government Tourism Office 4 (top); The Oxyrhynchus Papri Project, Oxford/Egypt Exploration Society 4 (bottom); ©2011 JupiterImages 5; ©iStockphoto.com/Hulton Archive 6, Corel Corporation 8, ASSOCIATED PRESS 9 (top); Institute of Human Origins 9 (center); © DeAgostini/ SuperStock 9 (bottom); "Singapore Skyline" by JeCCo/ Wikimedia Commons/GNUFDL 1.2/CC-BY-SA 3.0 10; ©2011 Jupiter Images/Photos.com All Rights Reserved. 11, 13 (top); Dr. Stewart Custer 13 (bottom); "Double Peaked Araratby" MEDIACRAT/Wikimedia Commons/GNUFDL 1.2/CC-BY-SA 3.0 15; Unusual Films/ Wade Ramsey 16

Chapter 2
Todd Bolen/BiblePlaces.com 18; ©iStockphoto.com/Eileen Morris 19 (top); "Sumerian 26th C Adab"/Wikimedia Commons/Public 19 (bottom); Wade Ramsey 20; ©North Wind Picture Archives. All Rights Reserved. 21; ©iStockphoto.com/Julia Chernikova 24; "Thutmosis III wien front" by Hay Kranen/ Wikimedia Commons/Public Domain 25; Egyptian Tourist Authority 26; "Rosetta Stone" by Hans Hillewaert/Wikimedia Commons/CC-BY-SA 3.0 27 (top); ©iStockphoto.com/ Hayley Easton 27 (bottom); "Hittite (bull) Rhyton at the Met" by Mark Randall Dawson/ Wikimedia Commons/CC 2.0 28; "Cypraea chinensis with partially extended mantle"/NOAA/ Wikimedia Commons/Public Domain 29 (top); "Cèdre du Liban Barouk 2005" by Olivier Bezes/Wikimedia Commons/ GNUFDL 1.2, CC-BY-SA 3.0 29 (bottom); Dia Karanough/Getty Images/iStockphoto/Thinkstock 30; Roberta Bianchi/Getty Images/iStockphoto/Thinkstock 32; Dennis Bollinger 33; Unusual Films/Wade Ramsey 36, 39 (top); "Persepolis 1" by GerardM/ Wikimedia Commons/ GNUFDL 1.2, CC-BY-SA 3.0 39 (bottom)

Chapter 3
PhotoDisc/Getty Images 42, 49; Viacheslav Khmelnytskyi/Getty Images/iStockPhoto/Thinkstock 43; www.HolyLandPhotos.org 44 (top); "Athena Parthenos Altemps Inv8622" by Marie-Lan Nguyen/Wikimedia Commons/Public Domain 45; ©iStockphoto.com/Leeman 48; "Thermopylae ancient coastline large"/Fkerasar/ Wikimedia Commons/ GNU FDL 1.2/CC BY-SA 3.0 50; "BattleofIssus333BC-mosaic-detail1"/Ruthven/Wikimedia Commons/Public Domain 53; ©iStockphoto.com/David Shawley 55; "Bust Socrates Musei Capitolini MC1163" by Marie-Lan Nguyen/Wikimedia Commons/Public Domain 56; "David-The Death of Socrates"/ Wikimedia Commons/Public Domain 57 (top); "Plato Silanion Musei Capitolini MC1377" by Marie-Lan Nguyen/CC 2.5/ Wikimedia Commons 57 (bottom); "Aristotle Altemps Inv8575"/Jastrow/Wikimedia Commons/Public Domain 58; Photos.com/Jupiter Images 60; Unusual Films/Wade Ramsey 61 (top); "Porch of Maidens" by Thermos/Wikimedia Commons/CC BY-SA 2.5 61 (bottom); ©iStockphoto.com/ Andreas Guskos 62 (left); ©iStockphoto.com/George Cairns 62 (center); ©iStockphoto.com/Marje Cannon 62 (right)

Chapter 4
Unusual Films/Wade Ramsey 64; Todd Bolen/ BiblePlaces.com 66; William L. Krewson/BiblePlaces.com 67 (top); "Arcades of the courtyard of Palazzo Pitti, Florence" by Giovanni Dall'Orto/Wikimedia Commons 70; PhotoDisc/Getty Images 72 (top); "Hannibal Slodtz Louvre MR2093" by Marie-Lan Nguyen/Wikimedia Commons/Public Domain 72 (bottom); ©iStockphoto.com/ Iwona Adamus 74; "Pompée Vaux" by Jebulon/Wikimedia Commons/Public Domain 78; "Julius Caesar Coustou Louvre MR1798" by Marie-Lan Nguyen/

Wikimedia Commons/Public Domain 79

Chapter 5

Detail of *Christ Leaving the Praetorium*, Gustave Doré, From the Bob Jones University Collection 82; "Bust of the Augustus Bevilacqua" by Bibi Saint-Pol, F l a n k e r/ Wikimedia Commons/ Public Domain 84; William L. Krewson/BiblePlaces.com 89 (top), 99 (bottom); Gerald Oskoboiny 89 (bottom and center); ©iStockphoto.com/ jamesbenet 90 (top); Unusual Films/Wade Ramsey 90 (bottom); ©2011 JupiterImages/ Photos.com. All Rights Reserved. 91 (top); Getty Images, Inc. 91 (bottom); Photo Office de Tourisme de Nimes, France 92 (top); ©iStockphoto.com/ Zastavkin 92 (bottom); "Marcus Aurelius Glyptothek Munich"/Bibi Saint-Pol/ Wikimedia Commons/Public Domain 93; "Baram033" by Ori~/Wikimedia Commons 94 (top); 2008 JupiterImages Corporation 94 (bottom); "Antonio Ciseri Ecce Homo" by Antonio Ciseri/Wikimedia Commons/Public Domain 95; www.HolyLandPhotos.org 96; Todd Bolen/BiblePlaces.com 97; "Nero 1" by Cjh1452000/ Wikimedia Commons/GNUFDL 1.2/CC-BY-SA 3.0 99 (top); "Diocletien Vaux1" by Jebulon/ Wikimedia Commons/Public Domain 99 (center); "MMA bust 02" by Katie Chao/Wikimedia Commons/CC-BY-SA 2.0 100; Unusual Films 102

Unit Two Opener

Getty Images/iStockphoto/ Thinkstock 106–7

Chapter 6

©iStockphoto.com/Murat Baysan 108, 111; PhotoDisc/ Getty Images 109; "Justinian I, San Vitale (Ravenna)"/The Yorck Project/Wikimedia Commons/ Public Domain 110 (left); "Empress Theodora and Her Court"/The Yorck Project/ Wikimedia Commons/ Public Domain 110 (right); ©iStockphoto.com/Eliana Dulinsky 112; Jupiter Images 114 (top); "Cyril and Methodius monument (Dmitrov)" by Amigovip/Wikimedia Commons/GNU FDL 1.2, CC-BY-SA 3.0 114 (bottom); Roman Barelko/Getty Images/ Thinkstock 115 (top); Mary, Tikhvinskaya, Theotokos (Bogoroditsa) Novgorod School, Mid 16th century, From the Bob Jones University Collection 115 (center); Mary, Iverskaya Theotokos (Bogoroditsa), Russian 20th century, From the Bob Jones University Collection 115 (bottom); "Cathedral of Christ the Saviour over Moscow River. Moscow" by Voytek s/Wikimedia Commons/ CC BY-SA 2.5 117; "Arabian Peninsula dust SeaWiFS", NASA/Goddard Space Flight Center, and ORBIMAGE/ Wikimedia Commons/Public Domain 118; "Cave Hira"/ Nazil/Wikimedia Commons/ Public Domain 119 (top); "Kaaba (1910)-2"/Library of Congress/ Wikimedia Commons/Public Domain 119 (bottom); "Kaaba mirror edit jj" by Muhammad Mahdi Karim/Wikimedia Commons/GNU FDL 1.2 121; Dick Doughty/Saudia Aramco World/SAWDIA 122; Todd Bolen/BiblePlaces.com 123; "Ijazah"/Library of Congress/ Wikimedia Commons/Public Domain 126 (top); "Badshahi Mosque July 1 2005 pic32" by Pale blue dot/Wikimedia Commons/CC BY-SA 2.5 126 (bottom)

Chapter 7

PhotoDisc/GettyImages 128, 129 (top), 138, 144; ©2011 JupiterImages/Photos.com. All Rights Reserved. 131, 143; "Buddha at Mulagandhakuti Vihara, Sarnath" by Wonker/ Wikimedia Commons/CC BY 2.0 132; "Ajanta caves, Maharashtra"/Soman/ Wikimedia Commons/ GNUFDL 1.2/CC-BY-SA 3.0 134; ©2011 JupiterImages/ Ablestock.com. All Rights Reserved. 135; "Confucius-templeapricotplatform" by Rolf Müller/Wikimedia Commons/ GNUFDL 1.2/ CC-BY-SA 3.0 137; "Cin Shihhuang Shaanxi statue" by Nat Krause/ Wikimedia Commons/Public Domain 139; "Terracotta Army Pit 1 - 7" by Maros Mraz/ Wikimedia Commons/GNUFDL 1.2/ CC-BY-SA 3.0 140; "Box with floral petals Asian Art Museum" by BrokenSphere/ Wikimedia Commons/ GNUFDL 1.2/CC-BY-SA 3.0 142; "Minamoto no Yoritomo"/ Wikimedia Commons/Public Domain 145; "Genghis Khan statue" by GenuineMongol/ Wikimedia Commons/Public Domain 146; "YuanEmperor-AlbumKhubilaiPortrait"/ Wikimedia Commons/Public Domain 147; "Bat Khan" by Enerelt/Wikimedia Commons/ GNUFDL 1.2/CC-BY-SA 3.0 148 (top); "Tamerlane"/Wikimedia Commons/Public Domain 148 (bottom); Photos.com/ JupiterImages 150; "Rome Stele" by Ondřej Žváček/Wikimedia Commons/GNUFDL 1.2/CC-BY-SA 3.0 151; Getty Images/ iStockphoto/Thinkstock 152; Edard Braekke/TrekEarth.com 153 (top); "Ekpokin-Musée ethnologique de Berlin" by Ji-Elle/Wikimedia Commons/ GNUFDL 1.2/ CC-BY-SA 3.0 153 (bottom)

Unit Three Opener

Getty Images/Hemera/ Thinkstock 156–7

Chapter 8

©iStockphoto.com/DemidBorodin 158; ©iStockphoto.com/Cristian Lupu159;©PeterWilli/SuperStock 161; "AachenerDomKarlsthron 1661" by Bojin/Wikimedia Commons/CC-BY-SA 3.0 162; "Aachen Cathedral North View at Evening" by Aleph/ Wikimedia Commons/CC-BY-SA 2.5 163 (top); "Freising manuscript"/Wikimedia Commons/Public Domain 163 (bottom); "Adoration-OfTheMagiOttebeurenC-ollectarBLYates"/Ottobeuren Collectar/Wikimedia Commons/Public Domain 166 (top); ©iStockphoto.com/ Craig Stanton 166 (bottom); "Musee-de-lArmee" by Rama/ Wikipedia/CeCILL, CC-BY-SA 2.0 167; ©Karen Hadley/ Shutterstock 168; "Kovář při práci (Velikonoční trhy na Václavském náměstí)" by Matěj Baťha/Wikimedia Commons/ CC BY-SA 3.0 170 (top); "Braine-le-Château" by Jean-Pol GRANDMONT/Wikimedia Commons/CC BY 2.0 170 (right); "Flour mill" by Jonas Bergsten/Wikimedia Commons/ Public Domain 170 (left); St. Jerome, Pietro Paolini, From the Bob Jones University Collection 172; ©iStockphoto.com/ Natalia Bratslavsky 173; ©iStockphoto.com/Peter Hibberd 174; ©iStockphoto.com/ Dale Robins 175; "Fra Angelico"/ The Yorck Project/Wikimedia Commons/Public Domain 176

Chapter 9

SEF/Art Resource, NY 178; Jupiter Images/Photo.com 181; Scala/Art Resource, NY 182; Réunion des Musées Nationaux/Art Resource, NY 184; ©Fotolia/Uwe Graf 185; "Weltliche Schatzkammer Wien" by Gryffindor/Wikimedia Commons/Public Domain 186; Anthony Baggett/Getty Images/ iStockphoto/Thinkstock 187; © Reading Museum (Reading Borough Council). All rights reserved. 188–89; Photos.com/ Getty Images/Thinkstock 190; Ian Poole/iStockphoto/ Getty Images/Thinkstock 191; Getty Images/Photos.com/ Thinkstock 194 (top); Art Renewal Center/Public Domain 194 (bottom); "Pope Urban" by Nelson Minar/Wikimedia Commons/CC BY-SA 2.0 195; ©iStockphoto.com/Witold Ryka 196; "Standbeeld Saladin Damascus" by Godfried Warreyn/Wikimedia Commons/ GNUFDL 1.2, CC-BY-SA 3.0 197; "Gustave dore crusades the childrens crusade"/Wikimedia Commons/Public Domain 198 (top); ©iStockphoto.com/ freephotoagency 198 (bottom)

Chapter 10

©iStockphoto.com/Emanuele Gnani 202; University of Bologna 203; bpk, Berlin/ Gemaeldegalerie, Staatliche Museen/Holbein, Hans the Younger/Art Resource, NY 205 (top); "Gouden florijn" by Fruitpunchline/Wikimedia/ Public Domain 205 (bottom); "The Moneylender and his Wife" by Quentin Matsys/Musée du Louvre, Paris/Web Gallery of Art/Wikimedia Commons/ Public Domain 206; Andrés Morya – Hinojosa 207; © 2006 JupiterImages/Ablestock.com. All rights reserved. 208; Science MuseumSSPL/© Science and Society/SuperStock 210; ©iStockphoto.com/marco bernes 211; "Anselmstatue-canterburycathedraloutside" by Ealdgyth/Wikimedia/CC-BY-SA 3.0 213; "Thomas Aquinas in Stained Glass" by Thomas Gun/ Wikimedia/CC-BY-SA-2.0 214 (top); Getty Images/Photos.com/ Thinkstock 214 (bottom), 215; Getty Images/iStockphoto/ Thinkstock 216 (top), 223; Pécs Cathedral Roman art era - Hungary by Takkk/Wikimedia/ GNUFDL 1.2/CC-BY-SA 3.0 216 (bottom); PhotoDisc/ Getty Images 217; ©Charles Stirling/Alamy 218; ©Pantheon/ SuperStock 219; Webb Hudspeth 222; Getty Images/iStockphoto/ Thinkstock 223

Unit Four Opener

Getty Images/iStockphoto/ Thinkstock 226–27

Chapter 11

2005 JupiterImages/ Photos.com. All rights reserved. 228; ©iStockphoto.com/Jocelyn Lin 229; ©iStockphoto.com/ Ogen Perry 230; Florentine 15th or 16th Century, probably after a model by Andrea del Verrocchio and Orsino Benintendi, Lorenzo de' Medici, Samuel H. Kress Collection, Image courtesy of the National Gallery of Art, Washington 231 (top); ©Scala/Art Resource, NY 231 (bottom); "Balthazar Castiglione, by Raffaello Sanzio"/Wikimedia Commons/Public Domain 232; From *The Praise of Folly*/Public Domain 234 (bottom); Getty Images/Thinkstock 235; "Title page William Shakespeare's First Folio" 1623/Wikimedia Commons/Public Domain 236; "Lorenzetti Ambrogio annunciation- 1344" by Ambrogio Lorenzetti/Wikimedia Commons/Public Domain 237 (top); "Sandro Botticelli - Adoration of the Magi" by Sandro Botticelli/Wikimedia Commons/Public Domain 237 (bottom left); "Sandro Botticelli" by Sandro Botticelli/Wikimedia Commons/Public Domain 237 (bottom right); "Savonarola monument, Ferrara"/ho visto nina volare/Wikimedia Commons/CC 2.0 238 (top); "Self-portrait by Raphael" by Raphael/Wikimedia Commons/Public Domain 238 (bottom); "Raffael 025 Madonna del Granduca" by Raphael/Wikimedia Commons/Public Domain 239 (bottom); Erich Lessing/Art Resource, NY 240 (top); ©Peter Barritt/SuperStock 241 (top); "Knight, Death and the Devil" by Durer/Wikimedia Commons/Public Domain 241 (bottom); ©SuperStock/SuperStock 242 (top); Scala/Art Resource, NY 242 (bottom); ©iStockphoto.com/Giorgio Magini 243 (top); "Bunelleschi"/Wikimedia Commons/Public Domain 243 (bottom); ©iStockphoto.com/rusm 244; PhotoDisc, Inc. 245

Chapter 12

©iStockphoto.com/Glen Rodgers 248; Webb Hudspeth 249; 'The English People Reading Wycliffe's Bible' (detail) oil on canvas by George Clausen, 1927. WOA 2603 ©Palace of Westminster Collection 250 (top); Stock Montage/Contributor/Archive Photos/Getty Images 250 (bottom); ©SuperStock/SuperStock 252; "Portrait of Pope Leo X and his cousins" by Raphael /Wikimedia Commons/Raffaello Sanzio/Public Domain 253 (top); "Johann Tetzel"/Wikipedia/Public Domain 253 (bottom); ©iStockphoto.com/Marc C. Johnson 254 (top); Wittenberg Culture, www.wittenberg.de 254 (bottom); "Johannes-Eck"/Wikimedia Commons/Public Domain 255 (top); "Porträt des Karl V. im Lehnstuhl"/Titian/Wikimedia Commons/Public Domain 255 (bottom); ©Edmund Nagele PCL/SuperStock 256 (top); ©iStockphoto.com/Duncan Walker 256 (bottom); Courtesy of Mark Sidwell 258; Public Domain 259; Library of Congress 260; DigitalSTOCK 261; JupiterImages 262 (top); Réunion des Musées Nationaux/Art Resource, NY 262 (bottom); ©Art Archive, The/SuperStock 263 (top); Nathan Benn 263 (bottom); Unusual Films 264; "Battle of Haarlemmermeer, 26 May 1573" by Hendrick Cornelisz Vroom/Wikimedia Commons/Public Domain 266; ©Robert Harding Picture Library/SuperStock 267 (top); ©2005 JupiterImages 267 (bottom); "William I (1533–1584), Prince of Orange, called William the Silent" by Adriaen Thomasz. Key/Wikimedia Commons/Public Domain 268 (top); François Dubois, Le Massacre de la Saint-Barthélemy, vers 1572–1584, Huile sur bois, 94 × 154 cm, Musée cantonal des Beaux-Arts de Lausanne 268 (bottom); Rèunion des Musèes Nationaux/Art Resource 269; ©Foto Marburg/ Art Resource 270; The New York Public Library 271

Chapter 13

Photo Courtesy of New Netherland Museum/www.newnetherland.org 274; "Ortelius - Maris Pacifici 1589" by Abraham Ortelius/Wikimedia Commons/Public Domain 276; ©Art Archive, The/SuperStock 279 (top left); "Bartolomeu Dias, South Africa House" by RedCoat/Wikimedia Commons/GNU FDL/CC-BY-SA-3.0 279 (top right); ©Art Archive, The/SuperStock 279 (bottom); ©iStockphoto.com/Michael Bischof 280 (top); "Monumento a Colón (Madrid)" by Luis García/Wikimedia Commons/CC-BY-SA-2.5 280 (bottom); "Landing of Columbus" by John Vanderlyn/Wikimedia Commons/Public Domain 281; Library of Congress 282; Getty Images/iStockphoto/Thinkstock 284, 285; ©iStockphoto.com/Nikki Bidgood 286; ©Image Asset Management Ltd./SuperStock 287 (top); ©iStockphoto.com/picture 287 (center); Architect of the Capitol 287 (bottom), 288; ©iStockphoto.com/DavidFreund 290 (top); Photo Courtesy of New Netherland Museum/www.newnetherland.org 290 (bottom); Courtesy of the APVA Preservation Virginia 291; Popperfoto/Contributor/Popperfoto/Getty Images 292; ©shirophoto-Fotolia.com 293; BJU Photo Services 294; "East Indiaman Warley" by Robert Salmon/Wikimedia Commons/Public Domain 295

Unit Five Opener

Theodor Josef Hubert Hoffbauer/The Bridgeman Art Library/Getty Images 298–99

Chapter 14

Library of Congress 300; ©iStockphoto.com/René Mansi 301; Getty Images/Photos.com/Thinkstock 302; Rèunion des Musèes Nationaux/Art Resource 303; ©iStockphoto.com/michel mory 304; ©iStockphoto.com/Ryan KC Wong 305; Swabian Tourism Bureau 306; "Antoine Pesne - Frederick the Great as Crown Prince" by Antoine Pesne/Wikimedia Commons/Public Domain 307; Erich Lessing/Art Resource 308 (top); Peter I the Great (1672–1725) 1838 (oil on canvas) (see also 144528) by Hippolyte Dearoche (Paul) (1797–1856) Hamburger Kunsthalle, Hamburg, Germany/The Bridgeman Art Library 308 (bottom); Erich Lessing/Art Resource 309; © Pantheon/SuperStock 310; "Charles I of England" by Antoon van Dyck/Wikimedia Commons/Public Domain 311 (top); ©2005 JupiterImages 311 (bottom); "Oliver Cromwell" by Robert Walker/Wikimedia Commons/Public Domain 312 (top); "King Charles II" by John Michael Wright or studio/Wikimedia Commons/Public Domain 312 (bottom); ©Huntington Library/SuperStock 313 (top); ©2005 JupiterImages 313 (bottom); "King William III of England, (1650–1702)" by Sir Godfrey Kneller/Wikimedia Commons/Public Domain 315 (left); *Portrait of Queen Mary II.* Sir Godfrey Kneller. From the Bob Jones University Collection 315 (right); Portrait of Sir Robert Walpole (1676–1745) Earl of Orford, 1743 (oil on canvas) by John Theodore Heins (1732–71) ©Norwich Castle Museum and Art Gallery/The Bridgeman Art Library 316; ©DeAgostini/SuperStock 317; "William Pitt, 1st Earl of Chatham" by William Hoare/Wikimedia Commons/Public Domain 318 (top); Library and Archives Canada/ C-139911 318 (bottom)

Chapter 15

©SuperStock/SuperStock 322; ©2009 JupiterImages Corporation 323; NASA 324 (top); Getty Images/Photos.com/Thinkstock 324 (bottom); "Justus Sustermans - Portrait of Galileo Galilei, 1636"/Wikimedia Commons/Public Domain 325; ©Science and Society/SuperStock 326 (top and bottom left); Collection of the University of Michigan Health System, Gift of Pfizer Inc. UMHS.23 327 (top); Stock Montage/Contributor/Archive Photos/Getty Images 327 (bottom left); James Sharpies/The Bridgeman Art Library/Getty Images 327 (bottom right); Collection of the University of Michigan Health System, Gift of Pfizer Inc. UMHS.19 328 (top); ©Photo Researchers/Alamy 328 (bottom); Stock Montage/Contributor/Archive Photos/Getty Images 329; Erich Lessing/Art Resource, NY 330 (top); ©Image Asset Management Ltd./SuperStock 330 (center); "Ivoire Montesquieu" by Siren-Com/Wikimedia Commons/GNU FDL/CC-BY-SA-3.0 330 (bottom); ©Peter Willi/SuperStock 331 (top); Library of Congress 331 (bottom), 334 (bottom), 336, 342 (top); Nicholaus Ludwig Count von Zinzendorf with the Daily Watchwords, 1761 (oil on panel) by Swiss School (18th century) Private Collection/The Bridgeman Art Library 333; BJU Press Files 334 (top); George Whitefield, by John Russell (died 1806), given to the National Portrait Gallery, London in 1917/Wikimedia Commons/Public Domain 335; ©SuperStock/SuperStock 338 (top), 339 (top and bottom); ©iStockphoto.com/Tiago Fernandes 338 (bottom); PhotoDisc, Inc. 340 (top); Ashmolean Museum, University of Oxford 340 (bottom); "George Frideric Handel" by Balthasar Denner/Wikimedia Commons/Public Domain 341 (top); Public Domain 341 (bottom); ©Photononstop/SuperStock 342 (bottom); "Daniel Defoe Kneller Style"/Wikimedia Commons/Public Domain 343 (left); "Edward Gibbon" by Henry Walton/Wikimedia Commons/Public Domain 343 (right)

Chapter 16

Library of Congress 346, 362 (top), 363, 368 (right); PhotoDisc, Inc. 347, 352; ©Ross Warner/Alamy 349; George R. Collins 350 (left and right); "Washington Crossing the Delaware" by Emanuel Gottlieb Leutze/Wikimedia Commons/Public Domain 351; "Louis16-1775" by Joseph-Siffred Duplessis/Wikimedia Commons/Public Domain 354; Erich Lessing/Art Resource, NY 355, 356; ©SuperStock/SuperStock 357; "Death of Marat" by David/Wikimedia Commons/Public Domain 359; ©2005 JupiterImages 360; Réunion des Musées Nationaux/Art Resource, NY 361; ©2009 JupiterImages Corporation 362 (bottom); ©National Maritime Museum, Greenwich, UK 364; Erich Lessing/Art Resource, NY 365; Napoleon's Retreat (oil on canvas) by Robert Alexander Hillingford (1825–1904) Private Collection/Photo © Bonhams, London, UK/The Bridgeman Art Library 367 (top); "Battle of Waterloo 1815" by William Sadler/Wikimedia Commons/Public Domain 367 (bottom); ©Image Asset Management Ltd./SuperStock 368 (left)

Unit Six Opener

"Sadie Pfeifer"/National Archives/Wikimedia Commons/Public Domain 370–371

Chapter 17

©2005 Hemera Technologies, Inc. All rights reserved. 372; "Portrait of Alexander I of Russia (1777–1825)" by Franz Kruger/Wikimedia Commons/Public Domain 373 (top); ©SuperStock/SuperStock 373 (bottom), 392 (right); Clipart.com/©2009 JupiterImages Corporation 374; "Louis-Philippe de Bourbon" by Franz Xaver Winterhalter/Wikimedia Commons/Public Domain 379; Nicolas Edward Gabe/The Bridgeman Art Library/Getty Images 380 (top); "Portrait of Napoleon III (1808–1873)" by Franz Xaver Winterhalter/Wikimedia Commons/Public Domain 380 (bottom); "Florence Nightingale three quarter length"/Wikimedia Commons/Public Domain 383 (top); "Seacole photo"/Wikimedia Commons/Public Domain 383 (bottom); Mark Sidwell 384 (left); Library of Congress 384 (right), 390 (bottom right); Scala/Art Resource, NY 385 (top); National Archives 385 (bottom); Evert A. Duyckinck, Portrait Gallery of Eminent Men and Women of Europe and America (New York: Johnson, Wilson and Company, 1873) 386; ©Image Asset Management Ltd./SuperStock 388; ©2005 JupiterImages 389 (left); "SamuelTaylorColeridge" by Pieter van Dyke/Wikimedia Commons/Public Domain 389 (center); "Portrait of Johann Wolfgang von Goethe" by Angelica Kauffmann/Wikimedia Commons/Public Domain 389 (right); ©Universal Images Group/SuperStock 390 (top and bottom left); "Lord Byron in Albanian dress" by Thomas Phillips/Wikimedia Commons/Public Domain 391; "Beethoven" by Joseph Karl Stieler/Wikimedia Commons/Public Domain 392 (left); ©2005 JupiterImages 393

Chapter 18

©iStockphoto.com/Chris Schmidt 396; Library of Congress 397, 401 (bottom), 402 (all), 404, 405, 407 (top and bottom right), 409 (top), 412 (center and bottom); "Portrait of Charles Townshend, 2nd Viscount Townshend (1674–1738)"/ National Portrait Gallery, London/Wikimedia Commons/Public Domain 398; "Bradford Industrial Museum" by Linda Spashett/Wikimedia Commons/CC-BY-3.0 399 (top); "Arkwright Water Frame (replica)" by Morio/Wikimedia Commons/GFDL/CC-BY-SA-3.0 399 (center); Getty Images/iStockphoto/Thinkstock 399 (bottom); ©Science and Society/SuperStock 400 (top); 2005 JupiterImages 401 (top); "Blucher engine"/Wikimedia Commons/Public Domain 401 (top inset); © 2009 JupiterImages Corporation/Photos.com 401 (bottom inset); "Edison and phonograph" by Levin C. Handy/Wikimedia Commons/Public Domain 403 (top); National Archives/Library of Congress 403 (bottom); Mark Sidwell 407 (bottom left); "AdamSmith" created by Cadell and Davies, John Horsburgh, or R.C. Bell/Wikimedia Commons/Public Domain 408; ©SuperStock/SuperStock 409 (bottom); Sword of the Lord 411; "George Muller"/Wikipedia/Public Domain 412 (top); "Charles Darwin seated" by Maull & Fox/Wikimedia Commons/Public Domain 413; ©2005 JupiterImages 414 (top); "Einstein 1921 portrait" by Ferdinand Schmutzer/Wikimedia Commons/Public Domain 414 (bottom); ©Universal Images Group/SuperStock 416 (top); ©Peter Willi/SuperStock 416 (bottom); "Renoir23"/Wikimedia Commons/Public Domain 417 (left); "Study of a Figure Outdoors: Woman with a Parasol, facing left" by Claude Monet/Wikimedia Commons/Public Domain 417 (right); "Still Life with a Curtain" by Paul Cezanne/Wikimedia Commons/Public Domain 418

Chapter 19

"China imperialism cartoon" by Henri Meyer/Wikimedia Commons/Public Domain 420; DOD 424 (top and bottom); PhotoDisc, Inc. 426 (bottom); John Bean 426 (top right and top left); Getty Images/iStockphoto/Thinkstock 427; "Battle of Bailen" by José Casado del Alisal/Wikimedia Commons/Public Domain 428; "CareyEngraving"/Wikimedia Commons/Public Domain 432 (top); ©North Wind Picture Archives. All Rights Reserved. 432 (bottom); Overseas Missionary Fellowship 433; Special Collections, Yale Divinity School Library 434 (top); Library of Congress/Harris & Ewing Collection 434 (center); Library of Congress 437 (top); Dundee Central Library, Mary Slessor Collection 437 (bottom); "Suez Canal Ismailia"/Library of Congress/Wikimedia Commons/Public Domain 440

Unit Seven Opener

"Astronaut-EVA"/NASA/Wikimedia Commons/Public Domain 444–45

Chapter 20

National Archives 446, 455 (Red Baron); Library of Congress 447, 449, 455 (zeppelin), 457, 460 (top left), 461; ©iStockphoto.com/Lisa Kyle Young 448; Punch Cartoon Library 450; © Armenian National Institute, Inc., courtesy of Sybil Stevens (daughter of Armin T. Wegner). Wegner Collection, Deutches Literaturarchiv, Marbach & United States Holocaust Memorial Museum. 451; "Franz ferdinand"/Library of Congress/Wikimedia Commons/Public Domain 452; "German infantry 1914" / Underwood & Underwood/Wikimedia Commons/Public Domain 453 (left); Morgan-Wells/Stringer/Hulton Archive/Getty Images 453 (right); "Vickers machine gun crew with gas masks"/Imperial War Museum Collection/Wikimedia Commons/Public Domain 455 (top); Getty Images/AbleStock.com/jupiterimages 455 (bottom); "RMS *Lusitania* coming into port, possibly in New York, 1907"/Library of Congress/Wikimedia Commons/Public Domain 456; Library of Congress 457; "John Pershing"/2d Lt. L J. Rode/Wikimedia Commons/Public Domain 459; US Army 460 (top right); "Stowers MOH ceremony - Palmer, Bowens and Bush" by Robert Ward, DOD PA/Wikimedia Commons/Public Domain 460 (bottom); National Archives/DOD 462; ©Photononstop/SuperStock 646 (bottom); Ed Richards 464 (top)

Chapter 21

Hugo Jaeger/Contributor/Time & Life Pictures/Getty Images 468; National Archives 469 (top), 476, 481, 483 (bottom), 484 (top right); "Ramsay MacDonald"/Library of Congress/Wikimedia Commons/Public Domain 469 (bottom); Three Lions/Stringer/Hulton Archive/Getty Images 470; Library of Congress 471 (top and bottom), 475 (right), 478, 484 (top left); Herbert Hoover Library 472; ©Fine Art Images/SuperStock 473; Topical Press Agency/Stringer/Hulton Archive/Getty Images 474 (top); "Alexander Kerensky"/Library of Congress/Wikimedia Commons/Public Domain 474 (bottom); Jupiter Images 475 (left); Russian Gospel Ministries 479; Courtesy of Calvin College 483 (top), 485 (bottom left, bottom center, and bottom right); "Reichstagsbrand"/National Archives/Wikimedia Commons/Public Domain 484 (bottom); United States Holocaust Memorial Museum 485 (top); ASSOCIATED PRESS 486 (top); ©Fine Art Images/SuperStock 486 (bottom); Courtesy of Western Pennsylvania Conservancy 487 (top); "Igor Stravinsky"/Library of Congress/Wikimedia Commons/Public Domain 487 (bottom); ©Pantheon/SuperStock 488

Chapter 22

"A Douglas SBD Dive Bomber over Wake Island, 1943" by Lt. Charles Kerlee/U.S. Navy/Wikimedia Commons/Public Domain 490; NARA/National Park Service 491 (top); Popperfoto/Contributor/ Popperfoto/Getty Images 491 (bottom); Harry S. Truman Library 492 (top); ASSOCIATED PRESS 492 (bottom); National Archives 493 (top), 496 (bottom), 505 (bottom), 507 (top and bottom), 508 (center, bottom), 509 (bottom), 510, 514 (top right, center), 515 (top); DOD 493 (bottom), 511, 513; Central Press/Stringer/Hulton Archive/ Getty Images 495, 497, 503 (top); ©SuperStock/SuperStock 496 (top); Keystone/Staff/Hulton Archive/Getty Images 499 (top); "Waffenstillstand von Compiègne, Hitler, Göring"/ Bundesarchiv, Bild 183-M1112-500 /Wikipedia/CC-BY-SA 3.0 Germany 499 (bottom); Library of Congress 500 (left), 502 (top and bottom), 514 (top left and bottom); ©Everett Collection/SuperStock 500 (right); Public Domain 501 (top and bottom), 505 (top left, top right); ©Stock Connection/ SuperStock 503 (bottom); US Holocaust Museum courtesy of Ralf Rossmeissl 504; BJU Press Files 506; "Yalta Conference (Churchill, Roosevelt, Stalin)"/ (US Department of Defense)/ Wikipedia/Public Domain 512; ©Belinda Images/SuperStock 515 (bottom)

Chapter 23

"BerlinWall-BrandenburgGate" by Sue Ream/Wikimedia Commons/CC 3.0 518; The National Churchill Museum Photographic Collection 520 (top); Library of Congress 520 (bottom), 526 (bottom), 528, 537; ASSOCIATED PRESS 522 (left), 526 (top right), 529 (top), 530 (bottom), 533 (bottom right), 538 (top); Reg Lancaster/Stringer/Hulton Archive/Getty Images 522 (right); "Mao and Jiang Qing 1946"/Wikimedia Commons/ Public Domain 525; DOD 526 (top left); National Archives 527, 531 (left); "Official Portrait of President Reagan 1981"/ Wikimedia Commons/Public Domain 531 (right); Courtesy of Ronald Reagan Presidential Library 532, 533 (top); German Information Center 533 (bottom left), 540 (bottom); William J. Clinton Library 534; ©age fotostock/SuperStock 538 (bottom); "Martin Luther King Jr"/ Library of Congress/Wikimedia Commons/Public Domain 539; "Bill Clinton"/Wikimedia Commons/Public Domain 540 (top); ©Culver Pictures, Inc./ SuperStock 541 (top); The White House 541 (bottom)

Chapter 24

©Simon Heaton/SuperStock 544; "George-W-Bush"/Eric Draper/Wikimedia Commons/ Public Domain 546 (top); "Official portrait of Barack Obama"/Pete Souza/Wikimedia Commons/CC-BY-3. 546 (center); "WORLD ECONOMIC FORUM ANNUAL MEETING 2009 - Tony Blair"/World Economic Forum/Wikimedia Commons/CC-BY-SA 2.0 Generic 546 (bottom); "Official-photo-cameron"/Wikimedia Commons/Open Government Licence v1.0 547 (top); "AM Juli 2010 - 3zu4" by Armin Linnartz/ Wikimedia Commons/CC-BY-SA 3.0 Germany 547 (center); "Nicolas Sarkozy (2008)" by (Aleph)/Wikimedia Commons/ CC-BY-SA 2.5 547 (bottom); REUTERS/Mainichi Shimbun 548; "USNWC Varyag02"/U.S. Navy/Wikimedia Commons/ Public Domain 549; "Vladimir Putin official portrait"/Kremlin.ru/Wikimedia Commons/CC-BY-SA 3.0 Unport 550 (top); "Dmitry Medvedev official large photo"/Kremlin.ru/Wikimedia Commons/CC-BY-SA 3.0 Unported 550 (bottom); ASSOCIATED PRESS 551 (top), 557, 558 (center), 559 (top right, top left), 560 (bottom); ©Science and Society/ SuperStock 551 (bottom); © Eye Ubiquitous/SuperStock 554; © Robert Harding Picture Library/SuperStock 555; "HugoChavez1824"/Agência Brasil/Wikimedia Commons/ CC-BY-SA 3.0 Brazil 556; "Mahmoud Ahmadinejad (Brazil 2009)"/Marcello Casal Jr/ABr/Wikimedia Commons/ CC-BY-SA 3.0 Brazil 558 (top); "Muammar al-Gaddafi at the AU summit"/U.S. Navy/Wikimedia Commons/Public Domain 558 (bottom); "1WTC DEC 23, 2011"/Renatus/Wikimedia Commons/CC-BY-SA 3.0 Unported 559 (bottom); "Hamid Karzai 2004-06-14-D-9880W-075"/U.S. Department of Defense/Wikimedia Commons/ Public Domain 560 (top)